The Problems of Aesthetics

THE PROBLEMS OF

AESTHETICS

A Book of Readings

EDITED BY

Eliseo Vivas

John Evans Professor of Moral and Intellectual Philosophy
Northwestern University

AND

Murray Krieger

Assistant Professor of English, University of Minnesota

Rinehart & Company, Incorporated

Publishers in New York and Toronto

Second printing   September, 1955

Preface

THIS VOLUME was projected in 1948 by the editors, who worked
on it continually through 1950, when the final selections were decided upon
and the manuscript in its present form, except for the introductory essay and
the several prefaces, was accepted by the publishers. The idea behind the
book was one which the senior editor had nurtured through many years of
teaching and research in aesthetics. For a long while he had hoped to organize
a book of readings as he had organized his course—about the central and heterogeneous problems which seemed to him to constitute the discipline of
aesthetics; and the majority of selections here included had been used successfully in the classroom with classes of various levels in several universities. The
junior editor's enthusiasm for organizing an anthology in this manner and with
these materials cleared the way for the creation of this volume.

These selections from the rich store of contemporary writings on the philosophy of art have been made not only on the basis of their intrinsic value
but also on the basis of the relevance with which they treat the problems about
which they are clustered, as these problems are discriminated in the introductory essay. The book, then, has been shaped in terms of a conception of the
nature of aesthetics and of the problems which constitute it, not in terms of a
more or less random collection of important essays in aesthetics included for
their own sakes. It is thus not only an anthology, though it may well serve as
that alone; it represents an analytic conception of what aesthetics is, a definition of the criteria in terms of which aesthetic theories—among which this
book need not discriminate—may be measured. For these reasons the editors hope that this reader will be a contribution to the teaching of aesthetics,
although they are convinced too that it will be useful to any teacher of aesthetics, regardless of his pedagogical approach or his philosophic affiliations.
They urge the reader to consult the introductory essay by the editors ("The
Nature, the Teaching, and the Problems of Aesthetics") and the prefaces to

the several sections, since these have been formulated to further the clarity and effectiveness of the organization.

Another aim of the editors has been to avoid restricting the selections to the most inevitable candidates for anthologies, to the obvious classics of recent aesthetics readily available in the English language. In a discipline developing as rapidly as aesthetics is at present in our country, they thought it desirable to include a number of essays of merit whose influence has been lessened by the fact that they have until now appeared only in journals. They also thought it desirable, for the same reason, to include a number of essays by younger aestheticians who have begun to make important contributions but who have not yet achieved the stature of writers of Croce's and Santayana's generation. In a total view of the best of contemporary aesthetics, these inclusions of periodical materials and of recent work by younger but mature theorists form an important supplement to the selections from established aestheticians whose work, while still rich in nutritive value, has already entered into the consolidated achievements broadly accepted by students of the field.

The editors also recognize the contributions to contemporary aesthetics which criticism in the arts, especially modern literary criticism, has made. Therefore they have included, along with more formally philosophical selections, some pieces of critical writing which have repercussions on aesthetics. The purposeful mingling of these materials, it is hoped, will show the reader that the barrier between these two closely related and mutually dependent disciplines is an artificial one. For similar reasons, the editors have tried also not to overlook the contributions which the self-conscious artist can make to the literature of aesthetics. They regret that limitations of space prevented them from including more work by critics and artists, without reference to which the philosopher may tend to lose touch with the actual problems of art of his day and merely concern himself with problems generated by his theoretical agreements and disagreements with other philosophers, thus running the risk of becoming abstract and aprioristic in the worst sense of these terms.

If a book of this kind is to attain its greatest usefulness, it has need of a careful and fairly exhaustive index to which the reader may turn with confidence. And a word is necessary here to explain the results of the editors' endeavors to index their material. The heterogeneity of the material collected, the limitations of space, and the desire to keep the index from extending itself until it became a minute and exhaustive analysis of each essay, forced the editors to resort to arbitrary criteria in order to determine what to include and what to leave out. While this arbitrariness will at times seem objectionable or even inconsistent to some readers, it can be urged in its defense that the editors sought to furnish an index in which the maximum of usability was joined with a minimum of wastefulness. And general rules of procedure to attain this end inevitably carry with them a certain unevenness in individual cases.

Almost all references in the text to aestheticians and critics can be found in the index. But those who are cited in the text merely as random examples of a class of thinkers and those who are merely glanced at in a footnote have been excluded. In the case of references to artists, since such references are innumerable in most theoretical essays concerned with the arts, these have been indexed only if the particular reference is sufficiently extensive to reward the reader who may be interested in what the writer has to say about the artist in question. However, with both aestheticians and artists, it is the man who is indexed and not his work, again for purposes of saving space. To mention titles as well as authors and artists would have almost doubled the size of the index. Thus, for example, a critical discussion of *Antony and Cleopatra* may be found only by tracing the various entries under Shakespeare in the index. The only titles to be found in the index are those of the books from which the selections were taken and those of the journal articles here included. To those whom the index does not serve as it was meant to, the editors can only plead that it was not a task whose importance was underestimated, nor a responsibility that was lightly assumed.

Finally the editors should like to express their gratitude to Professor Marvin Fox of The Ohio State University, who generously undertook the onerous job of furnishing translations of foreign phrases; and their profound indebtedness to their wives, Dorothy Vivas and Joan Krieger, who aided them continually in an editorial task whose unending complexity made such help as indispensable as it was demanding.

Northwestern University   ELISEO VIVAS
University of Minnesota   MURRAY KRIEGER
26 December 1952

Acknowledgments

The editors desire to thank all those whose permissions to reprint material owned by them made this reader possible. Individual acknowledgments will be found in the appropriate footnotes to the various selections.

However, the editors are here especially anxious to acknowledge their gratefulness to the following for their generosity in allowing the reprinting of material whose copyrights they control: Aristotelian Society, Bollingen Foundation, Brandt and Brandt, British Psychological Society, University of Chicago Press, Clarendon Press, Harper and Brothers, Johns Hopkins University Press, *Journal of Aesthetics and Art Criticism, Journal of Philosophy, Kenyon Review,* Museum of Modern Art, *Philosophical Review, Revue Internationale de Philosophie,* Routledge and Kegan Paul, and *Thought.*

Table of Contents

The Problems of Aesthetics

Section One

THE DISCIPLINE
OF AESTHETICS

THE EDITORS
The Nature, the Teaching, and the
Problems of Aesthetics

§ *1*

"AESTHETICS" IS THE NAME customarily given to the theoretical and systematic exploration of the questions which arise when men
reflect on their interest in the beauty of nature and the products of the fine
arts. It has traditionally been considered one of the philosophic disciplines;
but, as we shall see below, many of the questions which the aesthetician asks
refer to matters of fact which belong to the domain of science or gradually
fall into it, as science advances. However, aesthetics is not a "science" or
a collection of "sciences" in the sense in which modern physicists and most
American social scientists use the term, because the aesthetician is not
merely confronted with a "theoretical" task but with a "practical" one, in
the Aristotelian sense of these terms. He seeks, through his influence on
criticism and education, to guide the development of taste, and, more indirectly, to guide the activity of the creative artist. So long as positive science
remains a continuous development of what it is today, and so long as the
normative or practical aspect of aesthetics is recognized, it will be necessary
to distinguish it from the sciences.

Aesthetics presupposes two types of gifts which popular prejudice assumes to be more or less incompatible: on the one hand, some experiences with, and a genuine interest in beauty and art and, on the other, a need to formulate that experience in theoretical terms, to clarify it, and to give it order. The questions which the aesthetician asks are suggested to him by men's actual commerce with beauty and art; when they are not, they tend to be factitious or merely verbal in the dyslogistic sense; but these questions generate in the aesthetician's mind others, which are subsidiary and which must be settled if those that first arose are to be disposed of satisfactorily. If the aesthetician does not have some actual experience with beauty, he will not be likely to believe those who, like Plato or Tolstoy, have attributed to it strong powers over the soul. But he is not solely interested in answering discrete questions. He obeys the philosopher's impulse to coordinate his answers into a systematic whole which is not only adequate to the facts of beauty but which is also adequate to all the other data which his diverse experiences thrust into his purview. As he seeks to satisfy the demands of systematic construction, his original questions tend to be modified and to recede; and as the inquiry proceeds they tend to be restated in a progressively more technical terminology. This is not peculiar to aesthetics, of course, but happens in the development of any inquiry, whether philosophic or scientific; but it is a tendency that does not make the aesthetician popular with the artist, the critic, or the public.

There is another reason for his unpopularity. When God confounded men at Babel, it seems that He put a greater curse on aestheticians than he did on other men—a curse the historian did not record but which can be inferred from subsequent events. And the upshot is that what appears at first as an attempt at communication between the aesthetician and his readers often turns out to be, on scrutiny, pure soliloquy. Charity advises us to assume that these soliloquies are understood by those who utter them, but this is a hypothesis which we must hold on faith and sometimes in the teeth of the facts.

We cannot therefore altogether blame those who find the aesthetician an unpleasant companion. The artist is interested in making objects of beauty, and not in a thorough and systematic grasp of the meaning of his activity. The way in which his mind works, his habits and interests, keep him on the concrete and the particular, and tend to blind him to the large number of unexamined assumptions which influence his activity. The critic is also oriented toward particulars, since he is concerned with gaining a firmer possession of the object of beauty than can be gained without the aid of trained powers of discrimination. For the former the making of the object is a basic need, like eating or drinking. Such needs do not seem to him to call for an explanation from those who experience them, but for satisfaction.

It is natural that the artist resents the aesthetician, who does not seem to him to lead him directly to the satisfaction of his creative impulse, but routes him off along the unimproved side roads of philosophy, on an uncomfortable trip which does not seem to get anywhere. That without such tours his own creative activity and our commerce with his product would not be as rewarding as they are, could be demonstrated to him, but he does not have the patience to follow the proof. The critic is usually a little more tolerant. He has found that the aesthetician is sometimes helpful to him. But his interest in pure speculation soon flags. The pull of actual beauty is one he cannot and does not want to resist. The flights of the philosopher into a realm of abstractions seem to him as often to obfuscate as to help him grasp the "splendor of form shining on the proportionate parts of matter" which radiates from a Maillol or a Renoir. They do not seem to him always to justify the weariness they produce by improving in a noticeable way his capacity to capture his dream. The critic ends up by confessing that he can take the aesthetician in doses that must be small and far between.

The difficulty which we encounter when we try to justify the discipline of aesthetics increases the closer we look into its domain. For the man who undertakes its investigation needs a discouragingly large assortment of skills and of knowledge that very few men are versatile enough to possess. Unlike the physicist or the chemist, if the aesthetician is comprehensive in his interest, as he must be if he is to be systematic, he finds himself confronted by diverse questions which can only be attacked with a very wide range of information. He must ask questions about the nature of the talent which the artist possesses, about the structure of the object of beauty, and about the source of its power and its effects on the spectator. To answer even these few questions he requires versatile knowledge; he must be a psychologist, a sociologist, a critic of sorts, who has a working knowledge of what men like Barnes, Tovey, and Brooks discover about actual paintings and musical compositions and poems. Nor is this all, for insofar as beauty affects the life of men, the aesthetician must be acquainted with what Aristotle called the most authoritative art and that which is most truly the master art—the art of the moralist or legislator.

Some will argue that the aesthetician does not require the latter art, which gives him the authority to make normative judgments of value. For it is not his business, they will say, to do more than the physical scientist or the bacteriologist attempts: to keep rigorously within the range, so to speak, of purely descriptive questions—which is a way of saying that his business is not to tell us how we ought to respond, or what we ought to enjoy, or what we ought to exhibit, but what we do enjoy and exhibit, and the determining causes of our preferences and choices. Now this is, as such things go, a perfectly plausible conception of the burden that philosophers ought to assume, and it would seem that it is put forth on two grounds, either of which has undisputed strength. It is argued that the aesthetician, by keeping to what we have inadequately termed "purely descriptive questions," avoids the interminable wrangles about norms and thus gains in clarity what he may lose in legislative authority. And it is also argued that the "ought," whether aesthetic or moral, rests on attitudes which in the last analysis are themselves impervious to rational exploration and suasion. Those who take such a position have a formidable argument; but this Introduction is not the place to discuss its merits. Here it is enough to point to the controversy, for so long as it is not settled—so long as there exist different opinions, each of which has its own plausibility—honest editors are obliged to give the major representative positions an opportunity to present their cases.

Let us allow then that it is wise to consider the problem of the validity of objective normative judgments. But what shall we say in view of the multiplicity and heterogeneity of the problems which confront the aesthetician? Can we speak of one discipline? If we do so, what we do is dump a great number of heterogeneous problems in the lap of one man who, since he undertakes to be a jack of all trades, cannot be a master of any one of them. The best such a man can do is to build a pseudo-system, since he does not employ a single method consistently and since he builds with scraps of second-hand facts that do not stand rigorous investigation. Would it not be better to leave each problem to the science that can deal with it competently, waiting until each is ready to do so, instead of speculating on questions which are, or will some day be, susceptible of scientific solution? Were such a plan to be followed, there would still be enough work to keep the philosopher busy, since he would still have the problem of clarifying the language of aesthetics.

The advantage of handing over to scientists problems which can be satisfactorily solved only by their methods is, of course, obvious. The hope is that to the extent that facts are substituted for fancies as the coin of discourse the curse of Babel will be reduced and as a result a greater degree of substantive agreement on basic questions will be reached. It is an open question, however, and one too serious in its consequences to be solved without the most thorough investigation, whether the advantage envisaged may not be bought at too high a price—whether the disadvantages that would almost certainly have to be reckoned with would not wipe out the gains envisaged. Anyone who is acquainted with the meagre results of so-called "scientific" aesthetics since Fechner's day is justified in arguing that science can very frequently give us clear results which are nevertheless trivial. But whether it does or not, this much we can be fairly certain about—that if we were to hand over to scientists the various factual areas of our investigation and were to wait till they came back to us with their results, the hope of contriving a practical theory of art would have to be postponed to a distant future. The result would in turn be that criticism and the docent task would become even more incoherent than they are at the moment. While the importance of this problem, on which it is not at the moment possible to take dogmatic sides, cannot be overestimated, it is not one that can be settled here. Suffice to say that the editors have proceeded on what seemed to be the wisest editorial policy open to them and have assumed that aesthetics is a single discipline. The assumption is logically justified by the fact that the solution of any problem, whether speculative or factual, depends on the solutions arrived at for other problems. It is true that, so considered, aesthetics is made up of questions which belong to disparate disciplines. But it is at least desirable for practical reasons to keep them together, so to speak, under one tent.

The domain of aesthetics is, then, the heterogeneous conglomeration of questions which arise from a thinker's interest in beauty and in art. We shall try below to define these questions in general terms. Here it is desirable to emphasize that the student, confronted with so many and so diverse problems, ought not to expect to solve them in the same successful way in which the mathematician or the physicist solves his problems. The aesthetician seeks clarity, and to the best of his ability he tries to keep his eyes on the facts. But the facts in aesthetics cannot be exhibited unambiguously, nor can they be discovered by those who lack training and sensibility of a highly specialized kind. Nor is the aim of the aesthetician to discover invariant relations which can be formulated in such a way as to be open to test in terms of prediction. He seeks something else—something which seems much more refractory to satisfactory definition and which may remain, after our best efforts, ineradicably vague: he seeks an intellectual grasp, a comprehension, in the almost literal sense of the word, a gathering together in a single picture, of the various solutions to his several problems in their complex interrelations. If his results lack the quality of those achieved by the positive scientist, he can console himself by remembering what Aristotle said. There are some subjects, he said, that "admit of much variety and fluctuation of opinion," and in them "We must be content . . . to indicate the truth roughly and in outline," since we are "speaking about things which are only for the most part true and with premises of the same kind to reach conclusions that are no better." Aristotle goes on to say that the conclusions should be accepted in the spirit in which they are offered, "for it is the mark of an educated man to look for precision in each class of things just so far as the nature of the subject admits; it is evidently equally foolish to accept probable reasoning from a mathematician and to demand from a rhetorician scientific proofs." The fact that the discipline of aesthetics admits of much fluctuation of opinion does not make its teaching impossible, nor does it diminish the importance of the questions it poses. That importance is practical, and the man interested in the clarification of his commerce with art and in its guidance cannot wait till the discipline is perfected by the successful application of the methods of science to it. Until such perfection is achieved, he has to do with what help he can get, since the alternative would be to go without any.

§ 2

There seem to be three distinct ways in which aesthetics can be taught: historically; through the various "approaches" to the discipline, as represented by writers of prominent "schools"; and through an analysis of the distinct problems which, in their interrelatedness, constitute the domain of aesthetics. Each of these ways has its advantages and its inherent short-comings; each has its faithful advocates; and each is no doubt based on a defensible conception of the role which instruction in aesthetics ought to play in a liberal education. However the first two may be defended, the third, which is the way advocated by the editors of this reader, is grounded on the conviction that a course in aesthetics ought to attempt to develop the student's skill in dealing with the perplexities which he comes up against when he reflects seriously—or, in other words, theoretically—on the phe-nomenon of beauty and art. This is to say that a course in aesthetics ought to do for the student what any course in philosophy ought to do: it ought to develop the student's awareness of those intellectual difficulties of which he is as a rule unconscious or not deeply enough conscious, in any given area of human concern; and it ought to develop skill in dealing with these difficulties. The primary aim of a course in aesthetics ought not to be to impart to the student knowledge of the answers that have been proposed to the questions that have been asked; nor to impart knowledge of the succes-sion of schools that have arisen in the history of aesthetic speculation; nor of the one system that the teacher happens to favor as containing the true answers. The primary aim ought to be first, to develop the ability on the part of the student to recognize a problem where one exists, and then to impart to him knowledge of how to tackle it—how to isolate it before he proceeds to solve it, and yet how to keep it interrelated to the others, since the solution of any one affects the solutions of the rest. To this end knowledge of at least the highlights of the history of aesthetics and of the important systematic approaches to the subject is, in the long run, indispensable; but it must remain instrumental. Knowledge of those approaches which are significant because they are still influential can be imparted through a discussion of the important solutions that have been offered to the several problems; while the history of aesthetics can best be taught after the student has devel-oped an interest in the problems and is able to realize that the great thinkers of the past have, each in his own way, something of value to offer towards the solution of those problems with which he deals.

Ideally such a course would include not merely discussions of all the problems, but of all the influential basic solutions offered for each of these problems. What is meant by a "basic" solution in this context is one that is controlled by systematic methodological presuppositions. Thus such a course would constitute a comprehensive and comparative analysis of the various systems of aesthetics. It is clear therefore that the fulfillment of this ideal would require a linguistic equipment on the part of the student that he rarely possesses, time that the curriculum does not allow the teacher, and a library which only very few institutions are likely to be able to put at his disposal. A rough approximation to such an ideal, but in view of the difficulties under which we labor the only one possible, is to use a reader—a compilation of essays which offers a few typical discussions of each problem from philosophically contrasting points of view.

But a course which is content with less than the ideal runs instantly into a barrage of objections all launched from the ideal perimeter. For the compromises into which it is forced, like all compromises, are arbitrary, and at bottom remain unsatisfactory. This is all the more true of a book of readings, since it is not to be expected that it will satisfy the disparate demands that will be made of it. Such a book could achieve a high degree of organization if the discussions of the several problems were carried on from a limited number of points of view consistently represented in all the selections adopted. The result would be a treatment of all the problems of aesthetics in terms of the basic assumptions of a number of basic approaches, say, realism, materialism, idealism, pragmatism, positivism, Thomism, and other well defined philosophic "schools." But when the editors began to survey the field with the idea of making such selections, they soon discovered that it was not possible to turn up essays on each one of the problems written in terms of the several schools of philosophy that deserved to be represented in their book. Aestheticians, unless they write aesthetics "from above," are not always careful to examine their philosophic commitments, and the editors had difficulty enough finding contrasting discussions of each problem which, so to speak, kept relatively steadily on the target and which lent themselves to incorporation for other reasons in the reader. In view of this situation the editors decided to select several treatments of each problem which were sufficiently contrasting to envisage it from divergent perspectives, irrespective of whether the underlying assumptions of the writers selected were pure or hybrid, or whether they corresponded with the underlying assumptions of writers whose work was incorporated in another section.

Nor was this the only practical problem that the editors encountered when they decided to be satisfied with less than the ideal. They searched for more or less self-contained discussions of each problem; but aestheticians have seldom taken the trouble to analyze their domain in terms of the distinguishable problems which could be discerned within it. As a result, it is often difficult, and sometimes altogether impossible, to discover good treatments of a problem, which both keep the problem distinct and yet do not obfuscate its relations to other problems. We shall indicate below some of the reasons why aestheticians fail to unravel the various questions which can be distinctly asked. This is not to say that aestheticians are under obligation to elucidate all the problems of aesthetics. There is no methodological law prohibiting a man from restricting himself to the elucidation of one or two of them. And excellent essays have been written, like the classical contribution made by Hume *On the Standard of Taste,* which are discussions of single problems. Many essays confined to single problems are to be found in this book. But whatever the limited value of such efforts, ultimately the value of their contribution to the discipline will depend on the coherence and lucidity of their implicit assumptions. This value can in turn be tested by the way in which the assumptions allow for the systematic development of solutions to other problems with which the writer may not be concerned but which require solution in order to achieve a comprehensive theory of art.

Another difficulty which a less than ideal treatment of the subject in terms of problems has to face is of a different order. The selections compiled in this book represent treatments of the problems by various writers, and this makes it inevitable that they represent various degrees of relative difficulty to the student. Some can be read and digested without much labor on the student's part, but others will require some effort. It would be better if the selections all represented a more or less identical level of difficulty. But this could be secured—if at all—only by sacrificing quality and even content, frequently, to this desideratum; and it would have led in practice to passing over some excellent but difficult essays—for which adequate equivalents, written in a more elementary way, were not to be found. The editors decided to adopt selections which represented pointed discussions of the problems, disregarding the fact that a few of them are not elementary. They bethought themselves that the serious teacher would approve of this decision. For one of the objectives he may wish to realize in a course in aesthetics is that of introducing his students to readings that require some degree of effort to master. With some classes, however, the teacher may be forced to present his own analysis of some of these pieces as introduction to their being read; and it is even possible that with some classes he may be forced to skip some of the readings altogether because they are too difficult.

Another difficulty encountered by the editors, which was impossible to surmount, was the fact that all too frequently they had to exclude excellent essays because they were too long for the book and could not be cut. Their

inclusion would have led to the exclusion of others which the editors could
not bring themselves to sacrifice.

Again, the editors have confined themselves exclusively to contemporary
material. This is not a "difficulty" properly speaking, but it undeniably is
the result of an arbitrary choice which will be disapproved of by many
aestheticians. A full account of the grounds on which it was made cannot
be given here, nor would it be of interest to the reader. Suffice it to indicate
several practical advantages of choosing contemporary material. One is that
it lightens the burden of the teacher, who can confine his lexicographical
burden to a more or less manageable task. Another is that by keeping within
a single age or period the anthology gains in unity, because the various selections, however conflicting among themselves philosophically, all have a
greater similarity of tone than they would have if they ranged from Plato
to our day. There is one more advantage that ought to be mentioned; contemporary material possesses a greater degree of intrinsic interest than historical material. These are not grounds on which our choice could be adequately justified, but then, anthologies can only be put together on the basis
of arbitrary choices, nor can editors hope to please all readers in every respect.

In spite of all these difficulties the editors are convinced that the advantages of a book of readings organized in terms of problems more than
compensate for its inherent shortcomings. The teacher who is interested
seriously in aesthetics cannot ignore the systematic approach. But if the
student is taught a single system he is not taught to think but is indoctrinated.
Systematic coherence can be achieved in and through the analysis of various
solutions of the several problems which constitute the domain of the discipline. The claim, therefore, is made that a book of representative readings
on the problems of aesthetics can be taught by different kinds of teachers of
different philosophical affiliations, since the various readings can be presented
by any teacher in such a way as to bring out what he takes to be the best
solution of the problem. Nor does such a method deprive the teacher of
presenting his own point of view as the one which obviates the difficulties
which he sees in the others. The various essays included in each section converge on a given problem. And out of the variety of approaches the editors
believe that it is possible for the teacher to define the problem with a satisfactory degree of clarity and in its full density and complexity, much better
than he could do if he were dependent on the contributions of a single
writer. They also believe that it is thus possible for a teacher to disclose the
rich diversity of assumptions and presuppositions which aestheticians have
brought to bear on their perplexities.

Another advantage of a course taught in terms of problems is that it enables the student to acquire a comprehensive grasp of the whole field. Again

such a course ought to contribute to the methodological sophistication of the student; for in the analysis of each problem it is possible to show how the same subject matter is susceptible of treatment by several methods, and what the advantages and disadvantages of each one of these are. It is possible to show the student also how much remains to be done in aesthetics. For this must be said, in fairness, of the whole field: since it emerges out of a situation in which men of different interests—artists, critics, amateurs, historians, and moralists—find themselves when confronted by the ubiquitous and important yet elusive facts of beauty and art, the subject matter of the discipline has not yet been satisfactorily clarified. It is possible that it will continue to resist clarification for as far into the future as we can see. The facts are not yet in, but even if they were the variety of shifting interests which prompt inquiry in aesthetics constantly makes for confusion. It is true that the confusion can be easily exaggerated; but it is more harmful to dissimulate it or to underestimate it.

A course in aesthetics ought to leave the student with a keen sense that the questions of aesthetics are easier asked than answered, and that "canned" answers are of little value if the interest of the student is serious and his commerce with art is authentic. This, the editors believe, the "problems" method can accomplish. The problems method does not deal primarily with systems studied historically; nor with the mutual interrelatedness of the parts of a system. It deals with the questions as these arise naturally, and with reference to the data from which they arise. It focuses primarily on subject matter and not on what various thinkers have said of it. And it can provide intrinsically and not fortuitously a corrective against the inherent human tendency to see a large field in terms of a private perspective.

§ 3

The problems of aesthetics can be defined analytically and in general terms. This does not mean that they can be solved in an a priori fashion. Aesthetics is an empirical discipline. The solution of its problems cannot be excogitated by the philosopher from innate principles in the way in which, let us say, Spinoza thought he could pull the universe out of his definitions and axioms. If we are to make any headway in aesthetics we have to refer to the facts, and these, we know, are not yet fully explored. What is meant is that the field can be delimited and the main questions can be formulated. This is done by analyzing the factors or components which are required in order that art-objects be produced and used in human society, for these factors are by now well enough known. The central terms which, in their mutual interrelations, generate the problems are not in question. What is in question is what these terms involve: what they are or how they are constituted, and how they interact with one another to produce the phenomena which become the data of aesthetics. But we are not ignorant of the identity of the terms themselves and of their nature in a primary, rough, way. We can state them exhaustively. They are, "artist," "aesthetic object," "spectator," and "society."

The object to which the spectator responds is made by an artist; but both artist and spectator are considerably more than isolated individuals whose interests are exclusively focused on the object of art. They both live in a society which makes all sorts of demands of them and on which they themselves depend, not merely for their experience with art but for all their other needs and satisfactions. They are connected with a cultural tradition which has historical depth, from which they derive language, attitudes, values, and to a great extent the very sensibilities with which they are endowed. They are thus in a very important sense the product of their society. On the other hand, their activities as artists affect through their art the society which moulds them. The man who enters into commerce with art—whether as creator or spectator—is not endowed with a mind that is an unexposed film newly prepared for the moment of perception during which the object imprints its image. He brings to the aesthetic transaction what he is; and the appearance of the object for him depends on a personality which is not only the product of social factors, but which is also modified to some extent by the object during the moment of intercourse with it. There is thus a complex, more or less reciprocal, if not always obvious, interrelationship between a man's aesthetic interests and the rest of his interests and modes of behavior. Nor do the terms "artist," "object," "spectator," conceived as functioning within "a social medium" that has an historical depth, exhaust the data; for the society in which the transaction takes place consists of institutions which "inform" bio-physical nature. From these terms, then—from the interrelationships between them and among them—arise the questions which, related in a systematic fashion, mark the field of aesthetic inquiry. In the following diagram all these factors are exhibited, and the relations among them define the general problems which make up the divisions of our inquiry.[1]

Before going into an analysis of the diagram it is desirable to make explicit two reservations. The first refers to the exclusion from the selections of any treatment of the problem of natural beauty. The editors have narrowed the

---

[1] This diagram was used by one of the editors in his own course in aesthetics for many years before he went to the University of Chicago. A somewhat similar analysis in terms of "art," "work," and "audience" is or was employed by the "Chicago school of criticism." The Chicagoans do not include the social medium and they distinguish between "art" and "work," but there are important similarities between their approach and that which is suggested by the following diagram. In any case the writers are indebted to the Chicago critics for helping them refine the distinctions they employ. See *Critics and Criticism,* ed. R. S. Crane (Chicago: University of Chicago Press, 1952).

discipline of aesthetics to include only the relation between the artist, his artifact, and those interested in the latter, within the social process. But many thinkers insist that the problem of natural beauty is one of the legitimate problems of aesthetics. It would be an expression of superfluous and unjustifiable dogmatism on the part of the editors were they to deny the legitimacy of the problem. Nevertheless the editors decided not to include any selections dealing with this problem. They make, however, the claim that the problem of natural beauty can be included in the diagram, for the latter is intended merely to tell us what the problems of aesthetics are and not to give us their

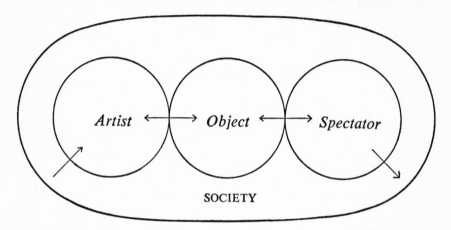

solution. The diagram cannot tell us who the maker of a given object is; and if an actual seascape, a rush of clouds over a mountain, a flower, a herd of browsing deer, are objects of aesthetic attention, as they may well be, there is a place for them under the circle labeled "object," even though it might precipitate a lively controversy among philosophers as to how they come by the aesthetic qualities which they exhibit. To be beautiful an object must needs possess certain traits or qualities, fundamental among which is the capacity of being grasped as an ordered whole. And it is a moot question whether these traits in a natural object can be grasped by a mind whose acquired habits of perception were not formed under the tutelage of aesthetic artifacts.

The second reservation refers to the exclusion of any selections on method as such. It was already asserted that the domain of aesthetics is conceived by the editors as including a number of heterogeneous disciplines. These can be classified into questions of meaning, normative problems and questions of fact. Nor do the latter fall under the domain of a single science; some pertain to psychology, some to physics, and still others fall within the purview of disciplines for which there is no single, widely used term, but whose data is distinctly historical. It can legitimately be argued that in a field that contains such bewildering heterogeneity of data the problem of method or methods of attack should necessarily loom large. This is not denied. Yet no selections on method have been included in this anthology. The reason for this is solely pedagogical. The editors are of the opinion that it would not have been profitable to give up their limited space to abstract discussions of method as such, since these are usually of little value from a teaching point of view. The teacher who is interested in introducing his students to methodological problems—and if he is a trained philosopher he cannot help but be—can bring to the attention of the students the various methods used by the various writers as he examines each writer's contributions.

The editors felt, however, that they had to deal with the problem which "psychological aesthetics" presents in a different manner. The serious and intense labor which psychologists have spent on aesthetics in the last seventy-five years cannot be ignored, even if, unfortunately, all this labor has panned out very little of genuine value to the aesthetician. On the other hand, the method—and it is the method, particularly in view of the paucity of the results, that would interest the serious student of aesthetics—cannot be exhibited by reproducing one or two articles. "Psychological aesthetics" is exemplified in this reader by the work on which Chandler reports and by many other writers, including Freud, Jung, Richards and others. But the field is so rich and what the psychologists attempt so varied that the editors thought it advisable to include Morgan's comprehensive article. The reader will find in it a useful survey of the work done in psychological aesthetics to date, a survey which is critical yet judicious, one which does not dismiss the potentialities of psychology for aesthetics, but which nevertheless points out clearly its weakness in the present stage of investigation. The reader seeking more knowledge than he can find in this article and its copious references will find it only in the experiments which are reported in the research journals.

These two reservations aside, we must turn to defining the problems of aesthetics through an analysis of our diagram. In this Introduction it is not necessary to define each of the problems in its full depth and complexity—that can be done only by a study of the selections under each heading, which are introduced by separate prefaces in which the problems are briefly sketched. What we need to do here is to analyze the diagram broadly in order to get a general view of the various problems with which the aesthetician is concerned. To do this let us read the diagram from left to right. We see that the first term that we encounter within the ellipse is the artist. He is first in order of history, since he is the maker of an object to which the spectator responds. With regard to him the student asks two types of questions, to which we can refer for convenience as "the intrinsic" and "the extrinsic." As regards the artist, the intrinsic questions seek light on his gifts and skills: what kind of talent is he endowed with, how does it differ from other talents; are his gifts innate or acquired; and by what kind of process is this experience transmuted and expressed in the work of art? We speak of the creative artist—do we intend to use the term "creative" literally, or does it merely stand for complex and subtle processes of association, whose laws still baffle us? It is a well known fact that we know very little more about the hidden way in which the artist transmutes his experience than did Plato, who seemingly offered in all seriousness the hypothesis that the poet was possessed as an explanation of his gift. We have considerably more factual data than Plato seems to have had access to. We know enough to reject with a modicum of confidence some hypotheses that once had some plausibility, such as that attributed to mechanists, according to which the creative activity is explained as a reorganizing or reshuffling of the data acquired from experience. This is too simple. But the heart of the mystery we have not yet succeeded in splitting: we know almost nothing about how the artist assimilates his experience and recreates it in a way that adds new forms and substance to the world as it offers itself to aesthetic attention.

The extrinsic questions as regards the artist refer to his nonaesthetic relations to those who, as Ducasse has it, "consume" his product, his art, and to the society which more or less generously sustains him and enables him to carry on. They are here chiefly questions about the moral obligation he has towards his society and that his society has towards him. But these obviously cannot be intelligently elucidated until we know the value of his product and the function it performs in culture. This is mentioned as an instance of the fact that while the problems of aesthetics can be distinguished and must be discussed each in its own terms and by means of its own method, they interilluminate one another.

Next in the diagram, still reading from left to right, we find the object of art—the product of the artist's activity and the means by which he conveys what he wishes to say. About it we can also ask two types of general questions, the intrinsic and the extrinsic. The former refers to the structure of the object, the aspects of it which observation can discriminate and to which, either singly or in interrelation, can be traced the complex burden of communication the artist accomplishes. But at this point it is necessary to draw a distinction between aesthetics and criticism. What inquiry seeks to elicit, if it is to be kept within the domain of aesthetics and not allowed to go into the domain of criticism, are the generic traits of all art objects, and the way in which these can be classified on the basis of their differentiae, the nature of the means of expression and of what is expressed and the relationship between the former and the latter. But while aesthetics must be distinguished from criticism, it would be injudicious to draw well-defined frontiers between the two activities as if they were *de jure* as separate as they sometimes tend to be *de facto*. Between aesthetics and criticism no separation ought to exist. It is true that if we observe the actual behavior of some critics and of some aestheticians we get the impression that there is an Iron Curtain between the two areas. But this curtain, like the other, is a political barrier; and one which works to the disadvantage of both criticism and aesthetics and to the advantage of no other discipline. The aesthetician goes or ought to go for his subject matter among others to the critic; he functions as critic when he goes for it to the art product directly available to him. And the critic uses conceptions which are examined and criticized by the aesthetician, but whose utility is tested by the critic. Custom, for reasons which are more or less obvious, assigns to aesthetics the region of abstract analysis and theoretical system building, and to criticism the discrimination of meanings and values expressed in actual objects of art in order to put them in the possession of the spectator.

In the history of aesthetics this was not always the practice and the question can be answered in two ways as to whether one of the earliest and most influential treatises on aesthetics that we possess in the West the *Poetics* of Aristotle, is a contribution to criticism, a handbook on how to write tragedies, or an unfinished treatise in the aesthetics of poetry. Somewhat similar remarks apply to Longinus. Nor is this true of the ancients only. Disregarding differences of accomplishment, it is no less true of contemporaries like Fry and Bell. It is also true of Bradley, and outside the English world, of innumerable figures, the most prominent of whom today is perhaps Croce. Thus there is no ground for the contempt that critics sometimes express for aesthetics. And it is to ignorance or neglect of aesthetics that we can frequently trace the failure of critics endowed with high powers of discrimination. As the result of such ignorance or neglect the critic often carries on his work in terms of theoretical assumptions which are sometimes mutually exclusive, sometimes altogether false, and more often than not too vague to be practically serviceable. But the critic's failure to notice his close dependence on theoretical issues is bound to increase if the aesthetician, on his part, yields to the tendency to atomize knowledge by separating linguistic analysis from normative problems and questions of fact.

It is desirable to note in passing that while the question as to the structure of the object constitutes a distinct problem, it is not one that can be solved in isolation from the question as to the nature of the aesthetic experience. Psychologists have attempted to classify "the varieties of the aesthetic experience." But whether there are several or only one, the question, "What is the nature of the aesthetic object?" cannot be settled satisfactorily until we are able to distinguish the aesthetic experience or experiences from the non-aesthetic, since it is obviously through the aesthetic experience that we determine whether an object possesses aesthetic quality or not. This, of course, does not prejudge the question as to whether the aesthetic values which characterize the object of the experience are subjective or objective.

As in the case of the artist, the extrinsic questions that we can ask about the object of art refer to the relationships that obtain between it and the society on which it has other than aesthetic effects. It is not difficult for contemporary man to see that the artist has a set of moral relations with his society which stem, not from his duty as citizen or as member of a family or church or the like, but from the fact that he demands of his society that it allow him to function as artist and that the society in some manner meet the demand. But it seems very difficult for a large number of men to see that the same is true of the object of art. It functions intrinsically as art when it becomes, as we say, the occasion of an aesthetic experience in the spectator. But it functions extrinsically when through the aesthetic experience it affects the spectator's values or his sensibilities or outlook. That art has such effects is today generally recognized. But art also functions extrinsically in another way. For a society that recognizes aesthetic activity as valuable—and Franz Boas tells us that there are no known societies that do not recognize the value of art—gives art some sort of place, usually a high place, in the hierarchy of the values it compels, or allows, its members to realize. The question as to what place art ought to have, and as a consequence, the practical question as to how much of the energy of the society ought to go into its cultivation and its maintenance—these and related questions fall distinctly within the field of moral speculation. -

The next term in the diagram is the spectator. As in the case of the artist and of the object, we can ask about the spectator both intrinsic and extrinsic questions. The intrinsic refer to his response to the object. These are psychological questions, and what they try to elicit is whether there are discriminable differences between our reaction to, or our experience of, an aesthetic object and our reactions to, or experiences of, other kinds of objects—moral, religious, cognitive. And if there are such differences, what do they consist of? But the impact of the art object on the spectator gives rise not only to a question about the nature of his response but also to one about the value of that response. This latter question is ambiguous and refers to two problems: for we may want to know what the value of the response or experience is considered in abstraction from other experiences of the same subject; and what the value of the effects of that experience is after the subject turns away from the object and goes about his other business. The former is an intrinsic problem, the latter an extrinsic one. However, this is too simple, for it is possible to ask these questions as mere questions of fact—as such they are difficult enough; but it is also possible to ask them as normative questions.

We can ask, What are in fact the values derived from commerce with art by an individual or a society; and we can also ask, What ought to be, under more or less clearly specified ideal conditions, the value derived from art?

We have suggested that as regards artist, object, and spectator, questions of both an intrinsic and an extrinsic nature arise. The readings, however, have not been placed in the order in which these questions have been discussed here. The intrinsic questions constitute Sections III, IV, V, and VI of the book, and the extrinsic, as explained in the Preface to Section VII, have been put together in one group. In what order these questions are taken up does not seem to be of moment. What is of importance is that the various questions be exhibited in their discreteness as well as in their organic relations to one another.

These, then, are the problems of aesthetics. It remains to point out succinctly what advantages are to be gained by analyzing them in advance of their resolution. A total grasp of the problems generated by the complex interrelationships between the terms which we placed in our diagram discourages the tendency to envisage the discipline in a partial manner. And it reveals with ease partiality on the part of others. Aesthetics, as it is cultivated, is usually envisaged from the exclusivistic standpoint of one of the terms—artist, object, spectator, or society. The result is not only incomplete analysis of the field but, frequently, confusion, which is a fault not of commission but of omission. Thus Croce, and with him other idealists, led by their philosophic assumptions, collapse the question of the nature of the created object, and thus minimize the importance of externalizing the aesthetic vision in or through matter, which other philosophies conceive to exist independently of the experiencing mind. When idealists face the problem of externalization of the creative vision they are forced to classify it as essentially a nonaesthetic problem. On the other hand, Matisse is an instance of a man who discusses aesthetics from the standpoint of a dominating interest. The editors selected his piece—which has many genuine merits and still retains its freshness after all these years—because it throws light on the nature of painting: they believe that it can be read to give the student in generic terms an idea of what a painting is. But it would be possible to make a good case for putting it in the section on the creative act. And the reason is that the author, writing as an artist on his art, views the object, naturally enough, not as the spectator looks at it, as a canvas hanging on a wall, but as it is produced by himself out of inward felt needs which he externalizes with materials that have to be manipulated technically. It is not altogether an exaggeration to say that Matisse, in considering the object which he makes, tends to be an idealist of sorts, since in his mind the distinction is blurred between the color—the colored paste which he squeezes out of a tube and daubs on the canvas—and his gradually growing inward vision of the picture, as he puts one color next to another already daubed on the canvas. Thus Matisse shuttles rather freely and sometimes even ambiguously, between the canvas and the vision or image that he is seeking to externalize, and for him, as painter, the two are one.

Other writers are so exclusively concerned with the public object that they have little or nothing to say of interest as regards either the creative activity of the artist or the aesthetic response, and the effects of the object on society. Prall seems to fall into this class. His chief contribution consists in his analysis of aesthetic surface and the way in which, through it, the object conveys what it does. He has very little to say on the nature of the aesthetic experience and his interest in the creative process is very limited. However, the statements he makes on these topics seem to be susceptible of systematic development. The limitations he sets on his investigations are not, therefore, open to criticism. Still other writers are interested in the intrinsic effects of the object on the spectator, to the exclusion of the after-effects. These are the men who in one way or another take a position of art for art's sake. Still others, of whom Tolstoy and the Marxists are perhaps the best examples, are exclusively interested in the extrinsic effects of art, and tend frequently to deny, as a consequence, the intrinsic value of the experience. Neither those who exclusively emphasize the intrinsic nor those who are exclusively interested in the extrinsic effects of art can successfully resolve the problem of morality and art.

Because a survey of the problems of aesthetics such as we have undertaken enables us to discover the selective emphasis of various writers, it leads us also to investigate the causes for this emphasis. Sometimes, as was noted in the case of Matisse, it seems plausible to suggest that the cause is practical and not theoretical. Doubtless, it is Matisse's dominating interest in his activity as painter that leads him to select the subject matter of his discussion. But in some cases the emphasis seems determined by philosophical considerations. And sometimes, of course, by both. It is clearly his philosophic presuppositions that lead Maritain to consider as mere means the manipulative activity of the artist in the creation of the object. And his presuppositions lead to Alexander's interest in the resistance of the material as a factor in the achieved expressiveness of the object. A case finally in which both philosophic and practical considerations cooperate to determine his selective emphasis seems to be that of Dewey. In *Art as Experience* the precise relation between artist-object-spectator is hard to disentangle. One of the reasons for this seems to be Dewey's interest in the problem of education and in the fact (intimately related, of course, to the foregoing) that he views the painter, whom he has chiefly in mind when he speaks of the artist, from the standpoint of the gallery goer. The other reason is that he brings to the solution of the aesthetic problems the ready-made epistemology of the objective-relativist. This is neither a fault nor a virtue. It is mentioned to explain the difficulty a man of different epistemological commitments has in understanding Dewey's analysis.

But perhaps the greatest advantage of a comprehensive grasp of all of the problems of aesthetics is that it enables us to perceive the futility of attempting to solve any one problem by itself without some sort of reference to the others. We have already seen in regard to some of the problems we have surveyed that their solutions depend on the solution of others. This is but a way of saying that in spite of the heterogeneity of the problems and the diversity of the methods which must be brought to bear on their solutions, aesthetics is not a collection of disparate disciplines, but a single, systematic one. Thus a systematic analysis of the problems of aesthetics is a critical tool by means of which one can be led to grasp what an author is about and exactly where his strength and his weaknesses lie. This constitutes the strongest claim that can be made for a course organized on such an analysis.

LOUIS ARNAUD REID

Artists, Critics, and Philosophers [1]

Few quarrels, it is said, are more bitter than family quarrels, and few jealousies more profound than those between parties who have, without always recognising it, some important cause in common. The very intensity of the interest in an end, produces an intensity of interest in the means to the end, so that when intellectual or other differences about means arise, they are apt to swamp all sense of common interest in the common object or good. We have only to think of the frequent violence of religious, or of political, opinions to furnish ourselves with ample illustration of this truth.

Three parties there are who may be said to have an interest, whether recognised or not, in the fact of aesthetic experience. [2] They are the artists,

---

[1] From Louis Arnaud Reid, *A Study in Aesthetics*, pp. 13–28. Copyright, 1931, by Unwin Brothers Ltd., and used by permission of The Macmillan Company and George Allen & Unwin Ltd. (Eds.)
[2] I will leave out the lover of "natural beauty" till Chapter XIV, which is reserved

the critics, and the aesthetic theorists, the theorists being either philosophers or psychologists, or both. It is indubitable that these three groups do have in common the fact of interest in aesthetic experience. On the other hand, their different relations respectively to this fact tend to obscure their community and their family relatedness to one another. It is not, as with those whose interest is mainly political, or religious, a matter of different opinions about means to a common end. It is rather a matter of different relations of different minds to the same thing. Very roughly, the artist desires to *feel* an aesthetic experience by making something beautiful, the critic desires to *recognise* it through beautiful art-objects, and the philosopher [3] desires to *comprehend* it. These interests are indeed so patently different that, in spite of the community of object between them, the artists, the critics, and the philosophers might be content to follow each their own paths were it not for a certain interrelation between their respective activities, concerning which a good deal of confusion, and often of resulting jealousy and friction, is apt to arise. As in these quarrels it is the philosopher who most frequently finds himself attacked, it is necessary, before entering upon any discussion of aesthetic philosophy, to remove, as far as may be, entangling and prejudicing misunderstandings.

The philosopher is sometimes attacked by the artist as an interfering meddler who tries to teach artists their proper business, by laying down a priori laws about matters concerning which he is unfit to judge. The artist has also been known to attack the critic for very much the same reasons, whilst the critic finds fault with the philosopher for meddling with *his* affairs. Let us investigate the grounds of these quarrels between artist and philosopher, artist and critic, and critic and philosopher.

The artist's complaint against the critic arises chiefly from temperament. The artist is creative, and in the glow of achievement he naturally tends to feel angry with the critic when the latter regards his work coldly or adversely. "What right has this fellow," he may say, "to find fault with me when he himself is (it may be) incompetent to compose a sonata or write a sonnet or a play, or put paint decently upon canvas?" The artist's complaint is natural, requires no explanation, and it is likely to vary with the smiles or the frowns of the critic.

With the philosopher, the artist as such has naturally less commerce. Artists may have their own philosophical views, but when they run across philosophers who chance to be interested in the philosophical problems underlying the artist's work and experience, they often find their jargon in-

---

for him. This exception holds good throughout, and may be made quite without prejudice to the question of "natural" beauty.

[3] I shall take the philosopher here as the type of aesthetic theorist. His relation to the psychologist will be discussed below.

comprehensible, or, if not wholly incomprehensible, either dull or wrong-headed. Artists there are, of course, who possess a *flair* for abstract inquiry. But the artist, *qua* artist, is concerned with making, and not with pulling ideas to pieces in abstract inquiry. Abstract inquiry, the artist tends to think, is a tedious business compared with the excitements of creating. If we are to theorise, let us do it quickly, and relevantly to the matter in hand, without introducing vague generalisations which can help nobody.

The artist's opinion of the philosopher is not of great importance, just because the artist's job is to produce art, and not to define or to attack philosophy (or indeed to discuss it at all). The artist is forgiven all irritabili-ties of temperament if only he does create well what it is in him to create. The critic's opinion of the philosopher (we need not here consider the critic's relation to the artist) is, on the other hand, more important, because, although the critic deals on the one hand with works of art, the critic is also a writer or a speaker, and deals in ideas about art. He thus approaches, if he does not at some points cover, the same ground as the philosopher.

That the interests of the critic and the philosopher very often overlap, I am going to suggest. But the critic is by no means always so aware as he ought to be of the close relation of his calling, on the one side of it, to philosophy. He has been known, as we said, to attack philosophy. There is a critic of a certain type who is only too ready to ask, Why should we analyse our experiences of beautiful things at all? Why should we not be content with our feelings and emotions about beautiful things? Is not each beautiful thing unique, and so elusive that it stands by itself? And is not the attempt to set up abstract standards or general principles only a revelation of ig-norance of the uniqueness of each beautiful thing? Is philosophical analysis not murdering to dissect?

This point of view is very clearly expressed by Walter Pater in the preface to his *Renaissance*. "Many attempts," he says, "have been made by writers on art and poetry to define beauty in the abstract, to express it in the most general terms, to find some universal formula for it. The value of these attempts has most often been in the suggestive and penetrating things said by the way. Such discussions help us little to enjoy what has been well done in art and poetry, to discriminate between what is more and what is less excellent in them, or to use words like beauty, excellence, art, poetry, with a more precise meaning than they would otherwise have. Beauty, like all other qualities presented to human experience, is relative; and the defi-nition of it becomes unmeaning and useless in proportion to its abstract-ness. To define beauty, not in the most abstract but in the most concrete terms possible, to find not its universal formula, but the formula which expresses most adequately this or that special manifestation of it, is the aim of the true student of aesthetics.

" 'To see the object as in itself it really is,' has been justly said to be the aim of all true criticism whatever." And he who does this distinctly, who can experience vividly, "has no need to trouble himself with the abstract question what beauty is in itself, or what is its exact relation to truth or experience—metaphysical questions, as unprofitable as metaphysical questions elsewhere. He may pass them all by as being, answerable or not, of no interest to him."

A more recent author [4] writes: "Into vague generalisations about 'Art' this is in any case no place to go. At best very little can be said that is worth saying, about things as different as a cathedral and a sonnet, a statue and a symphony." The same writer in another passage speaks [5] of Hegel's theory of tragedy as "one more instance of the rashness of metaphysicians who venture into regions where their speculations can for once be checked." These are certainly charges against philosophy. We shall return in a moment or two to consider how seriously they are to be taken, if they are to be taken seriously at all.

The philosopher, then, is attacked by the artist and the critic. If the philosopher in turn can be said to attack at all (apart from defending himself or retaliating) his attack is more of the nature of an assumption of a certain common ground or subject-matter between himself and the critic. He seldom presumes—and as philosopher he has never any right to presume—to interfere positively with the critic's business of intuitive judgment, even although he may be heard to murmur that he wishes that some art-critics occasionally had a little more philosophy in them.

The philosopher's attack, I have suggested, is of the nature of an assumption, and it is this assumption which is resented by the artist and the art-critic, chiefly by the latter. The assumption which is made by the philosopher is that he has some right to theorise about art and about aesthetic experience generally.[6] The critic is so far justified in his resentment in that this assumption has sometimes in fact been made by philosophers who have obviously been possessed of little first-hand experience of beautiful things.

In this matter it is of vital importance to be clear at the outset. It is of vital importance to be clear that generalisations about art and about aesthetic experience can only be justified when they are based upon immediately experienced aesthetic intuition. Without aesthetic intuition of individual beautiful things, generalisations about aesthetic experience are "but words and breath." Critics are right when they resent "high priori" ways of thinking and speaking of art. It may be possible to use the concept of beauty as the completion of a system of philosophy, as some philosophers have done; it

---

[4] F. L. Lucas, *Tragedy*, p. 14.
[5] *Ibid.*, p. 43.
[6] Including, once again, the possible aesthetic experience of nature.

may be even possible for the metaphysician to define beauty more or less correctly, out of a very general and vague sort of experience. But this kind of thing, even in the hands of genius, is not worth a great deal, unless it is based on experience of many beautiful things, and of many sorts of beautiful things. Aesthetic hypotheses have this in common with scientific ones, that they must be tried and tested and adjusted to suit the rich variety of particular facts. If anyone to-day exists who really believes that there is a purely deductive science, then it is certain that aesthetics can have nothing to do with it. Aesthetic generalisations must always be merely tentative, they must be hypotheses to be tested by experience, until by degrees the body of aesthetic theory grows into as coherent a system as we can make it. There must be the continual movement, familiar in science, from the individual facts to generalisation, and from generalisation back again to individual facts. And so on.

In this connection there is a common misunderstanding between artists and critics on the one hand, and philosophers on the other hand, which is typified in the use of the word "must." The philosopher is often heard to say, "The artist *must* do so and so." This sounds exactly as if the philosopher were laying down the law to the artist. But the philosopher is using the term "must" not in a normative sense, not in the sense of some categorical imperative, but rather as describing, as far as he can see, what *does* in fact happen with the best artists. The philosopher is puzzled; he talks aloud; he asks himself questions. "What is the explanation of this?" he asks. And after reflection he answers, *"This* is the explanation; this is what the artist *must* be doing." Of course the philosopher's discoveries through analysis *might* be, after many days, of practical value to the working artist. But that is another matter. The philosopher's business is to know, not to prescribe, and it is an injustice to think that, because he uses the word "must," he is laying down the law.

Having emphasised, then, that the business of the aesthetic philosopher is intellectual analysis and construction, and that, in order to analyse and construct to any purpose, he must also have first-hand acquaintance with beautiful things, we may now return to meet the objections already cited to the philosopher's making any attempt at all to analyse beautiful things.

The most direct—and perhaps the final—answer that can be given to the question, Why analyse? is that we have a fundamental impulse to do it, that we usually do it badly, and that if done at all it ought to be done well. Everyone has notions about what art or beauty is, even although these notions never become expressed in words. We do not merely feel, we think also. And it is unanalysed notions and preconceptions which, entering into our feelings about beautiful things, more often than not mislead us and induce false attitudes towards them. If we are to have preconceptions at all—and we can never avoid having them—then it is surely better, if opportunity offers itself, that we should take a little trouble in trying to acquire true preconceptions for future occasions. These true conceptions are worth acquiring for their own sake, for the sake of their truth, but it is almost certain that in the end they also help us to appreciate more truly.

Leaving this last point for the present, let us consider the main issue, in relation to that part of Pater's statement (given above) which denies that definitions do help us to use words liké beauty, art, etc., with more precise meaning. It is surely plain falsity that, in general, definitions do not aid mental precision. Pater's point however is that, in particular, it is *beauty* and its like which cannot be defined, because beauty is essentially an individual thing, and not a general concept. But though this has its truth, and though it may also be true, as Pater says, that beauty is in some sense relative to us, yet the fact that there are certain *kinds* of objects which many people agree in calling beautiful, and certain *kinds* of mental experience called aesthetic, is a sign that there is some quality—the aesthetic quality—common to all the particular instances. Whether or not this quality is relative to our minds, the whole history of criticism shows that it is, in some sense, describable, a describable quality. It is precisely this quality which it is the object of aesthetics to discover and to define. To say that we must define beauty, not in the most abstract, but in the most concrete terms possible, is to overlook the very nature of definition; it is to refuse to define at all. This is, of course, a procedure which is open to anyone who pleases, but he who adopts it, if he is to be consistent, must be content with the creation or enjoyment of this or that beautiful thing, and must entirely refrain from talking of it, from even murmuring the words "art," or "beauty." Even to murmur "art," "beauty," is to commit oneself to the supposition that there is some general "abstract" idea to which the words refer. Pater himself is—in his own individual way— undeniably an expert in the business of enjoying art, and he is always fascinating when he is acting what Oscar Wilde called "the Critic as Artist," when he is, through his own medium of artistic prose, making us *feel* beauty. (It may be questioned whether he is at these times a good *critic*.) The rest of the time he is continually violating his own principles and talking "abstractly." He has, strictly speaking, no right even to call his book *Studies in Art and Poetry,* because the terms "art" and "poetry" are abstract terms and therefore (to him) "meaningless." If it be replied, "Yes, that is all very well, but you know perfectly that Pater meant, not 'art' and 'poetry' in the abstract, but particular works of art and particular works of poetry," we may answer again, "Yes, but why call them all by the *name* of 'art' or 'poetry'? The terms must have some *general* meaning and they are without doubt hopelessly 'abstract.' " It is fortunate that Pater does violate his own principles, that his practice is better than his precept, for his generalisations are often illuminating. But it is a pity that he should have encouraged in himself and in so many of his admirers the old and muddled idea—so stupid as to be unworthy of attack, were it not for its prevalence —that to define is to destroy, that to try to form a clear general conception of anything is to do something which is much inferior to the act of direct perception. To generalise is not inferior, nor is it superior, to perceiving; it is simply different. It has a different aim and a different function, a function which has a directly theoretical object, and which has, indirectly perhaps, practical effects.

The same things are true of the quotation given from Mr. Lucas. It is no doubt the case that it is difficult to make general statements about things as different from one another as cathedrals, sonnets, statues, symphonies, and it is true that the difficulty of making generalisations tends to produce vagueness in the generalisations, and that good generalisations may *appear* vague because they are abstract and difficult to understand. But, once again, has the word "art" no meaning? Surely cathedrals and sonnets and statues and symphonies are, in at least one important respect, *more* like one another than they are like coal-heaving, sugar-selling, or taxi-driving? It is that which they have in common in which the philosopher is interested.

We have been saying that criticism involves abstraction. It may, however, be denied that the critic in any sense deals in abstractions, that his function is to discuss theories. There are, indeed, several views about the aims of criticism which it may be as well to enumerate now—without attempting neatness or detail of classification—before going on to speak of the relation of criticism to aesthetic philosophy.

The simplest kind of criticism, perhaps, is what is sometimes known as "signpost" criticism. Its aim is merely to point out what is good and what is bad in art. This has a useful function, largely the function of a guidebook or a good newspaper; it tells the uninitiated what to seek and what to avoid. It is hardly likely to be found by itself. Another kind of criticism is what may be called "technical" criticism; it is the kind of criticism which interests artists and others who are concerned with the processes of the actual building up of works of art. It is the kind of criticism which, applied to painting, includes comments on composition, on the balancing of lines, planes, and volumes, on tactual and colour values, on the expression of depth. In poetry this class of criticism is concerned with things like the disposition of vowel- and consonant-sounds, or of assonance and rhyme and rhythm and metre. Music also has its own technical jargon. "Technical" criticism is necessary and valuable in that it directs attention to the structural elements in art and their relation to the whole; without any such accurate discrimination, appreciation would be a vague and nebulous thing. "Historical" criticism (including what might be called "biographical" criticism) is another kind of criticism. This endeavours to evaluate works of art by showing them to be expressions of general classified tendencies in the history of art and also perhaps of circumstances in the private lives of artists. This again is, no doubt, of considerable value in helping us to understand the artist's point of view in its historical background. (It is part of what has been called, mainly in France, "scientific" criticism.) On the other hand, there is the danger that the historical or biographical critic may place what interests him historically before what is of intrinsic artistic importance.

There is, again, "artistic" criticism, described in Wilde's essay, *The Critic as Artist,* to which we referred in speaking of Pater. This is perhaps better known generally in this country and abroad as "impressionistic" criticism. Impressionism is in intention really a development of "signpost" criticism, with the great difference that the "signpost" becomes an impressionable living artist who records his impressions of a work of art, and who does not merely record them, but expresses them so intensely that a new, and literary, work of art is produced. The critic records his "adventures of the soul" in a lyric which in its own way may rival (as also it may not rival) the original object of appreciation. The main trouble with this kind of criticism is that it is apt to stop being criticism at all. The better an artist such a "critic" is, the more he may detach our attention from the original and fix it upon his own product. (Pater's lyricising on *La Gioconda* is an obvious example which comes to mind.) This may sometimes be very pleasant, and the end may justify the means. But it is not what we want when we go out to find criticism. It is like a geologist who should ask for a stone and be offered cakes and honey. In criticism the weekly newspaper signpost is better than this.

But indeed of criticism we ask something more than is given by any or all of the four kinds I have enumerated. All criticism implies good "taste," implies competence of aesthetic intuition. But this is not all that is required. Nor are technical, historical, and biographical knowledge, and the gift of literary expression, adequate supplements. Philosophy is required also. The interest of the critic is, of course, in individual works of art, and, as we have said, no amount of general knowledge is of the least use as a substitute for this. But surely it is also the business of the completely equipped critic to give reasons, if required, for the faith which is in him? I do not suggest that he must always be doing so, or that he is mainly concerned with theory. But he should be able to do so: his should be a *"thinking* study" of art. He can point, or he can talk round the issue, or he can sing as the poet sings. But as the complete critic he is, if he merely does these things, a comparative (not a complete) failure, for though he has likes and dislikes, though he may know *what* is good, he has no idea *why.* He is not interested in the question. All good critics must put to themselves from time to time such questions as, Why is this or that good? Why is this technical device to be preferred to that? Why is this or that historical development important? Such questions directly involve others, such as, What is the meaning of good, or of bad, in art? What is the difference between the "beautiful" and the "ugly," between the "great" and the "trifling," between the "tragic" and the "comic," between the "classical" and the "romantic"? And these are —however little this be realised by critics themselves—most emphatically *philosophical* questions.

This is not to say that criticism is the same thing as aesthetic philosophy. Rather criticism implies (and, of course, is implied by) aesthetic philosophy. The difference is perhaps one of the focus of interest. The critic as such may be compelled, willy-nilly, to enter into philosophy, but his main interest is in individual works of art. The aesthetic philosopher, on the other hand, though he should be competently acquainted with as great a variety of works of art as possible, is, as philosopher, interested chiefly in the theory. It ought not to be necessary to add that his interest in *general* theory carries with it no sort of implication that he denies that each work of art is in a real sense particular, individual, and unique, or that he is so completely foolish as to think that artists will successfully produce works of art from theories alone. It *ought* not, I say, to be necessary to add this. But in view of obstinate misunderstandings it is necessary to do so.

Our interest here will be aesthetic philosophy. But what of psychology? In discussing aesthetic philosophy it is impossible to avoid continually bordering upon psychology. As aesthetics is sometimes—wrongly, I think —identified with psychology, a word or two as to their relations may be in place here.

Psychology is concerned with mental processes, and to some extent with physiological processes so far as these have a bearing on mental processes and mental problems. (The subject-matter of aesthetic psychology is, broadly speaking, our processes of mind when we have aesthetic experience.) There are, as we know, two general methods of investigation which can be employed in psychology, one of them is direct or internal observation, or introspection, and the other is the external observation of behaviour. Both these methods may be used either in a freer, or in a more restricted and proscribed way. The introspecting subject may offer a running description of his experiences, or he may be asked to answer certain specific questions, carefully planned by the psychologist. Similarly, behaviour may be simply observed and recorded as it occurs, or it may be studied under definitely experimental conditions. A good deal of investigation has been carried out in these various ways in the psychology of aesthetics. Most stress has perhaps been laid upon experimental aesthetics, where the conditions can be controlled so that the experimenter is able to tabulate more accurately the results obtained either from introspection or from observation. This field of experimental aesthetics is a wide one and round the subject there has sprung up a considerable literature. What should be the relation of this experimental aesthetics to philosophy?

One part of the answer seems to me obvious. It is that aesthetic philosophy should take everything from the results of experiment it can make use of. An aesthetic philosophy which refuses to consider what psychology offers to it must indeed be blind and prejudiced. But two qualifications may be made. (*a*) One is that philosophy has a right, and a duty, to be sceptical. It must be critical of that which psychology offers to it. There is no possible objection to the principle of experimentation; but experimentation is difficult to manage, and the results of experimentation in a subject like aesthetics are perhaps not always so significant as its advocates sometimes imagine. Experiment may be conducted with some profit when the experimenter is concerned with experiences of simple colours and sounds, and the results obtained have undoubtedly their value, as I shall try to show, in helping us to discern some of the less complex characters of aesthetic experience. But it is a mistake to think of these simple experiences of colour and sound as typically aesthetic experiences. To understand aesthetic experience properly we have to go to the more complex examples of it, to the experience of works of art, of pictures, symphonies, poems, cathedrals. And in these cases, where the aesthetic experience is at its fullest and richest, the arrangement of experiment becomes most difficult of all. I do not in the least suggest that it is impossible to arrange experiments in such cases, or that it is unlikely that the technique of experiment will be greatly improved as time goes on. But it is certain that any mature aesthetic experience is a vastly complex concrete whole, and that the necessary isolation of elements, the selection of fundamental aspects to be tested, is extremely difficult, so difficult that it has probably not, up to the present, been successfully achieved. Further, this selection can only be arrived at after a very carefully reflective—and philosophic—study of private and personal aesthetic experiences as complex concrete wholes. In other words, experiment implies hypotheses, and hypotheses are the outcome of reflection upon direct, pre-experimental experience. And it is particularly the business of aesthetic philosophy to form hypotheses and to scrutinise the hypotheses behind all experimental work. One's general impression is that experimental aesthetics has tended to suffer from a too great eagerness to "get results," and that a more philosophic scrutiny of fundamentals is needed before really significant experiments can be devised. Aesthetic experience is so peculiarly susceptible to the danger of piece-meal treatment.

The results of the experimental psychology of aesthetics, then, must be received critically, though open-mindedly, by philosophy, and aesthetics cannot, for this reason, be identified with a part of experimental psychology. The second remark [7] (*b*) which may be made, is that aesthetics cannot be identified with psychology (or with any part of it) because psychology is concerned with processes of mind, whilst the field of aesthetics contains more than this. Aesthetics is concerned also with objects and products; it concerns the *things* which we call beautiful, ugly, sublime, ridiculous, and so on. With these objects pure psychology could, by the definition of its nature, have nothing to do. The nature of objects is, however—in a certain sense—the proper subject-matter of the part of philosophy called ontology. So again there arise problems of the relation of object to subject. These again fall outside psychology, but they are the very sphere of "epistemology," or the theory of knowledge. Logical questions there are, too, in aesthetics, as when it is said that tragedy is the expression of the "universal." Investigation in aesthetics, again, is essentially philosophical in that it treats these various problems not as separate, not as strictly speaking isolable, but as in relation to one another.

The chief and the fundamental aim of philosophy—in aesthetics or anywhere else—is truth. But philosophical aesthetics, like other philosophy, may in the long run affect our feelings, and affect practice. I have tried to show that the critic, if he is to be a complete critic, must call upon the aid of philosophy. Not only the intellectual explanations of the critic, however, but critical appreciation itself, may in the end be affected by philosophy. For aesthetic experience, as we have said, is not mere feeling; it is knowledge. And into knowledge there enters at any moment a vast complexity of assumptions and presumptions and past judgments. This needs little, if any, argument, since we all admit that aesthetic appreciation may be trained, and training means the direction of attention upon essentials which are in turn determined for us partly by analysis. As in the realm of perception we "see" the snow to be cold, so in the realm of aesthetic experience we may be said to "see" the thing in this or that *way,* because of a certain history, a certain training, a certain tradition, which is partly determined at every point by some sort of reflection. And if the reflection has been profound and thoroughgoing and true, surely the actual vision will be clarified? Pater is mistaken when he assumes that the only aim of trying to define is to help us to enjoy better; for definition, where possible, is a good in itself. It is overwhelmingly probable, however, that Pater is not only wrong in this assumption, but that he is wrong when he says that definitions help us very little to enjoy the best things in art and poetry. Definitions, to repeat, are no substitute for taste, but surely definitions, when they have become assimilated by our minds, must in some sense, and at some time, qualify the thing we call taste?

[7] See beginning of the last paragraph.

If this is true of appreciation, why should it not be true even of art-production itself? Of course, as we have said, the artist does not act in this or that way because he (consciously) *thinks* that a theory demands it. But surely even the artist, like the critic, is influenced by theories? We tend to accept grudgingly the idea that the artist can be helped by theories. And yet we are very ready to admit that his work is apt to be influenced by *bad* theories. For example, Wordsworth. But if bad theories affect, so may good theories affect. Why not as good theories as can be found?

Let us rid ourselves, then, of lingering prejudices. It is high time to be quit of irritating and elementary confusions about functions. There is no reason in the world why artists and critics and philosophers should not live peaceably and profitably together under the wide roof of heaven. As for aesthetic philosophy in particular, it is possible, necessary, good in itself, and probably, after many days, aesthetically useful. . . .

DOUGLAS N. MORGAN

Psychology and Art Today: A Summary and Critique [1]

For some 75 years, investigations into the psychology of art have been developing under that name, and for some 2300 years before that time some somewhat similar work was being done under the name of philosophy. I offer here no pseudo-comprehensive synopsis of this vast,

---

[1] From Douglas N. Morgan, "Psychology and Art Today: A Summary and Critique," *Journal of Aesthetics and Art Criticism,* X (1950), 81–96. Reprinted by permission. (Eds.)

This paper was read to the Psychology Colloquium of Northwestern University on January 30, 1950. It is intended as one contribution in partial fulfillment of Thomas Munro's reasonable request ("Methods in the Psychology of Art," *Journal of Aesthetics and Art Criticism,* March 1948, p. 226) for "more discussion of aims and methods." In this valuable article, Mr. Munro brings to the attention of American students the important work of Müller-Freienfels (*Psychologie der Kunst,* 3 vols., Leipzig 1923), Sterzinger (*Grundlinien der Kunstpsychologie,* Graz 1938), and Plaut (*Prinzipien und Methoden der Kunstpsychologie,* Berlin, 1935). The reader is referred to these books, and to Munro's article, for a survey of psychological approaches in Germany and Austria to 1935. Chandler's fine book, *Beauty and Human Nature,* (New York and London 1934) still contains interesting material; its approach is, however, almost wholly restricted to that called "experimental" in this paper. It goes without saying

rich range of material, but merely a brief summary and methodological criticism of some of the work being done today within the field. After a quick glance at certain psychological insights no longer being avidly pursued,[2] I shall try to classify in three broad groups the work being done now, offering examples of each approach in its application to various works of various arts. In the second part of my paper, I shall venture certain comments and criticisms—some new and some old—on ways and means by which, perhaps, somewhat more ground may be gained in our understanding of the psychology of the arts.

Following Fechner, who published his *Vorschule der Aesthetik* in 1876, and thereby founded experimental aesthetics, three major directions developed around three central and fertile ideas. The first of these, called "empathy," had grown from Aristotle [3] through Robert Vischer [4] to Lipps [5] and Lee.[6] Its central idea was an interpretation of the appreciative act in art as a kind of identification: a feeling-into or personification of the object by the spectator. The second central idea gave rise to a theory which stresses certain similarities found between the phenomenon of play and the act of creating or appreciating works of art. It descended from Schiller [7] through Herbert Spencer [8] to Karl Groos [9] and Konrad Lange.[10] The third of these ideas emerges from a concept of an aesthetically necessary "psychical distance" between spectator and aesthetic object, and finds its fullest statement in the work of Edward Bullough.[11] All three of these ideas: empathy, play, and psychical distance, have materially conditioned our present interpretations of art, but none of them seems to be receiving active attention from a significant number of psychologists now at work, at least in this country and in this language. The ideas appear to have performed their service and been set aside, at least for the time being; they are not in the main stream of the three approaches now being vigorously explored, espe-

---

that interested readers will refer to one of the masterpieces in the field by one of its masterworkers, the late Max Dessoir: *Aesthetik und allgemeine Kunstwissenschaft* (Stuttgart 1923).

[2] Except perhaps in France, and there only in an attenuated form. See the June 1949 issue of *Journal of Aesthetics and Art Criticism*. R. Bayer's article, "Method in Aesthetics," in this issue, contains a quasi-critical and quasi-poetic discussion of psychological methodology in aesthetics.

[3] 1411b, *34; Rhetoric* III, 2.

[4] *Das optische Formgefühl*, Tübingen 1873.

[5] *Aesthetik*, Hamburg and Leipzig 1903–1906.

[6] With C. Anstruther-Thompson, "Beauty and Ugliness," *Contemporary Review* 1897, pp. 72, 544–569; 669–688.

[7] *Letters upon the Aesthetical Education of Man*, 1793–94. More convenient is the 1905 London edition *Essays, aesthetical and philosophical*, etc.

[8] *The Principles of Psychology*, London 1870–72.

[9] *The Play of Animals*, New York 1898; *The Play of Man*, New York 1901.

[10] *Das Wesen der Kunst*, Berlin 1901.

[11] Miscellaneous articles in *British Journal of Psychology*, ca. 1913.

cially in America, England, and Italy. I am labelling these approaches respectively *psychoanalytic, Gestalt,* and *experimental,* for want of better terms. I now propose to characterize each of these approaches independently, in terms of what we may call its "core idea," to state its specifically aesthetic questions, and to offer examples of its research.[12]

§ 2

No extended or properly qualified epitomization of the core idea of psychoanalysis will be necessary or desirable before this audience; besides, I do not see that a philosopher need rush in where psychologists themselves fear to tread. In broad terms, let it simply be said that the psychoanalytic approach germinates out of the fundamental notion that man's behavior can be explained in terms of the working out of a complex of conscious and unconscious personality needs and drives, at least some of which are erotic, and all of which strive toward and often find symbolic expression, as in dreams and in the fine arts.

The most characteristic aesthetic question asked by the psychoanalysts is an inquiry into the personality factors which condition the creation and/or appreciation of works of art. It has developed from the "divine frenzy" of Plato's poet [13] who creates because of an irrational love-force; through the idea-dream-reality identification of Schopenhauer,[14] and the "Dionysiac" voluntarism of Nietzsche,[15] to the comprehensive contributions of Freud and his followers.[16] Today Edmund Bergler [17] has challenged the conventional psychoanalytic theory that the artist expresses through his work his unconscious wishes and fantasies in sublimated, symbolic form; Bergler urges instead that the artist is unconsciously *defending himself against* his own unconscious wishes and fantasies.

The general-theoretical development of this core-idea may be exemplified

---

[12] It should be noted that serious attempts have been made, and are still being made, to organize these various approaches into a unified program which will incorporate also discoveries contributed by anthropological, historical and sociological disciplines. See Munro, *op. cit.,* p. 233.

[13] *Phaedrus* 245.

[14] See Baudouin, *Psychoanalysis and Aesthetics* tr. by Paul, New York 1924, p. 29.

[15] *Das Geburt der Tragödie,* Leipzig 1872, available in translation; *The Will to Power,* 1878, New York 1924.

[16] Freud's own chief contributions to aesthetics include *Leonardo da Vinci,* New York 1916; *Wit and its Relation to the Unconscious,* New York 1916; *Dream and Delusion,* New York 1917; *Totem and Taboo,* New York 1918. The Jungian approach may be found in "Psychology and Literature," pp. 175–199 in *Modern Man in Search of a Soul* tr. by Dell and Baynes, New York 1934, and in *Contributions to Analytical Psychology,* London and New York 1928, pp. 225–249.

[17] *American Imago,* 1948, p. 200, and elsewhere. *The Writer and Psychoanalysis,* New York 1950.

in the work of Charles Baudouin [18] and of Harry B. Lee.[19] Baudouin stresses psychoanalytic factors in appreciation, offering an extended example in the analysis of the poetry of Verhaeren; Lee attempts, within a psychoanalytic framework, to describe factors leading up to artistic creation and explaining differential aesthetic responses. He makes frequent and interesting references to his own clinical experience.

Far more work is being done in the direction of detailed, applied interpretations of particular works of art. The attempt seems to be to read the work, in whatever field, symbolically, and to correlate these readings with whatever biographical data may be available, to the end that we understand more fully the personality of the creating artist, and that through this understanding light may be thrown upon the "mystery" of creation in the arts.

In literature, an enormous amount of analysis is being done; we take only a few, fairly random samples as typical. Hamlet has been a favorite subject for psychoanalysis,[20] King Lear was a narcissist;[21] Baudelaire and Poe are said to displace the death-bringing attributes of their fathers onto their mothers, as a result of infantile menstruation traumas.[22] The body images in the limericks of Edward Lear have been used as psychoanalytic data.[23] Charles Kingsley, author of *The Water Babies,* appears to have suffered from a respiratory neurosis, stammering asthma.[24] Lewis Carroll is said [25] to be the romantic, erotic, wish-fulfilling, schizic *alter ego* of the dignified mathematics professor Charles Dodgson. His heroine Alice is a phallus, and her adventures in Wonderland represent a trip back into the mother's womb.[26]

In music too this fertile idea has been generously applied. Perrotti [27] has

---

[18] *Op. cit.* We might almost take as a text Baudouin's quotation (p. 25) from Wagner's *Meistersinger:* "Poetry is nothing but the interpretation of dreams."

[19] "On the Esthetic State of Mind," *Psychiatry* 1947, pp. 281–306, and elsewhere.

[20] See, for only one example, Ernest Jones, *Hamlet,* London 1947, pp. 7–42.

[21] Abenheimer, "On Narcissism, etc.", *British Journal of Medical Psychology,* 1945, 20, pp. 322–329.

[22] Daly, "The Mother Complex in Literature," *Samiksa* 1947, 1, pp. 157–190. I am grateful to Dr. Edward Weiss of Chicago for his kindness in sharing his personal copy of this journal, and of those cited in notes 27 and 29 below.

[23] Reitman, "Lear's Nonsense," *Journal of Clinical Psychopathology and Psychotherapy,* 1946, 7, pp. 64–102.

[24] Deutsch, "Artistic Expression and Neurotic Illness," *American Imago* 1947, 64–102.

[25] Skinner, "Lewis Carroll's 'Adventures in Wonderland,' " *American Imago* 1947, pp. 3–31. The earliest article on this subject seems to be that of Schilder, "Psychoanalytic remarks on *Alice in Wonderland* and Lewis Carroll," *Journal of Nervous and Mental Diseases,* 1938, 87, pp. 159–168.

[26] Grotjohn, "About the Symbolization of Alice's Adventures in Wonderland," *American Imago* 1947, pp. 32–41.

[27] "La Musica, linguaggio dell'inconscio," *Psicoanalisi* 1945, pp. 60–82. He suggests that whereas ordinary verbal language tends to express cold, abstract concepts, music expresses the determinate "charge" (*carica*) of the unconscious.

exhumed Schopenhauer, suggesting that the mysteries of music may be explained in terms of the unconscious. The language of music is held to be a universal language in that the language of the unconscious is equally universal. Max Graf [28] has set boldly about the historical explanation of composition in terms of erotic powers and other impeti to creation; his ultimate conclusion is, unfortunately, somewhat mystical.

Freud himself presents the most extended analysis in painting, in his admittedly speculative but stimulating *Leonardo da Vinci*. Leonardo's childhood phoenix dream, the loss of his father and consequent intimacy with his mother, the details of his account book and manners with his assistants in the studio: all these and more are brought to bear upon the perennial question of why the Mona Lisa smiles. More recently, an Italian student [29] has done some interesting work in interpreting contemporary painting. He suggests, for example, that surrealism exhibits on a social plane what had hitherto been observed only clinically: a general tendency of the libido to regress from adult genitality to a pregenital phase of undifferentiated cell-activity; there is a consequent increase in forgetting and liberation of aggression tendencies. While psychoanalysts seek to *integrate* the self, surrealists seek its *disintegration*. Whether this hypothesis will prove ultimately satisfactory, I cannot say; but at least it seems to me more enlightening than the mountains of incoherent words which the surrealists themselves have had to utter in their own defense. Wight [30] interprets some of Goya's etchings. Bergler [31] suggests a highly stimulating psychoanalytic interpretation of one of Millais' paintings, in terms of the painter's loving sympathy for the frustrated wife of impotent John Ruskin, and argues for his interpretation in terms of material external evidence.

Even sculpture is coming within the purview of the psychoanalysts. If I may, however, I should like to defer my example for a few moments, when we shall be able to compare the psychoanalytic with the *Gestalt* interpretations of a given series of works.

§ 3

The hesitancy expressed earlier about the "core idea" of psychoanalysis holds also in connection with the Gestalt approach. Suppose that

[28] *From Beethoven to Shostakovich; The Psychology of the Composing Process* (New York 1947).

[29] Servadio, "Il Surrealismo: storia, dottrina, valutazione psicoanalitica," *Psicoanalisi* 1946, p. 77. See also Akin (or Atkin), "Psychological Aspects of Surrealism," *Journal of Clinical Psychopathology and Psychotherapy* 1945, pp. 35–41.

[30] "The Revulsions of Goya," *Journal of Aesthetics and Art Criticism*, 1946, 5, pp. 1–28.

[31] *Loc. cit.* Schneider also has done psychoanalyses of paintings: see his work on Picasso (*College Art Journal*, 1946, 6, pp. 81–95) and on Chagall (*ibid.*, pp. 115–124).

we characterize it, quite simply, as the belief that perception (and perhaps other psychological phenomena as well) can be explained in terms of neural factors tending to produce organized, though dynamically changing patterns or segregated groups of units, or "wholes." The application of these "functional concepts" to aesthetics follows quite clearly. Thinkers in this tradition ask, "What perceptual organizing factors condition the experience of seeing or hearing a work of art?"

We think, of course, of the work of Wertheimer,[32] Köhler,[33] and Koffka [34] in their general elaboration of the Gestalt thesis. The most recent full-scale development in aesthetics seems to be Schaefer-Simmern's study of art education.[35] Gestalt studies of aesthetic perception [36] also appear from time to time.

As has been the case with psychoanalysis, we find here also some extended attempts to apply the psychological categories to particular works of art, and to our experiences of them. Stephen Pepper [37] has given us many interesting working examples of figure-ground, positive-negative space relationships, and of the operation of sensory fusion, closure and sequence principles in actual paintings and works of sculpture. Hans Ruin [38] discusses the works of Monet, Cézanne, Gauguin, Munch, van Gogh and Matisse, suggesting that painters have, in their treatments of color, figure and structure, often anticipated theoretical Gestalt psychologists.

In music, Reymes-King [39] is studying the perceptual relationships of verbal and tonal stimuli as they are simultaneously presented in song. He asks whether any phenomenon analogous to sensory fusion may be found when stimuli come through different sense organs. Tentatively, he suggests that this is doubtful, but that a distinction among levels of perception may help to explain the differences between our responses to instrumental music and to song.

Even the movies are being studied by the Gestaltists. Rudolf Arnheim [40] examines the relationships between visual and auditory stimuli in the act of

---

[32] *Productive Thinking,* New York and London 1945.

[33] *Gestalt Psychology,* New York 1947.

[34] *Principles of Gestalt Psychology,* New York 1935. I cite only recent editions.

[35] *The Unfolding of the Artistic Activity,* Berkeley 1948.

[36] —as, for example, that of Koffka, "Problems on the Psychology of Art," *Bryn Mawr Notes and Monographs,* Bryn Mawr 1940, IX . . . cited by Heyl, *New Bearings in Esthetics and Art Criticism,* New Haven 1943, p. 110n.

[37] *Principles of Art Appreciation,* New York 1949.

[38] "La Psychologie Structurale et l'art moderne," *Theoria,* (Lund) 1949, pp. 253–275. "The holistic way of seeing," says Ruin (p. 259), "is, once and for all, innate in artists."

[39] —in an interesting but, so far as I can discover, still unpublished paper read at the 1949 meeting of the Society for Aesthetics in Oberlin, Ohio. It should be noted that my report is from memory; Reymes-King is not to be held responsible for these views.

[40] —also from an unpublished paper read at the 1949 meeting (see note 39). Arnheim is not to be held responsible for these views; they are quoted from memory.

perception, suggesting that one weakness in some sound movies (and, by extension, presumably also in television) may be a perceptual competition, and hence distraction, division, and loss of attention.

In summary of the discussion thus far, I should like to present two interpretations of what is essentially the same subject matter: the sculpture of Henry Moore. I choose first the recent analysis of a psychoanalytical critic, Frederick Wight.[41] For brevity I paraphrase.

Moore's figures have no soft parts or textures; he eviscerates his figures, eliminating hollow parts of the body, leaving only the bony structure. His father was a miner. Moore mines into the hollow of the breast, which is the feeding ground of the child. Subconsciously an infant cannibal, he eats away the flesh, feels himself inside his mother in image, regressing to the womb. But this is only the least profound of his subconscious interests. More subtly, he builds his sculpture for eternity. His drawings and his writings exemplify this need to transcend death. Everything temporal, soft, is wasted away. Nearly all figures are female. Is not the mine the grave? And is Moore not consigning his father to the mine forever, feeling his way *permanently* inside his mother? But death, as Moore presents it, is not revolting; it is almost dignified, after the British manner. The British national church is floored with graves; it is built on the serene acceptance of the dead underfoot; "for the Englishman the easy unrepugnant moldering of the dead exhales a rich philosophic savor." Not a Christian, Moore wants quite simply a particular image, a material and perhaps a national image, to survive.

We now turn to a Gestalt interpretation of the same material, selecting that of Arnheim,[42] and again paraphrasing. The problem of composing the human form has plagued sculptors for centuries; the solid trunk contrasts with the flying appendages. Moore transforms the trunk into a series of ribbons, and thus finds a common denominator for the whole. Plastic forms are dynamic: conic, pyramidal, ovoidal, rather than static cubes and cylinders. Brain-carrying heads are diminished in size; faces are placid; physical-subrational abdomens are emphasized in the characteristic reclining position. The holes, as perceived, are not merely dead and empty intervals but peculiarly substantial, as though they were filled out with denser air, puddles of semi-solid air hollowed out, scooped out by mostly concave surfaces. Principles of three-dimensional figure-ground relationships (concavity making for ground, convexity for figure; enclosed areas tending to be figure, enclosing areas tending to be ground, etc.) apply here also. Instead of pushing shapes out into space, Moore invites space inside his figures, adds to

---

[41] "Henry Moore: the Reclining Figure," *Journal of Aesthetics and Art Criticism*, 1947, pp. 95–105.

[42] "The Holes of Henry Moore," *Journal of Aesthetics and Art Criticism*, 1948, pp. 29–38.

their substance with space. The resulting deliberate figure-ground ambivalence results in a dynamic interplay between two figures in the same work, a lessening of importance of sharp boundaries, and a strong feeling for movement within the work.

Now it is apparent that these two criticisms do not contradict each other; they ask different questions about the aesthetic object, and arrive at different answers. I find both suggestive and interesting, and feel that they may well contribute side by side to our understanding of Moore's work, and of our responses to it.

§ 4

Finally, we come to our third principal approach to the problems of psychology of art: the approach which is usually labelled "experimental." An apology for the term is in order, since Gestaltists certainly also perform experiments. What I mean to indicate is the group of investigators sometimes loosely known as "behaviorists." Because I do not wish to limit the discussion to literal Watsonians, if there are any still around, or to "physicalists," I shall define this group as comprising those who distrust as "unscientific" or "merely philosophical" any investigations (including most of those already discussed) which make inferences on any basis other than precise mathematical measurements of behavior, and which make predictions to any other conclusions than those measurable in such precise terms.[43] The most recent experimental attempts at any kind of comprehensiveness in aesthetics seem to be those of Norman C. Meier,[44] who has outlined an elementary general interpretation of aesthetics and suggested an "interlinkage" theory of artistic creation, and of Albert Chandler.[45] The specific applications of experimentalism to aesthetics are too various to classify under one simple heading; let us rather discover the directions of work from particular examples, which I have very roughly classified as aptitude tests, physiological correlations (Wundt's "expression" category), and preference tests (Wundt's "impression"). A few investigations do not fit conveniently under any of these headings, and must be reserved for brief notation later.[46] Our examples, again, are fairly random samples from the vast contemporary literature, and represent only a fraction of the work being done. They are intended as typical, rather than as definitive.

---

[43] Consider, for example, the attitude expressed by Carl Seashore, *Psychology of Music,* New York 1938, p. 377.

[44] *Art in Human Affairs,* New York and London 1942.

[45] *Op. cit.* See note 1 above.

[46] I here deliberately set aside applied psychology experiments on the use of music in psychotherapy, and in increasing production in factories and chicken coops, the visual appearance of advertising layouts, and the like, since such experimenters generally make no claim to be contributing to our understanding of the arts.

Aptitude testing is fairly well advanced in music and in painting. The famous Seashore tests of pitch and tonal memory are, I understand, in use in schools today. The Tilson-Gretsch test, and others, have since been developed to measure tonal, harmonic and rhythmic discrimination. In painting and the plastic arts we have the McAdory Art Test, the Meier Art Judgment Test, the Knauber Test of Art Ability, and the Lewerenz tests in fundamental abilities of the visual arts. Color discrimination tests, line-drawing aptitude tests, and the like, have multiplied profusely. Perhaps the most difficult theoretical question in this field is whether the testers are testing aptitude or achievement: it is sometimes not easy to distinguish the two on experimental grounds. In either case, the practical value of the work is apparent; if we develop tests to the point where we can examine a youngster young enough, and decide what his prospects for a musical career might be, we ought to be able to make significant recommendations about his education, at least in a negative direction. Theoretical advantages of this work are perhaps not so immediately apparent.

Physiological testing is being done, primarily on subjects exposed to works of art, mainly works of music. Dreher [47] has observed that 33 college students trained in music sweat more when listening to certain pieces of piano music than do 33 students who are not so trained. There is some experimental correlation between physical characteristics of music and moods or feelings reported by listeners: music called "dignified" tends to be slow, low-pitched, and of limited orchestral range; music called "animated" tends to be fast, etc.[48]

Preference tests represent the major part of the work being done by experimental psychologists in aesthetics. Most of the work follows the by now well worn footsteps of Fechner. We take only a few samples from the wide range of literature.

In music, Olson [49] has concluded (by asking 1,000 people whether they prefer "this" to "that") that people prefer full frequency sound ranges over limited frequency ones. Pepinsky [50] modestly suggests that the emotion aroused by instrumental music depends partly on how the instrument is played, and not altogether on the physical characteristics of the tone or instrument.

---

[47] "The relationship between verbal reports and galvanic skin responses to music," abstract: *American Psychologist,* 1948, 3, p. 275.

[48] Gundlach, "Factors Determining the Characterization of Musical Phrases," 1935, 47, pp. 624–643.

[49] "Frequency range preference for speech and music," *Journal of Acoustical Society of America,* 1947, p. 549.

[50] "Musical Tone Qualities as a Factor in Expressiveness," *Journal of Acoustical Society of America,* 1947, p. 542. Pepinsky cites no actual experimental evidence; his inclusion in this classification is perhaps open to question.

In the field of painting, C. W. Valentine [51] has identified four distinct "types" of appreciators. From other workers [52] we learn that little boys prefer seascapes to landscapes, while little girls prefer pictures of people. Little children of both sexes like bright pictures. Children like bigger cardboard rectangles than adults do; preferred shapes approach the golden mean. [53] One of Great Britain's leading psychologists of art, R. W. Pickford, selected 45 pictures to include 10 aesthetic qualities. Eighteen judges who were interested in the psychology of art rated the pictures. Intercorrelations between the responses were factorized. The general conclusion was drawn that design, feeling, and rhythm were the "essence of art." [54] One of the most careful of recent experiments was performed by Sister Agnes Raley at Nazarene College. [55] Dissatisfied with speculative theories of humor, she set about psychometrics in this field. Twenty-eight cartoons were grouped into seven rows of four. A Thurston scale was developed, and a rank order preference technique explained to her students. Test retest correlation on the experiment ran .98. Probable error was computed at $+.007$ . . . a very high reliability. Sister Agnes suggests, on the basis of this experiment, that girls below the age of fifteen like different cartoons than do girls of sixteen, seventeen, and eighteen.

Rather less "preference" work has been done with literary or quasi-literary situations. I report only three experimental results. First: people of different ages aesthetically prefer familiar first names (Robert, Jean) over bizarre first names (Hulsey, Minna); children resent outlandish first names. [56] Second: a reader of poetry and prose is better understood if he speaks in a normal voice than he is if he talks through his nose. [57] Third: literary authors' punctuation habits differ; in poetry, fiction and drama, the use of the colon (counted per thousand marks of punctuation) is declining; punctuation profiles can be constructed, but are probably unreliable indices to total personality. [58]

Three last examples, which do not fit tidily under the headings listed

---

[51] *An Introduction to the Experimental Psychology of Beauty,* London and New York 1913.

[52] Dietrich and Hunnicutt, "Art content preferred by primary grade children," *Elementary School Journal,* 1948, pp. 557–559.

[53] Shipley, Dattman, Steele, "The influence of size on preferences for rectangular proportion in children and adults," *Journal of Experimental Psychology,* 1947, p. 333.

[54] Abstract: "Experiments with pictures," *Advancement of Science,* 1948, 5, p. 140.

[55] Abstract: *American Psychologist,* 1946, 1, p. 205.

[56] Finch, Kilgren, Pratt, "The Relation of First Name Preferences to Age of Judges or to Different Although Overlapping Generations," *Journal of Social Psychology,* 1944, 20, pp. 249–264.

[57] Glasgow, "The Effects of Nasality on Oral Communication," *Quarterly Journal of Speech,* 1944, 30, pp. 337–340.

[58] E. L. Thorndike, "The Psychology of Punctuation," *American Journal of Psychology,* 1948, 61, pp. 222–228.

above, will complete our "experimental" list. The first is quite an interesting experiment performed on a group of 100 college students to test the influence of prestige factors in directing affective response.[59] There does seem to be some such influence. Another investigator has shown that some music sounds funny, even without any program or title.[60] And finally, Paul Farnsworth, former president of the Esthetics Division of the A.P.A., among many other contributions to the psychology of music, has demonstrated [61] that there is some correlation among the following factors: the amount of attention certain eminent musicians receive in certain encyclopedias and histories of music (presumably measured in number of lines of type, so as to remain objective); the number of phonograph records of their music; the frequencies with which their names appear on the programs of certain symphony orchestras; and how well grade school, high school and college students say that they like the musicians' music. These materials are in turn correlated with the musicians' birthdays.

§ 5

Broadly, what contributions may each of these various approaches claim to have made to our understanding of the arts? What do its limitations seem at present to be?

We might first note, in an overview of all three positions, that none of them by any means definitely solves the *normative* problem—if there is any such problem—which has worried so many philosophers of art. Some, but not all, psychoanalysts frankly disavow any such interest, admitting that "bad" poems are equally revealing psychoanalytically as "good" ones.[62] The Gestaltists worry about the problem,[63] but I am not yet satisfied that their suggestions will prove ultimately satisfactory. The experimentalists, quite obviously, beg the normative question. This general scientific disinterest in aesthetic norms is, I believe, a healthy sign. A degree of philosophical naïveté is excusable and perhaps even desirable in a scientist; the converse, however, is not true. This whole question of the methodology of value-psychology needs consideration, but is much too extended to discuss here.

It seems, generally, that we owe to the psychoanalysts a broad set of categories, of hypothetical constants, of (charitably) "as if" personality

---

[59] Rigg, "Favorable versus Unfavorable Propaganda in the Enjoyment of Music," *Journal of Experimental Psychology*, 1948, pp. 78–81.

[60] Mull, "A Study of Humor in Music," *American Journal of Psychology*, October 1949, 62, pp. 560–566.

[61] Abstract: "Musical Eminence," *American Psychologist*, 1946, 1, p. 205.

[62] Stekel, *Die Träume der Dichter*, Wiesbaden 1932, p. 32; quoted by Langer, *Philosophy in a New Key*, Pelican ed., 1948, p. 168.

[63] See Köhler's *The Place of Value in the World of Facts*, New York 1938.

factors analogous to the "as if" constituents of the atom, which seem in some cases to help us partially account for what hitherto had appeared to be the "miracle" of creation. We have been provided with a very schematic picture of a "hidden mechanism" whose workings we are only beginning to understand. Miscellaneous groups of data, hitherto disorganized in our understanding, are brought under these categories and seen to have some kind of a common explanation, however broad. Some sort of "intellectual at-homeness" may be brought about in this way . . . although it may not be exactly the kind of a home of which we may be very proud.

In terms of these categories, certain very general generalizations do seem to be allowable, on an admittedly semi-speculative basis, as, for example, that erotic desires repressed by the censorial super-ego tend toward external vicarious or sublimated expression by means of art-symbols, analogous to dream-symbols. We find at least a serious attempt to give one kind of explanation of the symbols in art, and to bring together observed facts from various fields into a coherent explanation. There seems to be no reason why such explanations, when developed, may not warrant prediction; and their clinical efficacy seems fairly well established.

Among the many criticisms which have been levelled at the psychoanalytical approach to works of art I shall mention only a few. There are two naive and equally dogmatic rejections of the entire Freudian-Voluntaristic approach. The first of these is the lay rejection of the man in the street: "The whole business sounds cock-eyed. It must be crazy." To be sure, some of the speculative analyses do sound cock-eyed to the layman, but that is neither here nor there. Einstein's hypotheses, watered down to the lay level, sound cock-eyed too. It is a dogmatic and quite clearly extra-empirical demand that every scientific explanation make clear good sense to the man in the street. The question at issue is not whether Freudian interpretations sound far-fetched, but whether they are true, interesting and useful.

A second general criticism, less obviously naive but still, I think, dogmatic, amounts to little more than a blanket categorical refusal to grant the honorific title "science" to such enterprises, on grounds that they are not both experimental in a literal sense and quantitative in their data. This is the criticism we used to hear from the extreme behaviorists. Insofar as the dispute is a rather petty quibble over who has a right to the precious word "science," I do not find it enlightening. It is worth pointing out that many disciplines which we do ordinarily call by that name—astronomy, for example—do not feature literal experimentation. Similarly observational rather than literally experimental are all the so-called historical sciences of man, such as anthropology . . . sciences which (like psychoanalysis) take ranges of data and attempt generalizations on the basis of them. Nor is it the case that all of what we commonly call "sciences" constantly engage in statistical correlations: botany furnishes a familiar example.

There are, however, certain other criticisms which may be raised with perhaps somewhat more force. They are not intended as *a priori* categorical denunciations of a whole field of endeavor, but rather simply as requests. What Baudouin said in the twenties [64] remains true today: "The new doctrine requires criticism; but it is absurd, at this date, to regard psychoanalysis as null and void."

First, it would be helpful if it were possible for the psychoanalysts to clarify in empirical terms the grounding definitions of their categories: id, ego, super-ego, etc. Presumably we should be able to specify (or at least we should like to be able to specify) some sort of operational definitions for them, yet it seems to be exceedingly difficult to do so. We would like to be able to say, "If the painting contains this symbol, we see the artist's ego at work; if it contains that symbol, we see his super-ego." This demand may now be altogether impossible of fulfillment, because of the rich complexity of the subject matter with which the psychoanalyst is dealing. He himself assures us that all of the different factors are represented in our every action. Just exactly how, then (we would like to know) can we recognize the activity of the various personality factors when we meet them? How shall we even work *toward* precise measurement, granting that precision is impossible at the present time?

Furthermore, we are somewhat worried, on reviewing psychoanalytic-aesthetic literature, about an apparent tendency to reify categories, to make theoretical entities into "things out there." We are anxious to keep clearly before us in our analyses that the unconscious is a hypothetical construct, rather than a metaphysical entity; it is to be justified in use rather than to be intuited as a self-evident criterion and set up as an independent court of authority. We must be careful to use our categories as instruments of generalization *from* facts, rather than as prejudicial definitions of what kind of evidence will be admitted as factual.

And finally, we would like with psychoanalytic-aesthetic hypotheses, as with any other, some suggested pattern of verification. This will entail the presentation of specific predictions about human behavior, and it may be that we do not yet have adequate generalizations on which to base any far-

---

[64] *Op. cit.* p. 20. Baudouin claims (pp. 33–34) that psychoanalysts "have laid the foundations for the psychology of art, of a science of aesthetics which shall be genuinely scientific without thinking itself bound for that reason to approach art as a psychological 'case' or as a 'subject' to be catalogued, without succumbing to the danger of manifesting a sterile erudition, without losing contact with life, and without forfeiting the sense of beauty." Or again (p. 294) "Psychology is no longer (ca. 1922) content to make use of the methods proper to the physical sciences; it has sought out, and to a large extent has already found, methods proper to itself."

reaching predictions. But at least some of us will be happier when we see the way clear to a confirmation or disconfirmation of the hypotheses in terms of predictions fulfilled or frustrated. It seems fair to charge the proponents of any scientific theory with showing us at least in principle what kind of evidence will be accepted (when and if we can get it) as confirmatory, and what kind as disconfirmatory.

An estimate of the contributions of Gestalt psychology to our understanding of the arts would have to include our debt for several sensitive and enlightening criticisms of particular works of art, and for a set of principles, only now in process of fuller formulation, which seem to have widening application. Many of our actual experiences of familiar works can be enriched by looking for and finding these principles at work in our own perception. And again, we are always grateful for any fertile ideas which help us to organize into intelligible patterns miscellaneous ranges of data, to "make sense out of experience."

The naive criticisms of psychoanalysis in art have also been levelled against Gestaltism. Let our earlier comments apply here too.

A warning may, I think, be reasonably issued to the Gestaltists, analogous to one which is sometimes issued to the psychoanalysts, namely the stark and real possibility that the hypotheses may become so thin, in order to accommodate many various data, that they no longer say very much. It seems that some changes in this direction have taken place during the past twenty years . . . qualifications and refinements which rather dangerously broaden the scope. Any broad scientific or philosophical hypothesis runs this risk, of course; in striving for breadth, it becomes thin, just as, in striving for specificity, it becomes narrow.

Hardly anyone today doubts that the Gestalt is a good idea, but it has been suggested that at least some of its principles may already have done their work, have run their courses in art. We find in the arts magnificent textbook examples of fusion, closure, sequence, figure-ground principles, especially so long as we confine our attention to classical architecture and to sculpture. But, as Ehrenzweig points out,[65] the most persuasive Gestalt interpretations hinge quite naturally around those perceptual surfaces and depths in which the eye and the attention are expressly confined. But in much of contemporary painting and poetry, the eye and attention are invited to wander. There seem to be simply no well-defined wholes in perception. Figure and ground blend indistinguishably. The presented surface may as well be seen

---

[65] "Unconscious Form-Creation in Art," *British Journal of Medical Psychology,* 1948, pp. 185–214. Ehrenzweig attributes the basic idea to Herbert Read (*Art in Industry,* London, 1934), and points out that education both in creation and in appreciation often seems to contradict Gestalt principles: we learn, for example, to see ground, or negative space, as *figure,* as shaped.

as all figure, or all ground, or neither, like wallpaper. The Gestaltist can, of course, answer this criticism, but only by digging rather deep for evidence of the principles which he brings to the work of art. In no very clear sense does he find them "there" so to speak in the evidential work of art presented to him. To justify such "digging," overwhelming prior evidence, of a more direct sort, must warrant the hypothesis as highly probable. There is a suspiciously *ad hoc* feeling about any such extreme hypothetical extension; quite justifiably, I feel, it weakens our original, fresh faith in the hypothesis.

We come finally to an estimate of the contributions of what we have called the "experimental" approach to aesthetics. Here, I think, we may be most grateful for the aptitude tests, which are doing practical work every day. As for theoretical contributions to our understanding of the fine arts, however, I find myself (with few exceptions) [66] at a loss. Frankly, I don't think we have yet learned very much about art by the kind of experimentation and measurement which has been going on. If pressed, I will admit that I do not expect—unless we alter our approach somewhat—that we will learn a great deal more in this direction, at least within the next three thousand years. Beyond that I do not care to predict. Indirectly, of course, we in aesthetics have benefited materially from experimental psychology. Experiments in perception, learning and emotions have made some important contributions . . . but these investigations have, for the most part, been carried on outside the field of psychology of art.[67] Within that field, as practiced by the experimentalists, we have found some models of experimental technique, complete with control groups and probable error computations. We have found examples of highly refined statistical procedures and high-powered correlations; even factor analysis has found its way into this field.[68] And we have come out with fairly suggestive evidence quite strongly indicating that several things which we believed all along to be true are really true.

This latter-day sophisticated behaviorism in aesthetics seems to many of us to be frankly thin, to present results disappointing and even insignificant in proportion to the enormous labors which have been put into it. Why is this?

---

[66] —as sample exceptions, the investigations of Gundlach, Mull, and Rigg, cited above.

[67] Buswell, for example (*How People Look at Pictures,* Chicago 1935) presents relevant and important data on perception in art. He trained cameras on corneas and mapped out eye movement diagrams, timing fixations. Alschuler and Weiss (*Painting and Personality: A Study of Young Children,* Chicago 1947) present an intensive and fairly extensive study of the relations between creative expression and personality in children between the ages of two and five.

[68] Guilford and Holley, "A factorial approach to the analysis of variations in aesthetic judgments," *Journal of Experimental Psychology,* 1949, 39, pp. 208–218, an ingenious methodology applied to choices of designs of playing cards.

The naive answer to this question is one which perennially arises in cases of this sort: just because we find our scientific row difficult to hoe, some people deny the possibility of ever hoeing it, and illogically infer that the field is somehow forever "autonomous," "beyond science" in some mysterious sense in which the field of physics is not. "Art," it is argued, "is too pure, too unique, too otherworldly and intuitive to be a subject-matter for such 'atomistic' science." [69] I suppose that psychologists still have to listen to this sort of complaint from time to time, just as philosophers do. But I submit that it is vestigial 19th century romanticism and not worth taking seriously within the framework of our present-day lives and works. We cannot prove it false, because of the very nature of the position: it doesn't say anything explicit enough to be proved true or false. But in attempting a science of art, as in attempting a science of anything else, we must assume it to be false. Since this assumption seems (although admittedly extra-empirical) to be a condition of any knowledge about anything, I am willing to make it cheerfully, and I suggest that we all do so. I do not know of any evidence which could possibly prove our assumption to be mistaken, since it is at least primarily procedural rather than descriptive. The *analysis* of this assumption, by the way, I take to be one of the primary tasks of philosophy.

Three other answers however suggest themselves as possible explanations for our dissatisfaction with the results of experimental-quantitative aesthetics. The first of these points to the empirical fact that our experiences of works of art in appreciation, and artists' experience in creation, are admitted by all hands to be highly complex. A positively enormous number of variables enter into the perceptual situation; many, but not all, of these have been pointed out in philosophical analyses of art. The entire physical and psychological history of the percipient seems to condition his response, often in apparently irrelevant and certainly unexpected ways. A large number of the qualities of the work itself are clearly relevant. The physical and social environment of appreciation obviously plays an important part. The whole "as if" representational world of the visual and literary arts presents special psychological complexities. And all of these variable factors seem to fuse in extraordinarily complicated fashions. It is not at all evident, or perhaps it is even unlikely, that discrete observations gleaned in the sterile atmosphere of the usual psychological laboratory are now legitimate warrant for *any* very interesting or useful generalizations about the aesthetic experience. Responding to an El Greco on a museum wall simply isn't much like comparing cardboard rectangles in a classroom, and it is difficult to see from here how any number of such cardboard comparisons will ever pile

---

[69] See Jung, *Modern Man in Search of a Soul*, New York 1934, p. 177: "Any reaction to stimulus may be causally explained; but the creative act, which is the absolute antithesis of mere reaction will forever elude the human understanding."

up, one on top of another, to give a description of the aesthetic response. In order to get the problem into the laboratory, it has quite naturally been necessary to control the number of variables. It may be that this control has resulted in a fatal oversimplification of the problem.

Note that this is emphatically *not* a retreat into mysticism. I do not believe that these problems of aesthetics—or, for that matter, any real problems of description of any phenomena at all—are forever inevitably beyond the scientist. But I am not encouraged that they are now within the grasp of the quantitative experimentalist in anything closely approximating the rather cavalier attack we find in the books and journals of the nineteen forties. The counsel is one of caution rather than of surrender. Let us beware of the subtleties and complexities, lest we distort the problems into over-simplified caricatures in the name of empirical science.

As a second general observation, I suggest that at least in some cases in which aesthetic behavior patterns have been studied by experimentalists, the experimenters have apparently failed to ask significant and crucial questions *in advance of* experiment. Charles Darwin once remarked that he never heard of anything sillier than a man setting up an experiment without trying to prove or disprove something, just going into the laboratory to perform an experiment for the sake of the experiment. It does look sometimes as if some of these investigators into aesthetics have been willing to settle for just any old correlation between any old sets of behavioral data at all, so long as they are "objective." Small wonder that correlations are found: it is a tautology to say that *any* sets of data will correlate somewhere between —1.0 and +1.0. There are indeed behavioral correlations to be found; the trouble is that there are too many of them. In the psychology of art we must imaginatively select in advance of experiment *which* factors, when correlated, will give us interesting and important results. This requires some hard thinking, some imagination, some kind of a *theory,* however tentative, some "exploratory hypothesis" guessed at from earlier work, or from common sense observation, or wherever. *Mere* laboratory observations, however accurately made and acutely correlated, will never give us anything remotely resembling a scientific description of the aesthetic experience. Statistical calisthenics may be a fine exercise for a student of psychology; I expect it is; the études of Czerny are fine exercises for students of piano. But (to borrow a figure) we do not expect to hear Czerny études from the concert platform.

It may be that physics is indeed the proper model for psychology to emulate. But the emulation should be *methodological* rather than *material.* Psychologists of art may of course, but need not, make the rather extravagant assumption that every aesthetically relevant consideration is a space-time event measurable in physiological terms. And, as Köhler pointed out, if we are to take physics as our model, we might well remember that physics went through centuries of qualitative refinement before its quantitative methods became applicable. It is at least possible that our understanding of the psychology of art is still in a stone age, a period of pre-scientific or better "pre-quantitative" discrimination.[70] After all, even physics has occasionally had difficulty with its quantification techniques. I know of no one who would want to maintain seriously that the problems of psychology of art are simpler than those of physics . . . except where they have been made simpler by radical surgical excisions of important and relevant complexities. Frank recognition of these complexities is surely a prime duty of the empirical scientist.

This paper has included a summary, classification, and tentative criticism of psychology at work today among the arts. No moral need be drawn, but if one is requested, let it be simply this: we need hard-headed, cautious, clear scientific thinking about the arts; perhaps right now we need it most on the level of fundamental theory developed by trained psychologists who have a love for the arts and a healthy curiosity about what makes them tick.

---

[70] For examples of psychologists' critiques of psychological experimentations in aesthetics, see Max Dessoir, *op. cit.* pp. 17ff. R. M. Ogden, *The Psychology of Art,* New York 1938, p. 22, says: "A work of art eludes all efforts to quantify it in terms of a precise formula. 'Aesthetic measure' is a contradiction in terms." He refers, of course, to Birkhoff's *Aesthetic Measure,* Cambridge 1933. A more moderate, and I suspect, more nearly correct view, is that of Thomas Munro (*Scientific Method in Aesthetics,* New York 1928, pp. 15–17): "quantitative measurements . . . when erected into a fetish, as they have been by 'experimental aesthetics' . . . usually lead to premature inferences that have a specious air of certainty, and the neglecting of more fruitful methods of inquiry. . . . Too rigorous an insistence on absolute reliability and 'objectivity' of data, too impatient a zeal for universally valid generalizations, may be an obstacle in a field where these cannot be attained at once, if ever." See also Jung, *Modern Man,* p. 176.

Section Two

THE NATURE OF ART

Before proceeding to the cluster of problems which constitute the field of aesthetics, it is profitable to examine a few representative definitions of the general nature of aesthetic activity. There are several ways in which the nature of art may be defined. Writers who follow in the tradition of Aristotle would insist that art first be distinguished from nature, and no one since Aristotle has improved upon the pithy and lucid manner in which he formulates this distinction (see his *Physics* ii and *Metaphysics* vii). He characterizes the natural object as that which has its form, that is, the principle of its growth or movement, within itself. The form of an object of art, on the other hand, is imposed on the material from the outside by the artist. A distinction as far-reaching as this can be made only on the basis of a well worked out and complete philosophy, and for this reason an attempt to elucidate it and to present the grounds on which Aristotle justifies it would carry us far beyond the bounds of aesthetic discourse.

Contemporary aestheticians do not, for the most part, begin by distinguishing objects that grow or come about naturally from those that are manmade. Instead, they assume from the first that art is produced by human activity. Thus, in order to define art, they do not differentiate it from nature but, taking this distinction for granted, differentiate it from other possible modes of human activity. These distinctions also enable some writers to differentiate the so-called "fine" arts from the "useful" arts. Now it has been argued that the distinctions among the various modes of human activity and between the fine and the useful arts are not essential ones, and that only as a result of the specialization of the last several centuries has the

48

need for such distinctions become apparent. Such argument has some historical validity. It is well known, for example, that for a Greek citizen the presentation of a play was a religious, a civic, and an aesthetic affair all in one. The play was neither a less nor a more purely aesthetic object than were the ancient Greek temples. Indeed, a similar argument could be urged about many of the arts at least until the Renaissance.

It would thus not have been easy to make a distinction between the aesthetic, religious, and civic aspects of the public activities which involved the citizens, the guilds, and the church in the middle ages. The medieval artisan who built the church would hardly distinguish himself, as being a fine or a useful artist, from those who carved the statues. It may very well be that the integrated quality of their activities is the mark of the greatness of these ages, and, by contrast, that the specialization of social activities in our modern age and the social disintegration which some thinkers take to be the distinctive mark of our modernity are in some sense related. Whatever the cause, in our day it becomes possible and necessary to make the nice theoretical distinctions among the modes of human activity that have been suggested above. These are historical problems that solicit investigation. But regardless of what history may reveal about whether in the past these distinctions were or were not made, and why, its conclusions cannot invalidate the distinctions which, for purposes of aesthetic theory, are being made in this section on an analytical rather than an historical basis.

In the following selections, with the exception of that of Maritain, the distinction between fine art and useful art has been taken for granted. When the writers attempt to define art, we find that they do so in terms of one or more of the several factors distinguished in the diagram (see p. 12). They sometimes assume that art is best defined in terms of the artist's creative activity, which they proceed to explain by distinguishing it in some specific way from scientific or religious or moral-practical activity. They sometimes define art either in terms of the aesthetic effect it produces on the observer, an effect which they distinguish as a unique mode of response, or in terms of the moral-political effects it produces on its society at large. Or they define it in terms of the intrinsic make-up of the object which the artist creates and which produces the effects on the observer. Or, finally, they often define art in terms of any combination of these factors.

In the first selection, Maritain's definition of fine art touches on many of these factors. He first distinguishes all art, fine as well as useful, from science and wisdom on the one hand and prudence or morality on the other, in terms of the activity of the artist and the nature of the object. Then, by turning to the activity of the observer, he sees that there is a unique response to beauty as an end in itself which only the fine arts can arouse. Croce, distinguishing and even separating art from all other possible modes of activity, defines it solely in terms of the activity of the artist who produces it. As an idealist he conceives this activity, which he terms "intuition," to be purely spiritual. Parker criticizes many attempts at definition prior to his own. These he sees as erecting a single differentia to characterize art, although no one differentia, Parker claims, can be a sufficient as well as a necessary defining quality of art. His own definition is thus drawn in terms of the activity of the artist and a similar activity of the observer ("satisfaction in the imagination"), in terms of a certain quality of the object ("harmony"), and in terms of the need for society to provide both artist and observer with values and physical media which are socially shared ("social significance").

The last selection is that of Morris, who defines art in terms of the nature of the object. But he is primarily concerned with distinguishing among the various forms of discourse rather than among the various forms of human activity. Thus he treats the object as a means of communication in terms of a theory of signs. He distinguishes among the different kinds of signs and sign functions, differentiating the signs used in art from those used in scientific discourse and from those used in "technological" discourse, by which he means that form of discourse which induces action. It will be seen, however, that, while treating art as a kind of sign, the definition must refer to the various purposes of the users of the signs, since these purposes allow to signs their various functions. Thus we are once again returned to the distinctions among the modes of human activity, each of which, Morris claims, is to be more intelligently pursued on the discursive level once its objectives are clarified in semiotic terms.

Which of these definitions is preferable is something on which we may not expect any ready agreement. But certainly a knowledge of several of them is essential to us if we are to make our own choice among them. And while these definitions should help to mark off the field on which the discipline of aesthetics is to operate, they should serve also—if we look for the particular aesthetic problems from which the definitions are drawn—to introduce us to the necessity of seeing how interrelated are the various factors which make up this field.

JACQUES MARITAIN

A Definition of Art[1]

The Speculative Order and the Practical Order

THERE ARE VIRTUES of the mind whose *sole end is knowledge*. They belong to the *speculative* order.

Such are: The Understanding of first principles, which, once we have derived from the experience of our senses the ideas of Being, Causation, End, and the like, makes us perceive at once—through the active light which is in us naturally—the self-evident truths upon which all our knowledge depends; Science, which produces knowledge demonstratively, by attributing causes; Wisdom, which makes us contemplate first causes, wherein the mind embraces all things in the superior unity of a simple glance.

These speculative virtues perfect the mind in its peculiar function, in the activity in which it is purely itself: for the object of the mind, as such, is simply and solely knowledge. The mind is active and its action indeed is speaking absolutely, life *par excellence*: but it is an *immanent* action remaining wholly within the mind to make it perfect, and by means of it the mind, with insatiable voracity, seizes hold of being and draws it to itself, eats being and drinks it, so as to "become itself, in a way, all things." The speculative order is therefore its peculiar order: it finds its ease therein. The good or evil estate of the subject, its needs or convenience, are alike indifferent to it: it takes its joy in being and has eyes only for being.

The *practical* order differs from the speculative order because in practice man tends to something other than mere knowledge. If he has knowledge, it is not simply so that he shall rest in truth and enjoy it (*frui*); but rather

---

[1] Reprinted from *Art and Scholasticism* by Jacques Maritain, tr. J. F. Scanlan, New York, Charles Scribner's Sons, 1943, pp. 3–30, 32–35; used by permission of the publishers. Title by the editors.

The editors have found it impossible to keep all the numerous and valuable footnotes which the author of this selection appended to his text. They have translated between brackets only those quotations for which the author did not himself provide a rendering. The references given are the author's, although in some cases the editors did not succeed in verifying them. (Eds.)

to put what he knows to some use (*uti*), with a view to making or doing something.

Art belongs to the Practical Order. Its orientation is towards doing, not to the pure inwardness of knowledge.

There are, to be sure, speculative arts which are at the same time sciences, e.g. logic: such scientific arts perfect the speculative intellect, not the practical intellect; but the sciences in question retain in their *manner* an element of the practical, and are arts only because they involve *the making of a work*—in this case a work wholly within the mind, whose sole object is knowledge, a work which consists in putting order into our concepts, in framing a proposition or an argument. The result is then, that wherever you find *art* you find some action or operation to be contrived, some work to be done.

Making and Action

The Mind as a faculty is a complete self-subsisting whole, but it goes to work very differently according as it has knowledge for the sake of knowing or for the sake of doing.

The speculative intellect will find its perfect and infinitely superabundant joy only in the intuitive vision of the Divine Being: it is through it that man will then possess beatitude: *gaudium de Veritate* [joy about the truth]. It is very rarely exercised in absolute liberty on this earth except in the case of the philosopher, theologian or metaphysician, or the devotee of pure learning. In the great majority of cases the reason works in the practical order and for the various ends of human actions.

But the practical order is itself divided into two entirely distinct spheres which the Ancients termed Action (*agibile, πραχτόν*) and Making (*factibile, ποιητόν*).

Action, in the restricted sense in which the Schoolmen understood the word, consists in the *free* use (*free* being here emphatic) of our faculties or in the exercise of our free will considered not in relation to things themselves or the works of our hands, but simply in relation to the use to which we put our freedom.

This use depends upon our specifically human appetite or Will, which of itself does not tend to truth, but solely and jealously to the good of man, that only existing for the appetite which fulfils desire or love and increases the being of the subject or stands to the subject in the same relation as itself. This use is good if it conforms to the law governing all human acts and the true end of human life: and if it is good, the man so acting is himself good, purely and simply.

Action is thus ordered to the common end of all human life and it has a part to play in the perfection peculiar to the human being. The sphere of Action is the sphere of Morality or of human good as such. Prudence, a virtue of the practical intellect which keeps Action straight, is wholly confined within the limits of human conduct. Prudence is the queen of the moral virtues, of high lineage and born to command, because Prudence measures our acts in their relation to an ultimate end which is God Himself, the supreme object of love, but she retains nevertheless a savour of misery, because her province is the multitude of necessities, circumstances and occupations, the arena of human suffering, and because she imbues with humanity everything she touches.

As opposed to Action, the Schoolmen defined Making as *productive action,* considered not in relation to the use to which, assuming it, we put our freedom, but simply *in relation to the thing produced* or the work taken by itself.

This action is what it ought to be, is good of its kind, if it conforms to the rules and the end peculiar to the work to be produced: and the result to which it is directed, if it is good, is for the work in question to be good in itself. So Making is ordered to such-and-such a definite end, separate and self-sufficient, not to the common end of human life; and it relates to the peculiar good or perfection not of the man making, but of the work made.

The sphere of Making is the sphere of Art, in the most universal meaning of the word.

Art, therefore, keeping Making straight and not Action, remains outside the line of human conduct, with an end, rules, and values, which are not those of the man, but of the work to be produced. That work is everything for art—one law only governs it—the exigencies and the good of the work.

Hence the despotic and all-absorbing power of art, as also its astonishing power of soothing: it frees from every human care, it establishes the *artifex,* artist or artisan, in a world apart, cloistered, defined and absolute, in which to devote all the strength and intelligence of his manhood to the service of the thing which he is making. This is true of every art; the ennui of living and willing ceases on the threshold of every studio or workshop.

But if art is not human in the end which it pursues, it is human, essentially human, in its method of working. It involves the making of a man's work, stamped with the character of a man: *animal rationale.*

The work of art has been pondered before being made, has been kneaded and prepared, formed, brooded over, and matured in a mind before emerging into matter. And there it will always retain the colour and the savour of the spirit. Its *formal* element, what constitutes it of its kind and makes it what it is, is its being controlled and directed by the mind. If this formal element is in the least degree lacking, the reality of the art becomes correspondingly dissipated. *The work to be done* is merely the matter of art, the form of it is *undeviating reason*. *Recta ratio factibilium* [the right reason of that which is practicable]: I will try to translate into English this vigorous Aristotelian and Scholastic definition and define Art as the *undeviating determination of work to be done*.[2]

Art an Intellectual Virtue

To summarise now the teaching of the Schools concerning art in general, considered in the artist or the artisan and as peculiar to him:

1. Art is before all intellectual and its activity consists in impressing an idea upon a matter: therefore it resides in the mind of the *artifex,* or, as they say, it is subject in that mind. It is a certain *quality* of that mind.

2. The Ancients applied the term *habitus* (ἕξις) to qualities of a distinct and separate kind, essentially permanent conditions perfecting in the line of its own nature the subject they inform. Health and beauty are habits of the body, sanctifying grace a (supernatural) habit of the soul: other habits have for subject the faculties or powers of the soul, and as these naturally tend to action, the habits related to them perfect them in their very dynamism, are *operative* habits: such are the intellectual and moral virtues.

We acquire the last-mentioned kind of habit by exercise and customary use; but we must not therefore confuse habit in the present technical sense with the modern meaning of the word, namely, mere mechanical bent and routine: the two are utterly different and opposed. Customary habit, which attests the solid weight of matter, resides in the nerve centres. Operative habit, which attests the activity of the mind, resides chiefly in an immaterial faculty only, in the mind or the will. When the mind, for instance, originally indifferent in regard to any special object of knowledge, demonstrates some truth to its satisfaction, it makes use of its peculiar activity in a certain way, it arouses within itself a quality which makes it proportionate to, and commensurate with, such-and-such an object of speculation, which lifts it up to and keeps it on a level with that object; it acquires the habit of a science. Habits are interior growths of spontaneous life, vital developments which make the soul better in a given sphere and fill it full of a vigorous sap:

---

[2] Prudence on the other hand is the undeviating determination of acts to be done (*recta ratio agibilium*), and Science the undeviating determination of the objects of speculation (*recta ratio speculabilium*).

turgentia ubera animae [the swelling breast of the Soul] as John of St. Thomas calls them. And only the living (that is to say, minds which alone are perfectly alive) can acquire them, because they alone are capable of raising the level of their being by their own activity: they so possess, in such an enrichment of their faculties, secondary motives to action, which they bring into play when they want, and which make what is difficult in itself for them delightfully easy.

Habits are, as it were, metaphysical letters patent of nobility, and just as much as inborn talents make for inequality among men. The man with a habit has a quality in him for the lack of which nothing can compensate, as nothing can take its place; other men are defenceless, he is armour-clad, but his armour is the living armour of the spirit.

Habit again, properly so-called, is stable and permanent (*difficile mobilis* [difficult of movement]) *precisely because of the object* which specifies it; hence the difference between it and mere disposition, as for example opinion. The object in relation to which it perfects the subject is itself unchangeable,—such is, for the habit of Science, the infallible truth of demonstration,—and it is upon this object that the quality developed in the subject *catches*. Hence the strength and the rigidity of habits, their susceptibility,—they are irritated by any deviation from the straight line to their object,—their intransigence,—they are firmly fixed in an absolute: what possible concession could they make?—their boorishness in society. Men of the world, polished on every surface, dislike the man with a habit and his asperities.

Art is a habit of the practical intellect.

3. Such a habit is a *virtue,* that is to say a quality which, triumphing over the original indetermination of the intellective faculty, at once sharpening and hardening the point of its activity, raises it in respect of a definite object to a *maximum of perfection, and so of operative efficiency.* Every virtue being so determined to the utmost of which the faculty is capable, and every evil being a deficiency and a weakness, virtue can incline only to good: it is impossible to make use of a virtue to do evil: it is essentially *habitus operativus boni* [operative habit of the good].[3]

The presence of such a virtue in the workman is necessary to the goodness of the work, *for the manner of the action follows the disposition of the agent and, as a man is, so are his works.* For the work in hand to turn out well, there must correspond to it in the soul of the workman such a disposition as will produce between them the sort of congruence and intimate proportion which the Schoolmen termed *connaturality*: Logic, Music and

---

[3] *Sum. Theol.,* i–ii, q. 55, a. 3.

Architecture respectively graft the syllogism upon the logician, harmony upon the musician, and balance of masses upon the architect. Through the presence in them of the virtue of Art, they *are,* in a way, their work before they create it: to be able to form it, they have conformed to it.

But if art is a *virtue of the practical intellect,* and if every virtue inclines solely to the good (that is to say, in the case of a virtue of the intellect, to what is *true*), it necessarily follows that Art as such (Art, I say, and not the artist, whose actions often run contrary to his art) never makes a mistake and involves an *infallible correctness.* Otherwise it would not be a habit properly so called, stable by its very nature.

The Schoolmen debated at length this infallible correctness of art, and more at large the virtues of the practical intellect (Prudence in the sphere of Action, Art in the sphere of Making). How is it possible to make the intellect infallibly true in the domain of the individual and the contingent? They answered by making a fundamental distinction between *the truth of the speculative intellect,* which consists in *knowing,* in conformity with what is, and *the truth of the practical intellect,* which consists in *directing,* in conformity with what ought to be, according to the rule and the proper disposition of the thing to be done; if there can be no *science* except only of what is necessary, if there can be no infallible truth in *knowledge* of what can be other than it is, there can be infallible truth in *direction,* there can be *art,* as there is *prudence,* where contingencies are concerned.

But this infallibility of art concerns only the formal element in the operation, that is to say the regulation of the work by the mind. If the hand of the artist falters, if his tool proves inferior, if what he is working upon gives way, the defect thereby introduced into the result, into the *eventus,* in no way affects the art itself and is no evidence that the artist has fallen short of his art: as soon as the artist, in the act of judgement made by his intellect, determined the rule and proper disposition applicable to the particular case, no error, that is to say no misleading direction, occurred *in him.* The artist who has the habit of art and the quivering hand,

C'ha l'habito de l'arte e man che trema,

produces an imperfect work but retains a faultless virtue. The same thing may happen in the moral sphere: the event may fail, but the act resolved according to the rules of prudence will none the less have been infallibly direct. Although extrinsically and on the material side involving contingency and fallibility, in itself, that is to say on the formal side and so far as regulation by the mind is concerned, art does not fluctuate like opinion, but is firmly fixed in certitude.

Manual dexterity therefore is no part of art, but merely a material and extrinsic condition; the labour by which the virtuoso who "plays the harp" acquires agile fingers does not increase his art itself or produce any special form; it merely removes a physical impediment to the practice of the art: *non generat novam artem, sed tollit impedimentum exercitii ejus* [4]: art remains entirely by the side of the mind.

4. The better to define its nature, the Ancients compared it to Prudence, which also is a virtue of the practical intellect. By so distinguishing and contrasting Art and Prudence, they laid a finger upon a vital spot in the psychology of human actions.

Art, it has already been observed, is in the line of Making, Prudence in the line of Action. Prudence discerns and applies the means of attaining our moral ends, which are themselves subordinate to the ultimate end of all human life—that is to say, God. It may be described metaphorically as an art, but it is the art of *totum bene vivere* [living in true perfection], an art which the Saints alone fully possess, with supernatural Prudence and above all the Gifts of the Holy Ghost, which impel them to divine things in a divine *way* and made them act under the very direction of the Spirit of God and His loving art, by giving them the wings of eagles to help them walk upon the earth: *assument pennas ut aquilae, current, et non laborabunt, ambulabunt et non deficient.* [5] Art has no concern with our life, but only with such-and-such particular and extra-human ends which in regard to Art are an ultimate goal.

Prudence operates for the good of the worker, *ad bonum operantis,* Art operates for the good of the work done, *ad bonum operis,* and everything which diverts it from that end adulterates and diminishes it. The moment the artist works well—the moment the Geometer demonstrates—"it makes little difference whether he be in a good temper or in a rage." [6] If he is angry or jealous, his sin is the sin of a man, not the sin of an artist. [7] Art in no wise tends to make the artist good in his specifically human conduct; it would tend rather for the work produced, if that were possible, itself to make a perfect use in its own line of the artist's activity. But human art does not produce works which proceed to action of their own motion; God alone makes works of that kind, and so the Saints are truly and literally His masterpiece.

Again, as the artist is first a man and then an artist, it is easy to see what conflicts will rage in his heart between Art and Prudence, his character as Maker and his character as Man. Prudence, no doubt, which in all things

---

[4] John of St. Thomas, *Curs. Phil.,* Log. ii, q. 1, a. 5.
[5] *Isaias* xl. 31: "They that hope in the Lord shall renew their strength: they shall take wings as eagles: they shall run, and not be weary: they shall walk and not be faint."
[6] *Sum. Theol.,* i–ii, q. 57, a. 3.
[7] *Ibid.,* q. 21, a. 2, *ad* 2.

judges according to particular cases, will not apply the same rules to him as to a ploughman or a tradesman, will not require a Rembrandt or a Léon Bloy to produce works *which pay* in order to assure the material comfort of their families. The artist will nevertheless require a measure of heroism to keep always in the direct line of Action and not to sacrifice his immortal substance to the devouring idol in his soul. The truth is that such conflicts can be abolished only on condition that a deep humility make the artist as it were unconscious of his art, or if the all-powerful unction of wisdom imbue everything in him with the repose and peace of love. Fra Angelico felt no such inner vexation of spirit.

For all that, the pure artist considered in the abstract as such, is something completely unmoral.

Prudence perfects the mind only presupposing that the will is undeviating in its line of human appetite, that is to say in respect of its peculiar good, which is the good of every man: its business is simply to determine the *means* in regard to such-and-such particular concrete human ends already willed: it therefore presupposes that the appetite is well disposed in regard to such ends.

Art, on the contrary, perfects the mind without presupposing the correctness of the will in its own line of human appetite, the ends at which it aims being outside the line of human good. So "the motion of the appetite which spoils the calculation of prudence does not spoil the calculation of art any more than that of geometry." [8] The act of *using* our faculties (*usus*) depending upon the will in its peculiar dynamism of human appetite, it can be easily understood that Art confers only the power of making well (*facultas boni operis*), and not the *habitual practice* of making well. The artist, if he likes, can refrain from using or misuse his art, as the grammarian, if he likes, can commit a solecism; the virtue of art which is in him is no less perfect on that account. According to Aristotle's famous remark [9] (Aristotle, I feel sure, would have liked the fantasies of Erik Satie), an artist sinning against his art is not blamed, if his sin is wilful, as he would be if it were not, whereas a man sinning against prudence or against justice is blamed all the more for sinning wilfully than for sinning unwillingly. On this point the Ancients observed that Art and Prudence both have first to *judge* and then to *command,* but that the chief function of art is only to judge, whereas the chief function of Prudence is to command. *Perfectio artis consistit in judicando*.[10]

Prudence, again, having for matter not something to make, some object determined in being, but the pure use to which the subject puts his liberty, has no certain definite paths or fixed rules. Its fixed point is the direct end to

---

[8] Aristotle, *Eth. Nic.*, vi.
[9] *Eth. Nic.*, vi, 5.
[10] *Sum. Theol.*, i–ii, q. 47, a. 8.

which the moral virtues tend and its business is to determine the right means. But to attain this end and to apply the universal principles of moral science, its precepts and counsels, to the particular action to be produced, there are no ready-made rules; for the action in question is involved in a tissue of circumstances which give it an individual character and make it every time a really new case. In every particular case there will be a particular way of conforming to the end. It is for Prudence to discover that way, by using paths or rules subordinate to the will (for the will to make its choice as circumstance and opportunity occur), in themselves contingent and not pre-determined but determined with certainty and definitely laid down by the judgement or decision of the Prudent Man, and therefore by the Schoolmen termed *regulae arbitrariae* [contingent rules]. Particular in every particular case, the direction given by Prudence is none the less certain and infallible, as has been said before, because the truth of the prudential judgement is considered in relation to the undeviating intention (*per conformitatem ad appetitum rectum* [through conformity to right appetite]), not in relation to the event; and supposing a second case were to recur or an infinite variety of cases, *identical in every respect* with a given case, *the same direction* ought strictly to be given in all: but there never will be a single moral case absolutely identical with another.

Hence it is that no *science* can take the place of Prudence, for science, however casuistically complicated it may be supposed to be, never has any other than general and ascertained rules.

Hence also the absolute necessity for Prudence, in order to fortify its judgement, to have recourse to the manifold, groping exploration which the Ancients termed *consilium* (deliberation, counsel).

Art, on the other hand, whose matter is a thing to be done, proceeds by *certain, definite ways: imo nihil aliud ars esse videtur, quam certa ordinatio rationis, quomodo per determinata media ad determinatum finem actus humani perveniant* [art rather appears to be nothing else than an unerring ordering of reason by which human acts may come to a determinate end by determinate means].[11] The Schoolmen, following Aristotle, never tire of insisting upon it and make this possession of ascertained rules an essential characteristic of Art as such. Some observations will be made later on the subject of these fixed rules in the case of the Fine Arts. It will be sufficient for the present to bear in mind that the Ancients dealt with the virtue of Art considered in itself and all its relations, not in any particular one of its kinds, so that the simplest example of art so considered, one in which the generic concept of art is at once realised, had best be sought in the mechanical arts. The proper end of the art of the shipwright or the clockmaker is an invaria-

---

[11] St. Thomas, *in Poster. Analyt.* lib. i, lect. 1, l.

ble and universal end, determined by reason: to enable a man to sail the sea or to tell him the time—the thing to be made, ship or clock, being itself merely a matter to be adapted to such an end. And for that there are fixed rules, also determined by reason, as suitable to the end and to a certain set of conditions.

So the effect produced is no doubt individual, and in cases where the matter of the art is particularly contingent and susceptible of variation, as, for instance, in Medicine or Agriculture or Strategy, Art will find it necessary in order to supply its fixed rules to use contingent rules (*regulae arbitrariae*) and a sort of prudence, will find it necessary also to have recourse to deliberation, to *consilium*. None the less Art by itself derives its steadfastness from its rational and universal rules, not from *consilium,* and the soundness of its judgement derives not from circumstances and events, as is the case with Prudence, but precisely from the certain and determined ways which are peculiar to it. For this reason certain arts can be sciences—practical sciences such as Medicine or Surgery (*ars chirurgico-barbifica* it was still called in the seventeenth century), or even speculative sciences such as Logic.

5. To sum up: Art is therefore *more exclusively intellectual* than Prudence. Whereas the subject of Prudence is the practical intellect *in so far as it presupposes the undeviating will and depends upon it,* Art is not concerned with the proper good of the will and the ends it pursues in its line of human appetite; and if it presupposes a certain rectitude of the appetite, this is again in relation to some specifically intellectual end. Like Science, it is bound fast to an *object* (an object to be made, certainly, not an object of contemplation). It employs the circuit of deliberation and counsel only accidentally. Although it produces individual actions and results, it forms judgements only adventitiously, according to the contingencies of circumstance, and so takes less account than Prudence of the individuation of actions and the *hic et nunc.* In short, if, because of its matter, which is contingent, it accords with Prudence more than with Science, *according to its formal reason and in so far as it is a virtue* it accords with Science and the habits of the speculative intellect more than with Prudence: *ars magis convenit cum habitibus speculativis in ratione virtutis, quam cum prudentia* [if considered as virtue, then art has more in common with the habits of the speculative intellect than with prudence].[12] The Man of Learning is an Intellectual demonstrating, the Artist is an Intellectual operating, the Prudent Man is an intelligent Man of Will acting well.

---

[12] *Sum. Theol.,* i–ii, q. 57, a. 4, *ad* 2.

Such are the main features of the Scholastic theory of art. Not in Phidias and Praxiteles only, but in the village carpenter and blacksmith as well, the Schoolmen acknowledged an intrinsic development of reason, a nobility of the mind. They did not consider that the virtue of the *artifex* lay in strength of muscle or in nimbleness of fingers or in the rapidity of a chronometrised and taylorised gesture: nor was it a merely empirical dexterity (*experimentum*), taking shape in the memory and in the (cogitative) animal reason, and imitating art: art cannot dispense with such a talent, but it remains extrinsic to art. It was a virtue of the mind and endowed the humblest artisan with a certain perfection of the spirit.

In the normal type of human development and truly human civilisations, the artisan represents the average man. If Christ willed to be an artisan in an insignificant village, it was because He wanted to assume the common lot of humanity.

The Doctors of the Middle Ages did not, like so many of our introspecting psychologists, make town dwellers, bookworms and graduates the sole object of their studies; they were concerned also with the mass of mankind. But even so they did not neglect the study of their Master. Pondering the art or activity peculiar to the *artifex,* they pondered the activity which Our Lord chose to exercise throughout His hidden life; they pondered also, in a way, the activity even of the Father; for they knew that the virtue of art is to be predicated peculiarly of God, like Goodness and Justice, and that the Son, plying His poor man's trade, was still the image of the Father and of His action which never ceases: *Philippe, qui videt Me videt et Patrem* [oh Philip, who ever has seen Me has seen the Father also].

It is interesting to observe that the Ancients in their classifications allotted no separate place to what we call the Fine Arts.[13] They divided the arts into servile and liberal, according as they required corporal labour or not, or rather (for such a division, which is more far reaching than one would think, was derived from the very concept of Art, *recta ratio factibilium* [the right reason of that which is practicable]), according as the *work to be done* was in one case an effect produced in the matter (*factibile* properly so called), in the other a pure spiritual composition remaining in the soul. Sculpture and painting on that score belonged to the servile arts, music to the liberal arts where it had arithmetic and logic for neighbours—for the musician arranges intellectually the sounds in his soul, as the arithmetician

---

13 The truth is that the division of the arts into the arts of the beautiful (the Fine Arts) and the useful, however important it may be in other respects, is not what Logicians term an "essential" division; it derives from the end pursued, and the same art can quite well pursue usefulness and beauty at the same time. Such, *par excellence,* is the case with architecture.

numbers and the logician concepts. The oral or instrumental expression, which in the fluid successions of resonant matter transmits compositions thus completed in the spirit, is an extrinsic consequence and a simple means for such arts, and nothing more.

In the powerfully social structure of mediaeval civilisation the artist ranked simply as an artisan, and every kind of anarchical development was prohibited to his individualism, because a natural social discipline imposed upon him from without certain limiting conditions. He did not work for society people and the dealers, but for the faithful commons; it was his mission to house their prayers, to instruct their minds, to rejoice their souls and their eyes. Matchless epoch, in which an ingenuous folk was educated in beauty without even noticing it, as perfect religious ought to pray without being aware of their prayers; when doctors and painters lovingly taught the poor, and the poor enjoyed their teaching, because they were all of the same royal race, born of water and the Spirit!

More beautiful things were then created and there was less self-worship. The blessed humility in which the artist was situated exalted his strength and his freedom. The Renaissance was destined to drive the artist mad and make him the most miserable of men—at the very moment when the world was to become less habitable for him—by revealing to him his own grandeur and letting loose upon him the wild beast Beauty which Faith kept enchanted and led after it obedient, with a gossamer thread for leash.

Art and Beauty

1. St. Thomas, who was as simple as he was wise, defined the beautiful as what gives pleasure on sight, *id quod visum placet*.[14] The four words say all that is necessary: a vision, that is to say an *intuitive knowledge,* and a *joy.* The beautiful is what gives joy, not all joy, but joy in knowledge; not the joy peculiar to the act of knowing, but a joy superabounding and overflowing from such an act because of the object known. If a thing exalts and delights the soul by the bare fact of its being given to the intuition of the soul, it is good to apprehend, it is beautiful.

Beauty is essentially the object of *intelligence,* for what *knows* in the full meaning of the word is the mind, which alone is open to the infinity of being. The natural site of beauty is the intelligible world: thence it descends. But it also falls in a way within the grasp of the senses, since the senses in the case of man serve the mind and can themselves rejoice in knowing "the beautiful relates only to sight and hearing of all the senses, because these two are *maxime cognoscitivi* [the best of the senses that lead to knowledge]." [15] The

---

[14] *Sum. Theol.,* i, q. 5, a. 4, *ad* 1.
[15] *Sum. Theol.,* i–ii, q. 27, a. 1, *ad* 3.

part played by the senses in the perception of beauty becomes in our case enormous and well-nigh indispensable, because our mind is not intuitive like the angelic mind: it can perceive, no doubt, but only on condition of abstracting and discoursing. In man only knowledge derived through the senses possesses fully the intuivity necessary for the perception of the beautiful. So also man can certainly enjoy purely intelligible beauty, but the beautiful which is *connatural* to man is that which comes to delight the mind through the senses and their intuition. Such also is the peculiar beauty of our art, which works upon a sensible matter for the joy of the spirit. It would fain so persuade itself that paradise is not lost. It has the savour of the terrestrial paradise, because it restores for a brief moment the simultaneous peace and delight of the mind and the senses.

If beauty delights the mind, it is because beauty is essentially a certain excellence or perfection in the proportion of things to the mind. Hence the three conditions assigned to it by St. Thomas [16] : integrity, because the mind likes being; proportion, because the mind likes order and likes unity; lastly and above all brightness or clarity, because the mind likes light and intelligibility. A certain splendour is indeed according to all the Ancients the essential character of beauty,—*claritas est de ratione pulchritudinis* [17] [clarity is the essence of the beautiful], *lux pulchrificat, quia sine luce omnia sunt turpia* [18] [light makes things beautiful, because without light all things are ugly],—but it is a splendour of intelligibility: *splendor veri* [splendor of truth], said the Platonists, *splendor ordinis* [splendor of order], said St. Augustine, adding that "unity is the form of all beauty" [19]; *splendor formae* [splendor of form], said St. Thomas with a metaphysician's precision of language: for *form,* that is to say the principle determining the peculiar perfection of everything which is, constituting and completing things in their essence and their qualities, the ontological secret, so to speak, of their innermost being, their spiritual essence, their operative mystery, is above all the peculiar principle of intelligibility, the peculiar *clarity* of every thing. Every form, moreover, is a remnant or a ray of the creative Mind impressed upon the heart of the being created. All order and proportion, on the other hand, are the work of the mind. So, to say with the Schoolmen that beauty is the *splendour of form shining on the proportioned parts of matter* [20] is to say that it is a lightning of mind on a matter intelligently arranged. The mind rejoices in the beautiful because in the beautiful it finds itself again: recognizes itself, and comes into contact with its very own light. This is so true

---

[16] *Sum. Theol.,* i, q. 39, a. 8.

[17] St. Thomas, *Comment. in lib. de Devin. Nomin.,* lect. 6.

[18] St. Thomas, *Comment. in Psalm.* Ps. xxv. 5.

[19] *De Vera Religione, cap.* 41.

[20] *Opusc. de Pulchro et Bono,* attributed to Albertus Magnus and sometimes to St. Thomas.

that they especially perceive and particularly relish the beauty of things who, like St. Francis of Assisi, for example, know that they emanate from a mind and refer them to their Author.

Every sensible beauty, no doubt, implies a certain delight of the eye or the ear or the imagination: but there can be no beauty unless the mind also is in some way rejoiced. A beautiful colour "washes the eye" as a powerful scent dilates the nostrils: but of these two "forms" or qualities only colour is called "beautiful," because being received, as opposed to the perfume, in a sense capable of disinterested knowledge, it can be, even through its purely sensible brilliance, an object of joy to the mind. Again, the more highly developed a man's culture becomes, the more spiritual grows the brilliance of the form which ravishes him.

It is important, however, to observe that in the beauty which has been termed connatural to man and is peculiar to human art this brilliance of form, however purely intelligible it may be in itself, is apprehended *in the sensible and by the sensible,* and not separately from it. The intuition of artistic beauty so stands at the opposite pole from the abstraction of scientific truth. For in the former case it is precisely through the apprehension of sense that the light of being penetrates to the mind.

The mind then, spared the least effort of abstraction, rejoices without labour and without discussion. It is excused its customary task, it has not to extricate something intelligible from the matter in which it is buried and then step by step go through its various attributes; like the stag at the spring of running water, it has nothing to do but drink, and it drinks the clarity of being. Firmly fixed in the intuition of sense, it is irradiated by an intelligible light granted to it of a sudden in the very sensible in which it glitters; and it apprehends this light not *sub ratione veri* [by virtue of truth], but rather *sub ratione delectabilis* [by virtue of pleasure], by the happy exercise it procures for it and the succeeding joy in appetite, which leaps out to every good of the soul as its own peculiar object. Only afterwards will it more or less successfully analyse in reflection the causes of such joy.

So, although the beautiful is in close dependence upon what is metaphysically true, in the sense that every splendour of intelligibility in things presupposes some degree of conformity with that Intelligence which is the cause of things, the beautiful nevertheless is not a kind of truth, but a kind of good. The perception of the beautiful is related to knowledge, but by way of addition, "as its bloom is an addition to youth"; it is not so much a kind of knowledge as a kind of delight.

The beautiful is essentially delightful. Therefore by its very nature, by its very beauty, it stirs desire and produces love, whereas truth as such only illuminates. *"Omnibus igitur est pulchrum et bonum desiderabile et amabile et diligibile"* [21] [all people therefore think that what is beautiful and good is desirable and lovable]. It is for its beauty that Wisdom is loved. And it is for its own sake that every form of beauty is loved at first, even if later the too frail flesh is caught in the snare. Love in its turn produces ecstasy, that is to say, makes the lover beside himself: an ecstasy of which the soul experiences a lesser form when it is gripped by the beauty of a work of art, and the fullness when it is absorbed, like dew, by the beauty of God.

And of God Himself, according to Denys the Areopagite, one must be bold enough to say that He suffers as it were an ecstasy of love, because of the abundance of His goodness which makes Him give all things a share of His magnificence. But His love causes the beauty of what He loves, whereas our love is caused by the beauty of what we love.

2. The speculations of the Ancients concerning the nature of the beautiful must be taken in the most formal sense and their thought should not be materialised in any too narrow specification. The idea of *integrity* or perfection or complete execution can be realised not in one way only but in a thousand or ten thousand different ways. The lack of a head or an arm is a considerable defect in a woman but of much less account in a statue— whatever disappointment M. Ravaisson may have felt at being unable to *complete* the Venos of Melos. The slightest sketch of Leonardo's or even Rodin's is nearer to perfection than the most finished Bouguereau. And if it pleases a futurist to paint a lady with only one eye, or a quarter of an eye, nobody denies him such a right: all one is entitled to require—and here is the whole problem—is that the quarter eye is all the lady needs *in the given case.*

It is the same with proportion, fitness and harmony. They differ with the object and the end aimed at. Proportions good in a man are not good in a child. Figures constructed according to the Greek or the Egyptian canon are perfectly proportioned in their kind: but Rouault's yokels are also as perfectly proportioned in their kind. Integrity and proportion have no absolute significance and must be understood solely *in relation* to the end of the work, which is to make a form shine on the matter.

Last and most important: this very brilliance of form, the essence of beauty, shines on matter in an infinite variety of ways. [22]

---

[21] Denys the Areopagite, *De Divin. Nomin.,* cap. iv; St. Thomas, lect. 9. I shall continue to call the philosopher *the Areopagite,* from his age-old possession of the title. Modern critics call him *the pseudo-Denys.*

[22] By *brilliance of form* must be understood an *ontological* splendour which happens to be revealed to our minds, not a *conceptual* clarity. There must be no misunderstanding here: the words *clarity, intelligibility* and *light,* used to characterise the part played by *form* in the heart of things, do not necessarily indicate something clear and intelligible to *us,* but rather something which, although clear and luminous *in itself,* intelligible *in itself,* often remains obscure to our eyes either because of the matter in which the

At one time it is the sensible brilliance of colour or tone, at another the intelligible clarity of an arabesque, a rhythm or an harmonious balance, an activity or a movement, or again the reflection upon things of some human or divine thought, but above all it is the profound splendour of the soul shining through, of the soul which is the principle of life and animal energy or the principle of spiritual life, of pain and passion. There is also a more exalted splendour, the splendour of Grace, which the Greeks never knew.

Beauty therefore does not consist in conformity to a certain ideal and unchanging type, in the sense understood by those who, confusing the true and the beautiful, knowledge and delight, insist that to perceive beauty man shall discover "by the vision of ideas," "through the material envelope," "the invisible essence of things" and their "necessary type." St. Thomas was as far removed from this pseudo-Platonism as from the idealist fancy fair of Winckelman and David. Beauty for him begins to exist as soon as the radiation of any form over a suitably proportioned matter succeeds in pleasing the mind, and he is careful to warn us that beauty is in a manner *relative,* —not to the dispositions of the subject in the sense in which relativity is understood nowadays, but to the peculiar nature and end of the thing and to the formal conditions in which it is involved. *"Pulchritudo quodammodo dicitur per respectum ad aliquid. . . ."* [23] [Beauty is predicated in a certain way with respect to some things.] *"Alia enim est pulchritudo spiritus et alia corporis, atque alia hujus et illius corporis"* [24] [There is then a difference between the beauty of the soul and of the body, and also between the beauty of one body and that of another]. And however beautiful a created thing may be, it may appear beautiful to some and not to others, because it is beautiful only under certain aspects which some discover and others do not see: it is therefore "beautiful in one place and not beautiful in another."

---

form in question is buried or because of the transcendence of the form itself in the things of the spirit. The more substantial and profound this secret significance, the more concealed from us it is; so much so, in truth, that to say with the Schoolmen that form in things is the peculiar principle of *intelligibility* is to say at the same time that it is the peculiar principle of *mystery.* (There can in fact be no mystery where there is *nothing to know*: mystery exists where there is *more to be known* than is offered to our apprehension.) To define beauty by brilliance of form is at the same time to define it by brilliance of mystery.

It is a Cartesian error to reduce *absolute* brilliance to brilliance *for us.* Such an error produces academicism in art and condemns us to such a poor kind of beauty as can give only the meanest of pleasures to the soul.

If it be a question of the "intelligibility" of the work, I would add that if the *brilliance of form* can be apparent in an "obscure" as in a "clear" work, the *brilliance of mystery* can be as apparent in a "clear" work as in an "obscure." From this point of view neither "obscurity" nor "clarity" enjoys any privilege.

[23] St. Thomas, *Comment. in Psalm.,* Ps. xliv. 2.
[24] St. Thomas, *Comment. in lib. de Divin. Nomin.,* cap. iv, lect. 5.

3. If this be so, it is because the beautiful belongs to the order of *transcendentals*—that is to say, of concepts which surpass all limits of kind of category and will not suffer themselves to be confined in any class, because they absorb everything and are to be found everywhere. Like the one, the true and the good, it is *being* itself considered from a certain aspect, it is a property of being: it is not an accident super-added to being, it adds to being merely a relation of reason, it is being considered as delighting, by the mere intuition of it, an intellectual nature. So everything is beautiful as everything is good, at least in a certain relation. And as being is everywhere present and everywhere various, the beautiful likewise is scattered everywhere and everywhere various. Like being and the other transcendentals, it is essentially *analogous,* that is to say it is predicated for divers reasons, *sub diversa ratione,* of the divers subjects of which it is predicated: each kind of being *is* in its own way, is *good* in its own way, is *beautiful* in its own way.

Beauty therefore belongs to the transcendental and metaphysical order. For this reason it tends of itself to carry the soul beyond creation. Of the instinct for beauty, the *accursed* poet to whom modern art owes the recovery of the consciousness of the theological quality and the tyrannical spirituality of beauty, says, "it is that immortal instinct for the beautiful which makes us consider the world and its pageants as a glimpse of, a *correspondence* with, Heaven. The insatiable thirst for everything beyond, which life reveals, is the liveliest proof of our immortality. It is at once by poetry and *through* poetry, by music and *through* music that the soul perceives what splendours shine behind the tomb; and when an exquisite poem brings tears to the eyes, such tears do not argue an excess of enjoyment but rather attest an irritation of melancholy, some peremptory need of the nerves, a nature exiled in the imperfect which would fain possess immediately, even on this earth, a paradise revealed." [25]

4. Once we touch a transcendental, we touch being itself, a likeness of God, an absolute, all that ennobles and makes the joy of life: we enter the realm of the spirit. It is remarkable that the only real means of communication between human creatures is through being or some one of the properties of being. This is their only means of escape from the individuality in which they are enclosed by matter. If they remain on the plane of their sensible needs and their sentimental selves they tell their stories to one another in vain; they cannot understand each other. They watch each other and cannot see, each infinitely alone, however closely work or the pleasure of love may bind them together. But once touch the good and Love, like the

---

25 Baudelaire, *L'Art romantique.*

Saints, or the true, like an Aristotle, or the beautiful, like a Dante, a Bach or a Giotto, then contact is established and souls communicate. Men are only really united by the spirit: light alone gathers them together, *intellectualia et rationalia omnia congregans, et indestructibilia faciens.*[26]

Art in general tends to make a work. But certain arts tend to make a work of *beauty* and thereby differ essentially from all the rest. The work which involves the labour of all the other arts is itself ordered to the service of man and is therefore a mere means: it is completely enclosed in a definite material *genus* or kind. The work which involves the labour of the Fine Arts is ordered to beauty: in so far as it is beautiful it is an end, an absolute, self-sufficient; and if, as work to be done, it is material and enclosed in a kind, as beautiful it belongs to the realm of the spirit and dives deep into the transcendence and the infinity of being.

The Fine Arts therefore stand out in the *genus* art as man stands out in the *genus* animal. And like man himself they are like a horizon where matter comes into contact with spirit. They have a spiritual soul. Therefore they have many distinctive properties. Their association with the beautiful modifies in their case certain characteristics of art in general, notably, as I shall endeavour to show, all that concerns the rules of art. On the other hand it emphasises and carries to a kind of excess other generic characteristics of the artistic virtue, above all its intellectual character and its resemblance to the speculative virtues.

There is a curious analogy between the Fine Arts and wisdom. Like wisdom, they are ordered to an object transcending man and of value in itself, whose fullness is without limit, for beauty is as infinite as being. They are disinterested, pursued for their own sake, truly noble because their work considered in itself is not made to be used as a means, but to be enjoyed as an end, being a true fruit, *aliquid ultimum et delectabile* [something which is an end and pleasurable]. Their whole value is spiritual and their manner of being is contemplation. For if contemplation is not their activity, as it is the activity of wisdom, their object is nevertheless to produce an intellectual delight, that is to say a kind of contemplation, and they also presuppose in the artist a kind of contemplation, whence the beauty of the work ought to overflow. For this reason there may be applied to them, due allowance being made, the comparison drawn by St. Thomas between wisdom and games [27]: "The contemplation of wisdom is rightly compared with games for two things to be found in games. The first is that games give pleasure and the contemplation of wisdom gives the very greatest pleasure, according to what Wisdom says of itself in Ecclesiasticus: *My spirit is sweet*

---

[26] Denys the Areopagite, *De Divin. Nomin.*, cap. iv (St. Thomas, lect. 4).
[27] Opusc. lxviii, *in libr. Boetii de Hebdom.*, princ.

above honey. The second is that the movements in games are not contrived to serve another end but are pursued for their own sake. It is the same with the delights of wisdom. . . . Hence divine Wisdom compares its delight to games: *I was with him forming all things and was delighted every day, playing before him at all times: playing in the world."* [28]

But Art remains always essentially in the sphere of Making and it is by drudgery upon some matter that it aims at rejoicing the spirit. Hence for the artist a strange and pathetic condition, the very image of man's condition in the world, where he is condemned to wear himself out among bodies and live with minds. Although he reproaches the old poets for making the Divinity jealous, Aristotle admits that they were right in saying that to the Divinity alone is reserved the possession of wisdom as His true property: "The possession of it is beyond human power, for human nature in many ways is in bondage." [29] So the production of beauty belongs to God alone as His true property. And if the condition of the artist is more human and less exalted than that of the wise man, it is also more discordant and painful, because his activity is not wholly confined within the pure immanence of spiritual operations and does not consist in itself of contemplating, but of making. Unable to enjoy the substance and the peace of wisdom, he is caught by the harsh exigencies of the mind and the speculative life and condemned to every servile misery of temporal practice and production.

BENEDETTO CROCE

Art as Intuition [1]

Intuition and Expression

KNOWLEDGE HAS TWO forms: it is either *intuitive* knowledge or *logical* knowledge; knowledge obtained through the *imagination* or knowledge obtained through the *intellect*; knowledge of the *individual* or

---

[28] *Prov.,* viii, 31.
[29] *Metaph.,* lib. i, c. 2, 982 b.
[1] From Benedetto Croce, *Aesthetic,* tr. Douglas Ainslie, pp. 1–26, 32–36; copyright, 1909, by Macmillan and Company, Ltd., and used with The Macmillan Company's permission. (Eds.)

knowledge of the *universal*; of *individual things* or of the *relations* between them: it is, in fact, productive either of *images* or of *concepts*.

In ordinary life, constant appeal is made to intuitive knowledge. It is said that we cannot give definitions of certain truths; that they are not demonstrable by syllogisms; that they must be learnt intuitively. The politician finds fault with the abstract reasoner, who possesses no lively intuition of actual conditions; the educational theorist insists upon the necessity of developing the intuitive faculty in the pupil before everything else; the critic in judging a work of art makes it a point of honour to set aside theory and abstractions, and to judge it by direct intuition; the practical man professes to live rather by intuition than by reason.

But this ample acknowledgment granted to intuitive knowledge in ordinary life, does not correspond to an equal and adequate acknowledgment in the field of theory and of philosophy. There exists a very ancient science of intellectual knowledge, admitted by all without discussion, namely, Logic: but a science of intuitive knowledge is timidly and with difficulty asserted by but a few. Logical knowledge has appropriated the lion's share; and if she does not slay and devour her companion outright, yet yields to her but grudgingly the humble place of maid-servant or doorkeeper.—What can intuitive knowledge be without the light of intellectual knowledge? It is a servant without a master; and though a master find a servant useful, the master is a necessity to the servant, since he enables him to gain his livelihood. Intuition is blind; intellect lends her eyes.

Now, the first point to be firmly fixed in the mind is that intuitive knowledge has no need of a master, nor to lean upon any one; she does not need to borrow the eyes of others, for she has excellent eyes of her own. Doubtless it is possible to find concepts mingled with intuitions. But in many other intuitions there is no trace of such a mixture, which proves that it is not necessary. The impression of a moonlight scene by a painter; the outline of a country drawn by a cartographer; a musical motive, tender or energetic; the words of a sighing lyric, or those with which we ask, command and lament in ordinary life, may well all be intuitive facts without a shadow of intellectual relation. But, think what one may of these instances, and admitting further the contention that the greater part of the intuitions of civilized man are impregnated with concepts, there yet remains to be observed something more important and more conclusive. Those concepts which are found mingled and fused with the intuitions are no longer concepts, in so far as they are really mingled and fused, for they have lost all independence and autonomy. They have been concepts, but have now become simple elements of intuition. The philosophical maxims placed in the mouth of a personage of tragedy or of comedy, perform there the function, not of concepts, but of characteristics of such personage; in the same way as the red in a painted face does not there represent the red colour of the physicists, but is a characteristic element of the portrait. The whole is that which determines the quality of the parts. A work of art may be full of philosophical concepts; it may contain them in greater abundance and they may there be even more profound than in a philosophical dissertation, which in its turn may be rich to overflowing with descriptions and intuitions. But notwithstanding all these concepts the total effect of the work of art is an intuition; and notwithstanding all those intuitions, the total effect of the philosophical dissertation is a concept. The *Promessi Sposi* [2] contains copious ethical observations and distinctions, but does not for that reason lose as a whole its character of simple story or intuition. In like manner the anecdotes and satirical effusions to be found in the works of a philosopher like Schopenhauer do not deprive those works of their character of intellectual treatises. The difference between a scientific work and a work of art, that is, between an intellectual fact and an intuitive fact, lies in the difference of the total effect aimed at by their respective authors. This it is that determines and rules over the several parts of each, not these parts separated and considered abstractly in themselves.

But to admit the independence of intuition as regards concept does not suffice to give a true and precise idea of intuition. Another error arises among those who recognize this, or who at any rate do not explicitly make intuition dependent upon the intellect, to obscure and confuse the real nature of intuition. By intuition is frequently understood *perception,* or the knowledge of actual reality, the apprehension of something as *real.*

Certainly perception is intuition: the perceptions of the room in which I am writing, of the ink-bottle and paper that are before me, of the pen I am using, of the objects that I touch and make use of as instruments of my person, which, if it write, therefore exists;—these are all intuitions. But the image that is now passing through my brain of a me writing in another room, in another town, with different paper, pen and ink, is also an intuition. This means that the distinction between reality and non-reality is extraneous, secondary, to the true nature of intuition. If we imagine a human mind having intuitions for the first time, it would seem that it could have intuitions of actual reality only, that is to say, that it could have perceptions of nothing but the real. But since knowledge of reality is based upon the distinction between real images and unreal images, and since this distinction does not at the first moment exist, these intuitions would in truth not be intuitions either of the real or of the unreal, not perceptions, but pure intuitions. Where all

[2] By Alessandro Manzoni (1785–1873), translated into English as *The Betrothed Lovers.* (Eds.)

is real, nothing is real. The child, with its difficulty of distinguishing true from false, history from fable, which are all one to childhood, can furnish us with a sort of very vague and only remotely approximate idea of this ingenuous state. Intuition is the undifferentiated unity of the perception of the real and of the simple image of the possible. In our intuitions we do not oppose ourselves as empirical beings to external reality, but we simply objectify our impressions, whatever they be.

Those, therefore, who look upon intuition as sensation formed and arranged simply according to the categories of space and time, would seem to approximate more nearly to the truth. Space and time (they say) are the forms of intuition; to have an intuition is to place it in space and in temporal sequence. Intuitive activity would then consist in this double and concurrent function of spatiality and temporality. But for these two categories must be repeated what was said of intellectual distinctions, when found mingled with intuitions. We have intuitions without space and without time: the colour of a sky, the colour of a feeling, a cry of pain and an effort of will, objectified in consciousness: these are intuitions which we possess, and with their making space and time have nothing to do. In some intuitions, spatiality may be found without temporality, in others, *vice versa*; and even where both are found, they are perceived by later reflexion: they can be fused with the intuition in like manner with all its other elements: that is, they are in it *materialiter* and not *formaliter,* as ingredients and not as arrangement. Who, without an act of reflexion which for a moment breaks in upon his contemplation, can think of space while looking at a drawing or a view? Who is conscious of temporal sequence while listening to a story or a piece of music without breaking into it with a similar act of reflexion? What intuition reveals in a work of art is not space and time, but *character, individual physiognomy.* The view here maintained is confirmed in several quarters of modern philosophy. Space and time, far from being simple and primitive functions, are nowadays conceived as intellectual constructions of great complexity. And further, even in some of those who do not altogether deny to space and time the quality of formative principles, categories and functions, one observes an effort to unite them and to regard them in a different manner from that in which these categories are generally conceived. Some limit intuition to the sole category of spatiality, maintaining that even time can only be intuited in terms of space. Others abandon the three dimensions of space as not philosophically necessary, and conceive the function of spatiality as void of all particular spatial determination. But what could such a spatial function be, a simple arrangement that should arrange even time? It represents, surely, all that criticism and refutation have left standing—the bare demand for the affirmation of some intuitive activity in general. And is not this activity truly determined, when one single function is attributed to it, not spatializing nor temporalizing, but characterizing? Or rather, when it is conceived as itself a category or function which gives us knowledge of things in their concreteness and individuality?

Having thus freed intuitive knowledge from any suggestion of intellectualism and from every later and external addition, we must now explain it and determine its limits from another side and defend it from a different kind of invasion and confusion. On the hither side of the lower limit is sensation, formless matter, which the spirit can never apprehend in itself as simple matter. This it can only possess with form and in form, but postulates the notion of it as a mere limit. Matter, in its abstraction, is mechanism, passivity; it is what the spirit of man suffers, but does not produce. Without it no human knowledge or activity is possible; but mere matter produces animality, whatever is brutal and impulsive in man, not the spiritual dominion, which is humanity. How often we strive to understand clearly what is passing within us! We do catch a glimpse of something, but this does not appear to the mind as objectified and formed. It is in such moments as these that we best perceive the profound difference between matter and form. These are not two acts of ours, opposed to one another; but the one is outside us and assaults and sweeps us off our feet, while the other inside us tends to absorb and identify itself with that which is outside. Matter, clothed and conquered by form, produces concrete form. It is the matter, the content, which differentiates one of our intuitions from another: the form is constant: it is spiritual activity, while matter is changeable. Without matter spiritual activity would not forsake its abstractness to become concrete and real activity, this or that spiritual content, this or that definite intuition.

It is a curious fact, characteristic of our times, that this very form, this very activity of the spirit, which is essentially ourselves, is so often ignored or denied. Some confound the spiritual activity of man with the metaphorical and mythological activity of what is called nature, which is mechanism and has no resemblance to human activity, save when we imagine, with Aesop, that *"arbores loquuntur non tantum ferae"* [trees speak, not only beasts]. Some affirm that they have never observed in themselves this "miraculous" activity, as though there were no difference, or only one of quantity, between sweating and thinking, feeling cold and the energy of the will. Others, certainly with greater reason, would unify activity and mechanism in a more general concept, though they are specifically distinct. Let us, however, refrain for the moment from examining if such a final unification be possible, and in what sense, but admitting that the attempt may be made, it is clear that to unify two concepts in a third implies to begin with the admission of a difference between the two first. Here it is this difference that concerns us and we set it in relief.

Intuition has sometimes been confused with simple sensation. But since

this confusion ends by being offensive to common sense, it has more frequently been attenuated or concealed with a phraseology apparently designed at once to confuse and to distinguish them. Thus, it has been asserted
that intuition is sensation, but not so much simple sensation as *association*
of sensations. Here a double meaning is concealed in the word "association."
Association is understood, either as memory, mnemonic association, conscious recollection, and in that case the claim to unite in memory elements
which are not intuited, distinguished, possessed in some way by the spirit
and produced by consciousness, seems inconceivable: or it is understood as
association of unconscious elements, in which case we remain in the world
of sensation and of nature. But if with certain associationists we speak of an
association which is neither memory nor flux of sensations, but a *productive*
association (formative, constructive, distinguishing); then our contention is
admitted and only its name is denied to it. For productive association is no
longer association in the sense of the sensationalists, but *synthesis,* that is
to say, spiritual activity. Synthesis may be called association; but with the
concept of productivity is already posited the distinction between passivity
and activity, between sensation and intuition.

Other psychologists are disposed to distinguish from sensation something
which is sensation no longer, but is not yet intellectual concept: the *representation* or *image*. What is the difference between their representation or
image and our intuitive knowledge? Everything and nothing: for "representation" is a very equivocal word. If by representation be understood
something cut off and standing out from the psychic basis of the sensations,
then representation is intuition. If, on the other hand, it be conceived as
complex sensation we are back once more in crude sensation, which does not
vary in quality according to its richness or poverty, or according to whether
the organism in which it appears is rudimentary or highly developed and full
of traces of past sensations. Nor is the ambiguity remedied by defining representation as a psychic product of secondary degree in relation to sensation, defined as occupying the first place. What does secondary degree mean
here? Does it mean a qualitative, formal difference? If so, representation is
an elaboration of sensation and therefore intuition. Or does it mean greater
complexity and complication, a quantitative, material difference? In that
case intuition is once more confused with simple sensation.

And yet there is a sure method of distinguishing true intuition, true representation, from that which is inferior to it: the spiritual fact from the
mechanical, passive, natural fact. Every true intuition or representation is
also *expression*. That which does not objectify itself in expression is not
intuition or representation, but sensation and mere natural fact. The spirit
only intuites in making, forming, expressing. He who separates intuition
from expression never succeeds in reuniting them.

Intuitive activity possesses intuitions to the extent that it expresses them. Should this proposition sound paradoxical, that is partly because, as a general rule, a too restricted meaning is given to the word "expression." It is generally restricted to what are called verbal expressions alone. But there exist also non-verbal expressions, such as those of line, colour and sound, and to all of these must be extended our affirmation, which embraces therefore every sort of manifestation of the man, as orator, musician, painter, or anything else. But be it pictorial, or verbal, or musical, or in whatever other form it appear, to no intuition can expression in one of its forms be wanting; it is, in fact, an inseparable part of intuition. How can we really possess an intuition of a geometrical figure, unless we possess so accurate an image of it as to be able to trace it immediately upon paper or on the blackboard? How can we really have an intuition of the contour of a region, for example of the island of Sicily, if we are not able to draw it as it is in all its meanderings? Every one can experience the internal illumination which follows upon his success in formulating to himself his impressions and feelings, but only so far as he is able to formulate them. Feelings or impressions, then, pass by means of words from the obscure region of the soul into the clarity of the contemplative spirit. It is impossible to distinguish intuition from expression in this cognitive process. The one appears with the other at the same instant, because they are not two, but one.

The principal reason which makes our view appear paradoxical as we maintain it, is the illusion or prejudice that we possess a more complete intuition of reality than we really do. One often hears people say that they have many great thoughts in their minds, but that they are not able to express them. But if they really had them, they would have coined them into just so many beautiful, sounding words, and thus have expressed them. If these thoughts seem to vanish or to become few and meagre in the act of expressing them, the reason is that they did not exist or really were few and meagre. People think that all of us ordinary men imagine and intuite countries, figures and scenes like painters, and bodies like sculptors; save that painters and sculptors know how to paint and carve such images, while we bear them unexpressed in our souls. They believe that any one could have imagined a Madonna of Raphael; but that Raphael was Raphael owing to his technical ability in putting the Madonna upon canvas. Nothing can be more false than this view. The world which as a rule we intuite is a small thing. It consists of little expressions, which gradually become greater and wider with the increasing spiritual concentration of certain moments. They are the words we say to ourselves, our silent judgments: "Here is a man, here is a horse, this is heavy, this is sharp, this pleases me," etc. It is a medley of light and colour, with no greater pictorial value than would be expressed by a haphazard splash of colours, from among which one could barely make out a few special, distinctive traits. This and nothing else is what we possess in our ordinary life; this is the basis of our ordinary action. It is the index of a book. The labels tied to things (it has been said) take the place of the things themselves. This index and these labels (themselves expressions) suffice for small needs and small actions. From time to time we pass from the index to the book, from the label to the thing, or from the slight to the greater intuitions, and from these to the greatest and most lofty. This passage is sometimes far from easy. It has been observed by those who have best studied the psychology of artists that when, after having given a rapid glance at any one, they attempt to obtain a real intuition of him, in order, for example, to paint his portrait, then this ordinary vision, that seemed so precise, so lively, reveals itself as little better than nothing. What remains is found to be at the most some superficial trait, which would not even suffice for a caricature. The person to be painted stands before the artist like a world to discover. Michael Angelo said, "One paints, not with the hands, but with the brain." Leonardo shocked the prior of the Convent of the Graces by standing for days together gazing at the "Last Supper," without touching it with the brush. He remarked of this attitude: "The minds of men of lofty genius are most active in invention when they are doing the least external work." The painter is a painter, because he sees what others only feel or catch a glimpse of, but do not see. We think we see a smile, but in reality we have only a vague impression of it, we do not perceive all the characteristic traits of which it is the sum, as the painter discovers them after he has worked upon them and is thus able to fix them on the canvas. We do not intuitively possess more even of our intimate friend, who is with us every day and at all hours, than 'at most certain traits of physiognomy which enable us to distinguish him from others. The illusion is less easy as regards musical expression; because it would seem strange to every one to say that the composer had added or attached notes to a motive which was already in the mind of him who is not the composer; as if Beethoven's Ninth Symphony were not his own intuition and his intuition the Ninth Symphony. Now, just as one who is deluded as to the amount of his material wealth is confuted by arithmetic, which states its exact amount, so he who nourishes delusions as to the wealth of his own thoughts and images is brought back to reality, when he is obliged to cross the *Pons Asinorum* [Ass' Bridge—here, *test*] of expression. Let us say to the former, count; to the latter, speak; or, here is a pencil, draw, express yourself.

Each of us, as a matter of fact, has in him a little of the poet, of the sculptor, of the musician, of the painter, of the prose writer: but how little, as compared with those who bear those names, just because they possess the most universal dispositions and energies of human nature in so lofty a degree! How little too does a painter possess of the intuitions of a poet! And how little does one painter possess those of another painter! Nevertheless, that little is all our actual patrimony of intuitions or representations. Beyond these are only impressions, sensations, feelings, impulses, emotions, or whatever else one may term what still falls short of the spirit and is not assimilated by man; something postulated for the convenience of exposition, while actually non-existent, since to exist also is a fact of the spirit.

We may thus add this to the various verbal descriptions of intuition, noted at the beginning: intuitive knowledge is expressive knowledge. Independent and autonomous in respect to intellectual function; indifferent to later empirical discriminations, to reality and to unreality, to formations and apperceptions of space and time, which are also later: intuition or representation is distinguished as *form* from what is felt and suffered, from the flux or wave of sensation, or from psychic matter; and this form, this taking possession, is expression. To intuite is to express; and nothing else (nothing more, but nothing less) than *to express*.

Intuition and Art

Before proceeding further, it may be well to draw certain consequences from what has been established and to add some explanations.

We have frankly identified intuitive or expressive knowledge with the aesthetic or artistic fact, taking works of art as examples of intuitive knowledge and attributing to them the characteristics of intuition, and *vice versa*. But our identification is combated by a view held even by many philosophers, who consider art to be an intuition of an altogether special sort. "Let us admit" (they say) "that art is intuition; but intuition is not always art: artistic intuition is a distinct species differing from intuition in general by something *more*."

But no one has ever been able to indicate of what this something more consists. It has sometimes been thought that art is not a simple intuition, but an intuition of an intuition, in the same way as the concept of science has been defined, not as the ordinary concept, but as the concept of a concept. Thus man would attain to art by objectifying, not his sensations, as happens with ordinary intuition, but intuition itself. But this process of raising to a second power does not exist; and the comparison of it with the ordinary and scientific concept does not prove what is intended, for the good reason that it is not true that the scientific concept is the concept of a concept. If this comparison proves anything, it proves just the opposite. The ordinary concept, if it be really a concept and not a simple representation, is a perfect concept, however poor and limited. Science substitutes concepts for representations; for those concepts that are poor and limited it substitutes others, larger and more comprehensive; it is ever discovering new relations. But its method does not differ from that by which is formed the smallest universal in the brain of the humblest of men. What is generally called *par excellence* art, collects intuitions that are wider and more complex than those which we generally experience, but these intuitions are always of sensations and impressions.

Art is expression of impressions, not expression of expression.

For the same reason, it cannot be asserted that the intuition, which is generally called artistic, differs from ordinary intuition as intensive intuition. This would be the case if it were to operate differently on the same matter. But since the artistic function is extended to wider fields, yet does not differ in method from ordinary intuition, the difference between them is not intensive but extensive. The intuition of the simplest popular love-song, which says the same thing, or very nearly, as any declaration of love that issues at every moment from the lips of thousands of ordinary men, may be intensively perfect in its poor simplicity, although it be extensively so much more limited than the complex intuition of a love-song by Leopardi.

The whole difference, then, is quantitative, and as such is indifferent to philosophy, *scientia qualitatum* [science of qualities]. Certain men have a greater aptitude, a more frequent inclination fully to express certain complex states of the soul. These men are known in ordinary language as artists. Some very complicated and difficult expressions are not often achieved, and these are called works of art. The limits of the expression-intuitions that are called art, as opposed to those that are vulgarly called non-art, are empirical and impossible to define. If an epigram be art, why not a simple word? If a story, why not the news-jottings of the journalist? If a landscape, why not a topographical sketch? The teacher of philosophy in Molière's comedy was right: "whenever we speak, we create prose." But there will always be scholars like Monsieur Jourdain, astonished at having spoken prose for forty years without knowing it, who will have difficulty in persuading themselves that when they call their servant John to bring their slippers, they have spoken nothing less than—prose.

We must hold firmly to our identification, because among the principal reasons which have prevented Aesthetic, the science of art, from revealing the true nature of art, its real roots in human nature, has been its separation from the general spiritual life, the having made of it a sort of special function or aristocratic club. No one is astonished when he learns from physiology that every cell is an organism and every organism a cell or synthesis of cells. No one is astonished at finding in a lofty mountain the same chemical elements that compose a small stone fragment. There is not one physiology of small animals and one of large animals; nor is there a special chemical theory of stones as distinct from mountains. In the same way, there is not a science of lesser intuition as distinct from a science of greater intuition, nor one of ordinary intuition as distinct from artistic intuition. There is but one Aesthetic, the science of intuitive or expressive knowledge, which is the aesthetic or artistic fact. And this Aesthetic is the true analogue of Logic, which includes, as facts of the same nature, the formation of the smallest and most ordinary concept and the most complicated scientific and philosophical system.

Nor can we admit that the word *genius* or artistic genius, as distinct from the non-genius of the ordinary man, possesses more than a quantitative signification. Great artists are said to reveal us to ourselves. But how could this be possible, unless there were identity of nature between their imagination and ours, and unless the difference were only one of quantity? It were better to change *poeta nascitur* [the poet is born] into *homo nascitur poeta* [man is born a poet]: some men are born great poets, some small. The cult of the genius with all its attendant superstitions has arisen from this quantitative difference having been taken as a difference of quality. It has been forgotten that genius is not something that has fallen from heaven, but humanity itself. The man of genius who poses or is represented as remote from humanity finds this punishment in becoming or appearing somewhat ridiculous. Examples of this are the *genius* of the romantic period and the *superman* of our time.

But it is well to note here, that those who claim unconsciousness as the chief quality of an artistic genius, hurl him from an eminence far above humanity to a position far below it. Intuitive or artistic genius, like every form of human activity, is always conscious; otherwise it would be blind mechanism. The only thing that can be wanting to artistic genius is the *reflective* consciousness, the superadded consciousness of the historian or critic, which is not essential to it.

The relation between matter and form, or between *content* and *form,* as is generally said, is one of the most disputed questions in Aesthetic. Does the aesthetic fact consist of content alone, or of form alone, or of both together? This question has taken on various meanings, which we shall mention, each in its place. But when these words are taken as signifying what we have above defined, and matter is understood as emotionality not aesthetically elaborated, or impressions, and form as intellectual activity and expression, then our view cannot be in doubt. We must, that is to say, reject both the thesis that makes the aesthetic fact to consist of the content alone (that is, the simple impressions), and the thesis which makes it to consist of a junction between form and content, that is, of impressions plus expressions. In the aesthetic fact, expressive activity is not added to the fact of the impressions, but these latter are formed and elaborated by it. The impressions reappear as it were in expression, like water put into a filter, which reappears the same and yet different on the other side. The aesthetic fact, therefore, is form, and nothing but form.

From this was inferred not that the content is something superfluous (it is, on the contrary, the necessary point of departure for the expressive fact); but that *there is no passage* from the qualities of the content to those of the form. It has sometimes been thought that the content, in order to be aesthetic, that is to say, transformable into form, should possess some determined or determinable qualities. But were that so, then form and content, expression and impression, would be the same thing. It is true that the content is that which is convertible into form, but it has no determinable qualities until this transformation takes place. We know nothing about it. It does not become aesthetic content before, but only after it has been actually transformed. The aesthetic content has also been defined as the *interesting*. That is not an untrue statement; it is merely void of meaning. Interesting to what? To the expressive activity? Certainly the expressive activity would not have raised the content to the dignity of form, had it not been interested in it. Being interested is precisely the raising of the content to the dignity of form. But the word "interesting" has also been employed in another and an illegitimate sense, which we shall explain further on.

The proposition that art is *imitation of nature* has also several meanings. Sometimes truths have been expressed or at least shadowed forth in these words, sometimes errors have been promulgated. More frequently, no definite thought has been expressed at all. One of the scientifically legitimate meanings occurs when "imitation" is understood as representation or intuition of nature, a form of knowledge. And when the phrase is used with this intention, and in order to emphasize the spiritual character of the process, another proposition becomes legitimate also: namely, that art is the *idealization* or *idealizing* imitation of nature. But if by imitation of nature be understood that art gives mechanical reproductions, more or less perfect duplicates of natural objects, in the presence of which is renewed the same tumult of impressions as that caused by natural objects, then the proposition is evidently false. The coloured waxen effigies that imitate the life, before which we stand astonished in the museums where such things are shown, do not give aesthetic intuitions. Illusion and hallucination have nothing to do with the calm domain of artistic intuition. But on the other hand if an artist paint the interior of a wax-work museum, or if an actor give a burlesque portrait of a man-statue on the stage, we have work of the spirit and artistic intuition. Finally, if photography have in it anything artistic, it will be to the extent that it transmits the intuition of the photographer, his point of view, the pose and grouping which he has striven to attain. And if photography be not quite an art, that is precisely because the element of nature in it remains more or less unconquered and ineradicable. Do we ever, indeed, feel complete satisfaction before even the best of photographs? Would not an artist vary and touch up much or little, remove or add something to all of them?

The statements repeated so often, that art is not knowledge, that it does not tell the truth, that it does not belong to the world of theory, but to the world of feeling, and so forth, arise from the failure to realize exactly the theoretic character of simple intuition. This simple intuition is quite distinct from intellectual knowledge, as it is distinct from perception of the real; and the statements quoted above arise from the belief that only intellectual cognition is knowledge. We have seen that intuition is knowledge, free from concepts and more simple than the so-called perception of the real. Therefore art is knowledge, form; it does not belong to the world of feeling or to psychic matter. The reason why so many aestheticians have so often insisted that art is *appearance* (*Schein*), is precisely that they have felt the necessity of distinguishing it from the more complex fact of perception, by maintaining its pure intuitiveness. And if for the same reason it has been claimed that art is *feeling* the reason is the same. For if the concept as content of art, and historical reality as such, be excluded from the sphere of art, there remains no other content than reality apprehended in all its ingenuousness and immediacy in the vital impulse, in its *feeling,* that is to say again, pure intuition.

The theory of the *aesthetic senses* has also arisen from the failure to establish, or from having lost to view, the character of expression as distinct from impression, of form as distinct from matter.

This theory can be reduced to the error just indicated of wishing to find a passage from the qualities of the content to those of the form. To ask, in fact, what the aesthetic senses are, implies asking what sensible impressions are able to enter in aesthetic expressions, and which must of necessity do so. To this we must at once reply, that all impressions can enter into aesthetic expressions or formations, but that none are bound to do so of necessity. Dante raised to the dignity of form not only the "sweet colour of the oriental sapphire" (visual impressions), but also tactual or thermic impressions, such as the "dense air" and the "fresh rivulets" which "parch the more" the throat of the thirsty. The belief that a picture yields only visual impressions is a curious illusion. The bloom on a cheek, the warmth of a youthful body, the sweetness and freshness of a fruit, the edge of a sharp knife, are not these, too, impressions obtainable from a picture? Are they visual? What would a picture mean to an imaginary man, lacking all or many of his senses, who should in an instant acquire the organ of sight alone? The picture we are looking at and believe we see only with our eyes would seem to his eyes to be little more than an artist's paint-smeared palette.

Some who hold firmly to the aesthetic character of certain groups of impressions (for example, the visual and auditive), and exclude others, are nevertheless ready to admit that if visual and auditive impressions enter *directly* into the aesthetic fact, those of the other senses also enter into it, but only as *associated*. But this distinction is altogether arbitrary. Aesthetic expression is synthesis, in which it is impossible to distinguish direct and indirect. All impressions are placed by it on a level, in so far as they are aestheticized. A man who absorbs the subject of a picture or poem does not have it before him as a series of impressions, some of which have prerogatives and precedence over the others. He knows nothing as to what has happened prior to having absorbed it, just as, on the other hand, distinctions made after reflexion have nothing whatever to do with art as such.

The theory of the aesthetic senses has also been presented in another way; as an attempt to establish what physiological organs are necessary for the aesthetic fact. The physiological organ or apparatus is nothing but a group of cells, constituted and disposed in a particular manner; that is to say, it is a merely physical and natural fact or concept. But expression does not know physiological facts. Expression has its point of departure in the impressions, and the physiological path by which these have found their way to the mind is to it altogether indifferent. One way or another comes to the same thing: it suffices that they should be impressions.

It is true that the want of given organs, that is, of certain groups of cells, prevents the formation of certain impressions (when these are not otherwise obtained through a kind of organic compensation). The man born blind cannot intuite and express light. But the impressions are not conditioned solely by the organ, but also by the stimuli which operate upon the organ. One who has never had the impression of the sea will never be able to express it, in the same way as one who has never had the impression of the life of high society or of the political arena will never express either. This, however, does not prove the dependence of the expressive function on the stimulus or on the organ. It merely repeats what we know already: expression presupposes impression, and particular expressions particular impressions. For the rest, every impression excludes other impressions during the moment in which it dominates; and so does every expression.

Another corollary of the conception of expression as activity is the *indivisibility* of the work of art. Every expression is a single expression. Activity is a fusion of the impressions in an organic whole. A desire to express this has always prompted the affirmation that the work of art should have *unity*, or, what amounts to the same thing, *unity in variety*. Expression is a synthesis of the various, or multiple, in the one.

The fact that we divide a work of art into parts, a poem into scenes, episodes, similes, sentences, or a picture into single figures and objects, background, foreground, etc., may seem opposed to this affirmation. But such division annihilates the work, as dividing the organism into heart, brain, nerves, muscles and so on, turns the living being into a corpse. It is true that there exist organisms in which division gives rise to other living beings, but in such a case we must conclude, maintaining the analogy between the organism and the work of art, that in the latter case too there are numerous germs of life each ready to grow, in a moment, into a single complete expression.

It may be said that expression sometimes arises from other expressions. There are simple and there are *compound* expressions. One must surely admit some difference between the *eureka,* with which Archimedes expressed all his joy at his discovery, and the expressive act (indeed all the five acts) of a regular tragedy.—Not in the least: expression always arises directly from impressions. He who conceives a tragedy puts into a crucible a great quantity, so to say, of impressions: expressions themselves, conceived on other occasions, are fused together with the new in a single mass, in the same way as we can cast into a melting furnace formless pieces of bronze and choicest statuettes. Those choicest statuettes must be melted just like the pieces of bronze, before there can be a new statue. The old expressions must descend again to the level of impressions, in order to be synthesized in a new single expression.

By elaborating his impressions, man *frees* himself from them. By objectifying them, he removes them from him and makes himself their superior. The liberating and purifying function of art is another aspect and another formula of its character as activity. Activity is the deliverer, just because it drives away passivity.

This also explains why it is usual to attribute to artists both the maximum of sensibility or *passion,* and the maximum of insensibility or Olympian *serenity.* The two characters are compatible, for they do not refer to the same object. The sensibility or passion relates to the rich material which the artist absorbs into his psychic organism; the insensibility or serenity to the form with which he subdues and dominates the tumult of the sensations and passions.

Art and Philosophy

The two forms of knowledge, aesthetic and intellectual or conceptual, are indeed different, but this does not altogether amount to separation and disjunction, as of two forces each pulling in its own direction. If we have shown that the aesthetic form is altogether independent of the intellectual and suffices to itself without external support, we have not said that the intellectual can stand without the aesthetic. To describe the independence as *reciprocal* would not be true.

What is knowledge by concepts? It is knowledge of the relations of things, and things are intuitions. Concepts are not possible without intuitions, just as intuition is itself impossible without the matter of impressions. Intuitions are: this river, this lake, this brook, this rain, this glass of water; the concept is: water, not this or that appearance and particular example of water, but water in general, in whatever time or place it be realized; the material of infinite intuitions, but of one single constant concept.

But the concept, the universal, if it be no longer intuition in one respect, is intuition in another respect, and cannot fail of being intuition. The man who thinks has impressions and emotions, in so far as he thinks. His impression and emotion will be not love or hate, not the passion of the man who is not a philosopher, not hate or love for certain objects and individuals, but *the effort of his thought itself,* with the pain and the joy, the love and the hate joined to it. This effort cannot but assume an intuitive form, in becoming objective to the spirit. To speak is not to think logically; but to *think logically* is also to *speak.*

That thought cannot exist without speech, is a truth generally admitted. The negations of this thesis are all founded on equivocations and errors.

The first of the equivocations is that of those who observe that one can likewise think with geometrical figures, algebraical numbers, ideographic signs, without any word, even pronounced silently and almost insensibly within one; that there are languages in which the word, the phonetic sign, expresses nothing, unless the written sign also be examined, and so on. But when we said "speak," we intended to employ a synecdoche, by which was to be understood "expression" in general, for we have already remarked that expression is not only so-called verbal expression. It may or may not be true that certain concepts may be thought without phonetic manifestations. But the very examples adduced to show this also prove that those concepts never exist without expressions.

Others point out that animals, or certain animals, think and reason without speaking. Now as to how, whether, and what animals think, whether they be rudimentary men, like savages who refuse to be civilized, rather than physiological machines, as the old spiritualists maintained, are questions that do not concern us here. When the philosopher talks of animal, brutal, impulsive, instinctive nature and the like, he does not base himself on such conjectures as to dogs or cats, lions or ants; but upon observations of what is called animal and brutal in man: of the animal side or basis of what we feel in ourselves. If individual animals, dogs or cats, lions or ants, possess something of the activity of man, so much the better, or so much the worse, for them. This means that in respect to them also we must talk, not of "nature" as a whole, but of its animal basis, as being perhaps larger and stronger in them than the animal basis of man. And if we suppose that animals think and form concepts, what kind of conjecture would justify the assertion that they do so without corresponding expressions? Analogy with man, knowledge of the spirit, human psychology, the intrument of all our conjectures as to animal psychology, would constrain us on the contrary to suppose that if they think in any way, they also somehow speak.

Another objection is derived from human psychology, and indeed literary psychology, to the effect that the concept can exist without the word, for it is certainly true that we all know books *well thought and ill written*: that is to say, a thought which remains *beyond* the expression, or *notwithstanding* faulty expression. But when we talk of books well thought and ill written, we cannot mean anything but that in such books are parts, pages, periods or propositions well thought and well written, and other parts (perhaps the least important) ill thought and ill written, not really thought and so not really expressed. Where Vico's *Scienza nuova* is really ill written, it is also ill thought. If we pass from the consideration of big books to a short sentence, the error or inaccuracy of such a contention will leap to the eyes. How could a single sentence be clearly thought and confusedly written?

All that can be admitted is that sometimes we possess thoughts (concepts) in an intuitive form, which is an abbreviated or rather peculiar expression, sufficient for us, but not sufficient to communicate it easily to any other given person or persons. Hence it is incorrect to say that we have the thought without the expression; whereas we should rather say that we have, indeed, the expression, but in such a form that it is not easy to communicate it to others. This, however, is a very variable, relative fact. There are always those who catch our thought on the wing, prefer it in this abbreviated form, and would be wearied by the greater development of it required by others. In other words, the thought considered abstractly and logically will be the same; but aesthetically we are dealing with two different intuition-expressions, into which different psychological elements enter. The same argument suffices to destroy, that is, to interpret correctly, the altogether empirical distinction between an *internal* and an *external* language.

The most lofty manifestations, the summits of intellectual and of intuitive knowledge shining from afar, are called, as we know, Art and Science. Art and Science, then, are different and yet linked together; they meet on one side, which is the aesthetic side. Every scientific work is also a work of art. The aesthetic side may remain little noticed when our mind is altogether taken up with the effort to understand the thought of the man of science and to examine its truth. But it is no longer unnoticed when we pass from the activity of understanding to that of contemplation and see that thought either develop itself before us, limpid, exact, well-shaped, without superfluous or insufficient words, with appropriate rhythm and intonation; or confused, broken, embarrassed, tentative. Great thinkers are sometimes called great writers, while other equally great thinkers remain more or less fragmentary writers even if their fragments have the scientific value of harmonious, coherent, and perfect works.

We pardon thinkers and men of science their literary mediocrity. The fragments, the flashes, console us for the whole, because it is far easier to recover the well-arranged composition from the fragmentary work of genius, to liberate the flame latent in the spark, than to achieve the discovery of genius. But how can we pardon mediocre expression in pure artists? *"Mediocribus esse poetis non di, non homines, non concessere columnae."* [Not the gods nor men nor the book sellers allow poets to be mediocre.] The poet or painter who lacks form, lacks everything, because he lacks *himself*. Poetical material permeates the souls of all: the expression alone, that is to say, the form, makes the poet. And here appears the truth of the view which denies all content to art, just the intellectual concept being understood as content. In this sense, when we take "content" as equal to "concept" it is most true, not only that art does not consist of content, but also that *it has no content*.

The distinction between *poetry and prose* also cannot be justified, save as that between art and science. It was seen in antiquity that such distinction could not be founded on external elements, such as rhythm and metre, or on rhymed or unrhymed form; that it was, on the contrary, altogether internal. Poetry is the language of feeling, prose of the intellect; but since the intellect is also feeling, in its concreteness and reality, all prose has its poetical side.

The relation between intuitive knowledge or expression and intellectual knowledge or concept, between art and science, poetry and prose, cannot be otherwise defined than by saying that it is one of *double degree*. The first degree is the expression, the second the concept: the first can stand without the second, but the second cannot stand without the first. There is poetry without prose, but not prose without poetry. Expression, indeed, is the first affirmation of human activity. Poetry is "the mother tongue of the human race"; the first men "were by nature sublime poets." We assert this in another way, when we observe that the passage from soul to spirit, from animal to human activity, is effected by means of language. And this should be said of intuition or expression in general. But to us it appears somewhat inaccurate to define language or expression as an *intermediate* link between nature and humanity, as though it were a mixture of both. Where humanity appears, the other has already disappeared; the man who expresses himself, certainly emerges from the state of nature, but he really does emerge: he does not stand half within and half without, as the use of the phrase "intermediate link" would imply.

The cognitive spirit has no form other than these two. Expression and concept exhaust it completely. The whole speculative life of man is spent in passing from one to the other and back again.

Historicism and Intellectualism in Aesthetic

These relations between intuitive or aesthetic knowledge and the other fundamental or derivative forms of knowledge having been definitely established, we are now in a position to reveal the errors of a series of theories which have been, or are, presented as theories of Aesthetic.

From the confusion between the demands of art in general and the particular demands of history has resulted the theory (which has lost ground to-day, but was once dominant) of the *probable* as the object of art. As is generally the case with erroneous propositions, the meaning of those who employed and employ the concept of probability has no doubt often been much more reasonable than their definition of the word. By probability used really to be meant the artistic *coherence* of the representation, that is to say, its completeness and effectiveness, its actual presence. If "probable" be translated "coherent," a very just meaning will often be found in the discussions, examples, and judgements of the critics who employ this word. An improbable personage, an improbable ending to a comedy, are really badly-drawn personages, badly-arranged endings, happenings without artistic motive. It has been said with reason that even fairies and sprites must have probability, that is to say, be really sprites and fairies, coherent artistic intuitions. Sometimes the word "possible" has been used instead of "probable." As we have already remarked in passing, this word possible is synonymous with the imaginable or intuitible. Everything truly, that is to say coherently, imagined, is possible. But also, by a good many critics and theorists, the probable was taken to mean the historically credible, or that historical truth which is not demonstrable but conjecturable, not true but probable. This was the character which these theorists sought to impose upon art. Who does not remember how great a part was played in literary history by criticism based on probability, for example, censure of *Jerusalem Delivered*,[3] based upon the history of the Crusades, or of the Homeric poems, upon the probable customs of emperors and kings? Sometimes too the aesthetic reproduction of historical reality has been imposed upon art. This is another of the erroneous forms taken by the theory of the *imitation of nature*. Verism and naturalism also have afforded the spectacle of a confusion of the aesthetic fact with the processes of the natural sciences, by aiming at some sort of *experimental* drama or romance.

---

[3] Title of the English translation of an epic poem in twenty books by Torquato Tasso (1544–1595). It was published in 1581 as *Gerusalemme liberata* (Croce refers to it by its Italian title later in this selection). (Eds.)

Confusions between the methods of art and those of the philosophic sciences have been far more frequent. Thus it has often been held to be the task of art to expound concepts, to unite an intelligible with a sensible, to represent *ideas* or *universals*; putting art in the place of science, that is, confusing the artistic function in general with the particular case in which it becomes aesthetico-logical.

The theory of art as supporting *theses,* of art considered as an individual representation exemplifying scientific laws, can be proved false in like manner. The example, as example, stands for the thing exemplified, and is thus an exposition of the universal, that is to say, a form of science, more or less popular or vulgarizing.

The same may be said of the aesthetic theory of the *typical,* when by type is understood, as it frequently is, the abstraction or the concept, and it is affirmed that art should make the *species* shine in the *individual.* If individual be here understood by typical, we have here too a merely verbal variation. To typify would signify, in this case, to characterize; that is, to determine and to represent the individual. Don Quixote is a type; but of what is he a type, save of all Don Quixotes? A type, so to speak, of himself. Certainly he is not a type of abstract concepts, such as the loss of the sense of reality, or of the love of glory. An infinite number of personages can be thought of under these concepts, who are not Don Quixotes. In other words, we find our own impressions fully determined and realized in the expression of a poet (for example in a poetical personage). We call that expression typical, which we might call simply aesthetic. Thus poetical or artistic universals have sometimes been spoken of, only to show that the artistic product is altogether spiritual and ideal.

Continuing to correct these errors, or to clear up misunderstandings, we shall also remark that the *symbol* has sometimes been given as the essence of art. Now, if the symbol be conceived as inseparable from the artistic intuition, it is a synonym for the intuition itself, which always has an ideal character. There is no double bottom to art, but one only; in art all is symbolical, because all is ideal. But if the symbol be conceived as separable— if the symbol can be on one side, and on the other the thing symbolized, we fall back again into the intellectualist error: the so-called symbol is the exposition of an abstract concept, an *allegory*; it is science, or art aping science. But we must also be just toward the allegorical. Sometimes it is altogether harmless. Given the *Gerusalemme liberata,* the allegory was imagined afterwards; given the *Adone* of Marino,[4] the poet of the lascivious afterwards insinuated that it was written to show how "immoderate indulgence ends in pain"; given a statue of a beautiful woman, the sculptor can attach a

---

[4] Giambattista Marino (1569–1625), Neapolitan baroque poet. (Eds.)

label to the statue saying that it represents *Clemency* or *Goodness*. This allegory that arrives attached to a finished work *post festum* [after the feast] does not change the work of art. What then is it? It is an expression externally *added* to another expression. A little page of prose is added to the *Gerusalemme,* expressing another thought of the poet; a verse or a strophe is added to the *Adone,* expressing what the poet would like to make a part of his public believe; to the statue nothing but the single word: *Clemency* or *Goodness*.

But the greatest triumph of the intellectualist error lies in the theory of artistic and literary kinds, which still has vogue in literary treatises and disturbs the critics and the historians of art. Let us observe its genesis.

The human mind can pass from the aesthetic to the logical, just because the former is a first step in respect to the latter. It can destroy expression, that is, the thought of the individual, by thinking of the universal. It can gather up expressive facts into logical relations. We have already shown that this operation becomes in its turn concrete in an expression, but this does not mean that the first expressions have not been destroyed. They have yielded their place to the new aesthetico-logical expressions. When we are on the second step, we have left the first.

One who enters a picture-gallery, or who reads a series of poems, having looked and read, may go further: he may seek out the nature and the relations of the things there expressed. Thus those pictures and compositions, each of which is an individual inexpressible in logical terms, are gradually resolved into universals and abstractions, such as *costumes, landscapes, portraits, domestic life, battles, animals, flowers, fruit, seascapes, lakes, deserts; tragic, comic, pathetic, cruel, lyrical, epic, dramatic, chivalrous, idyllic facts,* and the like. They are often also resolved into merely quantitative categories, such as *miniature, picture, statuette, group, madrigal, ballad, sonnet, sonnet-sequence, poetry, poem, story, romance,* and the like.

When we think the concept *domestic life,* or *chivalry,* or *idyll,* or *cruelty,* or one of the quantitative concepts mentioned above, the individual expressive fact from which we started has been abandoned. From aesthetes that we were, we have changed into logicians; from contemplators of expression, into reasoners. Certainly no objection can be made to such a process. In what other way could science arise, which, if it have aesthetic expressions presupposed in it, must yet go beyond them in order to fulfil its function? The logical or scientific form, as such, excludes the aesthetic form. He who begins to think scientifically has already ceased to contemplate aesthetically; although his thought assumes of necessity in its turn an aesthetic form, as has already been said, and as it would be superfluous to repeat.

Error begins when we try to deduce the expression from the concept, and to find in what takes its place the laws of the thing whose place is taken; when the difference between the second and the first step has not been observed, and when, in consequence, we declare that we are standing on the first step, when we are really standing on the second. This error is known as the *theory of artistic and literary kinds.*

"What is the *aesthetic* form of domestic life, of chivalry, of the idyll, of cruelty, and so forth? How should these contents be *represented?*" Such is the absurd problem implied in the theory of artistic and literary classes, when it has been shorn of excrescences and reduced to a simple formula. It is in this that consists all search after laws or rules of classes. Domestic life, chivalry, idyll, cruelty and the like, are not impressions, but concepts. They are not contents, but logical-aesthetic forms. You cannot express the form, for it is already itself expression. For what are the words cruelty, idyll, chivalry, domestic life, and so on, but the expression of those concepts?

Even the most refined of such distinctions, which possess the most philosophic appearance, do not resist criticism; as when works of art are divided into subjective and objective kinds, into lyric and epic, into works of feeling and decorative works. In aesthetic analysis it is impossible to separate subjective from objective, lyric from epic, the image of feeling from that of things.

DE WITT H. PARKER

The Nature of Art [1]

THE ASSUMPTION UNDERLYING every philosophy of art is the existence of some common nature present in all the arts, despite their differences in form and content; something the same in painting and sculpture; in poetry and drama; in music and architecture. Every single work of art, it is admitted, has a unique flavor, a *je ne sais quoi* which makes it incomparable with every other work; nevertheless, there is some mark or set of marks which, if it applies to any work of art, applies to all works of art, and to nothing else—a common denominator, so to say, which constitutes the definition of art, and serves to separate, though not to isolate, the field of

[1] De Witt H. Parker, "The Nature of Art," *Revue Internationale de Philosophie,* Brussels, Belgium, Première année, No. 4 (July 15, 1939), 684–702. Reprinted by permission. (Eds.)

art from other fields of human culture. Consistent with this assumption is the experience that the study of one art throws light upon the study of the other arts—painting upon sculpture; music upon poetry and painting, and so on; expressed by the familiar habit of characterizing one art in terms of another art, as when we speak of architecture as frozen music; poetry as a picture; the poetry of architecture; the music of color and line; and the like.

The philosophy of art has however many things against it. The very possibility of a definition of art may be challenged, on at least two grounds. In the first place, it may be claimed that there is no significant nature common to all the arts which could serve as a basis for a definition. One may try to show that only confusion has resulted from the interpretation of one art in terms of another art; and to what a long history of fruitless controversy and darkening of counsel could one point as evidence with regard, for example, to Horace's famous phrase—*ut pictura poesis;* poetry like a picture. Each art, one might hold, since it makes use of a peculiar medium—color, tone, or what else—is subject to laws uniquely characteristic of it, and follows no others. Even such terms as "painting" are likely to be more misleading than useful; for water color is a different sort of thing from oil; and mural painting, from easel pictures; and there is all the difference in the world, say, between a Byzantine mosaic and a Renaissance nude. Or what have ceramics in common with music; a skyscraper with Michelangelo's *Day and Night?* And while there may be some convenience in using a term like literature to include both the novels of Sinclair Lewis and Baudelaire's *Fleurs du Mal,* let anyone beware of judging either by the standards of the other! It is equally convenient in the general delivery room of a postoffice to put all letters the names of whose addresses begin with B in one box, and those whose names begin with P in another box; but it does not follow that the owners of the letters in one box are more significantly like each other than they are like the owners of letters in the other box. Thus might one oppose a radical pluralism regarding the arts to the monism maintained by the philosophers.

The second ground for scepticism regarding the possibility of a definition of art is the difficulty of finding, not some nature common to all the arts, which was the first difficulty, but some criterion by means of which the sphere of art can be definitely separated from other human activities. It is interesting to recall that the Greeks never sharply distinguished the aesthetic arts from the other arts and crafts, using a single word, *techne,* for all; and that, for them, beauty and the good, which may be present in any experience, were identical. And until the beginning of the eighteenth century, expert opinion—barring certain prophetic exceptions—was against any absolute separation of art from other elements of culture, leaning in general to the view that beauty is a kind of truth, distinguishable from the truth of science or philosophy in no essential particular. When finally as a result of the reflexions of such men as Dubos, Vico, Kant, and Schiller there was promise of a genuine philosophy of art, the view that art has a unique nature and function came, not long after, in the middle of the last century, to be associated with the so-called theory of art for art's sake—a theory which, because it tended completely to isolate art from life, brought the whole philosophy of art into disrepute. Aside from its philosophic basis, the theory of art for art's sake was largely a reaction of sensitive minds against what seemed at the time to be the brutalities of industrialism and democracy. A vivid expression of this attitude is given by Th. Gauthier in the introduction to his poems: "My world is bounded by my window pane," he says, "I write poetry because I have nothing to do; and I have nothing to do in order that I may write poetry." In other words, art is a realm entirely separated from the interests of real life—a refuge for detached and gifted souls from sordid political and economic struggles.

It was thus the unhappy fate of the philosophy of art to become entangled with the point of view of the dwellers in the ivory tower. And it was inevitable that there should appear a counter-movement of ideas going to the opposite extreme, seeking not only to bring art back into connection with life, but to prove against the philosophers that art has no peculiar nature or function. The psychological motivation behind this attitude is interesting to notice; for it was the exact opposite of the motive that lay behind the theory of art for art's sake. For whereas that was expressive of a horrified retreat from life, this was expressive of an intense love of life, and a constant preoccupation with its larger social problems. While for the aesthetes the life of their own time was hateful; for the defenders of this counter point of view there was loveliness and fascination in all that was novel and characteristic of the present as compared with the past.[2] The railway carriage seemed to them an aesthetically more effective thing than the horse-drawn carriage; the steamboat than the sailboat; the factory than the shop; the open forum of democratic discussion than the stuffy cabinet of kings. Beauty, it was felt, is no privilege of art; but a pervasive property of our common experience. The doctrine of the aesthetes that art is a more perfect thing than life was reversed: in comparison with the zestful richness of life, art seemed a poor affair, winning for itself significance only through its connexion with life itself.

In our own day we find the same two opposing attitudes towards art. The one is well represented by such a statement as this from *Art* by Clive Bell: ". . . to appreciate a work of art we need bring with us nothing from

---

[2] The best example is the work of J. M. Guyau.

life, no knowledge of its ideas and affairs, no familiarity with its emotions." [3]
To represent the counter point of view I would quote from a young writer
on aesthetics as follows: "Anything in the world which satisfies any desire
may be regarded as beautiful . . . anyone who uses intelligence and skill
to fill a need is an artist; and every work of man which ministers to want
is a work of art." [4] And the same motive is at work as in the last century,
protesting against the effort to find some distinctive sphere for art and
beauty, namely, the wish to think well of life in its current form—to pro-
claim the beauty of its democratic texture and the glory of its mechanisms;
only instead of steamboats and steam engines we hear of motor cars and
airplanes. Or the motive may be associated with that of the reformer,
namely, the wish to transform life into a new and presumably better form,
that of socialism. This motive is well expressed by a distinguished veteran
in philosophic analysis, who has recently turned his attention from the
troubled ground of social theory to the quieter pastures of art, as follows:
"The hostility to association of fine art with normal processes of living is a
pathetic, even tragic commentary on life as it is ordinarily lived. Only because that life is usually so stunted, aborted, slack, or heavy laden, is the
idea entertained that there is some inherent antagonism between the process
of normal living, and creation and enjoyment of works of aesthetic art." [5]
Sometimes the doctrine that there is some feature distinctive of art as compared with an airplane, or some quality peculiar to beauty as compared
with ordinary satisfactory experience is deemed to be a superstition symptomatic of an aristocratic or bourgeois ideology that should long ago have
atrophied in the body-politic. And in this also history is repeating itself.

To find the motivation of a point of view is not to refute it; and no theory
is ever held for long by serious men, or recurs again and again in the history
of thought without some evidence in its favor. The student of aesthetic theories who watches the rhythmic reappearance of opposing ideas learns to look
for the facts covered by each, and to draw the moral that none was wrong, but
only inadequate. And while it is impossible to frame a satisfactory theory by
mere eclectic synthesis of opinions, it remains true that the aesthetician who
neglects the history of his subject runs the risk of proclaiming as new ideas
that are centuries old, or of overlooking some aspect of a subject-matter so
complex and subtle that no one mind is able to see around and into all of it.
There are two deductions from the study of ideas regarding art that leap to
the eyes with especial force. The first is the impossibility of finding some
simple formula that will serve as a definition of art. All the so popular brief
definitions of art—"significant form," "expression," "intuition," "objectified

---

[3] See below, p. 208. (Eds.)
[4] Van Meter Ames, *Introduction to Beauty*, p. xi.
[5] John Dewey, *Art as Experience*.

pleasure"—are fallacious, either because, while true of art, they are also true of much that is not art, and hence fail to differentiate art from other things; or else because they neglect some essential aspect of art. Art is itself so complex a fact that a satisfactory definition of it must also be complex, that is to say, must involve many characteristics. As the mathematicians would say, the characteristics must be not only necessary but sufficient. They must penetrate deep enough into the roots of art to meet the challenge of the pluralists and show that there is, after all, a significant sameness in all the arts,—despite their differences in technique and media,—connecting the fine with the applied arts, so far as the latter are beautiful, and the realistic with the fanciful and the idyllic. The other deduction is that however sharply art is differentiated from life, its deep connection with life must be revealed in any definition. This is the enduring truth underlying all criticism of the ivory tower. With these lessons from history in mind, I shall now briefly explain how I think a good account of art may be framed.

I begin with a truism, that a work of art has value; or, in other words, that it is a source of satisfaction. For a work of art is not a given thing, like a star or a tree, but a thing made by man, and for his pleasure. And I wish further to premiss that all value, as satisfaction, arises through the appeasement of what in a general way may be called desire. Desire in the broad sense in which I am using that term is at once the motivation of all experience, its inward drive, and the source of its value. And the truth underlying the opposition to every type of theory of art for art's sake is the fact that the substance of the aesthetic experience is the same as the substance of all experience, a satisfaction that is the result of the appeasement of identical desires. Almost any desire that urges man on in life reappears in his art. There are no peculiar elementary aesthetic interests or emotions. What is different is the mode by which desire is appeased. For while, in ordinary experience, desire is occupied with real objects and is satisfied through a course of action leading to a goal that involves interaction with the real environment physical or social, in the case of art, desire is directed upon immanent or fictitious objects, and is appeased, not through a course of action leading to a distant goal, but in present, given experience. This mode of satisfying desire I call satisfaction in the imagination. Such a use of the term imagination has been criticized on the ground that aesthetic appreciation is not always concerned with images or fictions, but in the case of music, or the color and line patterns of a picture, with sensory material. But such criticism betrays ignorance of the long use of the term in exactly the sense in which I am employing it in the history of critical writing. For example, in the *Spectator* Addison writes of the Pleasures of the Imagination, in which he includes the pleasures of a country landscape. But while it is true that in the aesthetic experience, sensory material is as important as imaginal, it is also true that all material there has the status of the image; that is to say, it has the same freedom from reference to the physical world of action that is possessed by images, as in a dream.

I can explain what I mean by imagination through a comparison between the experience to be derived from a still life picture and the experience which is had from the set-up from which it is painted. Let us suppose that the set-up contains a cup. Then the sensory material of our experience in each case with regard to the item of the cup is much the same—there is color and there is shape. And whatever satisfaction so dear to the connoisseur may be gained from the shape as shape and the color as color, will also be much the same. Moreover, the interpretation of this sensory material is the same in both cases: it is interpreted through the idea or meaning, cup. But observe now the differences between the two experiences. For while the interests that center in the real cup, such as filling it and drinking out of it, may be satisfied by a series of actions and interactions with it, these same interests cannot be so satisfied with regard to the picture of the cup. Yet they can be satisfied in a way, but only by the idea or appearance of the cup, as if the cup were seen in a dream. We can still *imagine* ourselves touching it and filling it and drinking out of it: to us it may be *as if* we were actually doing all these things with it; and in so imagining we may provide a satisfaction of a sort to the same habits or interests that would be satisfied if we were actually to handle it and drink from it. If we could give to a dream of a cup all the sensuous fullness and vividness characteristic of perception, then the aesthetic satisfaction which we could get out of the dream would be the same as that which we get out of the still life picture. In both cases the satisfacion would be a satisfaction in a given sensuous shape and in the immediacy of an idea or meaning, rather than a satisfaction in a course of action upon a real thing which this shape and this meaning might suggest. And this is what Kant meant when he said that aesthetic satisfaction is disinterested—a satisfaction in mere representation of objects, independent of anything that we can get out of the existence of the objects.

In imagination, ideas or meanings are as important as sensuous shapes. The denial of this is the grand error of our contemporary aesthetes. I have already quoted from the famous passage of Clive Bell in which this denial is expressed. Let me cite the whole of it. "The representative element in a work of art may or may not be helpful; always it is irrelevant. For to appreciate a work of art, we need bring with us nothing from life, no knowledge of its ideas and affairs, no familiarity with its emotions."

But could we say of any poetry, of such lines as these for example,

> O western wind, when wilt thou blow
> That the small rain down can rain?

> Christ, that my love were in my arms
> And I in my bed again.

that to appreciate their beauty we need bring with us nothing from life, no knowledge of its ideas and affairs, no familiarity with its emotions? It is true, of course, that without beauty of sensuous form there is no poetry; but it is equally true that without ideas, poetry is nothing but a sweet trivial jingle. One may object that Clive Bell was writing of painting, not of poetry; but it is no less false to the whole tradition and intent of painting to claim that the representative element, which is the element of meaning, is irrelevant. Significant indeed was the movement of modern art away from conventional and literal representation; but there is a valid middle ground, which all important painters have occupied, between the extremes of prosaic copying, and no representation at all. Universally significant for painting is the presence of object-meanings derived from nature and human life: the figure, the landscape, even the inner life as revealed through the face; the precise way in which such meanings are conveyed is unimportant, varying all the way from the schematism of early Christian art to the realism of a Masaccio; but the meanings as meanings have as legitimate a place in the art as rhythm, mass, space, light, and shade, and color. No one can fairly compare an abstraction of Braque with a painting by Renoir and fail to appreciate the rich value that is added by meaning: the former offers to the imagination an elemental satisfaction through the factors enumerated (Roger Fry's list); the latter, all of this, and a world besides. Music is the only art that can satisfy the hunger of the imagination through sensuous shape alone.

The necessity for the inclusion of meaning in imagination is proved by the case of architecture. As in a poem, there is a union of the sensuous beauty of formal pattern with underlying meaning, so in architecture there is a union of formal with functional layers of beauty. To eliminate either is arbitrarily to distort the simple facts of both creation and appreciation. The same truth holds for every work of the industrial and applied arts. The sole alternative to the recognition of the part that functional ideas play in the beauty of these things is to exclude them from the house of art altogether; but to do so with regard to, say pottery and basketry, would be as arbitrary as to deny beauty to Chartres or La Miniatura.[6] The industrial arts have always proved to be stumbling blocks to aesthetic theory. Is it said that the field of art is mere appearance, unreality, illusion: well, what is more real than a building or a pot? Or is it said that beauty has nothing to do with utility: well, is it not obvious that fitness of form to function plays a part in the beauty of pots, baskets, houses, and the like? The only way to solve

---

[6] Work by Frank Lloyd Wright.

the difficulty is to recognize that the practical meaning, as a pure meaning, does enter into the aesthetic experience of such things. It is of course true that the aesthetic value of a building is not the same as its practical value: one does not have to live in it or own it in order to appreciate its beauty. Or one does not have to wear a shoe in order to know that it is beautiful; "window shopping"—a good example of imaginative satisfaction—proves that this is so. Not that wearing the shoe or living in the house is a hindrance to appreciation; they may, on the contrary, be helps; but the value that arises from use is not the same as the aesthetic value. The aesthetic value is a transfer of the practical value to the plane of imagination. The beauty of the shoe is in the way the shoe looks, not in the way it feels; but it must look as if it would feel good. So the beauty of the house is not the living well in it; but the way it looks as if one could live well in it. It is in the memory or anticipation of its service—twin phases of imagination—that its beauty resides. The use is in action; the beauty in the pure meaning. The recognition that the practical meaning, as a pure meaning, may enter into the beauty of an object thus solves the paradox of the industrial arts, and reconciles the contention of those who insist on the connexion of art with life, with the disinterestedness of beauty proclaimed by the aesthetes and the philosophers.

Our first item in the definition of art is then the provision of satisfaction in the imagination, imagination being defined in a rich sense, inclusive of sensuous patterns and meanings, in the way indicated. But like other single-idea definitions, this criterion while necessary is not sufficient; for it does not serve to exclude from art things that we know do not belong there. It does not exclude the dream at night, the day-dream, and many kinds of play. The simplest of all examples of satisfaction through the imagination is perhaps the day-dream. If a politician seeking office by election allows himself to day-dream the ceremony whereby he is proclaimed the winner, it is clear that he is getting satisfaction, not by a real course of action that leads him in fact to his goal, but through a purely fictitious occurrence which he conjures up in his own mind, for himself. But, be it noted, the motivating desire is the same in both cases, as I have insisted; the difference lying in the method by means of which desire is satisfied. In the case of the dream at night—certainly when the dream is what we call a pleasant dream—there is again satisfaction of desire, but obviously not by means of a course of action leading to a goal—for the dreamer, fast asleep, acts not at all—but by means of images created by the desire itself. The same formula of satisfaction through the imagination holds for the phantasy play of the child. The lonely child that creates for itself a dream-companion, and carries on an animated conversation with it; the little girl playing, as we say, with a doll, but actually with an imaginary baby, are both satisfying an interest or habit through an ideal, substitute object; like the dreamer and the artist, they are creating a world out of fancies to meet their desires. It is correct therefore to speak of art as a dream—a waking dream—in both there is the same creativeness; the same absorption in immediacy; and yet it is clear that mere dreaming is not art.

The second criterion that I would propose in order that we may come closer to the distinctive nature of art, is that art is social. By this I mean, first negatively, that the satisfactions of art do not depend upon factors peculiar to an individual, but rather, positively, upon types of objects that may be present in the experience of anyone. The satisfaction that is taken in a keepsake—a lock of hair, a faded rose—illustrates a satisfaction that depends upon the special "conditioning" of the individual; so likewise does the satisfaction taken by the victor in a contest—impossible obviously for the vanquished. It is equally impossible for me to share your satisfaction in your dreams, because both the sources of satisfaction and the dream images which are the objects of the satisfaction, are private. But in the case of art, the satisfaction does not depend upon the peculiar circumstances and conditioning of the individual, but upon patterns of sensa and meanings that are potentially universal. You cannot dream the dream that I dream, but you can see the same pattern of color or hear the same harmonies and melodies that I hear; and you can understand the same meanings that I understand, when we both read a poem or look at a picture. I do not mean to deny, of course, the evident differences that exist among the experiences of the same work of art in the case of different individuals. When I read

> Son of man
> You cannot say or guess, for you know only
> A heap of broken images, where the sun beats

the associations aroused by each key word in my mind and in yours will differ; yet there will be a core of meaning that will be the same; and this sameness will grow greater and approximate the meaning of the poet, as we study the poem more carefully. Sometimes no definite meaning, but only a mood will be communicated, as when we read Gertrude Stein's *Portrait of Picasso,* a mood that the writer may mistake for the essence of the object—but that does not matter.

But when I say that art is social I mean even more than this. I mean not only that there are common factors in our enjoyment of it, but that our enjoyment depends partly upon our knowing that this is so. We may enjoy a work of art in loneliness, but afterwards we want to talk about it to our friends, and make sure that they too enjoyed it. I would even venture to assert that if some despot were to decree that no one should from this day forth speak or write or in any other way communicate with his fellows about books, pictures, plays, music, there would be an end to aesthetic creation and enjoyment. Art could not survive in a world of utter privacy and silence. The communicability of the value of art is, as Kant insisted, an essential fact about it. A work of art cannot be beautiful just for me, because its beauty, that is to say, its value, depends upon the possibility of sharing it.

Not only our pleasures, but also our standards with regard to art are social. In all aesthetic appreciation we can distinguish two phases, a primary phase of direct pleasure in what is offered us, and a secondary phase that arises through the fact that the work of art meets the standards which we bring to bear upon it. Without the direct appeal, the work of art is ineffective; but unless, besides, it measures up to our expectations, we are disappointed and disturbed. We come to every work of art with a fairly definite idea of what a work of art of that kind should be like; our approach is not naive, but critical and sophisticated. A good picture, a good play, a good musical composition, must be so and so; or so and so. In this respect, to be sure, art is not peculiar; for we bring to every type of experience a preconceived idea of excellence. Every smoker has his own idea of what makes a good smoke. For one, it is a briar pipe, with a certain brand of tobacco; for another, it is a fine Havana cigar; for a third, a Lucky Strike; for a fourth, a Camel. What is peculiar about art in comparison with, say, smoking, is that we claim for our standards social validity. If you like Camels, while I like Luckies; well, it is all right with me; we will agree to disagree, and that's the end of it; but if you don't like John Marin, I shall feel that there is something wrong with you, and I may call you a Philistine, and tell you that you are sadly in need of aesthetic education. And what you think of James Joyce is not a matter of indifference to me. If you give me provocation, I shall dispute with you about it until midnight. And unlike our standards of smoking, our standards for art are formed not merely on a basis of personal experience and comparison, but like our standards of manners and morals, on a basis of tradition and education. An aesthetic value is not a given thing, to take or to leave, but something to be educated into. What a long way we are from the mere dream! A work of art is part of the history and culture of a people; a dream is a transitory and trivial happening in an isolated brain. It would be an indignity to mention such commonplaces, were they not so flagrantly contradicted by certain "authorities."

Moreover, art is social not only for the appreciator, but also for the artist. A really fatal misunderstanding about this matter has arisen in certain quarters, in connexion with the definition of art as "expression." That art is expression or self-expression, no one would deny. It is a free creation of an imaginary world through which the artist finds surcease for his desires and a solution for his problems. But art is not self-expression the way a baby's cry or a bird's song is; it is not even what Wordsworth called poetry, a spontaneous overflow of powerful feelings. No genuine artist is content merely to give form to his feelings, burning desire clean in creation, and out of its flame warming his heart with a merely private joy. On the contrary, he is building something for his group from whom he demands sympathy and understanding. He is not trying to please the group; that is the last thing he wishes to do; rather he is insisting that his group find pleasure in what pleases him. The idea that art is mere expression is valid only for the work of amateurs and dilettantes. Such people are, in fact, just expressing themselves for the sake of expression; amusing, pleasing themselves. They do not care whether anyone likes what they do or not; that is no part of their purpose. The improviser does not need an audience; the amateur painter will not show his work except perhaps and grudgingly to his wife or intimate friend. How different is the artist! He stands for something in a group and insists that what he creates shall be known and valued as he values it.

A final implication of the social character of art is the necessity that imagination shall be embodied in some physical thing by means of which it may be reproduced in many minds and at many moments. So close in fact is the connexion between imagination and physical embodiment that common sense hardly knows how to distinguish between them. The unphilosophical mind means by the *Mona Lisa,* a canvas that hangs on a wall in the Louvre; by the *Venus de Milo* a sculptured block of marble set up in another room of the palace; and by a poem something he can find written on a certain page of a certain book. He is like the Pagan who believes that God can be found in a certain temple or even in a certain piece of wood in a shrine. If you remind him that the same poem can be found in many books; the same statue in many blocks of marble, of which the one in the Louvre was probably not the original; or ask how a landscape can hang on a wall, or Venus who dwells on Olympus can live in a museum; and enquire how it happens that the same music may be heard in Budapest that he is hearing in New York, he would probably be as much puzzled as the Pagan nurtured in a creed outworn would be if you were to ask him how God can inhabit so many shrines and temples at once. The solution of the problem is, of course, as follows: just as the theologian distinguishes between God, whom no man hath seen at any time, and the temple, shrine or icon, where God may be supposed to "appear"; so we can distinguish between the *aesthetic object* or experience—a sensuous form, together with meanings underlying the form, which exists only in the imagination, and what I would call the *aesthetic instrument,* which is the vehicle for the imagination, and a part of the physical world. The *Mona Lisa* as a pattern of color and shape, and a system of meanings that may enter the same into the minds of thousands, is what I am calling the aesthetic object; while the painted canvas that one can dust and carry about and steal and recover is the aesthetic instrument; the *Waste Land,* as a system of words and meanings that you and I and the generations after may hear and, with sufficient pains, understand, is an aesthetic object, while any printed page upon which the poem is written is an aesthetic instrument; the *Venus de Milo,* a gracious form beheld and adored by countless worshippers, is an aesthetic object, but the blocks of marble in which this form is incarnate are aesthetic instruments. But while it is important that this distinction be made and its validity recognized, one must not go the lengths of a Croce in affirming that the instrument has nothing to do with art. For the appreciator, the instrument is essential, because it makes the aesthetic experience communicable; and preserves it for future generations. Without the instrument it would be a mere dream, unknowable and ephemeral. Imagination and physical embodiment are two aspects of a single fact.

The physical aspect of a work of art is of supreme importance to the artist, also. It was said of Raphael that he painted with his mind, not with his hands; but however much truth this paradox contains, like all paradoxes, it conceals an equal amount of falsehood. For every painter knows that unless he has his vision in his fingers he cannot have it in his mind. His long effort to conquer the physical medium of his art is essential to the growth of his imagination. Michelangelo's conception of the form as lying sleeping in the marble was, as Bosanquet remarked, a truer account of the facts regarding sculpture than ever Vasari's was regarding painting. And what of the relation of the violinist to his instrument or the dancer's to hers—her own body? Does not the instrument enter into the very meaning of their art for them? There are, it is true, certain arts where it almost seems as if the creative, as distinguished from the merely receptive phase of the art, had acquired independence of the instrument, even as Aristotle thought that intellect could free itself of the body and so become immortal: poetry, where the use of pen and paper, or perhaps today the typewriter, appears so irrelevant; the poet sometimes composing his verses entirely in his head, as Goethe composed his *Wanderers Nachtlied* during a walk; the music of the composer, as contrasted with the music of the performer, which may be born complete in the head of a Mozart; for which reason every Platonizing philosopher has felt that these two arts were superior to such arts as painting, sculpture, and dancing, where the relation of the artist to his instrument seems to be essential, and where the activity of the artist, since it involves manual skill no less than imagination places him among the handicraftsmen. And following out this relationship between imagination and instrument, we might go on to distinguish between these same arts of poetry and music, on the one hand, where the preservation and communication of imagination depend indeed upon a physical instrument—the score of a sonata or the page of a book of poetry—yet may be multiplied a millionfold; and the beauty of a building or a dance, on the other hand, that are tied once and for all to unique materials of stone and steel, or of flesh and bones, and die with them; then, such intermediate arts as painting and sculpture, where reproduction is possible, but always imperfect. But interesting as these distinctions are, they are not important; the important matter is the fact that the full meaning of art includes its social and historical significance, which would be impossible without the material aesthetic instrument.

We come finally to the last of the marks by means of which I am seeking to define and distinguish art. There are a number of words, more or less synonymous, which have been used to designate what I have in mind—*harmony, form, pattern, design.* This is an absolutely universal characteristic of all works of art, of every kind. But while design is a necessary mark of art, it is not sufficient, for it is not a distinguishing mark. There are other things besides works of art that possess design. The human body possesses its design; so does any machine, an airplane or a motor car. Yet while this is true, it deserves to be pointed out that there are certain differences between the form of the human body and the machine, on the one hand, and the form of a work of art, on the other hand. In order to make this clear, I wish to distinguish between two types of design in aesthetic objects, which I shall call intrinsic form and extrinsic or representational form, respectively. By representational form, I mean structure that is determined by the meanings that underlie the sensuous surface. I can make this clear by asking whether even the most radical post-impressionist would be willing to have the part of a statue that represents a head attached to the part that represents the ankle; or in a picture whether he would be willing to have the shapes that represent the sky below those that represent the earth, and the tree tops touching the ground, with the trunks in the air. Whether, not in a fairy story, but in a novel, he would be willing to have the men look like women, the babes talk and the grown-ups babble; or whether in a line of verse, for example,

> Shall I compare thee to a summer's day?

it would be just as well to write,

> I shall compare thee to a summer's day.

In all such cases it is plain that part of the pattern of the work is determined by connexions between meanings, reproduced from nature and human life and thought. In other words, we demand of a work of art that represents nature or human life and thought, an analogous pattern of its parts. Now so far as this type of form in works of art is concerned, it is obviously closely similar to the form found in machines and the organism. Just as the purpose to represent a human body requires that such and such parts of a statue represent such and such portions of the human body, and with a certain comparable arrangement; so the embodied purposes of the organism itself demand the parts and organs necessary for the carrying out of this purpose. But notice that there is a difference. For whereas in the case of the human body or the machine, the various parts are meaningless and functionless, except with relation to an environment in which they operate—a foot in relation to the ground; an eye in relation to things to be seen; a mouth in relation to food; the wheel of an automobile in relation to a road; the seat in relation to passengers; on the other hand, in the case of a work of art, there is no relation of parts to an environment, but only of parts to parts within a whole. The foot of the statue rests, not on the ground, but on a pedestal; and while its eyes may be said to see, there is nothing for them to see, and if its mouth may be said to speak, there is no one to listen to what is said. Spencer defined life as a continual adjustment of inner relations to outer relations; and he might have defined a machine in much the same way. In a work of art, however, there are internal relations only; a part refers to other parts, within the whole, in accordance with the idea that is expressed there, but does not refer to anything outside itself. It is a microcosm, a self-sufficient little world of embodied, interrelated meanings, in need of nothing to give it life and significance, save only the mind of the spectator.

One might hope to make out a better case for the uniqueness of aesthetic form in regard to what I have been calling intrinsic form. This type of form is significant in complete independence of meanings. Absolute music is the best example, for there all form is intrinsic form. The rhythmic and harmonic structure of music is effective and intelligible wholly by itself; we understand why certain harmonies are present or certain dissonances resolved without any reference to the objects and events in nature or human life. In the same way we understand why in a picture a certain color demands its contrasting and complementary color, or a certain line its balancing line, independent of what the color is the color of, or the line the line of. In a poem, we know that a word of a certain length and sound texture is demanded, independent of its meaning, because of the necessities of rime and rhythm. And even in a statue, where it might seem as if every part had to be just what it is because of the laws of anatomy, there are relations of harmony and balance of line and mass that cannot be understood in *that* way, but are intelligible in their own way. I do not mean to imply that intrinsic and extrinsic form are as separate in any work of art as might appear from my discussion; for, on the contrary, there must be a fine adaptation of one to the other, for beauty. Yet I would insist that they are two very different types of form, springing from different roots; the one type following the objective laws of nature, and so creating in every work of art some semblance of truth; the other based on those subjective principles of human nature upon which depend all value or satisfaction. Elsewhere [7] I have tried to formulate these laws; but I have no room to go into the matter here. What is of immediate concern to us is the possibility of defining art in terms of intrinsic form. That intrinsic form is a universal factor in works of art, and for that reason belongs among the indispensable elements in any definition, can I think be proved. But that it is no exclusive characteristic, and cannot therefore function as a sufficient criterion, can also be shown. For all the activities of man, so far as they are valuable, display it. His walk is rhythmic, when he enjoys it; his body is beautiful to him when harmonious and well-balanced; even his life as a whole is happy when it possesses intrinsic form. It is true, I think, that intrinsic form is most perfect in works of art; because imagination is of all spheres the most plastic to desire, and because the technique of expression of the imagination in the medium of the arts, being vastly simpler than the technique of business or politics, has achieved a perfection there unmatched anywhere, except perhaps in mathematics. For this reason art will always seem to be the superlative example of form, even though, as has been shown, it be not the sole example.

In conclusion, let me summarize the chief points I have been making in regard to the definition of art. I have tried to show that there is no single and sufficient criterion by means of which art may be defined. There are single characteristics which apply to all works of art, but none which applies exclusively to art. The definition of art must therefore be in terms of a complex of characteristics. Failure to recognize this has been the fault of all the well-known definitions. The definition which I have proposed contains three parts: the provision of satisfaction through the imagination, social significance, and harmony. I am claiming that nothing except works of art possesses all three of these marks. By imagination is meant the whole realm of given experience, inclusive of sensations and meanings as well as of images, so far as it is under the control of desire, and capable of being viewed in independence of action and reality. By the social significance of art I have meant the fact that the satisfaction which art provides does not depend upon factors peculiar to the individual, but upon patterns of sensations and meanings which may become parts of the experience of many minds, and the further fact that an important element of aesthetic satisfaction comes from knowledge that other minds are having or may have a like satisfaction. We saw, in addition, that the possibility of the social significance

---

[7] *The Analysis of Art.* Yale University Press.

of art depends upon the fashioning of relatively permanent physical objects, called by us *aesthetic instruments,* which function as stimuli of the aesthetic experience for many minds and vehicles for its transmission to future generations. It is a peculiarity of the imagination of the artist that, despite its freedom, it seeks a local habitation, and a deathless name, in these instruments, and in creating them, the artist acts as both dreamer and artisan. What we call a work of art is on the one hand a thing; on the other hand, an experience. If we are asked to express the nature of this experience in a single sentence, we may venture to say of it that it is satisfaction of desire through a harmonious and socially significant imaginative object which, because it is superlatively harmonious and of more than personal significance, becomes the symbol of all order and all goodness.

CHARLES W. MORRIS

Science, Art and Technology [1]

§ 1

A CONSIDERATION OF SCIENCE, art, and technology is inevitably a study of basic human activities and their interrelations. The theme is an old one, and many pages by many writers in many centuries supply variations and commentary. Yet the theme is a timely one for an America that stands before decades of high promise and peril, and for this *Review* which has recently opened its pages to a discussion of the place of the arts in the unity of science movement. There also exists today an instrument—the theory of signs—which may prove of great power in meeting the recurrent demands for insight into the essentials of human culture. [2]

§ 2

The utilization of the theory of signs for an approach to cultural activities is grounded in the enormous rôle which signs play in human

---

[1] Charles W. Morris, "Science, Art and Technology," *The Kenyon Review,* I (1939), 409–423. Reprinted by permission. (Eds.)
[2] The reference is to pages 159–182 and 194–199 of the Spring 1939 number of *The Kenyon Review,* and *Foundations of the Theory of Signs (International Encyclopedia of Unified Science,* vol. I, no. 2), University of Chicago Press, 1938.

behavior. The use of certain properties of things as clues to further properties, and the functioning in behavior of subsidiary spoken or written languages correlated both with human activities and the things upon which the activities are directed, are distinctive features of human activity. This fact makes it possible to view human culture as a web of sign-sustained and sign-sustaining activities, and to utilize the different modes of sign-functioning as clues to the character of the different accompanying modes of activity. It is common, for instance, to distinguish various forms of discourse (scientific, poetic, mathematical, religious, metaphysical, philosophical, etc.); French and German would be different languages, but each of them permits of all such forms of discourse. The project naturally suggests itself of approaching the nature and relations between the dominant forms of human activity through a study of the forms of discourse which are components and products of the activities in question. This approach has the merit of concreteness, since in comparing, for instance, art and science it directs attention to the work of art and the piece of scientific writing, searching in them for the reflection of the differences between art and science as human activities.

§ 3

A form of discourse is a specialization of language for the better accomplishment of some specific purpose. The everyday language of a people is an amazingly complex sign structure performing a multitude of individual and social functions. Its very protean character is its strength, for it provides the matrix in which and through which all human activities are interlocked in symbolic expression as they are interlocked in practice. This strength, however, involves a fundamental weakness: the very multiplicity of functions performed prevents the adequate performance of any one specialized function. So it is that men have gradually devised certain specializations of their common language for the more adequate performance of various specific tasks. Such specializations are here referred to as forms of discourse.

Forms of discourse can be analyzed in terms of the functions they have been elaborated to perform, and light can be thrown on the characteristic human activities and their interrelations by a study of the nature of the forms of discourse which are the products and the instruments of these activities. In practice each approach aids the other, and both will be used in the account which follows.

It seems unlikely that all the characteristic forms of discourse are equally basic. A distinction can be made—analogous to that in the theory of colors —between primary and secondary forms of discourse. Secondary forms of discourse are those built up out of other forms of discourse; primary forms of discourse are those which are not a function of other forms of discourse. The present position is that there are three primary forms of discourse (the scientific, the aesthetic, and the technological), and that all other forms are secondary, that is, are a function of these primary forms.[3] A brief characterization of the three primary forms of discourse will provide an opportunity to show something of the interrelation of science, art, and technology, and to emphasize some of the cultural implications of these interrelations.

§ 4

The scientific form of discourse has received the most careful and elaborate analysis of any of the forms of discourse. Logicians have for the most part restricted their attention to the language of science; such a work as the *International Encyclopedia of Unified Science* is mainly devoted to such analysis.

It seems a fruitful hypothesis that the language of science is controlled primarily, and perhaps exclusively, by a single aim: to make possible accurate predictions. Beings living in a spatio-temporal structure of objects are dependent upon what happens at regions in this structure. It is important for such beings to be able to take account of what will occur in certain space-time regions on the basis of what is already found to occur in these or other space-time regions. For only if a being can predict with accuracy can it prepare itself for what it will encounter in its continued existence.

It is believed that detailed examination of scientific discourse would confirm this directive hypothesis; here only a point or two can be made. First, scientific discourse is rich in devices (such as coordinate systems) for accurate references to space-time regions and for elaborate descriptions as to what exists in those regions. It accordingly stresses the relation between signs and what they denote, and it controls its statement in terms of that relation. Thus the question whether a certain sign combination is true is the question whether it denotes something with the properties specified, and in the control of this question everything is rigorously excluded which is not evidence for the existence of the object in question. This means, as a

---

[3] The number of the primary forms of discourse corresponds to the three dimensions of sign functioning: scientific discourse brings into prominence the relation of signs to objects denoted (the semantical dimension), aesthetic discourse accents in a distinctive way the sign structure itself (the syntactical dimension), technological discourse emphasizes the efficacy of the signs in the practice of the users (the pragmatical dimension). The theory of discourse is thus one development of the general theory of signs (technically called semiotic).

second characteristic of scientific discourse, that it rests upon, and issues in, statements which are confirmable, i.e., statements upon whose truth or falsity empirical evidence can be brought to bear. Such statements (the scientific substructure) are not, however, the only statements within scientific discourse: the deriving of predictions from statements about the properties of certain space-time regions requires (in the third place) an apparatus for derivation (logic and mathematics) and statements from which the derived statements follow (scientific theories). Logico-mathematical statements and scientific theories may together be regarded as constituting the superstructure of the language of science; both are controlled by their relation to the essential task of science—to make possible accurate predictions. It is demanded of the tools of deduction that from true statements only true statements are obtained; even the demand that a scientific system be non-contradictory is related to the fact that from a contradictory system any statement whatever can be deduced, so that no specific prediction can be made. And it seems to coincide with scientific practice (though not all positivists have seen this) to admit any hypothesis such that from statements about the properties of specified space-time regions confirmable statements can be obtained about further properties of these regions or about the properties of other regions.

Scientific discourse is, in summary, statemental or predictive in character, and the statements are either confirmable (or disconfirmable) in terms of empirical evidence, or are statements used in obtained confirmable statements upon the basis of other confirmable statements.[4] Scientific discourse provides man with a map such that he can determine his expectations with increasing accuracy on the basis of what he encounters in direct experience. Science as an institution involves all the procedures by which such discourse is obtained; science as a habit of mind involves a preference for the scientific form of discourse and the procedures utilized in the control of such discourse. Science as a whole ministers to man's need to be able to determine correctly his expectations, and hence his activity, in terms of the evidence which lies at hand. It is in the realization of this purpose that scientific discourse has been evolved and is being progressively controlled.

§ 5

Men have, however, other needs than that of accurate prediction. As beings with needs, and so values, they are concerned with the vivid por-

---

[4] For the detailed development of such a view of scientific discourse—without however the emphasis on the control of predictions—see the writings of R. Carnap, especially *Foundations of Logic and Mathematics,* in the *International Encyclopedia of Unified Science,* vol. I, no. 3 (University of Chicago Press, 1939).

trayal of what they value, and in devices by which their needs can be satisfied. Aesthetic discourse ministers to the first interest; technological discourse to the second. By "aesthetic discourse" is meant that specialized type of language which is the actual work of art (the poem, the painting, the music); the term does not refer to discourse about art, unless, indeed, this discourse is itself aesthetic rather than scientific or technological.

That art is a language, that the work of art is in some sense a sign, is the basic doctrine of aestheticians from Plato to Dewey. It is an intelligible interpretation of the doctrine of "imitation" to regard it as a theory of the sign-character of the work of art. For "imitation" was never originally limited to literal reproduction of existing objects (thus Aristotle speaks of the imitation of what is or what men think to be or what ought to be); to affirm that the work of art was an imitation was to affirm that it was a sign, and, indeed, a sign of a specific character: an image or icon "imitating" what is designated by embodying in itself the characters of any object the sign could be said to denote. From this point of view it is possible to regard Aristotle's *Poetics* as a treatise in aesthetics written from the standpoint of the theory of signs. Thus the approach to art as a form of discourse is an ancient and common heritage in aesthetics; the modern theory of signs, in proportion as it is more precise and elaborate, should be able to make clear the foundational material which was hardly more than implicit in ancient formulations, should be able to make more specific the nature of aesthetic discourse, and should be able to free the sign theory of art from the Platonic metaphysics of universals which has enshrouded the doctrine from Plato to Schopenhauer and Santayana and which itself arose out of inadequacies in the existing theories of signs.[5]

If the work of art can be regarded as a sign, the central question is as to the nature of the designating sign and the nature of what is designated (in technical terms, the nature of the sign vehicle and the designatum). The view proposed is that the aesthetic sign designates the value properties of actual or possible situations and that it is an iconic sign (an "image") in that it embodies these values in some medium where they may be directly inspected (in short, the aesthetic sign is an iconic sign whose designatum is a value). To give content to this statement it would be necessary to analyze in detail the notion of value and the characteristics of iconic signs, but this is neither practical nor advisable in the present context. For whatever theory of value be maintained, it must be recognized that objects have value properties among their total set of properties (an object can be in-

---

[5] An article, "Aesthetics and the Theory of Signs," published in *The Journal of Unified Science* (formerly *Erkenntnis*), 1939, attempts to sketch an aesthetics based on the general theory of signs. I shall not in the present remarks on art attempt to cover the same ground or make use of the more precise terminology there developed. This theory had in genesis no connection with the classical doctrine of imitation.

sipid, sublime, menacing, oppressive, or gay in some contexts just as it may have a certain mass or length or velocity in other contexts), and that aesthetic media, since they themselves are objects, can embody certain value properties (a small piece of cork could hardly be sublime, but it could be insipid or even gay).

From this point of view the artist is one who molds some medium so that it takes on the value of some significant experience (an experience which may of course arise in the process of molding the medium and need not antedate this process). The work of art is a sign which designates the value or value structure in question, but has the peculiarity, as an iconic sign, that in spite of its generality of reference, the value it designates is embodied in the work itself, so that in perceiving a work of art one perceives directly a value structure and need not be concerned with other objects which the aesthetic sign might denote (technically, other denotata than the sign vehicle itself).[6] In works of art men and women have embodied their experience of value, and these experiences are communicable to those who perceive the molded medium. Art is the language for the communication of values.

If such is the function of art, detailed examination should show that aesthetic discourse is language specialized for the adequate accomplishment of this purpose. Since the work of art is an icon and not a statement, aesthetic discourse is not restricted to signs whose truth is confirmable, and it needs no elaborate set of indexical signs for accuracy in space-time references. Since the aim is not prediction, the requirements of consistency or non-contradictoriness take on a special form: it is only necessary that the component signs in the total sign structure be such as to build up the total icon with the value in question, and such consistency in the presentation of a value may even involve sign combinations which the logician of scientific discourse would class as contradictory. Since the aesthetic sign itself embodies the values it designates, in aesthetic discourse the perceptual properties of the sign vehicles themselves become of great importance, and the artist constantly experiments with special syntactical combinations of these signs to obtain desired value effects. Since the work of art does designate, and in many cases denotes the value properties of actual situations, aesthetic discourse is by no means a mere "expression of the emotions": value properties are objectively relative properties of objects and in dealing with them aesthetic discourse is concerned with the same world with which science and technology are concerned. It is for this reason that aesthetic discourse can often be given a paraphrase in scientific discourse, as in the prose restate-

---

[6] "Abstract" art (perhaps automorphic or metamorphic art would be a more exact name) might seem an exception to a sign theory of art. That this is not so is argued in the previously mentioned article, "Aesthetics and the Theory of Signs."

ment of the content of a poem. Nevertheless, the type of concern is different, for the presentation of value is not to be confused with making statements about value: science itself may make statements about values as about anything else. Art does not, except incidentally, make statements about values, but presents values for direct experience; it is not a language about values, but the language of value.

§ 6

The third form of primary discourse may be called technological discourse. It is distinguished by such signs as "ought," "should," "do," "do not." A sentence in technological discourse has in function, if not in fact, the form of a command; its purpose is not to report a situation or present a value but to induce a mode of action. Such a sentence ("Paint of this kind ought to be applied in this way") implies an accepted value, whether stated or not (the permanency of the painting, etc.); it may suggest a scientific statement ("This mode of application best realizes the value in question"); it has an irreducible rhetorical or imperative component ("Apply the paint in the way described!"). Various subdivisions of technological discourse are defined in terms of the ends for which techniques are indicated,—medical discourse, engineering discourse, agricultural discourse, and the like. Each profession has its own imperatives, its own *oughts,* relative to the values it seeks to control.

The question as to the relation of morality to technology may be put in terms of the relation of moral discourse to technological discourse. The simplest possibility would be to equate the two forms of discourse, so that any action is moral in so far as it aims to utilize techniques adequate to realize some value. While there is much to be said for such a position, it does not seem to correspond to general usage as well as a view which would make moral discourse a subspecies of technological discourse (and so morality a form of technology). The question then arises as to the basis of differentiation. The moral attitude may be held to arise when the endeavor is made to maximize the positive value of a situation in which values are in conflict. Morality would then become a technology of technologies, consisting of those techniques for the maximum integration and utilization of the various techniques which a community has available for the satisfaction of its interests. The community may of course be wrong in its belief as to which techniques do in fact perform this function, and it is here that the moral individual may feel forced to deviate from the moral techniques recognized by the community. Since morality is a technology, it will, when alive and vigorous, vary with changes in the component techniques of which it is a function. Yet, since it is a function of all techniques, it is not surprising that its changes should be slow, disappointingly slow, when measured in terms of the changes within specific technologies. Perhaps the technological conception of morality would aid in taking as seriously the problems set by the interaction of techniques upon one another as are now taken the problems which arise in special technological fields.[7]

§ 7

The three primary forms of discourse are simply the development of three basic functions found in the everyday language, which permits making statements, presenting values, and controlling behavior. The primary forms of discourse are related as these three basic human concerns are related. The purposes to be realized are distinct and the corresponding forms of discourse are irreducible. Proficiency in the use of one form of discourse by no means involves proficiency in the use of the others; indeed, in the life of the individual the forms of discourse are often in competition, both because of the differences in human abilities and because of the shortness of human life. But while the individual may have to make a choice, society as a whole need not, for the adequate accomplishment of each of the three basic purposes requires the fulfilment of the others.

If interests are to be satisfied and values realized it is helpful to present vividly what has been attained and what is being sought, and aesthetic discourse provides such presentation. It is also desirable to know the consequences of proposed courses of action under the conditions which have to be met, and scientific discourse favors such accuracy in prediction. Technological discourse gives the stimulation to act upon the techniques deemed effective in the realization of the values sought.

Scientific discourse does not entice by the presentation of value nor seduce to action by the advocacy of a technique; it represents the subordination of interest to the mapping of the structure of the existential. Yet it is clear that the direction of science is in a general sense determined by what values men at the time hold, and that science provides the basis for the control of all techniques, since the determination of whether a given procedure does or does not reach a certain goal is a scientific question. Further, the scientist may be helped in the scientific study of values by the vivid portrayal of the value whose conditions he endeavors to trace. He may obtain stimulation through the aesthetic presentation of the value of scientific activity and results. And as a scientist aiming to realize the ends of science,

---

[7] Though the present terminology is not used, important material bearing on what we have called technological discourse, and on its relation to scientific discourse, is found in the monograph by John Dewey, *Theory of Valuation* (*International Encyclopedia of Unified Science*, vol. II, no. 4), University of Chicago Press, 1939.

he is a technologist since he must develop and control the techniques adequate to his purposes. If science provides the basis for the control of technological discourse, it is also true that the development of science is inseparable from the development of technology.

Aesthetic discourse has as its field the presentation for direct inspection of the whole realm of values, negative as well as positive. Since men's values are a function of their interests and the world in which such interests arise and operate, the presentation of value will, by and large, require reference to persons and the world, so that aesthetic discourse may incorporate within itself and for its own purpose the statemental character of scientific discourse. It may, further, concern itself with the value of scientific and technological activity and their results. Its presentation of negative value might seem to endanger the work of the moralist, and indeed it does endanger encrusted moral customs. But if morality means the active endeavor to maximize positive values, the moralist needs to have before him for consideration all that interests, so that in the larger sense the free development of art is a vital aid in the development of a vigorous and progressive morality. Finally, the artist is himself technologist in that he must work his will upon some material or other. As technologist he can utilize whatever scientific knowledge can be obtained about his media and about the adequacy of his techniques to attain their ends.

The technologist in turn can only be grateful for the vivid presentation of the values whose status in nature he attempts to control, and for what scientific material he can draw upon to control the efficacy of his techniques. The same is true of the moral technologist. A vital morality can only be helped by a vigorous art and a courageous science which stop before no value or fact. For a morality which is not alert to all that men need and find good or evil is blind and fossilized, while a morality whose injunctions are not constantly corrected by scientific knowledge of the situations with which the injunctions deal, and of the adequacy of the commanded techniques in such situations, is dogmatic and superstitious.

The activities of the scientist, the artist, and the technologist are mutually supporting activities, and their differences and interrelations may be discerned in the differences and interrelations of scientific, aesthetic, and technological discourse.

§ 8

Perhaps the foregoing account may help to clarify some of the issues raised by Mr. Ransom in the Spring Number of this *Review* regarding the treatment of the arts in the unity of science program as represented in the *International Encyclopedia of Unified Science*. The position—and the fear—is there expressed that the sympathetic tone of the program towards the arts rests upon a fundamental misunderstanding of them as quasi-sciences. It is suggested that this mistaken position rests on the view that the arts, considered as languages, have all the three dimensions of scientific language (the semantical, syntactical, and pragmatical). The difference between the arts and the sciences seems then one of degree; the arts simply dress up diluted scientific knowledge in palatable form. Such an interpretation is then rejected and a counter-proposal made: "The Encyclopedists are talking about the language of science. I imagine that now is a splendid time for the aestheticians, inside or outside the Encyclopedia, to make an assertion which would be round, bold, metaphysical, just, and tactically perfect. To this effect: art has a language of its own; it is not the same as the language of science; its semantical meanings cannot be rendered in the language of science. Art fixes a kind of knowledge of which science has no understanding, and which gentlemen too confined within the scientific habit cannot approach intelligently. . . . They do not . . . . rise to a grasp of this kind of meaning, which is qualitatively unique and indivisible."

In terms of what has been said it is possible to state with some precision the points of agreement and disagreement with Mr. Ransom's views. It is true, I believe, that the aesthetic sign, in common with all signs, has all three dimensions of sign functioning; such a position seems a wise corrective to the common but too simple view that the artist simply "emotes" or "expresses himself" without any concern for actuality. Yet the recognition that art has a semantical aspect need not make art a quasi-science nor a metaphysical rival to scientific knowledge. In agreeing that art is a primary form of discourse, irreducible to the scientific, the positive kernel of Mr. Ransom's demand has been accepted; the reason for the metaphysical addition is not evident. It is true that in presenting values for experience, art provides the occasion for knowing about these values, and the easy transition from *having* to *knowing* is perhaps the source of the difference. But in so far as the knowledge of value which art gives is more than the having of value there is no reason to suppose that this knowledge is other than scientific in character. Controversy at this point easily becomes terminological. The work of art as such is an iconic sign and not a statement, and this distinguishes aesthetic discourse from scientific discourse and the aesthetic experience from scientific knowledge, even though icons have a semantic character as well as do statements.

If aesthetic discourse is not scientific discourse, then the arts as such could not be part of unified science nor be included in the *Encyclopedia of Unified Science*. Nevertheless, aesthetic discourse can itself be the subject of discourse. Sentences about a work of art may themselves be aesthetical, technological, or scientific discourse,—the babel of criticism lies in the confusion of the forms of discourse and the ways in which a form of discourse may be subject matter for other forms. The unity of science program would be concerned with the sentences in scientific discourse which are about aesthetic discourse and with the relation of these sentences to other scientific sentences. An activity must not be confused with statements made about it. Art as an activity is not the activity which is science, and art as such does not occur in a scientific treatise. But the difference between art and science, and their interrelations, can be stated scientifically, and such statements may be considered in their relation to other scientific statements. Art will not appear in the *Encyclopedia,* but aesthetics, and the place of aesthetics in the system of knowledge, should appear.

The unity of science movement is not without significance for the arts. The approach through the theory of signs gives the possibility of a scientific aesthetics, and a language in which to talk simply and clearly about art and its relations to other components of culture. This approach promises to throw light upon the current confusion of aesthetic criticism. The artist himself may gain release for his own activity if in an age of science and technology he can be made to see clearly the nature and importance of his own work, and to understand that in spite of irreducible and precious differences art, science, and technology are complementary and supporting activities.

§ 9

This country stands before an era of great promise. It is too early to know if that promise is to be fulfilled; indeed, the growing "paranoia-kinesis" of America (to borrow a term from Dali's recent manifesto) already shows the need of self-criticism and self-restraint. But if the promise is to be fulfilled it will require the full resources of scientists, artists, and technologists, proud and courageous in their own activities, with vision enough to see that each complements the other and that each requires of the others understanding, cooperation, and support.

Section Three

THE CREATIVE ACT

————

THE FIRST OF THE major problems to be treated concerns the nature of the relationship between the artist and the object he produces. This, after all, is the historical beginning of the aesthetic process. The writers on this problem seek to clarify the psychology of the creative imagination. Three general issues, closely interrelated, may be discriminated here. One may wonder, first, to what extent the mental activities of the creating artist are the same as, or different from, those of the non-artist. Can one say that a statesman who conceives a bold plan of action, or a scientist who makes a basic contribution, or a financier or industrialist who adds to the wealth of his nation, is "creative" in the same sense that the artist is? If he is not, how do the gifts of one and the other differ? Freud is centrally concerned with comparing the creative activity of the artist with that of other men, and Jung handles the problem by way of criticizing Freud. Again, Hulme's concept of the creative act rests completely on the difference in kind he establishes between ordinary perception and aesthetic perception.

There is a second group of questions which seek to discover what place the artist's previous experience in the world has in the finished product of his mind and skill. These questions have been a central concern of the aesthetician since Coleridge formulated, in idealistic terms, his distinction between Imagination and Fancy (*Biographia Literaria,* Chapter XIII) early in the nineteenth century. This distinction may be briefly summarized in the following manner: Imagination is that spontaneous power of mind which allows it to express itself in a literally creative way; through Imagination the mind infuses organic life into the lifeless mental impressions

116

it has gathered from a lifeless world. Fancy is the faculty which, while it also chooses among the many impressions stored by the mind, remains essentially passive; bound by the law of association, it can only add together mechanically the selections it has made from the mind's associative memories.

This statement left many questions for the probings of those who followed; these questions must be accepted as crucial if one is to understand the selections included here from James, Hulme, and Alexander. What relation has the object created by the artist to the data given him by the external world? Does the artist merely imitate or select from this data and superimpose an external form upon it? Or does his object reveal something which can in no way be accounted for in terms of what the artist's world has given him? To what extent, in other words, has the mind of the artist, in the creative process, added to the materials furnished it by experience? To what extent is the artist literally creative? Or, if, on the other hand, the object seems to correspond to the external world, does it answer to the reality given us by our senses or to a deeper, less attainable reality which art alone can give us? If it is the latter, can art in any strict sense be called "imitation"? Does the artist, then, really create his object or does he merely discover it?

To treat these questions is to examine the very heart of the creative process. It is to give us a theory of mind which will help us to understand the way the artist converts his experience into meaningful form. These considerations will also be valuable to us when we come to investigate the art object. For example, we shall have to re-examine such conventional categories of art as realism and symbolism to see whether a distinction between them retains any useful meaning in view of what we learn about the way all art is produced.

Thirdly, there are the questions clustered about the relation of the artist's medium to the mental processes revealed in the study of the second group of problems. We have already seen that Croce denies the artist's need to embody his intuitions in a pliable and yet recalcitrant material. In this section Alexander, Hulme, and Jung see the medium in which the objectification takes form as playing an important role in artistic creation. How completely, then, is the object predetermined by the original intentions of the artist? Or do the demands of the medium continually reshape these intentions so that the completed work in some sense stands apart from the mind of its creator as an independent entity? In other words, to what extent is the object obedient to the artist's preconceptions of it and to what extent to the controls and limitations imposed by a medium which has been conceived and developed by a tradition? Which of these two factors is the dominant one in the creative act, or is there rather a give-and-take struggle between them? May not the answers to these questions throw some light on the others we have raised about the creative act, so that we can see it as a unified process in which mental operations are carried on, not in terms of bodiless abstractions, but in the physical terms in which the object will finally be realized?

These are not all the questions that can be asked about the creative act, but the editors have tried to classify some of the more important ones that concern modern writers on aesthetics. An attempt to answer them introduces issues which may seem also to be allied to the nature of the object (the objective and formal demands of the artist's medium) and to the spectator's response (the artist's need to work in terms of a tradition shared by him and his audience, one that will permit the latter to react properly to his work). Although these problems are thus interrelated, there is nevertheless a clear enough sense in which it can be said that there is a more or less discrete problem of the creative activity, since the question, however it is answered, refers primarily to the nature of the gift of the man who produces art.

HENRY JAMES

The ''Germ'' of a Story[1]

I‌T WAS YEARS AGO, I remember, one Christmas Eve when I was dining with friends: a lady beside me made in the course of talk one of those allusions that I have always found myself recognising on the spot as "germs." The germ, wherever gathered, has ever been for me the germ of a "story,"

---

[1] This passage is from Henry James' own Preface to *The Spoils of Poynton*. It is reprinted from *The Art of the Novel*, by Henry James, edited by Richard P. Blackmur; pp. 119–125; copyright, 1934, by Charles Scribner's Sons; used by permission of the publishers. Title by the editors.

Like the other prefaces to the New York edition collected by Mr. Blackmur in this book, this one can be read by itself despite its references to the novel. *The Spoils of Poynton* is about a "row" between Mrs. Gereth and her son, Owen, over the exquisite "Things" which she has collected during her husband's lifetime, but which the son inherited upon the death of her husband. The misunderstanding is caused by the fact that Owen has become engaged to Mona, a woman who has no taste to appreciate the beauty of Poynton. Mrs. Gereth, rather than let the things fall into the hands of a vulgar woman, carries them off to the cottage her husband has left her. She plots to get Owen to break his engagement and marry Fleda, a girl capable of appreciating the "Things." Confident that her plot will succeed, by way of inducement she returns the things to Poynton. Owen himself is somewhat desirous of breaking his engagement to Mona, and most of the stories straining to shape under my hand have sprung from a single small seed, a seed as minute and wind-blown as that casual hint for *The Spoils of Poynton* dropped unwitting by my neighbour, a mere floating particle in the stream of talk. What above all comes back to me with this reminiscence is the sense of the inveterate minuteness, on such happy occasions, of the precious particle—reduced, that is, to its mere fruitful essence. Such is the interesting truth about the stray suggestion, the wandering word, the vague echo, at touch of which the novelist's imagination winces as at the prick of some sharp point: its virtue is all in its needle-like quality, the power to penetrate as finely as possible. This fineness it is that communicates the virus of suggestion, anything more than the minimum of which spoils the operation. If one is given a hint at all designedly one is sure to be given too much; one's subject is in the merest grain, the speck of truth, of beauty, of reality, scarce visible to the common eye—since, I firmly hold, a good eye for a subject is anything but usual. Strange and attaching, certainly, the consistency with which the first thing to be done for the communicated and seized idea is to reduce almost to nought the form, the air as of a mere disjoined and lacerated lump of life, in which we may have happened to meet it. Life being all inclusion and confusion, and art being all discrimination and selection, the latter, in search of the hard latent *value* with which alone it is concerned, sniffs round the mass as instinctively and unerringly as a dog suspicious of some buried bone. The difference here, however, is that, while the dog desires his bone but to destroy it, the artist finds in *his* tiny nugget, washed free of awkward accretions and hammered into a sacred hardness, the very stuff for a clear affirmation, the happiest chance for the indestructible. It at the same time amuses him again and again to note how, beyond the first step of the actual case, the case that constitutes for him his germ, his vital particle, his grain of gold, life persistently blunders and deviates, loses herself in the sand. The reason is of course that life has no direct sense whatever for the subject and is capable, luckily for us, of nothing but splendid waste. Hence the opportunity for the sublime economy of art, which rescues, which saves and hoards and "banks," investing and reinvesting these fruits of toil in wondrous useful "works" and thus making up for us, desperate spendthrifts that we all naturally are, the most princely of incomes. It is the subtle secrets of that system, however, that are meanwhile the charming study, with an endless attraction, above all, in the question —endlessly baffling indeed—of the method at the heart of the madness; the

---

but Fleda, while admitting she loves Owen, cannot accept the advantageous offer of marriage unless Mona willingly releases him. Mona, however, recognizing the practical advantages of the match, finally marries him and takes possession of Poynton and its beautiful things. The story ends with Fleda returning to Poynton in time to see it accidentally destroyed by fire. (Eds.)

madness, I mean, of a zeal, among the reflective sort, so disinterested. If life, presenting us the germ, and left merely to herself in such a business, gives the case away, almost always, before we can stop her, what are the signs for our guidance, what the primary laws for a saving selection, how do we know when and where to intervene, where do we place the beginnings of the wrong or the right deviation? Such would be the elements of an inquiry upon which, I hasten to say, it is quite forbidden me here to embark: I but glance at them in evidence of the rich pasture that at every turn surrounds the ruminant critic. The answer may be after all that mysteries here elude us, that general considerations fail or mislead, and that even the fondest of artists need ask no wider range than the logic of the particular case. The particular case, or in other words his relation to a given subject, once the relation is established, forms in itself a little world of exercise and agitation. Let him hold himself perhaps supremely fortunate if he can meet half the questions with which that air alone may swarm.

So it was, at any rate, that when my amiable friend, on the Christmas Eve, before the table that glowed safe and fair through the brown London night, spoke of such an odd matter as that a good lady in the north, always well looked on, was at daggers drawn with her only son, ever hitherto exemplary, over the ownership of the valuable furniture of a fine old house just accruing to the young man by his father's death, I instantly became aware, with my "sense for the subject," of the prick of inoculation; the *whole* of the virus, as I have called it, being infused by that single touch. There had been but ten words, yet I had recognised in them, as in a flash, all the possibilities of the little drama of my *Spoils,* which glimmered then and there into life; so that when in the next breath I began to hear of action taken, on the beautiful ground, by our engaged adversaries, tipped each, from that instant, with the light of the highest distinction, I saw clumsy Life again at her stupid work. For the action taken, and on which my friend, as I knew she would, had already begun all complacently and benightedly further to report, I had absolutely, and could have, no scrap of use; one had been so perfectly qualified to say in advance, "It's the perfect little workable thing, but she'll strangle it in the cradle, even while she pretends, all so cheeringly, to rock it; wherefore I'll stay her hand while yet there's time." I didn't, of course, stay her hand—there never *is* in such cases "time"; and I had once more the full demonstration of the fatal futility of Fact. The turn taken by the excellent situation—excellent, for development, if arrested in the right place, that is in the germ—had the full measure of the classic ineptitude; to which with the full measure of the artistic irony one could once more, and for the thousandth time, but take off one's hat. It was not, however, that this in the least mattered, once the seed had been transplanted to richer soil; and I dwell on that almost inveterate redundancy of the wrong, as opposed to the ideal right, in any free flowering of the actual, by reason only of its approach to calculable regularity.

If there was nothing regular meanwhile, nothing more so than the habit of vigilance, in my quickly feeling where interest would really lie, so I could none the less acknowledge afresh that these small private cheers of recognition made the spirit easy and the temper bland for the confused whole. I "took" in fine, on the spot, to the rich bare little fact of the two related figures, embroiled perhaps all so sordidly; and for reasons of which I could most probably have given at the moment no decent account. Had I been asked why they were, in that stark nudity, to say nothing of that ugliness of attitude, "interesting," I fear I could have said nothing more to the point, even to my own questioning spirit, than "Well, you'll see!" By which of course I should have meant "Well, *I* shall see"—confident meanwhile (as against the appearance or the imputation of poor taste) that interest would spring as soon as one should begin really to see *anything*. That points, I think, to a large part of the very source of interest for the artist: it resides in the strong consciousness of his seeing all for himself. He has to borrow his motive, which is certainly half the battle; and this motive is his ground, his site, and his foundation. But after that he only lends and gives, only builds and piles high, lays together the blocks quarried in the deeps of his imagination and on his personal premises. He thus remains all the while in intimate commerce with his motive, and can say to himself—what really more than anything else inflames and sustains him—that he alone has the *secret* of the particular case, he alone can measure the truth of the direction to be taken by his developed data. There can be for him, evidently, only one logic for these things; there can be for him only one truth and one direction —the quarter in which his subject most completely expresses itself. The careful ascertainment of how it shall do so, and the art of guiding it with consequent authority—since this sense of "authority" is for the master-builder the treasure of treasures, or at least the joys of joys—renews in the modern alchemist something like the old dream of the secret of life.

Extravagant as the mere statement sounds, one seemed accordingly to handle the secret of life in drawing the positive right truth out of the so easy muddle of wrong truths in which the interesting possibilities of that "row," so to call it, between mother and son over their household goods might have been stifled. I find it odd to consider, as I thus revert, that I could have had none but the most general warrant for "seeing anything in it," as the phrase would have been; that I couldn't in the least, on the spot, as I have already hinted, have justified my faith. One thing was "in it," in the sordid situation, on the first blush, and one thing only—though this, in its limited way, no doubt, a curious enough value: the sharp light it might project on that most modern of our current passions, the fierce appetite for the upholsterer's and joiner's and brazier's work, the chairs and tables, the cabinets and presses, the material odds and ends, of the more labouring ages. A lively mark of our manners indeed the diffusion of this curiosity and this avidity, and full of suggestions, clearly, as to their possible influence on other passions and other relations. On the face of it the "things" themselves would form the very centre of such a crisis; these grouped objects, all conscious of their eminence and their price, would enjoy, in any picture of a conflict, the heroic importance. They would have to be presented, they would have to be painted —arduous and desperate thought; something would have to be done for them not too ignobly unlike the great array in which Balzac, say, would have marshalled them: *that* amount of workable interest at least would evidently be "in it."

It would be wrapped in the silver tissue of some such conviction, at any rate, that I must have laid away my prime impression for a rest not disturbed till long afterwards, till the year 1896, I make out, when there arose a question of my contributing three "short stories" to *The Atlantic Monthly;* or supplying rather perhaps a third to complete a trio two members of which had appeared. The echo of the situation mentioned to me at our Christmas Eve dinner awoke again, I recall, at that touch—I recall, no doubt, with true humility, in view of my renewed mismeasurement of my charge. Painfully associated for me had *The Spoils of Poynton* remained, until recent re-perusal, with the awkward consequence of that fond error. The subject had emerged from cool reclusion all suffused with a flush of meaning; thanks to which irresistible air, as I could but plead in the event, I found myself—as against a mere commercial austerity—beguiled and led on. The thing had "come," the flower of conception had bloomed—all in the happy dusk of in-difference and neglect; yet, strongly and frankly as it might now appeal, my idea wouldn't surely overstrain a *natural* brevity. A story that couldn't pos-sibly be long would have inevitably to be "short," and out of the depths of that delusion it accordingly began to struggle. To my own view, after the "first number," this composition (which in the magazine bore another title) conformed but to its nature, which was not to transcend a modest amplitude; but, dispatched in instalments, it felt itself eyed, from month to month, I seem to remember, with an editorial ruefulness excellently well founded—from the moment such differences of sense could exist, that is, as to the short and the long. The sole impression it made, I woefully gathered, was that of length, and it has till lately, as I say, been present to me but as the poor little "long" thing.

It began to appear in April 1896, and, as is apt blessedly to occur for me throughout this process of revision, the old, the shrunken concomitants muster again as I turn the pages. They lurk between the lines; these serve for them as the barred seraglio-windows behind which, to the outsider in the glare of the Eastern street, forms indistinguishable seem to move and peer; "association" in fine bears upon them with its infinite magic. Peering through the lattice from without inward I recapture a cottage on a cliff-side, to which, at the earliest approach of the summer-time, redoubtable in London through the luxuriance of still other than "natural" forces, I had betaken myself to finish a book in quiet and to begin another in fear. The cottage was, in its kind, perfection; mainly by reason of a small paved terrace which, curving forward from the cliff-edge like the prow of a ship, overhung a view as level, as purple, as full of rich change, as the expanse of the sea. The horizon was in fact a band of sea; a small red-roofed town, of great antiquity, perched on its sea-rock, clustered within the picture off to the right; while above one's head rustled a dense summer shade, that of a trained and arching ash, rising from the middle of the terrace, brushing the parapet with a heavy fringe and covering the place like a vast umbrella. Beneath this umbrella and really under exquisite protection *The Spoils of Poynton* managed more or less symmetrically to grow.

HENRY JAMES

The Art of Fiction [1]

I OUGHT TO ADD, however, that if Mr. Besant says at the beginning of his essay that the "laws of fiction may be laid down and taught with as much precision and exactness as the laws of harmony, perspective, and proportion," he mitigates what might appear to be an extravagance by applying his remark to "general" laws, and by expressing most of these rules in a manner with which it would certainly be unaccommodating to disagree. That the novelist must write from his experience, that his "characters must be real and such as might be met with in actual life"; that "a young lady brought up in a quiet country village should avoid descriptions of garrison life," and "a writer whose friends and personal experiences belong to the lower middle-class should carefully avoid introducing his characters into society"; that one should enter one's notes in

---

[1] From Henry James, "The Art of Fiction," in *Partial Portraits* (London and New York: The Macmillan Company, 1888) pp. 386–390. James is here answering Walter Besant's lecture, "The Art of Fiction," and is criticizing his mechanical characterization of the relation of the creative imagination to experience. (Eds.)

a common-place book; that one's figures should be clear in outline; that making them clear by some trick of speech or of carriage is a bad method, and "describing them at length" is a worse one; that English Fiction should have a "conscious moral purpose"; that "it is almost impossible to estimate too highly the value of careful workmanship—that is, of style"; that "the most important point of all is the story," that "the story is everything": these are principles with most of which it is surely impossible not to sympathize. That remark about the lower middle-class writer and his knowing his place is perhaps rather chilling; but for the rest I should find it difficult to dissent from any one of these recommendations. At the same time, I should find it difficult positively to assent to them, with the exception, perhaps, of the injunction as to entering one's notes in a common-place book. They scarcely seem to me to have the quality that Mr. Besant attributes to the rules of the novelist—the "precision and exactness" of "the laws of harmony, perspective, and proportion." They are suggestive, they are even inspiring, but they are not exact, though they are doubtless as much so as the case admits of: which is a proof of that liberty of interpretation for which I have just contended. For the value of these different injunctions—so beautiful and so vague—is wholly in the meaning one attaches to them. The characters, the situation, which strike one as real will be those that touch and interest one most, but the measure of reality is very difficult to fix. The reality of Don Quixote or of Mr. Micawber is a very delicate shade; it is a reality so coloured by the author's vision that, vivid as it may be, one would hesitate to propose it as a model: one would expose one's self to some very embarrassing questions on the part of a pupil. It goes without saying that you will not write a good novel unless you possess the sense of reality; but it will be difficult to give you a recipe for calling that sense into being. Humanity is immense, and reality has a myriad forms; the most one can affirm is that some of the flowers of fiction have the odour of it, and others have not; as for telling you in advance how your nosegay should be composed, that is another affair. It is equally excellent and inconclusive to say that one must write from experience; to our supposititious aspirant such a declaration might savour of mockery. What kind of experience is intended, and where does it begin and end? Experience is never limited, and it is never complete; it is an immense sensibility, a kind of huge spider-web of the finest silken threads suspended in the chamber of consciousness, and catching every air-borne particle in its tissue. It is the very atmosphere of the mind; and when the mind is imaginative—much more when it happens to be that of a man of genius—it takes to itself the faintest hints of life, it converts the very pulses of the air into revelations. The young lady living in a village has only to be a damsel upon whom nothing is lost to make it quite unfair (as it seems to me) to declare to her that she shall have nothing to say about the military.

Greater miracles have been seen than that, imagination assisting, she should speak the truth about some of these gentlemen. I remember an English novelist, a woman of genius, telling me that she was much commended for the impression she had managed to give in one of her tales of the nature and way of life of the French Protestant youth. She had been asked where she learned so much about this recondite being, she had been congratulated on her peculiar opportunities. These opportunities consisted in her having once, in Paris, as she ascended a staircase, passed an open door where, in the household of a *pasteur,* some of the young Protestants were seated at table round a finished meal. The glimpse made a picture; it lasted only a moment, but that moment was experience. She had got her direct personal impression, and she turned out her type. She knew what youth was, and what Protestantism; she also had the advantage of having seen what it was to be French, so that she converted these ideas into a concrete image and produced a reality. Above all, however, she was blessed with the faculty which when you give it an inch takes an ell, and which for the artist is a much greater source of strength than any accident of residence or of place in the social scale. The power to guess the unseen from the seen, to trace the implication of things, to judge the whole piece by the pattern, the condition of feeling life in general so completely that you are well on your way to knowing any particular corner of it—this cluster of gifts may almost be said to constitute experience, and they occur in country and in town, and in the most differing stages of education. If experience consists of impressions, it may be said that impressions *are* experience, just as (have we not seen it?) they are the very air we breathe. Therefore, if I should certainly say to a novice, "Write from experience and experience only," I should feel that this was rather a tantalizing monition if I were not careful immediately to add, "Try to be one of the people on whom nothing is lost!"

T. E. HULME

Bergson's Theory of Art [1]

1. THE GREAT DIFFICULTY in any talk about art lies in the extreme indefiniteness of the vocabulary you are obliged to employ. The

---

[1] From T. E. Hulme, *Speculations* (London: Routledge and Kegan Paul, Ltd., 1936), pp. 143–169. Reprinted by permission. (Eds.)

concepts by which you endeavour to describe your attitude toward any work of art are so extraordinarily fluid. Words like creative, expressive, vital, rhythm, unity and personality are so vague that you can never be sure when you use them that you are conveying over at all the meaning you intended to. This is constantly realised unconsciously; in almost every decade a new catch word is invented which for a few years after its invention does convey, to a small set of people at any rate, a definite meaning, but even that very soon lapses into a fluid condition when it means anything and nothing.

This leads me to the point of view which I take about Bergson in relation to art. He has not created any new theory of art. That would be absurd. But what he does seem to me to have done is that by the acute analysis of certain mental processes he has enabled us to state more definitely and with less distortion the qualities which we feel in art.

2. The finished portrait is explained by the features of the model, by the nature of the artist, by the colours spread out of the palette; but even with the knowledge of what explains it, no one, not even the artist, could have foreseen exactly what the portrait would be. For to predict it would be to produce it before it was produced. Creation in art is not necessarily a mere synthesis of elements. In so far as we are geometricians we reject the unforeseeable. We might accept it assuredly in so far as we are artists, for art lives on creation and implies a belief in the spontaneity of nature. But disinterested art is a luxury like pure speculation. Our eye perceives the features of the living being merely as assembled, not as mutually organised. The intention of life—a simple movement which runs through the lines and binds them together and gives them significance—escapes it. This intention is just what the artist tries to regain in placing himself back within the object by a kind of sympathy and breaking down by an effort of intuition the barrier that space puts between him and his model. It is true that this aesthetic intuition, like external perception, only attains the individual, but we can conceive an inquiry turned in the same direction as art which would take life in general for its object just as physical science, following to the end the direction pointed out by external perception, prolongs the individual facts into general laws.

3. In the state of mind produced in you by any work of art there must necessarily be a rather complicated mixture of the emotions. Among these is one which can properly be called an essentially aesthetic emotion. It could not occur alone, isolated; it may only constitute a small proportion of the total emotion produced; but it is, as far as any investigation in the nature of aesthetics is concerned, the important thing. In the total body of effect produced by music, nine-tenths may be an effect which, properly speaking, is independent of the essentially aesthetic emotion which we get from it. The

same thing is most obviously true of painting. The total effect produced by any painting is most obviously a composite thing composed of a great many different kinds of emotions—the pleasure one gets from the subject, from the quality of the colour and the painting, and then the subsidiary pleasures one gets from recognition of the style, of a period or a particular painter. Mixed up with these is the one, sometimes small element of emotion, which is the veritable aesthetic one.

4. In order to be able to state the nature of the process which I think is involved in any art, I have had to use a certain kind of vocabulary, to postulate certain things. I have had to suppose a reality of infinite variability, and one that escapes all the stock perceptions, without being able to give any actual account of that reality. I have had to suppose that human perception gets crystallised out along certain lines, that it has certain fixed habits, certain fixed ways of seeing things, and is so unable to see things as they are.

Putting the thing generally—I have had to make all kinds of suppositions simply and solely for the purpose of being able to convey over and state the nature of the activity you get in art. Now the extraordinary importance of Bergson for any theory of art is that, starting with a different aim altogether, seeking merely to give an account of reality, he arrives at certain conclusions as being true, and these conclusions are the very things which we had to suppose in order to give an account of art. The advantage of this is that it removes your account of art from the merely literary level, from the level at which it is a more or less successful attempt to describe what you feel about the matter, and enables you to state it as an account of actual reality.

5. The two parts of Bergson's general philosophical position which are important in the theory of aesthetic are (1) the conception of reality as a flux of interpenetrated elements unseizable by the intellect (this gives a more precise meaning to the word reality which has been employed so often in the previous pages, when art has been defined as a more direct communication of reality); and (2) his account of the part played in the development of the ordinary characteristics of the mind by its orientation towards action.[2] This in its turn enables one to give a more coherent account of the reason for what previously has only been assumed, the fact that in ordinary perception, both of external objects and of our internal states, we never perceive things as they are, but only certain conventional types.

---

[2] Besides passages to be found scattered in Bergson's philosophical writings (see, for instance, *An Introduction to Metaphysics,* New York: G. P. Putnam's Sons, 1912), the work of Bergson in which he deals with aesthetic questions is *Le Rire,* translated into English as *Laughter: An Essay on the Meaning of the Comic* (New York: The Macmillan Company, 1911). (Eds.)

6. Man's primary need is not *knowledge* but *action*. The characteristic of the intellect itself Bergson deduces from this fact. The function of the intellect is so to present things not that we may most thoroughly understand them, but that we may successfully act on them. Everything in man is dominated by his necessity of action.

7. The creative activity of the artist is only necessary because of the limitations placed on internal and external perception by the necessities of action. If we could break through the veil which action interposes, if we could come into direct contact with sense and consciousness, art would be useless and unnecessary. Our eyes, aided by memory, would carve out in space and fix in time the most inimitable of pictures. In the centre of one's own mind, we should hear constantly a certain music. But as this is impossible, the function of the artist is to pierce through here and there, accidentally as it were, the veil placed between us and reality by the limitations of our perception engendered by action.

8. Philosophers are always giving definitions of art with which the artist, when he is not actively working but merely talking after dinner, is content to agree with, because it puts his function in some grandiose phraseology which he finds rather flattering. I remember hearing Mr. Rothenstein in an after-dinner speech say that "art was the *revelation of the infinite in the finite.*" I am very far from suggesting that he invented that phrase, but I quote it as showing that he evidently felt that it did convey something of the matter. And so it does in a way, but it is so hopelessly vague. It may convey the kind of excitement which art may produce in you, but it in no way fits the actual process that the artist goes through. It defines art in much the same way that saying that I was in Europe would define my position in space. It includes art, but it gives you no specific description of it.

This kind of thing was not dangerous to the artists themselves, because being familiar with the specific thing intended they were able to discount all the rest. When the infinite in the finite was mentioned, they knew the quite specific and limited quality which was intended. The danger comes from the outsiders who, not knowing, not being familiar with the specific quality, take words like infinite in the much bigger sense than is really intended.

9. To describe the nature of the activity you get in art, the philosopher must always create some kind of special vocabulary. He has to make use of certain metaphysical conceptions in order to state the thing satisfactorily. The great advantage of Bergson's theory is that it states the thing most nakedly, with the least amount of metaphysical baggage. In essence, of course, his theory is exactly the same as Schopenhauer's. That is, they both want to convey over the same feeling about art. But Schopenhauer demands such a cumbrous machinery in order to get that feeling out. Art is the pure

contemplation of the Idea in a moment of emancipation from the Will. To state a quite simple thing he has to invent two very extraordinary ones. In Bergson it is an actual contact with reality in a man who is emancipated from the ways of perception engendered by action, but the action is written with a small "a," not a large one.

10. The process of artistic creation would be better described as a process of discovery and disentanglement. To use the metaphor which one is by now so familiar with—the stream of the inner life, and the definite crystallised shapes on the surface—the big artist, the creative artist, the innovator, leaves the level where things are crystallised out into these definite shapes, and, diving down into the inner flux, comes back with a new shape which he endeavours to fix. He cannot be said to have created it, but to have discovered it, because when he has definitely expressed it we recognise it as true. Great painters are men in whom has originated a certain vision of things which has become or will become the vision of everybody. Once the painter has seen it, it becomes easy for all of us to see it. A mould has been made. But the creative activity came in the effort which was necessary to disentangle this particular type of vision from the general haze—the effort, that is, which is necessary to break moulds and to make new ones. For instance, the effect produced by Constable on the English and French Schools of landscape painting. Nobody before Constable saw things, or at any rate painted them, in that particular way. This makes it easier to see clearly what one means by an individual way of looking at things. It does not mean something which is peculiar to an individual, for in that case it would be quite valueless. It means that a certain individual artist was able to break through the conventional ways of looking at things which veil reality from us at a certain point, was able to pick out one element which is really in all of us, but which before he had disentangled it, we were unable to perceive. It is as if the surface of our mind was a sea in a continual state of motion, that there were so many waves on it, their existence was so transient, and they interfered so much with each other, that one was unable to perceive them. The artist by making a fixed model of one of these transient waves enables you to isolate it out and to perceive it in yourself. In that sense art merely reveals, it never creates.

11. Metaphors soon run their course and die. But it is necessary to remember that when they were first used by the poets who created them they were used for the purpose of conveying over a vividly felt actual sensation. Nothing could be more dead now than the conventional expressions of love poetry, the arrow which pierces the heart and the rest of it, but originally they were used as conveying over the reality of the sensation experienced.

12. If I say the hill is *clothed* with trees your mind simply runs past the word "clothed," it is not pulled up in any way to visualise it. You have no

distinct image of the trees covering the hill as garments clothe the body. But if the trees had made a distinct impression on you when you saw them, if you were vividly interested in the effect they produced, you would probably not rest satisfied until you had got hold of some metaphor which did pull up the reader and make him visualise the thing. If there was only a narrow line of trees circling the hill near the top, you might say that it was *ruffed* with trees. I do not put this forward as a happy metaphor: I am only trying to get at the feeling which prompts this kind of expression. You have continually to be searching out new metaphors of this kind because the visual effect of a metaphor so soon dies. Even this word *clothed* which I used was probably, the first time it was employed, an attempt on the part of a poet to convey over the vivid impression which the scene gave him. Every word in the language originates as a *live* metaphor, but gradually of course all visual meaning goes out of them and they become a kind of counters. Prose is in fact the museum where the dead metaphors of the poets are preserved.

The thing that concerns me here is of course only the *feeling* which is conveyed over to you by the use of fresh metaphors. It is only where you get these fresh metaphors and epithets employed that you get this vivid conviction which constitutes the purely aesthetic emotion that can be got from imagery.

13. From time to time in a fit of absent-mindedness nature raises up minds which are more detached from life—a natural detachment, one innate in the structure of sense or consciousness, which at once reveals itself by a virginal manner of seeing, hearing or thinking.

It is only by accident, and in one sense only, that nature produces someone whose perception is not riveted to practical purposes; hence the diversity of the arts. One applies himself to form, not as it is practically useful in relation to him, but as it is in itself, as it reveals the inner life of things.

In our minds—behind the commonplace conventional expression which conceals emotion—artists attain the original mood and induce us to make the same effort ourselves by rhythmical arrangements of words, which, thus organised and animated with a life of their own, tell us, or rather suggest, things that speech is not calculated to express.

14. *"Art should endeavour to show the universal in the particular."* This is a phrase that constantly recurs. I remember great play was made with it in Mr Binyon's little book on Chinese art. You are supposed to show, shining through the accidental qualities of the individual, the characteristics of a universal type. Of course this is perfectly correct if you give the words the right meaning. It seems at first sight to be the exact contrary to the definition that we have arrived at ourselves, which was that art must be always individual and springs from dissatisfaction with the generalised expressions of ordinary perception and ordinary language. The confusion simply springs

from the two uses of the word "universal." To use Croce's example. Don Quixote is a type, but a type of what? He is only a type of all the Don Quixotes. To use again my comparison of the curve, he is an accurately drawn representation of one of the individual curves that vary round the stock type which would be represented by the words loss of reality or love of glory. He is only universal in the sense that once having had that particular curve pointed out to you, you recognise it again.

15. From time to time, by a happy accident, men are born who either in one of their senses, or in their conscious life as a whole, are less dominated by the *necessities of action. Nature* has forgotten to attach their faculty for perception to their faculty for action. They do not perceive simply for the purposes of action: they perceive just for the sake of perceiving. It is necessary to point out here that this is taken in a profounder sense than the words are generally used. When one says that the mind is practical and that the artist is the person who is able to turn aside from action and to observe things as they are in a disinterested way, one should be careful to say that this does not refer to any conscious or controllable action. The words as they stand have almost a moral flavour. One might be understood as implying that one ought not to be so bound up in the practical. Of course the word *practical* is not used in this sense. It refers to something physiological and entirely beyond our control. This orientation of the mind towards action is the theory which is supposed to account for the characteristics of mental life itself, and is not a mere description of an avoidable and superficial habit of the individual mind.

When, therefore, you do get an artist, *i.e.* a man who either in one of his senses or in his mind generally is emancipated from this orientation of the mind towards action and is able to see things as they are in themselves, you are dealing with a rarity—a kind of accident produced by Nature itself and impossible of manufacture.

The artist is the man, then, who on one side of his nature is born detached from the necessities of action. According as this detachment is inherent in one or other of the senses or is inherent in the consciousness, he is painter, musician, or sculptor. If this detachment were complete—if the mind saw freshly and directly in every one of its methods of perception—then you would get a kind of artist such as the world has not yet seen. He would perceive all things in their native purity: the forms, sounds and colours of the physical world as well as the subtlest movements of the inner life. But this, of course, could never take place. All that you get is a breaking through of the surface-covering provided for things by the necessities of action in *one direction* only, *i.e.* in one *sense* only. Hence the diversity of the arts.

In one man it is the eye which is emancipated. He is able to see individual arrangements of line and colour which escape our standardised perceptions.

And having perceived a hitherto unrecognised shape he is able gradually to insinuate it into our own perception. Others again retire within themselves. Beneath the conventional expression which hides the individual emotion they are able to see the original shape of it. They induce us to make the same effort ourselves and make us see what they see; by rhythmical arrangements of words they tell us, or rather suggest, things that speech is not calculated to express.

Others get at emotions which have nothing in common with language; certain rhythms of life at the centre of our minds. By setting free and emphasising this music they force it upon our attention: they compel us willy-nilly to fall in with it like passers-by who join in a dance.

In each art, then, the artist picks out of reality something which we, owing to a certain hardening of our perceptions, have been unable to see ourselves.

One might express the differences in the mechanism, by which they do this most easily, in terms of the metaphor by which we have previously expressed the difference between the two selves. Some arts proceed from the outside. They notice that the crystallised shapes on the top of the stream do not express the actual shapes on the waves. They endeavour to communicate the real shapes by adding detail. On the other hand, an art like music proceeds from *the inside* (as it were). By means of rhythm it breaks up the normal flow of our conscious life. It is as if by increasing the flow of the stream inside it broke through the surface crust and so made us realise the real nature of the outline of the inner elements of our conscious life. It does this by means of rhythm which acts something like the means used to bring about the state of hypnosis. The rhythm and measure suspend the normal flow of our sensations by causing our attention to swing to and fro between fixed points and so take hold of us with such force that even the faintest imitation of sadness produces a great effect on us. It increases our sensibility, in fact.

16. What is the nature of the properly "aesthetic" emotion as distinct from the other emotions produced by art?

As I have said, I do not think that Bergson has invented any new theory on this subject, but has simply created a much better vocabulary. That being so, I think that the best way to approach this theory is to state first the kind of rough conception which one had elaborated for oneself, and then to show how it is all straightened up in his analysis. By approaching the theory gradually in this way one can get it more solidly fixed down.

Among all the varied qualities of good verse, and in the complex kind of emotion which it can produce, there is one quality it must possess, which can be easily separated from the other qualities and which constitutes this distinctively aesthetic emotion for which we are searching.

This peculiarly *aesthetic* emotion here, as in other arts, is overlaid with all kinds of other emotions and is only perceived by people who really understand verse. To get at what it is quite definitely, I only consider it in as far as it bears on the choice of epithets and images. The same quality is exhibited in the other parts of verse, in the rhythm and metre, for example, but it so happens that it is most easily isolated in the case of epithets.

17. Could reality come into direct contact with sense and consciousness, art would be useless, or rather we should all be artists. All these things that the artist sees exist, yet we do not see them—yet why not?

Between nature and ourselves, even between ourselves and our own consciousness, there is a veil, a veil that is dense with the ordinary man, transparent for the artist and the poet. What made this veil?

Life is action, it represents the acceptance of the utilitarian side of things in order to respond to them by appropriate actions. I look, I listen, I hear, I think I am seeing, I think I am hearing everything, and when I examine myself I think I am examining my own mind.

But I am not.

What I see and hear is simply a selection made by my senses to serve as a light for my conduct. My senses and my consciousness give me no more than a practical simplification of reality. In the usual perception I have of reality all the differences useless to man have been suppressed. My perception runs in certain moulds. Things have been classified with a view to the use I can make of them. It is this classification I perceive rather than the real shape of things. I hardly see an object, but merely notice what class it belongs to—what ticket I ought to apply to it.

18. Everybody is familiar with the fact that the ordinary man does not see things as they are, but only sees certain *fixed types*. To begin with, we see separate things with distinct outlines where as a matter of fact we know that what exists is merely a continuous gradation of colour. Then even in outline itself we are unable to perceive the individual. We have in our minds certain fixed conceptions about the shape of a leg. Mr Walter Sickert is in the habit of telling his pupils that they are unable to draw any individual arm because they think of it as an arm; and because they think of it as an arm they think they know what it ought to be. If it were a piece of almond rock you could draw it, because you have no preconceived notions as to the way the almonds should come. As a rule, then, we never ever perceive the real shape and individuality of objects. We only see stock types. We tend to see not *the* table but only *a* table.

19. One can sum up the whole thing by a metaphor which must not, however, be taken too literally. Suppose that the various kinds of emotions and other things which one wants to represent are represented by various curved lines. There are in reality an infinite number of these curves all differing

slightly from each other. But language does not and could not take account of all these curves. What it does do is to provide you with a certain number of standard types by which you can roughly indicate the different classes into which the curves fall. It is something like the wooden curves which architects employ—circles, ellipses, and so forth—by suitable combinations of which they can draw approximately any curve they want, but only approximately. So with ordinary language. Like the architect's curves it only enables us to describe approximately. Now the artist, I take it, is the person who in the first place is able to see an individual curve. This vision he has of the individuality of the curve breeds in him a dissatisfaction with the conventional means of expression which allow all its individualities to escape.

20. The artist has a double difficulty to overcome. He has in the first place to be a person who is emancipated from the very strong habits of the mind which make us see not individual things but stock types. His second difficulty comes when he tries to express the individual thing which he has seen. He finds then that not only has his mind habits, but that language, or whatever medium of expression he employs, also has its fixed ways. It is only by a certain tension of mind that he is able to force the mechanism of expression out of the way in which it tends to go and into the way he wants. To vary slightly my metaphor of the curves. Suppose that in order to draw a certain individual curve which we perceive, you are given a piece of bent steel spring which has a natural curvature of its own. To make that fit the curve you want you will have to press it to that curve along the whole of its length with all your fingers. If you are unable to keep up this pressure and at one end slacken the pressure, then at that end you will not get the curve you were trying to draw, but the rounded-off curve of the spring itself.

You can observe this actual process at work in all the different arts. You may suppose that in music, for example, a man trying to express and develop a certain theme in the individual form in which it appeared to him might, if he relaxed his grip over the thing, find that it had a tendency to slacken off into resemblances to already heard things. This comparison also illustrates what happens in the decay of any art. Original sincerity, which is often almost grotesque in its individuality, slackens off in the rounded curves of "prettiness."

21. The psychology of the process is something of this kind. You start off with some actual and vividly felt experience. It may be something seen or something felt. You find that when you have expressed this in straightforward language that you have not expressed it at all. You have only expressed it approximately. All the individuality of the emotion as you experienced it has been left out. The straightforward use of words always lets the individuality of things escape. Language, being a communal apparatus,

only conveys over that part of the emotion which is common to all of us. If you are able to observe the actual individuality of the emotion you experience, you become dissatisfied with language. You persist in an endeavour to so state things that the meaning does not escape, but is definitely forced on the attention of the reader. To do this you are compelled to invent new metaphors and new epithets. It is here, of course, that the popular misunderstanding about originality comes in. It is usually understood by the outsider in the arts that originality is a desirable quality in itself. Nothing of the kind. It is only the defects of language that make originality necessary. It is because language will not carry over the exact thing you want to say, that you are compelled simply, in order to be accurate, to invent original ways of stating things.

22. The motive power behind any art is a certain freshness of experience which breeds dissatisfaction with the conventional ways of expression because they leave out the individual quality of this freshness. You are driven to new means of expression because you persist in an endeavour to get it out exactly as you felt it.

You could define art, then, as a passionate desire for accuracy, and the essentially aesthetic emotion as the excitement which is generated by direct communication. Ordinary language communicates nothing of the individuality and freshness of things. As far as that quality goes we live separated from each other. The excitement of art comes from this rare and unique communication.

23. Creation of imagery is needed to force language to convey over this *freshness* of impression. The particular kind of art we are concerned with here, at any rate, can be defined as an attempt to convey over something which ordinary language and ordinary expression lets slip through. The emotion conveyed by an art in this case, then, is the exhilaration produced by the direct and unusual communication of this fresh impression. To take an example: What is the source of the kind of pleasure which is given to us by the stanza from Keats' "Pot of Basil," which contains the line

And she forgot the blue above the trees?

I do not put forward the explanation I give here as being, as a matter of fact, the right one, for Keats might have had to put trees for the sake of the rhyme, but I suppose for the sake of illustration that he was free to put what he liked. Why then did he put "blue above the trees" and not "sky"? "Sky" is just as attractive an expression. Simply for this reason, that he instinctively felt that the word "sky" would not convey over the actual vividness and the actuality of the feeling he wanted to express. The choice of the right detail, the blue above the trees, forces that vividness on you and is the cause of the kind of thrill it gives you.

24. This particular argument is concerned only with a very small part of the effects which can be produced by poetry, but I have only used it as an illustration. I am not trying to explain poetry, but only to find out in a very narrow field of art, that of the use of imagery, what exactly the kind of emotion you call aesthetic consists of. The element in it which will be found in the rest of art is not the accidental fact that imagery conveys over an actually felt visual sensation, but the actual character of that communication, the fact that it hands you over the sensation as directly as possible, attempts to get it over bodily with all the qualities it possessed for you when you experienced it.

The feeling conveyed over to one is almost a kind of instinctive feeling. You get continuously from good imagery this conviction that the poet is constantly in presence of a vividly felt physical and visual scene.

25. You can perhaps trace this out a little more clearly in a wider art, that of prose description, the depicting of a character or emotion. You are not concerned here with handing over any visual scene, but in an attempt to get an emotion as near as possible as you feel it. You find that language has the same defects as the metaphors we have just been talking about. It lets what you want to say escape. Each of us has his own way of feeling, liking and disliking. But language denotes these states by the same word in every case, so that it is only able to fix the objective and impersonal aspect of the emotions which we feel. Language, as in the first case, lets what you want to say slip through. In any writing which you recognise as good there is always an attempt to avoid this defect of language. There is an attempt, by the adding of certain kinds of intimate detail, to lift the emotion out of the impersonal and colourless level, and to give to it a little of the individuality which it really possesses.

26. Certain kinds of prose, at any rate, never attempt to give you any visual presentment of an object. To do so would be quite foreign to its purpose. It is endeavouring always not to give you any image, but to hurry you along to a conclusion. As in algebra certain concrete things are embodied in signs or counters which are moved about according to rule without being visualised at all in the process, so certain type situations and arrangements of words move automatically into certain other arrangements without any necessity at all to translate the words back into concrete imagery. In fact, any necessity to visualise the words you are using would be an impediment, it would delay the process of reasoning. When the words are merely counters they can be moved about much more rapidly.

Now any tendency towards counter language of this kind has to be carefully avoided by poetry. It always endeavours, on the contrary, to arrest you and to make you continuously see a physical thing.

27. Language, we have said, only expresses the lowest common denomi-

nator of the emotions of one kind. It leaves out all the individuality of an emotion as it really exists and substitutes for it a kind of stock or type emotion. Now here comes the additional observation which I have to make. As we not only express ourselves in words, but for the most part think also in them, it comes about that not only do we not express more than the impersonal element of an emotion, but that we do not, as a matter of fact, perceive more. The average person as distinct from the artist does not even *perceive* the individuality of their own emotions. Our faculties of perception are, as it were, crystallised out into certain moulds. Most of us, then, never see things as they are, but see only the stock types which are embodied in language.

This enables one to give a first rough definition of the artist. It is not sufficient to say that an artist is a person who is able to convey over the actual things he sees or the emotions he feels. It is necessary before that that he should be a person who is able to emancipate himself from the moulds which language and ordinary perception force on him and be able to see things freshly as they really are.

Though one may have some difficulty at first sight in seeing that one only perceives one's own emotions in stock types, yet the thing is much more easy to observe in the actual perception of external things with which you are concerned in painting.

28. I exaggerate the place of imagery simply because I want to use it as an illustration.

In this case something is physically presented; the important thing is, of course, not the fact of the visual representation, but the communication over of the actual contact with reality.

It is because he realises the inadequacy of the usual that he is obliged to invent.

The gradual conclusion of the whole matter (and only as a conclusion) is that language puts things in a stereotyped form.

This is not the only kind of effect produced on one by verse but it is (if one extends the same quality to the other aspects of verse I have left out) the one essentially aesthetic emotion it produces on us. Readers of poetry may attach more importance to the other things, but this is the quality the poets recognise among each other. If one wants to fix it down then one can describe it as a "kind of instinctive feeling which is conveyed over to one, that the poet is describing something which is actually present to him, which he realises visually at first hand."

Is there anything corresponding to this in Painting?

29. The essential element in the pleasure given us by a work of art lies in the feeling given us by this rare accomplishment of *direct communication*. Mr Berenson in his book on the Florentine painters expresses in a different

vocabulary what is essentially the same feeling. The part of the book I am thinking of is that where he explains the superiority of Giotto to Duccio. He picks out the essential quality of a painting as its *life-communicating* quality, as rendered by form and movement. Form in the figure arts gives us pleasure because it has extracted and presented to us the structural significance of objects more completely than we (unless we be also great artists) could have grasped them by ourselves. By emphasis the artist gives us an intimate realisation of an object. In ordinary life I realise a given object, say with the given intensity *two*. An artist realises this with the intensity *four* and by his manner of emphasising it makes me realise it with the same intensity. This exhilarates me by communicating a sense of increased capacity. In that sense it may be said to be life-communicating. This emphasis can be conveyed in various ways: by form as in Giotto, and by movement expressed in line, as in Botticelli. This is exactly what Bergson is getting at. But instead of saying that an artist makes you realise with intensity *four* what you previously realised with intensity *two,* he would say that he makes you realise something which you actually did not perceive before. When you come to the detailed application of this to art you find that they are both different ways of saying the same thing. They both agree in picking out this life-communicating quality as the essentially aesthetic one. And they both give the same analysis of the feat accomplished by the artist. The advantage of Bergson's account of the matter is that the expressions he uses are part of a definite conception of reality and not mere metaphors invented specially for the purpose of describing art. More than that, he is able to explain why it is that the ordinary man does not perceive things at all *vividly* and can only be made to do so by the artist. Both these things are of very little advantage as far as actual art criticism is concerned, but they are distinct advantages to anyone who wants to place art definitely in relation to other human activities.

S. ALEXANDER

The Creative Process in

the Artist's Mind [1]

THE ARTIST'S WORK belongs to the order of creative as distinguished from that of passive imagination. The second we have not only in ordinary memory or expectation, but in one species of what is commonly called constructive imagination, in day-dreams or reveries or in dreams in general, that is, the comparatively idle play of fancy—comparatively idle, for there are no hard and fast lines of distinction in these matters of the mind's action; and dreams in particular are, some of them at least, as is well established, directed by a hidden purpose. The difference of such passive imagination from the creative sort is the absence from it of purpose. In passive imagination, images flare up in the mind, more or less like the perceptions we have had, or in new combinations which have had and will have no real existence. In the creative imagination of art, on the other hand, a new reality is created (not to linger on what has been already urged) which possesses, or may, if successful, possess beauty. And it is done by moulding the material of the art to express a purpose. Not the purpose of creating beauty, for that is the last thing the artist thinks of. As the scientific inquirer aims not at truth but at the solution of his problem, the artist aims to express the subject which occupies his mind in the means which he uses. His purpose may be dictated by passion but is still a passionate *purpose*. The artist works spontaneously: the poet sings, indeed, like the bird because he must, but with a directed passion, not as the bird-wooer sings without forethought and predestinately in the pursuit of his natural ends. "Purpose" conceals no mystery. Even where it is most conscious it means that action, provoked from without, is controlled from within the agent's mind. Such controlling factors are present in the work of art, not necessarily and perhaps rarely in conscious form, most often as a dominant passion, which guides the artist more surely than conscious ideas, but yet unifying his choice of words or colours or sounds into an expressive whole.

---

[1] From S. Alexander, *Beauty and Other Forms of Value*. Copyright, 1933, by Macmillan and Company, Ltd., and used with The Macmillan Company's permission, pp. 53–74. (Eds.)

In attempting to trace his procedure in detail, we must begin by noting certain distinctions which may be regarded as provisional. The work of art consists of materials which assume a certain form, two things which are separable only in thought and not in reality. Further, in the actual substance or contents of the work of art, we note its topic or subject or subject matter or meaning, a face for instance, or a party at cards, or a landscape in storm, which occupies the artist's mind and is the stimulus to or occasion of his production. The subject may and does change between the inception of the work and its completion; in the final shape which it assumes it is embodied in the work of art. In representational art it is distinct from the rest of the work; in non-representational art like music, there may be no other subject but what is contained in the formed material itself. We may thus conveniently distinguish the mere subject of a work of art from what it means and says to the artist, or the spectator, though in non-representational art the two things coincide.

The topic or subject interests or agitates the artist and throws him into an excitement in which we can discriminate two sorts of elements, the passions appropriate to the subject and the passion proper to the artist. At the risk of some confusion in the double use of the word material, I shall call these respectively the material passions and the formal passion. The formal passion has been already identified. It is fed and controlled by the passions aroused by the subject, but is, though dependent on them, superadded to them, as their fine flowering into something they do not themselves contain. The difference is most obvious from illustrations. It is a long way from saying passionately "I love you and always shall" to saying

> As fair art thou, my bonnie lass,
>   So deep in love am I;
> And I will love thee still, my dear,
>   Till a' the seas gang dry,

where the words of the poem are not a mere half-practical gesture appropriate to the material passion, but are handled for their own sakes, and with that strangeness which enters into the proportion of beauty.

A second example is even more familiar:

> And Ruth said, Intreat me not to leave thee, or to return from following after thee: for whither thou goest, I will go; and where thou lodgest, I will lodge: thy people shall be my people, and thy God my God: where thou diest, will I die, and there will I be buried: the Lord do so to me, and more also, if aught but death part thee and me.

where the material passion of the devotion of the alien daughter to her husband's mother and the images and thoughts suggested by this emotion can be distinguished from the white heat of artistic excitement which, fed by these ideas and feelings, issues or, if the metaphor be pardoned, overflows into a perfection of words which reveals the situations appropriate to her devotion as perhaps she could not herself describe them.[2]

In conduct Aristotle has put the same point once for all when, in describing bravery, he contrasts that virtue with the impulse to show pluck and face danger, and says that in true courage there is the impulse towards the beautiful ($\tau\grave{o}$ $\kappa\alpha\lambda\acute{o}\nu$). It is this, I suppose, which is what the Herbartians meant when they spoke of the aesthetic and other feelings of value as formal. It is as necessary to recognise their special existence and status and the special impulses to which they belong as it is not to forget that, except in taking up and assimilating the impulses which feed them, they cannot operate. You cannot be generous without having something to give, were it only the widow's mite, and were the act only a thought or wish; nor pursue science without data; nor hardly indite a ballad to a mistress' eyebrow without some basic tenderness. I say hardly, for the material passions which gather round the subject and are felt by the artist himself may be replaced by thoughts or images he has of them, but need not feel himself except in sympathy. Not all poems are lyrical, and we cannot therefore accept the ruling of Mr. Croce that art is essentially lyrical; it is lyrical of the artistic impulse, but not necessarily except in lyrics and perhaps not always there lyrical of felt passions.[3] Some have even supposed that Shakespeare's sonnets were some of them exercises in gallantry after the Italian fashion of the time. Improbable as this may seem from the internal evidence of the sonnets themselves, the point is well taken, and as before explained there are whole regions of poetry where the poet cannot be supposed to experience in his own person the passions he describes, but only to know them by that divination which artists possess above other men.[4]

We have, then, to determine the part played in the artist's creation by images, and it is all the more needful to do so because of an opinion commonly entertained that the artist translates into material forms the images he has already in his mind.[5] Thus Mr. Lascelles Abercrombie (himself a poet and therefore particularly valuable to hear) writes [6]: "The moment of imaginative experience which possesses our minds the instant the poem is finished possessed the poet's mind the instant the poem began. For as soon

---

[2] From "Artistic Creation and Cosmic Creation," *Proceedings of the British Academy,* vol. xiii, 1927.
[3] See the selection from Croce, p. 69. (Eds.)
[4] Browning's comment on Wordsworth's sonnet on the sonnet is well known:
> *With this same key*
> *Shakespeare unlocked his heart.* Once more!
> Did Shakespeare? If so, the less Shakespeare he!
("House," *Collected Poems,* vol. ii, p. 479).
[5] From *Art and the Material,* Adamson Lecture. Manchester, 1925.
[6] *Theory of Poetry* (London, 1924), p. 58.

as there flashed into complete existence in his mind this many-coloured experience with all its complex passion, the poem which we know was *conceived* as an inspiration. . . . So that it is also possible to consider the inspiration of a poem as distinguishable from the verbal art of it: namely as that which the verbal art exists to convey, and which can be distinctly known as such, however impossible it may be to describe it or express it at all in any other words than those of the poet." Even Mr. Croce, who identifies the image or intuition of the artist (or anyone else) with expression, and laughs at those who fancy they could themselves be Raphaels or Shakespeares if they had but the skill to express their beautiful imaginations, still urges that the artistic experience, though it is essentially expression, is purely mental, and that the actual physical embodiment of the experience is a technical matter and merely serves the purpose of communication. I do not desire to press the words of these writers, and in what I shall say I shall sometimes say what they would take for granted. But I believe there is at least much obscurity in their doctrines and even in the end error.

It is vital to distinguish again among the images which have reference to the work of art images excited by the subject matter from images of the artistic product itself. Now as to the first set, there can be no doubt that such images precede in the artist's mind his work. The subject matter calls up such images in proportion to the artist's wealth of experience. They are images about the subject matter and along with them there may be unconscious thoughts or feelings which, like the express images, control and feed the constructive impulse. Here we note the relevance of what is said by psycho-analysis. Dante's love for Beatrice Portinari was part of the motives which supplied his art, and doubtless too the unrest hidden in an artist's unsatisfied life may be a reason unknown to himself for seeking satisfaction in a world of seeming.[7] Under this head of preliminary mental work about the subject belongs the stage through which the artist passes, which has been described so well by Graham Wallas as incubation, *à propos* not of art but of thought.[8] But all these images or thoughts or vague unconscious stirrings are but servants of the creative impulse, and they issue into outward expression in the material only *via* that impulse. There is no direct

---

[7] The reason why I apparently neglect the work of the psycho-analysts on art is not merely that it lies so much outside my capacity and knowledge, but a different one. In his *Introductory Lectures on Psycho-analysis* (Eng. transl., London, 1922) Mr. Freud speaks of the artist as seeking in art and phantasy a refuge from the unsatisfied longings of real life which he has not the power to gratify; and saving himself by true art from possible neurosis. I recognise the interest and importance of this, but it still leaves open the question why art is chosen for this purpose and what its nature is, and it is this I am concerned with.

[8] *The Art of Thought*, ch. iv, London, 1926.

road for them to voice or hand. Neither are they images of what the artist means to say or paint; they are not images of the artistic product; nor is it they which are translated into the material.

On the other hand, images of the product itself if they existed might be said to be translated into the material. But to speak generally (the qualifications must come later) there are no images of the product at all. The poem is not the translation of the poet's state of mind, for he does not know till he has said it either what he wants to say or how he shall say it. The imaginative experience supposed to be in his mind does not exist there. What does exist is the subject which detains him and fixes his thoughts and images and passions and gives his excitement a colour and direction which would be different with a different subject matter. Excitement caused and detained by this subject, and at once enlarged, enlightened and inflamed by insights into it, bubbles over into words or the movements of the brush or chisel. When the artist has achieved his product he knows from seeing it or hearing it what the purpose of his artistic effort was. He makes the discovery of what were the real directive forces of his action. All that he was aware of before, so far as he was aware of them, was the thoughts and emotions of the subject matter directly produced or indirectly suggested, and doubtless often presented in imaginative form. These combine with, or in part are identical with, the more or less unconscious movings and emotions yielded by his "vision and faculty divine" and with the gathered expertness of his technical flair, to guide his hand or his voice or speech into the movements which end in the material work of art.

Two conclusions follow from this statement, which have been anticipated. The external work being an organic part of the creative process, it ceases to be possible to hold that the external material is needed merely in order to communicate the artistic experience to others. That experience would not exist except for material embodiment, which may of course be replaced by finished imagination of it, about which more presently. Next,[9] it follows that Wordsworth was, I must believe, mistaken when he said that there are many poets in the world, who have "the vision and the faculty divine; yet wanting the accomplishment of verse"; as if verse were a charm superadded to the real poetic gift. His own words about the poet give a truer view: "he murmurs by the running brooks a music sweeter than their own." Poets and all artists, it will be admitted, are more sensitive to things and persons than ordinary men. Such greater sensitiveness does not, however, make them poets. You have only to compare the magnificent lines describing the mystical absorption of the youth in the spectacle of nature, in the

---

[9] The following pages of the chapter are taken in large part from *Brit. Journal of Psychology,* vol. iv., 1927, "The Creative Process in the Artist's Mind."

same poem,[10] with Spinoza's scientific account of the "intellectual love of God" in order to recognise that two great men may have like emotions and the one be a poet and the other a philosopher, and the expression of each be perfect in its kind, but that of the one a poet's work, and that of the other a philosopher and scientific man's. In the second case the words only catch fire from the subject matter; in the other the words are themselves on fire.

What the exact character of the excitement is which is the proper impulse to creation, it may be difficult to say. It may be something of a shock to realise how lowly in character it may be. To judge from the glow that accompanies productive work of inferior kinds, such as everyone has experience of who tries to write a brief essay, or even a letter, and make the result as artistic as is open to him, the excitement is mainly a feeling of unrest which keeps one in suspense, but a directed suspense like that we are aware of when we try to remember a name which we have forgotten but know that it is connected with this, that and the other circumstance, and we feel ourselves straining towards it but unattaining. Over and above this, the impulse is felt mainly in bodily repercussions, in the visceral organs and the organs of secretion, about the heart and down the back and all over the body. It is a directed restlessness for it varies according to the topic, but what it is the indication of, what hidden movings urge us forward into the customary outlet of words or other forms of artistic material, is not disclosed until we have in semi-blindness achieved the desired product.

The truth of the above description [11] of what goes on in the mind in artistic production may be tested in various ways, two of which are only approximations to a real test. We may take our own selves, all of us artists in our degree, and observe ourselves in modest efforts to produce something artistic or beautiful, say an ordinary essay of a student who tries to make a finished composition. He does not, if I may trust my own experience, try to think out his work in an artistic form, but steeps himself in the subject, "moons" over

---

10
　　　　　　　　　　Sound needed none,
Nor any voice of joy; his spirit drank
The spectacle; sensation, soul, and form,
All melted into him; they swallowed up
His animal being; in them did he live;
And by them did he live; they were his life.
In such access of mind, in such high hour,
Of visitation from the living God,
Thought was not; in enjoyment it expired.
No thanks he breathed, he proffered no request;
Rapt into still communion that transcends
The imperfect offices of prayer and praise,
His mind was a thanksgiving to the power
That made him; it was blessedness and love.

11 From *Art and the Material* to p. 63.

it, as we say, and when his interest is sufficiently strong lets himself go, and the words come of themselves. Anyone who happens to be blessed or cursed with the gift of humour, and practises it to some degree as a fine art, may test his own procedure. A person or topic releases within him a hidden spring of gaiety, flavoured perhaps with a slight sub-malicious ingredient, and the spring issues forth into jest. It is his gaiety which produces the words, and no image of what he means to say. Hence it is that the jester so rarely laughs at his own jest. His laughter has preceded the jest and has been done with; for him it is part of the cause of the jest, and not, as for the hearers, the effect.

Or he may take a finished piece of art, and, observing himself, think himself back into the artist's situation. Any work of art will serve as a test. For instance, the scene in Meredith's *Vittoria,* where the prima donna sings the song of Italian freedom in the opera-house of La Scala at Milan. In the agitation which such a passage throws us into (so violent that some readers can hardly proceed beyond this point in the book) it is perfectly possible to distinguish (however much they are interwoven) the passionate sympathy with the actors in the situation from the proper aesthetic excitement, felt in the fitness of the words both of the narrative and the song to express the situation. It is not necessary to suppose that Meredith or Shakespeare actually felt the emotions of his characters, but only that he understood them. Doubtless such emotional sympathy may be, and probably often is, present as well, but, if it is, it is present to add fuel to the excitement of the proper creative tendency, the tendency, I mean, to expression not in the ways of anger or remorse or love, but in the ways of speech or movements of the hand directing brush or chisel. Herein is the answer to the old controversy raised by Diderot (upon which Molière before him had expressed an opinion in the same sense as Diderot [12]) whether the actor should feel himself or not into the emotions of his personages. With different actors the conditions of success will vary. Some may be content with the semi-intellectual excitement of understanding their parts, another may be able more readily to imitate his part by feeling its emotions, or at least may have his imitative procedure heightened by the simulation of the passions themselves.

But the only satisfactory test is the judgment of artists themselves, helped out by observation of their behaviour in creation, and since it is the business of artists to create and not to psychologise, there may be difficulty in extracting their answer to questions which seem to them strange and perhaps unimportant or, in the old sense of that word, impertinent. An inductive inquiry of this sort I have failed to perform by direct inquiry from living artists. Artists have, however, left incidental reports of themselves, like the familiar

---

[12] *Impromptu de Versailles,* Sc. I: "You show what an excellent comedian you are by expressing so well a character contrary to your own humour."

ones of Mozart, and Goethe's comparison of his own condition in writing some of his poems to somnambulism, which favour the doctrine stated here. Other records of artists' experiences have been collected by M. Dessoir in his book.[13]

I have, however, to confess my own failure of energy in the research. Two young writers of imaginative literature whom I consulted told me that in their best work they do not know beforehand what they mean to say; one of them admits that sometimes the work is thought out consciously beforehand with much labour and never with so satisfactory a result.

An opportunity which I have had of observing an artist, and a great one, at work appeared to me to bear out my sketch of the creative process. The artist, a sculptor, was unacquainted with his sitter, and could hardly have formed any preconceived idea of the kind of character he was trying to produce in the clay. He in fact denied that he had, but declared that his sole object was to study the form of his sitter's head in every detail. To judge from his behaviour, which I was privileged to witness, he was utterly absorbed with the head he was modelling, and his excitement about it was manifest at every stage—first, when he was sketching the head each successive bit of clay was dabbed on to the growing shape, as if he were indulging in a violent pugilistic encounter with it, a gymnastic display which testified to his intentness on the exact delivery of each increment; and later when, the general form being modelled, the smaller knife was used to perfect the detailed structure, here removing clay or indenting lines, here adding tiny portions of liquid clay with as much delicacy as the painter uses with his brush, the sculptor's face marked the strenuous effort to transfer his subject into the clay. And yet this meticulous study of the sitter resulted in no literal copy of him but was full of the artist's vividness and rather a reading of the original than a transliteration of it. Plainly it was not only the aspect of the head which worked in the artist's mind; these forms were moulded by him, as if they passed through an alembic. His eyes saw differently from another man's and his hand was obedient to his eye. Therein lies, as I suppose, the personality of the artist, that he selects or adds or accentuates so as to bring out what is significant in the form. A direct answer to my question I could not elicit. But this particular artist seemed to think that both procedures might occur with him, both the semi-unconscious one I have suggested to be typical and the conscious forethought of some particular result, so far as he was guided by knowledge of the history of his art. My general impression was that I was witnessing absorbed observation of the sitter and that that observation, after filtration through what for want of a better word has to be called the artist's genius (for what this loose word means is mainly the un-

---

[13] M. Dessoir, *Aesthetik u. allg. Kunstw.*, Stuttgart, 1906, Pt. II. ch. i.

clear and undefined prompting of personality), ended in a creation which was far more significant than an ordinary observer like myself would have judged the original to be.

It is time to qualify the over simple account I have given of the artist's process of creation, which I have only suggested as an account of what happens in general and is the fundamental character of the artistic process. Even so far as I have gone in my inquisition it is clear that both processes are employed, execution by the relatively blind impulsion of the creative gadfly, and transcribing from pictures in the imagination. I set aside first, to repeat myself, those cases in which an artist of exceptional experience or skill produces his work in his head. Leonardo may have seen the picture of the Last Supper in all its details before he put the pigments on the wall; Wordsworth composed his poems on his walks, giving the simple peasants the impression of a mooning creature; the deaf Beethoven must have made the Choral Symphony in his imagination, and perhaps most musicians trust from the nature of the case to their imaginations. One eminent painter referred to in my correspondence formed so exact a picture in her mind of a portrait that when she came to put it on the canvas and desired to alter it, she found she could not. Is it not evident that the imagination in such cases is the work of art itself, and embodies the materials of the external work (I will not say the physical work) and possibly even the necessary movements of the hand? There is no more difference between it and the external work than there is between a sum done in the head or on paper. The question still arises, How is this image reached? You would not say from a precedent image of itself. And if not, then how? The case is irrelevant psychologically, for in such an image the work is already achieved.

I set aside such cases. Moreover, even when the artist does not do the whole work in his head, he may do parts of it in this way, and tends to do so the more in proportion to his experience and his acquaintance with the history of his art. But there is another way in which he may use images, not of the finished product, but of the subject matter, realised in such detail that it may seem he is merely transcribing his picture into words or colours in the same sense as a man of science describes a natural phenomenon or an animal form. Perhaps it is such cases which are in the minds of those who say that the external embodiment in the material form is merely a matter of technique. In other words the artist merely describes in his customary medium a fully realised picture of his subject matter. The supposed case is not so likely to occur in painting or sculpture, for there the more vividly the artist pictures his subject, say his landscape, or the person he is modelling or sculpturing in stone, the more his image approximates to a picture of the finished product, and the situation is the one already mentioned. In poetry, however, the poet often seems to be merely describing, as it were scientifically, a picture in his mind. It may be doubted whether even in purely descriptive poetry he really does so, unless exceptionally. In general the picture and the words mould each other: the picture may be transcribed in words, but the words as they flow alter the picture. One of my correspondents urges that when Wordsworth wrote of the daisy

> The beauty of its star-shaped shadow thrown
> On the smooth surface of this naked stone,

the picture preceded the words. *A* picture doubtless, but was even that not altered in the transcription? "Smooth" and "star-shaped" seem to exceed the mere picture. When Tennyson writes

> The lizard with his shadow on the stone
> Rests like a shadow,

the phrase "rests like a shadow" betrays the effort to turn the mere picture in the subject matter into words. If I am right, even these pictures fall back into the rank of subject matter in which the artist is absorbed but whose real character is only fully revealed when the words are spoken (or imagined). The lines which immediately follow the words quoted from Tennyson are:

> The purple flowers droop, the golden bee
> Is lily-cradled.

The poet is working from a picture; but is it likely that the "cradling" of the bee in the lily was part of the picture or suggested by a fresh one? It was wrung from him by his delight in his picture, and completes the feeling from which he worked.

Moreover, as the details are transcribed (and let it be granted they are literally transcribed) they affect and are affected by the rest of the composition, and either themselves must undergo change, or they alter the total. The sculptor I observed when he introduced a touch with his knife into the clay model's nose or eyes, found he had affected the unity of his model and so he was always working over the whole head at once.

The artist proceeds by stages, filling up his general impression into fulness. Partly, as I have said, he works from new images in the manner conceded. Partly he works by what a correspondent calls *tâtonnement* [groping], perpetually correcting the product. It may be asked, Does not his correction show that the work achieved falls short of his ideal, of some image in his mind of the perfect work? The answer I suggest is that it falls short of his ideal but not of the alleged image. If he had that image in his mind, his failure could only be a matter of technical unskill. He goes on correcting because his work does not satisfy the impulse which drives him into his work, with all those complicated sources from which that impulse is drawn which I have so inadequately sketched.

But it is precisely because the artist's working is so various that I desire to have more data. The variations of procedure attested at first hand are certain to be of more importance than rough and possibly incorrect or at least unguarded dogmas laid down by a person who is not himself an artist. Such material would be the only satisfactory basis of a thorough psychology of the matter.

There remains a further problem which arises from the existence of that "eidetic" imagery which has been so interesting and important a discovery of recent years. Children up to about fifteen in large numbers, and adults in much smaller numbers, appear to possess images of what they see which in some respects resemble the images of memory but in others resemble after-images. The image has the substantiality of a percept, the person sees the object or scene very much as if it were really before him; it has a hallucinatory character. Now it is natural to think that artists may be individuals who retain this gift which other persons lose after youth. "Many men," says Rossetti,

> Many men are poets in their youth,
> But for one sweet-strung soul the years prolong
> Even though all change the indomitable song.

And Mr. Kroh,[14] who gave the first systematic account (not the first account) of these facts, has made a study of certain German poets past and present, one of them being Goethe, and concluded on internal evidence that they were eidetics. It by no means follows that all artists are so; a passage is quoted describing Goethe's impatience with Schiller because when Goethe described the *Urpflanze* [15] from a vivid picture which he had in his mind, Schiller, who perfectly understood him, called Goethe's topic merely a notion. Let us assume, however, for the moment that all poets and other artists have such pictures in their minds. It might well be asked, Does the artist, does the poet for instance, do anything more than read off his image as a scientific man would read it off? I believe I have really answered the question in advance. The real problem would in the first place be to explain why the artist comes to possess such highly finished pictures; in other words the artistic creation lies behind the eidetic image used. In the next place, I incline to think that though eidetic artists have these vivid pictures which simulate reality, these pictures are but an additional gift they possess in conceiving the subject matter. The well-known case of Reynolds's friend who painted from a single sitting of his subjects is typical. The eidetic image took the place of the reality. There is even one case quoted of an engraver

---

[14] O. Kroh, *Subjektive Anschauungsbilder bei Jugendlichen*. Göttingen, 1922.
[15] Prototype of plants. Reference is made here to Goethe's botanical studies, *The Metamorphoses of Plants*. (Eds.)

who projected his image on to the plate and merely traced the outline with his tool. Whether the result was good or bad we are not told. But the case is surely exceptional. In general, when the artist paints from his image or describes it in words, he is moulding it, in the product itself, into something of which the image supplies him with the subject but whose complete idea is revealed in the product itself.

For completeness' sake, I will return for a moment to the organic character of the material work of art, confining myself to poetry. If the doctrine be correct, the mere sound of the words is vital to the art. Yet words have meaning and it is never possible to dissociate the meanings of words from the words themselves. Two conclusions follow which I may expound briefly by illustrations. In the first place, no subject however trivial or mean is beyond the reach of art. Success depends upon the handling, though no doubt the higher the subject the greater the work if the words are commensurate. To illustrate triviality of subject in a perfect poem I will cite a stanza from a well-known seventeenth-century poem, hardly daring to quote it because under our modern conditions it requires an effort to realise the picture:

> Her feet beneath her petticoat
> Like little mice stole in and out,
>   As if they feared the light.
> And oh! she dances such a way,
> No sun upon an Easter day
>   Is half so fine a sight.

Miss Austen's novels are compact of delicate trivialities, and how great is their art!

Secondly, there is a regular adjustment of sounds to meaning, and verse is far from being a superadded charm, but is an integral, possibly the chief constituent. The burden of Mr. Saintsbury's work on prosody is this theme. Metre and rhyme are not mere adjuncts of poetry. The periodic recurrence of sounds or groups of them is part of that process by which the unitary purpose of a work of art is effected in its material. We may take it that, as Mr. Middleton Murry says,[16] poetry differs from prose by its greater, at least its intenser, passion; that passion finding vent in words is ordered and controlled by rhythm and metre and rhyme. But I am more concerned with the blending of the delight of sounds, isolated or in their periods or in their cadence, with the thought or subject matter. Indeed it is mainly through poetry that we realise the charm of words. I come myself from no mean city but, its name suggesting smoke and damp, few persons perhaps think of the word as charming. They have only to repeat the words of the Jacobite song, "Farewell, Manchester, noble town farewell," to realise how beautiful a

---

[16] In his book *The Problem of Style.* London, 1922.

word it is. In good poetry there always is this consonance of thought and song. Where either element is found alone we have defect—the tinkle of words or the aridity of bare ideas. Illustration would be endless, but it would be taken, not from the deliberatively imitative passages,[17] where sound of word recalls sound of nature, but from great music like that of Prospero's speech in *The Tempest* or the cadence of Cleopatra's "Give me my robe," etc.; [18] from the rolling catalogues of names in Milton, or the organ music which accompanies Adam's prayer, or the fragrance and softness of the words themselves describing Eden in Book V. I will cite two examples; the first, to reprove Wordsworth's doctrine by his own practice, shall be the famous skating passage in the *Prelude:*

> So through the darkness and the cold we flew,
> And not a voice was idle; with the din
> Smitten the precipices rang aloud;
> The leafless trees and every icy crag
> Tinkled like iron; while far distant hills
> Into the tumult sent an alien sound
> Of melancholy not unnoticed, while the stars
> Eastward were sparkling clear, and in the west
> The orange sky of evening died away.

The second, where the purpose in the blending is more deliberate, is from the stanza describing the concert in the garden of Acrasia in the second book of the *Faery Queene* where the unison of sounds is expressed by the linkage of the lines:

> The joyous birdes, shrouded in chearefull shade,
> Their notes unto the voyce attempred sweet;
> Th' angelicall soft trembling voyces made
> To th' instruments divine respondence meet;
> The silver sounding instruments did meet
> With the base murmure of the waters fall;
> The waters fall with difference discreet,
> Now soft, now loud, unto the wind did call;
> The gentle warbling wind low answered to all.

I may summarise the preceding pages briefly thus: (1) The impulse to creation is based upon the material passions provoked by the subjects, but is distinguishable from them and is formal. (2) The process of creation arises from the excitement caused by the subject matter, and images play

---

[17]   *E.g.:* When Ajax strives some rock's vast weight to throw,
             The line too labours and the words move slow.

    or   The moan of doves in immemorial elms
             And murmur of innumerable bees.

[18] The remark comes from Mr. Murry.

a large part in the awareness of that subject. These are not images of the work of art, which are in general only got through actual production. (3) Images of parts of the work of art may precede the actual production, but that this is a subordinate feature of the creative process. When there is complete anticipation in idea or image, the work of art has been already produced. (4) Eidetic imagery which is probably frequent in artists belongs to the images of the subject matter not of the product. (5) The material of the art is a vital part of artistic process. In poetry for instance the sound of the words, their rhythm, metre, etc., are integral to the work, and perhaps the element of prior value.

Creativeness having been described, we can now advance to a "philosophical" feature of it [19] which is implied in what precedes. All cognition is discovery in which its object is revealed to the mind. The work of art being the expression or embodiment in material and contemplated for its own sake and not merely as a sign, however much it owes its form to the artist, reveals to him his own meaning, and the artistic experience is not so much invention as discovery. In sculpture, where the block already exists, it is easier to recognise the truth of this. In Michael Angelo's unfinished statues of slaves in the Academy at Florence we can feel the artist not so much making the figure as chipping off flakes of the marble from the figure which is concealed in it, and which he is laying bare (*vivos* ducunt *de marmore voltus*). Has he not said himself that there is no thought which the sculptor expresses in marble that does not exist there already? R. L. Nettleship [20] applies to the sculptor the words of Browning:

> The thousand sights and sounds that broke
> In on him at the chisel's stroke;

and the words describe how the sculptor's discovery, elicited by his own creative art, surprises him with the definition of his own mood of mind; in the same way as with no foreknowledge of the truth but with the passion to find it and to use the methods calculated to attain it, the scientific thinker is surprised by the discovery in nature of the law or fact which he is seeking. What is true of sculpture is true also of poetry. Shakespeare discovered *Hamlet* in the English language as the sculptor discovers his figure in the block. Full as that language is of the knowledge of nature and man for which it stands, of history and thought and emotion, Shakespeare, with his artistic excitement over the subject of Hamlet's story and with his profound insight into Hamlet's imagined nature, could discover there in the language of English folk the selection and combination of words which were

---

[19] From *Art and the Material*.
[20] In his essay on Plato's Education in *Hellenica*.

fitted to be the expression of his excitement, and in their turn surprised him as they surprise us with the imaginations they embody. Great artists know or believe that they are inspired from something outside themselves. Why should we suppose them to be deceived? It is true that to make the discovery the gifts of Shakespeare were needed; that is why great artists are rare. But equally the gifts and skill of Newton were needed to discover the law of gravitation in its first form, and other gifts and skill have been needed to discover that law in its later and preciser form. You cannot discover Hamlet unless you have Shakespeare's mind. But equally unless you have eyes you cannot discover the green trees. "Ripeness is all." Except for the features which make the artist's act creative, there is no difference in kind between the discovery of the tree by perception and the discovery of the Slave in the block or of Hamlet in the English language. The artist's creativeness conceals from us his real passivity. Every artist is in his degree like Shakespeare, who was a reed through which every wind from nature or human affairs blew music.

SIGMUND FREUD

The Relation of the Poet to

Day-Dreaming [1]

WE LAYMEN HAVE always wondered greatly—like the cardinal who put the question to Ariosto—how that strange being, the poet, comes by his material. What makes him able to carry us with him in such a way and to arouse emotions in us of which we thought ourselves perhaps not even capable? Our interest in the problem is only stimulated by the circumstance that if we ask poets themselves they give us no explanation of the matter, or at least no satisfactory explanation. The knowledge that not even the clearest insight into the factors conditioning the choice of imaginative material, or into the nature of the ability to fashion that material, will ever make writers of us does not in any way detract from our interest.

---

[1] First published in *Neue Revue*, I., 1908; reprinted in *Sammlung*, Zweite Folge. [Translated by I. F. Grant Duff.]

From Sigmund Freud, *Collected Papers* (London: Hogarth Press, Ltd., 1925), IV, 173–183. Reprinted by permission. (Eds.)

If we could only find some activity in ourselves, or in people like ourselves, which was in any way akin to the writing of imaginative works! If
we could do so, then examination of it would give us a hope of obtaining
some insight into the creative powers of imaginative writers. And indeed,
there is some prospect of achieving this—writers themselves always try to
lessen the distance between their kind and ordinary human beings; they so
often assure us that every man is at heart a poet, and that the last poet will
not die until the last human being does.

We ought surely to look in the child for the first traces of imaginative
activity. The child's best loved and most absorbing occupation is play. Perhaps we may say that every child at play behaves like an imaginative writer,
in that he creates a world of his own or, more truly, he rearranges the things
of his world and orders it in a new way that pleases him better. It would be
incorrect to think that he does not take this world seriously; on the contrary,
he takes his play very seriously and expends a great deal of emotion on it.
The opposite of play is not serious occupation but—reality. Notwithstanding the large affective cathexis [2] of his play-world, the child distinguishes it
perfectly from reality; only he likes to borrow the objects and circumstances
that he imagines from the tangible and visible things of the real world. It is
only this linking of it to reality that still distinguishes a child's "play" from
"day-dreaming."

Now the writer does the same as the child at play; he creates a world of
phantasy which he takes very seriously; that is, he invests it with a great deal
of affect, while separating it sharply from reality. Language has preserved
this relationship between children's play and poetic creation. It designates
certain kinds of imaginative creation, concerned with tangible objects and
capable of representation, as "plays"; the people who present them are
called "players." The unreality of this poetical world of imagination, however, has very important consequences for literary technique; for many
things which if they happened in real life could produce no pleasure can
nevertheless give enjoyment in a play—many emotions which are essentially painful may become a source of enjoyment to the spectators and
hearers of a poet's work.

There is another consideration relating to the contrast between reality and
play on which we will dwell for a moment. Long after a child has grown up
and stopped playing, after he has for decades attempted to grasp the realities
of life with all seriousness, he may one day come to a state of mind in
which the contrast between play and reality is again abrogated. The adult
can remember with what intense seriousness he carried on his childish play;
then by comparing his would-be serious occupations with his childhood's

---

[2] "Cathexis": the attachment of energy (sexual) to any object or idea. (Eds.)

play, he manages to throw off the heavy burden of life and obtain the great pleasure of humour.

As they grow up, people cease to play, and appear to give up the pleasure they derived from play. But anyone who knows anything of the mental life of human beings is aware that hardly anything is more difficult to them than to give up a pleasure they have once tasted. Really we never can relinquish anything; we only exchange one thing for something else. When we appear to give something up, all we really do is to adopt a substitute. So when the human being grows up and ceases to play he only gives up the connection with real objects; instead of playing he then begins to create phantasy. He builds castles in the air and creates what are called day-dreams. I believe that the greater number of human beings create phantasies at times as long as they live. This is a fact which has been overlooked for a long time, and its importance has therefore not been properly appreciated.

The phantasies of human beings are less easy to observe than the play of children. Children do, it is true, play alone, or form with other children a closed world in their minds for the purposes of play; but a child does not conceal his play from adults, even though his playing is quite unconcerned with them. The adult, on the other hand, is ashamed of his day-dreams and conceals them from other people; he cherishes them as his most intimate possessions and as a rule he would rather confess all his misdeeds than tell his day-dreams. For this reason he may believe that he is the only person who makes up such phantasies, without having any idea that everybody else tells themselves stories of the same kind. Day-dreaming is a continuation of play, nevertheless, and the motives which lie behind these two activities contain a very good reason for this different behaviour in the child at play and in the day-dreaming adult.

The play of children is determined by their wishes—really by the child's *one* wish, which is to be grown-up, the wish that helps to "bring him up." He always plays at being grown-up; in play he imitates what is known to him of the lives of adults. Now he has no reason to conceal this wish. With the adult it is otherwise; on the one hand, he knows that he is expected not to play any longer or to day-dream, but to be making his way in a real world. On the other hand, some of the wishes from which his phantasies spring are such as have to be entirely hidden; therefore he is ashamed of his phantasies as being childish and as something prohibited.

If they are concealed with so much secretiveness, you will ask, how do we know so much about the human propensity to create phantasies? Now there is a certain class of human beings upon whom not a god, indeed, but a stern goddess—Necessity—has laid the task of giving an account of what they suffer and what they enjoy. These people are the neurotics; among other things they have to confess their phantasies to the physician to whom they go in the hope of recovering through mental treatment. This is our best source of knowledge, and we have later found good reason to suppose that our patients tell us about themselves nothing that we could not also hear from healthy people.

Let us try to learn some of the characteristics of day-dreaming. We can begin by saying that happy people never make phantasies, only unsatisfied ones. Unsatisfied wishes are the driving power behind phantasies; every separate phantasy contains the fulfilment of a wish, and improves on unsatisfactory reality. The impelling wishes vary according to the sex, character and circumstances of the creator; they may be easily divided, however, into two principal groups. Either they are ambitious wishes, serving to exalt the person creating them, or they are erotic. In young women erotic wishes dominate the phantasies almost exclusively, for their ambition is generally comprised in their erotic longings; in young men egoistic and ambitious wishes assert themselves plainly enough alongside their erotic desires. But we will not lay stress on the distinction between these two trends; we prefer to emphasize the fact that they are often united. In many altar-pieces the portrait of the donor is to be found in one corner of the picture; and in the greater number of ambitious day-dreams, too, we can discover a woman in some corner, for whom the dreamer performs all his heroic deeds and at whose feet all his triumphs are to be laid. Here you see we have strong enough motives for concealment; a well-brought-up woman is, indeed, credited with only a minimum of erotic desire, while a young man has to learn to suppress the overweening self-regard he acquires in the indulgent atmosphere surrounding his childhood, so that he may find his proper place in a society that is full of other persons making similar claims.

We must not imagine that the various products of this impulse towards phantasy, castles in the air or day-dreams, are stereotyped or unchangeable. On the contrary, they fit themselves into the changing impressions of life, alter with the vicissitudes of life; every deep new impression gives them what might be called a "date-stamp." The relation of phantasies to time is altogether of great importance. One may say that a phantasy at one and the same moment hovers between three periods of time—the three periods of our ideation. The activity of phantasy in the mind is linked up with some current impression, occasioned by some event in the present, which had the power to rouse an intense desire. From there it wanders back to the memory of an early experience, generally belonging to infancy, in which this wish was fulfilled. Then it creates for itself a situation which is to emerge in the future, representing the fulfilment of the wish—this is the day-dream or phantasy, which now carries in it traces both of the occasion which engendered it and of some past memory. So past, present and future are threaded, as it were, on the string of the wish that runs through them all.

A very ordinary example may serve to make my statement clearer. Take the case of a poor orphan lad, to whom you have given the address of some employer where he may perhaps get work. On the way there he falls into a day-dream suitable to the situation from which it springs. The content of the phantasy will be somewhat as follows: He is taken on and pleases his new employer, makes himself indispensable in the business, is taken into the family of the employer, and marries the charming daughter of the house. Then he comes to conduct the business, first as a partner, and then as successor to his father-in-law. In this way the dreamer regains what he had in his happy childhood, the protecting house, his loving parents and the first objects of his affection. You will see from such an example how the wish employs some event in the present to plan a future on the pattern of the past.

Much more could be said about phantasies, but I will only allude as briefly as possible to certain points. If phantasies become over-luxuriant and over-powerful, the necessary conditions for an outbreak of neurosis or psychosis are constituted; phantasies are also the first preliminary stage in the mind of the symptoms of illness of which our patients complain. A broad by-path here branches off into pathology.

I cannot pass over the relation of phantasies to dreams. Our nocturnal dreams are nothing but such phantasies, as we can make clear by interpreting them.[3] Language, in its unrivalled wisdom, long ago decided the question of the essential nature of dreams by giving the name of "day-dreams" to the airy creations of phantasy. If the meaning of our dreams usually remains obscure in spite of this clue, it is because of the circumstance that at night wishes of which we are ashamed also become active in us, wishes which we have to hide from ourselves, which were consequently repressed and pushed back into the unconscious. Such repressed wishes and their derivatives can therefore achieve expression only when almost completely disguised. When scientific work had succeeded in elucidating the distortion in dreams, it was no longer difficult to recognize that nocturnal dreams are fulfilments of desires in exactly the same way as day-dreams are—those phantasies with which we are all so familiar.

So much for day-dreaming; now for the poet! Shall we dare really to compare an imaginative writer with "one who dreams in broad daylight," and his creations with day-dreams? Here, surely, a first distinction is forced upon us; we must distinguish between poets who, like the bygone creators of epics and tragedies, take over their material ready-made, and those who seem to create their material spontaneously. Let us keep to the latter, and let us also not choose for our comparison those writers who are most highly esteemed by critics. We will choose the less pretentious writers of romances, novels

---

[3] Cf. Freud, *Die Traumdeutung* [translated by A. A. Brill in 1913 as *The Interpretation of Dreams* (Eds.)].

and stories, who are read all the same by the widest circles of men and women. There is one very marked characteristic in the productions of these writers which must strike us all: they all have a hero who is the centre of interest, for whom the author tries to win our sympathy by every possible means, and whom he places under the protection of a special providence. If at the end of one chapter the hero is left unconscious and bleeding from severe wounds, I am sure to find him at the beginning of the next being carefully tended and on the way to recovery; if the first volume ends in the hero being shipwrecked in a storm at sea, I am certain to hear at the beginning of the next of his hairbreadth escape—otherwise, indeed, the story could not continue. The feeling of security with which I follow the hero through his dangerous adventures is the same as that with which a real hero throws himself into the water to save a drowning man, or exposes himself to the fire of the enemy while storming a battery. It is this very feeling of being a hero which one of our best authors has well expressed in the famous phrase, *"Es kann dir nix g'schehen!"* [4] It seems to me, however, that this significant mark of invulnerability very clearly betrays—His Majesty the Ego, the hero of all day-dreams and all novels.

The same relationship is hinted at in yet other characteristics of these egocentric stories. When all the women in a novel invariably fall in love with the hero, this can hardly be looked upon as a description of reality, but it is easily understood as an essential constituent of a day-dream. The same thing holds good when the other people in the story are sharply divided into good and bad, with complete disregard of the manifold variety in the traits of real human beings; the "good" ones are those who help the ego in its character of hero, while the "bad" are his enemies and rivals.

We do not in any way fail to recognize that many imaginative productions have travelled far from the original naïve day-dream, but I cannot suppress the surmise that even the most extreme variations could be brought into relationship with this model by an uninterrupted series of transitions. It has struck me in many so-called psychological novels, too, that only one person—once again the hero—is described from within; the author dwells in his soul and looks upon the other people from outside. The psychological novel in general probably owes its peculiarities to the tendency of modern writers to split up their ego by self-observation into many component-egos, and in this way to personify the conflicting trends in their own mental life in many heroes. There are certain novels, which might be called "excentric," that seem to stand in marked contradiction to the typical day-dream; in these the person introduced as the hero plays the least active part of anyone, and seems instead to let the actions and sufferings of other people pass him

---

[4] Anzengruber. [The phrase means "Nothing can happen to *me!*"—Trans. (*sic*)]

by like a spectator. Many of the later novels of Zola belong to this class. But I must say that the psychological analysis of people who are not writers, and who deviate in many things from the so-called norm, has shown us analogous variations in their day-dreams in which the ego contents itself with the rôle of spectator.

If our comparison of the imaginative writer with the day-dreamer, and of poetic production with the day-dream, is to be of any value, it must show itself fruitful in some way or other. Let us try, for instance, to examine the works of writers in reference to the idea propounded above, the relation of the phantasy to the wish that runs through it and to the three periods of time; and with its help let us study the connection between the life of the writer and his productions. Hitherto it has not been known what preliminary ideas would constitute an approach to this problem; very often this relation has been regarded as much simpler than it is; but the insight gained from phantasies leads us to expect the following state of things. Some actual experience which made a strong impression on the writer had stirred up a memory of an earlier experience, generally belonging to childhood, which then arouses a wish that finds a fulfilment in the work in question, and in which elements of the recent event and the old memory should be discernible.

Do not be alarmed at the complexity of this formula; I myself expect that in reality it will prove itself to be too schematic, but that possibly it may contain a first means of approach to the true state of affairs. From some attempts I have made I think that this way of approaching works of the imagination might not be unfruitful. You will not forget that the stress laid on the writer's memories of his childhood, which perhaps seems so strange, is ultimately derived from the hypothesis that imaginative creation, like day-dreaming, is a continuation of and substitute for the play of childhood.

We will not neglect to refer also to that class of imaginative work which must be recognized not as spontaneous production, but as a re-fashioning of ready-made material. Here, too, the writer retains a certain amount of independence, which can express itself in the choice of material and in changes in the material chosen, which are often considerable. As far as it goes, this material is derived from the racial treasure-house of myths, legends and fairy-tales. The study of these creations of racial psychology is in no way complete, but it seems extremely probable that myths, for example, are distorted vestiges of the wish-phantasies of whole nations—the age-long dreams of young humanity.

You will say that, although writers came first in the title of this paper, I have told you far less about them than about phantasy. I am aware of that, and will try to excuse myself by pointing to the present state of our knowledge. I could only throw out suggestions and bring up interesting points which arise from the study of phantasies, and which pass beyond them to the problem of the choice of literary material. We have not touched on the other problem at all, *i.e.* what are the means which writers use to achieve those emotional reactions in us that are roused by their productions. But I would at least point out to you the path which leads from our discussion of day-dreams to the problems of the effect produced on us by imaginative works.

You will remember that we said the day-dreamer hid his phantasies carefully from other people because he had reason to be ashamed of them. I may now add that even if he were to communicate them to us, he would give us no pleasure by his disclosures. When we hear such phantasies they repel us, or at least leave us cold. But when a man of literary talent presents his plays, or relates what we take to be his personal day-dreams, we experience great pleasure arising probably from many sources. How the writer accomplishes this is his innermost secret; the essential *ars poetica* lies in the technique by which our feeling of repulsion is overcome, and this has certainly to do with those barriers erected between every individual being and all others. We can guess at two methods used in this technique. The writer softens the egotistical character of the day-dream by changes and disguises, and he bribes us by the offer of a purely formal, that is, aesthetic, pleasure in the presentation of his phantasies. The increment of pleasure which is offered us in order to release yet greater pleasure arising from deeper sources in the mind is called an "incitement premium" or technically, "fore-pleasure." I am of the opinion that all the aesthetic pleasure we gain from the works of imaginative writers is of the same type as this "fore-pleasure," and that the true enjoyment of literature proceeds from the release of tensions in our minds. Perhaps much that brings about this result consists in the writer's putting us into a position in which we can enjoy our own day-dreams without reproach or shame. Here we reach a path leading into novel, interesting and complicated researches, but we also, at least for the present, arrive at the end of the present discussion.

SIGMUND FREUD

Neurotic and Artist[1]

Before you leave to-day I should like to direct your attention for a moment to a side of phantasy-life of very general interest. There is, in fact, a path from phantasy back again to reality, and that is—art. The artist has also an introverted disposition and has not far to go to become neurotic. He is one who is urged on by instinctual needs which are too clamorous; he longs to attain to honour, power, riches, fame, and the love of women; but he lacks the means of achieving these gratifications. So, like any other with an unsatisfied longing, he turns away from reality and transfers all his interest, and all his libido too, onto the creation of his wishes in the life of phantasy, from which the way might readily lead to neurosis. There must be many factors in combination to prevent this becoming the whole outcome of his development; it is well known how often artists in particular suffer from partial inhibition of their capacities through neurosis. Probably their constitution is endowed with a powerful capacity for sublimation and with a certain flexibility in the repressions determining the conflict. But the way back to reality is found by the artist thus: He is not the only one who has a life of phantasy; the intermediate world of phantasy is sanctioned by general human consent, and every hungry soul looks to it for comfort and consolation. But to those who are not artists the gratification that can be drawn from the springs of phantasy is very limited; their inexorable repressions prevent the enjoyment of all but the meagre day-dreams which can become conscious. A true artist has more at his disposal. First of all he understands how to elaborate his day-dreams, so that they lose that personal note which grates upon strange ears and become enjoyable to others; he knows too how to modify them sufficiently so that their origin in prohibited sources is not easily detected. Further, he possesses the mysterious ability to mould his particular material until it expresses the ideas of his phantasy faithfully;

---

[1] From *A General Introduction to Psychoanalysis* by Sigmund Freud, tr. Joan Riviere; published by Liveright Publishing Corporation, New York, pp. 327–328. Copyright Edward L. Bernays, 1935. Reprinted by permission of Liveright Publishing Corporation and George Allen & Unwin, Ltd. In the previous selection Freud has identified the artist with the common neurotic; in this selection he distinguishes between the two. Title by the editors. (Eds.)

and then he knows how to attach to this reflection of his phantasy-life so strong a stream of pleasure that, for a time at least, the repressions are out-balanced and dispelled by it. When he can do all this, he opens out to others the way back to the comfort and consolation of their own unconscious sources of pleasure, and so reaps their gratitude and admiration; then he has won—through his phantasy—what before he could only win in phantasy: honour, power, and the love of women.

CARL G. JUNG

On the Relation of Analytical Psychology to Poetic Art [1]

NOTWITHSTANDING ITS manifold difficulties, the task of discussing the relation of analytical psychology to poetic art provides me with a not unwelcome occasion for defining my standpoint in regard to a much debated question; namely, the relation between psychology and art in general. In spite of their incommensurability both provinces are closely inter-related, and these connexions cannot remain unexplored. For they originate in the fact that art in practice is a psychological activity, and, in so far as this is the case, it actually requires a psychological consideration. Art, like every other human activity proceeds from psychic motives, and from this angle, it is a proper object for psychology. But this conclusion also involves a very obvious limitation in the application of the psychological view-point: only that aspect of art which consists in the process of artistic form can be an object of psychology; whereas that which constitutes the essential nature of art must always lie outside its province. This other aspect, namely, the problem what is art in itself, can never be the object of a psychological, but only of an aesthetico-artistic method of approach.

A like distinction must also be made in the realm of religion; there also a psychological consideration is permissible only in respect of the emotional and symbolical phenomena of a religion, where the essential nature of religion is in no way involved, as indeed it cannot be. For were this possible,

---

[1] From Carl G. Jung, *Contributions to Analytical Psychology*, tr. H. G. and Cary F. Baynes (London: Routledge and Kegan Paul, Ltd., 1928), pp. 225–249. Reprinted by permission of the Bollingen Foundation, Inc. (Eds.)

not religion alone, but art also could be treated as a mere subdivision of psychology. In saying this I do not mean to affirm that such an encroachment has not actually taken place. But whoever trespasses in this way clearly forgets that a similar fate can easily befall psychology, the specific value and essential quality of which is at once obliterated as soon as it is regarded as a mere brain activity, thus bringing it into line with other glandular activities as a mere subdivision of physiology. In actual fact, this depreciation has already occurred.

Art, by its very nature, is not science, and science is essentially not art; both provinces of the mind, therefore, have a reservation that is peculiar to them, and that can be explained only from themselves. Hence when we speak of the relation between psychology and art, we are treating only of that aspect of art which without encroachment can be submitted to a psychological manner of approach. Whatever psychology is able to determine about art will be confined to the psychological process of artistic activity, and will have nothing whatever to do with the innermost nature of art itself. It is as powerless in this respect as is the capacity of the intellect to present or even apprehend the nature of feeling. Moreover these two things could have no kind of existence as separate entities had not their essential difference long since challenged recognition. The fact that in the child, the "war of faculties" not yet having declared itself, we find artistic, scientific, and religious possibilities still slumbering tranquilly together; or that with the primitive, dispositions towards art, science, and religion still maintain an undifferentiated co-existence in the chaos of a magical mentality; or that, finally, with animals no trace of "mind" can as yet be discerned, but merely "natural instinct,"—all these facts hold no shadow of evidence for that essential unity in the nature of art and science which alone could justify a reciprocal subsumption, or in other words, a reduction of the one into the other. For if we go back far enough in the state of mental development for the essential differences of the individual provinces of the mind to have become altogether invisible, we have not thereby reached a deeper principle of their unity, but merely an earlier evolutionary state of undifferentiation in which neither province has as yet any existence at all. But this elementary state is not a principle from which any conclusion regarding the nature of later and more highly developed states might be inferred, notwithstanding, as is of course always the case, that a direct descent can be demonstrated. The scientific attitude will naturally and constantly tend to overlook the nature of a differentiation in favour of its causal derivation, and will strive to subordinate the former to an idea that is certainly more general, but at the same time more elementary.

These reflections seem to me not inappropriate at the present time, for there have been frequent demonstrations of late of the way in which poetic art-works in particular may be submitted to an interpretation that is neither more nor less than a reduction to elementary conditions. Granted that the determinants of the artistic creation, the material and its individual treatment, for instance, can be traced back to the personal relations of the poet with his parents. Yet nothing is gained by this procedure for the understanding of his art, since we can perform the same reduction in every other possible case, and not the least in cases of pathological disorder. Neuroses and psychoses are also reducible to infantile relations with the parents, as are good and bad habits, convictions, qualities, passions, especial interests and so forth. But we are surely not entitled to assume that all these very different things must, therefore, have one and the same explanation; for were this so, we should be driven to conclude that they were actually one and the same thing. Thus, if a work of art and a neurosis are explained in precisely similar terms, either the art-work must be a neurosis, or the neurosis a work of art. As a paradoxical play upon words such a *façon de parler* [manner of speaking] might pass muster, but a healthy human reason must assuredly revolt at the notion of art-work and neurosis being placed in the same category. To take the most extreme case, only an analysing physician viewing a neurosis through the spectacles of a professional bias could come to regard it as a work of art. But it would never occur to a thinking lay mind to confound art with a morbid phenomenon, in spite of the undeniable fact that the origin of a work of art must confess to similar psychological preconditions as a neurosis. This is only natural, since certain psychic preconditions are universally present, and furthermore, because of the relative similarity of human conditions of life these are constantly the same, whether in the case of a nervous intellectual, a poet, or a normal human being. All, doubtless, have had parents, all have a so-called father and mother-complex, all have the onus of sexuality and, therewith, certain general and typical human difficulties. That one poet is influenced more by the relation to the father, another by the tie to the mother, while a third reveals unmistakable traces of repressed sexuality in his works—all this can be said equally well not only of every neurotic, but also of every normal human being. Hence nothing specific is thereby gained for the judgment of a work of art. At most our knowledge of the historic preconditions will have been somewhat broadened and deepened. The school of medical psychology inaugurated by Freud has certainly tended to inspire the literary historian to bring certain qualities of the individual work of art into relation with the personal and intimate life of the poet. But in so doing nothing more has been said than what the scientific treatment of poetic works had long since revealed, namely, the presence of certain threads, woven by the personal and intimate life of the poet—whether with or without conscious intention—into the fabric of his work. But the works of Freud may conceivably enable a more penetrating and exhaustive demonstration of these influences, reaching back even as far as earliest childhood, that so often affect the artistic creation.

When employed with taste and common sense, such treatment often provides an attractive general picture of the way in which the artistic creation is interwoven in the personal life of the artist, and also in a sense arises from it.

To this extent the so-called psycho-analysis of art-works differs in no essential way from a penetrating and skilfully shaded psychologico-literary analysis. The difference is at most a question of degree, although it may occasionally astound us by indiscreet conclusions and references that a rather more delicate touch, or a certain sense of tact might easily have avoided. This lack of delicacy in dealing with the all-too-human element, which seems to be a professional peculiarity of the medical psychologist, was perfectly understood by Mephistopheles: "So may you finger everything and welcome, round which another prowls for years and years"—although unfortunately not always to his own advantage. The possibility of daring conclusions may easily lead the way to flagrant lapses of taste. A slight touch of scandal often flavours a biography, but a little more becomes a nasty inquisitiveness, a catastrophe of good taste beneath the cloak of science. Our interest is unwittingly diverted from the work of art and gets lost in the mazy, labyrinthine confusion of psychic preconditions, the poet becomes a clinical case, even serving on occasion as a curious example of *psychopathia sexualis*. But therewith the psycho-analysis of the art-work has also turned aside from its objective, and the discussion has strayed into a province that is as broad as mankind, and not in the smallest degree specific for the artist; it therefore possesses even less relevance to his art.

This kind of analysis brings the work of art into the sphere of general human psychology, whence everything else besides art may proceed. An explanation of a work of art obtained in this way is just as great a futility as the statement that "every artist is a narcissist." Every man who pursues his own line to the limit of his powers is a "narcissist"—if indeed it is at all permissible to use a concept so specifically coined for the pathology of neuroses in this wider application—hence such a statement says nothing; it merely elicits surprise in the style of a *bon-mot*.

Because this kind of analysis is in no sense concerned with the art-work itself, but is always striving with the instinct of a mole to bury itself as quickly as possible in the murky back-ground of the human psyche, it always finds itself in the same common earth that unites all mankind. Accordingly its explanations possess an indescribable monotony—that same tedious recital, in fact, which can daily be heard in certain medical consulting rooms.

The reductive method of Freud is purely a method of medical treatment that has for its object a morbid and unsuitable structure. This morbid structure has taken the place of normal accomplishment, and hence must be broken down before the way can be cleared for a sound adaptation. In this case the process of leading-back to a general human basis is entirely appropriate. But when applied to the work of art this method leads to the results depicted above. From beneath the shimmering robe of art it extracts the naked commonness of the elementary *homo sapiens,* to which species the poet also belongs. The golden semblance of sublime creation we were about to discuss is blotted out; for its essence is lost when we treat it with the corrosive method which has to be used for the deceptive phantasms of hysteria. The product obtained by this mordant technique is, of course, interesting and might conceivably possess the same kind of scientific value as for instance a post-mortem examination of the brain of Nietzsche, which might certainly teach us the particular atypical form of paralysis from which he died. But what would this have to do with Zarathustra? Whatever may have been its subterranean background, is this not a world in itself, beyond the human, all-too-human imperfections, beyond the world of migraine and cerebral atrophy?

I have spoken hitherto of Freud's reductive method without stating with any particularity in what the method consists. It has to do with a medico-psychological technique for the investigation of morbid psychic phenomena. This technique is exclusively occupied with ways and means for circumventing or peering through the conscious foreground in order to reach the so-called unconscious, or psychic background. It is based upon the assumption that the neurotic patient is repressing certain psychic contents from consciousness because of their incompatibility or inconsistency with conscious values. This incompatibility is regarded as a moral one; accordingly, the repressed contents must bear a correspondingly negative character, namely, infantile-sexual, obscene, or even criminal. It is these qualities that render them so distasteful to consciousness. Since no man is perfect, it is clear that everyone must possess such a background whether the fact be admitted or not. Hence it can be disclosed in all cases if only we apply the technique of interpretation elaborated by Freud.

I cannot, of course, enter here into the details of the technique. A few intimations as to its nature must suffice. The unconscious background does not remain inactive, but betrays itself by certain characteristic effects upon the conscious contents. For example, it creates phantasy-products of a peculiar character, which are in most cases easily referable to certain subterranean sexual representations. Or it effects certain characteristic disturbances of the conscious process, which are likewise reducible to repressed contents. A most important source of the knowledge of unconscious contents is provided by dreams, which are direct products of the activity of the unconscious. The essential factor of Freud's reductive method consists in the fact, that it collects all the circumstantial evidence of the unconscious backgrounds, and, through the analysis and interpretation of this material, reconstructs the elementary, unconscious, instinctive processes. Those conscious contents which give us a clue, as it were, to the unconscious backgrounds are by Freud incorrectly termed symbols. These are not true symbols, however, since, according to his teaching, they have merely the rôle of signs or symptoms of the background processes. The true symbol differs essentially from this, and should be understood as the expression of an intuitive perception which can as yet, neither be apprehended better, nor expressed differently. When, for example, Plato expresses the whole problem of the theory of cognition in his metaphor of the cave, or when Christ expresses the idea of the Kingdom of Heaven in his parables, these are genuine and true symbols; namely, attempts to express a thing, for which there exists as yet no adequate verbal concept. If we were to interpret Plato's metaphor in the manner of Freud we should naturally come to the uterus, and we should have proved that even the mind of Plato was deeply stuck in the primeval levels of "infantile sexuality." But in doing so we should also remain in total ignorance of what Plato actually created from the primitive antecedents of his philosophical intuition; we should, in fact, carelessly have overlooked his most essential product, merely to discover that he had "infantile" phantasies like every other mortal. Such a conclusion could possess value only for the man who regards Plato as a super-human being, and who is therefore able to find a certain satisfaction in the fact that even Plato was also a man. But who would want to regard Plato as a god? Surely only a man who is afflicted by the tyranny of infantile phantasies, in other words, a neurotic mentality. For such an one the reduction to universal human truths is profitable on medical grounds. But this would have nothing whatever to do with the meaning of the Platonic parable.

I have purposely lingered over the relation between medical psycho-analysis and the work of art, because I want to emphasize the point that this kind of psycho-analysis is, at the same time, also the Freudian doctrine. Freud himself by his rigid dogmatism has seen to it that the two fundamentally different things should be regarded by the public as identical. Yet this technique may be employed with benefit in certain medical cases without any corresponding necessity to exalt it to the level of a doctrine. Indeed against this doctrine we are bound to raise vigorous objections. The assumptions it rests upon are quite arbitrary. In no sense, for example, are neuroses exclusively based upon sexual repression, and the same holds good for the psychoses. There is no foundation for saying that dreams merely contain repressed wishes the incompatibility of which requires them to be disguised by a hypothetical dream-censor. The Freudian technique, in so far as it remains under the influence of its own one-sided and, therefore, erroneous hypotheses, is patently arbitrary.

Before analytical psychology can do justice to the work of art it must entirely rid itself of medical prejudice; for the art-work is not a morbidity, and therefore demands a wholly different orientation from the medical. The physician must naturally seek the prime cause of a sickness in order to eradicate it, if possible, by the roots; but just as naturally must the psychologist adopt an exactly opposite attitude towards the work of art. He will not raise the question, which for the art-work is quite superfluous, concerning its undoubted general antecedents, its basic human determinants; but he will inquire into the meaning of the work, and will be concerned with its preconditions only in so far as they are necessary for the understanding of its meaning. Personal causality has as much and as little to do with the work of art, as the soil with the plant that springs from it. Doubtless we may learn to understand some peculiarities of the plant by becoming familiar with the character of its habitat. And for the botanist this is, of course, an important component of his knowledge. But nobody will maintain that he has thereby recognized all the essentials relating to the plant itself. The personal orientation that is demanded by the problem of personal causality is out of place in the presence of the work of art, just because the work of art is not a human being, but essentially supra-personal. It is a thing and not a personality; hence the personal is no criterion for it. Indeed the especial significance of the genuine art-work lies in the fact, that it has successfully rid itself of the restraints and blind alleys of the personal and breathes an air infinitely remote from the transitoriness and short-winded excursions of the merely personal.

I must confess from my own experience that it is by no means easy for the physician to lay aside his professional spectacles when considering the work of art, and at the same time to clear his judgment of the current biological causality. But I have come to learn that although a psychology with a purely biological orientation can with a certain measure of justification be applied to men, it can never be applied to the true work of art, and still less to man as creator. A purely causalistic psychology is only able to reduce every human individual to a member of the species *homo sapiens,* since its entire range is limited to what is either transmitted or derived. But the art-work is not merely transmitted or derived—it is a creative reorganization of those very determinants to which a causalistic psychology must always reduce it. The plant is not a mere product of the soil; but a living creative process centred in itself, the essence of which has nothing to do with the character of the soil. In the same way the art-work must be regarded as a creative formation, freely making use of every precondition. Its meaning and its own individual particularity rests in itself, and not in its preconditions. In fact one might almost describe it as a being that uses man and his personal dispositions merely as a cultural medium or soil, disposing his powers according to its own laws, while shaping itself to the fulfilment of its own creative purpose.

But here I am anticipating somewhat, since I have in mind a particular class of art-work which I must first introduce. For not every work of art is produced under this constellation. There are works, verse as well as prose writings, that proceed wholly from the author's intention and resolve to produce this or that effect. In this case the author submits his material to a definite treatment that is both directed and purposeful; he adds to it and substracts from it, emphasizing one effect, modifying another, laying on this colour here, that there, with the most careful weighing of their possible effects, and with constant observance of the laws of beautiful form and style. To this labour the author brings his keenest judgment, and selects his expression with the most complete freedom. In his view his material is only material, and entirely subject to his artistic purpose; he wills to present this and nothing else. In this activity the poet is simply identical with the creative process, whether he has willingly surrendered himself as the head of the creative movement, or whether this has so entirely seized upon him as a tool or instrument that all consciousness of the fact has escaped him. He is the creative process itself, standing completely in it and undifferentiated from it with all his aims and all his powers. There is no need, I think, to bring before you examples of this identity, either from the history of literature or from the poets' own confessions.

Doubtless, also, I am saying nothing new when I speak of the other class of art-works, that flow more or less spontaneous and perfect from the author's pen. They come as it were fully arrayed into the world, as Pallas Athene sprang from the head of Zeus. These works positively impose themselves upon the author; his hand is, as it were, seized, and his pen writes things that his mind perceives with amazement. The work brings with it its own form; what he would add to it is declined, what he does not wish to admit is forced upon him. While his consciousness stands disconcerted and empty before the phenomenon, he is overwhelmed with a flood of thoughts and images which it was never his aim to beget and which his will would never have fashioned. Yet in spite of himself he is forced to recognize that in all this his self is speaking, that his innermost nature is revealing itself, uttering things that he would never have entrusted to his tongue. He can only obey and follow the apparently foreign impulse, feeling that his work is greater than himself, and therefore has a power over him that he is quite unable to command. He is not identical with the process of creative formation; he is himself conscious of the fact that he stands as it were underneath his work, or at all events beside it, as though he were another person who had fallen within the magic circle of an alien will.

When we are speaking of the psychology of a work of art, before all else we must bear in mind these two entirely different possibilities of the origin of a work, since much that is of the greatest importance for psychological judgment hangs upon this discrimination. This antithesis was also sensed by Schiller; he sought, as we know, to embrace it with the concept, sentimental and naïve. The choice of his expression is probably based upon the fact that he had mainly the poetic activity in view. Psychologically we term the former kind introverted, the latter extraverted. The introverted attitude is characterized by an upholding of the subject with his conscious ends and aims against the claims and pretensions of the object; the extraverted attitude, on the contrary, is distinguished by a subordination of the subject to the claims of the object. In my view, Schiller's dramas give a good idea of the introverted attitude to material, as do most of his poems. The material is mastered by the aim of the poet. For the opposite attitude the second part of *Faust* gives us a good illustration. Here the material distinguishes itself by its refractory obstinacy. A still more striking example is Nietzsche's *Zarathustra* wherein the author himself observes how "one became two."

You will perhaps have discerned in the foregoing presentation that a considerable displacement of psychological standpoint has taken place, for now I am no longer speaking of the poet as a person, but of the creative process that moves him. The accent of interest has been shifted to the latter factor, while the former comes into consideration, as it were, only as a reacting object. When the consciousness of the author is not identical with the creative process this is at once clear, but in the first-mentioned instance the opposite appears at first to be the case. Here the author is apparently the creator himself, of his own free will and without the smallest compulsion. He is perhaps fully convinced of his own freedom, and will not be disposed to allow that his creation is not also his will, from which, in conjunction with his knowledge, he believes it to be exclusively derived.

Here we are faced with a question that we are quite unable to answer from what the poet himself tells us about the manner of his creating. It is really a scientific problem that psychology alone can solve. For it might also be the case, as I have already hinted, that the poet, while apparently creating consciously and spontaneously out of himself and producing only what he intends, is nevertheless, in spite of his consciousness, so caught up by the creative impulse that he is as little aware of an "alien" will, as the other type can be said to have any direct appreciation of his own will in the apparently foreign inspiration, and this notwithstanding the fact that it is manifestly the voice of his own self. In this case his conviction of the unconditioned freedom of his creating would be an illusion of consciousness—he fancies he is swimming, whereas an invisible stream bears him along.

In no sense is this doubt an airy phantasy; it is founded upon the experience of analytical psychology. For analytical investigation of the unconscious has disclosed an abundance of possibilities in which consciousness is not only influenced by the unconscious, but is actually led by it. The doubt therefore is justified. Yet where may we find evidence for the possible assumption that a conscious poet may also be taken captive by his work? The proof may be of two kinds, direct or indirect. Direct proof would be found in those cases where the poet, in what he believes he is saying, actually and patently says more than he himself is aware of. Many such instances could be cited. Indirect proof would be found in cases, where behind the apparent spontaneity of the production there stands a higher "must," that reveals the imperative nature of its demand if the creative activity is renounced voluntarily, or in those difficult psychic complications which immediately ensue in the event of an arbitrary interruption of the artistic production.

Practical analysis of artists invariably shows not only the strength of the creative impulse springing from the unconscious, but also its splenetic and arbitrary character. We have only to turn to any of the biographies of the great artists to find abundant evidence of the way in which the creative urge works upon them; often it is so imperious that it actually absorbs every human impulse, yoking everything to the service of the work, even at the cost of health and common human happiness. The unborn work in the soul of the artist is a force of nature that effects its purpose, either with tyrannical might, or with that subtle cunning which nature brings to the achievement of her end, quite regardless of the personal weal or woe of the man who is the vehicle of the creative force. The creative energy lives and waxes in the man as a tree in the earth from which it takes its nourishment. It might be well, therefore, to regard the creative process as a living thing, implanted, as it were, in the souls of men. In terms of analytical psychology this is an autonomous complex. It is in fact a detached portion of the psyche that leads an independent psychic life withdrawn from the hierarchy of consciousness, and in proportion to its energic value or force, may appear as a mere disturbance of the voluntarily directed process of consciousness, or as a superordinated authority which may take the ego bodily into its service. The latter case, therefore, would be the poet who is identified with the creative process and who at once acquiesces whenever the unconscious "must" threatens. But the other poet to whom the creative element appears almost as a foreign power, is unable for one reason or another to acquiesce, and is, accordingly, caught by the "must" unawares.

It might be expected that this heterogeneity in its motivation would also be felt in a work of art. For in one case we have to do with a purposeful production that is accompanied and directed by consciousness, and to the making of which every consideration as to the form and effect intended has been freely given. Whereas in the other we are dealing with an event proceeding from unconscious nature; something that achieves its aim without the smallest contribution from human consciousness, and often imposing its form and effect quite arbitrarily in spite of the latter. Thus we should expect in the former case, that nowhere would the work transcend the limits of conscious understanding, that its effect would, as it were, be spent within the framework of the author's intention, and that in no way would its expression exceed the author's deliberate purpose. In the latter case we should have to conceive of something of a supra-personal character that transcends the range of conscious understanding in the same degree as the author's consciousness is withheld from the development of his work. We should expect a certain strangeness of form and shape, thoughts that can only be apprehended by intuition, a language pregnant with meanings, expressions that would have the value of genuine symbols, because they are the best possible expressions of something as yet unknown—bridges thrown out towards an invisible shore.

These criteria are, on the whole, decisive. Wherever it is a question of an admittedly intended work with consciously selected material it should correspond to the first-named qualities, and similarly in the latter case. The familiar example of Schiller's dramas, on the one hand, and the second part of *Faust,* on the other, or better still *Zarathustra,* should illustrate what has been said. I would not, however, pledge myself to place the work of an unknown poet into either of these classes without previously having made a rather searching inquiry into the poet's personal relation to his work. The knowledge as to whether a poet belongs to the introverted or to the extraverted type of man is not enough; since both types have the possibility of creating at one time in the extraverted, and, at another, in the introverted attitude. This can be observed with Schiller, in the difference between his poetical and his philosophical works; with Goethe in the contrast between his perfectly formed poems and his obvious struggle in the shaping of his material in the second part of *Faust;* with Nietzsche in the difference between his aphorisms and the coherent stream of *Zarathustra.* The same poet may have quite different attitudes towards his various works, and the particular standard to be applied must be made dependent upon the particular relation prevailing at the time of production.

This question, as we now see, is infinitely complicated. But the complication is still further aggravated when our judgment must also include the above-mentioned considerations concerning the case of the poet who is identical with the creative impulse. Should it chance that the conscious and purposeful manner of production with all its apparent consciousness of intention is nevertheless a mere subjective illusion of the poet, then his work will also possess the same symbolical qualities, passing into the indefinable and thus transcending contemporary consciousness. But in this case these qualities would remain hidden; for the reader would likewise be unable to reach beyond the limits of the author's consciousness, which are themselves fixed by the spirit of his time. He too moves within the limits of contemporary consciousness, with small hope of availing himself of some Archimedian point outside the orbit of his world by which he could raise, as it were, his contemporary consciousness off its hinges. For nothing short of this would enable him to recognize the symbol in a work of this kind; the symbol being the possibility and intimation of a meaning higher and wider than our present powers of comprehension can seize.

This question, as we remarked, is somewhat delicate. Indeed, I am raising it only that the possible significance of a work of art might not be fettered or restricted by my typification, even though apparently it intends neither to be nor to say anything except what it obviously is and says. It happens moreover quite frequently that a poet long dead is suddenly rediscovered. This may occur when our conscious development has reached a higher level, from which standpoint the ancient poet can tell us something new. It was always present in his work, but it remained a hidden symbol that only a renewal of the spirit of the time permits us to read and to understand. It demanded other and fresher eyes, just because the old ones could see in it only the things they were accustomed to see. Experiences like these should prompt us to be circumspect, since they give a certain justification for the view I developed above; whereas the admittedly symbolic work does not demand this subtlety. In its prophetic language it almost seems to say: I am really meaning more than I actually say, my meaning carries further than my words. Here we may lay our hand upon the symbol, although a satisfying solution of the riddle still escapes us. The symbol remains a perpetual reproach to our subsequent thoughts and feelings. Surely this explains the fact that the symbolical work is more stimulating, drives, as it were, more deeply into us, and therefore seldom permits us a purely aesthetic enjoyment of it. Whereas the work that is manifestly not symbolical appeals much more vividly to our aesthetic sensibility, because it offers us an harmonious vision of fulfilment.

But, you may ask, what contribution can analytical psychology make to the root-problem of artistic "creation," that is, the mystery of the creative energy? All that we have spoken of hitherto has been merely psychological phenomenology. Inasmuch as "no created mind can penetrate the inner soul of Nature," you will surely not expect the impossible from our psychology, namely, a valid explanation of that great mystery of life, that we immediately feel in the creative impulse. Like every other science psychology has only a modest contribution to make towards the better and deeper understanding of the phenomena of life; it is no nearer than its sisters to absolute knowledge.

We have spoken so much of the significance and meaning of the work of art, that one can hardly suppress the theoretical doubt whether in fact art does "signify." Perhaps art itself does not intend to "signify," contains no sort of "meaning," at least not in the sense in which we are now speaking of "meaning." Perhaps it is like nature, which simply is, without any intention to "signify." Is "meaning" necessarily more than mere interpretation "secreted" into it by the need of an intellect hungry for meaning? Art—one might say—is beauty, and therein it finds its true aim and fulfilment. It needs no meaning. The question of meaning holds nothing productive for art. When I enter the sphere of art I must certainly submit to the truth of this statement. But when we are speaking of the relation of psychology to the work of art we are standing outside the realm of art, and here it is impossible for us not to speculate. We must interpret; we must find meaning in things, otherwise we should be quite unable to think about them. We must resolve life and happenings, all that fulfils itself in itself, into images, meanings, concepts; and thereby we deliberately detach ourselves from the living mystery. As long as we are caught up in the creative element itself we neither see nor understand; indeed we must not begin to understand, for nothing is more damaging and dangerous to immediate experience than cognition. But for the purpose of cognition we must detach ourselves from the creative process and regard it from without; only then does it become a picture that expresses meanings. Then we not only may, but indeed must speak of "meaning." And in so doing, what was before pure phenomenon, becomes something that in association with other phenomena has meaning; it plays a definite rôle, serves certain ends, brings about effects fraught with meaning. And when we can see all this we get the feeling of having understood and explained something. Thus is the need of science recognized.

When just now we likened the art-work to a tree growing from the nourishing earth, we might with equal justice have chosen the still more familiar metaphor of the child in its mother's womb. But there is a certain lameness about all comparisons; in places of metaphors, therefore, let us make use of the more precise terminology of science. You will remember that I described the work existing *in statu nascendi* [in the state of being born] as an autonomous complex. This concept is used to distinguish all those psychic formations which at first are developed quite unconsciously, and only from the moment when they attain threshold-value are able to break through into consciousness. The association which they then make with consciousness has not the importance of an assimilation, but rather of a perception; which means to say, that the autonomous complex, although certainly perceived, cannot be subjected to conscious control, whether in the form of inhibition or of voluntary reproduction. The autonomy of the complex reveals itself in the fact that it appears or vanishes when and in such guise as accords with its own intrinsic tendency; it is independent of the option of consciousness. The creative complex shares this peculiarity with every other autonomous complex. It is, moreover, at this point that the possibility of an analogy with morbid psychic processes presents itself, for the latter class (and mental disorders in particular) are especially distinguished by the appearance of autonomous complexes. The divine frenzy of the artist has a perilously real relation to morbid states without being identical with them. The analogy consists in the presence of an autonomous complex. The fact of such a presence, however, proves nothing either for or against the morbid hypothesis, since normal men have also to submit either temporarily or permanently to the tyranny of autonomous complexes. This fact is simply one of the normal peculiarities of the psyche, and for a man to be unaware of the existence of an autonomous complex merely betrays a rather high degree of unconsciousness. For instance every typical attitude that is to a certain extent differentiated shows a tendency to become an autonomous complex, and in the majority of cases actually becomes one. Every instinct too has more or less the character of an autonomous complex. In itself, therefore, there is nothing morbid in an autonomous complex, only its stored-up energy and its disturbing appearance on the scene may often involve suffering or illness.

How does an autonomous complex arise? From some cause or another—a closer investigation of which would at this point lead us too far afield—a hitherto unconscious region of the psyche is thrown into activity, and this activation undergoes a certain development and extension through the inclusion of related associations. The energy employed in this operation is naturally withdrawn from consciousness, unless the latter prefers to identify itself with the complex. But where this is not the case there results what Janet has termed an *"abaissement du niveau mental"* [abasement of the mental level]. The intensity of conscious interests and activities gradually fades, whereupon, either an apathetic inactivity—a condition very common with artists—or a regressive development of the conscious functions takes place, namely, a descent to their infantile or archaic prestages; hence something akin to a degeneration. The *"parties inférieures des fonctions"* [the lower elements of the functions] force themselves to the front, the instinctive rather than the ethical, the naïvely infantile instead of the deliberated and mature, the unadapted in place of the adapted. This also is shown in the lives of many artists. From the energy thus withdrawn from the conscious control of the personality the autonomous complex develops.

But in what does the autonomous creative complex consist? Of this we can know next to nothing so long as the completed work offers us no insight into its foundations. The work gives us a finished picture in the widest sense. This picture is accessible to analysis just in so far as we are able to appreciate it as a symbol. But if we are unable to discover any symbolic value in it, we have thereby ascertained that, for us at least, it means no more than what it obviously says—in other words, so far as we are concerned it is no more than it seems. I use the word "seems," because it is conceivable that our own bias forbids a wider appreciation of it. At all events in the latter case we can find no motive and no point of attack for analysis. In the former case, however, a phrase of Gerhart Hauptmann will come to our minds almost with the force of an axiom: "Poetry means the distant echo of the primitive word behind our veil of words." Translated into psychological language our first question should run: to what primordial image of the collective unconscious can we trace the image we see developed in the work of art?

This question demands elucidation in more than one respect. As already observed, the case I have assumed is that of a symbolical art-work; a work, therefore, of which the source is not to be found in the personal unconscious of the author, but in that sphere of unconscious mythology, the primordial contents of which are the common heritage of mankind. Accordingly, I have termed this sphere the collective unconscious, thus distinguishing it from a personal unconscious which I regard as the totality of those psychic processes and contents that are not only accessible to consciousness, but would often be conscious were they not subject to repression because of some incompatibility that keeps them artificially suppressed beneath the threshold of consciousness. From this sphere art also receives tributaries, dark and turbid though they be; but if they become a major factor they make the work of art a symptomatic rather than a symbolical product. This kind of art might conceivably be left without injury or regret to the Freudian purgative method.

In contrast to the personal unconscious, which in a sense is a relatively superficial layer immediately below the conscious threshold, the collective unconscious is quite unadapted for consciousness under normal conditions, and hence by no analytical technique can it be brought to conscious recollection, being neither repressed nor forgotten. In itself the collective unconscious cannot be said to exist at all; that is to say, it is nothing but a possibility, that possibility in fact which from primordial time has been handed down to us in the definite form of mnemic images, or expressed in anatomical formations in the very structure of the brain. It does not yield innate ideas, but inborn possibilities of ideas, which also set definite bounds to the most daring phantasy. It provides categories of phantasy-activity, ideas *a priori* as it were, the existence of which cannot be ascertained except by experience. In finished or shaped material they appear only as the regulative principle of its shaping, *i.e.,* only through the conclusion derived *a posteriori* from the perfected work of art are we able to reconstruct the primitive foundation of the primordial image. The primordial image or archetype is a figure, whether it be a daemon, man, or process, that repeats itself in the course of history wherever creative phantasy is freely manifested. Essentially, therefore, it is a mythological figure. If we subject these images to a closer investigation, we discover them to be the formulated resultants of countless typical experiences of our ancestors. They are, as it were, the psychic residua of numberless experiences of the same type. They depict millions of individual experiences in the average, presenting a kind of picture of the psychic life distributed and projected into the manifold shapes of the mythological pandemonium. These mythological forms, however, are in themselves themes of creative phantasy that still await their translation into conceptual language, of which there exist as yet only laborious beginnings. These concepts, for the most part still to be created, could provide us with an abstract scientific understanding of the unconscious processes that are the roots of the primordial images. Each of these images contains a piece of human psychology and human destiny, a relic of suffering or delight that has happened countless times in our ancestral story, and on the average follows ever the same course. It is like a deeply graven river-bed in the soul, in which the waters of life, that had spread hitherto with groping and uncertain course over wide but shallow surfaces, suddenly become a mighty river. This happens when that particular chain of circumstances is encountered which from immemorial time has contributed to the laying down of the primordial image. The moment when the mythological situation appears is always characterized by a peculiar emotional intensity; it is as though chords in us were touched that had never resounded before, or as though forces were unloosed; of the existence of which we had never even dreamed. The struggle of adaptation is laborious, bcause we have constantly to be dealing with individual, *i.e.* atypical conditions. No wonder then, that at the moment when a typical situation occurs, we feel suddenly aware of an extraordinary release, as though transported, or caught up as by an overwhelming power. At such moments we are no longer individuals, but the race; the voice of all mankind resounds in us. The individual man is never able to use his powers to their fullest range, unless there comes to his aid one of those collective presentations we call ideals that liberates in his soul all the hidden forces of instinct, to which the ordinary conscious will alone can never gain access. The most effective ideals are always more or less transparent variants of the archetype. This is proved by the fact that these ideals lend themselves so readily to allegorization, *e.g.* the motherland as the mother. In this kind of figurative expression the allegory itself has not the smallest motive-power; this has its source in the symbolic value of the motherland-idea. The corresponding archetype in this case is the so-called *"participation mystique"* [mystical participation] of the primitive with the soil on which he dwells, and which alone contains the spirit of his ancestors. Exile spells misery.

Every relation to the archetype, whether through experience or the mere spoken word, is "stirring," *i.e.* it is impressive, it calls up a stronger voice than our own. The man who speaks with primordial images speaks with a thousand tongues; he entrances and overpowers, while at the same time he raises the idea he is trying to express above the occasional and the transitory into the sphere of the ever-existing. He transmutes personal destiny into the destiny of mankind, thus evoking all those beneficent forces that have enabled mankind to find a rescue from every hazard and to outlive the longest night.

That is the secret of effective art. The creative process, in so far as we are able to follow it at all, consists in an unconscious animation of the archetype, and in a development and shaping of this image till the work is completed. The shaping of the primordial image is, as it were, a translation into the language of the present which makes it possible for every man to find again the deepest springs of life which would otherwise be closed to him. Therein lies the social importance of art; it is constantly at work educating the spirit of the age, since it brings to birth those forms in which the age is most lacking. Recoiling from the unsatisfying present the yearning of the artist reaches out to that primordial image in the unconscious which is best fitted to compensate the insufficiency and one-sidedness of the spirit of the age. The artist seizes this image, and in the work of raising it from deepest unconsciousness he brings it into relation with conscious values, thereby transforming its shape, until it can be accepted by his contemporaries according to their powers.

The nature of the work of art permits conclusions to be drawn concerning the character of the period from which it sprang. What was the significance of realism and naturalism to their age? What was the meaning of romanticism, or Hellenism? They were tendencies of art which brought to the surface that unconscious element of which the contemporary mental atmosphere had most need. The artist as educator of his time—much could be said about that to-day.

People and times, like individual men, have their peculiar tendencies or attitudes. The very word "attitude" betrays the necessary one-sidedness that every definite tendency postulates. Where there is direction there must also be exclusion. But exclusion means that certain definite psychic elements that could participate in life are denied their right to live through incompatibility with the general attitude. The normal man can endure the general tendency without much injury. But the man who takes to the by-streets and alley-ways because, unlike the normal man, he cannot endure the broad high-way, will be the first to discover those elements that lie apart from the main streets, and that await a new participation in life.

The artist's relative lack of adaptation becomes his real advantage; for it enables him to keep aloof from the high-ways, the better to follow his own yearning and to find those things of which the others are deprived without noticing it. Thus, as in the case of the single individual whose one-sided conscious attitude is corrected by unconscious reactions towards self-regulation, art also represents a process of mental self-regulation in the life of nations and epochs.

I am aware that I have only been able to give certain intuitive perceptions, and these only in the barest outlines. But I may perhaps hope that what I have been obliged to omit, namely, the concrete application to poetic works, has been furnished by your own thoughts, thus giving flesh and blood to my abstract intellectual frame.

THE AESTHETIC
OBJECT

THE NEXT PROBLEM to be discussed concerns the nature of the object which the artist has created and which the observer is to experience. This section naturally divides itself into two parts. After six selections which treat the generic traits of the aesthetic object, we arrive at the specific arts and have one selection each on the literary work, the plastic work, and the musical composition. While it would be desirable to add analyses of the other arts, limitations of space prevent the editors from doing so.

In treating the generic traits of the aesthetic object, the editors have tried to discriminate the three main levels of traits with which, they believe, any complete consideration of this problem must be concerned. Starting with the immediate level and moving to those which are more buried, we find, first, "aesthetic surface"; secondly, form; and, finally, that which is expressed through the form, or the "substance," to use Bradley's term. While some writers think of these terms as referring to components that can be conceived independently of one another and can be additively put together, others—the majority, perhaps, today—argue that they are levels that should not be thought of as separate or as mechanically superimposed, one on the other. Rather, these writers claim, they should be conceived as organically interrelated, although they may be distinguished for purposes of analysis.

The selection from Prall is concerned with what he calls "aesthetic surface"; that is, with the immediate sensuous properties of a medium. Form underlies these properties and is dependent on them, since it is through the artist's ability to order them that he is in the first instance able to create form. Therefore Prall must show what order, intrinsic to them, allows them to be formed. To this end he distinguishes among the various senses, first differentiating the higher from the lower senses according to their having or not having a discriminable order which can be aesthetically shaped, and then differentiating among the higher senses according to the kind of discriminable order they have. The question whether the purely sensuous elements are in any way expressive, moves us to consider the other levels of the object.

Contemporary discussions of form must be viewed with an awareness of the fact that the word has at least two different meanings as it is employed by modern aestheticians. For Gotshalk and for Bell (and for others, too; for instance, for Prall, although we are not including his discussion of form) form is composition or the manner in which the physical properties of the medium are arranged. These writers see the properties of the object more or less mechanistically, so that form for them often seems to stand as a self-sufficient entity to which content, if there is to be any, is superadded. On the other hand, writers like Isenberg and Bradley (whose selection we have included, for reasons later to be given, in Section VII—see p. 480) have more organic theories. It may seem to be a matter of degree, but they see form as the manner in which everything that is to be found in the object is put together, as the total interrelation of whatever is discriminable (the expressive as well as the formal elements) in the object. Form is for them, obviously, much more than mere composition, and they have to deny the possibility of making any dichotomy between form and content. Thus it is that modern discussions of content usually do not occur independently but are made part of organic treatments of form, and that form is treated independently only by those who conceive it to be no more than composition.

In this section, then, Prall's discussion of "aesthetic surface" is followed by Gotshalk's analysis of the general formal or compositional features which are common to all aesthetic objects. Bell, also concerned with composition, but insisting on it to the exclusion of everything else, denies that there is any noncompositional element which is legitimately aesthetic, and even denies that the formal elements are expressive in any currently accepted use of the term. Isenberg and Bradley counter this so-called formalism, Isenberg by trying to show that what is expressed and the technique of "informing" it are perceptually inseparable in the art object, and Bradley by making his important distinction between "subject" and "substance." Both the formal and the expressive elements are also treated in the analyses of Ritchie and Mrs. Hungerland, which, while conflicting, are alike (and different from the others) in that both are drawn in terms of a theory of signs. Once the generic traits of the aesthetic object have been revealed, we turn to the various arts in which these traits show themselves and, thus, to the selections by Wellek and Warren, Matisse, and Hadow; on the nature of literature, painting, and music, respectively.

It has already been noted that the problems of aesthetics cannot be completely separated from one another. The questions raised in this section may

seem to give the lie to this claim, for it seems possible to talk of the object
in isolation from the creative act or the aesthetic response. However, what
the object is taken to be depends, it could be shown, on how it is to be
responded to and how it is conceived to be created. By definition the aesthetic object exists for an observer, and everything we can possibly say
about its traits presupposes this observer, his senses, and his sensitivity to
these traits, which a tradition has helped to fashion. And we see also, especially in writers like Ritchie and Matisse, how decidedly a conception of
the creative act can mold one's treatment of the aesthetic object. Thus even
in this section, while the problem may at first seem more distinct and less
dependent on other problems than were those we discussed earlier, the advantage is specious. The various problems of aesthetics are so interrelated
that, even when we try to isolate a single one in the interests of analytical
clarity, we find it cannot long remain completely separated from its fellows.

Generic Traits

D. W. PRALL

The Elements of Aesthetic Surface in General [1]

1. Aesthetic elements that lack intrinsic order, and composition in
nature. 2. Elements defined in an intrinsic order as the condition of
human composition. 3. The orders intrinsic to elements of sound,
color, and spatial form.

§ 1

DISCRIMINATING PERCEPTION focused upon an object as it appears directly to sense, without ulterior interest to direct that perception
inward to an understanding of the actual forces or underlying structure giv-

[1] From D. W. Prall, *Aesthetic Judgment* (New York: Thomas Y. Crowell Company,
1929), pp. 57–75. Reprinted by permission. (Eds.)

ing rise to this appearance, or forward to the purposes to which the object may be turned or the events its presence and movement may presage, or outward to its relations in the general structure and the moving flux—such free attentive activity may fairly be said to mark the situation in which beauty is felt. It is the occurrence of such activity that makes possible the records put down in what we have called aesthetic judgments. Only the red that has really caught our attention fully, and upon which that attention has actually rested, is more than merely red—bright or glaring or hard or stirring, or lovely and rich and glowing, or fresh and clear and happy, or harsh or muddy or dull or distressing, ugly or beautiful in any one of a thousand determinate and specific meanings of those words.

But though these variations are indefinitely great in number, they are after all limited, as appearing upon the aesthetic surface of our world, by the limitations of the variations in that surface itself.[2] There is a limited range of hues to see, a limited range of sounds to hear, and even a limit to the dimensions of shapes perceived or imagined. Not that the number of possible variations in color, for example, is the number of the possible beauties of color, for the beauty of color is not simply its specific hue or shade or tint or intensity or saturation, but that specific color as upon an object, and not merely as distinguished there by vision, or noted in passing or for further reference as the color it appears to be, but also as appreciated, as felt to be delightful or the reverse to the perceiving subject. And this is plainly indicated, this relational character of the situation in which the beauty of sense elements is present, a relation involving feeling, in the long list of typical words used in describing such elements.

As we pass from the perceptually discriminated quality, taken as sensed, to the intuited beauty immediately felt, we pass from terms like bright and clear and red, to warmly red, pleasantly bright, charmingly clear, or to attractive or lovely or fascinating. As the aesthetic nature of the judgment is more and more unambiguously expressive of beauty as against ugliness, the terms used to describe it more and more definitely assert the relation to the perceiving subject which is attracted or interested or fascinated by it, or who finds it lovely as he loves it. Not that all qualities are not found in a relation to a subject who finds them, but that strictly aesthetic qualities involve not merely this finding, but such quality as is found, such quality as is perhaps only constituted at all, when the feelings of the subject are involved in its relation to the object. But the range of possibilities for delightful or ugly color, for example, bears some relation to the range of possible variations intrinsic to color as perceived; and if we are to know what we mean

---

[2] By aesthetic surface Prall means "the objectively discriminable sensuous presentations" (*Aesthetic Analysis,* New York: Thomas Y. Crowell Company, 1936, p. 11); that is, the data of sense or of immediate intuition, the color of the world as color, the sound as sound, etc. See also Chapter III of *Aesthetic Judgment.* (Eds.)

when we assert that colors are beautiful or ugly, we should know first a little about color itself.

So of the other elements of sensuous content; so of all the materials of aesthetic experience, sounds and shapes, textures and lines, and as it would also seem, so of tastes and smells and various recognizable kinds of bodily feelings which have distinctive character of their own. But if aesthetic character is properly limited to the object of attention, which takes on as directly apparent to sense its own specific beauty, felt in intuition but felt as a quality of itself, it is clear enough that fully appreciable beauty must be that of objects upon which this beauty actually shines as their own nature when we perceive them. Now we do perceive fruits, for example, as clearly upon the palate as upon the retina, although as the rationalists would say, not so distinctly; clearly, in that the taste is present as what it seems to be, indistinctly, in that what it seems to be, what it appears as, is not in its own essential nature rationally transparent, self-explanatory, native to mind as understandable by intellect. We are using the distinction within a field where historical rationalism did not make it, but the distinction itself, as we do make it, is exactly parallel, and worth putting into these old terms to show how troublesome, though in the end fruitless, this kind of distinction has been for all thinking. In our example, the exquisite aroma and taste of rich, ripe strawberries, marked by the palate and the organs of smell, are qualities exactly parallel in perception to their visual qualities, their specific form and color and texture as discriminated by the eye. And there is no doubt either that strawberries or foaming milk, or cabbages, for that matter, have clearly characteristic savour. But these sense qualities, subtle and specific and characteristic and objective as they are, seem to lack just the possibility of giving such fully satisfying aesthetic experience as is given by colors and shapes and sounds.

It is not that they are unworthy because they are so close to our bodies. The palate is no more internal than the ear, and the taste of strawberries is no more a function of the human body than their color or their shape. It would be a very determined esoteric theorist indeed who should deny that the fragrance of roses or gardens or orchards or perfumes was not merely not part of their visual beauty but not part of their beauty at all, even as its richness. And it is not their intimate connection with our vital bodily processes and motions that makes tastes less characteristically aesthetic than sounds or colors or shapes. Part of the appreciation of form itself, as in jars, or vases, is without question incipient motions or motor tendencies in our own bodies, and the beauty of the morning is in part the freshness of our vital functioning as well as of our perceptive faculties. We cannot rule out the specific character of tastes and of bodily feelings and of smells from the materials of genuine aesthetic experience on any clear ground. Certainly the fact that we usually consume what we taste but not what we see or hear does not furnish such a ground; for we do not need to consume and absorb it in order to taste it, though, as with tobacco or incense, we sometimes appreciate its savour best by passing the smoke of its destruction intimately over the organs by which we apprehend it. Such distillations of beauty are common enough even with rose or lavender, with the resin of pines or the oil of bays. It is only accident, then, that bodily consumption is the means to the full aesthetic flavor of objects, and this without any relation, either, to biological needs or interests. Appetite is not hunger, of course, and even appetite need not precede enjoyment except as a tendency or possibility or natural disposition of the human body and its organs, scarcely different on principle from the disposition of the eyes to see or the ears to hear. Moreover, we could be nourished by our food perfectly well, though our senses were anaesthetized. And in any case the perception of tastes or odors is never as such the devouring of them. We devour the substance, not the quality. And the smell of boiled cabbage, as of blooming roses, is a distinctly discriminated and easily remembered quality, eternally a quality to delight in or be offended by, were all the cabbages in the world consumed, and all the roses dead forever.

Nor does the transitoriness of smells and tastes in their occurrence rule them out as materials of aesthetic pleasure. Nothing is more transitory than sound. And what is more transitory than beautiful expressions upon human faces, or than beautiful young human bodies themselves?

But the fact remains that we do not say of the taste of even the most subtly blended salad or the most delicately flavored ice that it is beautiful. Hence it is clear that smells and tastes and vital feelings are not the materials of beauty in the sense that colors are, or sounds or forms, or even textures, for they are obviously not the contents of typical aesthetic judgments. If they are not to be ruled out on grounds of their nearness to the body, or their destruction by consumption, which is contemporaneous with and sometimes necessary to the very act of perception, or because of their transitoriness of occurrence, or because they are associated in our minds with fulfilling biological needs, or because of any lack of objectivity or specificity of quality, we must find some other ground for the obvious fact that though they occur in delighted perception, though attention may be focussed on them, as specific qualities directly apprehended in sense experience, they are not usually pronounced beautiful, do not become the content of aesthetic judgments, and thus apparently are not the characteristic materials of the aesthetic experience that such judgments record.

Now this ground is not far to seek, and when we stop to notice just what it is, it will offer us three points of clarification for general aesthetic theory. In the first place, smells and odors are unquestionably and emphatically sensuously delightful, and so far are elements of aesthetic experience, however elementary. In the second place much of the beauty of nature is made up of just such elementary sensuous materials, which also enter into complex natural beauties just as truly as other elementary materials, more commonly called beautiful. But in the third place, smells and odors do not in themselves fall into any known or felt natural order or arrangement, nor are their variations defined in and by such an intrinsic natural structure, as the variations in color and sound and shape give rise to in our minds. Hence our grasp of them, while it is aesthetic very clearly, since they may be felt as delightful, is the grasp in each case upon just the specific presented nonstructural quality, which is as absolutely different, unique, simple, and unrelatable to further elements intrinsically through its own being, as anything could be. One smell does not suggest another related smell close to it in some objective and necessary order of quality or occurrence or procedure, nor does one taste so follow another. There are apparently more or less compatible and incompatible smells and tastes, but there is no clearly defined order of smells and tastes, or any structure of smells and tastes in which each has its place fixed by its own qualitative being. Our experience of these elements is always of elements properly so-called, but also aesthetically elementary, of course.

Tastes may be subtly blended, and so may odors. Cooks and perfumers are in their way refined and sensitive artists, as tea-tasters and wine-tasters are expert critical judges. But such art and such criticism have no intelligible, or at least so far discovered, structural or critical principles, simply because the elements they work with have neither intelligible structure nor apparently any discoverable order in variation. It is this lack that rules them out of the characteristically aesthetic realm, not any lack of spatial distance from the body, nor of objectivity in themselves as specific characterized elements; nor is it their admitted occurrence in the consumption of the objects of which they are qualities. Their extremely transitory occurrence only marks them as not suitable elements for aesthetic structures that are to remain long before us. They do have a degree of distance after all, as great, if measured from our minds, as the distance of any sense quality; and it is the mind or the mind-body, not the body as such to which they are present at all. They have complete and well-defined objective native character, clearly discriminable specific natures, often even very subtle and refined and exciting. If they are more fleeting in their occurrence than some other beauties, they are no more fleeting than the colors of sunset, nor than many beautiful forms, and they are just as readily reproducible or more so. No beauty is more than a little lasting, for whatever occurs at all, to present us with any quality, also by its very nature passes away.

But relations objectively clear in given orders and a defining structure of variation, tastes and odors and bodily feelings do not have, and it is for this reason that we call them not merely the bare materials of beauty—colors and sounds and shapes are also only materials of beauty—but elementary aesthetic materials. For they remain merely elements, refusing to become for us, in any kind of intelligible human arts, within relational structures or movements or processes, that is, such composed and complex and elaborated beauties as we build up out of shapes and colors and lines and sounds.

Before we turn to these latter it is important to repeat with emphasis the fact that, while taste and smell are not the aesthetic senses *par excellence*, they are capable of aesthetic experience merely by virtue of being senses at all. For like all sense presentations, smells and tastes can be pleasant to perception, can be dwelt on in contemplation, have specific and interesting character, recognizable and remembrable and objective. They offer an object, that is, for sustained discriminating attention, and in general they fulfill the conditions necessary for aesthetic experience recorded in aesthetic judgments. While they remain only elements in such experience, like bodily feelings, and offer no intrinsic structure or formal relations in variation or combination by which they might become the materials of conscious arts of smell and taste, they are still beauties, the elementary materials of certain limited aesthetic experiences.

They do also enter into higher, that is, less elementary, aesthetic experiences, if not of all the arts at least of some representative art, and without forcing themselves upon attention they help compose beauties definitely expressive, the recognized elements of which are forms and colors and sounds. Organ tones depend without question, for even their strictly aesthetic effect, at least in part on the feelings not due to hearing and ears, but stirred by quite other bodily processes. The beauty of flowers is enriched by fragrance, the beauty of Catholic ceremonials by the odor of incense. Thus while they are only elementary aesthetic qualities, they are in exactly the same sense as sounds and shapes the materials of beauty and even of complex structural beauty. While they themselves are but elements, they are materials of more than elementary beauties. So far science and art have discovered in them no order or structural principles by which to compose with them, so that they remain either separately appreciated bare elements, or, if they go to make up beauties apprehended in the main by other senses, they enter as hidden or unconsciously employed constituents, with no apparently necessary relations to or in the structures of such non-elementary, that is composed or complex beauty.

Since tastes and smells and vital feelings reveal no principles of ordered variation, it is obvious that the compositions into which they do as a matter of fact enter are cases of natural or representative beauty; for the beauties of art as such, being forms created by man on some principle or other, however vaguely known or crudely followed, require such objectively established relations. Human composing is doing something with elementary materials that are capable of being composed, and elements cannot be put together at all unless in themselves and by their very nature they are capable of sustaining structural relations to one another, relations of contrast, balance, rhythmic sequence, form in general. These relations must be at least dimly discerned by any artist if he is to use the materials of beauty at all. But there is no such system of smells and tastes, and what relations and contrasts we do notice in such matters seem fairly arbitrary and accidental: apples with pork, perhaps, and perhaps not sour wine with sweets; certain blendings of tea and of spices, certain combinations toned into each other with sugar, or toned in general with garlic; but no structure, or any very clear general principles, though the whole matter is in all probability not so formless and accidental as it may seem, as current psychology is beginning to discover. One is indeed tempted to look for articulate principles here as elsewhere, if only to dignify to obstinately verbal minds whole realms of expert activity which seem to them too natural and domestic to be important and interesting, and too illiterate, it may be thought, to have any full moral status in the society of the arts.

What we are to point out here is that natural beauty in general is so largely of just this unprincipled sort, whether in its rank, unchaste profusion, or in its natural but unintelligible selection and composition. Nature at some places, at least, and at various times, without men's efforts, assumes lovely aspects, unintelligibly composed and unreasonably fine. In fact much of what men, artists particularly, know of color combination has been learned not out of any knowledge or perception of the orders and structures that color and line and shapes inherently possess by being color and line and shape, but from the purely accidental and familiar success of such combinations as nature has exhibited to them, in rocks under sunlight, birds and flowers against trees and sky, hills beyond running streams, metals or jewels against human flesh, and the thousand other happy accidents of natural beauty. If we do not know enough of perfumes or colors or sounds to compose with all of them at once, this is not to say that all these may not in nature go to make up rare beauty, nor that nature may not with impunity paint the lily with its own fragrance and add as integral elements in natural beauties the aesthetic materials of the despised senses of smell and taste.

If there is a beauty of August nights, or beauty in the rareness of a June day, or the fresh loveliness after rain, if there is ripe and languorous beauty in the mist and mellow fruitfulness of autumn, or a hard, cold beauty of glittering winter frosts, such beauty is not all for the eye and ear, and if we do not ourselves know how to blend smells and tastes with sound and form and color to compose such beauties, we need not foist our limitations upon nature. The saltiness of the breeze is as integral to the beauty of the sea as the flashing of the fish or the sweep of the gulls or the thunder of the surf or the boiling of the foam. If we know no modes of arranging smells or tastes or vital feelings or even noises in works of art, nature does not hesitate to combine the soughing of pines, the fragrance of mountain air, and the taste of mountain water or its coolness on the skin, with dazzling mountain sunlight and the forms and colors of rocks and forests, to make a beauty intense and thrilling in an unexpected purity and elevation, almost ascetic in its very complexity and richness. The greatest beauties of nature are concrete and full. Nature appears to have no aesthetic prejudices against any sort of elementary aesthetic materials, nor to lack insight into the principles of their combination in the greatest variety. Only human limitations may miss some of these elements and human insight fail to recognize any principles of structure or form to hold them so firmly together and make them often so transcendently beautiful.

But what happens in nature is not, of course, art, and an artist must work with materials that have relations, degrees of qualitative difference, established orders of variation, structural principles of combination. While we must be careful to include in the materials of beauty sense elements of all sorts, since all the senses, by virtue of being senses, may take such pleasure in their specific objects as is in all rigor to be called aesthetic pleasure, we must admit that these elements of smell and taste remain mere elements, except where natural occurrences happen to combine them, and through familiarity sometimes to sanctify the combination to men and to art, on no principles intelligible or available to human beings, but as some of the richest of natural or of representative beauties. As aesthetic materials they remain for us elementary in the simple sense of being elements, specifically aesthetic in quality, but still merely elements, not amenable to composition through intrinsically established orders.

§ 2

For less elementary aesthetic experience the materials are sound and shapes and color and line. The simple distinction that marks these materials is that they present objective structural orders intrinsic to their qualitative variation, through which we have control over them to build them into the complex formal beauties characteristic of the human arts and no longer the beauties of elements alone or of merely accidental natural combinations. If nature loves tastes and smells and vital feelings as well as she does colors and sounds and shapes, we may be ready enough to appreciate the beauty both of her materials and of her compositions; but in our own human compositions we are limited to such materials as order and arrange themselves by their own intrinsic nature. And to know even a little of humanly made beauties or even of natural ones involving these intrinsically ordered elements, we must know their order and their formal variation, and learn from this the possibilities they furnish, not for mere fortuitous, if often felicitous, combinations, but for composition in which the principles of such order and form have been consciously employed or at least intuitively discerned.

The essential nature of these orders or structural principles, which are intrinsic to the materials as such, which lie embedded in the very nature of color or sound or shape and line, vary of course with the varying materials, since it is just the defining nature of the material that is its falling into that sort of order that it has, that unique kind of relation that establishes the place of any one given determinate color or sound or shape in the range of colors or sounds, or the structural possibilities of lines and shapes and masses. It is clear that what is peculiar to color, for example, is not any quality that sounds can have; what is peculiar to sound is impossible to color; and spatial form as such is simply spatial, not colored or resonant. Thus no intrinsic order or structure of colors can be the order intrinsic to sounds or shapes, much less to smells or tastes or muscular imagery.

There are also, of course, orders common to several materials. Clearly enough, sounds occur and in occurring involve temporal sequence; and if they occur in throats, they involve the feelings of muscular coördinations and activities besides. Clearly enough, also, colors are found in shapes, along lines, and in general in spatial order. What we must look for here is that peculiar order in color which is not temporal, and for that order in shapes that is uniquely spatial. Time orders we shall find common to the occurrence of any color, any sound, any shape, and so, available for composing with them and making structures out of them, but not intrinsic to them and their nature in the sense in which the order of hue is intrinsic to color, the order of pitch intrinsic to sound, and geometrical structure intrinsic to line and shape.

While all this directs us to these intrinsic orders as fundamental, it indicates clearly enough that still more fundamental factor in all aesthetic experience, a factor in all occurrence and therefore in all experience of form or color or sound, in all the experience to be had in an existing—that is, temporally occurring—world. This most fundamental fact of order and arrangement is of course rhythm, and rhythm, as we shall see, is applicable to composition with *any* materials whatever. But that which rhythmically occurs is in itself aesthetic material, and, though sound embodies it more obviously than line or shape—for even space is temporal in all motion—shapes, too, may be rhythmical, though not unless their spatial nature defines them as what moves rhythmically or progresses in a pattern. Rhythm is all-pervasive in its application, since all there is in the world moves to its own peculiar

measure, rocks and trees as well as waves of sand or of ocean, or drum-
beats or dances or songs, or laboring bodies or machines themselves. But
only perceptible rhythm is aesthetic, and for perception motion on too great
or too small a scale is rest.

To complicate matters even here, however, perception and feeling, occurring as they do in time, have their own rates, and these may introduce
rhythm into movements or spatial structure where it would not otherwise
be felt. But it will be easier to grasp both the nature and the significance of
this possibly all-pervasive and absolutely—even metaphysically, perhaps—
fundamental character of aesthetic experience and of all objects of such
experience, all manifestations in beauty, after we have surveyed those intrinsically present orders of the very materials of beauty that manifest
rhythms so variously, faintly or clearly, directly or indirectly, making rhythm
sometimes a primary, and sometimes scarcely even a secondary, consideration.

§ 3

Before we pass to a detailed account of these intrinsic and unique
orders in the very materials of beauty, we may here mention them briefly
and then leave this general account to turn to more specific description of
the separate kinds of aesthetic material in their peculiarities, their possibilities of variation on the one hand and of combination and composition on
the other.[3] It is clear at once that in color the intrinsic variation, peculiar and
unique, is what we call difference in hue, so that absence of color in the rich,
lively meaning of the word means absence of hue. We contrast colored surface, colored walls, colored toys, colored glasses, colored light, with white
or black or gray primarily, not with absence of all visual sensation. The
colors of the rainbow are what we mean by colors, the breaking of the white
radiance into the discriminably different hues from red to violet. Colors vary
in other ways, of course, but it is variation in hue, and combinations and
contrasts of hue, that are intrinsic to color and nowhere else to be found.

This is what is sometimes called the specificity of sensation. It is the fact
that color, being color, being the specific hue that it is in any case, is just
uniquely its own quality for vision; and if we apply loosely the term color to
musical sounds, or mental states of depression or the reverse, or if we speak
of the colors of tones or the toning of color, we go beyond what we mean by
color itself, to apply terms not in their specific literal senses, but either by
analogy, and often vaguely and with resulting confusion as well as the sug-

---

[3] The detailed account is taken up in subsequent chapters of *Aesthetic Judgment*.
(Eds.)

gestiveness intended, or else by letting these terms color and tone carry as their meaning the principles of order and variation common to both but not uniquely present in either. For color or sound may vary also not in specific hue or pitch but in intensity, for example, although even here the specific intensity is in the one case brightness or darkness, in the other, loudness or softness, and these are not directly but only indirectly or even only analogously comparable.

In sound it is clear enough that pitch, differences in pitch or combinations of pitch, is the uniquely ordering quality. Sounds may vary in intensity too, as we just noted, as colors also may; but as color has no pitch, so sound has no hue, and nowhere but in the aesthetic materials called sounds do we find an intrinsic order of pitch established. We may use abstract terms such as value in its technical meaning for painters, and say that as color-value is higher or lower, so pitches are higher and lower; but here the confusion of the parallel is obvious and the work mostly of words. What we mean by high in pitch depends entirely on the meaning of pitch itself, which simply is this specific way in which sounds differ from each other more or less, and in which colors do not, the way in which a high note is above a lower note, not the way in which a high color value is above a lower one of the same or another hue. For this last is a difference in what is usually, but after all ambiguously, called saturation, a way of differing peculiar to color not to pitch; so that while there is an analogy between higher and lower color value and louder and softer sounds, there is an equally good analogy, perhaps a better one, between higher and lower color-value and differences in timbre, the difference, for example, between brass and strings, and only a rather faint analogy between pitch differences and differences in color-values. Even these analogies find little but abstract words to base themselves upon, words which refer to abstracted aspects of what in reality are full concrete qualities, the abstraction being sometimes useful enough to make a comparison, and forceful and enlightening enough as indicating in both fields genuine structural possibilities, but as applied to the materials themselves and their specific intrinsic orders established by their unique qualitative specificity with which we are all so familiar, only analogies, which, since there is no common principle involved, no identity of these two structural modes of variation, but only the fact that in both cases the variations are ordered, lead almost inevitably to confusion and often to actual error.

When we come to lines and space-forms, the intrinsically ordering feature is harder to name, but is after all clear enough except that it is two-fold. We have two principles, which we may call that of simple extension or extendedness itself—shape perhaps is the best term—and that of geometrical order, which permits what we call different perspectives of the same spatial configuration, such different perspectives being often not merely geometrically correlated but apparent to vision as the same. While the geometrical identity may remain, however, a change in perspective may result in such great changes in the spatial appearance that for vision there is no identity recognizable, but only a difference. It will be necessary to explain the two principles and differentiate them not only from each other but from other meanings suggested by the terms we seem forced to employ. But mathematics is, in its strictly geometrical, non-analytical methods, at least in part visually intuitive, and we have therefore to seek the intrinsic orders of the aesthetic materials of spatial form not only in obvious appearances but in the mathematical nature of spatial order. So far as we can give any clear account of all this, it is to be deferred to a later chapter. For the present we may be content with illustrations that suggest the difficulties.

A shift in perspective makes the circular elliptical, the vertical horizontal, and so on. But also the eye sometimes sees the elliptical as circular, sometimes not. Thus the character of shapes and lines may or may not vary while the strictly geometrical order remains the same, as a mathematically defined conic section may in limiting cases be a line or a point, and still possess all its geometrical order and the corresponding properties. So too lines or surfaces or solids lose none of their mathematically ordered properties by being revolved through angles or referred to a new system of coördinates or moved to greater distances or projected upon planes or solids at various angles. But for aesthetic perception such shifts are often all-important. A circle is one shape, an ellipse another. A group of horizontal parallels is one appearance, a group of vertical parallels another. Shapes and directions and sizes are absolute for our sight and not to be confounded with one another simply because geometrically they may be mere transformations in reference not affecting intrinsic mathematical order or structure.

In fact spatial form itself is one of the striking illustrations that any beauty is absolutely its unique self only in relation to the perceiving subject, his spatial orientation and habits in general, and his space location in particular. But for such a subject, so constituted and placed, the spatial characters of objects and their visible beauty are what they are uniquely and absolutely. Objects are of one specific size and shape and proportion, they lie in one direction, and the lines themselves have the direction they have and no other. Obviously the unique and intrinsic ordering quality and structural principles of spatial form are a complex and difficult matter, but we have at least seen that they are present, and their uniqueness is plain. Colors have as hues neither shape nor direction but only hue, sounds may move in space and time, but only sounds have pitch, and pitch itself has neither dimensions nor shape nor direction, nor is even duration of sound its actual intrinsic quality. Thus we have marked and distinguished from one another these three orders of variation, each intrinsic to its own realm.

D. W. GOTSHALK

Form [1]

I. Art and Form

FINE ART AT ITS BEST, we might say, is a selection, refinement, and vivification for intrinsic attention of perceptible material aspects of nature and the social world. It selects and refines these material aspects so that we are given a purified revelation of their perceptual properties, possibilities, and values on the aesthetic level. But we might equally say that fine art at its best is a selection, refinement, and vivification for intrinsic attention of perceptible unities or forms. In ordinary experience we usually perceive only confused and fragmented unities. Rarely do things or scenes, people or deeds, stand forth in highly organized and seemingly self-complete connections. In works of art, however, all this is shown abundantly. The unities of the world are reconstructed in miniature, so that we apprehend in ideal simplicity formal properties and values usually evident only obscurely, if at all, in ordinary experience. So much is this the case that fine art is often described as pre-eminently concerned with unity or form. Fine art is a process of introducing a certain novel fineness of form into the welter of incoherent fragments that enter our experience. Such a view is, of course, oversimple as a complete theory of fine art. But it does point to one of the salient achievements of art and to one of the basic aspects of the public object.

Works of art are highly unified entities. To begin with, they are space-time systems. Works of art exhibit togetherness in space and successiveness in time. In the so-called "static" arts of painting, sculpture, and architecture, the space is most highly organized. But the works of these arts also exist in time, sometimes briefly but often for long historical epochs. In the so-called "dynamic" arts of music, the dance, and literature the time is most intricately organized. But the works of these arts also exist in space, and

---

[1] From D. W. Gotshalk, *Art and the Social Order* (Chicago: University of Chicago Press, 1947), pp. 108–126. Reprinted by permission. (Eds.)

sometimes, as in group dancing and in the acted drama, the space is extensively organized. Besides space and time, causality and teleology are present in works of art. The most obvious illustrations of cause-effect and telic structure are in the representational arts, especially opera, the dance, the drama, the novel, and the short story, where represented actions are depicted as in causal and telic patterns. But we shall find numerous other instances of causality and teleology in artistic creations.

Space and time, causality and teleology, however, are universal forms. They are the structure of all existence, not merely of works of art. Space and time are the bounding forms of the entire world of events and things; causality is as ubiquitous as events; and teleology, at least in the sense of self-determinacy, is as world-wide as continuants or things.[2] In its uniqueness, artistic form is clearly more than mere spatiotemporal, causo-telic structure. Artistic form employs these universal cosmic forms, and, separately or together, they constitute the general framework of works of art as they do of all other entities. But in its specific character artistic form at its best is rather a purification and vivification on a small scale of these cosmic forms in the direction of added intrinsic perceptual interest. It is enhanced spatiotemporal, causo-telic structure, the form of the world reconstructed and heightened in a certain area for multiple aesthetic effects.

II. Principles of Artistic Form

By what principles does the artist transcend "nature" and enhance existential structure in the direction of greater intrinsic perceptual interest? There are a number of these principles. Harmony is one of them. Two items together in space, for example, which also harmonize with each other are much more closely and complexly united for perception than are two such items which are merely spatially coexistent. And this is also true of two items successive in time, or of items connected causally or teleologically. As a principle of enhancing existential unity, harmony may be secured by two methods. The first is repetition or recurrence of so-called "complete similars," e.g., separated areas of green of the same value and intensity in a painting, successive tonic chords in a musical figure, a pointed-arch form repeated in a building, the repetition at a later stage of an earlier action in a drama. The second method of securing harmony is partial similarity, e.g., vigorous colors and vigorous lines in a painting, a tonic succeeded by its fifth in a musical figure, a smaller triforium arcade surmounting the lower larger arcade, an action in a later part of a drama similar in motivation but otherwise very different from an earlier action. Gradation, a green surface,

---

[2] D. W. Gotshalk, *Structure and Reality* (New York: Dial Press, 1937), chaps. iv, v, vi.

for example, with ever so slight differences in "value" or intensity between adjacent areas of the green; modulation, changing to a new musical key through a passage retaining something of the old key; theme and variation, restating a color, shape, line, or musical figure in various guises, are three well-known methods of linking diverse items by partial similarity and thereby attaining a harmony.

Balance is a second principle for building enhanced existential unity. Like harmony, balance can be secured by two methods. The first is by symmetry, the balance of so-called "similars," e.g., two equal and similar groups of figures converging toward the central figures in a late medieval Madonna and child or two similarly dressed dancers of equal stature approaching each other from opposite sides of the stage and executing the same pattern of movement. The second type of balance is secured by asymmetry, the balance of so-called "dissimilars," e.g., good and evil forces in a drama, theme and countertheme in a musical composition, a small compact group of figures on one side of a painting and a larger, looser group on the other side converging toward an area off center, as in Giotto's "Bewailing of Christ" (Arena Chapel, Padua).

Harmony achieves unity by recurrence, by items echoing each other partly or wholly, sometimes again and again, throughout a work. Balance achieves unity by contrast, by items opposing and equilibrizing each other. The opposing items form a system of complementary and neutralizing tensions, resulting in a complete and stable unity. Abstractly, balance and harmony are the reverse of each other. Balance emphasizes diversity in unity, and harmony emphasizes unity in diversity. Nevertheless, harmony and balance are effective collaborators and are often found together in works of art. A musical composition may exhibit numerous balances and harmonies—a balance of melody and countermelody or of theme and theme or of section and section, a harmony of tones within a melody or theme, a recurrence of a melody or theme or section. In combination, however, either harmony or balance tends to dominate over the other. In general, harmony tends to dominate in the so-called "temporal" arts, and balance in the so-called "spatial" arts. The temporal arts are by nature dynamic; and the tranquilizing principle of harmony tends to give them a stability and firmness of form which both amplifies and steadies for perception their intrinsically dynamic nature. On the other hand, the spatial arts are by nature static; and balance, by throwing opposites against one another, tends to give these arts a dynamic power which adds vitality to their form and enlivens their intrinsically static nature. Music and poetry are par excellence the arts of harmony, while painting, sculpture, and architecture are par excellence the arts of balance.

A very important principle of artistic form arising from a collaboration of balance and harmony or recurrence is rhythm. A rhythm is an organization of materials so that they possess or suggest patterned movement. It may be achieved in numerous ways, e.g., by quantities (long-short, large-small) distributed over the material in space or time, or by accents (beats, emphases) similarly distributed, or by both. The material may be colors, lines, shapes, tones, dance-movements, word-syllables. In any case the quantities or accents or whatever are so distributed that the material falls into measures either in the conventional sense, such as the ONE-two of a march rhythm, or in the sense of "figures," such as the up-and-down thrust of a horizontal, zigzag line. Regular rhythm is the occurrence in sequence of measures that are alike or only slightly different. It is achieved by repetition or by recurrence of the "same" measure pattern. Irregular rhythm is the occurrence in sequence of measures of greater diversity—e.g., a small zigzag, followed by a long curved line, followed by a large zigzag, etc. It is achieved by the occurrence of measure patterns that are very diverse. But occurrence in sequence of measures of some sort, or recurrence of measure, is a basic trait of all rhythms organizing artistic creations, since a single measure is never extensive enough to constitute any but a fragmentary or negligible work of art.

Balance, however, is as fundamental in rhythm as is harmony or recurrence of measure. Balance exists primarily within the measure, as recurrence exists between measures. In most ordinary measures the balance is asymmetrical. Thus in accentual rhythm the ordinary measure is usually a combination of accent and balancing unaccent or unaccents: ONE-two, ONE-two-three, one-TWO, one-two-THREE, and so on. The accented item receives more stress than the unaccented item or items. But this greater stress is offset by the greater relaxation of the nonstressed or unaccented item or items. There is a balance within the measure of stress-relaxation or relaxation-stress. A similar analysis would apply to rhythm based on quantity, where the balance within the measure would be a balance of speed and delay, short and long. Incidentally, the peculiar balancing of items within the measure accounts for the characteristic phrasing and pulsation of a rhythmic unit. Thus rhythm is a combination of balance and recurrence. Balance is primarily the internal principle of the measure. Recurrence of measure is the principle of the larger measured movement.

A third major principle of artistic organization is the principle of centrality. This principle is employed when an ensemble of items is so connected that one item or group is given aesthetic dominance over the others which remain important but subordinate to it, e.g., Giotto's "Madonna Enthroned" (Uffizi Gallery, Florence) with its dominant mother and child; the statuary in the east pediment of the Temple of Zeus (Olympia) with its dominant figure of Zeus. This principle may govern the form of details as well as the form of an entire work. In a musical figure a certain tone or chord may dominate over the others, e.g., the chord for oboes in the third measure of the four-measure figure that opens Wagner's *Tristan* Prelude. As a principle part or whole, however, centrality is not to be confused with mere spatial or temporal centrality. In the Giotto and the Greek work cited above, it is true, the Madonna and the Zeus are at the spatial mid-point of the ensemble. But centrality even in the spatial arts can be attained without this. For example, in Giotto's "Bewailing of Christ," the center of the composition, toward which everything else in the picture converges, is the head of the reclining Christ, which is located to the left of the spatial mid-point of the fresco. Centrality means aesthetic centrality, confluence of perceptual interest to, or dominance of perceptual interest at, a point. Spatial or temporal centrality may promote this but it not necessarily identical with it. Other ways of promoting it are to endow an item with greater size or fuller embellishment or intenser color or superior expressive power and dramatic significance, or to make it the focus of subordinate harmonies, balances, and rhythms.

In some works of art centrality seems to be totally absent. These works have no high spot, no focal point. Such works may be constructed solely of certain harmonies or balances or rhythms as a stylized relief in which reiteration or rhythmic recurrence of the "same" figure is the chief formal principle. Compositions lacking centrality, however, may differ from such stylized works by unfolding not a series of similar figures but a single unstylized idea, pattern, or figure. A short story may have neither a dominant high point nor a balance or recurrence of similars. It may merely reveal progressively and without points of emphasis a character, a dilemma, a mood, or a situation. Bit by bit the composition may evolve a pattern or expression in which everything used is needed but nothing is merely repeated or balanced or markedly outstanding. Such compositions seem to require the recognition of a principle of organization different not only from centrality but also from harmony and balance. This new principle might be called the "principle of development," and its most striking illustrations are in the temporal arts, where the elements of a work are set in a pattern of directional change and unified as successive steps in a progression.

This principle may be combined with harmony, balance, and centrality in varying degrees, e.g., in a drama. But it is distinct from them. Thus it is distinct from harmony. Harmony is based on repetition, on partial or complete reiteration of the similar. It is a harking backward, not a growth—a staying within the bounds of the past and the previous. Development is based on novelty, on partial or complete advance to the nonsimilar. It is a going forward, a growth, a leaving behind of the past and the previous. Development is also different from balance. Balance is based on equilibrium, on the meeting and neutralizing of opposites, on deadlock and stabilization. Development is based on disequilibrium, on the transforming of opposites into directional movement, on progression and the conversion of the primarily static into the primarily progressive. Finally, development is unlike centrality. Centrality is based on hierarchical order, on a superordination and subordination of items, on dominance. But the basis of development is an arrangement of items as prior and posterior, not as superior and inferior. It is based on sequence, not on rank, and may be carried forward solely by equals, as in the example cited, without the aid of items markedly superior or inferior in rank.

III. Two Levels of Form

The four principles of harmony, balance, centrality, and development, with their associates and derivatives—recurrence, similarity, gradation, variation, modulation, symmetry, contrast, opposition, equilibrium, rhythm, measure, dominance, climax, hierarchy, and progression—are probably the chief formal principles used by the imagination of artists for the purification and enhancement of existential structure in works of art.[3] Employing these principles, artists build up perceptually vivid spatial, temporal, causal, and telic unities in the details and the over-all designs of their works.

Before considering this achievement, it should be noted that artists may use the four major principles of design and their associates and derivatives on two levels: the presentational and the representational. In a painting there may be a harmony or balance between colors or shapes or lines. But there may also be a harmony or balance between suggested actions or attitudes or between represented personages within a scene or between the glint in the eye and the gesture of an arm of a single represented personage. The representational side of the painting may be as composed, as harmonized, as balanced, as are the lines or shapes or colors. Centrality and development may be similarly employed on the two levels. In a statute there may be a dominance of a certain shape over others, but there may also be a dominance of a certain represented attitude. In Rodin's "La Pensée" (Musée Rodin, Paris), the head shape is not only dominant over the block, but the reflective attitude represented in the face is dominant in the head and central to the statue. As to development, it may appear merely on the presentational

---

[3] *Cf.* DeWitt Parker, *The Analysis of Art* (New Haven: Yale University Press, 1926), chap. ii; D. W. Prall, *Aesthetic Analysis* (New York: Thomas Y. Crowell Co., 1936), chaps. ii, iii, iv; T. M. Greene, *The Arts and the Art of Criticism* (Princeton, N.J.: Princeton University Press, 1940), chap. vii ff.; S. C. Pepper, *Aesthetic Quality* (New York: Charles Scribner's Sons, 1937, 1938), chaps. v–viii; Leo Stein, *ABC of Aesthetics* (New York: Boni & Liveright, 1927), chaps. xii, xiii. The preceding section is greatly in debt to all these works but particularly to the excellent chapter in Parker's *Analysis of Art*.

level as in the progressive unfolding of an abstract dance pattern or a pattern of musical sounds. But it may equally appear on the representational level in the progressive unfolding of a character, a course of action, or an idea in a drama, an opera, or a novel.

This fact—the operation on two levels of the principles of design—is important not merely for understanding the nature of artistic form but also for the light it throws on the problem of representation in fine art. Writers who have contended that the sole business of art is the creation of form have sometimes maintained that representation is irrelevant to art. But if representation itself is a field for the operation of the principles of form, it would seem contradictory to call representation irrelevant to art, at least on a theory that described the business of art as the creation of form. If the operation of formal principles on the representational level necessarily conflicted with their use on the presentational level, the case might be different. But this is not true. In a painting, such as Renoir's "Three Bathers" (Cleveland Museum of Art), a balanced organization of expressive subject matter may amplify, prolong, and enrich the balanced organization of colors, lines, and planes; and the balanced organization of colors, lines, and planes may give sensuous depth, complexity, and enlargement to the balanced organization of expressive subject matter. It is, indeed, a question as to whether the operation of formal principles on the representational level is not absolutely necessary to enable such arts as painting and sculpture to compete in formal power with such an art as music, as formalists wish them to do. After describing the marvelous complexity of musical form, Abell writes: "To attain a similar richness, painting and sculpture must definitely avoid abstraction. Only when they employ their innate resources of spontaneously evoked meanings do they present a sufficient variety of elements, a sufficient range and complexity of relations, to make possible the achievement of forms worthy to compare with symphonic music in exalted beauty." [4]

The chief merits of the polemics of formalists such as Clive Bell and Roger Fry have been to call greater attention to "abstract" or presentational form and to deprecate nonaesthetic sentimental "life"-attitudes toward subject matter, especially in painting. But to restrict art to abstract form and to dismiss representation as irrelevant to art because it may be used to indulge sentimental nonaesthetic life-attitudes, as Bell does,[5] is, to put it mildly, a paradoxical procedure. Bell admits, it is true, that the representation of the third dimension or of deep space in painting gives opportunity for greater formal realizations and is therefore permissible. Here would seem to be the principle to hold to. In the end the basic artistic consideration regarding

---

[4] W. Abell, *Representation and Form* (New York: Charles Scribner's Sons, 1936), p. 168.
[5] Clive Bell, *Art* (London: Chatto & Windus, 1914), p. 225.

representation in art is certainly this: Does the introduction of representation into art permit the creation of works which provide richer aesthetic experiences? And even if we accept the formalist restriction of aesthetic experience to the experience of form, the answer would seem to be affirmative. Representation opens a vast field for the operation of formal principles, and this operation can be synchronized with the operation of these principles on the merely abstract or presentational level, so that there is not merely an extension but also an enrichment all around of the form of the work of art.

IV. Over-All Design

What is to be understood by "artistic form" taken as a dimension of the public object? Artistic form in this sense might be described as the system of relations uniting the materials of the public object into a perceptual whole or the system of patterns pervading and organizing the presentational and representational levels of the materials of a work of art. This will be its primary descriptive meaning in our account. We have, however, described artistic form at its best in different language, viz., as enhanced existential form. It is the form of all material existence—space, time, causality, teleology, one or all—transformed in a certain area by the application of such principles as harmony, balance, centrality, development, and their associates and derivatives. More precisely, artistic form at its best is such a unification of materials that all the conflicting ramifications and loose ends of ordinary existential patterns are eliminated and a certain systematic self-completeness is installed in the work of art. Every material item is connected so subtly and amply with other material items that the work of art becomes for perception a tiny island universe. Such a complex, thoroughgoing, and self-complete unity of the materials is, of course, an ideal not necessarily exemplified by every work of art, and even flagrantly violated by some works of art which are of very great merit in other respects.

The descriptive meaning of artistic form as the total system of relations in the materials of the work of art is not to be confused with two other meanings. The first is pattern—the pattern of colors or lines in a painting, the pattern of shapes or masses in a statue or a building, the pattern of words or actions in a novel, poem, drama, or opera. Such patterns are true forms, but they are only fragments of artistic form in our sense. Artistic form is rather the system of such patterns found in any given creation. The second meaning defines artistic form as the total body of relations in a work of art. Artistic form includes not only the total system of relations of the materials but also the relation of this system to expression, function, and materials, and the relation of these dimensions to each other and to the system of material relations. Artistic form is the interdimensional system of relations as well as a dimension of the public object.

In our sense, artistic form is a dimension only and is exactly coextensive with the other dimensions, e.g., the dimension of material. Artistic materials, as we have seen, have a sensory-intuitive and an imaginative-intellectual side as well as an affective side, which is evident upon sensory intuition (non-"associational" reaction) and fully disclosed upon imaginative intellection ("associational" reaction). When artistic materials are placed in a composition and the sensory-intuitive-affective side of them is composed by rhythm, harmony, development, and so on, the work of art presents certain relations or relational patterns, and these are what we have called "artistic form on the presentational level." When the imaginative-intellectual-affective or associational side of the material is similarly composed and its suggestions or connotations are organized into a coherent and meaningful system, the work of art represents, as well as presents, certain relations or relational patterns, namely, relations or patterns in the "subject" represented; and these are what we have called "artistic form on the representational level." Thus artistic form as the system of relations pervading the presentational and representational levels of a work of art has a point-for-point correspondence to the multiple sides of artistic materials. It is simply the organization installed in the major perceptual aspects of these materials, and it extends only so far as and in the degree that, these aspects are composed into definite features of the artistic creation.

As the system of patterns pervading the presentational and representational levels of a work of art, artistic form might be called over-all form or over-all design. The magnitude of this design will vary with the artistic creation. In a simple work devoid of definite representational form or content, such as an abstract two-dimensional painting, the basic over-all design will be merely the pattern of lines, shapes, and colors as integrating into a unitary scheme. In a simple work with definite representational form and content, such as a short story by Bret Harte or Poe, the basic over-all design will be the pattern of incidents, characters, and moods, together with such presentational patterns as have been contrived by placing words in relations governed by rhythm, balance, recurrence, and similar formal principles. In a complex work of art the detailed wealth of relations constituting the over-all design may stagger comprehension. In the first movement of a great symphony the themes and the relation of the other sections as expositions, extensions, variations, developments, and repetitions of these themes may become clear upon careful study and hearing. But the detailed relationships within the components of the movement, even the total rhythmic, melodic, harmonic, coloristic, and dynamic relations between the tones and chords of the themes, may be grasped only in the most summary and incomplete fashion by all except the most expert and tenacious musical analyst.

One of the delightful paradoxes of great art, however, is that, with all the dense and infinite complexity of design it frequently has, it tends, upon familiarity, to create an impression of singular formal simplicity. The reason for this is that the highly complex detailed orders in great works, although they are the basis of the works' extraordinary formal strength, are usually organized by the imagination of the artist as incidental strands within large sections. They are like the threads in a tapestry, whose individual convolutions elude us, although the broad design of the tapestry itself seems perfectly clear. In each case microscopic details are fused into a few macroscopic unities, such as the musical themes and sections just mentioned; the fine complexity becomes absorbed in the larger simplicities and is grasped in terms of these simplicities instead of in terms of its own separate and perplexing diversity.

The study of the over-all design of particular works of art belongs to history and criticism, not to philosophical analysis. But a few additional general remarks about over-all design may not be out of place before we consider more specifically its characteristics and uses as a dimension of the public object.

V. Type Designs

Every over-all design, simple or complex, is as individual and unique as the work of art possessing it. To reproduce the design of a picture by Tintoretto, one would have to copy the shapes and lines and colors in the various patterns given them by the painter and the personages represented in their dramatic relationships, since these also enter into the total structure put there by the artist. Change a shape, substitute in Tintoretto's "Miracle of the Slave" or "Miracle of St. Mark" (Academy, Venice) a tiny rigid body for the great St. Mark, and the pattern of the shapes is perceptibly altered. Change a personage, substitute Christ for the executioner, and the structure of the drama is perceptibly altered. To reproduce the over-all design of a work with absolute completeness, one must reproduce the work itself with absolute completeness. To alter any feature is immediately to alter the presentational or representational relations radiating from that feature and so to alter the precise over-all design that the artist has given to his work.

Nevertheless, designs can be considered at a certain level of abstraction as mere schemata, or, more exactly, patterns within designs can be so regarded. In this sense the "same" design may occur again and again in the works of an artist. The swirl pattern in the "Miracle of St. Mark" recurs in one form or another in innumerable Tintoretto compositions. Artists generally tend to reuse similar patterns. As an artist matures, he develops a characteristic manner of organizing the aspects of his materials. "Each artist creates his own type of co-ordination, it is special to himself, it is his own personal language." [6] The artist uses this personal method of co-ordination again and again, usually suitably varied, in diverse works. The terse, monumentally simple linear patterns of Giotto; the vertically elongated shape patterns of El Greco; the dense, weighty, color rhythms of the later Titian, are repeated by these artists in different pictures with endless modifications. Similar type patterns are used by creators in the other arts. A person may recognize an excerpt from a poem as a quotation from Whitman or Dante by the rhythm of the language or by other formal features of the verse. A person may equally recognize a piece of music as by Bach or Beethoven or Wagner by its rhythmic, melodic, or harmonic structure. The characteristic form traits that artists impart to their diverse individual designs, it is true, often change considerably over time. Historians speak of the early, middle, and late manner of a Titian, a Beethoven, or a Wagner. An artist's manner of construction, like any habit, may be discarded for a new one or for a very different one. Still it is usually possible to abstract a set of recurrent formal traits from some group of any great artist's individual designs. Manners may change, but a manner is a manner and results in a type of form.[7]

Type patterns, however, include much more than type forms peculiar to individual artists. Indeed, the most familiar of all type patterns are traditional forms, often obscure in origin, that are employed equally in the work of numerous artists. Illustrations are the sonnet and ballad, the minuet and mazurka, the sonata and fugue and *passacaglia* and rondo, the orders of Greek architecture, the canons of Greek sculpture, the formal conventions of Byzantine or Japanese painting.

Type designs, individual and traditional, are important to all concerned with the arts. To the ordinary perceptive person they can be the starting-point of an apprehension of the total individual design of a creation. The swirl of a Tintoretto, the *terza rima* of a Dante, the sonata form of the first movement of a Haydn symphony, can be tools for entering more fully into the over-all design and apprehending it in great detail. They supply a spacious frame which can be clothed in the flesh and blood of the individual form. To be sure, type patterns can be used by percipients as mere tags of identification and can become the dead ends of devitalized perception instead

---

[6] Vernon Blake, *The Art and Craft of Drawing* (London: Oxford University Press, 1927), p. 65.

[7] Ernest Newman, *The Unconscious Beethoven* (New York: Alfred A. Knopf, 1927), is a good example of an interesting detailed study of a creative artist's peculiar habits and unconscious traits of construction.

of tools to implement detailed appreciation. Often they are no more than this in so-called "appreciation courses" in colleges. But, if type patterns are used as instrumentalities instead of as finalities and as methods for starting on the quest of an over-all design, they can open up the general outlay of an individual structure and become the dim beginnings of aesthetic wisdom regarding form.

The critic and the historian of art can also make good use of type designs. Not only can these designs serve as starting-points for that full appreciation of form which should precede the distinctive critical and historical tasks, they can also be used in the critical and historical tasks themselves.

The critic, for example, can use type patterns as a basis for judging the originality of an artist. Has this artist merely borrowed a stencil from tradition and filled it with timely commonplaces or inconsequential novelties? Has he given new and glowing life to a traditional form that seemed played out and dead before he revived it? Has he invented a powerful type form peculiarly his own? Often the difference between a genius and a hack is revealed more clearly in the difference of the handling of a traditional type pattern or in the difference of strength of their individual type patterns than in any other formal difference or in any differences in the material, expressive, or functional features of their works.

As to the historian of art, he can use type patterns as tools of clarification and correlation of individual designs. A type pattern, such as a sonata or an epic, is a schema of recurrent formal traits. In his analysis of form, the main business of the historian, I believe, is the analysis of concrete forms, not of schemata. But type patterns, as schemata of recurrent formal traits, can highlight generic formal features of concrete forms and formal similarities between different concrete forms. The general pattern of the sonata can help to point up certain general properties of a Beethoven or a Mozart sonata and supply a language in terms of which to compare the individual design of this Beethoven sonata with that, or this Mozart sonata with this Beethoven sonata. Thus, while the analysis of type patterns is not the main concern of the historian, these patterns can supply bases for the clarification and correlation of individual designs, which is his main business, and so make a substantial contribution to his analysis of form.

Type patterns, finally, can be of considerable service to the creative artist. To the apprentice in an art, traditional type patterns can provide good discipline. They can require him to hew to a line while allowing him a certain freedom of invention of details. They can teach him general conceptions of artistic ordering and can help to inculcate precision and a certain amount of elementary technical facility. To the alert apprentice they can even be means to the discovery of new forms by stirring his imagination to conceive alternatives and variants of traditional forms.

To the mature artist, traditional type patterns can equally be an asset. Such types as the ode and ballad and prose epic in literature or the sonata and theme and variations and fugue in music can serve as fruitful bases of original productions. A certain superior richness of inventive imagination and a certain temperament are probably required to create works in such traditional forms that are outstanding and permanently valuable. But when artists with these qualities do take over these forms, they can usually make something very fine out of them. In literature there have been myriad examples of artists of this sort from the Greek poets to Fielding and Coleridge and Keats. In music, Bach is an obvious example. "Bach was one of the most conventional composers who ever existed. He accepted forms and formulas ready-made from his predecessors, chiefly German and Italian, but French and English also, and he was none the worse for it, because he succeeded, in spite of these self-imposed blinkers to his fancy, in making something greater out of precedent than it had ever been before." [8] An artist less virile than Bach, or a slavish copyist who took traditional type patterns as rigid schemata and traditional examples as absolute models, would be unlikely to turn traditional forms to very significant account. But an artist who extracted their principles, adapted them to his own needs, and filled them with rich new matter from his own abundant fancy would be perennially able to find them profitable.

Besides traditional forms, individual type patterns or the characteristic formal twists that artists employ in designing their works have an obvious creative usefulness. Ordinarily, these patterns are developed as a consequence of the artist's personality maturing and gaining stability. Their usefulness to the artist is similar to the usefulness of a habit in everyday life. Our habits of walking and running facilitate our everyday responses to stimuli. The individual type patterns of artists, at least as technical "manners" or traits, can facilitate artistic responses to stimuli. They can constitute mechanisms of action ready to cope with creative impulses, and they can enable the artist to ride the crest of his inspiration by supplying devices adequate to his personality that automatically shape the energy going into his work.

It should certainly be added that type patterns, traditional and individual, can be a disadvantage and even a danger to the creative artist. An ambitious apprentice may be handcuffed and ill at ease writing drama in neoclassic patterns or music in seventeenth-century forms and may produce only undistinguished work in these molds. A change to designs of his own invention, adapted to some compelling contemporary purpose, may release unsuspected creative powers, and the young artist may eventually become the founder of

---

[8] Eric Blom, *The Limitations of Music* (New York: Macmillan Co., 1928), p. 114.

a new type of drama or musical form. In the work of a mature artist who lacks fertility of invention, the use of traditional type patterns may not curb his creativity, but it may underline his mediocrity. His Greek-temple banks and memorials, his statues of grand antique design, his facile heroic couplets, or his carefully classical sonatas and fugues may have the slickness of high-grade studio pieces. Flavored by a cool or dulcet personality, they may even have a mild gracious charm. But in the end they will bespeak a feebleness of imagination, and their charm will be clouded by recognition of the hackneyed, derivative, out-of-date, otiose, and irrelevant.

One of the most frequent uses of traditional type forms is as easy short cuts. A veneer of novelty spread upon a tried and true artistic pattern usually produces a very salable product. The monetarily successful hackworks of the great often follow this formula. So do many of the popular songs of the commercial theater, which sell immensely, then vanish immediately. Motion pictures frequently use for plots stereotyped dramatic forms which have been spruced up by novelties of setting and dialogue, by popular actors, and the like. Such works are entertaining when their additions are lively or clever, but they usually do not stand up under close or repeated scrutiny. To the gifted professional artist, traditional type patterns can be a means to quick commercial success but also to quick artistic death or to low-grade creative performance.

Nor are individual type patterns free of disadvantages and perils for the creative artist. A painter such as Corot may hit upon a type of composition warmly approved by the public and, deserting his earlier and more solid work, spend his days repeating his new formula. For any number of reasons the manner of any artist may degenerate into a conscious mannerism or, remaining unconscious, be used too profusely or mechanically. People there are who would gladly do without some of the more synthetic of Haydn's compositions or some of the more pretentious of Liszt's forms. Others would gladly forego some of the patterns of sweet *bambini* of the Della Robbias or some of the clouds of corpulent nudes garnishing the more lush works of Rubens or pupils of Rubens. Every artist—a Bach as well as a Haydn or a Liszt, a Michelangelo as well as a Rubens or a Della Robbia—has a limited set of gestures manifesting his personality and modifying his forms; and no artist has a personality so profoundly complex that these gestures are without danger, upon occasion, of protruding too insistently and, by so doing, marring the aesthetic effectiveness of his forms.

With these remarks about type patterns, their importance to the ordinary perceptive person, the critic, and the historian, and their uses and perils to the creative artist, we must return to the discussion of over-all designs or concrete individual form. Type patterns are partial forms, abstractions from concrete forms. In the public object, it is the concrete form, the total individual system of relations pervading the materials of the work of art, that is artistic form in the fullest sense. What roles does this concrete form have in the public object? What are the chief aesthetic properties and values to be found in it? The correct answers to these questions are similar, I believe, to the answers already given to similar questions regarding materials. In the public object artistic form has instrumental properties and terminal properties. It is related to the other dimensions as means to an end and can have— and in the best works does have—considerable value as instrumental to the other dimensions; and it is itself an aesthetic end and can have—and in the best works does have—considerable terminal value as an end to which the other dimensions are subordinate.

CLIVE BELL

The Aesthetic Hypothesis[1]

LET NO ONE IMAGINE that representation is bad in itself; a realistic form may be as significant, in its place as part of the design, as an abstract. But if a representative form has value, it is as form, not as representation. The representative element in a work of art may or may not be harmful; always it is irrelevant. For, to appreciate a work of art we need to bring with us nothing from life, no knowledge of its ideas and affairs, no familiarity with its emotions. Art transports us from the world of man's activity to a world of aesthetic exaltation. For a moment we are shut off from human interests; our anticipations and memories are arrested; we are lifted above the stream of life. The pure mathematician rapt in his studies knows a state of mind which I take to be similar, if not identical. He feels an emotion for his speculations which arises from no perceived relation between them and the lives of men, but springs, inhuman or superhuman, from the heart of an abstract science. I wonder, sometimes, whether the appreciators of art and of mathematical solutions are not even more closely allied. Before we feel an aesthetic emotion for a combination of forms, do we not perceive intellectually the rightness and necessity of the combination? If we do, it would explain the fact that passing rapidly through a room we recognise a picture to be good, although we cannot say that it has provoked much emo-

---

[1] From Clive Bell, *Art* (London: Chatto & Windus, 1914), Section I, Chap. I. Reprinted by permission. (Eds.)

tion. We seem to have recognised intellectually the rightness of its forms without staying to fix our attention, and collect, as it were, their emotional significance. If this were so, it would be permissible to inquire whether it was the forms themselves or our perception of their rightness and necessity that caused aesthetic emotion. But I do not think I need linger to discuss the matter here. I have been inquiring why certain combinations of forms move us; I should not have travelled by other roads had I inquired, instead, why certain combinations are perceived to be right and necessary, and why our perception of their rightness and necessity is moving. What I have to say is this: the rapt philosopher, and he who contemplates a work of art, inhabit a world with an intense and peculiar significance of its own; that significance is unrelated to the significance of life. In this world the emotions of life find no place. It is a world with emotions of its own.

To appreciate a work of art we need bring with us nothing but a sense of form and colour and a knowledge of three-dimensional space. That bit of knowledge, I admit, is essential to the appreciation of many great works, since many of the most moving forms ever created are in three dimensions. To see a cube or a rhomboid as a flat pattern is to lower its significance, and a sense of three-dimensional space is essential to the full appreciation of most architectural forms. Pictures which would be insignificant if we saw them as flat patterns are profoundly moving because, in fact, we see them as related planes. If the representation of three-dimensional space is to be called "representation," then I agree that there is one kind of representation which is not irrelevant. Also, I agree that along with our feeling for line and colour we must bring with us our knowledge of space if we are to make the most of every kind of form. Nevertheless, there are magnificent designs to an appreciation of which this knowledge is not necessary: so, though it is not irrelevant to the appreciation of some works of art it is not essential to the appreciation of all. What we must say is that the representation of three-dimensional space is neither irrelevant nor essential to all art, and that every other sort of representation is irrelevant.

That there is an irrelevant representative or descriptive element in many great works of art is not in the least surprising. Why it is not surprising I shall try to show elsewhere. Representation is not of necessity baneful, and highly realistic forms may be extremely significant. Very often, however, representation is a sign of weakness in an artist. A painter too feeble to create forms that provoke more than a little aesthetic emotion will try to eke that little out by suggesting the emotions of life. To evoke the emotions of life he must use representation. Thus a man will paint an execution, and, fearing to miss with his first barrel of significant form, will try to hit with his second by raising an emotion of fear or pity. But if in the artist an inclination to play upon the emotions of life is often the sign of a flickering inspiration, in the spectator a tendency to seek, behind form, the emotions of life is a sign of defective sensibility always. It means that his aesthetic emotions are weak or, at any rate, imperfect. Before a work of art people who feel little or no emotion for pure form find themselves at a loss. They are deaf men at a concert. They know that they are in the presence of something great, but they lack the power of apprehending it. They know that they ought to feel for it a tremendous emotion, but it happens that the particular kind of emotion it can raise is one that they can feel hardly or not at all. And so they read into the forms of the work those facts and ideas for which they are capable of feeling emotion, and feel for them the emotions that they can feel—the ordinary emotions of life. When confronted by a picture, instinctively they refer back its forms to the world from which they came. They treat created form as though it were imitated form, a picture as though it were a photograph. Instead of going out on the stream of art into a new world of aesthetic experience, they turn a sharp corner and come straight home to the world of human interests. For them the significance of a work of art depends on what they bring to it; no new thing is added to their lives, only the old material is stirred. A good work of visual art carries a person who is capable of appreciating it out of life into ecstasy: to use art as a means to the emotions of life is to use a telescope for reading the news. You will notice that people who cannot feel pure aesthetic emotions remember pictures by their subjects; whereas people who can, as often as not, have no idea what the subject of a picture is. They have never noticed the representative element, and so when they discuss pictures they talk about the shapes of forms and the relations and quantities of colours. Often they can tell by the quality of a single line whether or no a man is a good artist. They are concerned only with lines and colours, their relations and quantities and qualities; but from these they win an emotion more profound and far more sublime than any that can be given by the description of facts and ideas.

This last sentence has a very confident ring—overconfident, some may think. Perhaps I shall be able to justify it, and make my meaning clearer too, if I give an account of my own feelings about music. I am not really musical. I do not understand music well. I find musical form exceedingly difficult to apprehend, and I am sure that the profounder subtleties of harmony and rhythm more often than not escape me. The form of a musical composition must be simple indeed if I am to grasp it honestly. My opinion about music is not worth having. Yet, sometimes, at a concert, though my appreciation of the music is limited and humble, it is pure. Sometimes, though I have a poor understanding, I have a clean palate. Consequently, when I am feeling bright and clear and intent, at the beginning of a concert for instance, when something that I can grasp is being played, I get from music that pure aesthetic emotion that I get from visual art. It is less intense, and the rapture is evanescent; I understand music too ill for music to transport me far into the world of pure aesthetic ecstasy. But at moments I do appreciate music as pure musical form, as sounds combined according to the laws of a mysterious necessity, as pure art with a tremendous significance of its own and no relation whatever to the significance of life; and in those moments I lose myself in that infinitely sublime state of mind to which pure visual form transports me. How inferior is my normal state of mind at a concert. Tired or perplexed, I let slip my sense of form, my aesthetic emotion collapses, and I begin weaving into the harmonies, that I cannot grasp, the ideas of life. Incapable of feeling the austere emotions of art, I begin to read into the musical forms human emotions of terror and mystery, love and hate, and spend the minutes, pleasantly enough, in a world of turbid and inferior feeling. At such times, were the grossest pieces of onomatopoeic representation—the song of a bird, the galloping of horses, the cries of children, or the laughing of demons—to be introduced into the symphony, I should not be offended. Very likely I should be pleased; they would afford new points of departure for new trains of romantic feeling or heroic thought. I know very well what has happened. I have been using art as a means to the emotions of life and reading into it the ideas of life. I have been cutting blocks with a razor. I have tumbled from the superb peaks of aesthetic exaltation to the snug foothills of warm humanity. It is a jolly country. No one need be ashamed of enjoying himself there. Only no one who has ever been on the heights can help feeling a little crestfallen in the cosy valleys. And let no one imagine, because he has made merry in the warm tilth and quaint nooks of romance, that he can even guess at the austere and thrilling raptures of those who have climbed the cold, white peaks of art.

ARNOLD ISENBERG

Perception, Meaning, and the Subject-Matter of Art[1]

I PROPOSE, IN THESE pages, to examine the distinction that is drawn between the content and the form of a work of art—a distinction with

[1] Arnold Isenberg, "Perception, Meaning, and the Subject-Matter of Art," *The Journal of Philosophy*, XLI (1944), 561–575. Reprinted by permission. (Eds.)

which all are dissatisfied but no one, apparently, is ready to dispense. Commonly, it is given a psychological significance—for example, by Franz Boas: "It is essential to bear in mind the twofold source of artistic effect, the one based on form alone, the other on ideas associated with form." [2] This alludes to the ordinary classification of art objects as formal and representative; but the *principle* of classification is extraordinary. A composition is based on the repetition of a spiral motive, or on a scheme of interlocking lozenges, or on elements placed with exact symmetry on a rectangular field; in another there appears a mountain, a face, a tree. The first is called an abstract or pure design; in the second, called a representation, we find—I will not say a *familiar* form because the abstract figure is perhaps familiar in its way —the form which is characteristic of a familiar sort of object or situation lying about us in the world. Now comparing the rug on the floor with the picture on the wall, we are instantly aware of a difference which would seem to be *anterior* in the order of obviousness to the categories of psychology; and a child, we might suppose, who should be asked to explain the difference between these objects would wonder why they should be expected to be *alike*—so great is the disparity of visible form. Yet Boas has taken no account of this disparity. He finds that the examples are in one respect similar, since each presents a certain form to the eye, but that there is added something to the second in the nature of a contribution which it extorts from the mind; and it is implied that if this increment were somehow obviated, there would remain no fundamental difference to be marked. This implication is made explicit, in an essay designed to establish the esthetic significance of subject-matter, by Professor Walter Abell:

> Were we to limit painting and sculpture to elements provided in complete form by vision, then color, line, shape, and size would be the only elements available to them. . . . [Subject-matter] cannot be legitimately excluded unless we wish to limit ourselves to visual stimuli uninterpreted by *any* of their meanings, in which case we should have to restrict art to the sphere of geometrical pattern.[3]

If painting and sculpture, in short, were perfectly formal, they would be perfectly abstract.

Appreciation is an activity that runs its course within the psychological framework. The question must therefore arise, what functions or faculties does it call into play; and what, in particular, is the rôle of direct perception on the one hand and of meaning, association, or thought on the other? There has also existed a controversy, from an early time, between the *Form-aesthetiker,* as Fechner called them, and the *Inhaltsaesthetiker,* over the

---

[2] *Primitive Art,* p. 13.
[3] *Representation and Form,* pp. 97–98.

element of subject-matter in the arts. The singular feature of the analysis from which I have quoted is that it combines the two issues by assuming that subject-matter is imported through associative processes into the experience of art. It affirms the importance of the representative factor in art and, simultaneously, of the higher mental action in esthetic experience. (Modern formalism joins issue very squarely on this ground, rejecting the double thesis in a single breath.[4]) Originating within the limits of a psychology of consciousness, it tends to adopt an account of meaning in terms of sensory datum and associated image; but the same assumption has been couched in the terminology of behaviorism and in quasi-epistemological terms like "designation," "construction," and "reference." [5] It will not be material to my argument what theory of interpretation we may choose to endorse.

I shall argue that an all but complete analysis of "subject-matter" can be given by a *presentational* esthetic; and that we may, therefore, continue to identify the esthetic with the immediate without submitting to the reductions of formalism. It will be convenient to press this thesis in a one-sided fashion, leaving the necessary qualifications to the end.

I must give notice that I shall be unable to propose definitions that will satisfy *every* element in the complicated usage of our leading terms. "Form" we may here define with Santayana as "sensuous elements in combination."

§ *1*

We have a picture in which the moon is seen shining through leaves upon figures in a garden. If associations can be said to contribute to the effect of this scene, they must be called upon to bring the absent into the present—to render certain ingredients available that are not directly given to sense. But the moon could not be one of these, because it is already included within the direct impression. Nor any of these leaves—for the same reason; and I believe that we can pronounce them *sere* or *fragile* with a certainty equal to that with which we can say that they are *yellow* or *symmetrical*. In fact, if I may say so, the whole picture is already in the picture: since there is no question of a response on our part to outlying extensions of the picture landscape, there can be no need that these extensions (which do not even exist) should be made known to us.

It will be said that there are no leaves in the picture and no moon, but a collection of shapes—a geometrical pattern. Now nothing that exists in two

---

[4] "To appreciate a work of art we need bring with us nothing from life, no knowledge of its ideas and affairs . . . nothing but a sense of form and color and a knowledge of three-dimensional space." Clive Bell, *Art,* pp. 25–27.

[5] I number among English and American partisans of this view Santayana, Bosanquet, Dewey, Alexander, Ducasse, Parker, Morris, Barnes, Bowers, and others.

dimensions or in three is not a shape and a geometrical pattern; but it may be just as arbitrary as it is accurate to describe it so. A leaf is a geometrical, a botanical, a foliar, and finally a uniquely individualized pattern. But the point is otherwise well taken: there is of course no leaf in the picture but something that looks like a leaf—a leaf-like shape. (Not some *other* shape, be it noted, such as a triangle; nor does the moon reduce itself to a "yellow disk"; nor does the painting as a whole assume the slightest tendency to resemble a composition by Kandinsky.) Not to confuse the "shape" (that is, the sense-datum) with the object, I shall refer to the first, whenever necessary, in quotation marks—as, the "leaf," the "moon."

The inside and the other side, the physical dimensions—in a word, the substance—of the moon finds no place in the representation. Let us therefore turn to the moon itself, which we will imagine ourselves to be admiring. The same associations, be it admitted, which are demanded of us by *this* situation will be demanded by the other. (We must suppose, in the interest of our problem, that the sense-data are exactly alike in the two cases—a condition that is perhaps never fulfilled.) Now it is not essential to the present argument that associations be ruled out of *either* situation: we are concerned with the question of associations only in so far as that question is raised in a *special* form by the topic of artistic representation. Yet it does appear to be just the peculiarity of the esthetic outlook on nature that the normal processes of interpretation are in abeyance for its duration. To *admire* a natural object is to contract one's interest to its appearance; or, conversely, we may say that the appearance, relinquishing its several sign functions, achieves an intrinsic importance; so that precisely that substance which is lacking in the imitation is ignored in the original, where it really exists. All this, to be sure, is more easily said than understood, for the *analysis* of the esthetic attitude is somewhat complicated. But a conception can be sound without being precise, and this is a conception upon which modern writers, with few exceptions, converge, saving their differences for the refinements. When they deal with the esthetic experience *in general,* they find nothing to distinguish it save the aspect of absorption in the immediate. But the subject-matter of *art,* as they insist, is drawn from nature. Do the forms, then, with which in nature we are said to traffic directly become symbolical and referential when they are translated into the experience of art?

The moon is said to be *represented* by a sense-datum, an impression. In the same sense, though less directly, it may be represented by a photograph or a drawing, for on such a figure we may base certain calculations concerning the moon. The function of representation in this sense, I suppose it granted, is utterly antagonistic to esthetic appreciation. There remains only the sense in which the picture of the moon may be said to represent, not the moon itself, but the original impression. But why should the picture need to *represent* the "moon" when *ex hypothesi* it *is* the "moon"? What would in that case account for the ability of the original to act on us as it does? The "moon" as it appears to us this evening is certainly not unique—we have seen the "same thing" before. Yet no one will say that the present impression represents, or recalls, a past impression, much less a painting. The scene being here and now laid out before us with all its elements, there is nothing which recollection is needed to supply. But the same condition is met by the representation. We can not, perhaps, explain why certain cloud forma- tions, hovering before the moon, should affect us with a sense of mystery; but no special problem, surely, is created by the same form (still supposing that it were the same) when it appears in painting.

To treat with a representative is to aim at a principal; but the esthetic datum, artificial or natural, acts for itself alone, and our response is appro- priate not to what the form may stand for but to what the form may *be*. Art, then, in its esthetic capacity, is not representation; and we shall continue to refer to "representations" by that name only in the way that a senator retains his title when he leaves his office. Works of art may indeed retain their *power* of representation in so far as, being connected by a chain of events with various incidents or persons, they can form the basis of an in- ference respecting the latter. The so-called *iconic* emblem, such as a portrait, which bears a certified resemblance to an original, can tell us something about the appearance and character of that original. And this use to which the object lends itself has its familiar satisfactions, more renowned, per- haps, than those of beauty. A portrait of Erasmus possesses an interest which stems from the "subject," as we say, meaning the sitter; but if that interest could be said to contribute to the beauty of the picture, then its beauty would be subject to impairment, e.g., by documentary evidence, which might show that the portrait was spurious. Which is absurd.

Does it follow that we must ignore what undubitably is *in* the picture, an aspect of its form—the human countenance with its moral expression, its smile, the light in the eye? Must we speak only of color areas, volumes, the relationship of planes?

We have by no means exhausted the question of the dependence of ap- preciation upon past experience, for past experience may function in recog- nition as well as in interpretation and recall. The concept of recognition, however, is ambiguous. One is said to have recognized somebody in a crowd. This implies a conviction of that person's physical presence. The act of recognition, in this sense, is predictive: it is equivalent to an act of inference. But it embodies a necessary first stage in which one "recognizes" a typical form, as one might in the case of a portrait; without this the inference would not be possible. I will reserve the term "recognition" for the preliminary act by which we identify a mere impression as belonging by its character to a certain class. This act can occur without its customary sequel, and *does* occur, e.g., when we recognize a figure on the blackboard as a circle or a musical interval as a fifth. Here the *name* that we use, e.g., "circle," has a meaning; but it will not be urged, on that account, that the circle has a meaning. What the shape or the tone may be *like* is one thing—its resemblance to certain other forms suffices to give it a name; what it *stands for* is something else. What we bring to the datum is one thing; it is another thing where we go from there. Interpretation digresses beyond the datum; while in the act of recognition the form which is being classified can remain the final *object* of attention.

Recognizability is hardly the differentia of subject-matter, since it is a prerequisite for the apprehension of any form whatsoever.[6] Percepts without concepts are blind; and while there can hardly exist such a thing in mature experience as absolute failure of recognition, since there is nothing that we can not classify under one head or another, yet a form which is at once original, complicated, and abstract will be greeted with bewilderment. But this difficulty is met simply by repeated exposure: we familiarize ourselves, say, with the style of a Mondrian as we digested long ago the abstract motives of an older art. To speak accurately, then, we can not say that the abstract motive is unfamiliar but only that it has not been rendered familiar through our experience of nature—and there lies the basis for a definition of subject-matter. A form may be entitled a "subject" if it bears a resemblance, in specific respects, to certain *natural* forms. "Form" refers to what is in the picture and "subject-matter" to a resemblance borne by this form to some aspect of the real environment. "Representations" are works containing forms which are in certain respects like the forms of nature.

There is also a negative requirement. If we could make a genuine tree, as pins are made in the factory, on the model of those which exist already, it would not be called a representation. Artistic imitation exists by defect as well as by likeness. The representation will bear a double relationship to its model—a resemblance in appearance and a deficiency of the substance.

This criterion suggests the following remarks:

(i) The criterion is not precise, for it is well known that the naturalistic grades off into the abstract. Resemblance is a matter of respects and degrees. A simple circle with a line extending beneath—is it a "flower"? The rigidly rectilinear "snake" pattern of an Indian basket—does it resemble a snake? The animal motive is "formalized," the flanks are brought into exact balance, the tail describes a regular scroll. Between the perfect oval and the

---

[6] "For eyes unpracticed in the discriminating perceiving of shapes and lines, one Gothic arch will look much like another; it will not be felt in its own specific individual character; its felt character for discriminating eyes will not be expressed to the organism whose eyes do not discriminate."—D. W. Prall, from an unpublished manuscript.

human head a series of forms can be inserted; and whole styles—whole arts, one might say—flourish in this particular limbo.

(ii) The criterion is based on a circumstance extraneous to the form. It requires that a form shall (*a*) be similar to a form which (*b*) is natural. But natural forms are distinguished as a class by nothing save their connection with natural objects. The subjects of representation are as remote from one another as from various classes of abstractions; and if we had to define subject-matter on the basis of intrinsic quality, we could proceed only by enumeration. It is an accident, so to speak, that there are no real musicians who resemble Picasso's. There may today exist seemingly abstract forms in painting which in fact have been adapted from little known fishes or plants.

(iii) It follows that subject-matter is not an esthetic category. This point must not be misinterpreted. It is not a matter of indifference that heads and bodies should appear in painting rather than cubes and cones; and I can see no reason why the human shape, regarded purely as a shape, should be expected to affect us like a checkerboard. *What* the form may be that nature may contribute is significant; but it is immaterial that *nature* should be the source. Nature works as a purely decorative designer in the tortoise-shell, the skin of reptiles, the plumage of birds; in the honeycomb and the snowflake it develops the geometrical style. To imitate such an aspect of nature is to deal with "reality"—but the effect is formalistic, minute, and precise. A tendency to abstraction, on the other hand, in some of the Italian painters is responsible for broadly structural and expressive values. Indeed, abstract compositions are themselves objects of nature and are, accordingly, imitable. Architecture, pottery, and dress are examples of formal design, which lean upon the naturalistic not at all. Let any such object be photographed and *pouf!* it is subject-matter. What has happened? Nothing has been added, nothing has been altered. Something has been *omitted*—the physical body of the building or gown. But whatever was the esthetic quality of the original, it will be held intact in the representation. It is therefore impossible to agree with those who, confusing an accident with the essence, hold that the decorative is to the expressive as the immediate to the "real." [7] Esthetic distinctions (with a class of exceptions presently to be noted) are distinctions of quality *within* the field of the immediate.

To generalize this thesis somewhat beyond the present topic: If it had been Plato's intention to stifle the analysis as well as the production of art, he could not have adopted a better expedient than that conception of the archetype which he fixed on esthetic theory. Let me briefly examine a single

---

[7] "The expressive inclines to the side of meaning, the decorative to that of sense."—Dewey, *Art as Experience*, p. 124.

"Expressive form, in other words, always involves the perception of something real. . . . The 'decorative arts' proper depend wholly on such qualities as are immediately apprehended."—Barnes, *The Art in Painting*, pp. 14–16.

application of that idea. It is believed that there exists a realistic motive in art which is the antithesis of the motive of expression through design. I will take the example of Shakespearean acting. The last speeches of the dying Hamlet can be organized, in performance, into a rhythmic unity in which, with due emphasis and subordination, a range of feeling culminates and is brought to rest. *Or* they can be punctuated with stertorous gasps, heavy breathing, a death rattle, etc., gaining "conviction" of a sort but with a sacrifice in point of dramatic design. There is an example of the constructive versus the merely imitative aim. But the inferiority of the realistic version stems from the pattern of the original—the natural death, as it happens, is not designed for esthetic effect and seldom comes off very well. At bottom we have a contrast not between imitation and design but between one design and another. There is design in nature (if I am permitted the pun)— only that design is not always to our liking. Imitation reproduces, as imagination invents; and the significance of each lies in the nature of the content which it brings into art. A literally literal realism, if that could exist, would be raw and shapeless, vital or dull, according to the phase of nature which it duplicated; and if we search for the real effort of criticism beneath the label of "realism" which it attaches to this trend or that, we find that it seeks to discriminate a particular *kind* of topic or of treatment—low subjects, minute detail, intimate emotions, casual arrangement. Certainly a work is not less momentous because its issues, its forms, are also to be found in the world that surrounds it. Art perpetually discloses value and significance that had existed independently in nature but had lain unnoticed; and I make no doubt that this connection is part of the special relevance borne by certain works to our lives. But such a *correspondence* between one experience and another is not a relationship of *dependence,* and it can not begin to account for the beauty of either.

§ 2

Our language contains a number of *sensory terms*—those which refer to elements or forms that can be given in direct experience—as well as the wider *physical* vocabulary. Examples of the first are the names of the plane figures, musical tones, colors, tastes, and smells. (This could be called the language of recognition.) Now we are said to see "ourselves" in the mirror or to have seen a "friend" in a dream or, in a picture, a "group of fighting men." Here we wish to describe a specific appearance for which no sensory name exists, and it is convenient to borrow the name of the physical object with which that appearance is associated. Clearly, the name has dropped its physicalist function and is being used as a sensory term. Physical terms so imported into the sensory language make up what we shall call the language of subject-matter.

Now appreciative criticism is subject inevitably to this limitation, that while form is individual and determinate, language is general and (in W. E. Johnson's sense) merely determinable. "In composition," wrote Emerson, "the *What* is of no importance compared with the *How.*" [8] But the *How* is nothing but the determinate *What.* The language of subject-matter can not express the *How* because it touches upon only those characteristics of the form which it shares with certain whole classes of forms. A swerve in the outline, the slightest variation in the shading, of a head represents the gulf between the master and the dub, but no ready distinction of language corresponds to it. *Formalism* strives to repair this deficiency with the help of an explicitly sensory vocabulary—"line," "plane," "color," "light," and their derivatives. The formalistic analysis of painting has often demonstrated its utility. The eye is arrested in its perfunctory grasp of the familiar form and persuaded, as if by a pointer, to follow the determinate course of the design. But the language of formalism, we must observe, is itself general and determinable. The following comment—a model of elucidation—on Seurat's *Poudreuse* employs a formalistic terminology combined with references to subject-matter: "Table, plant, mirror, stylized bow are all conceived according to a succession of curves that are continued both in the color pattern of the wall behind and the form of the woman herself. The skirt is modeled by a series of curves that not only repeat the shapes of arms and shoulder-straps but complete the circular pattern of the shadows on the wall." [9] It is still necessary to look at the picture—we could not construct it from the description. Language does not communicate the determinate—"color pattern" and "curves" get us hardly closer to the actual form than "female figure," "table," and "skirt." [10] *In the presence of the picture* certain geometrical designations (as for that matter certain figurative comparisons—"flame-like," "gem-like," "serpentine," etc.) may assist our vision to grasp the unique design where an inventory of subject-matter would leave it fixed on the general type of object or situation.

When we speak of emaciated or swollen bodies, gnarled or pudgy fingers, grass, foliage, the bark of trees, we are talking about areas, colors, and lines.

---

[8] Quoted from Emerson's *Journals* by F. O. Matthiessen, *American Renaissance.*

[9] Robert J. Goldwater, "Some Aspects of the Development of Seurat's Style," *Art Bulletin,* Vol. XXIII, p. 120.

[10] I do not raise the question whether it is *in principle* possible to communicate an esthetic content by means of language. With the help of a set of co-ordinates like the color solid one can no doubt determine an exact shade of any color. But such precision is still impossible *in practice,* that is, where we are dealing with a form of the slightest complexity.

The countenance is pale or florid, grim or gaunt, according to the relationship of colors, the arrangement of planes. To say that Brouwer's figures are "stunted," Greco's "elongated," Tura's "contorted," Signorelli's "flayed"— these are limited but genuine expressions of esthetic value *because they designate formal character*. The terminology of formalism represents simply another selection from the sensory language, convenient perhaps for further specification. It does not represent a distinct set of esthetic attributes, to be set off as the "design" from the "material" values of subject-matter. The very same form—often, indeed, the same characteristic of the form—can be designated in either way. The movement which engages the Three Graces in the *Primavera* is a linear rhythm. It is also a "lovely gesture of concord." We are not talking about different things—we are grouping the same thing either with one class of forms or another. Undoubtedly there might be another "gesture of concord" which had little in common with this; but so are there linear rhythms which do not resemble this one. If the line were altered here, the gesture would not be the same; and if the gesture were altered, it would not be the same line.

Let us suppose there was a group of figures which served as the model for this detail. That group had its lines, its colors, its volumes, its shadows and lights. Composition, relation, pattern, proportion are *everywhere!* The significance of the act of imagination is that it brings *new* colors, new lines, new arrangements in place of the original qualities, that is, that it creates new "objects." The notion is preposterous that line, light, color, space are a set of properties peculiar to art, to be superimposed upon a formless matter supplied by nature. Yet Roger Fry could write: "The moment representation is introduced forms have an entirely new set of values. Thus a line which indicated the bend of a head in a certain direction would have far more than its mere value as line in the composition because of the attraction which a marked gesture has for the eye." [11] As if the attraction which a gesture has for the eye were conceivable apart from the *line* which it describes! As if a line could have a value "merely as line" and not as that determinate line which automatically takes membership in the class of "gestures"! Mr. Fry was no doubt thinking about the value of the gesture in isolation as against its value in the total composition; but that is a distinction of part and whole, of figure drawing and space-composition. Representation introduces an entirely new set of forms. It contributes new designs. It does not intrude itself, with an effect of disturbance, into the midst of a set of abstract forms, which somehow hang on as pure line and color and shape.

I will submit two further examples of the same confusion: "As Mr. R. G. Collingwood has wittily said, a painter may be interested either in the vol-

---

[11] *Vision and Design,* p. 35.

umes of a woman or in her femininity." [12] No painter, we may safely affirm, has ever been interested in a femininity without volumes. But there are painters who study volumes that are rather familiar to us from everyday life and there are painters who render relatively abstract, or fantastic, or stylized volumes. The volumes, in any two painters, are not alike.

"Whistler's *Mother* was called by the artist *Arrangement in Grey and Black,* but it has seldom been looked at simply as a pattern of colors." [13] But to look at the pattern of colors that Whistler painted is to see a "woman seated in a chair."

It will be observed, finally, that we do not align ourselves with those who insist that form and content are inseparable or, according to the appeal of the phrase, "inextricably intermingled," "indissolubly blended," or "indistinguishably fused." At bottom this formula represents an obscurantist protest against the comparison and analysis of different forms. "Content," according to our definition, refers to certain general or class characteristics of the form. Now it is not senseless—though it is for various reasons pretty futile—to ask whether a class of forms may not be marked as a class by a particular value, whether "nudes" are not nobler than "apples," in other words, whether the "subject" does not contribute something to the effect. This question, to be sure, is apt to be complicated by another. For many people esthetic forms are merely the pretext for the release of feelings which belong to the corresponding *objects. Any* mother or baby or sheep dog or venerable old man, any *Nativity* or *Crucifixion,* regardless of the individual treatment, elicits the stereotyped sentiment; and popular criticism, when it considers whether a *subject* is edifying or offensive, is thinking about the *thing portrayed.* Now the esthetic value of a form does not necessarily correspond to the value which its bearer enjoys in real life. There may be representations of humanity which are grander than any rendering of still life, but not because of the superior station of the former in some non-esthetic hierarchy of excellence. The painter who takes the heavenly choir or the Supreme Court for his subject does not start with the slightest advantage on that account, and we observe that religious pictures, figure studies, landscapes, interiors range all the way from supreme achievement to utter failure. Formalism is justified in seeking to eliminate this source of sentimental and didactic irrelevancy. But popular taste suffers from another limitation which is more nearly excusable. Children, horses, flowers, mountains, and waves do after all possess inherent esthetic quality, and that quality will be carried into any reproduction. But that quality is apt to be trivial, elementary, crude. An area of shadow thrown over one side of a head, a relationship between the head and the positions of the hands, may create a mightier organization than any-

---

[12] Samuel Alexander, *Beauty and Other Forms of Value,* p. 79.
[13] George Boas, *A Primer for Critics,* p. 62.

thing known to us from nature: it may absorb, it may cancel whatever value the model may have possessed in isolation. The emphasis upon subject-matter, the demand for the reproduction of "beautiful things," is therefore seen to represent a fixation upon the isolated detail and a blindness to the values of the total synthesis; an arrest at the *elementary* esthetic quality and an insensibility to great achievement; a predilection for the standardized and an incapacity to comprehend the original. Genuine issues figure here, but they are issues of formal analysis. A thousand problems of formal analysis are agitated under the heading of subject-matter versus form.

§ 3

The depth effect, whether in nature or in painting, is measurably dependent upon habits of perception. The cube, drawn correctly on a piece of paper, can hardly be seen as another pattern on a plane with the square— it seems to have assumed a new dimension; and the conditions of this effect are not all innate. A large number in the list of elements which contribute to our sense of the bulk and location of objects in space—overlapping, perspective, distribution of light—could not function with that result apart from acquired adjustments of the optical mechanism. Meaning interpenetrates with sense to give the visual effect: it may be said that in the visual perception of space the datum is itself a function of learning. The depth phenomenon, incidentally, is not unique in this respect—the apparent color of a heavily shaded sheet of white paper, which is white when it "should" be gray, testifies equally to the influence of learning upon immediate effect.

The question we have to settle is a simple one. Suppose that we are standing on the seashore, looking out to a group of islands. Now the field is organized for us very differently from that field which might exist for a man who had just gained his vision, for the first time, by surgical means—for whom the islands might stand merely *above* the water in the vertical plane. Ours is a fuller experience of space, and it is at least in some degree our past experience that is our advantage. But we may further be led to judge that the islands are just two miles out, and in this we may turn out to have been mistaken. Our perception will then have been proved "illusory"; but, returning to our position on the beach, we find that the visual field has not changed. When we have once come to the end of one of those stair-cases or avenues of columns which are contrived to look longer than they are, our muscular preparation will not be the same another time round: the same phenomenal distance now "means" a shorter physical stretch. The habits which condition the visual phenomenon are not affected by the revision of those later judgments, relating to traversible distance and physical size, which are *based* on the visual phenomenon. All of the last are canceled, in the case of painting, by good and sufficient knowledge; yet the effect of depth and of solidity persists. Without intending to obscure the difference in kind between the flat and the "deep" order of composition, I hold, then, that the space which matters esthetically is given and that the space which is not given does not count; or, in other words, that "volume" and "mass" are what we have called sensory terms in their application to painting.

Yet those who argue, on the strength of the depth effect, for a factor of interpretation in the appreciation of painting are thinking not of the "space" which indubitably appears in the picture but of the space which does not exist within it.[14] The meanings for which they plead are not those which, e.g., help to create perspective but those which operate normally to correct perspective in the interest of physical action upon the environment. That a surface which exists in two dimensions should manage to express a third is a paradox in their eyes, to be resolved only by an appeal to the supplementary action of the mind. But to say that we are dealing with volumes and masses when we know that there is only a plane is not a paradox but a contradiction; on the other hand it is but an axiom that a scene which only *seems* to recede does seem to recede. To utilize untouched resources of their direct experience, to duplicate upon wood or canvas the complete *appearance* of physical nature, was the task projected by those fifteenth-century masters who first achieved the conquest of naturalistic space.

We can now understand the strategy which is followed by representationalist and formalist alike, for the example of the third dimension is typical of the entire issue. Painting, they feel, so far as it is a matter of direct perception, *ought* to appear flat. So *in general* the first step is to conceive an impoverished caricature of the immediate: at the level of "sensation," we are told, there are only colors and lines and shapes. This causes us to imagine, in place of the obvious landscape or interior, a patch-work of abstractions. The formalist rests at this point, convinced of the supremacy of formal relationships—by which he secretly understands some other than the *given* scheme of relationships. Thus Birkhoff, seeking to apply his mathematical analysis to the art of painting, proposes to ignore the "connotative" factor, that is, the factor of meaning. As it turns out, what he ignores are those irregularities of the forms—by which we recognize them as "kneeling figures," "warriors," "slaves"—which refuse to fit into a purely *abstract* or geometrical analysis. The moment is ripe for someone to interpose with emphasis that we perceive not "isolated" colors and lines but the *real* objects

---

[14] "[Subject-matter] is *never immediately experienced as a whole,* but consists in part of qualities and relations whose presence can only be *inferred* or *assumed.* This is true if only because the subject-matter of all representational painting includes three-dimensional objects whereas the pictorial surface itself is necessarily two-dimensional."— D. F. Bowers, "The Role of Subject-Matter in Art," (*Journal of Philosophy*), Vol. XXXVI (1939), p. 618. My italics.

of which they are qualities.[15] Meaning is invoked to supply what has been expelled from sense—a task which is beyond its power; for, if we saw nothing to begin with but a twisted system of planes, the mind would be impotent to assemble them into the form of a man.

Representation borrows the forms of nature without the substance, and that is everywhere the main source of confusion. For criticism seems unable to conceive a medium between real objects and abstract forms. Finding that space, body, reality are not included within the work, it does not concede the obvious—that these are not required for what the work is meant to do—because that seems to ignore the significant difference between representations and abstractions. In the face of material nature it is ready to admit the possibility of an esthetic approach: where the reality is granted, we can readily see how it might be forgotten. Art is conceded no such independence, precisely because in art the form stands alone! Hence the appeal to an *extra* faculty to account for the *negative* factor, the factor of absence—that is, the esthetically immaterial.

It may be well at this point to underscore our admission that to the extent to which a natural effect depends upon association, the representation of that effect does too. It is far from my purpose to deny, e.g., that tactile quality is apprehended through the medium of vision. In general, the claim of this paper is positive: it seeks to show how much of what we understand by the subject-matter of art can be rescued for the province of sense-perception, what an enormous range of esthetic feeling can be explained through the power of form—not the "pure" pleasure of formalistic arrangement merely but the awe, the mystery, the excitement inherent in Greco's landscape or the shadows and perspectives of Chirico or the quiver and vibration of Van Gogh's form. It would be quite a different matter to urge that associations are illicit, to banish the factor of meaning from the conception of esthetic experience. I believe that almost any representation will excite at least a penumbral activity of meaning. The figures of men and women are not cut off at the edges; an arm which passes behind another body is not, for our feeling, thereby amputated. Moreover, the element of drama, which involves a sequence of incidents in time, can be condensed into the experience of painting only through a significance which attaches to the presented form. But painting *does* occasionally exploit the values of narrative and of drama; and it is only by a sacrifice of its own competence that a criterion of the esthetic can dismiss this factor as irrelevant.

Esthetic theory will now have to show how meanings, admitted as legitimate, can be reconciled with the conditions that define the esthetic experience as such. Otherwise, it must continue to fluctuate between intolerable

---

[15] Cf., for instance, Dewey, *Art as Experience*, pp. 86–89.

extremes, whereby the field is either reduced to the field of *sense,* with undue restriction of its scope, or assimilated to a mode of *cognition,* with consequent impairment of the very marks which delimit the esthetic. In other words, it must establish the existence of interpretations which are not fundamentally inferential and predictive. This task has been recognized—the recognition is embodied in such expressions as "immanent reference"—but it has not been executed; and it can not be executed here. But we may say that meaning functions, in esthetic experience, so as to expand the field on which attention rests. The essential condition of the esthetic experience is that attention should *rest* on a certain content. It is by no means essential that that content be supplied by sense. The fundamental thing is the nature of the attitude that is aroused. What renders an attitude practical rather than esthetic is not the fact that it is based on past experience: it is the fact that it turns away from a given content to obtain or avoid what it does not yet possess. But in the contemplation of things which we do not see but only imagine, we definitely possess those things. Hence the *immediate* can not be identified with the *sensuous.* Through the play of meaning, a veritable universe can figure as an object of contemplation. And we reach the conception of the total imaginative experience, or the total *content* of the work, in which questions of source are transcended.

BENBOW RITCHIE

The Formal Structure of the

Aesthetic Object[1]

THIS PAPER PROPOSES to investigate the formal structure of the aesthetic object. At the outset let us assume the distinction between those values of the aesthetic object which are formal and those which are extra-formal. A *formal value* satisfies an interest which has been aroused by some aspect of the aesthetic object. An *extra-formal value* satisfies an interest

―――――――――

[1] Benbow Ritchie, "The Formal Structure of the Aesthetic Object," *Journal of Aesthetics and Art Criticism,* III, Nos. 11–12 (n.d.), 5–14. Reprinted by permission.

This article and the following may be profitably read in the light of the article by Mr. Morris, p. 105. For a definition of terms like semantics, syntactics, pragmatics, which are necessary for the reading of these articles, see Morris, p. 107, note 3; for a definition of icon see p. 109. (Eds.)

which has been brought ready-made to the object. For example, the satisfaction we gain from the way that Shakespeare treats politics in *Julius Caesar* is a satisfaction of an extra-formal interest, an interest we bring with us. On the other hand the satisfaction we derive from Anthony's funeral oration is of a different kind. Here the satisfied interest is one which was aroused by a variety of factors which are inextricably bound up with the plot and characters. It is obvious that this distinction between formal and extra-formal values lacks precision in its present form. It is hoped that this paper will enable us to sharpen that distinction. At any rate, it is clear that the formal values of the aesthetic object in some sense set the framework within which the total aesthetic response takes place. How this framework is created is, then, the subject of our discussion.

Since aesthetic activity is a kind of activity which creates value, we must begin with a short analysis of how value is created. A human organism is a system of potential and actual activities, each of which under specifiable circumstances tends to pursue its own career within the total environment. As changes take place within this environment the activities tend to change also. Thus, an activity is said to adjust itself to a change in the environment if it selects an appropriate way of pursuing its career within the new environmental situation. In a similar fashion activities tend to adjust themselves to each other, so that each activity can follow its own career within the total environment. When all the activities of the organism are adjusted both to each other and to the environment, then we shall say that they are in *equilibrium,* a condition in which each activity finds a state of affairs within the total environment suitable to its career. It is this tendency, as we shall see, of an organism to maintain an equilibrium among its activities, that constitutes the ground for the creation of value.

An activity is frustrated, blocked or checked (1) if the conditions in the environment demand that it become overt, and (2) if, at the same time, its environment is unfavorable to the carrying on of the activity. When such frustration takes place the equilibrium is upset, and in reaction to this distortion of the equilibrium a new activity begins. Considered solely as a reaction to the distortion, such newly initiated activity is called impulsive, and the act viewed in its raw, primitive, "reactive" stage is called an impulse. Such raw activity is dispersive and without clear direction. The activity becomes "purposive" or gains direction only when the effects which it has upon the environmental situation are taken as signs of future situations, and thus signs of future stages of activity. When the human organism has begun to take account of its activity in this manner, and to symbolize to himself *plans of action,* then the activity has become interested activity. Throughout the ensuing complex act we may say that the impulse remains the same only if the activities which were originally frustrated remain so. That is, the impulse remains constant only so long as (1) the conditions that demand the activities, and (2) their unsuitable environments remain constant. When either of these factors are removed the impulse is fulfilled, the equilibrium is restored. Furthermore, the plans of action when regarded as relevant to the fulfilment of an impulse, are called *interests*. Any member of the class of modifications which tend to be effected by repeated enactment of an interest, is a product of that interest. Such a product is the object of the interest, the *value* which satisfies that interest. When a value of a complex of values succeeds in fulfilling an impulse this value of a value-complex is a *good*. Consequently, an interest is said to be relevant to an impulse if its value will either produce a partial or total fulfilment of the impulse.

Although it is not apparent at first sight, the domain of values and goods, as here defined, largely conforms to the domain set by common sense. Anything is a value when it is believed to be relevant to the fulfilment of an impulse. Anything is a good when it does in fact fulfill the impulse. Although the pursuance of a course of action is generally required for the occurrence of a good, it is not logically necessary. Occasionally happenings, such as lightning bolts, sunsets, or earthquakes, take place and, although they are not causally connected with our activities, nevertheless succeed in removing our distortions. Such events then, are genuine goods. This is the status, in this view, of those pleasures which traditional value theory calls "contemplative."

Such in stark outline is the way in which values and goods are created. But this outline is so bare that it demands a somewhat detailed example in order to make what is involved concrete. Sherlock Holmes was a comparatively simple system of activities (pipe-smoking, violin-playing, and crime-solving) organized in a highly delicate equilibrium. Thus, whenever Dr. Watson would tell him of some new crime Holmes would jump up impulsively and stalk about the room. Then after a moment or two of dispersive bafflement he would begin to sort clues out of the jumbled mass of facts. From these clues he would draw up tentative plans of action. He would become interested in one of these plans (i.e., he would regard the plan as relevant to his impulse) and plunge into action. The enactment of this plan would bring forth further clues (i.e., values) and from these he would form further plans of action. Eventually he would find the final clue and the culprit would be discovered. Thus Holmes' equilibrium would be established again, and he could return to Baker Street and resume his customary activities which had been dislocated by the original distortion.

The creation of an aesthetic object is, I believe, similar in many important ways to the crime-solving of Mr. Holmes. In both cases the activity begins with an impulse resulting from a disorder in the environment and consists of converting this disorder into an order which is a good. The order develops *in* the experience; it evolves as the experience progresses. In the typical aesthetic experience this order develops as the material of the medium is worked upon and yields clues of what to expect, and therefore, of what to do. The direction is pointed out by signs which arise during the process. The man who orders the furniture in his room according to customary formula is performing a drudgery. The man who begins by changing the position of one piece of furniture with the idea of discovering from this change clues, signs, ideas for further changes, creates an order, and in doing so, creates an aesthetic object. There is no essential difference between this process and that involved in the writing of *Paradise Lost* or the composition of a Bach fugue.

To be able to create the latter kind of aesthetic object, a work of art, the artist must know a great deal about the structural properties of his medium. Thus, a painter like Matisse, who uses color as a unifying principle must have an extensive knowledge of the "spatial" peculiarities of colors. Since so little is known about these matters by those of us who are not artists, it is impossible here to give a detailed account of the structural uses of color. We do, however, know perhaps some of the elementary facts; namely, that certain shades of red tend to overrun their boundaries, to expand and surge forward to the front of the painting, while various shades of blue tend to recede and contract. Other colors have similar spatial peculiarities. Certain shades of yellow, for example, are spatially ambivalent. Suppose, for example, that we have a patch of this yellow between a red and a blue patch. When the yellow is perceived in relation to the red patch it seems to share the "aggressive" character of the red. On the other hand when it is perceived in relation to the blue patch, it seems to share the latter's "cool reticence."

An artist begins a painting with a large body of such knowledge funded in his painting habits. The situation is similar in many respects to the beginning of a game of chess by an experienced player. The latter has knowledge (1) of the permissible moves (the structural properties of the medium) and (2) of the characteristics of the various openings in relation to further plans of action (the relation of certain initial combinations of plastic elements to further possible combinations).

A painter begins then by searching for a combination of colors which will be satisfactory, which will be a partial good.[2] In his search he may hit upon a vivid red which seems peculiarly exciting. He puts a patch of this red upon the canvas, and then gives himself up to the enjoyment of the warmth of this color. For some reason he feels that this particular red patch

---

[2] Compare this discussion of the way a painter works with Matisse's *Notes of a Painter,* p. 258. As in Matisse's essay, in this section Mr. Ritchie approaches the object from the point of view of the creative artist. (Eds.)

is "just right"; "it hits the mark!" During this phase of enjoyment he begins to realize vaguely "what he's after"; that is, he begins to realize what kind of a painting he is trying to ex-press. The feeling of direction becomes stronger and stronger until he realizes that it will be a painting in which this red patch will be restrained by a soft blue line. Somehow he feels that the vigor of the red patch demands the restraint of a cool blue. He puts the blue line on the canvas, and at once the combination "clicks." He marvels anew at the fitness of the combination. Then out of this marvelling phase comes a further clarification of the painting he is trying to ex-press. He gains another hint about how to proceed. This process continues until finally a certain patch or line completes the painting. Nothing more is demanded and nothing more can be added.

This description of the painter's procedure is intended to illustrate the psychological process involved in the interaction between the artist and his medium. Thus, we do not intend to overlook the fact that there is a great deal of individual variation in the concrete ways in which artists may set about their work. The main point is, however, that the artist's impulses are always controlled by him in terms of their consequences in a specific medium.

We may now describe the general structure of the aesthetic experience. It begins like any other experience, with a blind search for value, for a color combination that will be satisfactory. The ensuing process is continuous but contains two kinds of activity which succeed each other in dominating the experience. First comes an exploration of the stuff of the medium (a mixing of the pigments on the palette). In this exploration some of the stuff is so formed that it is made to satisfy some interest which is partially relevant to the impulse which initiated the experience. This forming of the stuff of the medium (the putting of the red patch on the canvas) has created a thing with value which is a partial good. Succeeding and growing out of this phase of active exploration comes one of enjoyment and contemplation, in which the value (the exciting red patch) is scrutinized and studied. First, it is studied in relation to the impulse or distortion (to whatever made the painter feel that he had "a painting in him to ex-press"). In this manner the direction of the original impulse is made more specific by viewing it in relation to the value which has just been created. Second, as a result of this specification of the direction of the original impulse we get a rough indication of the general kind of values for which we are searching. That is, expectations are aroused of further similar values (further colored patches and lines which will also "hit the mark") latent within the unexplored and unformed stuff remaining.

The newly formed value (the red patch) is now taken to be a sign since it is perceived and used as a link between the aroused expectations and further values. The designatum of this sign consists of all those values which will satisfy the interested expectations aroused by the sign. Further active exploration into the stuff of the medium is now guided by the designation which this sign supplies. The search for value which at the outset was blind, has grown more definite by being converted into a search for the denotatum of this sign. Then with the creation of a new value (the blue line which has the restraint demanded by the red patch) comes another phase of enjoyment. During it we gain a still more precise indication of the kind of values for which we are searching. Consequently, this second value (the blue line) is converted into a sign of further values to be extracted from the remaining stuff. As the experience progresses, the two phases interplay continuously. The expectations aroused become more and more precise until the experience ends with the creation of a total complex value which fulfills the impulse. No further interests or expectations are aroused for the experience has been consummated and is at an end.

In describing this process we have referred to the creation of value and the embodying of value in the stuff of the medium. These statements suffer from a certain ambiguity due to the fact that values are often regarded as mentalistic phenomena which are, in Santayana's terms, somehow "objectified" and made to seem as properties of perceptual objects. In our view, on the contrary, values are not mentalistic, they are merely properties of objects relative to organisms with the relevant interests. There is a common objection to this which maintains that the perception of values lacks the "immediacy" or "intimacy" which characterizes the perception of colors and shapes. The latter properties seem to have unambiguous spatial location and extent, and are in some sense "surface" properties. Values on the other hand lack this spatial specificity and thus appear ephemeral and ghostly. But this objection can hardly be taken seriously for it would make ghosts out of such primary properties as weight, hardness, elasticity, and so forth. The empirical fact seems to be that only a few of nature's many properties have spatial spread and thus are surface properties. The rest are properties which pervade and suffuse their objects, and are without trace of surface spread.

Furthermore, to say merely that "our expectations are satisfied" is to be guilty of another serious ambiguity. At first sight such a statement seems to deny the obvious fact that much of our enjoyment is derived from surprises, from betrayals of our expectations. The solution to this paradox is to find some ground for a distinction between "surprise" and "frustration." Roughly, the distinction can be made in terms of the effects which the two kinds of experiences have upon us. Frustration blocks or checks activity. It necessitates new orientation for our activity, if we are to escape the *cul de sac*. Consequently, we abandon the frustrating object and return to blind impulsive activity. On the other hand, surprise merely causes a temporary cessation of the exploratory phase of the experience, and a recourse to intense contemplation and scrutiny. In the latter phase the surprising elements are seen in their connection with what has gone before, with the whole drift of the experience, and the enjoyment of these values is then extremely intense. Finally, it appears that there must always be some degree of novelty or surprise in all these values if there is to be a progressive specification of the direction of the total act.

In reading a poem, in listening to a quartet, or in looking at a picture, we follow the development of the object by discriminating a texture of interrelated values. "A temporal work of art is developed," says Mr. Pepper, "inductively from the qualities of the detail to the qualities of the whole. A spatial work of art is developed deductively from a sense of the general character of its totality to confirmations of this throughout all the details." [3] But both the temporal and the spatial arts exhibit the same general formal value structure. The difference between them that Mr. Pepper points out, is important but not fundamental, since both the temporal and spatial arts are created "inductively," and any aesthetic experience tends to exhibit a continuous interplay between "deductive" and "inductive" operations. To make clear what is involved in these "deductive" and "inductive" procedures we must give a precise account of the formal structure of the aesthetic object. To do this we must first specify in what sense the elements of the object are signs, that is, we must show what kind of signs they are.

From what I have said so far, it is clear that what the red patch denotes is the value of the blue line, and not the blue line as such. The primary problem then is: "In what way does the red patch denote this value?" It certainly does not denote the value in the same sense that the word "good" denotes some value which is a good. Secondly, it does not denote merely by directing our attention to the value, as would an indexical gesture of pointing. Thus, we must conclude that if the red patch is a sign it must be an icon denoting the value of the blue line in somewhat the same way that a map denotes a certain geographical area. The semantical rule of usage for icons such as these states that the icon denotes any object which has certain of the properties of the icon. That is to say, anything which is interpreted as a sign of some other thing by virtue of a relation of similarity between the two things, is an icon. Our red patch, however, is a special kind of icon and differs from a diagram or a map, since the only similar property that the blue line must have, in order to be denoted by it, is the same value property. In short, the blue line must partially fulfill the same impulse as is fulfilled by the red patch if the two are to have the same value. And, as we

---

[3] Stephen C. Pepper, *Aesthetic Quality* (New York: Charles Scribner's Sons, 1937), p. 45. (Eds.)

have pointed out earlier, the impulse remains the same in so far as the originally frustrated activities remain frustrated. Such signs are called *icons of value*.

Now, both formal and extra-formal signs in a work of art may be icons of value. Mr. Morris has discussed at length the iconic character of extra-formal signs. The main point of his discussion is that "representative" or extra-formal signs in an aesthetic object must be values, rather than merely suggestions of values. If the painted flowers in a Matisse merely symbolically indicate the value of actual flowers, they do not perform an aesthetic function, for the attention and interest go straight through the sign-vehicle to what is designated. But since icons of value have the values of the things they designate we can fix our attention upon the value of the painted flowers. Put in other words "when an interpreter apprehends directly an iconic sign-vehicle he apprehends directly what is designated."

Mr. Morris makes little reference, however, to formal signs, other than to acknowledge them as a sort of "secondary symbolism . . . serving to direct the attention . . . from one part of the aesthetic sign-vehicle to another." [4] He adds that these signs are neither iconic nor aesthetic. However, from what we have said thus far, it is clear that formal signs as well as extra-formal signs are iconic of value. The difference between them, and this difference is fundamental, is that formal icons have within the aesthetic object other denotata than themselves. The painted flowers, on the other hand, when considered as iconic of the value of flowers, can have no denotatum within the aesthetic object other than themselves. Thus, the denotata of extra-formal icons are external to the object in the sense that in order to know what value is designated by painted flowers, we must at same time have had direct enjoyment of the value of unpainted, botanical flowers. On the other hand, we can know what value the red patch designates merely by turning to and enjoying the value of the blue line. Acquaintance with all other values is irrelevant.

At the beginning of this paper we made a rough distinction between formal and extra-formal values, by stating that a formal value is one which satisfies some interest aroused by some aspect of the aesthetic object, while an extra-formal value is one which satisfies an interest which we bring ready-made to the object. This rough distinction can now be made more precise by stating that *formal values are the denotata of formal icons, while extra-formal values are identical with extra-formal icons*.

Mr. Morris makes some very suggestive remarks about the possibility of aesthetic syntactics. In our terms, aesthetic syntactics would be a study of the syntactical relations between formal icons of value. From a study of

---

[4] Charles W. Morris, "Esthetics and the Theory of Signs," *Journal of Unified Science,* VIII (1939), 139. (Eds.)

the "structural" properties of any medium we ought to be able to construct various syntactical systems. These systems would be analogous to mathematical systems, or systems of logic. In each of these systems certain sign-vehicles would be "primitive terms." "Formation rules" would determine the possible combinations of these sign-vehicles, while "transformation rules" would determine the possible transitions from one sign-vehicle combination to another. Consequently, with an adequate knowledge of the structural properties of the various media, we could describe any particular work of art as a certain kind of syntactical system, and further, we could show the relation of this system to certain wider and more general systems such as traditions.

In this paper I have attempted to describe what I believe to be the genesis and nature of the formal structure of the aesthetic object. From this analysis we can draw several conclusions. First, the germs of such formal aesthetic structures are to be found in every activity which produces a good. All the elements in such an activity function to fulfill the impulse partially, and consequently have similar values. When these elements are interpreted in this way and are viewed in abstraction from all but their similar value properties, these elements as organized, constitute a formal aesthetic structure. The main reason that ordinary experience is so rarely perceived aesthetically is that it is generally shot through with stereotypes. Recognition, as Mr. Dewey puts it, takes the place of aesthetic perception.

Second, any combination of formal values is *sui generis* and untranslatable in the sense that it is a constituent of a particular syntactical system, and such systems are autonomous. This emphasizes the fact that formal values satisfy unique interests, interests aroused by the formal icons of the object.

Third, since the formal structure of any work of art is an autonomous system this structure will be common to the aesthetic experiences of all those who know the primitive terms, and the formation and transformation rules of the system. Thus, although the interest bias which the perceiver brings to the aesthetic object will have a serious effect upon the enjoyment of the extra-formal values, it will have no bearing upon the enjoyment of the structure of formal values. All that is required for an enjoyment of the latter values is an adequate training in the structural properties of the medium.

Finally, we can understand that the status of a work of art must be determined in terms of the status of the formal value structure. It is obvious that we cannot legitimately criticize an aesthetic object because it fails to have certain extra-formal values. All that we can do is to criticize the way in which its elements are related.

ISABEL CREED HUNGERLAND

Iconic Signs and Expressiveness [1]

M R. RITCHIE HAS presented a very lucid development of C. W. Morris's view that the work of art can be defined as an iconic sign that designates values. He has also shown how Morris's definition can be based upon Dewey's account of the aesthetic experience as a unified experience which achieves a restoration of equilibrium between organism and environment, the equilibrium having been upset by an environmental thwarting of an impulse. In this brief essay I wish, not to disagree with the account presented by Mr. Ritchie of the aesthetic experience and the work of art, but to indicate certain omissions, certain directions in which supplementation is needed, if the views of Dewey and Morris are taken as *definitive* of, respectively, aesthetic experience and the work of art. In what follows I shall limit myself mainly to the situation in which an organism appreciates aesthetic values, concentrating on the values which may be found in works of art.

The Deweyan account of aesthetic experience, so far as it concerns creative processes, leaves no place for the works of art (and there seem to be such) which are the *celebrations* of an equilibrium achieved and thus not themselves worked out in the struggle to maintain equilibrium.[2] Nor is there a place for the work of art which may result from a "playing around" with a medium whose structures and potentialities for novel combinations fascinate the artist. Again, in connection with the appreciator, as distinguished from the creator of aesthetic values, the kind of unsought for, accidentally encountered, yet often intense aesthetic experience of natural object remains to be explained. A mere chance turn of the head, and an aesthetic value may be realized, apparently as independent of our struggling with our environment as the gift of grace in the old church doctrine. Dewey's organism, in whatever context he considers it, seems forever struggling, forever earnest and unrelaxed in its endeavor to maintain itself; yet the

---

[1] Isabel Creed Hungerland, "Iconic Signs and Expressiveness," *Journal of Aesthetics and Art Criticism,* III, No. 11–12 (n.d.), 15–21. Reprinted by permission. This article is a critical commentary of the preceding selection by Mr. Ritchie. (Eds.)

[2] See our selection from Mr. Dewey's *Art as Experience,* p. 325. (Eds.)

complete and integrated experience which Dewey has in many respects so well described often appears to come without the genesis which is included by him in its definition. I do not maintain that the apparent exceptions cannot be reduced to the general rule in question, but their reduction would presumably involve the noticing of additional conditions which might turn out to be of extreme importance in understanding aesthetic phenomena.

In order not to limit too narrowly the generating conditions of aesthetic experience, I shall adopt a broader conception of "interests" than that of Mr. Ritchie—making them equivalent to *any* motor-affective attitude or behavioral pattern, i. e. any attending to or turning away from environmental objects, whether or not generated by frustration. Values, I shall interpret, as properties of objects correlative to any such attitudes.[3] On the basis of this broader conception, I wish to supplement Mr. Ritchie's account of the work of art in two interrelated directions: first, in indicating the multiplicity of interests which may be evoked and organized by the work of art, and secondly, in making out how the many interests are organized, in particular how so-called "formal" and "extra-formal" values are integrated.

The work of art is experienced as a perceptual structure, the features of which are gradually grasped by the percipient in a series of perceptions having a cumulative character. (The old distinction between the spatial and temporal arts is useful if referred to differences in the way in which a perceptual grasp of the work of art as a whole is built up.) In so far as the aesthetician considers only that aspect of the perceptual experience which is focused on sensuous qualities and their organization, the values realized are usually called "formal." However, the term "formal" fails to indicate that the sensuous aspect of the perceptual object has an expressive as well as a structural character. As Mr. Ritchie's account of the red-blue combination makes clear, the two colors are perceived not only as contrasting (and, I would add, as creating tensions) in terms of their distance, in a color scheme, from one another, but also in terms of the exciting quality of the particular red and the soothing quality of the particular blue, i. e. in terms of the contrasting expressive qualities.

Expressiveness is a concept of pragmatics, not of semantics. It may be roughly defined in the following way. When X expresses Y for an organism Z, X does not designate, or represent Y. Rather, Y is some emotional quality, mood, feeling-tone, idea, type of behavior, or way of functioning, which through some process of fusion, has come to characterize X itself for Z. Thus, a certain configuration of the human face is expressive to us of anger, another of joy—that is, the face is perceived *as angry* or *as joyful*. If, however, the facial configuration becomes for the percipient a sign of certain psychological

---

[3] Values may be said to be "realized" in an object when an object satisfies an interest.

processes in the possessor, anger is not an expressive quality of the face but a designatum.

The values realized in the perceptual grasp of expressive and dynamic organizations of sensuous qualities, I shall call "aesthetic," rather than "formal," using "aesthetic" in the context of this paper more or less in its etymological meaning. Aesthetic values may then be said to be basic to the total grasp of a work of art and to possess the greatest degree of immediacy in the following senses of these terms. Aesthetic values are basic in that the realization of other values in a way relevant to the work of art presupposes the realization of the values of an organization of sensuous qualities. They possess the greatest degree of immediacy in that their realization is least dependent upon the mediation of cognition and the various kinds of past, non-aesthetic experience which the organism brings to the work of art.[4]

Next in the scheme are what I shall call "artistic values." Unless one believes in a Platonic God, these values are absent in aesthetic enjoyment of natural objects. They may be described as the satisfying of interests in the skillful exploitation of the aesthetic possibilities of a medium. Media have two characteristics which distinguish them from mere totalities of discriminable sensory qualities and structures. First, they are these totalities as ordered by the various schemes of selection or scales and rules for combination which constitute artistic traditions. Secondly, there is a reference in the meaning of "medium" to the physical and chemical materials and instrumental means involved in producing certain aesthetic effects for percipients. Thus, the medium of music consists in musical tones, ordered in one scale or another, and produced by pianos, violins, etc. The medium of the dance consists in motions in definite space performed by a human body and these motions have been ordered by various selections of principles of the dynamics of the human body—and so on for the other arts.

The competent percipient whom I shall assume in this paper brings to the work of art a knowledge of the structure of its medium as explored by various traditions and a knowledge of the various physical means and techniques of producing certain perceptual effects. He will notice, for example, that Peter Breughel has fused into a perceptual unity two diverse traditions in treating spatial forms, namely the painterly and the linear. He will be interested in the quality of color, possible to oil, which Breughel has achieved. In watching a dance, he will be aware of the system of movements within which the work is constructed, (for example, the developments of the principle of fall and recovery as used by Doris Humphrey) and he will be interested in the extent to which this principle is basic in bodily motions

---

[4] It should be kept in mind that the experience of a work of art is a process and hence that the various values which the work may have are realized gradually and realized together as attention shifts from one aspect of the work to another.

and has been consistently and fully developed by the choreographer. (Also, in the arts where a performer is required, the degree to which the potentialities of the composition are fulfilled becomes important to the percipient.)

The interests which I have just described are obviously different from aesthetic interests and far more conditioned by cognition. When these interests enter the aesthetic situation there is, of course, a danger that the perceptual structure becomes a sign merely of various techniques and traditions and that attention wanders off to them as designata. However, since the skillful exploitation of the aesthetic potentialities of a medium is actualized in the perceptual structure, the interests generative of artistic values, though broader than the interests generative of aesthetic values, may remain centered upon the perceptual structure. The structure then becomes expressive, rather than designative, of traditions and techniques, and artistic values reinforce rather than disrupt aesthetic ones.

I wish now to consider the practically limitless set of interests which may be stimulated when the work of art is perceived as representing familiar kinds of objects and situations. Morris's definition of the work of art makes it in every case an iconic sign, but an iconic sign of values. Apart from the difficulty of placing values in the semantic dimension, rather than the pragmatic, Morris's definition takes no account of the work of art as an iconic sign of properties other than value—properties of more or less familiar activities and objects, that is, of representation as that term is commonly used in connection with the arts. Obviously, the media of the various arts differ in regard to their capacities for being iconic of things of our everyday life. The medium of music cannot designate iconically the visual and tactual properties of our environment. It is dubious whether any resemblances to things outside the medium, other than resemblances to rhythms and tempos of various activities, are of much importance in music. The values appropriate to music seem to be largely artistic and aesthetic.

However, since the objects upon which are directed our practical, moral and cognitive interests are defined for us mainly in terms of visual and tactual qualities and forms, the media of painting and sculpture have great capacities for iconic designation. The questions which I wish to consider now are: 1. What are the characteristics of iconic designation in art? 2. Are the interests stimulated by such designation essentially destructive of aesthetic and artistic values or do they provide a possible source of further enrichment of aesthetic experience?

In regard to the first question, Morris's definition of an iconic sign as a sign which has properties in common with what it designates must be supplemented if it is to be useful in this context. The differences are as important as the resemblances when an iconic sign is a work of art. The basic difference between sign and designatum in art results from the fact that in art properties of objects are presented in a medium—the object itself is not reproduced. Secondly, the resemblances to familiar things rarely if ever consist in the repetition of identical qualities, but in approximate and often weak similarities. The artist selects certain properties of a familiar object and suppresses others. He distorts familiar shapes and properties—he takes shapes and colors from familiar contexts and presents them in new and strange contexts in his work. All these devices, of course, can be interpreted as mere devices for achieving perceptual unity in the work, and hence as generative only of aesthetic and artistic values. The resemblances which remain, however weak, may seem unavoidable facts which should be disregarded as far as possible because stimulative of interests antagonistic to aesthetic and artistic values. There are two true statements at the basis of this position. First, the interest in recognizing iconic signs of familiar objects is cognitive in character and, considered alone, is irrelevant to aesthetic values. The pleasure of merely identifying familiar shapes in a painting has no more to do with aesthetic values than the pleasure of identifying an old school friend in a photograph. Secondly, the interests aroused by noting resemblances, unless transformed by the aesthetic perceptual experience, are as antagonistic to aesthetic interest as the sentimental reveries that may be evoked by the recognition of the old school friend.

But the resemblances, together with the differences involved in the iconic character of a work of art can be instrumental in enriching both aesthetic and artistic values in the following ways. The interests aroused by the resemblance are modified or transformed by the differences. They can achieve an outlet or satisfaction *in* the work of art if the associations evoked are molded by the perceptual structure and become part of its expressiveness, an expressiveness which can reinforce or work together with the expressiveness of line, shape, or color. Thus, in Barlach's sculpture *The Avenger,* the outlines and volume seen as abstract, if that be possible, would be perceived as moving strongly in one direction. There would still be a quality of harshness, severity, and strength in the three-dimensional design. But the recognition of the iconic character of the form reinforces the movement and the emotions appropriate to the fiercely moving avenger are felt as characteristics of the perceptual form, not as designata or characteristics of designata. Further, the perceptual structure is not the bearer of an isolable, general feeling which without change might have another bearer. The feelings which become part of the expressiveness of the work are transformed and shaped by the individual perceptual structure itself. They are, as felt in the aesthetic situation, a function of that structure and cannot be specified or described except in terms of it. In addition, the blending and mutual reinforcing of the expressiveness of the design as abstract and the design as iconic is a source of further artistic values. Paul Klee's *Winter Garden* would serve as a good example here. In this work, the delicate fantastic quality of color, line, and design blend so as to be almost indistinguishable from the delicacy and phantasy expressed by means of the work's iconic character. The two examples given illustrate only one kind of fusion between the expressiveness of a work of art as abstract design and its expressiveness as iconic, namely, a fusion through similarity alone. The fusion and reinforcement may be one containing at least partially contrasting elements, as in Breughel's *The Blind*.

The work of art, then, is an exceedingly complicated perceptual object. It can satisfy in its own way, i. e. in terms of its medium, a practically limitless set of interests so far as they are transformed and governed by its perceptual structure.

Various Arts

RENÉ WELLEK and
AUSTIN WARREN
The Analysis of the Literary
Work of Art [1]

THE NATURAL AND SENSIBLE starting point for work in literary scholarship is the interpretation and analysis of the works of literature themselves. After all, only the works themselves justify all our interest in the life of an author, in his social environment and the whole process of literature.

---

[1] From *Theory of Literature* by René Wellek and Austin Warren, copyright, 1942, 1947, 1949, by Harcourt, Brace and Company, Inc., pp. 139–158. Reprinted by permission.

The editors have found it impossible to keep all the numerous and valuable footnotes which the authors of this selection appended to their text. The student interested in either verifying the authors' ideas or further reading is advised to consult the excellent notes and bibliography found in *Theory of Literature*. (Eds.)

But, curiously enough, literary history has been so preoccupied with the setting of a work of literature that its attempts at an analysis of the works themselves have been slight in comparison with the enormous efforts expended on the study of environment. Some reasons for this overemphasis on the conditioning circumstances rather than on the works themselves are not far to seek. Modern literary history arose in close connection with the Romantic movement, which could subvert the critical system of Neo-Classicism only with the relativist argument that different times required different standards. Thus the emphasis shifted from the literature itself to its historical background, which was used to justify the new values ascribed to old literature. In the nineteenth century, explanation by causes became the great watchword, largely in an endeavor to emulate the methods of the natural sciences. Besides, the breakdown of the old "poetics," which occurred with the shift of interest to the individual "taste" of the reader, strengthened the conviction that art, being fundamentally irrational, should be left to "appreciation." Sir Sidney Lee, in his inaugural lecture, merely summed up the theory of most academic literary scholarship when he said: "In literary history we seek the external circumstances—political, social, economic—in which literature is produced." [2] The result of a lack of clarity on questions of poetics has been the astonishing helplessness of most scholars when confronted with the task of actually analyzing and evaluating a work of art.

In recent years a healthy reaction has taken place which recognizes that the study of literature should, first and foremost, concentrate on the actual works of art themselves. The old methods of classical rhetoric, poetics, or metrics are and must be reviewed and restated in modern terms. New methods based on a survey of the wider range of forms in modern literature are being introduced. In France the method of *explication de textes,* in Germany the formal analyses based on parallels with the history of fine arts, cultivated by Oskar Walzel, and especially the brilliant movement of the Russian formalists and their Czech and Polish followers have brought new stimuli to the study of the literary work, which we are only beginning to see properly and to analyze adequately. In England some of the followers of I. A. Richards have paid close attention to the text of poetry and also in this country a group of critics have made a study of the work of art the center of their interest. Several studies of the drama which stress its difference from life and combat the confusion between dramatic and empirical reality point in the same direction. Similarly, many studies of the novel are not content to consider it merely in terms of its relations to the social structure but try to analyze its artistic methods—its points of view, its narrative technique.

The Russian Formalists most vigorously objected to the old dichotomy of

---

[2] Sir Sidney Lee, *The Place of English Literature in the Modern University,* London, 1913 (reprinted in *Elizabethan and Other Essays,* London, 1929, p. 7).

"content versus form," which cuts a work of art into two halves: a crude content and a superimposed, purely external form. Clearly, the aesthetic effect of a work of art does not reside in what is commonly called its content. There are few works of art which are not ridiculous or meaningless in synopsis (which can be justified only as a pedagogical device). But a distinction between form as the factor aesthetically active and a content aesthetically indifferent meets with insuperable difficulties. At first sight the boundary line may seem fairly definite. If we understand by content the ideas and emotions conveyed in a work of literature, the form would include all linguistic elements by which contents are expressed. But if we examine this distinction more closely, we see that content implies some elements of form: e.g., the events told in a novel are parts of the content, while the way in which they are arranged into a "plot" is part of the form. Dissociated from this way of arrangement they have no artistic effect whatsoever. The common remedy proposed and widely used by Germans, i.e., the introduction of the term "inner form," which originally dates back to Plotinus and Shaftesbury, is merely complicating matters, as the boundary line between inner and outer form remains completely obscure. It must simply be admitted that the manner in which events are arranged in a plot is part of the form. Things become even more disastrous for the traditional concepts when we realize that even in the language, commonly considered part of the form, it is necessary to distinguish between words in themselves, aesthetically indifferent, and the manner in which individual words make up units of sound and meaning, aesthetically effective. It would be better to rechristen all the aesthetically indifferent elements "materials," while the manner in which they acquire aesthetic efficacy may be styled "structure." This distinction is by no means a simple renaming of the old pair, content and form. It cuts right across the old boundary lines. "Materials" include elements formerly considered part of the content, and parts formerly considered formal. "Structure" is a concept including both content and form so far as they are organized for aesthetic purposes. The work of art is, then, considered as a whole system of signs, or structure of signs, serving a specific aesthetic purpose.

How, more concretely, can we envisage an analysis of this structure? What is meant by this totality, and how can it be analyzed? What is meant by saying that an analysis is wrong or mistaken? This raises an extremely difficult epistemological question, that of the "mode of existence" or the "ontological situs" of a literary work of art (which, for brevity's sake, we shall call a "poem" in what follows). What is the "real" poem; where should we look for it; how does it exist? A correct answer to these questions must solve several critical problems and open a way to the proper analysis of a work of literature.

To the question what and where is a poem, or rather a literary work of art in general, several traditional answers have been given which must be criticized and eliminated before we can attempt an answer of our own. One of the most common and oldest answers is the view that a poem is an "artifact," an object of the same nature as a piece of sculpture or a painting. Thus the work of art is considered identical with the black lines of ink on white paper or parchment or, if we think of a Babylonian poem, with the grooves in the brick. Obviously this answer is quite unsatisfactory. There is, first of all, the huge oral "literature." There are poems or stories which have never been fixed in writing and still continue to exist. Thus the lines in black ink are merely a method of recording a poem which must be conceived as existing elsewhere. If we destroy the writing or even all copies of a printed book we still may not destroy the poem, as it might be preserved in oral tradition or in the memory of a man like Macaulay, who boasted of knowing *Paradise Lost* and *Pilgrim's Progress* by heart. On the other hand, if we destroy a painting or a piece of sculpture or a building, we destroy it completely, though we may preserve descriptions or records in another medium and might even try to reconstruct what has been lost. But we shall always create a different work of art (however similar), while the mere destruction of the copy of a book or even of all its copies may not touch the work of art at all.

That the writing on the paper is not the "real" poem can be demonstrated also by another argument. The printed page contains a great many elements which are extraneous to the poem: the size of the type, the sort of type used (roman, italic), the size of the page, and many other factors. If we should take seriously the view that a poem is an artifact, we would have to come to the conclusion that every single copy is a different work of art. There should be no *à priori* reason why copies in different editions should be copies of the same book. Besides, not every printing is considered by us, the readers, a correct printing of a poem. The very fact that we are able to correct printer's errors in a text which we might not have read before or, in some rare cases, restore the genuine meaning of the text shows that we do not consider the printed lines as the genuine poem. Thus we have shown that the poem (or any literary work of art) can exist outside its printed version and that the printed artifact contains many elements which we all must consider as not included in the genuine poem.

Still, this negative conclusion should not blind us to the enormous practical importance, since the invention of writing and printing, of our methods of recording poetry. There is no doubt that much literature has been lost and thus completely destroyed because its written records have disappeared and the theoretically possible means of oral tradition have failed or have been interrupted. Writing and especially printing have made possible the con tinuity of literary tradition and must have done much to increase the unity and integrity of works of art. Besides, at least in certain periods of the history of poetry, the graphic picture has become a part of some finished works of art.

In Chinese poetry, as Ernest Fenollosa has shown, the pictorial ideograms form a part of the total meaning of the poems. But also in the Western tradition there are the graphic poems of the *Greek Anthology,* the "Altar" or the "Church-floor" of George Herbert, and similar poems of the Metaphysicals which can be paralleled on the Continent in Spanish Gongorism, Italian Marinism, in German Baroque poetry, and elsewhere. Also modern poetry in America (e. e. cummings), in Germany (Arno Holz), in France (Apollinaire), and elsewhere has used graphic devices like unusual line arrangements or even beginnings at the bottom of the page, different colors of printing, etc. In the novel *Tristram Shandy,* Sterne used, as far back as the eighteenth century, blank and marbled pages. All such devices are integral parts of these particular works of art. Though we know that a majority of poetry is independent of them, they cannot and should not be ignored in those cases.

Besides, the role of print in poetry is by no means confined to such comparatively rare extravaganzas; the line-ends of verses, the grouping into stanzas, the paragraphs of prose passages, eye-rhymes or puns which are comprehensible only through spelling, and many similar devices must be considered integral factors of literary works of art. A purely oral theory tends to exclude all considerations of such devices, but they cannot be ignored in any complete analysis of many works of literary art. Their existence merely proves that print has become very important for the practice of poetry in modern times, that poetry is written for the eye as well as for the ear. Though the use of graphic devices is not indispensable, they are far more frequent in literature than in music, where the printed score is in a position similar to the printed page in poetry. In music such uses are rare, though by no means non-existent. There are many curious optical devices (colors, etc.) in Italian madrigal scores of the sixteenth century. The supposedly "pure" composer Handel wrote a chorus speaking of the Red Sea flood where the "water stood like a wall," and the notes on the printed page of music form firm rows of evenly spaced dots suggesting a phalanx or wall.

We have started with a theory which probably has not many serious adherents today. The second answer to our question puts the essence of a literary work of art into the sequence of sounds uttered by a speaker or reader of poetry. This is a widely accepted solution favored especially by reciters. But the answer is equally unsatisfactory. Every reading aloud or reciting of a poem is merely a performance of a poem and not the poem itself. It is on exactly the same level as the performance of a piece of music by a musician.

There is—to follow the line of our previous argument—a huge written literature which may never be sounded at all. To deny this, we have to subscribe to some such absurd theory as that of some behaviorists that all silent reading is accompanied by movements of the vocal cords. Actually, all experience shows that, unless we are almost illiterate or are struggling with the reading of a foreign language or want to articulate the sound whisperingly on purpose, we usually read "globally," that is, we grasp printed words as wholes without breaking them up into sequences of phonemes and thus do not pronounce them even silently. In reading quickly we have no time even to articulate the sounds with our vocal cords. To assume besides that a poem exists in the reading aloud leads to the absurd consequence that a poem is non-existent when it is not sounded and that it is recreated afresh by every reading. Moreover, we could not show how a work like Homer's *Iliad,* or Tolstoy's *War and Peace,* exists as a unity, as it can never be read aloud all in one sitting.

But most importantly, every reading of a poem is more than the genuine poem: each performance contains elements which are extraneous to the poem and individual idiosyncrasies of pronunciation, pitch, tempo, and distribution of stress—elements which are either determined by the personality of the speaker or are symptoms and means of his interpretation of the poem. Moreover, the reading of a poem not only adds individual elements but always represents only a selection of factors implicit in the text of a poem: the pitch of the voice, the speed in which a passage is read, the distribution and intensity of the stresses, these may be either right or wrong, and even when right, may still represent only one version of reading a poem. We must acknowledge the possibility of several readings of a poem: readings which we either consider wrong readings, if we feel them to be distortions of the true meaning of the poem, or readings which we have to consider as correct and admissible, but still may not consider ideal.

The reading of the poem is not the poem itself, for we can correct the performance mentally. Even if we hear a recitation which we acknowledge to be excellent or perfect, we cannot preclude the possibility that somebody else, or even the same reciter at another time, may give a very different rendering which would bring out other elements of the poem equally well. The analogy to a musical performance is again helpful: the performance of a symphony even by a Toscanini is not the symphony itself, for it is inevitably colored by the individuality of the performers and adds concrete details of tempo, rubato, timbre, etc., which may be changed in a next performance, though it would be impossible to deny that the same symphony has been performed for the second time. Thus we have shown that the poem can exist outside its sounded performance, and that the sounded performance contains many elements which we must consider as not included in the poem.

Still, in some literary works of art (especially in lyrical poetry) the vocal side of poetry may be an important factor of the general structure. Attention can be drawn to it by various means like meter, patterns of vowel or consonant sequences, alliteration, assonance, rhyme, etc. This fact explains —or rather helps to explain—the inadequacy of much translating of lyrical poetry, since these potential sound-patterns cannot be transferred into another linguistic system, though a skillful translator may approximate their general effect in his own language. There is, however, an enormous literature which is relatively independent of sound-patterns, as can be shown by the historical effects of many works in even pedestrian translations. Sound may be an important factor in the structure of a poem, but the answer that a poem is a sequence of sounds is as unsatisfactory as the solution which puts faith in the print on the page.

The third, very common answer to our question says that a poem is the experience of the reader. A poem, it is argued, is nothing outside the mental processes of individual readers and is thus identical with the mental state or process which we experience in reading or listening to a poem. Again, this "psychological" solution seems unsatisfactory. It is true, of course, that a poem can be known only through individual experiences, but it is not identical with such an individual experience. Every individual experience of a poem contains something idiosyncratic and purely individual. It is colored by our mood and our individual preparation. The education, the personality of every reader, the general cultural climate of a time, the religious or philosophical or purely technical preconceptions of every reader will add something instantaneous and extraneous to every reading of a poem. Two readings at different times by the same individual may vary considerably either because he has matured mentally or because he is weakened by momentary circumstances such as fatigue, worry, or distraction. Every experience of a poem thus both leaves out something or adds something individual. The experience will never be commensurate with the poem: even a good reader will discover new details in poems which he had not experienced during previous readings, and it is needless to point out how distorted or shallow may be the reading of a less trained or untrained reader.

The view that the mental experience of a reader is the poem itself leads to the absurd conclusion that a poem is non-existent unless experienced and that it is recreated in every experience. There thus would not be one *Divine Comedy* but as many Divine Comedies as there are and were and will be readers. We end in complete skepticism and anarchy and arrive at the vicious maxim of *De gustibus non est disputandum*. If we should take this view seriously, it would be impossible to explain why one experience of a poem by one reader should be better than the experience of any other reader and why it is possible to correct the interpretation of another reader. It would mean the definite end of all teaching of literature which aims at enhancing the understanding and appreciation of a text. The writings of I. A. Richards, especially his book on *Practical Criticism,* have shown how much can be done in analyzing the individual idiosyncrasies of readers and how much a good teacher can achieve in rectifying false approaches. Curiously enough, Richards, who constantly criticizes the experiences of his pupils, holds to an extreme psychological theory which is in flat contradiction to his excellent critical practice. The idea that poetry is supposed to order our impulses and the conclusion that the value of poetry is in some sort of psychical therapy lead him finally to the admission that this goal may be accomplished by a bad as well as a good poem, by a carpet, a pot, a gesture as well as by a sonata.[3] Thus the supposed pattern in our mind is not definitely related to the poem which caused it.

The psychology of the reader, however interesting in itself or useful for pedagogical purposes, will always remain outside the object of literary study —the concrete work of art—and is unable to deal with the question of the structure and value of the work of art. Psychological theories must be theories of effect and may lead in extreme cases to such criteria of the value of poetry as that proposed by A. E. Housman in a lecture, *The Name and Nature of Poetry* (1933), where he tells us, one hopes with his tongue in his cheek, that good poetry can be recognized by the thrill down our spine. This is on the same level as eighteenth-century theories which measured the quality of a tragedy by the amount of tears shed by the audience or the movie scout's conception of the quality of a comedy on the basis of the number of laughs he has counted in the audience. Thus anarchy, skepticism, a complete confusion of values is the result of every psychological theory, as it must be unrelated either to the structure or the quality of a poem.

The psychological theory is only very slightly improved by I. A. Richards when he defines a poem as the "experience of the right kind of reader." [4] Obviously the whole problem is shifted to the conception of the *right* reader —and the meaning of that adjective. But even assuming an ideal condition of mood in a reader of the finest background and the best training, the definition remains unsatisfactory, as it is open to all the criticism we have made of the psychological method. It puts the essence of the poem into a momentary experience which even the right kind of reader could not repeat unchanged. It will always fall short of the full meaning of a poem at any given instance and will always add inevitable personal elements to the reading.

A fourth answer has been suggested to obviate this difficulty. The poem, we hear, is the experience of the author. Only in parenthesis, we may dis-

---

[3] I. A. Richards, *Principles of Literary Criticism,* London, 1924, pp. 125, 248. Cf. *Practical Criticism,* London, 1929, p. 349.

[4] Richards, *Principles,* pp. 225–227.

miss the view that the poem is the experience of the author at any time of his life after the creation of his work, when he rereads it. He then has obviously become simply a reader of his work and is liable to errors and misinterpretations of his own work almost as much as any other reader. Many instances of glaring misinterpretations by an author of his own work could be collected: the old anecdote about Browning professing not to understand his own poem has probably its element of truth. It happens to all of us that we misinterpret or do not fully understand what we have written some time ago. Thus the suggested answer must refer to the experience of the author during the time of creation. By "experience of the author" we might mean, however, two different things: the conscious experience, the intentions which the author wanted to embody in his work, or the total conscious and unconscious experience during the prolonged time of creation. The view that the genuine poem is to be found in the intentions of an author is widespread even though it is not always explicitly stated. It justifies much historical research and is at the bottom of many arguments in favor of specific interpretations. However, for most works of art we have no evidence to reconstruct the intentions of the author except the finished work itself. Even if we are in possession of contemporary evidence in the form of an explicit profession of intentions, such a profession need not be binding on a modern observer. "Intentions" of the author are always "rationalizations," commentaries which certainly must be taken into account but also must be criticized in the light of the finished work of art. The "intentions" of an author may go far beyond the finished work of art: they may be merely pronouncements of plans and ideals, while the performance may be either far below or far aside the mark. If we could have interviewed Shakespeare he probably would have expressed his intentions in writing *Hamlet* in a way which we should find most unsatisfactory. We would still quite rightly insist on finding meanings in *Hamlet* (and not merely inventing them) which were probably far from clearly formulated in Shakespeare's conscious mind.

Artists may be strongly influenced by a contemporary critical situation and by contemporary critical formulae while giving expression to their intentions, but the critical formulae themselves might be quite inadequate to characterize their actual artistic achievement. The Baroque age is an obvious case in point, since a surprisingly new artistic practice found little expression either in the pronouncements of the artists or the comments of the critics. A sculptor such as Bernini could lecture to the Paris Academy expounding the view that his own practice was in strict conformity to that of the ancients and Daniel Adam Pöppelmann, the architect of that highly rococo building in Dresden called the Zwinger, wrote a whole pamphlet in order to demonstrate the strict agreement of his creation with the purest principles of Vitruvius. The metaphysical poets had only a few quite inadequate critical formulae (like "strong lines") which scarcely touch the actual novelty of their practice; and medieval artists frequently had purely religious or didactic "intentions" which do not even begin to give expression to the artistic principles of their practice. Divergence between conscious intention and actual performance is a common phenomenon in the history of literature. Zola sincerely believed in his scientific theory of the experimental novel, but actually produced highly melodramatic and symbolic novels. Gogol thought of himself as a social reformer, as a "geographer" of Russia, while, in practice, he produced novels and stories full of fantastic and grotesque creatures of his imagination. It is simply impossible to rely on the study of the intentions of an author, as they might not even represent a reliable commentary on his work, and at their best are not more than such a commentary. There can be no objections against the study of "intention," if we mean by it merely a study of the integral work of art directed towards the total meaning. But this use of the term "intention" is different and somewhat misleading.

But also the alternative suggestion—that the genuine poem is in the total experience, conscious and unconscious, during the time of the creation—is very unsatisfactory. In practice, this conclusion has the serious disadvantage of putting the problem into a completely inaccessible and purely hypothetical x which we have no means of reconstructing or even of exploring. Beyond this insurmountable practical difficulty, the solution is also unsatisfactory because it puts the existence of the poem into a subjective experience which already is a thing of the past. The experiences of the author during creation ceased precisely when the poem had begun to exist. If this conception were right, we should never be able to come into direct contact with the work of art itself, but have constantly to make the assumption that our experiences in reading the poem are in some way identical with the long-past experiences of the author. E. M. Tillyard in his book on *Milton* has tried to use the idea that *Paradise Lost* is about the state of the author when he wrote it, and could not, in a long and frequently irrelevant exchange of arguments with C. S. Lewis, acknowledge that *Paradise Lost* is, first of all, about Satan and Adam and Eve and hundreds and thousands of different ideas, representations, and concepts, rather than about Milton's state of mind during creation.[5] That the whole content of the poem was once in contact with the conscious and subconscious mind of Milton is perfectly true; but this state of mind is inaccessible and might have been filled, in those particular moments, with millions of experiences of which we cannot find a trace in the poem itself. Taken literally, this whole solution must lead to absurd speculations about the exact duration of the state of mind

[5] E. M. Tillyard and C. S. Lewis, *The Personal Heresy: A Controversy*, London, 1934; Tillyard's *Milton*, London, 1930, p. 237.

of the creator and its exact content, which might include a toothache at the moment of creation. The whole psychological approach through states of mind, whether of the reader or the listener, the speaker or the author, raises more problems than it can possibly solve.

A better way is obviously in the direction of defining the work of art in terms of social and collective experience. There are two possibilities of solution, which, however, still fall short of solving our problem satisfactorily. We may say that the work of art is the sum of all past and possible experiences of the poem: a solution which leaves us with an infinity of irrelevant individual experiences, bad and false readings, and perversions. In short, it merely gives us the answer that the poem is in the state of mind of its reader, multiplied by infinity. Another answer solves the question by stating that the genuine poem is the experience common to all the experiences of the poem. But this answer would obviously reduce the work of art to the common denominator of all these experiences. This denominator must be the *lowest* common denominator, the most shallow, most superficial and trivial experience. This solution, besides its practical difficulties, would completely impoverish the total meaning of a work of art.

An answer to our question in terms of individual or social psychology cannot be found. A poem, we have to conclude, is not an individual experience or a sum of experiences, but only a potential cause of experiences. Definition in terms of states of mind fails because it cannot account for the normative character of the genuine poem, for the simple fact that it might be experienced correctly or incorrectly. In every individual experience only a small part can be considered as adequate to the true poem. Thus, the real poem must be conceived as a structure of norms, realized only partially in the actual experience of its many readers. Every single experience (reading, reciting, and so forth) is only an attempt—more or less successful and complete—to grasp this set of norms or standards.

The term "norms" as used here should not, of course, be confused with norms which are either classical or romantic, ethical or political. The norms we have in mind are implicit norms which have to be extracted from every individual experience of a work of art and together make up the genuine work of art as a whole. It is true that if we compare works of art among themselves, similarities or differences between these norms will be ascertained, and from the similarities themselves it ought to be possible to proceed to a classification of works of art according to the type of norms they embody. We may finally arrive at theories of genres and ultimately at theories of literature in general. To deny this as it has been denied by those who, with some justification, stress the uniqueness of every work of art, seems to push the conception of individuality so far that every work of art would become completely isolated from tradition and thus finally both incommunicable and incomprehensible. Assuming that we have to start with the analysis of an individual work of art, we still can scarcely deny that there must be some links, some similarities, some common elements or factors which would approximate two or more given works of art and thus would open the door to a transition from the analysis of one individual work of art to a type such as Greek tragedy and hence to tragedy in general, to literature in general, and finally to some all-inclusive structure common to all arts.

But this is a further problem. We, however, have still to decide where and how these norms exist. A closer analysis of a work of art will show that it is best to think of it as not merely one system of norms but rather of a system which is made up of several strata, each implying its own subordinate group. The Polish philosopher, Roman Ingarden, in an ingenious highly technical analysis of the literary work of art,[6] has employed the methods of Husserl's "Phenomenology" to arrive at such distinctions of strata. We need not follow him in every detail to see that his general distinctions are sound and useful: there is, first, the sound-stratum which is not, of course, to be confused with the actual sounding of the words, as our preceding argument must have shown. Still, this pattern is indispensable, as only on the basis of sounds can the second stratum arise: the units of meaning. Every single word will have its meaning, will combine into units in the context, into syntagmas and sentence patterns. Out of this syntactic structure arises a third stratum, that of the objects represented, the "world" of a novelist, the characters, the setting. Ingarden adds two other strata which may not have to be distinguished as separable. The stratum of the "world" is seen from a particular viewpoint, which is not necessarily stated but is implied. An event presented in literature can be, for example, presented as "seen" or as "heard": even the same event, for example, the banging of a door; a character can be seen in its "inner" or "outer" characteristic traits. And finally, Ingarden speaks of a stratum of "metaphysical qualities" (the sublime, the tragic, the terrible, the holy) of which art can give us contemplation. This stratum is not indispensable, and may be missing in some works of literature. Possibly the two last strata can be included in the "world," in the realm of represented objects. But they also suggest very real problems in the analysis of literature. The "point of view" has, at least in the novel, received considerable attention since Henry James and since Lubbock's more systematic exposition of the Jamesian theory and practice. The stratum of "metaphysical qualities" allows Ingarden to reintroduce questions of the "philosophical meaning" of works of art without the risk of the usual intellectualist errors.

It is useful to illustrate the conception by the parallel which can be drawn from linguistics. Linguists such as the Geneva School and the Prague Lin-

---

[6] Roman Ingarden, *Das literarische Kunstwerk,* Halle, 1931.

guistic Circle carefully distinguish between *langue* and *parole,* the system of language and the individual speech-act; and this distinction corresponds to that between the individual experience of the poem and the poem as such. The system of language is a collection of conventions and norms whose workings and relations we can observe and describe as having a fundamental coherence and identity in spite of very different, imperfect, or incomplete pronouncements of individual speakers. In this respect at least, a literary work of art is in exactly the same position as a system of language. We as individuals shall never realize it completely, for we shall never use our own language completely and perfectly. The very same situation is actually exhibited in every single act of cognition. We shall never know an object in all its qualities, but still we can scarcely deny the identity of objects even though we may see them from different perspectives. We always grasp some "structure of determination" in the object which makes the act of cognition not an act of arbitrary invention or subjective distinction but the recognition of some norms imposed on us by reality. Similarly, the structure of a work of art has the character of a "duty which I have to realize." I shall always realize it imperfectly, but in spite of some incompleteness, a certain "structure of determination" remains, just as in any other object of knowledge.[7]

Modern linguists have analyzed the potential sounds as phonemes; they can also analyze morphemes and syntagmas. The sentence, for instance, can be described not merely as an *ad hoc* utterance but as a syntactic pattern. Outside of phonemics, modern functional linguistics is still comparatively undeveloped; but the problems, though difficult, are not insoluble or completely new: they are rather restatements of the morphological and syntactical questions as they were discussed in older grammars. The analysis of a literary work of art encounters parallel problems in units of meaning and their specific organization for aesthetic purposes. Such problems as those of poetic semantics, diction, and imagery are reintroduced in a new and more careful statement. Units of meaning, sentences, and sentence structures refer to objects, construct imaginative realities such as landscapes, interiors, characters, actions, or ideas. These also can be analyzed in a way which does not confuse them with empirical reality and does not ignore the fact that they inhere in linguistic structures. A character in a novel grows only out of the units of meaning, is made of the sentences either pronounced by the figure or pronounced about it. It has an indeterminate structure in comparison with a biological person who has his coherent past. These distinctions of strata have the advantage of superseding the traditional, misleading distinction between content and form. The content will reappear in close contact with

---

[7] Cf. E. Husserl's *Méditations Cartésiennes,* Paris, 1931, pp. 38–39.

the linguistic substratum, in which it is implied and on which it is dependent.

But this conception of the literary work of art as a stratified system of norms still leaves undetermined the actual mode of existence of this system. To deal with this matter properly we should have to settle such controversies as those of nominalism versus realism, mentalism versus behaviorism—in short, all the chief problems of epistemology. For our purposes, however, it will be sufficient to avoid two opposites, extreme Platonism and extreme nominalism. There is no need to hypostatize or "reify" this system of norms, to make it a sort of archetypal idea presiding over a timeless realm of essences. The literary work of art has not the same ontological status as the idea of a triangle, or of a number, or a quality like "redness." Unlike such "subsistences," the literary work of art is, first of all, created at a certain point in time and, secondly, is subject to change and even to complete destruction. In this respect it rather resembles the system of language, though the exact moment of creation or death is probably much less clearly definable in the case of language than in that of the literary work of art, usually an individual creation. On the other hand, one should recognize that an extreme nominalism which rejects the concept of a "system of language" and thus of a work of art in our sense, or admits it only as a useful fiction or a "scientific description," misses the whole problem and the point at issue. The narrow assumptions of behaviorism define anything to be "mystical" or "metaphysical" which does not conform to a very limited conception of empirical reality. Yet to call the phoneme a "fiction," or the system of language merely a "scientific description of speech-acts," is to ignore the problem of truth. We recognize norms and deviations from norms and do not merely devise some purely verbal descriptions. The whole behaviorist point of view is, in this respect, based on a bad theory of abstraction. Numbers or norms are what they are, whether we construct them or not. Certainly I perform the counting, I perform the reading; but number presentation or recognition of a norm is not the same as the number or norm itself. The pronouncement of the sound *h* is not the phoneme *h*. We recognize a structure of norms within reality and do not simply invent verbal constructs. The objection that we have access to these norms only through individual acts of cognition, and that we cannot get out of these acts or beyond them, is only apparently impressive. It is the objection which has been made to Kant's criticism of our cognition, and it can be refuted with the Kantian arguments.

It is true we are ourselves liable to misunderstandings and lack of comprehension of these norms, but this does not mean that the critic assumes a superhuman role of criticizing our comprehension from the outside or that he pretends to grasp the perfect whole of the system of norms in some act of intellectual intuition. Rather, we criticize a part of our knowledge in the light of the higher standard set by another part. We are not supposed to put ourselves into the position of a man who, in order to test his vision, tries to look at his own eyes, but into the position of a man who compares the objects he sees clearly with those he sees only dimly, makes then generalizations as to the kinds of objects which fall into the two classes, and explains the difference by some theory of vision which takes account of distance, light, and so forth.

Analogously, we can distinguish between right and wrong readings of a poem, or between a recognition or a distortion of the norms implicit in a work of art, by acts of comparison, by a study of different false or incomplete realizations. We can study the actual workings, relations, and combinations of these norms, just as the phoneme can be studied. The literary work of art is neither an empirical fact, in the sense of being a state of mind of any given individual or of any group of individuals, nor is it an ideal changeless object such as a triangle. The work of art may become an object of experience; it is, we admit, accessible only through individual experience, but it is not identical with any experience. It differs from ideal objects such as numbers precisely because it is only accessible through the empirical part of its structure, the sound-system, while a triangle or a number can be intuited directly. It also differs from ideal objects in one important respect. It has something which can be called "life." It arises at a certain point of time, changes in the course of history, and may perish. A work of art is "timeless" only in the sense that, if preserved, it has some fundamental structure of identity since its creation, but it is "historical" too. It has a development which can be described. This development is nothing but the series of concretizations of a given work of art in the course of history which we may, to a certain extent, reconstruct from the reports of critics and readers about their experiences and judgments and the effect of a given work of art on other works. Our consciousness of earlier concretizations (readings, criticisms, misinterpretations) will affect our own experience: earlier readings may educate us to a deeper understanding or may cause a violent reaction against the prevalent interpretations of the past. All this shows the importance of the history of criticism or, in linguistics, of historical grammar, and leads to difficult questions about the nature and limits of individuality. How far can a work of art be said to be changed and still remain identical? The *Iliad* still "exists"; that is, it can become again and again effective and is thus different from a historical phenomenon like the battle of Waterloo which is definitely past, though its course may be reconstructed and its effects may be felt even today. In what sense can we, however, speak of an identity between the *Iliad* as the contemporary Greeks heard or read it and the *Iliad* we now read? Even assuming that we know the identical text, our actual experience must be different. We cannot contrast its language with the everyday language of Greece, and cannot therefore feel the deviations from colloquial langauge on which much of the poetic effect must depend. We are unable to understand many verbal ambiguities which are an essential part of every poet's meaning. Obviously it requires in addition some imaginative effort, which can have only very partial success, to think ourselves back into the Greek belief in gods, or the Greek scale of moral values. Still, it could be scarcely denied that there is a substantial identity of "structure" which has remained the same throughout the ages. This structure, however, is dynamic: it changes throughout the process of history while passing through the minds of its readers, critics, and fellow artists. Thus the system of norms is growing and changing and will remain, in some sense, always incompletely and imperfectly realized. But this dynamic conception does not mean mere subjectivism and relativism. All the different points of view are by no means equally right. It will always be possible to determine which point of view grasps the subject most thoroughly and deeply. A hierarchy of viewpoints, a criticism of the grasp of norms, is implied in the concept of the adequacy of interpretation. All relativism is ultimately defeated by the recognition that "the Absolute is in the relative, though not finally and fully in it." [8]

The work of art, then, appears as an object of knowledge *sui generis* which has a special ontological status. It is neither real (like a statue) nor mental (like the experience of light or pain) nor ideal (like a triangle). It is a system of norms of ideal concepts which are intersubjective. They must be assumed to exist in collective ideology, changing with it, accessible only through individual mental experiences based on the sound-structure of its sentences.

We have not discussed the question of artistic values. But the preceding examination should have shown that there is no structure outside norms and values. We cannot comprehend and analyze any work of art without reference to values. The very fact that I recognize a certain structure as a "work of art" implies a judgment of value. The error of pure phenomenology is in the assumption that such a dissociation is possible, that values are superimposed on structure, "inhere" on or in structures. This error of analysis vitiates the penetrating book of Roman Ingarden, who tries to analyze the work of art without reference to values. The root of the matter lies, of course, in the phenomenologist's assumption of an eternal, non-temporal order of "essences" to which the empirical individualizations are added only later. By assuming an absolute scale of values we necessarily lose contact with the relativity of individual judgments. A frozen Absolute faces a valueless flux of individual judgments.

The unsound thesis of absolutism and the equally unsound antithesis of relativism must be superseded and harmonized in a new synthesis which makes the scale of values itself dynamic, but does not surrender it as such.

---

[8] Cf. Ernst Troeltsch's "Historiography," in Hastings' *Encyclopaedia of Religion and Ethics*, Edinburgh, 1913, Vol. VI, p. 722.

"Perspectivism," as we have termed such a conception, does not mean an anarchy of values, a glorification of individual caprice, but a process of getting to know the object from different points of view which may be defined and criticized in their turn. Structure, sign, and value form three aspects of the very same problem and cannot be artificially isolated.

HENRI-MATISSE

Notes of a Painter[1]

A PAINTER WHO addresses the public not in order to present his work but to reveal some of his ideas on the art of painting exposes himself to several dangers. In the first place, I know that some people like to think of painting as dependent upon literature and therefore like to see in it not general ideas suited to pictorial art, but rather specifically literary ideas. I fear, therefore, that the painter who risks himself in the field of the literary man may be regarded with disapproval; in any case, I myself am fully convinced that the best explanation an artist can give of his aims and ability is afforded by his work.

However, such painters as Signac, Desvallières, Denis, Blanche, Guérin, Bernard, etc. have written on such matters in various periodicals. In my turn I shall endeavor to make clear my pictorial intentions and aspirations without worrying about the writing.

One of the dangers which appears to me immediately is that of contradicting myself. I feel very strongly the bond between my old works and my recent ones. But I do not think the way I thought yesterday. My fundamental thoughts have not changed but have evolved and my modes of expression have followed my thoughts. I do not repudiate any of my paintings but I would not paint one of them in the same way had I to do it again. My destination is always the same but I work out a different route to get there.

[1] Originally published as "Notes d'un Peintre" in *La Grande Revue,* Paris, December 25, 1908. Reprinted here from *Henri-Matisse,* Introduction by Alfred H. Barr, Jr., Notes by the Artist. Museum of Modern Art, W. W. Norton & Co., Inc., New York. Copyright, November, 1931, The Museum of Modern Art, New York, pp. 29–36. Used with permission of The Museum of Modern Art.
Through this selection is illustrated what painting is as object of art. But it will easily be seen that its author does not distinguish clearly between what is objectively exhibited on the canvas and the subjective processes of his own creative activity. (Eds.)

If I mention the name of this or that artist it will be to point out how our manners differ so that it may seem that I do not appreciate his work. Thus I may be accused of injustice towards painters whose efforts and aims I best understand, or whose accomplishments I most appreciate. I shall use them as examples not to establish my superiority over them but to show clearly through what they have done, what I am attempting to do.

What I am after, above all, is expression. Sometimes it has been conceded that I have a certain technical ability but that, my ambition being limited, I am unable to proceed beyond a purely visual satisfaction such as can be procured from the mere sight of a picture. But the purpose of a painter must not be conceived as separate from his pictorial means, and these pictorial means must be the more complete (I do not mean complicated) the deeper is his thought. I am unable to distinguish between the feeling I have for life and my way of expressing it.

Expression to my way of thinking does not consist of the passion mirrored upon a human face or betrayed by a violent gesture. The whole arrangement of my picture is expressive. The place occupied by figures or objects, the empty spaces around them, the proportions, everything plays a part. Composition is the art of arranging in a decorative manner the various elements at the painter's disposal for the expression of his feelings. In a picture every part will be visible and will play the rôle conferred upon it, be it principal or secondary. All that is not useful in the picture is detrimental. A work of art must be harmonious in its entirety; for superfluous details would, in the mind of the beholder, encroach upon the essential elements.

Composition, the aim of which is expression, alters itself according to the surface to be covered. If I take a sheet of paper of given dimensions I will jot down a drawing which will have a necessary relation to its format —I would not repeat this drawing on another sheet of different dimensions, for instance on a rectangular sheet if the first one happened to be square. And if I had to repeat it on a sheet of the same shape but ten times larger I would not limit myself to enlarging it: a drawing must have a power of expansion which can bring to life the space which surrounds it. An artist who wants to transpose a composition onto a larger canvas must conceive it over again in order to preserve its expression; he must alter its character and not just fill in the squares into which he has divided his canvas.

Both harmonies and dissonances of color can produce very pleasurable effects. Often when I settle down to work I begin by noting my immediate and superficial color sensations. Some years ago this first was often enough for me—but today if I were satisfied with this my picture would remain incomplete. I would have put down the passing sensations of a moment; they would not completely define my feelings and the next day I might not recognize what they meant. I want to reach that state of condensation of sensations which constitutes a picture. Perhaps I might be satisfied momentarily with a work finished at one sitting but I would soon get bored looking at it; therefore, I prefer to continue working on it so that later I may recognize it as a work of my mind. There was a time when I never left my paintings hanging on the wall because they reminded me of moments of nervous excitement and I did not like to see them again when I was quiet. Nowadays I try to put serenity into my pictures and work at them until I feel that I have succeeded.

Supposing I want to paint the body of a woman: First of all I endow it with grace and charm but I know that something more than that is necessary. I try to condense the meaning of this body by drawing its essential lines. The charm will then become less apparent at first glance but in the long run it will begin to emanate from the new image. This image at the same time will be enriched by a wider meaning, a more comprehensively human one, while the charm, being less apparent, will not be its only characteristic. It will be merely one element in the general conception of the figure.

Charm, lightness, crispness—all these are passing sensations. I have a canvas on which the colors are still fresh and I begin work on it again. The colors will probably grow heavier—the freshness of the original tones will give way to greater solidity, an improvement to my mind, but less seductive to the eye.

The impressionist painters, Monet, Sisley especially, had delicate, vibrating sensations; as a result their canvases are all alike. The word "impressionism" perfectly characterizes their intentions for they register fleeting impressions. This term, however, cannot be used with reference to more recent painters who avoid the first impression and consider it deceptive. A rapid rendering of a landscape represents only one moment of its appearance. I prefer, by insisting upon its essentials, to discover its more enduring character and content even at the risk of sacrificing some of its pleasing qualities.

Underneath this succession of moments which constitutes the superficial existence of things animate and inanimate and which is continually obscuring and transforming them, it is yet possible to search for a truer, more essential character which the artist will seize so that he may give to reality a more lasting interpretation. When we go into the XVII and XVIII century sculpture rooms in the Louvre and look for instance at a Puget, we realize that the expression is forced and exaggerated in a very disquieting way. Then, again, if we go to the Luxembourg the attitude in which the painters seize their models is always the one in which the muscular development will be shown to greatest advantage. But movement thus interpreted corresponds to nothing in nature and if we catch a motion of this kind by a snapshot the image thus captured will remind us of nothing that we have seen. Indication of motion has meaning for us only if we do not isolate any one sensation of movement from the preceding and from the following one.

There are two ways of expressing things; one is to show them crudely, the other is to evoke them artistically. In abandoning the literal representation of movement it is possible to reach towards a higher ideal of beauty. Look at an Egyptian statue: it looks rigid to us; however, we feel in it the image of a body capable of movement and which despite its stiffness is animated. The Greeks too are calm; a man hurling a discus will be shown in the moment in which he gathers his strength before the effort or else, if he is shown in the most violent and precarious position implied by his action, the sculptor will have abridged and condensed it so that balance is re-established, thereby suggesting a feeling of duration. Movement in itself is unstable and is not suited to something durable like a statue unless the artist has consciously realized the entire action of which he represents only a moment.

It is necessary for me to define the character of the object or of the body that I wish to paint. In order to do this I study certain salient points very carefully: if I put a black dot on a sheet of white paper the dot will be visible no matter how far I stand away from it—it is a clear notation; but beside this dot I place another one, and then a third. Already there is confusion. In order that the first dot may maintain its value I must enlarge it as I proceed putting other marks on the paper.

If upon a white canvas I jot down some sensations of blue, of green, of red—every new brushstroke diminishes the importance of the preceding ones. Suppose I set out to paint an interior: I have before me a cupboard; it gives me a sensation of bright red—and I put down a red which satisfies me; immediately a relation is established between this red and the white of the canvas. If I put a green near the red, if I paint a yellow floor, there must still be between this green, this yellow and the white of the canvas a relation that will be satisfactory to me. But these several tones mutually weaken one another. It is necessary, therefore, that the various elements that I use be so balanced that they do not destroy one another. To do this I must organize my ideas; the relation between tones must be so established that they will sustain one another. A new combination of colors will succeed the first one and will give more completely my interpretation. I am forced to transpose until finally my picture may seem completely changed when, after successive modifications, the red has succeeded the green as the dominant color. I cannot copy nature in a servile way, I must interpret nature and submit it to the spirit of the picture—when I have found the relationship of all the tones the result must be a living harmony of tones, a harmony not unlike that of a musical composition.

For me all is in the conception—I must have a clear vision of the whole composition from the very beginning. I could mention the name of a great sculptor who produces some admirable pieces but for him a composition is nothing but the grouping of fragments and the result is a confusion of expression. Look instead at one of Cezanne's pictures: all is so well arranged in them that no matter how many figures are represented and no matter at what distance you stand, you will be able always to distinguish each figure clearly and you will always know which limb belongs to which body. If in the picture there is order and clarity it means that this same order and clarity existed in the mind of the painter and that the painter was conscious of their necessity. Limbs may cross, may mingle, but still in the eyes of the beholder they will remain attached to the right body. All confusion will have disappeared.

The chief aim of color should be to serve expression as well as possible. I put down my colors without a preconceived plan. If at the first step and perhaps without my being conscious of it one tone has particularly pleased me, more often than not when the picture is finished I will notice that I have respected this tone while I have progressively altered and transformed the others. I discover the quality of colors in a purely instinctive way. To paint an autumn landscape I will not try to remember what colors suit this season, I will only be inspired by the sensation that the season gives me; the icy clearness of the sour blue sky will express the season just as well as the tonalities of the leaves. My sensation itself may vary, the autumn may be soft and warm like a protracted summer or quite cool with a cold sky and lemon yellow trees that give a chilly impression and announce winter.

My choice of colors does not rest on any scientific theory; it is based on observation, on feeling, on the very nature of each experience. Inspired by certain pages of Delacroix,[2] Signac is preoccupied by complementary colors and the theoretical knowledge of them will lead him to use a certain tone in a certain place. I, on the other hand, merely try to find a color that will fit my sensation. There is an impelling proportion of tones that can induce me to change the shape of a figure or to transform my composition. Until I have achieved this proportion in all the parts of the composition I strive towards it and keep on working. Then a moment comes when every part has found its definite relationship and from then on it would be impossible for me to add a stroke to my picture without having to paint it all over again. As a matter of fact, I think that the theory of complementary colors is not absolute. In studying the paintings of artists whose knowledge of colors depends only upon instinct and sensibility and on a consistency of their sensations, it would be possible to define certain laws of color and so repudiate the limitations of the accepted color theory.

What interests me most is neither still life nor landscape but the human

---

[2] See *The Journal of Eugène Delacroix*, trans. Walter Pach, New York, Crown, 1948.

figure. It is through it that I best succeed in expressing the nearly religious feeling that I have towards life. I do not insist upon the details of the face. I do not care to repeat them with anatomical exactness. Though I happen to have an Italian model whose appearance at first suggests nothing but a purely animal existence yet I succeed in picking out among the lines of his face those which suggest that deep gravity which persists in every human being. A work of art must carry in itself its complete significance and impose it upon the beholder even before he can identify the subject matter. When I see the Giotto frescoes at Padua I do not trouble to recognize which scene of the life of Christ I have before me but I perceive instantly the sentiment which radiates from it and which is instinct in the composition in every line and color. The title will only serve to confirm my impression.

What I dream of is an art of balance, of purity and serenity devoid of troubling or depressing subject matter, an art which might be for every mental worker, be he business man or writer, like an appeasing influence, like a mental soother, something like a good armchair in which to rest from physical fatigue.

Often a discussion arises upon the value of different processes, and their relation to different temperaments. A distinction is made between artists who work directly from nature and those who work purely from their imagination. I think neither of these methods should be preferred to the exclusion of the other. Often both are used in turn by the same man; sometimes he needs tangible objects to provide him with sensations and thus excite his creative power; at other times when his pictorial sensations are already present in his mind he needs contact with reality before he can organize them into a picture. However, I think that one can judge of the vitality and power of an artist when after having received impressions from nature he is able to organize his sensations to return in the same mood on different days, voluntarily to continue receiving these impressions (whether nature appears the same or not); this power proves he is sufficiently master of himself to subject himself to discipline.

The simplest means are those which enable an artist to express himself best. If he fears the obvious he cannot avoid it by strange representations, bizarre drawing, eccentric color. His expression must derive inevitably from his temperament. He must sincerely believe that he has only painted what he has seen. I like Chardin's way of expressing it: "I put on color until it resembles (is a good likeness)," or Cezanne: "I want to secure a likeness," or Rodin: "Copy nature!" or Leonardo, "He who can copy can do (create)." Those who work in an affected style, deliberately turning their backs on nature, are in error—an artist must recognize that when he uses his reason his picture is an artifice and that when he paints he must feel that he is copying nature—and even when he consciously departs from nature he must do it with the conviction that it is only the better to interpret her.

Some will object perhaps that a painter should have some other outlook upon painting and that I have only uttered platitudes. To this I shall answer that there are no new truths. The rôle of the artist, like that of the scholar, consists in penetrating truths as well known to him as to others but which will take on for him a new aspect and so enable him to master them in their deepest significance. Thus if the aviators were to explain to us the researches which led to their leaving earth and rising in the air they would be merely confirming very elementary principles of physics neglected by less successful inventors.

An artist has always something to learn when he is given information about himself—and I am glad now to have learned which is my weak point. M. Peladon in the "Revue Hébdomadaire" reproaches a certain number of painters, amongst whom I think I should place myself, for calling themselves *"Fauves"* (wild beasts) and yet dressing like everyone else so that they are no more noticeable than the floor walkers in a department store. Does genius count for so little? In the same article this excellent writer pretends that I do not paint honestly and I feel that I should perhaps be annoyed though I admit that he restricts his statement by adding, "I mean honestly with respect to the Ideal and the Rules." The trouble is that he does not mention where these rules are—I am willing to admit that they exist but were it possible to learn them what sublime artists we would have!

Rules have no existence outside of individuals: otherwise Racine would be no greater genius than a good professor. Any of us can repeat a fine sentence but few can also penetrate the meaning. I have no doubt that from a study of the works of Raphael or Titian a more complete set of rules can be drawn than from the works of Manet or Renoir but the rules followed by Manet and Renoir were suited to their artistic temperaments and I happen to prefer the smallest of their paintings to all the work of those who have merely imitated the "Venus of Urbino" or the "Madonna of the Goldfinch." Such painters are of no value to anyone because, whether we want to or not, we belong to our time and we share in its opinions, preferences and delusions. All artists bear the imprint of their time but the great artists are those in which this stamp is most deeply impressed. Our epoch for instance is better represented by Courbet than by Flandrin, by Rodin better than by Fremiet. Whether we want to or not between our period and ourselves an indissoluble bond is established and M. Peladon himself cannot escape it. The aestheticians of the future may perhaps use his books as evidence if they get it in their heads to prove that no one of our time understood a thing about the art of Leonardo da Vinci.

W. H. HADOW

Outlines of Musical Form [1]

ALL MUSIC WHICH is worthy of serious regard must be the spontaneous outcome of a natural and healthy emotion. But this is clearly not the last word in the matter: if it were, we should be threatened with the *reductio ad absurdum,* that all genuine music is of equal value. Nor can the distinction be entirely explained by the fact that some emotional states are deeper and more serious than others: for, in the first place, such a classification of our feelings is almost impossible; and, in the second, even if it were effected, it would carry us but a little way towards a solution. The emotional basis of Beethoven's Eighth Symphony is lighter than that of Berlioz' *Symphonie Fantastique,* but Beethoven's is undoubtedly the greater work. We have, in short, the whole question of formal beauty to discuss, the whole analysis of those intellectual laws on which it has been already suggested that artistic perfection ultimately depends. It must be remembered that music is not only the expression, but the idealisation of feeling, and that its true worth will be largely conditioned by the qualities of abstract beauty which such an idealisation implies.

These qualities may roughly be classified under the two heads of style and structure. By structure in music is meant the general distribution of ideas in a work or movement: the contrast and recurrence of themes, the organisation of the key system, the whole architectural plan which aims at the establishment of coherence and stability. By style is meant the due arrangement of the phraseology; the right melodic curve, the proper degree of richness and transparency in the harmonisation, the feeling for the special capacities of the different voices or instruments. No doubt the two cannot be sharply separated: they are in a great measure interdependent, and are more or less determined by the same ultimate principles. But as complementary aspects they may at any rate be logically distinguished, and in some cases may even suggest different lines of criticism. In some early sonata movements, for instance, the structure is coherent, but the phraseology deficient in force and

---

[1] From W. H. Hadow, *Studies in Modern Music,* Second Series, pp. 32–56, copyright, 1907, by Seeley and Company, Ltd., and used with permission of The Macmillan Company, New York, and of Seeley, Service & Company, Ltd. (Eds.)

contrast. In some works of our romantic period the phraseology is admirable, but the importance of key-relationship almost entirely disregarded. It is much the same with a play or a novel; the story cannot be perfectly told unless the characters are perfectly drawn; we may even add, unless the author has entire command of the right word and the telling phrase. But short of this ideal proportion the balance may swing to the side of plot or to the side of characterisation, to boldness of invention or delicacy of treatment. It is only in the greatest work that the form is, on both sides, entirely satisfying.

Now, the highest type of formal perfection which our minds are capable of conceiving, is that of unity in diversity. The discovery of this principle in Nature, as a whole, was the main problem of Greek philosophy; its discovery in different departments of Nature is the entire problem of modern science. Knowledge is the unification of isolated facts under a single law: truth, which is the correlative of knowledge, finds its climax in the existence of law and the inter-relation of facts. More especially is this the case with that particular form of unification which we call organic; that in which the details are absolutely diverse in character, but all play interdependent parts in one single economy. The organism is not only our supreme example of physical structure, it is the type of all human society and all natural order.

Again, our great evolutionist philosopher has told us that an organism must possess three main attributes.[2] First, it must be definite, clear in outline, complete in substance, and filling with unbroken continuity the fixed limits by which it is circumscribed. Secondly, it must be heterogeneous: composed, that is, of a plurality of parts, each of which has its own special function, and no two of which are interchangeable. Thirdly, it must be coherent: holding this plurality in exact balance and equipoise, so that each part, incapable by itself of maintaining the whole body, is yet essential to the due health and efficiency of the others. Illustrations of this principle are the primary facts of biology. They may be traced in steady gradation from the earliest and most rudimentary forms of animal life until they culminate in the ordered complexity of the human frame. And a line of similar development runs through all political history, from the primitive tribe to the communities of our present civilisation.

Mutatis mutandis, this scientific ideal is also the ideal of art. When we speak of a great picture, a great poem, a great novel, we mean one that groups its diverse elements round a central principle, one in which variety is never chaotic and unity never monotonous; one in which every stroke tells and every touch is essential. No doubt, in the representative arts, this principle is qualified by other considerations,—poetry has to criticise life, painting has to represent nature; but in both the element of formal perfection is of

---

[2] Herbert Spencer, 1820–1903. (Eds.)

vital importance, and in both formal perfection means perfection of organism. A bad composition in pictorial art means one in which some detail can be obliterated without loss to the whole. A bad composition in literature means one which contains superfluous digressions and "passages that lead to nothing." Virgil is the great epic artist, Sophocles the great artist in drama, for precisely the same reasons that teach us to see extravagance in Wiertz' scenes from the *Iliad,* or make us laugh, not without pity, at Nat Lee's Bedlam Tragedy "in Twenty-five Acts and some Odd Scenes." Again the flexibility of fine verse simply means the organic inter-relation of different metrical devices. If we examine a dozen lines of Shakespear, or Milton, or Keats, or Tennyson, we shall recognise that their beauty of sound depends partly on the harmonious juxtaposition of words, each of which finds its natural complement in the rest, partly on the varieties of stress which balance and compensate one another throughout the whole. Take away the variety, and we get verse like that of Hoole's *Tasso.* Take away the compensation, and we get the misshapen prose of Byron's *Deformed Transformed.*

Lastly, among all arts, it is to Music that the law of organic proportion most intimately applies. In Painting and Literature, an emotional state gives rise to a thought which gives rise to an appropriate form of expression: in Music, the state of emotion gives rise to a melody which is thought and form in one. While, therefore, with the representative arts, we can sometimes criticise the idea and the expression as two separate factors, with Music it is only in the expression that the idea can be ascertained. Again, the musician has a far more opulent command of formal resource than his brother artists. Contrasts of *timbre* and tone are at least as various as contrasts of colour: the complexity of musical rhythm is far beyond anything that language can achieve; while, in the devices of harmony, and still more of polyphony and counterpoint, the composer occupies a position which is virtually unique in human experience. Hence we may naturally expect that, in their highest development, the style and structure of Music should present the most complete examples of artistic organism: that they should be, as Mr Pater has described them, the perfect type to which it is the glory of other arts to conform.

Before we proceed to test this hypothesis by reference to the practice of the great masters, there is one preliminary consideration on which it is advisable to lay some emphasis. Music assumes so many forms, and is devoted to so many purposes, that it would be idle to expect the same kind of organic perfection in all. The melodies of the dance and the ballad are, for obvious reasons, compelled to a certain uniformity of rhythm and stanza; and it is impossible that they should exhibit the same diversity as a work which is not bound by their restrictions. Again, a continuously recurrent figure may be used with admirable effect in a short pianoforte piece, or in the accompaniment of a song, though it would grow monotonous and wearisome if maintained through the whole length of a symphonic movement. In Music as in Poetry, the heterogeneity of a work will be in great measure conditioned by its extent and scale; only, as no composition is large enough to justify incoherence, so none is small enough to dispense with diversity altogether. Look at Heine's *Du bist wie eine Blume* simply as a matter of phrase and versification. The unity of the lyric is beyond all question, but we may note how the extra syllables come pressing into the more impassioned stanza, and how the style of the whole is perfected by the exquisite inversion in the last line.

It is precisely the same with a lyric tune like 'Barbara Allen.' [3] Here the stanza is prescribed by the exigencies of the ballad-form, in which the alternate strains answer each other perforce. But it is worth remarking, that although there is little variety in the rhythmic figure, there is almost perfect organisation in the notes that constitute the melodic curve. It is not too much to say that after the first phrase every detail in the tune is inevitable, made requisite either by some preceding gap which the ear desires to fill, or by some swing of metre which the mind desires to balance. Another and more highly organised instance may be found in the great tune from the finale of the Ninth Symphony. [4] Here the curve is as broad and simple as that of a Volkslied, filling its limit with entire and satisfying completeness, while the rhythm is perhaps the most marvellous example in Music of organic effect produced from the plainest and most elementary materials. In the first part only two rhythmic figures are employed, one of which is a bare statement of the tempo, while the other differs from it only by a dotted note, yet they are so presented that there is no sense of monotony in the stanza. The first two strains of the second part present a new set of figures, of which each is developed out of its predecessor, while the last two complete the unity of the tune as a whole, by recalling the first stanza and recapitulating its close. Still more, in cases where there is no external requisition of metre, shall we find the unity of the melodic organism qualified by the diversity of its parts. In the first movement of Mozart's G Minor Quintett, there is an admirable instance; [5] the first two bars balance in rhythm, but differ in curve and harmony; the third intervenes with a new figure in strong contrast; and the fourth closes the half-stanza by recalling the second. Then comes the most beautiful point of style in the whole tune. The figure of the third bar, which, hitherto, has only been used for contrast . . . is answered and compensated by the fifth bar, which itself leads directly into the cadence-phrase. And thus every part is made vital, and differences themselves co-

---

[3] *See* Example A.
[4] *See* Example B.
[5] *See* Example C.

EXAMPLES

ordinated into uniformity of result. Finally, as a climax, we may take two more examples from Beethoven: the melody on which is founded the slow movement of the Pathétique,[6] and the opening theme of the Violoncello Sonata in A.[7] The former contains six different rhythmic figures in eight bars, the latter is composed of disparate elements, no two of which bear any resemblance to each other; and yet both alike are complete melodic stanzas, as definite and coherent in their total effect as any dance-tune of Strauss, or any ballad-tune of Schumann. It is impossible for the organisation of melody to be carried to a higher pitch. Unity may be easily enough attained by an exact balance of similar phrases, but only a master can produce it from the interplay of factors so diverse and so incongruous.

The earliest known method of harmonising a melody was a continuous series of consecutive intervals, produced when the same passage is sung simultaneously by two voices of different pitch. Here we have the first proto-plasmic germ of this particular musical device, absolutely homogeneous in style, and therefore inartistic. Art in harmony began with organisation; that is, with the discovery that unity of effect might be combined with individu-ality in the part writing: that each voice might have a separate character, each chord be determined by some intelligible law of sequence, and yet the whole be developed into a coherent system. So rose the old counterpoint of Lassus and Palestrina, bound by certain conventional restrictions, but, within their limits, as highly organised as genius could make it: so in course of time grew the freer polyphony of Bach and Brahms and Wagner, which stands to the earlier method as the Romance languages to Latin. Thus there are two main tests of good harmony,—first, whether each part taken by itself is in-teresting; second, whether each chord can be explained and justified by its context. For instance, the setting of the words "Und seinem Heil'gen Geist" from the chorale in the *Lobgesang* is badly harmonised; the last chord is simply out of balance, and it is only necessary to open any page of Bach to see the contrast. Of course, in song and drama, and, to a certain extent, even in sonata and symphony, it may be necessary to break the law of organism in some particular detail in order to obtain a special poetic effect. But in that case the passage in question must be regarded as a factor in the total result: the principle of criticism is not altered, but only applied to a wider area. And, at any rate, on all occasions where drama is out of place, and purity of tone the first requisite, the rule of organisation in harmony may be taken as paramount. There is no need to multiply instances; two lie ready to hand in our collection of *Hymns Ancient and Modern*. The second tune assigned in that volume to the "Litany of the Incarnate Word" is a compendium of almost every fault of style which harmony can commit: the setting of "Nun

---

[6] *See* Example D.
[7] *See* Example E.

danket alle Gott" is as near perfection as it is possible for our system to attain.

So far we have considered musical style in relation to isolated strains or melodies: and thus have led up to the more important question of its nature in the range of a continuous composition. It is obviously easier to write a good sentence than a good paragraph or chapter, even though all three are amenable to the same laws: and we can find many an artist who, like Horace's coppersmith, has skill enough in details, but remains

> Infelix operis summâ, quia ponere totum
> Nescit.[8]

Indeed, the preservation of balance and unity in a large work is an achievement that requires high gifts cultivated by long and patient training: every cadence gives a hostage to fortune, every phrase offers a pledge that must ultimately be redeemed. It is not surprising that composers have often been too fully proccupied with the elaboration of single points to notice the due inter-relation of parts by which style in the whole is constituted.

For instance, there can be no question of Grieg's genius. His lyric pieces for the pianoforte are almost uniformly charming: his songs are among the greatest possessions of the art. But as soon as Grieg attempts to fill a larger canvas, his imperfections of style begin to appear, and the work becomes either incoherent, as in the String Quartett, or monotonous, as in the first two numbers of the incidental music to *Peer Gynt*. Gounod, again, has some admirable qualities, but among them is not included any great gift for uniformity, beyond the limits of a Berceuse or a Serenade. The "Calf of Gold" song in *Faust* opens with a magnificent phrase, and then degenerates into an anticlimax of pure irrelevance. The choruses in the *Redemption* and the *Mors et Vita* set out, for the most part, with a pompous fugue exposition, and discard counterpoint at the moment when its difficulties begin. Grant that the change of manner is due to deliberate choice and not to deficiency in technical skill; no plea of purpose can palliate the error. It would be just as reasonable for a dramatist to write the first act of his tragedy in Elizabethan English and drop to the nineteenth century for the other four.

We shall find a more interesting example if we compare the two versions of Brahms' B major Trio. In the first, possibly misled by an apparent analogy from Beethoven,[9] Brahms allowed himself to spoil the opening movement with an incident of sheer incongruity: in the second he has completely re-written the passage and reduced it to entire harmony with its surroundings. Not that the latter version is deficient in contrast, but it makes contrast subservient to coherence. And it is certainly a striking fact that the great master

---

[8] Infelicitous at the highest level, because he does not know how to deal with a whole. (Eds.)

[9] Finale of the A major Sonata, Op. 101.

should have recalled his early work in order to correct the one offence against organism of style, which it may be held to contain.

But we need look no further than Beethoven if we wish to see this principle in its most perfect embodiment. The opening movements of the two Sonatas, which he has numbered as Op. 27, stand on the outside verge of organic style: the former contains the maximum of diversity without being indefinite; the latter the maximum of unity without being monotonous: and between their bounds lie all those marvellous examples of contrast and antithesis, of variation and development, of firm outline and steadfast plan, which have placed his work as far beyond rivalry as that of Angelo or Shakespear. See how the stormy opening of the *Waldstein* is soothed and quieted by the melody of the second subject: how the bleak majesty of the first theme in the *Appassionata* finds its complement in the warm, rich tune that enters upon the change of key. Look at the balance of phrase in the first Rasoumoffsky Quartett, in the fifth Symphony, in the *Emperor* Concerto. But indeed the fact is too patent to need illustration, even if the selection of instances were possible. One might as well try to pick out examples of Milton's dignity and Goethe's wisdom, or direct attention to evidences of skill in Titian and Velasquez. Even the few imperfections may readily be condoned. The finale of the first Sonata is a legacy from an alien system: that of the *Eroica* an obvious experiment, that of the Sonata in A major an instance of the curious devotion to counterpoint which Beethoven specially manifested at the end of his career. And it should be noted that his comparative failures are always steps in a new direction, and are almost always followed by some conspicuous victory on the same lines. In any case, they may be counted on the fingers of a single hand. There is certainly no musician, there is probably no artist, whose work as a whole is so varied and yet so masterly.

A complete discussion of musical structure would involve a history of the art from the year 1600. It must therefore suffice for the present purpose to note the main stages of development, and to analyse the chief types, first as they appear in single movements, then as they are combined into the complex organisms of sonata and symphony. Before the Florentine revolution there was virtually no such thing as a system of key-relationship, no recognition of the important effects of contrast which may be produced in a work by the alternation of different tonics. Music during the Ecclesiastical period was entirely homogeneous in structure, bound within the limits of the mode, or, at most, transcending them for a moment of tentative audacity wholly different from the firm definite scheme of modern modulation. When the change came, it was only natural that the first consequence should be a period of chaos. The lay-brothers who had broken loose from the monastery went roaming about the world with no settled plan or direction, turning along any path which promised adventure, and ending their journey wherever they happened to stop at nightfall. The Moresca in Monteverde's *Orfeo* [10] is a good example of the reaction against uniformity. It can hardly be described without anachronism in our modern terminology, but, if the attempt must be made, we may analyse it as a single melodic phrase, beginning on dominant harmony and ending on tonic, repeated four times in four different keys. In other words, it is as deficient in structural coherence as the preceding method in structural diversity.

But as our scale came into established use, and brought with it an intelligible system of related tonic notes, the value of key distribution began *pari passu* to be recognised. Men refused any longer to acquiesce in mere indefiniteness or mere monotony, and set themselves to find some means of organising the form of composition by combining different tonal centres into a coherent system. Scientific composers, loyal to the traditions of counterpoint, endeavoured to solve their problem by the elaboration of the fugue in which unity of style is secured by the recurrent subject, and diversity of structure by the free modulation. This form, which may be said to start with the Gabrielis, and to culminate in Sebastian Bach, is of the highest interest to musicians as an attempt to make style and structure play into each other's hands: the former possessing too little diversity, the latter too little coherence to stand as separate organisms. But as it is factitious in its origin, so it is liable to become rigid and mechanical in its results; an exercise of barren ingenuity, not a warm vital expression of true emotion. Bach no doubt could breathe poetry into it, as Corneille could fill with his splendid rhetoric the hard outlines of the classical drama, but both results are great in spite of their form, not in consequence of it. Considered merely as examples of fugue structure, Bach's compositions are not greater than those of a hundred kapellmeisters of his time: they owe their greatness to the purity of their themes, and to the unapproachable perfection of their harmony. But lay aside all questions of melody and harmony, everything, in short, which can be classed under the head of style, and Beethoven's sonatas will still remain supreme in virtue of their structure. Fugue form is an artificial thing which a man can learn: sonata form is a living thing which a man must feel.

Hence it is interesting to notice that all the forms most intimately associated with the sonata may be directly traced to one primitive type of Volkslied. [11] The simplest possible contrast of key which man can adopt without falling into incoherence, is that of a melody in three strains: the first assert-

---

[10] Quoted in Grove's *Dictionary*, Vol. ii, p. 501.

[11] The term sonata is here employed in the sense which it has borne since the time of Haydn. If it is widened so as to include composers of the 17th and early 18th century, we must start from two primitive types in place of one.

ing the tonic, the second leading to some related key, the third repeating the tonic in order to complete the outline. Now, if we imagine the first strain given in duplicate, so as to suit the requirements of a four-line stanza of verse, we shall find ourselves with a melodic form of which "The Bluebells of Scotland" and "The Vicar of Bray" may be taken as familiar examples. It is probable that the immediate reiteration of the first phrase is a concession to the poet rather than a point of musical structure: in any case, the essential element of the form is to be found in the three clauses, assertion, contrast, and reassertion. "Of this simple type," says Dr. Parry, "there are literally thousands of examples." It is, indeed, the most natural form of melodic sentence which the popular songs of any nation can assume: it is the living germ from which all our most complex musical organisms are developed.

At the outset there are two possible lines of evolution. First, the clause of contrast and the clause of reassertion may be repeated alternately so as to extend the number of strains to five or seven, or whatever is required by the exigencies of the words. Thus we get the primitive type of rondo, which may be illustrated by Burns' "John Hielandman," or by the Skye Boat Song, or by our well-known hymn for Palm Sunday. A further stage of development is reached when the number of clauses is fixed at five: and when the fourth, instead of being an exact repetition of the second, affords a change of contrast by presenting a new episode in a new key. This gives us the rondo form as used by Rameau and Purcell, Haydn and Mozart, and occasionally Beethoven himself. We need only compare the exquisite song, "I attempt from Love's sickness to fly," with the Adagio of the Sonata Pathétique to see that in point of structure they are identical. No doubt there were some experiments on the way. Haydn tried the form as a vehicle of variations; Mozart opened a new path in his Piano Sonata in A minor: but all these were only variants of the established type which either left its structure unaltered, or remained as exceptions. It was not until the time of Beethoven that the rondo passed into its third stage of development, and even with him the earlier form is of not infrequent occurrence.[12]

Secondly, the number of clauses may be restricted to the original three, and each strain by itself organised into a higher degree of diversity. In its simplest form, which may be exemplified by the minuets of many early sonatas, the first strain ends with a full close in the tonic, and thus, while it fulfils the function of asserting its key, does so at the expense of complete detachment from the second. Hence it is a step towards organisation if the

---

[12] The development may be illustrated if we take alphabetical letters to represent the clauses. The primitive ballad form is ABA: each verse being a unit, and therefore the whole song inorganic. The primitive rondo form is ABABABA, etc., the whole song being a unit, and therefore slightly organised. The form of Purcell's song is ABACA, and therefore the most highly organised of the three.

first strain is made to end with a half close, or even to modulate to the key from which the second is going to start. If this is so, the cadence of the third clause will have to be modified—since the tune must end with a full close in the key in which it began—and thus a new element of diversity is introduced into the work as a whole. Of this stage an instance may be found in the Minuet of Haydn's Piano Sonata in D (No. 6), where the first strain is divided into two sub-clauses, one in the tonic, the other in the dominant, and the third strain transposes the latter back and presents both of them in the same key. Here another point offers itself for consideration. If the clause of assertion has been allowed to modulate, and still more, if it has been allowed to dwell upon a key other than the tonic of the piece, it is obvious that the clause of contrast must be allowed still freer modulation—otherwise its purpose will remain unaccomplished. And by this time our clauses have grown in size and extent until it is not appropriate to call them clauses any longer. They have become sentences, or even paragraphs, each with its own subdivisions, its own structural character, and its own function in the general economy of the whole movement. For instance, in the Minuet of Mozart's Piano Sonata in A major, the first part consists of a 10-bar tune in A followed by an 8-bar tune in E: the second begins in B minor, drops to A minor, and then passes through an augmented sixth to the dominant of A, while the third brings the work to a logical conclusion by repeating the two sections of the first in the tonic key.[13]

In its present stage of development the form is admirably suited to the short lyric movements in which it usually appears. Taken by itself it typifies the classical minuet, the air for variations, and the majority of such pianoforte pieces as the Kinderscenen and the Poetische Tonbilder. Extended by the addition of a second example, and completed by a restatement of the first, it gives us the minuet and trio of our sonatas and the common structure of the march and the polonaise. But, as the form grows in bulk and importance, as it discovers new functions and adapts itself to a new environment, so it will naturally submit to certain changes of organism. The two sections of which the first part is composed, appear at present in a direct juxtaposition which will seem crude and disconnected if the movement be increased to a larger size: and it will therefore be advisable to join them by a link of modulation that shall carry the ear gradually over the change of key. Again, the sections of contrast in the second part have hitherto fulfilled

---

[13] The analysis of the Mozart Minuet may be tabulated as follows:—

FIRST PART.	SECOND PART.	THIRD PART.
(a) Melody in A major.	(a) New episode in B minor.	(a) Repetition of first melody in A major.
(b) Melody in E major.	(b) The same repeated in A minor.	(b) Repetition of second melody in A major.
	(c) New cadence-phrase to dominant of A.	

their purpose by a complete digression, not only presenting new keys but using them to exhibit new material; and it is obvious that, after the limit of a few bars, such a digression will be fatal to the unity of the work as a whole. Now the variety of key in this part is, as we have already seen, a structural necessity: and thus the readiest means of unification will be attained if we minimise the novelty of material, and use the sections of contrast, either wholly or mainly, to express phrases and themes that have been already stated in the first part of the composition. Lastly, we may notice that the third part ends by repeating in the tonic precisely the same melodic cadence which the first part ended by asserting in the dominant; and it will sometimes happen, that the clause which served admirably as the finish of a paragraph may appear abrupt or inconclusive as the finish of a chapter. In such cases the composer can extend his third part by the addition of an epilogue or coda, completing and rounding off the outline, which would otherwise be left imperfect. It must be remembered that, as a point of structure, the existence of the coda is optional. The composer may wish, for certain reasons of style, to make the first part of his work conclusive, or the last inconclusive: and in either event the need of an epilogue disappears. But, as a general rule, it may be said that the more highly organised the movement the more it will require the employment of this particular device. Continuity is best secured if all the parts of the work be made interdependent, and in that case it is only by a coda that any real climax of phraseology can be attained.

One more detail and the organism is complete. Among the many experiments in structure which mark the course of musical evolution, one of the most important is the so-called French Overture. The main feature of this form, which may be readily illustrated by the Overture to the *Messiah,* was its habit of prefacing the chief division with an introduction or prologue in slower tempo; and this device has been adopted by the great cyclic composers, and especially by Beethoven, in order to prepare the hearer for movements of unusual importance or solemnity. Like the coda, the introduction is optional in its use: depending not on the structure of the work, but on the manner of its thought and the style of its expression. In Beethoven we find three principal types: the first merely calling attention to the key of the piece, either by directly asserting it, as in the Piano Sonata in F sharp major, or by rousing expectation, as in the third Rasoumoffsky Quartett, the second containing in addition some melodic phrase which is to be employed in the succeeding movement, as in the Sonata Pathétique or the Piano Trio in E flat; and the third, as in the A major Symphony, foreshadowing the key-system, not only of the opening allegro, but of the whole work. It is hardly fantastic to compare the respective prologues of *Henry VIII.,* of *Pericles,* and of *Romeo and Juliet.*

This, then, is the highest type of structural development to which Music has yet arrived. The three clauses of the primitive ballad-tune have grown into three cantos, all different in character and function, all working together in the maintenance of a single economy. The first, technically known as the Exposition, presents two subjects or paragraphs, diverse in key, and connected by a short episodical link of modulation: the second, technically known as the Development Section, consists of a fantasia on themes or phrases of the first, with such freedom of key as the composer chooses to adopt: the third, technically known as the Recapitulation, repeats the two subjects with any minimum of change that may be implied in the transposition of the second to the tonic key. Finally, if the style of the movement require it, the whole may be introduced by a Prologue and summed up by an Epilogue.[14] It is hardly necessary to point out that the principle of perfect symmetry embodied in this form is precisely the same as that on which is constructed a great drama or a great novel. At the outset our attention is divided between two main centres of interests; as the work proceeds the plan is complicated by the introduction of new centres; at its close the complications are cleared away and the interests identified. For instance, the *Alcestis* of Euripides opens with the bare contrast of life and death, continues with those of youth and age, of mourning and hospitality, of vacillating weakness and genial strength, and finally returns to its two first themes, and unifies them by restoring its heroine from the grave. But the parallel is hardly a matter for further illustration. The exact balance and proportion of the structure will best be exhibited if we epitomise its three parts under their appropriate

---

[14] As a simple instance of the form, we may take the first movement of Beethoven's Piano Sonata in G major, Op. 14, No. 3:—

Prologue or Introduction.	First Canto or Exposition.	Second Canto or Development Section.	Third Canto or Recapitulation.	Epilogue or Coda.
None.	(a) First Subject in G major (bars 1–8). (b) Transition modulating to D major (bars 9–25). (c) Second Subject, consisting of four sections, in D major (bars 26–63).	(a) Treatment of First Subject, G minor to B flat major (bars 64–73). (b) Treatment of Second Subject in B flat major (bars 74–80). (c) Treatment of First Subject in A flat, G minor, F minor and E flat (bars 81–106). (d) New Episode on dominant pedal of G, and anticipation of First Subject (bars 107–123).	(a) First Subject in G major (bars 124–131). (b) Transition extended so as to lead back to G major (bars 132–151). (c) Second Subject in G major (bars 152–186).	Final reminiscence of First Subject (bars 187–199).

abstract names:—duality for the first, plurality for the second, unity for the third.

Omitting a few rare exceptions, such as the Finale of the Hammerclavier Sonata, we may say that all movements in so-called Classical form represent some definite stage in this line of evolution. No doubt experiments were tried by Schumann and Chopin and other composers of the Romantic School, but even these are not so much new discoveries as variants of the established type, sometimes due to carelessness or indifference, and sometimes to deliberate plan. It must be remembered that the generation which succeeded Beethoven paid much less attention to structure than to expression. The essays of Berlioz and Schumann, admirable in most respects, are almost entirely silent on the subject of musical form, and their work, considered from this standpoint, is not an advance but a retreat. Schumann, of course, was far the greater of the two; yet even with him we feel that deliberation has not always brought counsel. The introduction to his A minor Quartett, and still more the first movement of his C major Symphony, are really steps away from organism, condoned in part by undeniable beauties of style, but at the same time needing condonation as structural errors. Even in the shorter narrative forms of ballade and impromptu, of fantasia and novellette, the same rule holds good. Their structure will be found satisfactory in proportion as it is organic, it will be found organic in proportion as it conforms to this law of natural development.

There remains a word to be said about the combination of different numbers or movements into a continuous work. The complete sonata-form, like the Trilogies or Tetralogies of the classical drama, is a complex organism of which each part is itself organic, a corporate body composed of separate but interdependent members. Hence we should naturally expect that in the earliest examples there would be a comparative homogeneity of melodic style and key system, and that this homogeneity would be gradually differentiated as the form advanced towards perfection. This is precisely what has happened. In the first pianoforte sonata of Haydn all the movements are in the same key, as they were in the suites and partitas of a previous age; then, by steps which are readily traceable, the form progressed and developed until it reached its structural climax in Brahms. So also with the style of the work as a whole, by which is meant the selection of different organic types in its constituent members. Out of all possible alternatives—the minuet, the rondo, the air with variations, the fully-developed "ternary" form—it is clearly the composer's business to choose specimens which will afford the most complete contrast and yet combine into the most organic unity. The gradual application of this rule is simply another name for the growth of the sonata form. One has only to compare Haydn's first quartett with one of the Rasoumoffskys to see the advance; one has only to compare the *Eroica* Symphony with Chopin's B-flat minor Sonata to see the retrogression. In this, as in other respects, Brahms has restored the balance and has adapted the traditions of Beethoven to the language of the present day.

Enough has been said to show that this principle of organic growth not only explains the style and structure of all great Music, but answers to a fundamental need in human nature. Its laws are not mere grammatical rules, framed in one generation to be broken in the next; it makes no transitory appeal to faculties that change with every mood and every condition: if there be anything permanent and abiding in the mind of man, it is here that it will find its counterpart. Not, of course, that the present stage of development is to be regarded as final: there is probably no such thing as finality in any art. But progress is not change, it is a kind of change, and one which, from its very nature, points to a fixed ideal. We, with our limited capacities of knowledge, and our limited appreciation of beauty, may still be far behind the position that is to be occupied in future ages. But, unless the teaching of History be wholly false, we may predict with some security the direction in which that position will lie. It is as inconceivable in art as it is in physical nature, that the process of organic evolution should revert or turn aside. No doubt there will be further modification of detail—some "Shakspearian convention" abandoned, some scheme of artistic composition revised; but every step that brings greater freedom will bring greater responsibility, and will shift the issue from artificial laws to the great code of human intelligence. We cannot suppose that the generations which look back upon our own masters will ever rest satisfied with incoherence or shapelessness or monotony. There will be new methods in the days to come, but the principles of art will remain unaltered.

THE AESTHETIC
EXPERIENCE

THE CONSIDERATION of the spectator's response to the aesthetic object returns us to the realm of psychology. Certainly the response differs greatly with every individual; but even if we can establish similarities among responses, can we do more than group them into several classes? For we find that individual experiences of the object are radically different from, or even opposed to, one another. In the face of overwhelmingly disparate evidence, can we hope to approach a definition of the aesthetic experience or even a group of alternative definitions for which we can claim any validity? If men differ so widely from one another in their response to art and beauty, how can we say that one man's response is proper or correct and that another's is not?

Nietzsche, in his early work, *The Birth of Tragedy* (1871), first distinguished between the static, distanced, and dreamlike calm of Apollonian art and the dynamic, orgiastic striving of Dionysian art. Although he drew the distinction largely from the standpoint of the creative act and of the object (even suggesting that each form of art was capable of eliciting its own kind of response), psychological aestheticians have, from his time, increasingly addressed themselves to evidence which points to important differences in reactions to the aesthetic object. The work of William James on the varieties of religious experience may also have had its influence on psychological investigations of the varieties of aesthetic experience. In dealing with these varieties, psychologists have usually worked in terms of the dichotomy

277

which Delacroix, at least, sees as analogous to that drawn by Nietzsche, between objective and subjective responses.

Each of the writers in the first part of this section seeks to enumerate several varieties of aesthetic response. As psychologists they are concerned with a scientific problem; they need only do justice on the descriptive level to the various possibilities inherent in the situation of the spectator. It is not their business to affirm or deny the value of any of the types of response which they discover. They have merely to classify them. While Delacroix studies the responses of the observer from a broadly speculative point of view, the psychologists on whom Chandler reports, and Vernon Lee, are concerned with a more experimental method. Chandler transcribes the results of the efforts of several psychologists to systematize the findings of various preference tests, and Lee uses a very detailed questionnaire in which her subjects carefully examine their reactions during the aesthetic experience.

But one may legitimately wonder whether it is possible to choose among the various possibilities suggested by these psychologists. Thus, in moving from the first to the second part of this section, we move from descriptive to normative issues. Here the writers, instead of concerning themselves with the problem of classifying the several observable modes of response, try to establish the superiority of a single mode, at the expense of other possible modes, as the proper aesthetic attitude. The selections in this part, which represent many, but not all, of the more influential current interpretations of the aesthetic experience, should indicate how varied are the approaches to this problem.

We have organized this part in terms of the different mental attitudes according to which the writers define the true or proper aesthetic experience. Yet another organizational scheme could be imposed on this part. The authors could be divided into two groups, irrespective of the quality by which they define the experience: those who see the experience of the spectator as essentially similar to that which the artist undergoes during the act of creation and those who carefully distinguish between the two. For example, Collingwood, Ducasse, and Pepper are all included under emotionalist interpretations; yet Collingwood's expression theory makes every observer of art an artist, while Ducasse differentiates the artist's objectification of feeling from the observer's reception of it, and, similarly, Pepper maintains the distinction between the expression and the arousal of emotion. Thus, with respect to conceiving the experience of the observer as similar to, or different from, that of the artist, Collingwood, for instance, is closer to Dewey than he is to the other exponents of emotionalist theories here included: Dewey's all-inclusive end, experience, also must make the activity of the observer similar to that of the artist; the former is to recreate the work furnished him by the latter. Consequently, the reader will discover, in the selections in which the aesthetic experience is not differentiated from the creative act, that the author often uses much of the space allotted him here to discussions of artistic creation. Thus a great part of the selection from Collingwood may seem to belong more appropriately under the creative act. This situation, the editors must claim, is not due to their misplacing the selections or to a faulty organizational scheme; rather, it is a blurring, on the part of some authors, of two of the problems of aesthetics—a blurring inherent in the theories which underlie these selections. It is claimed by the editors that one of the advantages of the organization of this book is that it reveals such a collapsing of problems. Thus, besides judging these various interpretations of the aesthetic experience according to the psychological attitude which the authors maintain to be proper to it, we can judge their adequacy in treating the problem as one which is unique and valid in the study of aesthetics.

Varieties of Aesthetic Experience

HENRI DELACROIX
Varieties of Aesthetic Experience[1]

ACCORDING TO SCHOPENHAUER, aesthetic contemplation begins with the effacement of the self. The pure subject of knowledge no longer contains anything of the subjective; he escapes from the vicissitudes of his own life and the predetermination of his character. He forgets his own fortunes and becomes the eternal subject, mirror of the eternal Idea. Two eternities confront each other.

On the contrary, does not observation make us realize, in certain aesthetic states at least and particularly, perhaps, with certain subjects, that the contemplator is completely charged with the story of his own life, his capacities and affective habits, his inclinations and his dreams; completely animated

---

[1] From Henri Delacroix, *Psychologie de l'Art*. (Paris: Librairie Felix Alcan, 1927), pp. 116–127. Translated for this volume by Joan Krieger and used by permission of Presses Universitaires de France. (Eds.)

too with the strange life which stimulates him, enriching itself as it enriches him. If our imagination and feelings are to be awakened, is it not necessary that the work speak to us, that it stir our emotions and our memories? If it is to speak to us, must it not be face to face with us like a strange life? The awakening, the thrill, the shock we feel before a work, has its secret origins at the root of our being and in the rapport of our being with that which speaks to us.

There are, then, several stages and several possible varieties of aesthetic contemplation. We would have to distinguish them as follows: (1) The subject who tells himself his own life-story; (2) the subject who tells himself a story; (3) he who forgets all stories in order to lose himself in the object itself; (4) he who forgets the exactness and distinctness of the object in favor of the profound emotion that it arouses.[2]

In effect, experience shows us a large enough variety of attitudes; theories have only to attach themselves to one or another of these varieties and treat it as the only one possible. In particular, no one can deny that there are subjects in art who dream about themselves; others whom animating sympathy transports into the strange life of things; others who answer the calmer, more serene and more objective description of Schopenhauer; others, finally, who at the very least, in the paroxysm of aesthetic emotion, lose themselves in an exalted confusion.

Such also is the self of the poet, rich in varied manifestations: now the abstract, anonymous and yet collective personality, now the concrete and multi-colored personality, now the pure self that dominates all experience.

Karl Groos had formerly distinguished the passive contemplation which is forgetful of itself, "Zufühlung," and active contemplation which sees itself in the object, "Einfühlung."

Müller-Freienfels has revived this distinction; his "participant" (*Mitspieler*) and his "spectator" (*Zuschauer*) answer the description of Karl Groos. These two types represent two extremes; for the direct participation in the aesthetic experience ought to be accompanied—at the cost of being no longer aesthetic—by less direct attention. And, inversely, to understand implies to sympathize. There is either a mixture or alternation of these two kinds of contemplation. The observer who experiences the torments of Desdemona and shares them, nevertheless enjoys them, since he experiences with regard to them some feelings which Desdemona does not; it is precisely

---

[2] In a very penetrating passage of *Données immédiates* (translated into English by F. L. Pogson under the title *Time and Free Will*, N.Y., 1916—eds.), Bergson shows that there are distinct phases in the progression of an aesthetic sentiment. Now the suggested feeling scarcely interrupts the severed tissue of psychological facts which make up our history; now it detracts our attention from them without however making us lose sight of them; now finally it substitutes itself for them, absorbs us and monopolizes our entire being.

. this surplus which supports the entire aesthetic attitude. On the other hand, for aesthetic contemplation one must also realize and live the spectacle.

The following comment shows us clearly that all the vehemence, all the ardent naiveté of this participation conforms very well to the doctrine of *Einfühlung*.

> I completely forget that I am in the theater. I forget my personal existence. I only experience the feelings of the characters. Now I rave with Othello, now I tremble with Desdemona. Now too I would wish to intervene and save them. I pass so quickly from one state to another that I cannot control myself, above all in the modern plays. Yet, in *King Lear*, I have noticed that by the end of the play, out of terror I have latched onto a friend.[3]

And here is the passive and slightly "dry" spectator:

> I am seated in front of the scene as one seated before a picture. I am continually aware that this is not reality. I do not forget for a moment that I am seated in the orchestra. Granted that I feel the emotions or the passions of the characters, but they are only material for my own aesthetic feeling. I do not feel the emotions represented but rather feel beyond them. My judgment remains awake and clear. My emotions are always conscious. There is no involvement, or if there should be, I would find it discomfiting. Art begins when one forgets the *Was* [the 'what'] and interests himself only in the *Wie* [the 'how'].[4]

Müller-Freienfels states that the "participant" finds himself especially in poetry and in the arts of action; the "spectator" in ornamental art and architecture. I am not sure of this. We can participate as vehemently whether looking at a palace or a cathedral or an arabesque. *Einfühlung* claims the second group as well as the first . . . and it easily would find the testimonials in order to ascertain its claim.

The "participant," according to Müller-Freienfels, is primarily active, affective, at times a bit confused—a Dionysian. He lives in the alive world of play. The "spectator" is above all sensuous and rational. He is an Apollonian. He lives in a dream world. The first is subjective and the second objective. The first type gives us, in the creative act, the art of expression; the second, the art of form.

---

[3] Müller-Freienfels, *Psychologie der Kunst,* I, 66. In a much more subtle fashion Balzac writes in *Facino Cane* (it is a question with him of a method of study): "With me the observation had become intuitive, it penetrated the soul without neglecting the body; or rather it grasped so well the external details that it went onto the field beyond; it gave me the faculty of living the life of the individual on which it trained itself, in permitting me to substitute myself for him." (*Facino Cane* is a well-known story by Balzac, published in 1837—Eds.)

[4] Müller-Freienfels, *op. cit.,* I, 67.

The spectator of Müller-Freienfels never forgets himself; but there are more objective spectators to whom the description of Schopenhauer also applies. We return to the distinctions that we proposed earlier: the aesthetic state framed in the feeling of the self; the aesthetic state freed from the feeling of the self; the state in which external matter intrudes; the state of ecstasy in which the subject as well as the object of contemplation seems to disappear.

These are distinctions of degree rather than of kind; but still certain subjects have certain tendencies for a given response that seem to reveal certain psychological capacities. They are also stages—the same subject can go through several of the above states. Do we not often go through a period of excitement and effervescence before arriving at a calmer and more passive stage? They are also reactions which are apt to turn to this or that aspect of art.

The true subjective type is not at all the *Mitspieler* of Müller-Freienfels; he is the one who tells himself his own life-story.

It is very true that, with many people, aesthetic contemplation deviates into the contemplation of themselves. To tell their own stories, to evoke in a game of ghosts their own potentialities, to dream of themselves—these are all the pleasures of art for many people. The work arouses, directs, intensifies and restores this reverie. It prevents them from an escape into complete freedom. They borrow from the artist some few of his themes and discover themselves in some one of his characters.

To take an example from literature, we may recall Madame Bovary at the theater of Rouen. How often we find the pleasure particularly alive when a direct correspondence is established between the observer and the hero of the drama, between the reader and the poem! The observer or reader takes himself for the hero. It is a fusing of two characters. The one is anxious to recognize himself in the other. We know the adolescent's preference for love poems.

The pleasure of the novel, nearly always, is to communicate to us this imaginary life, to put us in the place of the hero, to give us the illusion of living an adventure.

We willfully invent our own novel on the theme that the artist supplies us or on the rhythm of his work. We will see later that a certain way of enjoying music is nothing but this. It pleases Stendhal, not for itself, but as a symbol of his passions. "One really plays music only for the reveries that it inspires." "This music that makes one dream of a thing that at the moment occupies his mind."

For some excellent aestheticians the poetic pleasure is nothing but this. According to Souriau, the proper poetic pleasure—of course an abstraction brought about by the technical pleasure of beautiful verse—is a state of sentimental dreaming which appears to us with a certain quality of beauty, one that the workmanship of the poem, no less than its theme, can arouse.[5]

Hytier has taken up and developed this view. The poetic pleasure, produced by the play of images, is very clearly distinguished from aesthetic pleasure, aroused by the technical value of the versification. The poetic pleasure is "a play of images freely systematized for a profound emotional satisfaction." It is life according to the heart. Thus the poetic pleasure differs from aesthetic pleasure in that it exacts only the feeling and the play of images around an affective theme. Poetic pleasure, then, can exist without aesthetic value. The least valuable work contains a potential dream.

No one can deny the power of suggestion in works of art. All of them, in effect, contain a possible dream. But their value perhaps depends upon keeping the dream in a potential state. The theory to which we are referring distorts a fact. It is true that there is about aesthetic contemplation a margin of reverie, a halo at once vague and yet definite that encircles emotional depth, a grouping of all our powers in response to a song. But the impression is more poetic if this dream does not clearly display itself, if it does not reveal itself explicitly in images, if it remains in a musical state. Or if it should become explicit, it must not do so in a haphazard fashion. Upon the poetic music the words and images which are chosen must not be placed at random. They must be born and must develop according to the poetry itself, obedient to its rhythm and its deep meaning. This half-hidden commentary must scarcely formulate itself and must always be ready to vanish. It must not delight in itself but must be content to mark the emotion of sensitivity. Is it not in the bearing of the reverie toward the work, in its return to the impression that art arouses, that it earns the right to call itself poetic? But this last remark does not deny the value of the fact that these theories describe for us. These theories spring from an exact observation. Indeed, many subjects feel and behave in the manner claimed by them.

There are subjective and objective types in art. For many artists, whether they are concerned with confession, expression or impression, art is always in the service of the self. All that they feel, all that flows from them takes plastic, verbal or tonal form. Without doubt the history of art shows us the progressive development of subjectivity.

For the others, objects, their relationships and actions, possess a value in themselves. The self of the artist intervenes only in order to effect as

---

[5] Étienne Souriau, like Jean Hytier, to whom reference is made in the next paragraph, is a contemporary French aesthetician. The works here referred to are Souriau, *La rêverie esthétique,* and Hytier, *Le plaisir poétique* and "L'Activité Poétique et L'Activité Esthétique," *Journal de Psychologie,* 1926, pp. 160–182. (Eds.)

faithful an adaptation as possible. It is a means through which aesthetic reality takes shape.

As a matter of fact, the subjective often pierces through the masque of objectivity. *Booz endormi* seems to us a great poem in which the author has lost himself in his character. And yet more attentive investigation reveals to us his own character, his own life.[6]

I need not return to contemplation itself. It satisfies this state of harmony and equilibrium that we have already described. Contemplation is the accord of divergent functions, the marvelous result of which is that we no longer exist; all that exists is the object which is the symbol of this accord. From this state comes the feeling of so close an adaptation that the work takes the place of our personality and seems to fulfill all our wishes and answer all our desires; and from this state comes the appearance of necessity and eternity.

We can live the work itself in its totality and in the hierarchy of its elements. We can be particularly sensitive to its formal structure, to its symbolic value, to the impressive power of its sensuous elements. In all these cases we remain in the framework of the work itself.

But our affective life can also liberate itself and take itself for the object, so that we tell our own story or are lost in the story of another.

Finally, we can fall into ecstasy, and we will shortly study these states of depersonalization in connection with musical feeling.[7]

Art arouses, in certain subjects and at certain moments, intense, violent or profound feelings, ecstasy or rapture where the object of contemplation seems to disappear; a kind of intuition without formula or illumination without explanation.

All this comes to pass here as in religious ecstasy, where the divine presence suddenly substitutes itself for the prayer. All the sensuous or intellectual determinations disappear at the same time as the subject's consciousness becomes free of itself. And still, in a confusion of richness, the ecstatic one has the impression of possessing much more than that which he has lost. God and he have become one substance.

Similarly, in aesthetic ecstasy, the work is forgotten and yet present. Ecstasy remains directed toward itself and gravitates around itself.

The study of the artist would bring us, we will see, to very analogous results.

These ecstatic states, in the course of creation, are very frequently de-

---

[6] *Booz endormi* is a famous poem by Victor Hugo. Delacroix claims as authority for this remark Marcel Proust's discussion of this poem early in his essay, "A Propos de Baudelaire," *La Nouvelle Revue Française,* XVI (1921), see pp. 641ff. (Eds.)

[7] Studied by Delacroix in Part II of the book from which this passage has been taken. (Eds.)

scribed. There are some artists who express themselves, and only themselves, in their work. There are those who live the content of the work, lose themselves in the forms, in the different characters. There are those with whom the work, in its technical purity, erases the artist and his desire, and with whom ascetism and intoxication with the form predominate by turns.

Through affective memory does not any aesthetic object whatever evoke profound echoes deep within us?

An affective remembrance, it seems, is the reappearance of a moment lost to the self, the resurrection of a forgotten past, the sudden intrusion, the irresistible invasion of the soul by some one of its older forms, "the *manes* of our dead emotions."

The work of art can at times arouse the acute evocation of a moment of our life. But, most of the time, it is under an anonymous and confused form that our affective states order themselves about the present impression. Our affective experience inflates the present moment with fullness. Certain of the selves which we are and have been become more transparent. It is at times like a rebirth of the juvenile sensibility, although there rarely are precise remembrances. The representations or feelings which the artist arouses are brought into conjunction with our experience. And when they renew themselves, when the work becomes familiar to us, it is charged with a good part of our life. We love ourselves in it and love our old meetings and former friendships.

ALBERT R. CHANDLER

Types of Response to Color [1]

Bullough's Experiments

B ULLOUGH FIRST PUBLISHED a study on the apparent heaviness of colors. [2] This study showed the importance of other effects besides pleasantness and revealed the presence of different types of observers. The inter-

---

[1] Reprinted from *Beauty and Human Nature*, by Albert R. Chandler, pp. 97–103, 230–236, by permission of Appleton-Century-Crofts, Inc. Copyright, 1934, by D. Appleton–Century Company, Inc. Title by the editors. For purposes of consistency we have changed the form of the author's footnotes to our own. (Eds.)

[2] E. Bullough, "On the Apparent Heaviness of Colors," *British Journal of Psychology*, II (1907), 111–152.

play of color with shapes and areas also received attention. The material he used was a series of plates each containing two isosceles triangles of 12 cm. base and 20 cm. legs. In each triangle the upper part was of one color, the lower of another. The division was not at exactly the same height in all, but averaged 8.02 cm. (He admits that this gives the larger area to the lower color.) Six plates contained different shades of the same color above and below; six others had different hues above and below. The background was gray or black. Fifty observers participated. Each observer viewed the figures two at a time and stated which figure he preferred as a whole. He also gave his reasons for his preference, as far as he could.

As it turned out, many motives besides "weight" were cited by the observers, and a statistical summary would have been meaningless. There were nine observers who chose pretty consistently on the basis of weight; twenty-one others did so to a considerable extent; that leaves twenty others with whom, if the pun be permitted, "weight" had little weight.

Those who *did* choose on the basis of weight almost always preferred the *darker* colors in the lower position; but even here there were exceptions; one observer preferred the heavy color at the apex of the triangle, because that emphasized the triangularity of the figure.

Other criteria were as follows:

    (a) Landscape associations, as sea and sky color, the more plausible arrangement being preferred.

    (b) Preference for one color, which was therefore placed in the lower section having (in the triangle) the larger area. Here again one dissenter placed the favorite color at the apex, as being the focus of the figure.

    (c) Other obscure criteria.

The notable feature of this article, as compared with previous studies, is its recognition of the rights of the minority. The dissenting judgment is not to be swept aside by statistical methods as an insignificant aberration. It is to be recognized as having equal psychological significance with the majority or plurality judgments.

The problem of surveying and classifying the manifold effects of color and the varying susceptibility of different persons to different groups of effects was carried further by Bullough's article on "The Perceptive Problem in the Aesthetic Appreciation of Single Colors," published in 1908.

Thirty-five colored papers were used of which actual samples are pasted upon Plate X of his report. Unfortunately he relied upon gas-light and frankly admits the resulting loss of saturation for many hues. Thirty-five persons served as observers, all being university students and all but three of them men. The colors were judged one by one, a method which Bullough thought more nearly approximated an aesthetic appreciation than the methods calling for a comparison. A disk of color, 14 cm. in diameter, was viewed through a funnel to minimize the effect of background. The observer was asked whether he liked or disliked the color and encouraged to give a full introspective report as to why he liked or disliked it.

Bullough found many aspects in the appreciation of color. He classified them into four main groups: objective, physiological, associative, and "character" aspects. He also classified his observers into four "perceptive types," according as one or another of these aspects predominated in their appreciation of color.

First of all, the objective and physiological aspects of color may be treated together and correlated with the aspects of the stimulus which give rise to them.[3]

  I. Hue determines
    (a) Purity, in its first sense
    (b) Stimulation
    (c) Temperature-effects
  II. Saturation determines Purity, in its second sense.
  III. Luminosity determines
    (a) Heaviness
    (b) Brightness
  IV. and V. Saturation and luminosity, or these two plus hue, determine Strength.

Purity in its first sense rests on comparison with standards which the observer supposes himself to bear in mind. A color is condemned as "impure" if it is thought of as a standard hue reduced in saturation or luminosity by the admixture of another tone. But one cannot predict what an observer will regard as "pure"; a bluish red may be called impure by the same observer who called a reddish purple pure.

Purity in its second sense is a matter of saturation; it is "fine" or "good" color as opposed to "dingy," "poor," "insipid," or "indefinite" color. "Even pale and broken shades such as purples, mauves, pinks, light blues and greens, may therefore be found pleasant on the ground of purity, as showing the best saturation possible for that particular tint." (Here I suppose we must interpret *tint* as a specific value or luminosity of a specific hue.)

Stimulation depends on hue but also presupposes a fair degree of saturation. Red, in Bullough's opinion, is "well known" to be exciting even to animals.[4] This, however, has been challenged by Stratton, on the basis of experiments.[5] Orange and yellow are also stimulating but in less degree.

---

[3] E. Bullough, "The Perceptive Problem in the Aesthetic Appreciation of Single Colors," *British Journal of Psychology*, II (1908), 419.

[4] *Ibid.*, 422.

[5] G. M. Stratton, "The Color Red, and the Anger of Cattle," *Psychological Review*, XXX (1923), 321–325.

Green is variable, perhaps "gently stimulating"; blue is soothing; purple is neutral, except that blue-purple (what others call violet?) is often depressing.

As to temperature, red, orange, and yellow seem warm; green is variable; blue is cold, especially if unsaturated.

Strength, Bullough maintains, is not identical with purity. Purity is relative and is coolly discriminated; strength is absolute and, as it were, hits us. Highly saturated and luminous colors of any hue may have it, but more especially certain saturated tones of red, orange, and yellow.

Weight and brightness both depend on luminosity or value. But in weight the color is thought of as having more or less body or substance—the darker values seeming heavier—while in brightness the color is thought of as more or less illuminating or radiant. The same high value may be disliked as thin or unsubstantial, but liked when thought of as luminous.

The associative aspect of color-experience is manifold and variable. Color contributes so little to the firm identification of objects that all sorts of multiple and fluctuating associations can be retained with it. Some associations rest on very widespread experience, as the association of green with vegetation, blue with sky and water, orange and yellow (shown in these experiments as disks) with the sun or moon, and—more rarely—the association of red, orange, or yellow with fire. Other associations are peculiar to the individual, as the color of a medicine once taken. Associations of the former type may be regarded as more "objective" and more "aesthetic"; those of the latter type are more "subjective," but often have a stronger emotional tone.

The "character" aspect of color is the one most emphasized by Bullough. It is "the appearance in a color or the expression by a color of what, in the case of a human being, would be called his character, or mood, or temperament. . . ." Bullough insists that there is marked agreement as to the "character" of each group of colors among those who report the character aspect at all. . . .

We may, however, summarize Bullough's description of the character of different groups of colors. The main division is between colors containing red, which are affectionate and frank, and colors containing blue, which are reserved and distant, though not necessarily repellent; the red type is active, the blue type is contemplative, reposeful, spacious. Yellow is cheerful and sparkling, not serious, not massive. Orange mingles the characters of red and yellow, but thereby suggests a sort of duplicity. Green has a solid, "bourgeois" character; unlike red, it is restful; unlike blue, it is jovial. The effect fluctuates because of frequent admixtures of yellow or blue. . . . Purples unite the contrasting characters of red and blue, yet without duplicity; there is an inclination to morbidness, especially in the blue-purples (violets). ". . . a fully saturated blue-purple possesses a degree of stateliness and depth, which, combined with the somewhat abnormal, many-faceted temperament, produces the impression of a mysterious not easily fathomed personality; one of the subjects (No. 35) described a color of this kind very pertinently as 'a person with a past.' " [6]

Bullough is inclined to explain the character aspect as the transformation of the physiological aspect by projecting the effects into the object; for example, "the stimulating effect of the scarlet is . . . objectivated . . . as *its* strength." Similarly warmth is translated into "affectionate openness and sympathy." [7] Such processes are forms of empathy.

Bullough claims that most of his observers showed the predominance of one or another of these types of appreciation, though rarely without admixture of others. In any one judgment the types are incompatible, or nearly so—a single experience is seldom compound in this respect.

In the objective type of observer the attitude is intellectual and critical, not emotional. The judgments are mainly comparative, resting on conformity to type or lack of such conformity.

The physiological type is responsive to stimulation and warmth and their opposites. "The preferences are determined in the last analysis by the general constitution of the individual, according as he likes being stimulated or soothed, or prefers warmth or coolness."

In the associative type the effects of pleasantness and unpleasantness are as variable as the associations which determine them.

Observers of the character type are reluctant to state preferences; each character has its own interest—one may like to contemplate even a disagreeable character (as is often the case in fiction).

Conceiving aesthetic value in terms of objectified emotion, Bullough regards the character type of observer as the most aesthetic; the others he ranks in the following order: type with fused associations; objective type; type with non-fused associations; physiological type. In a preliminary experiment Bullough had found two observers of each type. Of the thirty-five in the final experiment, two were objective, thirteen physiological, ten associative, and ten "character," according to Bullough's reckoning. He lays his cards very completely on the table by summarizing the reports of every observer on every color. After examining the ten reports which he assigns to the character type, it seems to me that only three of them give more than a few scattering answers of the kind he describes.

Bullough in 1910 reported the results of his experimentation with pairs of colors.[8] For this purpose he used bits of Liberty silk about 1 by 2 inches;

---

[6] E. Bullough, "The Perceptive Problem in the Aesthetic Appreciation of Single Colors," *British Journal of Psychology,* II (1908), 438.

[7] *Ibid.,* 447.

[8] E. Bullough, "The Perceptive Problem in the Aesthetic Appreciation of Simple Color Combinations," *British Journal of Psychology,* III (1910), 406–447.

these he displayed against a background of neutral-tinted Holland, by day-light. He used eight reds, eight yellows and oranges, eight greens, seven blues, five purples, two browns.

In this first series of experiments he showed to the observer thirty-eight pairs formed from the above colors. The pairs were shown one at a time. The observer had to state whether the pair of colors was pleasant or not and to give his reasons.

In his second series the observer had to form a combination. Given successively a red, a yellow, a green, a blue, a purple, and a brown, the observer had, in each case, to select three of the remaining thirty-seven colors which would make good combinations with it and to give his reasons for liking the combinations.

Bullough gives an elaborate analysis of the criteria used by the observers in judging the combinations in the first series, under four main heads and twenty subheads. Among these various grounds for acceptance or rejection were the following: acceptance because of unification through a common element in the colors; acceptance because of compensation of character, e.g., "a sad brown . . . enlivened by collocation with a cheerful yellow"; acceptance because the pair consisted of two values of the same hue, or rejection for the same reason.

In the first series, of 760 pairs judged, twenty-nine were unpleasant although both components were pleasant; ten were pleasant although both components were unpleasant.[9] In the second series the task of selecting other colors to go with a given color was found very difficult by many observers, some of whom had to try all combinations and eliminate the unpleasing ones.

ALBERT R. CHANDLER

Types of Listeners

IT IS OBVIOUS that different listeners vary widely in their response to music, and it is natural to try to classify them in this respect. Myers applied to listeners the same general classification which Bullough had applied to observers of color.[1] This classification recognizes four types of ob-

---

[9] *Ibid.*, 422.

[1] All references to Myers and Ortmann are from *The Effects of Music*, ed. M. Schoen (New York: Harcourt, Brace and Company, 1927), pp. 10–37, 38–76.

servers: objective, intra-subjective, associative, and "character" types. A listener of the objective type reports the quality of tones, the defects of instrument or technique, picks out the different instruments in the orchestra; in short, he is concerned with the most objective features of the music. This is illustrated by the responses of a professional musician who was one of Myers's subjects. "I noticed the second horn was too loud. . . ." "As always in Beethoven, one must notice the tremendous . . . contrasts, especially dynamic contrasts." "I now nearly always view music from the critical standpoint. . . . I always want to know how the conductor is getting effects if it is a *new* work, and what will be his rendering if it is an old one. . . . I never think of 'programme' unless it is suggested to me. . . . To me music is never sad or joyful. I only get aesthetic impression." (His meaning of *aesthetic* must be interpreted in the light of the preceding remarks.)

A listener of the intra-subjective type reports real or apparent changes within his own organism which may or may not be regarded as emotions or moods. One of Myers's observers, in listening to tuning forks, reported, "I felt a touch on the tympanum." "I felt warm in the ear." "I had a lazy feeling." In listening to phonograph records the same observer reported "a restful feeling throughout . . . like one of going downstream while swimming."

A listener of the associative type reports scenes, events, persons as being associated with the music. Of Myers's fifteen observers in an experiment with phonograph records, ten reported associations of dancing; eight reported associations of sexual character; six, a stage full of moving people; six, outdoor scenes; five, associations involving an orchestra, conductor or a musical instrument. "The influence of sexual experience and of juvenile imagination is shown in the fact that the commonest figures evoked . . . were those of lovers, dancers, soldiers, savages, fairies, fauns, and goblins." Associations were rarely reported by the most musical observers, who either took a critical (objective) attitude, or else listened to the music "for its own meaning and beauty." When, however, a highly musical observer finds the music unreal, meretricious, or vulgar, associations sometimes crop up; so long as the music is rich enough to satisfy him, associations are inhibited; if the music falls below his standard, they come in.

A listener of the character type imputes to the music itself moods, traits, and activities which he may or may not share. ". . . the art material may be personalized and characterized as morbid, jovial, insincere, dainty, mystic, reckless, playful, etc., without necessarily having previously evoked, or consequently evoking morbid, jovial, etc. feelings in the listener." One observer reports, "The piece sounded cheerful in certain parts. But I felt in a contrary grain all the time."

Myers, in accord with Bullough, regards the character type as the most aesthetic. The experience of the objective type is too cold, of the intra-subjective type too primitive, of the associative type, too variable and irrelevant.

Ortmann classifies responses to music according to their psychological level as sensorial, perceptual, and imaginal. According to his classification ". . . the sensorial response is limited to the unsystematized and ungrouped sensory material; the perceptual to the organized or grouped sensory material immediately present objectively to sense; and the imaginal to the re-creation of this perceptive material through memory activity, or the creation of newly elaborated and varied material through the action of the so-called productive imagination."

Sensorial effects would include the pleasantness or unpleasantness of tones and chords in so far as these are uninfluenced by melodic and harmonic sequence. This he regards as "the typical response of young children, untrained adults, and untalented pupils." The perceptual and imaginal forms of response are characteristic of more talented listeners and trained musicians. His discussion of perceptual and imaginal response need not detain us, but we may well raise the question whether the three types of response represent three grades of development. Ortmann himself recognizes that the sensorial response is not absent from the most specialized musicians. "Kreisler or Thibaut need but draw a single down bow, Galli-Curci but sustain a single tone for sheer beauty of tone to become operative in the response of the musician. A vocal teacher, upon hearing a famous baritone sustain a single tone in a production of Rigoletto, exclaimed: 'That tone alone is worth the price of admission.' "

It seems to me we must go further and recognize that appreciation of beauty of tone is not a primitive stage left behind in musical development, but something that normally grows with our growth in other forms of appreciation. The best musicians wish to hear music played on the best instruments or sung by the best voices, in either case controlled by a technique which secures as much beauty of tone as is consistent with demands of expression. The keenest judge of sheer tonal beauty is not a child but a mature expert. Pratt insists on the importance of "material" in music. He warns against "the silly conceit that the sensuous stuff of experience is lowly and base," and declares that "the very protoplasm of [musical] enjoyment begins to disintegrate whenever the quality of tone ceases to be important." [2]

To me it seems that the highest type of response to music is the type which most adequately discriminates among different compositions and performances, puts us most thoroughly in *rapport* with the intentions of the composer, and gives us the greatest satisfaction in the music, as contrasted with satisfaction in reverie occasioned by the music. Such response is not char-

[2] C. C. Pratt, *The Meaning of Music* (New York: McGraw-Hill Book Company, Inc., 1931), pp. 71–76.

acterized by the predominance of any one of Ortmann's factors (sensorial, perceptual, imaginal) but by an adequate development of all, in proportion as the nature of the music demands it.

Similarly in regard to Bullough's types, it seems to me that the most adequate response need not always be of the "character" type. So long as the movements and moods reported are congruous with the music, I do not see that it is important whether the observer localizes them in himself or in the music (intra-subjective *vs.* character type). The "objective" factor is indispensable to the material and framework of the musical experience. Myers is doubtless right in deprecating trains of association that lead to ignoring the music itself.

Types of listeners are really as numerous as the types of musical capacity plus musical experience. To answer the question, "What kind of a listener is so-and-so?" we should have to measure his responsiveness to the various aspects of music. Table I, though necessarily incomplete, will suggest what I mean.

TABLE I

QUALITIES OF LISTENERS

1. Responsiveness to the materials of music
     a. Pitch: how well can the listener tell whether a melody is played or sung in tune?
     b. Timbre: how well can he distinguish good and poor tone-quality and how well can he distinguish the timbres expressive of different emotions?
     c. Intensity and Duration: (almost every one discriminates these well enough for musical purposes)
     d. Melody: how responsive and discriminating is he with reference to melody in its different varieties, such as folk-song, art-song, and jazz?
     e. Consonance: what stage has he reached in the evolution of consonance? (compare the previous discussion)
     f. Harmony and polyphony: to what degree of complexity and to what types is he responsive?
     g. Rhythm: to what degree of rhythmic complexity is he responsive, and to what varieties, such as classical and jazz types?
2. Responsiveness to form
     To what degree of formal complexity is the listener responsive, and to what types, such as simple song or dance forms, sonata, operatic, and polyphonic forms?

294 The Aesthetic Experience

3. Associations
   Does the listener indulge in reverie or stick to the music, in hearing some or all types of music?
4. Appreciation of expression
   How well does the listener catch the dramatic and emotional
   expressiveness of music, in its various types?
5. Adaptability
   To what extent can the listener adapt himself to varied types of
   music?

With quantitative answers to these questions—supposing such measurements possible—we could make a diagram for each individual showing his
profile of responsiveness, similar to Seashore's charts of musical talent.[3]
The lover of coloratura singing would have peaks at purity of tone and agility
of performance and hollows at dramatic expression, harmonic sequence, and
other factors; for a lover of Wagnerian opera these peaks and hollows would
be interchanged. But we have the further complication that some people are
of sufficiently catholic taste to enjoy both types of opera. Such persons
sharpen their ears for what each type of opera offers and deafen them to
what it does not offer. In the "Mad Scene" from *Lucia* they listen for the
bell-like tones and agile melodic flights of the coloratura and graciously overlook the tame and banal harmonic effects and the lack of dramatic expression. In listening to *Tristan* they do not expect Italian suavity of tone but
yield to the surging harmonic and dramatic expression. The listener's profile
of responsiveness would represent his maximum responsiveness to the several musical factors, but to enjoy specific works he must often ignore certain
factors to a large extent. Here adaptability is needed. The listener must re-
tract his profile of responsiveness to fit the profile of effect in the work in
question.

But there may be limits to this retraction or tolerance. In *La Traviata*
the soprano is supposed to die of tuberculosis. On her deathbed she coughs,
to be sure, but coughs musically and sweetly; and sings an aria which requires the lungs and throat to be in the most perfect condition. To the early
nineteenth century "consumption" was a romantic disease—a mysterious
affliction which carried off the fairest flowers of humanity in their prime. But
now that we know something of the causes of tuberculosis and the best modes
of treating it, we find nothing romantic in an obese prima donna singing
florid arias on a tubercular deathbed. A modern music-lover may make al-
lowances enough to enjoy coloratura singing in general, but he will be likely
to draw the line at this falsification of dramatic effect.

[3] C. E. Seashore, *The Psychology of Musical Talent* (New York: Silver, Burdett and
Company, 1919), pp. 19–26.

The profile of responsiveness which an individual develops depends largely on his musical environment. Native capacity presents an array of possibilities which are realized in different degrees according to the opportunities and demands of the environment. Children who attend church and sing hymns at home develop one type of appreciation. Young people who frequent dance-halls and other places where jazz music predominates develop a different appreciation. Persons who attend operas or concerts usually develop responsiveness to the type of music they hear. Lessons in singing or in playing some instrument develop musical responsiveness in various directions. The violinist or vocalist must be more attentive to slight differences of pitch than the pianist, but the pianist is more rapidly initiated into the complexities of rhythm and harmony. Playing in a band or orchestra or singing in a chorus gives more discipline in tempo and rhythm than solitary playing or singing. The teacher, by determining what music his pupils shall study, exerts a great influence on the development of their taste. The musician who conducts has motives for many-sided development. The composer's responsiveness must be greatly enhanced for music akin to the type which he composes.

The most useful classification of listeners is one such as we use in describing one music-lover to another: "He loves the old-fashioned Italian operas." "He is a trained violinist and a devotee of Beethoven." "He cares for nothing but jazz." "He is a keen musical critic but can't tolerate the moderns."

The following classification indicates roughly the chief types of Occidental music which are cultivated by more or less separate social groups. They constitute different musical environments in which the individual may grow up, or with which he may sooner or later come in contact.

Elementary	*Advanced*
Hymns	Complex ecclesiastical music
Popular songs and ballads	"Art song"
Musical comedy	Opera
Jazz	————
Military music	————
Simple instrumental music	Piano and other instrumental solo music; chamber and orchestral music

Of course the social groups which cultivate these types of music are not walled off from one another, and the individual may at some time be a member of several of them. The types of music in the first column are appreciated by persons who give little attention to music, but take it as it comes. Those in the second column require more attentive listening or definite training in technique or theory. In any of these more advanced fields there is room for the individual to develop an appreciation of more and more complex or subtle music, at a rate determined by his capacity and enthusiasm. Persons may differ either in the degree or in the field of their appreciation. The first difference is illustrated by two persons, of whom one is just beginning to like Wagnerian opera and the other is a fine conductor of such operas. The second difference is illustrated by two persons of whom one is a devotee of early church music and the other a devotee of the German symphonic composers; their musical culture may be equal in degree, but is different in kind.

After all, the only way to describe a music-lover is to tell what music he likes.

VERNON LEE

Varieties of Musical Experience[1]

"ALL ART," WROTE PATER, summarising Hegel, "tends to the nature of music." This saying had long haunted me; and with it the suspicion that knowledge of the nature of music would afford the best clue to the aesthetics of other arts less simple in their tasks and less seemingly intimate in their processes. Now what is the nature of music? To one who deals with aesthetics not as part of *a priori* philosophy, but as a branch of empirical psychology, the nature of music, like the nature of anything else we can discuss with any profit, is merely another way of saying: its actions and reactions as they can be discerned and foretold by us. From this point of view the nature of music would be most profitably studied not so much by analysing and comparing various works of art, for that would acquaint us only with the evolution of various styles and the influence of individual masters, as by examining the effects of music in general on its audience. Since, from the psychologist's point of view, an art is not the material collection of objectively existing pictures, statues, poems or musical compositions, but the summing up of a set of spiritual processes taking place in the mind of the artist and in the mind of him who receives the artist's gift. Or rather, the work of art is the junction between the activities of the artist and those of the beholder or hearer. Indeed, musical aesthetics ought to be the clue to

---

[1] From *Music and Its Lovers*, by Vernon Lee, published by E. P. Dutton & Co., Inc., New York, 1933, pp. 23–34. Reprinted by permission. (Eds.)

study of all other branches of art, first and foremost because the evanescence of music's material makes it more evident that the work of art really is the special group of responses which it is susceptible of awakening in the mind of its audience, including the composer himself, who mentally hears his own work in the process of building it up and taking stock of its whole and its parts.

The enquiry what music *is,* therefore resolves itself, for those thinking like myself, into an enquiry as to what music does in the mind of the hearer; or, more correctly, of what the mind of the hearer does in response to the music which he hears. But the "mind of the hearer" is not an individual entity; it is only a convenient average of the phenomena common to all or most minds of all hearers under examination. And the first result of such examination is to reveal that these hearers' minds, although similar in one or two main points which oblige us to classify them as *hearers of music,* are in other respects dissimilar, indeed so dissimilar that we are obliged to consider them as belonging to opposed classes. Therefore, before being able to say how music acts upon mankind as a whole, we have to enquire how music acts upon different categories of human beings; which, as already remarked, is another way of saying how the minds of various categories or types of hearers act in response to the music they hear. Ever since Galton and Charcot, empirical psychology has dealt more or less scientifically with certain types whose names at least, the visual, the auditory, the motor, the verbal type and their cross-breeds, have become familiar to most readers. But it is not this classification I have applied to our subject. For although it becomes apparent that the visualising and the verbal endowment may produce special responses to music: and although we may suspect that the motor type, that enigma and *deus ex machina* of experimental psychology, may be at the bottom of other kinds of responses, yet the phenomena we are studying are of a far less elementary nature than those determining such classifications, and the method of tackling them is not that of the artificially simplified experiments of the psychological laboratory; but, on the contrary, a method starting from the extremely complex data furnished by everyday experience and thence working its way by comparison and analysis to the simpler, more intelligible, facts underlying these first-hand, and often puzzling, facts of experience.

Starting from such everyday experience, we are immediately obliged to notice that there are persons in whose life music means a great deal, others in whose life it means less, and others in whose life it means nothing worth reckoning. These last-named people we will, for the moment, leave out of our enquiry, although subsequent sifting of this rejected material may lead, even in these musical nullities, to discoveries shedding light on the modes of being of persons in whose life music does mean something.

This convenient, though slovenly, form of words affords a short-cut into our field of study; and more particularly into the method, whose technical details would demand a separate essay, by which I have endeavoured to deal with it. For in the successive Questionnaires, written and verbal interrogations, by means of which I have tapped the musical experiences of nearly a hundred and fifty subjects, there has recurred a query which has always received two apparently irreconcilable sets of answers.[2] This query, altered as has been its actual wording (in English, French and German, besides successive versions) and implied (though cunningly inexplicit) in many other questions presented to my subjects, can be summarised as follows: When music interests you at all, has it got for you a meaning which seems beyond itself, a message? or does it remain *just music?* And here before dealing with these conflicting answers, I must explain that such enquiries have to steer between opposite dangers: they can avoid the Scylla of suggesting an answer, in so far worthless, which the interrogated subject would not have otherwise come by, only by running into the Charybdis of being answered by a person who does not really understand what is being asked. And of all the whirlpools of cross purposes, over whose darkness the present enquirers have strained their psychological eyesight, none is so baffling as the one of which *meaning* is in itself the obscure, the perpetually shifting, centre. However, by dint of indefatigable watching round that maelstrom, fishing for any broken items found whirling in its obscurity, my eyes and those of my fellow-investigator have been able to discern the cause of its baffling but (as afterward became apparent) quite regular eddies. As already remarked, the word "meaning" is one whose own meaning is apt to vary. And it was by following up its two chief meanings in the present connection that we were able to make our first working classification of the persons who had been good enough to answer my Questionnaires. One of these two meanings of "meaning" is embodied in my previous sentence: "persons in whose life music means a great deal," which is only another way of saying "persons in whose life music occupies much attention"; for "meaning" is here used as a measure of importance, and importance, when we are dealing with mental life, means importance for the attention, or as we call it, interest. I would beg my readers to bear in mind this connection between "meaning" as here employed and "attention"; for musical attention is going to be one of the chief items of our enquiry.

But "meaning" can also be taken as roughly implying a message, as in my query:—"Does music seem to you to have a message, a meaning beyond

---

2 In this selection, Vernon Lee summarizes the results of the Questionnaires to which reference is made here. In the rest of the book, several types of response to music are carefully analyzed. The Questionnaires, to which frequent references are made in this selection, are reprinted in pp. 563–567 of the book. (Eds.)

itself?" And half the persons interrogated did answer precisely that undoubtedly music *had* a meaning beyond itself; many adding that if it had not it would constitute only sensual enjoyment, and be unworthy of their consideration; some of them moreover indignantly taking in this sense my words about music remaining *just music.* That for these persons music did not remain *just music,* but became the bearer of messages, was further made certain by a good deal of often unexpectedly explicit or eloquent writing which attempted to describe the nature of that message, to describe the things it dealt with and the more or less transcendental spheres whence that message of music seemed to come.

So far for one-half of the Answerers. The other either explicitly denied or disregarded the existence of such a message; insisted that music had not necessarily any meaning beyond itself, and far from taking the words "remains just music" as derogatory to the art or to themselves, they answered either in the selfsame words or by some paraphrase, that when they cared for music it remained *just music.* And, in the same way that the believers in "meaning" as "message" often gave details about the contents of that message, so, on the other hand, the subjects denying the existence of a message frequently made it quite clear that for them the meaning of music was in the music itself, adding that, when really interested in music, they could think of nothing but the music.

Now this latter answer, repeated as it was in every form of words, suggests a possibility if not of reconciling two diametrically opposed views concerning the nature of music, at all events of understanding what such an opposition implies and depends on. For distributed throughout the Questionnaires in such a manner as to prevent their being interpreted into a theory which might impair the spontaneity of the answers, was a whole set of questions bearing upon the nature of that alleged message, of that meaning beyond itself, which music might assume for its hearers: In listening or remembering music, especially music unaccompanied by words or suggestive title, did the Answerers *see* anything, landscapes, people, moving pictures or dramatic scenes, in their mind's eye? Did the music strike them as expressing the emotions or life-history of the composer or performer, or their own? Or else was such emotional expression merely recognised as existing in the music without being referred to any particular persons? The affirmative answers, covering sometimes several pages, showed that according to individual cases the "message" was principally of one of these kinds, visual or emotional, abstract or personal, but with many alterations and overlappings. But fragmentary, fluctuating, and elusive as it was oftenest described as being, and only in rare cases defining itself as a coherent series of pictures, as a dramatic sequence or intelligible story, the message was nevertheless always a message, inasmuch as it appeared to be an addition made to the hearer's previous thoughts by the hearing of that music; and an addition due to that music and ceasing with its cessation. Now comes an important point: while half of the interrogated subjects declared that such a meaning or message constituted a large part of music's attraction, some persons actually admitting that they went to hear music for the sake of the images, emotions, trains of thought with which it enriched them, the other half of the Answerers by no means denied the existence of a meaning in music, often indeed remarking that without such a meaning it would be mere sound: but they furthermore claimed that such meaning resided inseparably in the music itself: and added that whenever they found music completely satisfying, any other meaning, anything like visual images or emotional suggestions, was excluded or reduced to utter unimportance. Indeed, this class by a great majority answered that so far as emotion was concerned, music awakened in them an emotion *sui generis,* occasionally shot with human joy or sadness, but on the whole analogous to the exaltation and tenderness and sense of sublimity awakened by the beautiful in other arts or in nature, but not to be compared with the feelings resulting from the vicissitudes of real life. It was nearly always persons answering in this sense who explicitly acquiesced in the fact that music could remain, in no derogatory sense but quite the reverse, *just music.*

I must here interrupt our comparison of these two main classes of answers, those which affirmed music to have a message, and those which acquiesced in its remaining just music, and explain that a large part of our Questionnaires consisted in queries attempting to classify the Answerers themselves. To what extent were they musical? This question, like all the main ones of our enquiry, was not left to the direct decision of the subjects interrogated, most of whom would have been incapable and perhaps unwilling to write themselves down as more or less musical than average mankind about whose precise endowment they would probably feel ignorant. Conformably therefore to the rest of my method, the Questionnaire contained sets of queries which, taken together, constituted an objective criterion of the degree of musical endowment and cultivation: queries dealing principally with memory for musical sequences (melody) and especially for musical combinations (harmony and orchestral timbre) along with the capacity and habit of taking stock (analysis) of the tone-relations constituting the music they were hearing; finally, the capacity for finding accompaniments and for extemporising, these being a proof either of special musical endowment or of special musical cultivation. By this means it became possible to ascertain how far the conflicting answers about music having a message or remaining *just music* correspond with the musical status, if I may be allowed this expression, of the individuals by whom they were furnished.

Two other sets of queries dealt respectively with memory of and interest in visible objects, and with interest in the drama; but especially with such tenacity of emotional memory as enable painful past associations to spoil opportunities of present happiness; all of which queries were intended to obtain some insight into the imaginative and emotional dispositions of each Answerer. For my whole enquiry had started with the working hypothesis that the tendency to attribute to music an emotional message (i.e. the expression of the emotional vicissitudes either of the Answerer or of the composer or of some third person) might be due to the greater predominance of emotional interest in the Answerer's usual inner life. This hypothesis speedily broke down: some people were obviously very emotional who yet persisted in answering that music had no message for them; others utterly rejected the *just music* alternative without revealing any particular emotional bias, or, for that matter, any particular development of visual imagination either. Still less was it possible to connect musical endowment and cultivation with the presence or the lack of any specially emotional disposition. But while this first, and insufficiently complex, view of the problem utterly broke down, the sifting of the evidence which led to its rejection left us quite unexpectedly in presence of what has, I think, proved a real clue to the matter.

For although there seemed no direct relation between the degree of emotional disposition and the question whether music had or had not a message, a meaning beyond itself, this question showed itself in an obvious relation to what I have called the musical *status* of the Answerers. The more musical Answerers were also those who repudiated the message, who insisted that music had a meaning in itself, in fact, that it remained for them "just music." A certain number of highly musical Answerers not only declared this to be the case with themselves, but foretold that we should find it so with every other sufficiently musical hearer. Their own experience was that the maximum interest and maximum pleasure connected with music can leave no room for anything else. And this answer led to the framing of queries bearing upon musical attention: queries which elicited some very unexpected information. For the distinctly musical Answerers proved to be those who admitted without hesitation that their musical attention was liable to fluctuations and lapses. They were continually catching themselves thinking of something else while hearing music. They complained of their own inattention and divagation. But—and this is the important point in the evidence— these lapses were regarded by them as irrelevancies and interruptions: the music was going on, but their attention was not following it. On the other hand, the less musical Answerers, those precisely who found in music a meaning beyond itself, seemed comparatively unaware of such lapses or interruptions. From some of their answers one might have gathered that rather unmusical people could sit through two hours of a concert with unflagging enjoyment; but further sets of queries revealed that although un-

broken by boredom, restlessness or the conscious intrusion of irrelevant matters, that enjoyment was not confined to the music. When asked whether the
music suggested anything, they abounded in accounts of inner visions, trains
of thought and all manner of emotional dramas, sometimes most detailed
and extensive, which filled their minds while, as they averred, they were
listening to the music; indeed some of which, they did not hesitate to admit,
constituted the chief attraction of music.

Putting their statement opposite that of the more musical Answerers,—
namely, that musical appreciation left room for nothing else, and that although musical attention could and did frequently lapse, it could never be
simultaneously divided between the heard music and anything else,—the
conclusion became obvious that there existed two different modes of responding to music, each of which was claimed to be the only one by those
in whom it was habitual. One may be called *listening* to music; the other
hearing, with lapses into merely *over-hearing* it. *Listening* implied the most
active attention moving along every detail of composition and performance,
taking in all the relations of sequences and combinations of sounds as regards pitch, intervals, modulations, rhythms and intensities, holding them
in the memory and coordinating them in a series of complex wholes, similar
(this was an occasional illustration) to that constituted by all the parts,
large and small, of a piece of architecture; and these architecturally coordi-
nated groups of sound-relations, i.e. these audible shapes made up of intervals, rhythms, harmonies and accents, themselves constituted the meaning
of music to this class of listeners; the meaning in the sense not of a message
different from whatever conveyed it, but in the sense of an interest, an importance, residing in the music and inseparable from it.

This is what we gather about that which I have called *listening to music.
Hearing music,* as it is revealed by our Answerers, is not simply a lesser
degree of the same mental activity, but one whose comparative poverty from
the musical side is eked out and compensated by other elements. The answers to our Questionnaires show that even the least attentive "Hearers"
have moments, whose frequency and duration depend both on general
musical habits and on the familiarity with the particular piece or style of
music, of active listening; for they constantly allude to their ability to follow
or grasp, as they express it, the whole or only part of what they happen to
hear. But instead of constituting the bulk of their musical experience (in
such a way that any other thought is recognised as irrelevant) these moments
of concentrated and active attention to the musical shapes are like islands
continually washed over by a shallow tide of other thoughts: memories,
associations, suggestions, visual images and emotional states, ebbing and
flowing round the more or less clearly emergent musical perceptions, in such
a way that each participates of the quality of the other, till they coalesce,

forming a homogeneous and special contemplative condition, into whose blend of musical and non-musical thoughts there enters nothing which the "Hearer" can recognise as inattention, for which, on the contrary, the concentrated musical "Listener" recognises the lapses and divagations whereof he complains. Moreover, in this kind of *hearing the music* there really seem fewer intrusions from everyday life. Musical phrases, non-musical images and emotions are all welded into the same musical day-dream, and the trains of thought are necessarily harmonious with the music, for if they were conflicting, the music (which is heard though not always listened to) would either drive them away or (as in the lapses of the more musically attentive) cease to play any part. For these intermittently and imperfectly perceived sequences and combinations of sound *do* play a very important part in these day-dreams. By their constancy, regularity and difference from anything else, they make and enclose a kind of inner ambience in which these reveries live their segregated and harmonious life. It must be remembered that while the eye (to which psychology adds the motor sense) is unceasingly building up a spatial world which is the scene of our everyday existence, the usual dealings of the ear are with intermittent and heterogeneous impressions, so that only music can surround us with a continuous and homogeneous world of sound, a world foreign to what we call real life, and therefore excluding from its magic enclosure all real life's concerns, save when they have been stripped of all reality, accidents and urgencies, and been transfigured by a bath, if not of oblivion, at least of harmonious contemplation.

The above summing up of the evidence of those Answerers who admitted that they did not always follow or grasp, i.e. actively listen to, the music they were hearing, and who alleged that for them music has a message—a meaning beyond itself—has taken us much further into the question of the nature of music than is warranted by the limits of this introduction. A detailed examination of the answers to my Questionnaires will follow up these first indications, and first and foremost deal with the other category of Answerers, those whose attention is engrossed by the music, and who allege that for them music remains *just music.*

But at the bottom of all these varieties of musical experience, and of the many subdivisions and crosses thereof, lies the question of musical attention. And the first fruits of my Questionnaires have therefore been the establishing of a distinction between listening to music and merely hearing it; between a response to music such as implies intellectual and aesthetic activity of a very intense, bracing and elevating kind; and a response to music consisting largely of emotional and imaginative day-dreams, purified from personal and practical preoccupations and full of refreshing visions and salutary sentimental satisfactions. These are the two ways of impersonal, contemplative happiness in which music can benefit mankind. And they explain the two kinds of "meaning" which are ascribed to music and which music can have in our lives.

The following study of the data elicited by my Questionnaires shows furthermore how these two main modes of responding to music overlay and enrich one another; it may even suggest how the desire for music as something to be listened to has gradually evolved out of a primitive need for music as something to stir inert, or release pent-up, emotions and to induce such daydreams as restore and quicken the soul.

Interpretations of Aesthetic Experience

AS PLEASURE

HENRY RUTGERS MARSHALL
The Aesthetic Experience as Pleasure [1]

The Field of Aesthetics: Introductory Summary

A GREAT DEAL OF attention has been given by thinkers in the past to the subject of Aesthetics, but for all that we find ourselves to-day without any Sciences of Aesthetics, and without any Philosophy of Art which is comprehensive and widely acknowledged as valid. This is probably due principally to the fact that thinkers of importance have found themselves called upon to deal primarily with theories of knowledge and of activity in relation to their fellows; and have turned to the discussion of Aesthetics with preconceived notions and settled formula, to which they have subordinated the facts forced upon them from the realm of art.

---

[1] From Henry Rutgers Marshall, *Pain, Pleasure, and Aesthetics* (New York: The Macmillan Company, 1894), pp. 106–111, 148–158. Title by the editors. (Eds.)

Attempts have been made by many writers, who have taken example from Aristotle, to discover some special qualities in beautiful objects which determine their beauty. These efforts have invariably failed. The same objective tendency is observed in the many efforts made by the best of thinkers to describe and account for certain absolutes or universals of beauty to which our individual experiences relate. No agreement between thinkers in this direction has been reached, however, and we must acknowledge that no satisfactory resting-place for art theory has thus been attained.

Better results seem to be within the reach of those who study the subject from the subjective side, examining the mental state of the observer of the beautiful in nature and art product; looking within for some principles of unity upon which to base a philosophic treatment of the subject.

The usual sensational initiative of aesthetic psychoses has attracted attention to the sensational aspect, but it has been found impossible to discover any sensation, or group of sensations, to which the aesthetic is limited, nor do we find that the aesthetic is determined solely by sensational experience.

Emotional states seem to be very closely allied to the aesthetic; but we find upon consideration that we cannot limit the aesthetic to emotional psychoses without counting sensation of no effect.

The field of intellectual activity has also been presented as the special field of aesthetics. But this view would exclude the prominent sensational and emotional elements,—a proceeding which is indefensible. We find no distinctly intellectual *product* without which an aesthetic state of mind becomes impossible, nor does an examination of the intellectual *processes* themselves bring us any more satisfactory result. We find no special movement of thought, nor any distinct formal arrangement of thought elements, with which we can identify the aesthetic state of mind.

One bond of unity we do find in the hedonic quality of the aesthetic state. Whatever else they are, however much they may differ in other respects, aesthetic psychoses are always pleasurable. But it cannot be claimed that all pleasures are aesthetic, therefore it is quite proper to consider whether any special class of pleasures can be eliminated from the aesthetic field.

We find upon examination that it is impossible to cut off the sense pleasures or, on the other hand, to limit aesthetics to them. In like manner we find it impossible to limit aesthetic pleasures to either emotional or intellectual fields, and equally impossible to cut off either pleasure field from effectiveness for aesthetic result. An attempt has been made by Kant and others to limit aesthetic delights to elements of disinterestedness, but this position is opposed by other thinkers, and seems to be controverted by the importance allowed by the highest authorities to the principle of usefulness. Others have emphasised the passive pleasures, holding them to be alone aesthetic; but this view appears unsatisfactory when we consider, first, that all receptivity in the system involves reaction, and, secondly, that many so-called passive pleasures are not judged to be aesthetic, *e.g.* the cooling effect of a breeze on a hot day.

It has been claimed that the aesthetic pleasures are different in quality, are "higher" in grade, than the non-aesthetic pleasures; but this seems to be merely the statement of an identical proposition, for it cannot be shown that there is any other criterion for the valuation of pleasure *quâ* pleasure than that of intensity. No two men agree in their grading of pleasures, and the differences of grading which we find seem to be determined by differences of that mental field in which pleasure is strongest or most permanently strong. Immediacy of pleasure getting and width of pleasure getting have been suggested as possible aesthetic criteria, but neither of the suggestions has brought conviction to many thinkers.

The Separation of Aesthetics from Hedonics

We have thus far found no basis of unification amongst all aesthetic states of mind other than their pleasure quality. There appears no difficulty in conceiving that the complex and varied aesthetic psychoses may be determined in some manner by pleasure, provided we look upon pleasure as a general quality which may, under the proper conditions, belong to any mental element; . . .

Our study thus far seems to show clearly that the connection between aesthetics and hedonics is too close to be superficial—a fact that is emphasised by the observation that aesthetic fields vary from race to race and from individual to individual, and that they differ as the mental habits vary in different races and individuals. Inasmuch as mental habits determine our pleasure fields, it is easy to see that divergence of standard is compatible with the aesthetic-hedonic theory, and this point is made more emphatic when we note that aesthetic theorists have evidently been influenced in their views by their individual mental tendencies. But notwithstanding this evidence of closeness of connection between aesthetics and hedonics, we are confronted by a great difficulty in the fact already noted, that while all aesthetic states of mind are pleasurable, not all states that we call pleasurable are called aesthetic; and that notwithstanding the study which has been given to this subject, no agreement has been reached as to the grounds for the separation of the aesthetic and pleasure fields. Until the *rationale* of this separation can be explained it will not be thoroughly satisfactory to treat aesthetics as a branch of hedonics.

One point has become clear in what has preceded this, viz. that very many powerful thinkers have looked upon beauty as a fixity; an Absolute or a Universal. If pleasure is the basis of aesthetics, then there must be a quality of fixity, of permanence, about it, unless these careful thinkers have read their experience incorrectly.

But pleasures are notably evanescent; and it cannot be claimed that there is a class of pleasures, which are permanent in themselves, that make up the aesthetic field. There are states of mind, however, which may remain pleasant for long periods in consequence of shifting of the field of interest; other cases where an effect of permanency is produced by the fact that the mental state is always pleasant when it is presented and disappears before it becomes painful. The varieties of effect produced in us by beautiful objects, and the capacities that we have in connection with all art works of shifting attention before we tire, seem to point to a possibility that this seeming permanence, this relative fixity, may be the basis of the separation of aesthetic from non-aesthetic pleasures. This leads to the adoption of the following hypothesis: *That object is to be considered beautiful which produces a psychosis that is permanently pleasurable in revival. Each pleasure may form an element of impression in an aesthetic complex; but only those pleasures are judged to be aesthetic which (relatively speaking) are permanently pleasurable in memory:* the non-aesthetic, so-called, pleasures of memory being merely pleasures in name, psychoses non-pleasurable in themselves in revival, but to which, for one reason or another, the word "pleasure" still clings. We are led also to the further conclusion that *that object is to be considered ugly which produces a psychosis that is permanently disagreeable in revival.*

If this hypothesis be true we should expect the aesthetic field to vary from race to race and from individual to individual, and in the same individual from year to year, as we find that it does; for these variations involve differences and changes of the mental elements of consciousness such as are natural to man.

Under this hypothesis, besides (A) the wide field of aesthetic impression, above spoken of, which admits all pleasures, we should look for (B) a field of individual judgment *of the moment,* determined by the momentary effect upon us of an art work or of a beautiful natural object; (C) a *relatively stable* field of aesthetic individual judgment, determined by the elements which persist pleasurably more than momentarily, this field marking our individual taste; (D) a still more fixed and objective field, viz. that of the highly-cultivated man as we conceive him, this field determining our judgment when we take the attitude of the philosophic critic.

This view does not exclude the ideal aesthetic field (F), which must vary from individual to individual; which is not the vision of an Absolute, as usually conceived, towards the attainment of which we weakly aim, but a field which differs from the average field, and which each of us feels the world ought to adopt.

This view thus enables us to explain on a basis of relativity the facts of aesthetic judgment as we find them. It enables us, furthermore, to account for the differences of theory to which we have above referred, as due to differences of individual mental constitution in the theorists themselves.

It appears, then, that the theory above discussed indicates that it may not be impossible to explain the only serious difficulty which presented itself to the acceptance of the hedonic-aesthetic view. . . .

The Differentiation of Aesthetics from Hedonics

§ 8. We conclude, then, that there is no kind or description of pleasure which is not, for one person or another, part of what makes up the aesthetic psychosis; that there is no pleasure or class of pleasures which we are able to say must be excluded from the aesthetic field in its widest sense, as it is shown to exist in the experience of the race. On the other hand, there seem to be for each individual certain pleasures which he individually does exclude from his own aesthetic field. So far as I can judge from an examination of my own consciousness, I can say that no pleasure-for-me at any moment fails to become a component part of the aesthetic complex of that moment. There is no particular pleasure which I was experiencing a moment ago that I can say stood apart from the pleasures which during that moment thrilled me in what I recognised as an aesthetic state of mind. Common speech upholds this view, for we find the word "beautiful" applied to all sorts and kinds of objects which give us the most ephemeral of pleasures. The Germans use *schön* in the same way, and the French their more varied phrases in similar manner. On the other hand, however, I clearly do with others call certain states pleasant which are excluded from the aesthetic field, and this aesthetic field therefore I do separate in thought from the hedonic field. Why or how this separation is made is a question which must be answered before hedonistic aesthetics can be felt to be satisfactory or tenable.

We must note at the start that in undertaking this inquiry we change our standpoint in no small respect. No longer do we consider the make-up of the psychosis of aesthetic impression, but we are dealing with the matter of aesthetic judgment and the standards which judgment implies. The question before us, then, appears in this shape. If any species of pleasure whatever may be an element of an aesthetic psychosis, how does it happen that we come to judge any pleasure to be non-aesthetic?

In the course of examination of others' thought which has preceded this, I have already referred to one characteristic of the aesthetic field, viz. that of permanency. This characteristic is worthy of note because it is directly opposed to the nature of the hedonic field as it is generally conceived. The ephemeral nature of pleasure is the theme of the pessimist; is recognised by the optimist as a fact to be accounted for. The aesthetic field, on the other hand, is felt to be opposed to the pleasure field on this very ground, as is evidenced by the great number of theorists who uphold universality, absoluteness, almost Platonic idealism, as the basis of aesthetics; how could they do so did not their experience give them knowledge of something permanent in the psychoses which they discuss? The aesthetic hedonist then is confronted with the question whether there be any such thing as non-ephemeral pleasure; whether there be a permanent pleasure field which is the aesthetic field, and to which is opposed the ordinarily recognised field of pleasure.

It seems to me clear that there is no such thing as a permanent pleasure. Pleasure, as elsewhere shown, is a quality which may attach to any element of consciousness; but not permanently. It is a quality which always fades away under unchanged relations of activity and capacity in the organ involved; the more vivid is the pleasure, other things being equal, the more rapid the fading; the outcome of the fading being either what is called "indifference" or pain. On the other hand, it seems to me equally clear that complexes of mental elements may in arising so arrange themselves by a shifting of the field of contents as to yield new pleasures to take the place of those which fade away, so that a relative permanence may be reached. This permanence, however, will still be only apparent, not real, close examination showing the impossibility of retaining the enjoyment connected with such a complex indefinitely. This kind of pleasure permanence, I think it will be agreed, is in some degree possessed by all important aesthetic objects.

But there is another manner in which an effect of pleasure permanency may be produced, and one of very great importance to this consideration. There are likely to occur cases where a content is pleasurably presented whenever it is presented at all; *and where the revival is pleasurable at the moment of its appearance, and does not at any time become painful.* Not that it might not be indifferent or painful under the proper conditions, but that in fact it never is, but is withdrawn from consciousness whenever painful and for the most part even when indifferent. Such appearance of stability may readily obtain if the source of stimulus be within our control, so that we may avoid the stimulation as soon as it brings other than pleasure to us; this condition obtains in all fields of art, and pre-eminently so with the arts dependent upon the organ of sight, which thus have an advantage over the arts connected with the ear, where stimulation cannot be controlled by covering the organ (as with the eyelid) or by simply turning the head, but only by much more complex and less automatic moments.

It seems not unlikely that we have here the basis of the distinction which is made between the aesthetic and the hedonic. This distinction is noted in reflection and is due to comparison of revivals. It may be that those pleasures in revival which are permanent (relatively speaking) are termed aesthetic; and that those pleasures that are not thus relatively permanent are termed non-aesthetic. When we ask ourselves the question, "Is this aesthetic or is it not?" we clearly are dealing with comparison within the fields of revival; the lately presented is compared with a standard, and included with or excluded from its class, as the case may be. If this view be correct, it is what we call "the lately presented pleasure" which is compared, and that with which it is compared is a field which relatively is permanently pleasurable in revival.

But if the "lately presented pleasure" is in any case excluded from this field of pleasurable revival, it must be because it is in reality no longer a pleasure. How comes it then that we call it a pleasure? Pleasures obtained by direct stimulation are not necessarily pleasures in revival.[2] This change, however, is not always connected with a corresponding dislocation of the word "pleasure," which may, and often does, continue to cling to much that no longer brings pleasure for us in revival. Much that is brought up in revival spontaneously when we think of "pleasure," or when we make recognition of the enjoyments of others, is no longer a pleasant revival for ourselves. These revivals to which the name "pleasure" still clings, but which are not pleasant in themselves, it appears to me are what we cast out as non-aesthetic.

For me apparently the process is this: 1st, I class all that as aesthetic which is pleasurable in revival, with no painful and little indifferent tendency; in other words, *the relatively permanent field of pleasure in revival* is that which I call my aesthetic field; all else is non-aesthetic. What is indifferent in revival I tolerate only as an adjunct; what is painful in revival I cast out of my aesthetic field entirely; I do not always judge a work non-aesthetic because of a painful element in its revival, but I exclude that element as non-aesthetic. 2nd, Those revivals I call hedonic and not aesthetic to which the name "pleasure" clings in any way (either because I remember the original to have been pleasant or because of the recognition of the enjoyment which they bring to others), but which for me in revival are not pleasant but indifferent or positively painful.

Now all this refers to and describes the field of aesthetic judgment, but, as already noted, is, strictly speaking, apart from the field of actual aesthetic presentation. Every argument, in my opinion, goes to show that in the latter field any pleasure which is a pleasure at the time for the one to whom the aesthetic object is presented, does have to do with the make-up of the

---

[2] It must be noted here, . . . that a revival is not necessarily pleasurable, because the impression of which it is a revival was pleasurable; nor was the original impression necessarily pleasurable because the revival is so; the pleasurableness of any mental element depends upon conditions which may alter from time to time, so that recurrence of a content does not necessarily imply the recurrence of the pleasure-pain quality which held with any one impression of that content.

essential nature of the aesthetic effect. The difficulty which we have been considering would, therefore, appear to arise from a failure to distinguish the field of aesthetic impression from the field of aesthetic judgment. From the former no pleasure that occurs for an individual at a given moment can be excluded. From the latter all that is not pleasurable in revival is to be excluded, and this cuts off much to which the name "pleasure" persistently clings: the pleasures of the so-called "lower senses," for instance.

The relative permanency of the aesthetic field, as opposed to the ephemeral nature of ordinary pleasure thus explained, gives us then apparently a solution of the difficulty which remained in the defence of hedonic aesthetics, and we are led to the general statement: *For each person the aesthetic field to which he refers in making judgments as to beauty is his relatively permanent pleasure-field of revival.*[3]

I say *relatively* permanent, because it is very evident from the nature of pleasure that true permanence here is impossible of realisation. If each individual pleasure is ephemeral, so must the pleasures of revival be ephemeral *per se;* there will, however, always be revivals which are pleasant for the time, and objects which are judged to be aesthetic will be those which in reflection are pleasurable at the time of their revival. It will be apparent, therefore, that this aesthetic field, if I have described it correctly, must be constantly changeable as we have found it to be. It must alter with those conditions that render variable the nature of the revivals we are to find pleasurable. The racial changes from age to age which development implies, with the necessarily connected alterations of mode of life and habit of thought; the differences of national life, of education, of occupation, between tribes and families; the differences of environment, of habitat, of wealth; the differences of individual life, and, in that life, of years—all should show us differences of standard as to what is aesthetic; for each will show differences in the character of the mental revivals, which will be pleasurable. Who can deny that just such alterations of the aesthetic standard are to be found varying in relation to the differences of life and thought thus sketched out? For each man there is indeed, for the time during which he is engaged in an examination of his mental life, a semi-permanent field of contents which remain pleasurable in revival, and which are revived when he questions himself as to what is his aesthetic field. But even this field of the time, when reviewed in restrospect, shows its alteration in comparison with what he can remember to have made up the the content of his aesthetic field of the past: to the fact of this real non-permanency, it seems to me, is due the difficulty which is found in defining the field, so that in reality its description

---

[3] The reader will bear with me if I again remind him that this is not the same as the field of the revival of pleasures as often understood, *i.e.* of contents once pleasurable, but which in revival may not be pleasurable at all.

is usually indirect by the statement that one object is, and another is not, within its bounds.

§ 9. This matter of aesthetic standards we must consider more at length. As we have already seen, under this view, the field of aesthetic impression is a very different thing from the field of aesthetic judgment. From the *field of aesthetic impression* (A) we are able to exclude no pleasure, whatever be its character, unless it bring in with it *at the time* an overbalance of pain. Any pleasure which can in any way be brought into connection with the pleasurable complex, so that it forms part of the co-presentation or follows in its associative train, by this fact becomes part of the field of aesthetic impression. The field will be wider and more vivid than that of aesthetic judgment. It will be notably "presentative," as this word is commonly understood in opposition to "representative." The pleasures of sense will enter notably into its complexes, as they are the most vivid of pleasures; but, on the other hand, the pleasures of revival will not be excluded from the field. Many impressions which are pleasant in themselves but not pleasurable in revival, and which, therefore, will be excluded from the field of aesthetic judgment, will be included in the field of aesthetic impression as part and parcel of the totality.

The field of aesthetic impression is of far less interest, however, than the field of aesthetic judgment; the ephemeral nature of pleasure, and the variation which this implies in the character of the revivals from which we are able to gain pleasure, would lead us to look for a *field of individual aesthetic judgment of the moment* (B), covering any complex, wide or narrow, which for the individual gives a pleasant revival at any special time. This must in its nature be very variable; it is the field of revival made use of when we make offhand judgments in aesthetic matters. But this field will be recognised as abnormal so far as it differs from the *relatively stable aesthetic field of the individual* (C), which is the basis of the judgments we make after reflection, and which determines our personal taste. From this field will naturally be cast out all that reflection shows us to be painful in any well-recognised case, or indifferent in all but unusual cases. To this field we look in the careful comparison which goes with the analysis of a work of art, while the aesthetic field of the moment is the basis of our casual everyday judgments.

It must be noted that we are still dealing with a field which is only relatively permanent, which is liable to change from year to year, and in a lesser degree from day to day. Few of us ever realise this variability of individual taste, but as soon as we do we refuse to be satisfied; we ask for something more certain and stable. We do not care so much what a person's individual judgment is, as what it ought to be. It is here that the opponents of hedonism make their most vigorous attack. Hedonism, say they, shows us no difference between taste as it is and taste as it should be; if pleasure be your criterion you must give us a guide as to what *ought* to please; otherwise you sweep away all difference between what gratifies you and the true and noble beauty. I am perfectly willing to grant that this objection is well made against any aesthetic hedonism which would at the same time defend absoluteness of aesthetic standard; but the weight of the objection bears against absolutism in aesthetics and not against aesthetic hedonism. I grant that if one is to be a hedonist in aesthetics then he is compelled to abandon absolutism psychologically, whatever position he may take from a metaphysical standpoint. But the hedonist in aesthetics is not at a loss for a standard. His standard, to be sure, is more liberal, is less dogmatic than that which the absolutist aims to describe, but it has an existence of very decided vitality; it has an objective stability at any special moment which gives it worth, and I find it not less, but more valuable, than the absolutist finds the hypothetical *quasi*-platonic ideals which he aims to approach. To reach this aesthetic "ought" of the hedonist is no very simple matter. The average man never reaches it. He is unwittingly the most ardent of absolutists. His own personal taste he believes to be a reflection of this certain fixed absolute, and if others differ from him it is, in his view, because they are thoughtless or are led by other than aesthetic influences, or are not sufficiently cultivated to appreciate what is good. What we have just here described he is content to do always, viz. to deal entirely with his own subjective standard; when he would have something more stable than individual taste, he canonises his own taste and makes that the standard. The logical hedonist, when he feels the need of a more stable criterion than his own taste, turns from his own field to an objective field; the *field of the highly cultivated man as he conceives him* (D); the field which every philosophic critic must acknowledge apart from his own individual taste if he is to treat art subjects with any breadth. The individual peculiarities of his own field, whilst none the less effective for himself, must be treated as individual rather than general; and his criticism be determined by reference to a broader field which contains all that is common to those for whom he speaks. It must be noted, however, that it is not often that he himself recognises the non-personal nature of this standard.

This standard, it will be seen, is still changeable, unstable; but it is *relatively* unchangeable and stable. It must vary with width of experience, of education, of refinement. It changes as a person limits his notions of life and of the universe, or as his views become broader and more sympathetic. It alters with his change of conception as to what is worthy in the world surrounding him, and as to the sincerity and value of other people's beliefs, and in the end it will be found to be largely determined by his ethical conceptions. As Wundt says, "Effectiveness of higher aesthetic representations depends always upon the arousal of moral or religious ideas." [4] It is thus that Taine, though no hedonist, would have us measure a work of art by its importance and beneficence—that is, its power to develop and preserve the individual and the group in which he is comprehended.[5] It is thus that Fechner would have us make our own final standard of aesthetic valuation dependent upon our conception of what on the whole has the best outcome for the well-being of mankind for time and eternity.[6]

In emphasising the value of the recognition of others' standards, however, we must not overlook the fact that individuality of field is none the less important, for upon it is dependent *the ideal aesthetic field* (E). This ideal field, from our standpoint, must be a variable one, differing for each individual; no absolute as usually conceived; no fixed objective Platonic ideal towards which we weakly strain, but the field which in some direction differs from the normal field; and in this direction the individual feels that the world *ought* to agree with him. Each one of us, however prosaic, has some sort of an ideal field of this kind; non-agreement with it in others looks like aesthetic error. So firmly rooted is this belief in one's own ideal that intolerance is proverbial among artists and connoisseurs; intolerance which is often amusing to one who looks at the subject from a student's standpoint. Once in a while an individual ideal when expressed enlightens the world of art. The artistic genius is the prophet who shows to others an ideal field which they recognise as effective for themselves, and which but for him would have been unknown to them. To express his own ideal must the artist work. He must indeed produce effective results in the field of presentative aesthetic enjoyment (A), but if his work is to be of importance it must go beyond the momentary effect; it must compel recognition as part and parcel of the stable field of pleasurable revival (C), and must not stand opposed to the objective standard which is given by recognition of the value of the opinion of others whose cultivation entitles them to speak with authority (D); if, however, the work of an artist is to be recognised as that of a master it must express an ideal (E) which the common mortal, however highly cultivated, does not and cannot reach of himself, but which he will recognise when it is reached by another as an enlightenment of his own duller conceptions.

---

[4] *Elements of Phy. Psy.*, ii. p. 221.
[5] "Ideal in Art."
[6] Cf. *Vors. d. Aest.*, end of vol. i.

AS EMPATHY

HERBERT SIDNEY LANGFELD

Empathy [1]

§ 1. The Motor Response in Perception

IT IS NOT NECESSARY to lift a stone in order to know that it is heavy. The visual perception of the size and nature of the stone is sufficient to arouse within us, through association with previous experiences of lifting, the muscle sensations or motor set which would accompany the actual process of lifting. Without such previous experience, there would be no perception of weight. The word itself would be without meaning. All of our perceptions are dependent upon the motor attitudes that are assumed toward the object. The eye measures the extent of a line by moving over it, or there is an incipient revival within us of the muscular sensations of some other part of the body, such as the hand or the leg; that is, we think of the movement of that member along the line, and thus have the clue to the length of the line. The perception obtained by the roundness of an object or other factors of shape, depends upon similar processes. When we notice the smooth curves of a marble torso, we can probably, if we observe carefully, get a fleeting image of our hands moving in imagination around the figure. Combined with this sense of movement, there will probably be fancied the coldness of the marble and the quality of the touch. The true distance of objects from us, their shape, and the nature of lines are also given in terms of movement. The meaning of facial expression is learned from the movement of one's own face, or a tendency toward such movement as suggested by the lines of the face observed.[2]

When we listen to a song, we have a tendency to move in time to the

---

[1] From *The Aesthetic Attitude,* by H. S. Langfeld, copyright, 1920, by Harcourt, Brace and Company, Inc., pp. 109–127, 136–138. Reprinted by permission. (Eds.)

[2] See the author's "The Judgment of Emotions from Facial Expressions," *Journal of Abnormal Psychology,* August, 1918.

rhythm, and to repeat the notes with accompanying tension in the throat. In silent reading, the tendency to movement often goes over into actual movement of the lips or muscles of the larynx. The act of unity itself, fundamental to experience, is conceived in motor terms as a bringing of things together. It will rightly be objected that in many instances of perception there is no consciousness of such movement, not even of the faintest tendency toward such imitation of facial expression as that just described. The answer is that these motor sets may be, and in fact most frequently are, subconscious. The object observed, whether through the eye, ear, or another of the senses, arouses the memory of former movements, which are so revived that they form a nervous pattern; that is, the nerve paths going to the necessary muscle groups are opened, and those to opposed muscles groups are closed, and this pattern, which is ready on additional stimulation to produce actual movement, is sufficient to give us our perception of space, weight, form, smoothness, delicacy, and many of our other experiences. Accordingly one must for the most part explain this tendency to movement in physiological rather than psychological terms.

We can readily prove to our satisfaction that we do assume a motor attitude to the object of our perception, even though such an attitude is carried in unconscious terms, by performing a simple experiment. If we look successively at two pictures which are identical, except that one is reversed as in a mirror, the difference in the direction of the lines of the figures will be felt distinctly as a physical jar, such as is produced by a sudden change in the direction of a voluntary movement. In this case as in many other actual experiences, the motor set assumed toward the object is not noticed until there is some transition to an attitude that conflicts with the former one. This may also be readily observed in regard to our motor set toward the familiar arrangement of objects about us, such as those of our room. There is a very faint glow of familiarity about those possessions which we perceive every day of the year, and this sense of the accustomed is carried in terms of ease of adjustment through long practice; but let one thing be removed or disarranged and instantly there is felt an uneasiness and motor restlessness, as we should describe it. We feel that there has been a change even though at times we are unable to identify it. When motion is suggested to us, the motor tendency is even more noticeable, as for example when we are directed to go down the street one block, turn to the right, then to the left, etc. There are many who will, in order to understand and remember the directions, act them out in imagination so vividly that there will be felt in the body and extremities a tug to the right or the left. When an actual motion is visually perceived, the movement is still more vividly felt. In watching a football game, we suddenly realize that in the excitement of following our team, we have been unconsciously pushing against our neighbor on the bench. The prestidigitator has no difficulty in directing the attention away from the sleight of hand by simply pointing toward the innocent hand with the fingers of the hand which is to do the palming.

There are two main forms of motor attitude that may be assumed in regard to an object, one of which particularly concerns aesthetics, the other not. The one is an adjustment toward, the other an adjustment in the object. When one sees a tree swaying in the sunshine, one can either have the motor impulse to put out one's hand to stop the motion, which is in a sense a defensory attitude, or one may have the impulse to sway with the moving tree and thus to realize the true nature of its motion. It is this latter form of adjustment that has been described by Lotze, and it will probably be recognized from what has gone before that it is such a reaction that is found in aesthetic enjoyment. It will be recalled that two attitudes may be assumed toward the outstretched hand of a statue: either one of grasping the hand, or of feeling the "outstretching" of the hand. It is through this latter attitude, which gives us the feeling of the tension and the weight of the arm, the angle at which it is raised, and the bend at the elbow and wrist, that we can get the true aesthetic effect. We can feel these qualities of form and motion only by carrying out the movements or experiencing somewhere in the organism a tendency to such muscular adjustments and movements. It is only by such a movement within ourselves that we can have the experience of the aesthetic pleasantness or unpleasantness of things.

§ 2. *Lipps' Theory of Empathy*

This fact of the dynamic quality of perceptions has been described by Lotze and F. T. Vischer [3] and has even appeared earlier in the literature, but the wider application of the principle to aesthetics was made clear by Theodor Lipps. He termed this phenomenon "Einfühlung" (feeling into), a word which had already been casually used by Lotze, and which has been translated by Professor Titchener as "empathy." [4]

Lipps has illustrated his meaning by examples from the appreciation of architecture, vases, etc., and has used the principle also as an explanation of optical illusions. In his first description of his theory of empathy he says: "The Doric column rises [literally rears itself up] as does every column. . . . This self-raising of the column is its 'intrinsic activity.' The word activity is used in the fullest sense of exertion, striving, expenditure of energy; at the same time expenditure as energy through which something is achieved. Such activity is not without opposing activity or resistance, which must be overcome. This [resistance] is here occasioned by the weight. . . . But

---

[3] *Das Schöne und die Kunst,* p. 70.
[4] *Experimental Psychology of the Thought Processes,* p. 21.

upon our observing the column and seeing it raise itself to a certain height above the ground, this [resistance] does not prevent the force which is directed against the weight from appearing to us as the actual activity; the force and not the weight will in our eyes seem to perform the act with which we are here concerned or through which the column appears to gain its peculiar property." [5] The manner in which this dynamic quality of inanimate objects is apprehended is explained by Lipps as follows: "A similar way of considering things can be noticed whenever we speak of a 'force' residing in an object; more clearly even whenever we realize a 'tendency' or 'striving' in anything that happens, whenever we realize any 'doing' or 'being done to,' any 'activity' or 'passivity.' All such vivifying of our surrounding realities comes about, and can come about only as we attribute to outer things our own feeling of force, our own feeling of striving or willing, our own activity and passivity. . . . The column seems to brace itself and raise itself, that is to say, to proceed in the way in which I do when I pull myself together and raise myself, or remain thus tense and erect, in opposition to the natural inertness of my body. It is impossible for me to be aware of the column without this activity seeming to exist directly in the column of which I am aware." [6] That is, when we see an object such as a column or a spiral or an arch, we realize from our previous experience how it was constructed. We have an idea of the forces, tensions, etc., involved. There are then induced in our muscles and joints sensations of strain and movement similar to those which we should have if we built such objects. The ideas of these sensations are then projected into the object and these give it life. They are no longer our own sensations but attributes of the object. It is not a mere perception of the form which directly calls up ideas of one's activity and which in turn is projected into the object; for Lipps it is first necessary that we have this knowledge of the process of construction, before we can have the ideas of movement. The perception of movement, however, is first identified in the object and not in one's self. There is the immediate perception of the rearing of a column, the span of the arch, the motion of the spiral. "Briefly, in the act of empathy I do not supply any form to the spiral or to the manner in which it seems to have been constructed, but it is the forces through which its form has originated to which I attach this personal quality. Nor is it at all necessary that I should have ever realized this form within myself. Inasmuch as this personal quality is added to the form of this definite mechanical process or is incorporated in it, this quality naturally appears as a quality of a mechanical process which is spatially so

---

[5] *Raumaesthetik und Geometrisch-Optische Täuschungen*, pp. 3–4. Vernon Lee and C. Anstruther-Thomson published a similar theory under the title of "Beauty and Ugliness" in the *Contemporary Review*, Oct. and Nov., 1897.

[6] *Op. cit.*, pp. 6–7.

constituted as to form a spiral." [7] This is the essence of Lipps' theory. He has enlarged upon it in his subsequent writings,[8] but has become more metaphysical in his amplifications, especially in his insistence upon the idea that the projection of our movements is a projection of our ego into the object. Lipps has insisted that there is not in us the actual sensation of muscular effort. He believes in a purely mental process without any sensational basis, an idea which is entirely free from actual experiences of bodily processes, a mystical mind substance, and it is the ideas of movement within us in this, as he would perhaps say, "spiritual sense" that give the inanimate objects dynamic force and cause us to realize their true form and shape.

§ 3. Movements and Tendencies to Movements

Professor Karl Groos among others, called attention, on the other hand, to the fact that there are often actual sensations of movements of the organism when perceiving shapes, etc. He called his theory "inner mimicry," [9] and as it was contrary to Lipps' spiritual theory, it was bitterly opposed by the latter. The majority of modern experimental psychologists, however, agree with the contentions of Professor Groos. In fact, such actual movements can be detected in the laboratory during experiments upon perception. Lipps, however, is correct in so far that during aesthetic contemplation such experiences are not felt as sensations within the body. In fact, they do not come to consciousness as sensations of our own movements at all, but influence the perception in such a way that the lines and figures themselves seem to have the force which is actually in us. As soon as we are conscious of our own sensations, we are no longer contemplating the beauty of the object, for the words "our own sensations" in themselves denote that we are no longer enjoying the object, but that our aesthetic attitude has broken down under the distraction of the bodily processes. Indeed, as soon as our attention is upon such processes, there can be no identification of such movements with the lines, no fusion of the sensations with the object, and so even empathy itself is impossible. This fact suggests a further reason why it is so difficult to assume an aesthetic attitude toward objects which are perceived through the lower senses. When one chews and swallows, the sensations from the muscles of the jaw and throat are relatively strong and come readily into consciousness. The same is true of the sensations from the muscles of the nose in smelling, especially when we are interested in the quality of the odor, that is when we sniff carefully. In obtaining touch and

---

[7] "Aesthetische Einfühlung," *Zeitschrift für Psych., u. Phys. der Sinnes-organe,* vol. 22, 1900, pp. 439–440.

[8] See *Zur Einfühlung.*

[9] See *Die Spiele des Menschen.*

temperature stimulations there are also strong sensations from the various muscles of the body, for they are generally moved during the perception. The attention then is partly at least upon the process; things *taste* good, *smell* good, *feel* good. On the other hand, it is seldom that one feels the tension in the eyes or the ears, and so the color *is* pretty, the sound *is* agreeable, etc.[10] The fact that there are sensations of bodily movements or tendencies toward such movements is not learned directly at the time of the spontaneous aesthetic experience, but only when one is definitely set for analytical introspection or else through objective records obtained under experimental conditions.

In discussing the possibility of the accompaniment of eye movements in certain perceptions of form, Vernon Lee writes: "This phenomenon is *hidden,* can be watched only in especial experiments like those made by my collaborator as the result of specially trained attention, and is, by the very fact of normal aesthetic attention being withdrawn from the perceiving subject and fixed upon the perceived object, translated at once into qualities of the visible shape (*Beauty and Ugliness,* p. 546). Our attention has become engaged, not with the change in ourselves productive of the sense of height, or roundness, or symmetry, but with the objective external causes of these changes; and the formula of perception has become, not 'I *feel* roundness, or height, or symmetry,' but 'this or that object *is* round, or high, or symmetrical.' " [11]

When her collaborator, Miss C. Anstruther-Thomson, made the observations upon which to base the following description, she was for the most part a psychologist and not an aesthetician: "My eye falls on the Venus of Milo. . . . The pressure of my feet on the ground is pressure that I see in a marked degree in the feet of the statue. The lift-up of my body I see done more strongly and amply in her marble body, and the steadying pressure of my head I see in a diminished degree in the poise of the statue's beautiful head. These movements I may be said to imitate, but I should find them and imitate them equally in a Renaissance monument or a mediaeval chalice. They are at the basis of all art. Another connexion that I feel with her is by the balance and shifting of my weight from side to side in order to follow her balance." [12] The analysis of our motor attitude, however, increases such participation in future aesthetic situations, and these add to the depth and richness of our immediate experience, sharpen the critical function, and heighten the power of discrimination.

Professor Groos believes that there are three different stages in our em-

---

[10] It is probably this projection of our feeling into the object which is the basis of Professor Santayana's definition of beauty as "pleasure objectified." *The Sense of Beauty,* p. 52. See also James' *Essays in Radical Empiricism,* pp. 143–144.

[11] *Beauty and Ugliness,* p. 135.

[12] *Op. cit.,* p. 119.

pathic response. When the bodily feelings, etc., are not perceived as localized in the body, they seem to fill the object; when these sensations are still too weak to induce our attention to wander from the object, but are sufficiently strong to have a decided effect on consciousness, there is a projection of ourselves in the object; if they are still stronger, they will be definitely realized and then there is no longer this projection.[13] The first and last stages are in agreement with what has been said above, and the description is important for an adequate knowledge of the nature of empathy and its relation to the immediate aesthetic appreciation. The existence of a second stage, that of the consciousness of the "projection of ourselves," just as that of Lipps' "projection of the ego," is doubtful. It seems to be a theoretical assumption and not a fact discernible in experience. If we are conscious of such projection then we are also aware of ourselves; that is, that the sensations are our own sensations, and that therefore they cannot be located in the object, which is what such projection implies. The object seems to have force, to live; that is a fact of experience. It is discovered that such a perception is due to one's own muscle sensations, although at the time of the perception they seem to be a quality of the object. This latter is also a fact of experience. These two facts are empirical and important. It is then, however, assumed that because these muscle sensations condition the quality of the object, there must be some awareness at times of the fact of the projection itself, which is not necessarily true, and is not borne out by experience. In other words, the idea seems to be a logical assumption and not an empirical fact. It has seemed necessary to discuss this point at some length, because it is typical of descriptions which so frequently occur in aesthetic literature, and which in the case of empathy have tended to express in metaphysical terms a perfectly honest and clean-cut experience.

The phenomenon of empathy is not so complicated as one is led to suppose from descriptions like that by Lipps. When we see a form such as a spiral, memories of movements corresponding to the spiral are touched off, probably memories of the movements of the hand in drawing such a figure. If it is an unknown shape, one first seeks the experience of actually tracing the form in order to perceive its quality. These memories are expressed either in actual motor responses or merely in tendencies to movement. The degrees of response vary greatly. A tendency toward movement may be described as a motor set or pattern which must precede any overt action. It must be emphasized that it is not necessary that we should first have the idea of the formation of such a figure, and that we then imitate in ourselves such a process as Lipps and others have contended. An idea of mechanical construction as "mere idea" is meaningless. Even if the idea

---

[13] "Das Aesthetische Miterleben," *Zeitschrift für Aesthetik,* etc., Vol. IV, part 2, p. 181.

of construction were a necessary link, it would itself have to be expressed in motor set and accompanying sensations, for that is the only way in which it could be understood.

Further, these sensations of movement or tendencies to movement are projected into the lines and shapes. They are not felt as movements of our body, but fuse with the object as visual, auditory, or other form of perception, giving character and meaning to the object as will be shown by examples. They are also the cause of the accompanying enjoyment or affective tone. The objects cannot be pleasing unless they give rise to unified empathic responses because the nervous set requires such unification, and that is the ultimate reason why unity in the object is essential to beauty. The degree of unity required in the object for the greatest pleasure, however, depends upon the total situation, and the exact nature of the empathic response, which the particular object induces, and of the consequent perception depends upon the experience and total state of the observer's organism at the time.

It is evident that mere adaptation to the situation, quickly and readily attained through previous familiarity with the perceived objects, would soon lose its interest for us. We do not find pleasure in the accustomed. There must be something present in our relation to the environment that requires a new effort on our part.[14] It may be stated then that a *new* and *successful* adaptation is a necessary and fundamental factor of the pleasure in aesthetic creations.

The following is a description of the motor set from the physiological side. Dr. E. J. Kempf writes: "This is virtually saying that we think with our muscles, because the kinesthetic impulses . . . arising from the embedded proprioceptors are much more numerous than all the others. For example, if we allow ourselves to become aware of the visual image of a moving automobile, the awareness of its movement is furnished by extrinsic muscles of the eye-ball as they shift the image by shifting their postural tensions. Overt movements are not necessary unless we desire a very vivid image, then, also, the muscles of the neck may contribute by moving the head. If the image of the moving automobile is one of ourselves pushing it, then the muscles of the body come into play to furnish the images . . . and, if it is to include pushing it through a cold, wet, muddy road, the sensations of coldness and wetness arise from the tactile receptors of the skin of our legs. If the description of the experience includes the reproduction of an

---

[14] Professor R. S. Woodworth has stated, in his *Dynamic Psychology,* p. 102, "Action that is too easy because all difficulties have been smoothed away or already subjugated by well-formed habits is automatic rather than interesting, and action that meets with unsurmountable obstacles is distinctly annoying; but action that encounters resistance but overcomes it without resorting to the last ounce of effort is distinctly interesting."

accident (say slipping), we feel the image of the movement of the slipping in our legs first, the remainder of the body then adjusting and coördinating to the change of posture." [15] The possibility of the shifting of tensions in muscles without overt movement gives a physiological explanation of what is meant by the change in tendency to movement and in motor set. This is particularly important, because it has been argued against empathy that the time of perception is often too short for actual movements, and yet within that time effects are observed which are claimed to be caused by an empathic attitude. If it were necessary to make actual movements in order to empathize, then there would be a justified skepticism in regard to the validity of the theory, for it is more than probable that in the majority of instances of empathy no overt action can be detected. Dr. Kempf has written further on this point: "Apparently we may have such changes in the postural tonus as reciprocally increasing or decreasing tonus between the flexors and extensors, pronators and supinators, abductors and adductors of a limb or several limbs without overt movement of the limb; as when one makes his arm give him the sensations of wielding a tennis racket without going through visible movements; and as the sensations of such movements are made more vivid the overt movements begin to appear." [16]

Another argument that has been made against empathy is that it is often impossible to move in the way that perceived shapes suggest. Particular reference has been made to eye movements, the importance of which has perhaps been somewhat overemphasized. It was supposed at one time that we experienced the quality of lines and judged the degree of their gracefulness, etc., by following them with the eyes. Professor G. M. Stratton performed the experiment of photographing the movements of the eyes while they were following a curved line. It was found that they could not trace the curved line but moved in jerks, forming a line with sharp angles which no one could fail to consider disagreeable.[17] That the eye does ordinarily move in jerks has been substantiated by other investigators. That it cannot possibly move in smooth curves does not seem to have as yet been conclusively proven. However, these results do not minimize the importance of empathy. It is not necessary to empathize with the eyes any more than it is necessary to imagine ourselves walking in a spiral in order to appreciate the curves. A tendency to move any part of the body that is capable of moving in the way suggested is sufficient. Just what part of the body is used depends upon conditions. We may have the impulse to trace the line with the foot or with the whole leg, or with the hand. We may incline the body

---

[15] "The Autonomic Functions and the Personality," *Nervous and Mental Disease Monograph,* series 28, 1918, p. 23.

[16] *Op. cit.,* p. 21.

[17] "Eye-Movements and the Aesthetics of Visual Form," *Philosophische Studien,* vol. 20, pp. 336–359.

or merely the head to one side, we may beat the rhythm with the foot, the head, the hand, or the finger, or the response may come through the change in breathing. The perception of weight may be due to strain in all the muscles of the body which would ordinarily be used to lift an object like the one perceived, or the strain may be in only one small muscle group, such as that which moves the finger.

It must be repeated, in order that there shall be no misunderstanding, that in all such instances, the impulses may be so far in the initial stage that there is no movement produced and frequently not even a consciousness of strain or of other similar sensations. The nervous set is capable of influencing perception, even though it remains completely unconscious and is discoverable only when the conditions are suddenly altered, as in the example on page 111. Professor Titchener, who believes that the effect of empathy can be the result of unconscious processes has written in another connection: "We have learned, again, that physiological conditions may produce their effect not within but upon consciousness; that nervous sets and tendencies may direct the course of conscious processes without setting up new and special processes of their own. . . ." [18]

§ 4. Description of Empathy by Art Critics

. . . Probably one of the most vivid experiences of empathy that we can have is in perceiving an object that we realize is not well-balanced and may fall at any moment, as for instance, in witnessing one acrobat balancing another at the end of a long pole. As the acrobat in the air sways back and forth on the verge of plunging head first into the orchestra, the audience goes through at low tension all of his contortions.[19] Whenever the balance is insecure, the empathic response will, as a rule, be of an unpleasant nature, a fact which the artist does not always bear sufficiently in mind. Even Michael Angelo, in his superb de Medici monument, did not make the support for the limbs of the recumbent figures on the tomb of Lorenzo de Medici sufficiently evident, so that for some observers the figures seem about to slip off the incline.

In the drama, the empathy is always very strong, and for the correct aesthetic attitude, we should empathize in all the characters as they in turn take up the action. This usually happens when one is entirely absorbed in the play. At times, however, the character is portrayed in a manner foreign to our experience or understanding. In that case it is impossible for us to

---

[18] *Experimental Psychology of the Thought Processes,* p. 32.

[19] Adam Smith in his chapter on "Sympathy" has described the writhing and twisting of a mob in watching a slack-rope dancer. He does not, however, develop this idea further in the direction of empathy. (*Moral Sentiments,* sec. 1, chap. 1.)

respond empathically, that is, to live in the character. The effect on the observer is unpleasant. The character is judged to be badly drawn and untrue to life.

The term "sympathy" may be used by some persons uncritically in instances such as that just described. We may say that we are not in sympathy with the play or the actors, but strictly speaking, sympathy should not be confused with empathy. The latter is feeling in the object. One's own personality is merged and fused in that of some external thing. Sympathy is feeling with; instead of being merged in the object, our feelings run, so to speak, parallel with the object. The difference between the one sympathizing and the object of sympathy is always somewhat present in consciousness. The ego is to some extent represented in consciousness in the form of self-satisfaction, so that the sympathetic response can never be an aesthetic one. One's sympathy is usually expressed in terms of subject and object: "I sympathize sincerely with you," while one's empathy is in terms of the object: "the man walks awkwardly."

AS EXPERIENCE

JOHN DEWEY

Having an Experience [1]

EXPERIENCE OCCURS CONTINUOUSLY, because the interaction of live creature and environing conditions is involved in the very process of living. Under conditions of resistance and conflict, aspects and elements of the self and the world that are implicated in this interaction qualify experience with emotions and ideas so that conscious intent emerges. Oftentimes, however, the experience had is inchoate. Things are experienced but not in such a way that they are composed into *an* experience. There is distraction and dispersion; what we observe and what we think, what we desire and what we get, are at odds with each other. We put our hands to the plow and turn back; we start and then we stop, not because the experience

---

[1] From *Art as Experience,* by John Dewey, Chap. III. Copyright, 1934, by John Dewey. Courtesy of G. P. Putnam's Sons. (Eds.)

has reached the end for the sake of which it was initiated but because of extraneous interruptions or of inner lethargy.

In contrast with such experience, we have *an* experience when the material experienced runs its course to fulfillment. Then and then only is it integrated within and demarcated in the general stream of experience from other experiences. A piece of work is finished in a way that is satisfactory; a problem receives its solution; a game is played through; a situation, whether that of eating a meal, playing a game of chess, carrying on a conversation, writing a book, or taking part in a political campaign, is so rounded out that its close is a consummation and not a cessation. Such an experience is a whole and carries with it its own individualizing quality and self-sufficiency. It is *an* experience.

Philosophers, even empirical philosophers, have spoken for the most part of experience at large. Idiomatic speech, however, refers to experiences each of which is singular, having its own beginning and end. For life is no uniform uninterrupted march or flow. It is a thing of histories, each with its own plot, its own inception and movement toward its close, each having its own particular rhythmic movement; each with its own unrepeated quality pervading it throughout. A flight of stairs, mechanical as it is, proceeds by individualized steps, not by undifferentiated progression, and an inclined plane is at least marked off from other things by abrupt discreteness.

Experience in this vital sense is defined by those situations and episodes that we spontaneously refer to as being "real experiences"; those things of which we say in recalling them, "that *was* an experience." It may have been something of tremendous importance—a quarrel with one who was once an intimate, a catastrophe finally averted by a hair's breadth. Or it may have been something that in comparison was slight—and which perhaps because of its very slightness illustrates all the better what is to be an experience. There is that meal in a Paris restaurant of which one says "that *was* an experience." It stands out as an enduring memorial of what food may be. Then there is that storm one went through in crossing the Atlantic— the storm that seemed in its fury, as it was experienced, to sum up in itself all that a storm can be, complete in itself, standing out because marked out from what went before and what came after.

In such experiences, every successive part flows freely, without seam and without unfilled blanks, into what ensues. At the same time there is no sacrifice of the self-identity of the parts. A river, as distinct from a pond, flows. But its flow gives a definiteness and interest to its successive portions greater than exist in the homogenous portions of a pond. In an experience, flow is from something to something. As one part leads into another and as one part carries on what went before, each gains distinctness in itself. The enduring whole is diversified by successive phases that are emphases of its varied colors.

Because of continuous merging, there are no holes, mechanical junctions, and dead centers when we have *an* experience. There are pauses, places of rest, but they punctuate and define the quality of movement. They sum up what has been undergone and prevent its dissipation and idle evaporation. Continued acceleration is breathless and prevents parts from gaining distinction. In a work of art, different acts, episodes, occurrences melt and fuse into unity, and yet do not disappear and lose their own character as they do so—just as in a genial conversation there is a continuous interchange and blending, and yet each speaker not only retains his own character but manifests it more clearly than is his wont.

An experience has a unity that gives it its name, *that* meal, that storm, that rupture of friendship. The existence of this unity is constituted by a single *quality* that pervades the entire experience in spite of the variation of its constituent parts. This unity is neither emotional, practical, nor intellectual, for these terms name distinctions that reflection can make within it. In discourse *about* an experience, we must make use of these adjectives of interpretation. In going over an experience in mind *after* its occurrence, we may find that one property rather than another was sufficiently dominant so that it characterizes the experience as a whole. There are absorbing inquiries and speculations which a scientific man and philosopher will recall as "experiences" in the emphatic sense. In final import they are intellectual. But in their actual occurrence they were emotional as well; they were purposive and volitional. Yet the experience was not a sum of these different characters; they were lost in it as distinctive traits. No thinker can ply his occupation save as he is lured and rewarded by total integral experiences that are intrinsically worth while. Without them he would never know what it is really to think and would be completely at a loss in distinguishing real thought from the spurious article. Thinking goes on in trains of ideas, but the ideas form a train only because they are much more than what an analytic psychology calls ideas. They are phases, emotionally and practically distinguished, of a developing underlying quality; they are its moving variations, not separate and independent like Locke's and Hume's so-called ideas and impressions, but are subtle shadings of a pervading and developing hue.

We say of an experience of thinking that we reach or draw a conclusion. Theoretical formulation of the process is often made in such terms as to conceal effectually the similarity of "conclusion" to the consummating phase of every developing integral experience. These formulations apparently take their cue from the separate propositions that are premises and the proposition that is the conclusion as they appear on the printed page. The impression is derived that there are first two independent and ready-made entities that are then manipulated so as to give rise to a third. In fact, in an experience of thinking, premisses emerge only as a conclusion becomes manifest. The experience, like that of watching a storm reach its height and gradually subside, is one of continuous movement of subject-matters. Like the ocean in the storm, there are a series of waves; suggestions reaching out and being broken in a clash, or being carried onwards by a coöperative wave. If a conclusion is reached, it is that of a movement of anticipation and cumulation, one that finally comes to completion. A "conclusion" is no separate and independent thing; it is the consummation of a movement.

Hence *an* experience of thinking has its own esthetic quality. It differs from those experiences that are acknowledged to be esthetic, but only in its materials. The material of the fine arts consists of qualities; that of experience having intellectual conclusion are signs or symbols having no intrinsic quality of their own, but standing for things that may in another experience be qualitatively experienced. The difference is enormous. It is one reason why the strictly intellectual art will never be popular as music is popular. Nevertheless, the experience itself has a satisfying emotional quality because it possesses internal integration and fulfillment reached through ordered and organized movement. This artistic structure may be immediately felt. In so far, it is esthetic. What is even more important is that not only is this quality a significant motive in undertaking intellectual inquiry and in keeping it honest, but that no intellectual activity is an integral event (is *an* experience), unless it is rounded out with this quality. Without it, thinking is inconclusive. In short, esthetic cannot be sharply marked off from intellectual experience since the latter must bear an esthetic stamp to be itself complete.

The same statement holds good of a course of action that is dominantly practical, that is, one that consists of overt doings. It is possible to be efficient in action and yet not have a conscious experience. The activity is too automatic to permit of a sense of what it is about and where it is going. It comes to an end but not to a close or consummation in consciousness. Obstacles are overcome by shrewd skill, but they do not feed experience. There are also those who are wavering in action, uncertain, and inconclusive like the shades in classic literature. Between the poles of aimlessness and mechanical efficiency, there lie those courses of action in which through successive deeds there runs a sense of growing meaning conserved and accumulating toward an end that is felt as accomplishment of a process. Successful politicians and generals who turn statesmen like Caesar and Napoleon have something of the showman about them. This of itself is not art, but it is, I think, a sign that interest is not exclusively, perhaps not mainly, held by the result taken by itself (as it is in the case of mere efficiency), but by it as the outcome of a process. There is interest in completing an experience. The experience may be one that is harmful to the world and its consummation undesirable. But it has esthetic quality.

The Greek identification of good conduct with conduct having proportion, grace, and harmony, the *kalon-agathon,* is a more obvious example of distinctive esthetic quality in moral action. One great defect in what passes as morality is its anesthetic quality. Instead of exemplifying wholehearted action, it takes the form of grudging piecemeal concessions to the demands of duty. But illustrations may only obscure the fact that any practical activity will, provided that it is integrated and moves by its own urge to fulfillment, have esthetic quality.

A generalized illustration may be had if we imagine a stone, which is rolling down hill, to have an experience. The activity is surely sufficiently "practical." The stone starts from somewhere, and moves, as consistently as conditions permit, toward a place and state where it will be at rest—toward an end. Let us add, by imagination, to these external facts, the ideas that it looks forward with desire to the final outcome; that it is interested in the things it meets on its way, conditions that accelerate and retard its movement with respect to their bearing on the end; that it acts and feels toward them according to the hindering or helping function it attributes to them; and that the final coming to rest is related to all that went before as the culmination of a continuous movement. Then the stone would have an experience, and one with esthetic quality.

If we turn from this imaginary case to our own experience, we shall find much of it is nearer to what happens to the actual stone than it is to anything that fulfills the conditions fancy just laid down. For in much of our experience we are not concerned with the connection of one incident with what went before and what comes after. There is no interest that controls attentive rejection or selection of what shall be organized into the developing experience. Things happen, but they are neither definitely included nor decisively excluded; we drift. We yield according to external pressure, or evade and compromise. There are beginnings and cessations, but no genuine initiations and concludings. One thing replaces another, but does not absorb it and carry it on. There is experience, but so slack and discursive that it is not *an* experience. Needless to say, such experiences are anesthetic.

Thus the non-esthetic lies within two limits. At one pole is the loose succession that does not begin at any particular place and that ends—in the sense of ceasing—at no particular place. At the other pole is arrest, constriction, proceeding from parts having only a mechanical connection with one another. There exists so much of one and the other of these two kinds of experience that unconsciously they come to be taken as norms of all experience. Then, when the esthetic appears, it so sharply contrasts with the picture that has been formed of experience, that it is impossible to combine its special qualities with the features of the picture and the esthetic is given an outside place and status. The account that has been given of experience dominantly intellectual and practical is intended to show that there is no such contrast involved in having an experience; that, on the contrary, no experience of whatever sort is a unity unless it has esthetic quality.

The enemies of the esthetic are neither the practical nor the intellectual. They are the humdrum; slackness of loose ends; submission to convention in practice and intellectual procedure. Rigid abstinence, coerced submission, tightness on one side and dissipation, incoherence and aimless indulgence on the other, are deviations in opposite directions from the unity of an experience. Some such considerations perhaps induced Aristotle to invoke the "mean proportional" as the proper designation of what is distinctive of both virtue and the esthetic. He was formally correct. "Mean" and "proportion" are, however, not self-explanatory, nor to be taken over in a prior mathematical sense, but are properties belonging to an experience that has a developing movement toward its own consummation.

I have emphasized the fact that every integral experience moves toward a close, an ending, since it ceases only when the energies active in it have done their proper work. This closure of a circuit of energy is the opposite of arrest, of *stasis*. Maturation and fixation are polar opposites. Struggle and conflict may be themselves enjoyed, although they are painful, when they are experienced as means of developing an experience; members in that they carry it forward, not just because they are there. There is, as will appear later, an element of undergoing, of suffering in its large sense, in every experience. Otherwise there would be no taking in of what preceded. For "taking in" in any vital experience is something more than placing something on the top of consciousness over what was previously known. It involves reconstruction which may be painful. Whether the necessary undergoing phase is by itself pleasurable or painful is a matter of particular conditions. It is indifferent to the total esthetic quality, save that there are few intense esthetic experiences that are wholly gleeful. They are certainly not to be characterized as amusing, and as they bear down upon us they involve a suffering that is none the less consistent with, indeed a part of, the complete perception that is enjoyed.

I have spoken of the esthetic quality that rounds out an experience into completeness and unity as emotional. The reference may cause difficulty. We are given to thinking of emotions as things as simple and compact as are the words by which we name them. Joy, sorrow, hope, fear, anger, curiosity, are treated as if each in itself were a sort of entity that enters full-made upon the scene, an entity that may last a long time or a short time, but whose duration, whose growth and career, is irrelevant to its nature. In fact emotions are qualities, when they are significant, of a complex experience that moves and changes. I say, when they are *significant,* for otherwise they are but the outbreaks and eruptions of a disturbed infant. All emotions are qualifications of a drama and they change as the drama develops. Persons are sometimes said to fall in love at first sight. But what they fall into is not a thing of that instant. What would love be were it compressed into a moment in which there is no room for cherishing and for solicitude? The intimate nature of emotion is manifested in the experience of one watching a play on the stage or reading a novel. It attends the development of a plot; and a plot requires a stage, a space, wherein to develop and time in which to unfold. Experience is emotional but there are no separate things called emotions in it.

By the same token, emotions are attached to events and objects in their movement. They are not, save in pathological instances, private. And even an "objectless" emotion demands something beyond itself to which to attach itself, and thus it soon generates a delusion in lack of something real. Emotion belongs of a certainty to the self. But it belongs to the self that is concerned in the movement of events toward an issue that is desired or disliked. We jump instantaneously when we are scared, as we blush on the instant when we are ashamed. But fright and shamed modesty are not in this case emotional states. Of themselves they are but automatic reflexes. In order to become emotional they must become parts of an inclusive and enduring situation that involves concern for objects and their issues. The jump of fright becomes emotional fear when there is found or thought to exist a threatening object that must be dealt with or escaped from. The blush becomes the emotion of shame when a person connects, in thought, an action he has performed with an unfavorable reaction to himself of some other person.

Physical things from far ends of the earth are physically transported and physically caused to act and react upon one another in the construction of a new object. The miracle of mind is that something similar takes place in experience without physical transport and assembling. Emotion is the moving and cementing force. It selects what is congruous and dyes what is selected with its color, thereby giving qualitative unity to materials externally disparate and dissimilar. It thus provides unity in and through the varied parts of an experience. When the unity is of the sort already described, the experience has esthetic character even though it is not, dominantly, an esthetic experience.

Two men meet; one is the applicant for a position, while the other has the disposition of the matter in his hands. The interview may be mechanical, consisting of set questions, the replies to which perfunctorily settle the matter. There is no experience in which the two men meet, nothing that is not a repetition, by way of acceptance or dismissal, of something which has happened a score of times. The situation is disposed of as if it were an exercise in bookkeeping. But an interplay may take place in which a new experience develops. Where should we look for an account of such an experience? Not to ledger-entries nor yet to a treatise on economics or sociology or personnel-psychology, but to drama or fiction. Its nature and import can be expressed only by art, because there is a unity of experience that can be expressed only as an experience. The *experience* is of material fraught with suspense and moving toward its own consummation through a connected series of varied incidents. The primary emotions on the part of the applicant may be at the beginning hope or despair, and elation or disappointment at the close. These emotions qualify the experience as a unity. But as the interview proceeds, secondary emotions are evolved as variations of the primary underlying one. It is even possible for each attitude and gesture, each sentence, almost every word, to produce more than a fluctuation in the intensity of the basic emotion; to produce, that is, a change of shade and tint in its quality. The employer sees by means of his own emotional reactions the character of the one applying. He projects him imaginatively into the work to be done and judges his fitness by the way in which the elements of the scene assemble and either clash or fit together. The presence and behavior of the applicant either harmonize with his own attitudes and desires or they conflict and jar. Such factors as these, inherently esthetic in quality, are the forces that carry the varied elements of the interview to a decisive issue. They enter into the settlement of every situation, whatever its dominant nature, in which there are uncertainty and suspense.

There are, therefore, common patterns in various experiences, no matter how unlike they are to one another in the details of their subject matter. There are conditions to be met without which an experience cannot come to be. The outline of the common pattern is set by the fact that every experience is the result of interaction between a live creature and some aspect of the world in which he lives. A man does something; he lifts, let us say, a stone. In consequence he undergoes, suffers, something: the weight, strain, texture of the surface of the thing lifted. The properties thus undergone determine further doing. The stone is too heavy or too angular, not solid enough; or else the properties undergone show it is fit for the use for which it is intended. The process continues until a mutual adaptation of the self and the object emerges and that particular experience comes to a close. What is true of this simple instance is true, as to form, of every experience. The creature operating may be a thinker in his study and the environment with which he interacts may consist of ideas instead of a stone. But interaction of the two constitutes the total experience that is had, and the close which completes it is the institution of a felt harmony.

An experience has pattern and structure, because it is not just doing and undergoing in alternation, but consists of them in relationship. To put one's hand in the fire that consumes it is not necessarily to have an experience. The action and its consequence must be joined in perception. This relationship is what gives meaning; to grasp it is the objective of all intelligence. The scope and content of the relations measure the significant content of an experience. A child's experience may be intense, but, because of lack of background from past experience, relations between undergoing and doing are slightly grasped, and the experience does not have great depth or breadth. No one ever arrives at such maturity that he perceives all the connections that are involved. There was once written (by Mr. Hinton) a romance called "The Unlearner." It portrayed the whole endless duration of life after death as a living over of the incidents that happened in a short life on earth, in continued discovery of the relationships involved among men.

Experience is limited by all the causes which interfere with perception of the relations between undergoing and doing. There may be interference because of excess on the side of doing or of excess on the side of receptivity, of undergoing. Unbalance on either side blurs the perception of relations and leaves the experience partial and distorted, with scant or false meaning. Zeal for doing, lust for action, leaves many a person, especially in this hurried and impatient human environment in which we live, with experience of an almost incredible paucity, all on the surface. No one experience has a chance to complete itself because something else is entered upon so speedily. What is called experience becomes so dispersed and miscellaneous as hardly to deserve the name. Resistance is treated as an obstruction to be beaten down, not as an invitation to reflection. An individual comes to seek, unconsciously even more than by deliberate choice, situations in which he can do the most things in the shortest time.

Experiences are also cut short from maturing by excess of receptivity. What is prized is then the mere undergoing of this and that, irrespective of perception of any meaning. The crowding together of as many impressions as possible is thought to be "life," even though no one of them is more than a flitting and a sipping. The sentimentalist and the day-dreamer may have more fancies and impressions pass through their consciousness than has the man who is animated by lust for action. But his experience is equally distorted, because nothing takes root in mind when there is no balance between doing and receiving. Some decisive action is needed in order to establish contact with the realities of the world and in order that impressions may be so related to facts that their value is tested and organized.

Because perception of relationship between what is done and what is undergone constitutes the work of intelligence, and because the artist is controlled in the process of his work by his grasp of the connection between what he has already done and what he is to do next, the idea that the artist does not think as intently and penetratingly as a scientific inquirer is absurd. A painter must consciously undergo the effect of his every brush stroke or he will not be aware of what he is doing and where his work is going. Moreover, he has to see each particular connection of doing and undergoing in relation to the whole that he desires to produce. To apprehend such relations is to think, and is one of the most exacting modes of thought. The difference between the pictures of different painters is due quite as much to differences of capacity to carry on this thought as it is to differences of sensitivity to bare color and to differences in dexterity of execution. As respects the basic quality of pictures, difference depends, indeed, more upon the quality of intelligence brought to bear upon perception of relations than upon anything else—though of course intelligence cannot be separated from direct sensitivity and is connected, though in a more external manner, with skill.

Any idea that ignores the necessary rôle of intelligence in production of works of art is based upon identification of thinking with use of one special kind of material, verbal signs and words. To think effectively in terms of relations of qualities is as severe a demand upon thought as to think in terms of symbols, verbal and mathematical. Indeed, since words are easily manipulated in mechanical ways, the production of a work of genuine art probably demands more intelligence than does most of the so-called thinking that goes on among those who pride themselves on being "intellectuals."

I have tried to show in these chapters that the esthetic is no intruder in experience from without, whether by way of idle luxury or transcendent ideality, but that it is the clarified and intensified development of traits that belong to every normally complete experience. This fact I take to be the only secure basis upon which esthetic theory can build. It remains to suggest some of the implications of the underlying fact.

We have no word in the English language that unambiguously includes what is signified by the two words "artistic" and "esthetic." Since "artistic" refers primarily to the act of production and "esthetic" to that of perception and enjoyment, the absence of a term designating the two processes taken together is unfortunate. Sometimes, the effect is to separate the two from each other, to regard art as something superimposed upon esthetic material, or, upon the other side, to an assumption that, since art is a process of creation, perception and enjoyment of it have nothing in common with the creative act. In any case, there is a certain verbal awkwardness in that we are compelled sometimes to use the term "esthetic" to cover the entire field and sometimes to limit it to the receiving perceptual aspect of the whole operation. I refer to these obvious facts as preliminary to an attempt to show how the conception of conscious experience as a perceived relation between doing and undergoing enables us to understand the connection that art as production and perception and appreciation as enjoyment sustain to each other.

Art denotes a process of doing or making. This is as true of fine as of technological art. Art involves molding of clay, chipping of marble, casting of bronze, laying on of pigments, construction of buildings, singing of songs, playing of instruments, enacting rôles on the stage, going through rhythmic movements in the dance. Every art does something with some physical material, the body or something outside the body, with or without the use of intervening tools, and with a view to production of something visible, audible, or tangible. So marked is the active or "doing" phase of art, that the dictionaries usually define it in terms of skilled action, ability in execution. The Oxford Dictionary illustrates by a quotation from John Stuart Mill: "Art is an endeavor after perfection in execution" while Matthew Arnold calls it "pure and flawless workmanship."

The word "esthetic" refers, as we have already noted, to experience as appreciative, perceiving, and enjoying. It denotes the consumer's rather than the producer's standpoint. It is Gusto, taste; and, as with cooking, overt skillful action is on the side of the cook who prepares, while taste is on the side of the consumer, as in gardening there is a distinction between the gardener who plants and tills and the householder who enjoys the finished product.

These very illustrations, however, as well as the relation that exists in having an experience between doing and undergoing, indicate that the distinction between esthetic and artistic cannot be pressed so far as to become a separation. Perfection in execution cannot be measured or defined in terms of execution; it implies those who perceive and enjoy the product that is executed. The cook prepares food for the consumer and the measure of the value of what is prepared is found in consumption. Mere perfection in execution, judged in its own terms in isolation, can probably be attained better by a machine than by human art. By itself, it is at most technique, and there are great artists who are not in the first ranks as technicians (witness Cézanne), just as there are great performers on the piano who are not great esthetically, and as Sargent is not a great painter.

Craftsmanship to be artistic in the final sense must be "loving"; it must care deeply for the subject matter upon which skill is exercised. A sculptor comes to mind whose busts are marvelously exact. It might be difficult to tell in the presence of a photograph of one of them and of a photograph of the original which was of the person himself. For virtuosity they are remarkable. But one doubts whether the maker of the busts had an experience of his own that he was concerned to have those share who look at his products. To be truly artistic, a work must also be esthetic—that is, framed for enjoyed receptive perception. Constant observation is, of course, necessary for the maker while he is producing. But if his perception is not also esthetic in nature, it is a colorless and cold recognition of what has been done, used as a stimulus to the next step in a process that is essentially mechanical.

In short, art, in its form, unites the very same relation of doing and undergoing, outgoing and incoming energy, that makes an experience to be an experience. Because of elimination of all that does not contribute to mutual organization of the factors of both action and reception into one another, and because of selection of just the aspects and traits that contribute to their interpenetration of each other, the product is a work of esthetic art. Man whittles, carves, sings, dances, gestures, molds, draws and paints. The doing or making is artistic when the perceived result is of such a nature that *its* qualities *as perceived* have controlled the question of production. The act of producing that is directed by intent to produce something that is enjoyed in the immediate experience of perceiving has qualities that a spontaneous or uncontrolled activity does not have. The artist embodies in himself the attitude of the perceiver while he works.

Suppose, for the sake of illustration, that a finely wrought object, one whose texture and proportions are highly pleasing in perception, has been believed to be a product of some primitive people. Then there is discovered evidence that proves it to be an accidental natural product. As an external thing, it is now precisely what it was before. Yet at once it ceases to be a work of art and becomes a natural "curiosity." It now belongs in a museum of natural history, not in a museum of art. And the extraordinary thing is that the difference that is thus made is not one of just intellectual classification. A difference is made in appreciative perception and in a direct way. The esthetic experience—in its limited sense—is thus seen to be inherently connected with the experience of making.

The sensory satisfaction of eye and ear, when esthetic, is so because it does not stand by itself but is linked to the activity of which it is the consequence. Even the pleasures of the palate are different in quality to an epicure than in one who merely "likes" his food as he eats it. The difference is not of mere intensity. The epicure is conscious of much more than the taste of the food. Rather, there enter into the taste, as directly experienced, qualities that depend upon reference to its source and its manner of production in connection with criteria of excellence. As production must absorb into itself qualities of the product as perceived and be regulated by them, so, on the other side, seeing, hearing, tasting, become esthetic when relation to a distinct manner of activity qualifies what is perceived.

There is an element of passion in all esthetic perception. Yet when we are overwhelmed by passion, as in extreme rage, fear, jealousy, the experience is definitely non-esthetic. There is no relationship felt to the qualities of the activity that has generated the passion. Consequently, the material of the experience lacks elements of balance and proportion. For these can be present only when, as in the conduct that has grace or dignity, the act is controlled by an exquisite sense of the relations which the act sustains—its fitness to the occasion and to the situation.

The process of art in production is related to the esthetic in perception organically—as the Lord God in creation surveyed his work and found it good. Until the artist is satisfied in perception with what he is doing, he continues shaping and reshaping. The making comes to an end when its result is experienced as good—and that experience comes not by mere intellectual and outside judgment but in direct perception. An artist, in comparison with his fellows, is one who is not only especially gifted in powers of execution but in unusual sensitivity to the qualities of things. This sensitivity also directs his doings and makings.

As we manipulate, we touch and feel, as we look, we see; as we listen, we hear. The hand moves with etching needle or with brush. The eye attends and reports the consequence of what is done. Because of this intimate connection, subsequent doing is cumulative and not a matter of caprice nor yet of routine. In an emphatic artistic-esthetic experience, the relation is so close that it controls simultaneously both the doing and the perception. Such vital intimacy of connection cannot be had if only hand and eye are engaged. When they do not, both of them, act as organs of the whole being, there is but a mechanical sequence of sense and movement, as in walking that is automatic. Hand and eye, when the experience is esthetic, are but instruments through which the entire live creature, moved and active throughout, operates. Hence the expression is emotional and guided by purpose.

Because of the relation between what is done and what is undergone, there is an immediate sense of things in perception as belonging together or as jarring; as reënforcing or as interfering. The consequences of the act of making as reported in sense show whether what is done carries forward the idea being executed or marks a deviation and break. In as far as the development of an experience is *controlled* through reference to these immediately felt relations of order and fulfillment, that experience becomes dominantly esthetic in nature. The urge to action becomes an urge to that kind of action which will result in an object satisfying in direct perception. The potter shapes his clay to make a bowl useful for holding grain; but he makes it in a way so regulated by the series of perceptions that sum up the serial acts of making, that the bowl is marked by enduring grace and charm. The general situation remains the same in painting a picture or molding a bust. Moreover, at each stage there is anticipation of what is to come. This anticipation is the connecting link between the next doing and its outcome for sense.

What is done and what is undergone are thus reciprocally, cumulatively, and continuously instrumental to each other.

The doing may be energetic, and the undergoing may be acute and intense. But unless they are related to each other to form a whole in perception, the thing done is not fully esthetic. The making for example may be a display of technical virtuosity, and the undergoing a gush of sentiment or a revery. If the artist does not perfect a new vision in his process of doing, he acts mechanically and repeats some old model fixed like a blue print in his mind. An incredible amount of observation and of the kind of intelligence that is exercised in perception of qualitative relations characterizes creative work in art. The relations must be noted not only with respect to one another, two by two, but in connection with the whole under construction; they are exercised in imagination as well as in observation. Irrelevancies arise that are tempting distractions; digressions suggest themselves in the guise of enrichments. There are occasions when the grasp of the dominant idea grows faint, and then the artist is moved unconsciously to fill in until his thought grows strong again. The real work of an artist is to build up an experience that is coherent in perception while moving with constant change in its development.

When an author puts on paper ideas that are already clearly conceived and consistently ordered, the real work has been previously done. Or, he may depend upon the greater perceptibility induced by the activity and its sensible report to direct his completion of the work. The mere act of transcription is esthetically irrelevant save as it enters integrally into the formation of an experience moving to completeness. Even the composition conceived in the head and, therefore, physically private, is public in its significant content, since it is conceived with reference to execution in a product that is perceptible and hence belongs to the common world. Otherwise it would be an aberration or a passing dream. The urge to express through painting the perceived qualities of a landscape is continuous with demand for pencil or brush. Without external embodiment, an experience remains incomplete; physiologically and functionally, sense organs are motor organs and are connected, by means of distribution of energies in the human body and not merely anatomically, with other motor organs. It is no linguistic accident that "building," "construction," "work," designate both a process and its finished product. Without the meaning of the verb that of the noun remains blank.

Writer, composer of music, sculptor, or painter can retrace, during the process of production, what they have previously done. When it is not satisfactory in the undergoing or perceptual phase of experience, they can to some degree start afresh. This retracing is not readily accomplished in the case of architecture—which is perhaps one reason why there are so many ugly buildings. Architects are obliged to complete their idea before its translation into a complete object of perception takes place. Inability to build up simultaneously the idea and its objective embodiment imposes a handicap. Nevertheless, they too are obliged to think out their ideas in terms of the medium of embodiment and the object of ultimate perception unless they work mechanically and by rote. Probably the esthetic quality of medieval cathedrals is due in some measure to the fact that their constructions were not so much controlled by plans and specifications made in advance as is now the case. Plans grew as the building grew. But even a Minerva-like product, if it is artistic, presupposes a prior period of gestation in which doings and perceptions projected in imagination interact and mutually modify one another. Every work of art follows the plan of, and pattern of, a complete experience, rendering it more intensely and concentratedly felt.

It is not so easy in the case of the perceiver and appreciator to understand the intimate union of doing and undergoing as it is in the case of the maker. We are given to supposing that the former merely takes in what is there in finished form, instead of realizing that this taking in involves activities that are comparable to those of the creator. But receptivity is not passivity. It, too, is a process consisting of a series of responsive acts that accumulate toward objective fulfillment. Otherwise, there is not perception but recognition. The difference between the two is immense. Recognition is perception arrested before it has a chance to develop freely. In recognition there is a beginning of an act of perception. But this beginning is not allowed to serve the development of a full perception of the thing recognized. It is arrested at the point where it will serve some *other* purpose, as we recognize a man on the street in order to greet or to avoid him, not so as to see him for the sake of seeing what is there.

In recognition we fall back, as upon a stereotype, upon some previously formed scheme. Some detail or arrangement of details serves as cue for bare identification. It suffices in recognition to apply this bare outline as a stencil to the present object. Sometimes in contact with a human being we are struck with traits, perhaps of only physical characteristics, of which we were not previously aware. We realize that we never knew the person before; we had not seen him in any pregnant sense. We now begin to study and to "take in." Perception replaces bare recognition. There is an act of reconstructive doing, and consciousness becomes fresh and alive. *This* act of seeing involves the coöperation of motor elements even though they remain implicit and do not become overt, as well as coöperation of all funded ideas that may serve to complete the new picture that is forming. Recognition is too easy to arouse vivid consciousness. There is not enough resistance between new and old to secure consciousness of the experience that is had. Even a dog that barks and wags his tail joyously on seeing his master return is more fully alive in his reception of his friend than is a human being who is content with mere recognition.

Bare recognition is satisfied when a proper tag or label is attached, "proper" signifying one that serves a purpose outside the act of recognition —as a salesman identifies wares by a sample. It involves no stir of the organism, no inner commotion. But an act of perception proceeds by waves that extend serially throughout the entire organism. There is, therefore, no such thing in perception as seeing or hearing *plus* emotion. The perceived object or scene is emotionally pervaded throughout. When an aroused emotion does not permeate the material that is perceived or thought of, it is either preliminary or pathological.

The esthetic or undergoing phase of experience is receptive. It involves surrender. But adequate yielding of the self is possible only through a controlled activity that may well be intense. In much of our intercourse with our surroundings we withdraw; sometimes from fear, if only of expending unduly our store of energy; sometimes from preoccupation with other matters, as in the case of recognition. Perception is an act of the going-out of energy in order to receive, not a withholding of energy. To steep ourselves in a subject-matter we have first to plunge into it. When we are only passive to a scene, it overwhelms us and, for lack of answering activity, we do not perceive that which bears us down. We must summon energy and pitch it at a responsive key in order to *take* in.

Every one knows that it requires apprenticeship to see through a microscope or telescope, and to see a landscape as the geologist sees it. The idea that esthetic perception is an affair for odd moments is one reason for the backwardness of the arts among us. The eye and the visual apparatus may be intact; the object may be physically there, the cathedral of Notre Dame, or Rembrandt's portrait of Hendrik Stoeffel. In some bald sense, the latter may be "seen." They may be looked at, possibly recognized, and have their correct names attached. But for lack of continuous interaction between the total organism and the objects, they are not perceived, certainly not esthetically. A crowd of visitors steered through a picture-gallery by a guide, with attention called here and there to some high point, does not perceive; only by accident is there even interest in seeing a picture for the sake of subject matter vividly realized.

For to perceive, a beholder must *create* his own experience. And his creation must include relations comparable to those which the original producer underwent. They are not the same in any literal sense. But with the perceiver, as with the artist, there must be an ordering of the elements of the whole that is in form, although not in details, the same as the process of organization the creator of the work consciously experienced. Without an act of recreation the object is not perceived as a work of art. The artist selected, simplified, clarified, abridged and condensed according to his interest. The beholder must go through these operations according to his point of view and interest. In both, an act of abstraction, that is of extraction of what is significant, takes place. In both, there is comprehension in its literal signification—that is, a gathering together of details and particulars physically scattered into an experienced whole. There is work done on the part of the percipient as there is on the part of the artist. The one who is too lazy, idle, or indurated in convention to perform this work will not see or hear. His "appreciation" will be a mixture of scraps of learning with conformity to norms of conventional admiration and with a confused, even if genuine, emotional excitation.

The considerations that have been presented imply both the community and the unlikeness, because of specific emphasis, of *an* experience, in its pregnant sense, and esthetic experience. The former has esthetic quality; otherwise its materials would not be rounded out into a single coherent experience. It is not possible to divide in a vital experience the practical, emotional, and intellectual from one another and to set the properties of one over against the characteristics of the others. The emotional phase binds parts together into a single whole; "intellectual" simply names the fact that the experience has meaning; "practical" indicates that the organism is interacting with events and objects which surround it. The most elaborate philosophic or scientific inquiry and the most ambitious industrial or political enterprise has, when its different ingredients constitute an integral experience, esthetic quality. For then its varied parts are linked to one another, and do not merely succeed one another. And the parts through their experienced linkage move toward a consummation and close, not merely to cessation in time. This consummation, moreover, does not wait in consciousness for the whole undertaking to be finished. It is anticipated throughout and is recurrently savored with special intensity.

Nevertheless, the experiences in question are dominantly intellectual or practical, rather than *distinctively* esthetic, because of the interest and purpose that initiate and control them. In an intellectual experience, the conclusion has value on its own account. It can be extracted as a formula or as a "truth," and can be used in its independent entirety as factor and guide in other inquiries. In a work of art there is no such single self-sufficient deposit. The end, the terminus, is significant not by itself but as the integration of the parts. It has no other existence. A drama or novel is not the final sentence, even if the characters are disposed of as living happily ever after. In a distinctively esthetic experience, characteristics that are subdued in other experiences are dominant; those that are subordinate are controlling—namely, the characteristics in virtue of which the experience is an integrated complete experience on its own account.

In every integral experience there is form because there is dynamic organization. I call the organization dynamic because it takes time to complete it, because it is a growth. There is inception, development, fulfillment. Material is ingested and digested through interaction with that vital organization of the results of prior experience that constitutes the mind of the worker. Incubation goes on until what is conceived is brought forth and is rendered perceptible as part of the common world. An esthetic experience can be crowded into a moment only in the sense that a climax of prior long enduring processes may arrive in an outstanding movement which so sweeps everything else into it that all else is forgotten. That which distinguishes an experience as esthetic is conversion of resistance and tensions, of excitations that in themselves are temptations to diversion, into a movement toward an inclusive and fulfilling close.

Experiencing like breathing is a rhythm of intakings and outgivings. Their succession is punctuated and made a rhythm by the existence of intervals, periods in which one phase is ceasing and the other is inchoate and preparing. William James aptly compared the course of a conscious experience to the alternate flights and perchings of a bird. The flights and perchings are intimately connected with one another; they are not so many unrelated lightings succeeded by a number of equally unrelated hoppings. Each resting place in experience is an undergoing in which is absorbed and taken home the consequences of prior doing, and, unless the doing is that of utter caprice or sheer routine, each doing carries in itself meaning that has been extracted and conserved. As with the advance of an army, all gains from what has been already effected are periodically consolidated, and always with a view to what is to be done next. If we move too rapidly, we get away from the base of supplies—of accrued meanings—and the experience is flustered, thin, and confused. If we dawdle too long after having extracted a net value, experience perishes of inanition.

The *form* of the whole is therefore present in every member. Fulfilling, consummating, are continuous functions, not mere ends, located at one place only. An engraver, painter, or writer is in process of completing at every stage of his work. He must at each point retain and sum up what has gone before as a whole and with reference to a whole to come. Otherwise there is no consistency and no security in his successive acts. The series of doings in the rhythm of experience give variety and movement; they save the work from monotony and useless repetitions. The undergoings are the corresponding elements in the rhythm, and they supply unity; they save the work from the aimlessness of a mere succession of excitations. An object is peculiarly and dominantly esthetic, yielding the enjoyment characteristic of esthetic perception, when the factors that determine anything which can be called *an* experience are lifted high above the threshold of perception and are made manifest for their own sake.

AS EMOTION

EXPRESSION OF EMOTION

R. G. COLLINGWOOD

The Expression of Emotion [1]

Expressing Emotion and Arousing Emotion

OUR FIRST QUESTION is this. Since the artist proper has something to do with emotion, and what he does with it is not to arouse it, what is it that he does? It will be remembered that the kind of answer we expect to this question is an answer derived from what we all know and all habitually say; nothing original or recondite, but something entirely commonplace.

Nothing could be more entirely commonplace than to say he expresses them. The idea is familiar to every artist, and to every one else who has any acquaintance with the arts. To state it is not to state a philosophical theory or definition of art; it is to state a fact or supposed fact about which, when we have sufficiently identified it, we shall have later to theorize philosophically. For the present it does not matter whether the fact that is alleged, when it is said that the artist expresses emotion, is really a fact or only supposed to be one. Whichever it is, we have to identify it, that is, to decide what it is that people are saying when they use the phrase. Later on, we shall have to see whether it will fit into a coherent theory.

They are referring to a situation, real or supposed, of a definite kind. When a man is said to express emotion, what is being said about him comes

---

[1] From R. G. Collingwood, *The Principles of Art* (Oxford: Clarendon Press, 1938), pp. 109–119, 308–318, 323–324. Reprinted by permission. Title by the editors; subtitles are Mr. Collingwood's. (Eds.)

to this. At first, he is conscious of having an emotion, but not conscious of what this emotion is. All he is conscious of is a perturbation or excitement, which he feels going on within him, but of whose nature he is ignorant. While in this state, all he can say about his emotion is: "I feel. . . . I don't know what I feel." From this helpless and oppressed condition he extricates himself by doing something which we call expressing himself. This is an activity which has something to do with the thing we call language: he expresses himself by speaking. It has also something to do with consciousness: the emotion expressed is an emotion of whose nature the person who feels it is no longer unconscious. It has also something to do with the way in which he feels the emotion. As unexpressed, he feels it in what we have called a helpless and oppressed way; as expressed, he feels it in a way from which this sense of oppression has vanished. His mind is somehow lightened and eased.

This lightening of emotions which is somehow connected with the expression of them has a certain resemblance to the "catharsis" by which emotions are earthed through being discharged into a make-believe situation; but the two things are not the same. Suppose the emotion is one of anger. If it is effectively earthed, for example by fancying oneself kicking some one down stairs, it is thereafter no longer present in the mind as anger at all: we have worked it off and are rid of it. If it is expressed, for example by putting it into hot and bitter words, it does not disappear from the mind; we remain angry; but instead of the sense of oppression which accompanies an emotion of anger not yet recognized as such, we have that sense of alleviation which comes when we are conscious of our own emotion as anger, instead of being conscious of it only as an unidentified perturbation. This is what we refer to when we say that it "does us good" to express our emotions.

The expression of an emotion by speech may be addressed to some one; but if so it is not done with the intention of arousing a like emotion in him. If there is any effect which we wish to produce in the hearer, it is only the effect which we call making him understand how we feel. But, as we have already seen, this is just the effect which expressing our emotions has on ourselves. It makes us, as well as the people to whom we talk, understand how we feel. A person arousing emotion sets out to affect his audience in a way in which he himself is not necessarily affected. He and his audience stand in quite different relations to the act, very much as physician and patient stand in quite different relations towards a drug administered by the one and taken by the other. A person expressing emotion, on the contrary, is treating himself and his audience in the same kind of way: he is making his emotions clear to his audience, and that is what he is doing to himself.

It follows from this that the expression of emotion, simply as expression, is not addressed to any particular audience. It is addressed primarily to the speaker himself, and secondarily to any one who can understand. Here again, the speaker's attitude towards his audience is quite unlike that of a person desiring to arouse in his audience a certain emotion. If that is what he wishes to do, he must know the audience he is addressing. He must know what type of stimulus will produce the desired kind of reaction in people of that particular sort; and he must adapt his language to his audience in the sense of making sure that it contains stimuli appropriate to their peculiarities. If what he wishes to do is to express his emotions intelligibly, he has to express them in such a way as to be intelligible to himself; his audience is then in the position of persons who overhear him doing this. Thus the stimulus-and-reaction terminology has no applicability to the situation.

The means-and-end, or technique, terminology too is inapplicable. Until a man has expressed his emotion, he does not yet know what emotion it is. The act of expressing it is therefore an exploration of his own emotions. He is trying to find out what these emotions are. There is certainly here a directed process: an effort, that is, directed upon a certain end; but the end is not something foreseen and preconceived, to which appropriate means can be thought out in the light of our knowledge of its special character. Expression is an activity of which there can be no technique.

Expression and Individualization

Expressing an emotion is not the same thing as describing it. To say "I am angry" is to describe one's emotion, not to express it. The words in which it is expressed need not contain any reference to anger as such at all. Indeed, so far as they simply and solely express it, they cannot contain any such reference. The curse of Ernulphus, as invoked by Dr. Slop on the unknown person who tied certain knots, is a classical and supreme expression of anger; but it does not contain a single word descriptive of the emotion it expresses.[2]

This is why, as literary critics well know, the use of epithets in poetry, or even in prose where expressiveness is aimed at, is a danger. If you want to express the terror which something causes, you must not give it an epithet like "dreadful." For that describes the emotion instead of expressing it, and your language becomes frigid, that is inexpressive, at once. A genuine poet, in his moments of genuine poetry, never mentions by name the emotions he is expressing.

Some people have thought that a poet who wishes to express a great variety of subtly differentiated emotions might be hampered by the lack of a

---

[2] Laurence Sterne, *Tristram Shandy*, Book III, Chap. 11. (Eds.)

vocabulary rich in words referring to the distinctions between them; and that psychology, by working out such a vocabulary, might render a valuable service to poetry. This is the opposite of the truth. The poet needs no such words at all; the existence or nonexistence of a scientific terminology describing the emotions he wishes to express is to him a matter of perfect indifference. If such a terminology, where it exists, is allowed to affect his own use of language, it affects it for the worse.

The reason why description, so far from helping expression, actually damages it, is that description generalizes. To describe a thing is to call it a thing of such and such a kind: to bring it under a conception, to classify it. Expression, on the contrary, individualizes. The anger which I feel here and now, with a certain person, for a certain cause, is no doubt an instance of anger, and in describing it as anger one is telling truth about it; but it is much more than mere anger: it is a peculiar anger, not quite like any anger that I ever felt before, and probably not quite like any anger I shall ever feel again. To become fully conscious of it means becoming conscious of it not merely as an instance of anger, but as this quite peculiar anger. Expressing it, we saw, has something to do with becoming conscious of it; therefore, if being fully conscious of it means being conscious of all its peculiarities, fully expressing it means expressing all its peculiarities. The poet, therefore, in proportion as he understands his business, gets as far away as possible from merely labelling his emotions as instances of this or that general kind, and takes enormous pains to individualize them by expressing them in terms which reveal their difference from any other emotion of the same sort.

This is a point in which art proper, as the expression of emotion, differs sharply and obviously from any craft whose aim it is to arouse emotion. The end which a craft sets out to realize is always conceived in general terms, never individualized. However accurately defined it may be, it is always defined as the production of a thing having characteristics that could be shared by other things. A joiner, making a table out of these pieces of wood and no others, makes it to measurements and specifications which, even if actually shared by no other table, might in principle be shared by other tables. A physician treating a patient for a certain complaint is trying to produce in him a condition which might be, and probably has been, often produced in others, namely, the condition of recovering from that complaint. So an "artist" setting out to produce a certain emotion in his audience is setting out to produce not an individual emotion, but an emotion of a certain kind. It follows that the means appropriate to its production will be not individual means but means of a certain kind: that is to say, means which are always in principle replaceable by other similar means. As every good craftsman insists, there is always a "right way" of performing any operation. A "way" of acting is a general pattern to which various individual actions may conform. In order that the "work of art" should produce its intended psychological effect, therefore, whether this effect be magical or merely amusing, what is necessary is that it should satisfy certain conditions, possess certain characteristics: in other words be, not this work and no other, but a work of this kind and of no other.

This explains the meaning of the generalization which Aristotle and others have ascribed to art. We have already seen that Aristotle's *Poetics* is concerned not with art proper but with representative art, and representative art of one definite kind.[3] He is not analysing the religious drama of a hundred years before, he is analysing the amusement literature of the fourth century, and giving rules for its composition. The end being not individual but general (the production of an emotion of a certain kind) the means too are general (the portrayal, not of this individual act, but of an act of this sort; not, as he himself puts it, what Alcibiades did, but what anybody of a certain kind would do).[4] Sir Joshua Reynold's idea of generalization is in principle the same; he expounds it in connexion with what he calls "the grand style," which means a style intended to produce emotions of a certain type.[5] He is quite right; if you want to produce a typical case of a certain emotion, the way to do it is to put before your audience a representation of the typical features belonging to the kind of thing that produces it: make your kings very royal, your soldiers very soldierly, your women very feminine, your cottages very cottagesque, your oak-trees very oakish, and so on.

Art proper, as expression of emotion, has nothing to do with all this. The artist proper is a person who, grappling with the problem of expressing a certain emotion, says, "I want to get this clear." It is no use to him to get something else clear, however like it this other thing may be. Nothing will serve as a substitute. He does not want a thing of a certain kind, he wants a certain thing. This is why the kind of person who takes his literature as psychology, saying "How admirably this writer depicts the feelings of women, or bus-drivers, or homosexuals . . . ," necessarily misunderstands every real work of art with which he comes into contact, and takes for good art, with infallible precision, what is not art at all.

Selection and Aesthetic Emotion

It has sometimes been asked whether emotions can be divided into those suitable for expression by artists and those unsuitable. If by art one means art proper, and identifies this with expression, the only possible

---

[3] See *The Principles of Art,* pp. 50–52. (Eds.)
[4] *Poetics* 9, 1451ª36–1452ª11. (Eds.)
[5] See Sir Joshua Reynolds, *Discourses on Art,* especially Discourses III and IV. (Eds.)

answer is that there can be no such distinction. Whatever is expressible is expressible. There may be ulterior motives in special cases which make it desirable to express some emotions and not others; but only if by "express" one means express publicly, that is, allow people to overhear one expressing oneself. This is because one cannot possibly decide that a certain emotion is one which for some reason it would be undesirable to express thus publicly, unless one first becomes conscious of it; and doing this, as we saw, is somehow bound up with expressing it. If art means the expression of emotion, the artist as such must be absolutely candid; his speech must be absolutely free. This is not a precept, it is a statement. It does not mean that the artist ought to be candid, it means that he is an artist only in so far as he is candid. Any kind of selection, any decision to express this emotion and not that, is inartistic not in the sense that it damages the perfect sincerity which distinguishes good art from bad, but in the sense that it represents a further process of a nonartistic kind, carried out when the work of expression proper is already complete. For until that work is complete one does not know what emotions one feels; and is therefore not in a position to pick and choose, and give one of them preferential treatment.

From these considerations a certain corollary follows about the division of art into distinct arts. Two such divisions are current: one according to the medium in which the artist works, into painting, poetry, music, and the like; the other according to the kind of emotion he expresses, into tragic, comic, and so forth. We are concerned with the second. If the difference between tragedy and comedy is a difference between the emotions they express, it is not a difference that can be present to the artist's mind when he is beginning his work; if it were, he would know what emotion he was going to express before he had expressed it. No artist, therefore, so far as he is an artist proper, can set out to write a comedy, a tragedy, an elegy, or the like. So far as he is an artist proper, he is just as likely to write any one of these as any other; which is the truth that Socrates was heard expounding towards the dawn, among the sleeping figures in Agathon's dining-room.[6] These distinctions, therefore, have only a very limited value. They can be properly used in two ways. (1) When a work of art is complete, it can be labelled *ex post facto* as tragic, comic, or the like, according to the character of the emotions chiefly expressed in it. But understood in that sense the distinction is of no real importance. (2) If we are talking about representational art, the case is very different. Here the so-called artist knows in advance what kind of emotion he wishes to excite, and will construct works of different kinds according to the different kinds of effect they are to produce. In the

---

[6] Plato, *Symposium*, 223 D.

case of representational art, therefore, distinctions of this kind are not only admissible as an *ex post facto* classification of things to which in their origin it is alien; they are present from the beginning as a determining factor in the so-called artist's plan of work.

The same considerations provide an answer to the question whether there is such a thing as a specific "aesthetic emotion." If it is said that there is such an emotion independently of its expression in art, and that the business of artists is to express it, we must answer that such a view is nonsense. It implies, first, that artists have emotions of various kinds, among which is this peculiar aesthetic emotion; secondly, that they select this aesthetic emotion for expression. If the first proposition were true, the second would have to be false. If artists only find out what their emotions are in the course of finding out how to express them, they cannot begin the work of expression by deciding what emotion to express.

In a different sense, however, it is true that there is a specific aesthetic emotion. As we have seen, an unexpressed emotion is accompanied by a feeling of oppression; when it is expressed and thus comes into consciousness the same emotion is accompanied by a new feeling of alleviation or easement, the sense that this oppression is removed. It resembles the feeling of relief that comes when a burdensome intellectual or moral problem has been solved. We may call it, if we like, the specific feeling of having successfully expressed ourselves; and there is no reason why it should not be called a specific aesthetic emotion. But it is not a specific kind of emotion preexisting to the expression of it, and having the peculiarity that when it comes to be expressed it is expressed artistically. It is an emotional colouring which attends the expression of any emotion whatever.

The Artist and the Ordinary Man

I have been speaking of "the artist," in the present chapter, as if artists were persons of a special kind, differing somehow either in mental endowment or at least in the way they use their endowment from the ordinary persons who make up their audience. But this segregation of artists from ordinary human beings belongs to the conception of art as craft; it cannot be reconciled with the conception of art as expression. If art were a kind of craft, it would follow as a matter of course. Any craft is a specialized form of skill, and those who possess it are thereby marked out from the rest of mankind. If art is the skill to amuse people, or in general to arouse emotions in them, the amusers and the amused form two different classes, differing in their respectively active and passive relation to the craft of exciting determinate emotions; and this difference will be due, according to whether the artist is "born" or "made," either to a specific mental endowment in the artist, which in theories of this type has gone by the name of "genius," or to a specific training.

If art is not a kind of craft, but the expression of emotion, this distinction of kind between artist and audience disappears. For the artist has an audience only in so far as people hear him expressing himself, and understand what they hear him saying. Now, if one person says something by way of expressing what is in his mind, and another hears and understands him, the hearer who understands him has that same thing in his mind. The question whether he would have had it if the first had not spoken need not here be raised; however it is answered, what has just been said is equally true. If some one says "Twice two is four" in the hearing of some one incapable of carrying out the simplest arithmetical operation, he will be understood by himself, but not by his hearer. The hearer can understand only if he can add two and two in his own mind. Whether he could do it before he heard the speaker say those words makes no difference. What is here said of expressing thoughts is equally true of expressing emotions. If a poet expresses, for example, a certain kind of fear, the only hearers who can understand him are those who are capable of experiencing that kind of fear themselves. Hence, when some one reads and understands a poem, he is not merely understanding the poet's expression of his, the poet's, emotions, he is expressing emotions of his own in the poet's words, which have thus become his own words. As Coleridge put it, we know a man for a poet by the fact that he makes us poets. We know that he is expressing his emotions by the fact that he is enabling us to express ours.

Thus, if art is the activity of expressing emotions, the reader is an artist as well as the writer. There is no distinction of kind between artist and audience. This does not mean that there is no distinction at all. When Pope wrote that the poet's business was to say "what all have felt but none so well express'd," we may interpret his words as meaning (whether or no Pope himself consciously meant this when he wrote them) that the poet's difference from his audience lies in the fact that, though both do exactly the same thing, namely express this particular emotion in these particular words, the poet is a man who can solve for himself the problem of expressing it, whereas the audience can express it only when the poet has shown them how. The poet is not singular either in his having that emotion or in his power of expressing it; he is singular in his ability to take the initiative in expressing what all feel, and all can express.

The Audience as Understander

What is meant by saying that the painter "records" in his picture the experience which he had in painting it? With this question we come to the subject of the audience, for the audience consists of anybody and everybody to whom such records are significant.

It means that the picture, when seen by some one else or by the painter himself subsequently, produces in him (we need not ask how) sensuous-emotional or psychical experiences which, when raised from impressions to ideas by the activity of the spectator's consciousness, are transmuted into a total imaginative experience identical with that of the painter. This experience of the spectator does not repeat the comparatively poor experience of a person who merely looks at the subject; it repeats the richer and more highly organized experience of a person who has not only looked at it but has painted it as well.

That is why, as so many people have observed, we "see more in" a really good picture of a given subject than we do in the subject itself. That is why, too, many people prefer what is called "nature" or "real life" to the finest pictures, because they prefer not to be shown so much, in order to keep their apprehensions at a lower and more manageable level, where they can embroider what they see with likes and dislikes, fancies and emotions of their own, not intrinsically connected with the subject. A great portrait painter, in the time it takes him to paint a sitter, intensely active in absorbing impressions and converting them into an imaginative vision of the man, may easily see through the mask that is good enough to deceive a less active and less pertinacious observer, and detect in a mouth or an eye or the turn of a head things that have long been concealed. There is nothing mysterious about this insight. Every one judges men by the impressions he gets of them and his power of becoming aware of these impressions; and the artist is a man whose life's work consists in doing that. The wonder is rather that so few artists do it revealingly. That is perhaps because people do not want it done, and artists fall in with their desire for what is called a good likeness, a picture that reveals nothing new, but only recalls what they have already felt in the sitter's presence.

How is any one to know that the imaginative experience which the spectator, by the work of his consciousness, makes out of the sensations he receives from a painting "repeats," or is "identical" with, the experience which the artist had in painting it? That question has already been raised about language in general [7] and answered by saying that there is no possibility of an absolute assurance; the only assurance we can have "is an empirical and relative assurance, becoming progressively stronger as conversation proceeds, and based on the fact that neither party seems to the other to be talking nonsense." The same answer holds good here. We can never absolutely know that the imaginative experience we obtain from a work of art is identical

---

[7] See *The Principles of Art*, Chap. XI, Section 5. (Eds.)

with that of the artist. In proportion as the artist is a great one, we can be pretty certain that we have only caught his meaning partially and imperfectly. But the same applies to any case in which we hear what a man says or read what he writes. And a partial and imperfect understanding is not the same thing as a complete failure to understand.

For example, a man reading the first canto of the *Inferno* may have no idea what Dante meant by the three beasts. Are they deadly sins, or are they potentates, or what are they? he may ask. In that perplexity, however, he has not completely lost contact with his author. There is still a great deal in the canto which he can understand, that is to say, transmute from impression into idea by the work of his consciousness; and all this, he can be fairly confident, he grasps as Dante meant it. And even the three beasts, though he does not understand them completely (something remains obstinately a mere untransmuted impression) he understands in part; he sees that they are something the poet dreads, and he imaginatively experiences the dread, though he does not know what it is that is dreaded.

Or take (since Dante may be ruled out as allegorical and therefore unfair) an example from modern poetry. I do not know how many readers of Mr. Eliot's poem *Sweeney among the Nightingales* have the least idea what precisely the situation is which the poet is depicting. I have never heard or read any expression of such an idea. Sweeney has dropped asleep in a restaurant, vaguely puzzled by the fact that the Convent of the Sacred Heart, next door, has reminded him of something, he cannot tell what. A wounded Heart, and waiting husbandless women. As he snores all through the second verse a prostitute in a long cloak comes and sits on his knees, and at that moment he dreams the answer. It is Agamemnon's cry—"O, I am wounded mortally to the heart"—wounded to death at his homecoming by the false wife he had left behind. He wakes, stretching and laughing (tilting the girl off his knee), as he realizes that in the queer working of his mind the hooded husbandless nuns and the cloaked husbandless girl, waiting there like a spider for her prey, are both Klytaemnestra, the faithless wife who threw her cloak (the "net of death") round her lord and stabbed him.

I quote this case because I had known and enjoyed the poem for years before I saw that this was what it was all about; and nevertheless I understood enough to value it highly. And I am willing to believe that the distinguished critic who thinks that the "liquid siftings" of the nightingales were not their excrement, but their songs, values it highly too, and not everywhere so unintelligently as that sample would suggest.[8]

The imaginative experience contained in a work of art is not a closed

---

[8] And it was not until a few days after I had written the above, that I recognized "gloomy Orin" as a borrowing from Marlowe's *Dido*—another tragedy about a husbandless woman.

whole. There is no sense in putting the dilemma that a man either understands it (that is, has made that entire experience his own) or does not.
Understanding it is always a complex business, consisting of many phases,
each complete in itself but each leading on to the next. A determined and
intelligent audience will penetrate into this complex far enough, if the work
of art is a good one, to get something of value; but it need not on that account think it has extracted "the" meaning of the work, for there is no such
thing. The doctrine of a plurality of meanings, expounded for the case of
holy scripture by St. Thomas Aquinas, is in principle perfectly sound: as he
states it, the only trouble is that it does not go far enough. In some shape or
other, it is true of all language.

The Audience as Collaborator

The audience as understander, attempting an exact reconstruction in its own mind of the artist's imaginative experience, is engaged on an
endless quest. It can carry out this reconstruction only in part. This looks as
if the artist were a kind of transcendent genius whose meaning is always too
profound for his audience of humbler mortals to grasp in a more than fragmentary way. And an artist inclined to give himself airs will no doubt interpret the situation like that. But another interpretation is possible. The artist
may take his audience's limitations into account when composing his work;
in which case they will appear to him not as limitations on the extent to
which his work will prove comprehensible, but as conditions determining
the subject-matter or meaning of the work itself. In so far as the artist feels
himself at one with his audience, this will involve no condescension on his
part; it will mean that he takes it as his business to express not his own private emotions, irrespectively of whether any one else feels them or not, but
the emotions he shares with his audience. Instead of conceiving himself as a
mystagogue, leading his audience as far as it can follow along the dark and
difficult paths of his own mind, he will conceive himself as his audience's
spokesman, saying for it the things it wants to say but cannot say unaided.
Instead of setting up for the great man who (as Hegel said) imposes upon
the world the task of understanding him, he will be a humbler person, imposing upon himself the task of understanding his world, and thus enabling
it to understand itself.

In this case his relation to his audience will no longer be a mere by-product
of his aesthetic experience, as it still was in the situation described in the
preceding section; it will be an integral part of that experience itself. If
what he is trying to do is to express emotions that are not his own merely,
but his audience's as well, his success in doing this will be tested by his audience's reception of what he has to say. What he says will be something that

his audience says through his mouth; and his satisfaction in having expressed what he feels will be at the same time, in so far as he communicates this expression to them, their satisfaction in having expressed what they feel. There will thus be something more than mere communication from artist to audience, there will be collaboration between audience and artist.

We have inherited a long tradition, beginning in the late eighteenth century with the cult of "genius," and lasting all through the nineteenth, which is inimical to this second alternative. But I have already said that this tradition is dying away. Artists are less inclined to give themselves airs than they used to be; and there are many indications that they are more willing than they were, even a generation ago, to regard their audiences as collaborators. It is perhaps no longer foolish to hope that this way of conceiving the relation between artist and audience may be worth discussing.

There are grounds for thinking that this idea of the relation is the right one. . . . We must look at the facts; and we shall find that, whatever airs they may give themselves, artists have always been in the habit of treating the public as collaborators. On a technical theory of art, this is, in a sense, comprehensible. If the artist is trying to arouse certain emotions in his audience, a refusal on the part of the audience to develop these emotions proves that the artist has failed. But this is one of the many points in which the technical theory does not so much miss the truth as misrepresent it. An artist need not be a slave to the technical theory, in order to feel that his audience's approbation is relevant to the question whether he has done his work well or ill. There have been painters who would not exhibit, poets who would not publish, musicians who would not have their works performed; but those who have made this great refusal, so far as one knows them, have not been of the highest quality. There has been a lack of genuineness about their work, corresponding to this strain of secretiveness in their character, which is inconsistent with good art. The man who feels that he has something to say is not only willing to say it in public: he craves to say it in public and feels that until it has been thus said it has not been said at all. The public is always, no doubt, a circumscribed one: it may consist only of a few friends, and at most it includes only people who can buy or borrow a book or get hold of a theatre ticket; but every artist knows that publication of some kind is a necessity to him.

Every artist knows, too, that the reception he gets from his public is not a matter of indifference to him. He may train himself to take rebuffs with a stiff lip, and go on working in spite of bad sales and hostile reviews. He must so train himself, if he is to do his best work; because with the best will in the world (quite apart from venality in reviewers and frivolity in readers) no one enjoys having his unconscious emotions dragged into the light of consciousness, and consequently there is often a strongly painful element in a genuine aesthetic experience, and a strong temptation to reject it. But the reason why the artist finds it so hard to train himself in this way is because these rebuffs wound him not in his personal vanity, but in his judgment as to the soundness of the work he has done.

Here we come to the point. One might suppose that the artist by himself is in his own eyes a sufficient judge of his work's value. If he is satisfied with it, why should he mind what others think? But things do not work like that. The artist, like any one else who comes before an audience, must put a bold face on it; he must do the best he can, and pretend that he knows it is good. But probably no artist has ever been so conceited as to be wholly taken in by his own pretence. Unless he sees his own proclamation, "This is good," echoed on the faces of his audience—"Yes, that is good"—he wonders whether he was speaking the truth or not. He thought he had enjoyed and recorded a genuine aesthetic experience, but has he? Was he suffering from a corruption of consciousness? Had his audience judged him better than he judged himself?

These are facts which no artist, I think, will deny, unless in that feverish way in which we all deny what we know to be true and will not accept. If they are facts, they prove that, in spite of all disclaimers, artists do look upon their audiences as collaborators with themselves in the attempt to answer the question: is this a genuine work of art or not? But this is the thin end of a wedge. Once the audience's collaboration is admitted thus far, it must be admitted farther.

The artist's business is to express emotions; and the only emotions he can express are those which he feels, namely, his own. No one can judge whether he has expressed them except some one who feels them. If they are his own and no one else's, there is no one except himself who can judge whether he has expressed them or not. If he attaches any importance to the judgment of his audience, it can only be because he thinks that the emotions he has tried to express are emotions not peculiar to himself, but shared by his audience, and that the expression of them he has achieved (if indeed he has achieved it) is as valid for the audience as it is for himself. In other words, he undertakes his artistic labour not as a personal effort on his own private behalf, but as a public labour on behalf of the community to which he belongs. Whatever statement of emotion he utters is prefaced by the implicit rubric, not "I feel," but "we feel." And it is not strictly even a labour undertaken by himself on behalf of the community. It is a labour in which he invites the community to participate; for their function as audience is not passively to accept his work, but to do it over again for themselves. If he invites them to do this, it is because he has reason to think they will accept his invitation, that is, because he thinks he is inviting them to do what they already want to do.

In so far as the artist feels all this (and an artist who did not feel it would not feel the craving to publish his work, or take seriously the public's opinion of it), he feels it not only after his work is completed, but from its inception and throughout its composition. The audience is perpetually present to him as a factor in his artistic labour; not as an anti-aesthetic factor, corrupting the sincerity of his work by considerations of reputation and reward, but as an aesthetic factor, defining what the problem is which as an artist he is trying to solve—what emotions he is to express—and what constitutes a solution of it. The audience which the artist thus feels as collaborating with himself may be a large one or a small one, but it is never absent.

Aesthetic Individualism

The understanding of the audience's function as collaborator is a matter of importance for the future both of aesthetic theory and of art itself. The obstacle to understanding it is a traditional individualistic psychology through which, as through distorting glasses, we are in the habit of looking at artistic work. We think of the artist as a self-contained personality, sole author of everything he does: of the emotions he expresses as his personal emotions, and of his expression of them as his personal expression. We even forget what it is that he thus expresses, and speak of his work as "self-expression," persuading ourselves that what makes a poem great is the fact that it "expresses a great personality," whereas, if self-expression is the order of the day, whatever value we set on such a poem is due to its expressing not the poet—what is Shakespeare to us, or we to Shakespeare?—but ourselves.

It would be tedious to enumerate the tangles of misunderstanding which this nonsense about self-expression has generated. To take one such only: it has set us off looking for "the man Shakespeare" in his poems, and trying to reconstruct his life and opinions from them, as if that were possible, or as if, were it possible, it would help us to appreciate his work. It has degraded criticism to the level of personal gossip, and confused art with exhibitionism. What I prefer to attempt is not a tale of misdeeds, but a refutation.

In principle, this refutation is simple. Individualism conceives a man as if he were God, a self-contained and self-sufficient creative power whose only task is to be himself and to exhibit his nature in whatever works are appropriate to it. But a man, in his art as in everything else, is a finite being. Everything that he does is done in relation to others like himself. As artist, he is a speaker; but a man speaks as he has been taught; he speaks the tongue in which he was born. The musician did not invent his scale or his instruments; even if he invents a new scale or a new instrument he is only modifying what he has learnt from others. The painter did not invent the idea of painting pictures or the pigments and brushes with which he paints them. Even the most precocious poet hears and reads poetry before he writes it. Moreover, just as every artist stands in relation to other artists from whom he has acquired his art, so he stands in relation to some audience to whom he addresses it. The child learning his mother tongue, as we have seen, learns simultaneously to be a speaker and to be a listener; he listens to others speaking, and speaks to others listening. It is the same with artists. They become poets or painters or musicians not by some process of development from within, as they grow beards; but by living in a society where these languages are current. Like other speakers, they speak to those who understand.

The aesthetic activity is the activity of speaking. Speech is speech only so far as it is both spoken and heard. A man may, no doubt, speak to himself and be his own hearer; but what he says to himself is in principle capable of being said to any one sharing his language. As a finite being, man becomes aware of himself as a person only so far as he finds himself standing in relation to others of whom he simultaneously becomes aware as persons. And there is no point in his life at which a man has finished becoming aware of himself as a person. That awareness is constantly being reinforced, developed, applied in new ways. On every such occasion the old appeal must be made: he must find others whom he can recognize as persons in this new fashion, or he cannot as a finite being assure himself that this new phase of personality is genuinely in his possession. If he has a new thought, he must explain it to others, in order that, finding them able to understand it, he may be sure it is a good one. If he has a new emotion, he must express it to others, in order that, finding them able to share it, he may be sure his consciousness of it is not corrupt.

This is not inconsistent with the doctrine, stated elsewhere in this book, that the aesthetic experience or aesthetic activity is one which goes on in the artist's mind. The experience of being listened to is an experience which goes on in the mind of the speaker, although in order to its existence a listener is necessary, so that the activity is a collaboration. Mutual love is a collaborative activity; but the experience of this activity in the mind of each lover taken singly is a different experience from that of loving and being spurned. . . .

The conclusion of this chapter may be summarized briefly. The work of artistic creation is not a work performed in any exclusive or complete fashion in the mind of the person whom we call the artist. That idea is a delusion bred of individualistic psychology, together with a false view of the relation not so much between body and mind as between experience at the psychical level and experience at the level of thought. The aesthetic activity is an activity of thought in the form of consciousness, converting into imagination an experience, which, apart from being so converted, is sensuous. This activity is a corporate activity belonging not to any one human being but to a community. It is performed not only by the man whom we individualistically call the artist, but partly by all the other artists of whom we speak as "influencing" him, where we really mean collaborating with him. It is performed not only by this corporate body of artists, but (in the case of the arts of performance) by executants, who are not merely acting under the artist's orders, but are collaborating with him to produce the finished work.[9] And even now the activity of artistic creation is not complete; for that, there must be an audience, whose function is therefore not a merely receptive one, but collaborative too. The artist (although under the spell of individualistic prejudices he may try to deny it) stands thus in collaborative relations with an entire community; not an ideal community of all human beings as such, but the actual community of fellow artists from whom he borrows, executants whom he employs, and audience to whom he speaks. By recognizing these relations and counting upon them in his work, he strengthens and enriches that work itself; by denying them he impoverishes it.

AS EMOTION

RECEPTIVITY TO FEELING

CURT JOHN DUCASSE

The Aesthetic Attitude[1]

In the last chapter, the contention was set forth that art essentially consists in consciously objective expression of feeling; and expression was defined as being objective when its product is such that, *in contemplation,* it reflects back accurately the feeling which was to be expressed. The notion of aesthetic contemplation being thus involved in the conception of art formulated, it is necessary to inquire next more particularly what aesthetic contemplation is.

---

[9] Sections which Collingwood here summarizes and which have been omitted from this selection as irrelevant to our problem are "Collaboration between Artists" (pp. 318–320) and "Collaboration between Author and Performer" (pp. 320–321). (Eds.)

[1] Reprinted from *The Philosophy of Art,* by Curt J. Ducasse, pp. 134–147, 189–201, by permission of The Dial Press, Inc. Copyright, 1929, by The Dial Press. (Eds.)

§ *1*

The receptive, effective, and judgmental attitudes. Three funda-mental possible orientations, directions of interest, or attitudes in respect to any given object of attention may be distinguished,—the receptive, the effective or practical, and the judgmental. These three sorts of orientation may be discerned not only in the life of man as artist, but also in his life as a worker, as a playing being, and as a being carrying on various automatic activities. The characters differentiating from one another, play, art, work, and automatism, have been discussed in the last two chapters, and the con-clusions reached summarily expressed in respect to the notion of telism, by describing automatic activities as such as atelic, play as autotelic, work as ectotelic, and art as endotelic.[2] It is no part of the task of the present volume to discuss the forms under which the receptive, effective, and judgmental orientations appear in play, in work, and in the automatic life; but only to consider the phenomena to which they give rise in the endotelic life.

§ *2*

Art-creation is the effective aspect of the endotelic life; which, however, has also a judgmental aspect, viz., Criticism; and a receptive, viz., Contemplation. As to this, we must now note that art-creation is not the whole of endotelic life, but constitutes only its effective or practical aspect. Contemplation and Criticism are the other two aspects of it, corresponding to the receptive and the judgmental orientations in it. These three aspects of the endotelic life are not, indeed, mutually insulated. We have already seen that in art-creation, a contemplative and a critical moment are involved, although they are not there the central thing.[3] Each, however, is capable of being made central: Contemplation is made central in the life of the "consumer" of

---

[2] In these earlier chapters (pp. 99–100, 105–109) Mr. Ducasse has distinguished these four modes of activity according to the way they serve as means to ends. Since auto-matic activity involves no consciousness of our purpose in performing it, it has no place in this teleological scheme and is classified as *atelic.* The other three are said to be *telic,* and the end is consciously sought. Play is *autotelic* (that is, having its own pur-pose) because it is "the systematic pursuit of an end set up or accepted expressly for the purpose." Thus it is "activity, telic in form only, performed for its own sake." Art and work are differentiated from play in that they are seriously undertaken and have a "real end" to which an obligation is owed. But in art the end is "internal" and "cate-gorical," while in work it is "external and conditional." In art one feels the obligation to come from oneself as creator, while in work it is imposed from the outside. The end is known beforehand in work, so that the real object copies the object imagined by us to be needed as a means to that end. The art-object, however, can copy nothing, since the object, like the internal end it serves, is known only when the creative process is completed. Art, having an end internal to itself, is *endotelic;* work, serving an external end, is *ectotelic.* (Eds.)

[3] See Chapter VII of *The Philosophy of Art,* particularly Section 3, pp. 114–116. (Eds.)

works of art and other aesthetic objects; and Criticism, naturally, in the life of the critic,—the other two aspects in these cases, being not absent, but present as necessary means or conditions only, as were contemplation and criticism in art-creation.

The word Practical is somewhat ambiguous, and owing to this it may sound strange to hear the artist's activity referred to as practical. It is not practical in the sense of attempting to create something "useful"; but it is practical in the sense of *effective*, i.e., it produces effects in or upon things: the painter effects changes in the surface of his canvas, the sculptor in the shape of his marble, the musician in the audible environment, etc. This is so whether the stuff in which creation takes place be perceptual or purely imaginal stuff. But it is not so when one's orientation is, instead of the effective, the receptive or the judgmental. Effectiveness, although, as stated, present then also, does not then consist in creativeness.

§ 3

Aesthetic contemplation is endotelic receptivity to feeling. In the light of the foregoing considerations, contemplation, or the contemplative attitude, may be defined as *the receptive orientation in the endotelic life.* But that to which one holds oneself receptive may, as we have seen, be either will-impulse, meaning, or feeling.[4] Therefore *endotelic receptivity to feeling,* constitutes an accurate definition of what is called *aesthetic contemplation,* or the aesthetic attitude. That aesthetic contemplation actually has the endotelic character will be shown later on. It is enough here to point out that, like art-creation, it *contains* a true end, which is not as in play the mere pleasure of the process going on, nor, as in work, external and useful to something beyond.

Inasmuch as aesthetic contemplation alone is directly connected with aesthetic art, with which primarily we are here occupied, I shall from the present point on claim the privilege of using for short the single words Contemplation, Contemplative, etc., instead of the longer Aesthetic Contemplation, Aesthetically Contemplative, etc., whenever it is convenient,—giving on the contrary some special indication if occasion arises to use the word Contemplation in the generic or in one of its other two specific senses.

§ 4

Some empirical descriptions of aesthetic contemplation. From this brief outline of the setting of aesthetic contemplation in a theory of art

---

[4] See Chapter VII, Section 2, pp. 112–114 of *The Philosophy of Art.* (Eds.)

in general, we may now pass to an empirical examination of that much-discussed state. One of the best accounts of it in the classical literature is that given by Schopenhauer. Divested of technical terminology and of references to particular doctrines of that philosopher's system, it would read substantially as follows: If a man relinquishes the common way of looking at things, which is always ultimately concerned with their relations to desires and purposes; if he thus ceases to consider the where, the when, the why, and the whither of things, and looks simply and solely at the *what;* if, further, he does not allow himself to think of them conceptually (e.g., as things to be recognized, distinguished, classified, etc.), but instead of all this, gives the whole power of his mind to perception, sinks himself entirely in this, and so yields himself to the quiet contemplation of the object present that he loses himself in this object,—then his state is that of aesthetic contemplation, and the object of it is the aesthetic object.[5]

The following passage from Spencer's *Principles of Psychology* [6] is rather differently worded but is more or less to the same effect: "Throughout the whole range of sensations, perceptions, and emotions which we do not class as aesthetic, the states of consciousness serve simply as aids and stimuli to guidance and action. They are transitory, or if they persist in consciousness some time, they do not monopolize the attention: that which monopolizes the attention is something ulterior, to the effecting of which they are instrumental. But in the states of mind we class as aesthetic, the opposite attitude is maintained towards the sensations, perceptions, and emotions. These are no longer links in the chain of states which prompt and guide conduct. Instead of being allowed to disappear with merely passing recognitions, they are kept in consciousness and dwelt upon."

A more recent writer, Vernon Lee,[7] effectively contrasts the contemplative attitude with the practical and the scientific by reporting an imaginary conversation between three persons on the top of a hill, one of whom dwells on the economic possibilities of what lies before them, and another on its geological and geographical aspects, while the third on the contrary is intent only on beholding it and letting its aesthetic aspect affect him as it may.

The contrast between contemplation and the ectotelic life is dwelt upon also in the following passage from a recent French work: [8] "Its essence is always to set aside useful signs, conventional appearances, all that masks the reality itself, in order to set before us the existence of the object of art, wholly concrete and nevertheless devoid of empirical existence." [9]

---

[5] *The World as Will and Idea.* Trans. Haldane and Kemp, vol. I, p. 231.
[6] Vol. II, pp. 646–647.
[7] *The Beautiful,* Ch. II.
[8] H. Delacroix, *Psychologie de l'Art,* p. 67.
[9] The documents by which Professor Delacroix endeavors to support his contention that there are several varieties of aesthetic contemplation, seem to me to show only

§ 5

Comments on the terminology of these descriptions. In the light of the careful distinctions made in this and earlier chapters and embodied in technical terms having exact meanings, it is obvious that such accounts as the foregoing, of the contrast between the contemplative, the practical, and the scientific attitudes, although essentially sound, nevertheless leave room for a good deal of confusion. This is largely owing to the ambiguity pointed out above, of the word Practical, which, as most commonly used, means having an end (usually economic), external to the process that seeks it, i.e., being what we have called Ectotelic; but which means also very properly, simply *Effective*,[10] without implication as to whether the effectiveness is connected with the ectotelic life, or with life of one of the other sorts distinguished. Owing to this ambiguity of the word Practical, we may agree here to use it as a rule for the more popular of the two senses, whenever the technical term Ectotelic would be merely pedantic; and to use the word Effective for the other sense whenever there might be any doubt as to what is meant if Practical were used.

If now, for the sake of theoretical precision, the reader will forgive a very brief indulgence in technical terminology, the "practical" man of Vernon Lee's account will have to be described as ectotelically judgmental, for as she represents him to us he is not *effecting* anything, but *judging* with reference to certain external (and economic) ends. The word "scientific," on the other hand, when used to describe an orientation contrasted with the effective and the receptive, means only *judgmental,* i.e., judgment-forming, cognitive, but it does not indicate that the judging activity has the endotelic character usually thought of when the "scientific interest" or "pure science" are spoken of, rather than the ectotelic character which on the contrary belongs to the judging activity of the engineer as such.

§ 6

Aesthetic contemplation is a "listening" with our capacity for feeling. Let us now pass to a direct empirical examination of the state of aesthetic contemplation. It is, we may note first, a *throwing oneself open*

---

that the response of some people to works of art is not aesthetic contemplation but something else. For instance, he himself says that the enjoyment derived from reading novels is usually that of giving us the illusion of living through the adventures described. But obviously then, this enjoyment is that of vicarious adventure, which is no more aesthetic than the precisely similar pleasure of watching a football game, a thrilling rescue, or a dramatic escape. (loc. cit. p. 118.) (C. J. D.) See above, p. 282. (Eds.)

[10] The word Practical being from πράσσειν, to do, to effect.

to the advent of something, and in this respect it resembles the endeavor to understand. But whereas in the latter it is to the advent of meaning, that one throws oneself open, in aesthetic contemplation it is to the advent *of feeling*. What takes place is something analogous to listening. That is, the attention is withdrawn from everything other than the object of aesthetic contemplation, and inwardly the ground is cleared for the reception of the import of feeling of that object. This clearing of the ground means the elimination, as complete as possible, of any antecedent feeling. Aesthetic contemplation may thus be described as (*endotelic*) *"listening," or "looking," with our capacity for feeling*. The words "listening," or "looking," are of course figurative, but they are nevertheless perfectly accurate if only so much of their meaning is kept as remains after leaving out their special reference to the faculties of hearing and seeing and to impressions of sound and light. There is no general term in the language (other than the term Contemplation) to denote without special reference to kind of impression and kind of faculty, the attitude of *directed but contentless receptiveness;* but if the present explanation is kept in mind, the use of the word, "listening," to designate that attitude, is adequately descriptive without being misleading.

§ 7

Aesthetic contemplation is not attention, but presupposes it. To this account of the nature of aesthetic contemplation, it is, however, necessary to add that the "listening" with our capacity for feeling, is a "listening" *for,* not a "listening" *to.* That is, it is not to be confused with merely attending, for it *presupposes a content of attention,* towards which it is that the aesthetic attitude is taken. It is *to* that content that our attention is directed, but it is *for* the feeling import of it that we "listen," i.e., make ourselves receptive. This essential point is made clearer still if we note that, given attention to the very same content, we might have "listened" not for feeling, but instead for meaning or for will-impulse. The fact of rapt attention is thus not peculiar to the aesthetic attitude. What differentiates the latter, is what we "listen" for and with, (viz., feeling and our capacity for feeling), when we attend (endotelically) to the given content. That contemplation is something more than attention is obvious in the case of reading. Attention to the words on the page is necessary, but in addition, a throwing oneself open to their meaning has to take place (and constitutes lectical or logical contemplation of them, as distinguished from aesthetic).[11]

---

[11] The term "lectical art" is explained here, and earlier defined by the author, as one of the three species of endotelic art, the other two being aesthetic art and heuristic art. Lectical art is used to designate the objective expression of meanings, aesthetic art the objective expression of feelings, and heuristic art the conscious objectification of will. (Eds.)

To say, however, that in the sort of "listening" which constitutes aesthetic contemplation, we "listen" *for* a feeling, is not to be taken as meaning that our attitude is describable as contemplative *only up to* the advent of the aesthetic feeling to be obtained through it. It means only that it is then that the aesthetic attitude, as distinguished from its fruit, can best be studied introspectively. But the feeling that we obtain is aesthetic feeling only so long as our attitude remains the aesthetic; and this means, only so long as our interest, our aim, is in feeling itself as such. "What we are interested in," and "What we attend to," cannot therefore here be regarded as synonymous expressions. Spinoza pointed out that emotional states cannot be attended to without being destroyed, and modern psychologists, e.g., Titchener, having confirmed this. But it is possible to make feelings or emotional states as such, what one aims at; it is possible to make them the center of one's *interest,* i.e., to treat them not scientifically, as states to be compared, studied, etc., but as states to be simply "tasted" to the full and in all their most subtle nuances. And this is precisely what occurs in successful aesthetic contemplation. Our *attention* is, say, on the pattern and color of a fabric, but our *interest* is in its feeling-import to us. And if our interest at the moment is on the contrary in the origin, or history of that pattern, and such feelings as we have in the presence of it are then merely by the way, (incidents but not ends), then our attitude is not the aesthetic, and the feelings are not aesthetic feelings.

§ 8

Aesthetic contemplation has the endotelic character. Lastly, the "listening" with our capacity for feeling, which constitutes aesthetic contemplation, is endotelic; that is, this throwing oneself open to the advent of feeling is for the sake of the feeling to be obtained, which is treated not as something to be recognized or compared; nor as something leading to or furnishing a drive for some act; but solely as something to be tasted, and as it were, rolled under one's emotional tongue. In aesthetic contemplation, feeling is then the end, and the occurrence of it constitutes the completion, the success, of the contemplation, which is thus truly endotelic.

§ 9

Aesthetic contemplation is not a rare, esoteric state, but a common and familiar one. Almost any attempt to give an analysis of the nature of aesthetic contemplation is likely to convey the impression that it is some strange state, difficult of attainment, and, like the mystic trance, accessible only to the elect. It is therefore not amiss to emphasize the fact that, on the contrary, it is a state in which every normal person has entered countless times, even if only for brief moments; and that only a little introspection is needed to render him aware of that fact, and to place him in position to decide for himself as to the accuracy of the description of it given above. The occasions upon which the persons who have any doubt concerning their own acquaintance with that state are most likely to have truly entered it, are not so much visits to art galleries, as cases where they have had to formulate some simple but genuine judgment of taste. To judge, for instance, whether the color of a given necktie "goes with" that of the suit with which it is to be worn, is to judge whether the feeling obtained in the aesthetic contemplation of the color combination is pleasant or not. But virtually everyone is aware of having made judgments of this sort, which would have been impossible had one been incapable of aesthetic contemplation. To observe for oneself the nature of that state, one but needs to report oneself to the moment when one was giving one's attention to the color combination, but had not yet obtained from it the inner experience, (viz., the feeling) which, when obtained, was judged, as the case may have been, pleasant or unpleasant.

Aesthetic contemplation is an attitude which would seem to have little if any biological utility; and it is therefore natural that our capacity for it should be far less developed than for the attitudes connected with the ecto-telic, so-called practical, life. The immediate consequence of this is that it is only in the absence of any temptation to take those other, more practiced attitudes, that aesthetic contemplation becomes possible. As Spencer justly observes, before the sort of action of our faculties can arise, which is characteristic of the states of mind we class as aesthetic, "it is necessary that the needs to be satisfied through the agency of sensational, perceptional, and emotional excitements shall not be urgent. So long as there exist strong cravings arising from bodily wants and unsatisfied lower instincts, consciousness is not allowed to dwell on these states that accompany the actions of the higher faculties: the cravings continually exclude them." [12]

The taking of so-called practical dispositions, the satisfying of so-called practical and to some extent of "idle" curiosity, occupy most persons most of the time. Ordinary life is for the most part lived among objects which we do not contemplate but merely use, or, to some extent, study for use, whether as themselves instruments or as signs informing us of matters of practical concern that we cannot at the time directly perceive. It is thus that we may paradoxically say of a town, for instance, that the more we see of it, the less we see it. On the other hand, when we travel and first come to a town new to us, a given building in it cannot be treated by us as mere sign of the

---

[12] *Principles of Psychology.* Vol. II, p. 647.

nearness of the shoe-store around its corner, for we do not yet know that one is there. And because there is thus little temptation, and if we be in funds, little need to take the town practically, it is correspondingly easy to take it aesthetically. As Schopenhauer and others have pointed out, this absence of practical relation of the object to us is one of the chief sources of the pleasure of travel, of the glamour of distant times and places or other objects from which we are in some way insulated for any practical purpose. Such interest as we take in things of this sort can then hardly be other than of the endotelic sort, whether contemplative, (i.e., receptive), or judgmental; with the consequence that, for the time being, we find ourselves free from the specter of fear which ever more or less discreetly lurks through the so-called practical life.

The fact that the possibility of taking the aesthetic attitude depends to so great an extent upon the absence of practical relation between ourselves and the object, explains why the terms "detachment" and "psychical distance" are sometimes used in accounts of the nature of the aesthetic attitude.[13] Distance in time or space is the typical bar to action upon us by a thing or upon a thing by us, and is the typical factor which discourages or inhibits the practical interest. It is therefore natural that the word "distance," and for analogous reasons the word "detachment," should have come to be used figuratively in attempted characterizations of the aesthetic attitude, which is fundamentally non-practical. These words, however, do not point in the aesthetic attitude to anything additional to what has been said in the account of it given above; nor do they stand for either the whole or any part of the *positive* description of the attitude. Their import is essentially negative, since all they really say is that the aesthetic attitude is fundamentally non-practical.

In addition to the negative conditions facilitating aesthetic contemplation, already considered, there exist also certain possible positive inducements to prolong it. The chief of them is to be found in beauty of the object offered to contemplation, i.e., in pleasantness of the feelings obtained in contemplating the object. That the beautiful is so much easier to contemplate at any length than the ugly, which on the contrary requires of us an effort, is one reason for the fact that, on the whole, beauty is expected in works of art by almost everyone in spite of its being, as we have seen, not in the least implied by art. Therefore, as already remarked, it would be very nearly true to say that, for most people, beauty is the condition of the "aesthetic visibility" of anything. For the ugly does not, like the beautiful, bribe and encourage contemplation, but immediately punishes and discourages it, and thus tends to become aesthetically quasi-nonexistent.

On the other hand, so far as the artist is concerned, the fact that on the

---

[13] Respectively, by Münsterberg in his *Principles of Art Education,* and by Bullough in an article on Psychical Distance. (C. J. D.) See p. 396. (Eds.)

whole his works have beauty rather than ugliness is due partly to the selection exercised, among the feelings he might attempt to express, by the extraneous desire that his work shall be thus aesthetically visible to the public; and partly to the fact that unpleasant feelings, by themselves, (i.e., when not somehow tied up with others that are pleasant), tempt one to ectotelically effective action, that is, to interference with their real or fancied external occasion, rather than to objectification by art. But when for any reason remedy by practical action is impossible and the unpleasant feeling yet cannot be dismissed, it may then receive expression through art by the creation of the ugly. Examples of art thus predominantly ugly are at times to be found in propagandist art, which, whatever the merits of the cause it is used to promote, often in the very nature of the case springs from rebellious, harsh, bitter feeling.

The negative aids to contemplation, so far as artificial, consist of all the devices which make difficult or impossible the actual establishment of a practical relation to the object; or which inhibit practical or idle curiosity concerning it. Thus, the frame of a picture sharply differentiates it from the objects of practical moment that surround it. The framing and raising of the stage in the theater achieves the same result, and as other writers have noted, the separation of it from the audience contributes to the inhibiting of such impulses as might arise in its members to rescue the heroine in distress. Again, the requirement that a work of art must be a self-sufficient whole implies among other things that one's curiosity must not be tempted to supply missing elements. Nor must the work of art, for the same reason, contain anything in the nature of a puzzle. If it is representative, it should be so unambiguously. If the representative element, on the contrary, is either absent or merely incidental, the giving to the work a title that invites the beholder to perform an act of recognition or identification only hinders his taking towards it the aesthetic attitude. The name of a painting, therefore, should either be a mere identification tag, for instance, as in music, "Opus No. —," or else, if descriptive at all, it should be such as immediately to focus the beholder's attention on the essential aspect of the work. "Landscape," "Woman seated," "Portrait of a Young Man," would be good titles for such subjects. But something which is intended to be primarily a woman seated, but includes say a red cigarette box, should not just for oddity be called "The red cigarette box." For a wholly or partly "abstract" picture, on the contrary, such titles would be bad, inasmuch as their effect would be to present the picture to us not as an object for aesthetic contemplation, but as a picture-puzzle challenging us for instance to "find the young man." For abstract or semi-abstract pictures, titles such as "synchromy," "composition," "study in blue and green," "arrangement of solids," etc., would be appropriate in that they would at once force the beholder's attention to the aspect which the artist means him to contemplate. The title of a work of art, in short, should not pique our curiosity, but on the contrary anticipate it and set it at rest from the very start, so that nothing remains for us to do but to contemplate the work aesthetically.

CURT JOHN DUCASSE
The Aesthetic Feelings

§ 1

Aesthetic feeling is any feeling obtained in contemplation. The question how aesthetic feelings differ from others has received considerable attention from writers on aesthetics. Some have attempted to differentiate the aesthetic feelings from the non-aesthetic on the basis of the sense organs through which the objects yielding the feelings are perceived,— the eye and the ear alone being considered "aesthetic senses." Others have proposed disinterestedness and universality, as distinguishing marks of the feelings called aesthetic and of aesthetic pleasure. These attempts to formulate the distinction between aesthetic and other feelings, however, have all been effectively criticized by various writers,[1] and need not be reviewed in detail here. On the basis of what has now been said concerning the nature of the state of aesthetic contemplation, aesthetic feelings may be defined simply as follows: *Any feeling whatever which is obtained in aesthetic contemplation, is aesthetic feeling;* and no feeling is aesthetic feeling, which we experience while our attitude is other than the aesthetically contemplative. In other words, feeling is aesthetic feeling whenever its status is neither that of a mere incitement to or accompaniment or result of practical activity, nor that of an accessory or by-product of cognition, but is on the contrary the status of something being sought or entertained for itself, and simply *"tasted."*

§ 2

Under certain conditions, any feeling-quality may acquire the aesthetic status. The aesthetic feelings are thus not qualitatively different from the non-aesthetic, and this involves that there is no sort of feeling which

---

[1] See for instance, Santayana, *Sense of Beauty,* part I.

may not on occasion acquire the aesthetic status, or which art may not attempt to objectify. Spencer rightly observes that "The aesthetic feelings and sentiments are not, as our words and phrases lead us to suppose, feelings and sentiments that essentially differ in origin and nature from the rest. . . . The same agencies are in action; and the only difference is in the attitude of consciousness towards its resulting states." [2]

As concerns intensity rather than kind, it is obvious that feeling of a given sort may without losing the aesthetic status have any degree of intensity which will not preclude the maintaining of the aesthetic attitude towards the object; for it is one and the same thing to say that the feeling is experienced in that attitude, and that the feeling is aesthetic feeling.

To say that feelings of any sort may, at least theoretically, be aesthetic, is of course also to say that any subject may be treated by the artist, if he is able to present it in a manner which will invite, or at least permit aesthetic contemplation. Thus the problem of the conditions of aesthetic contemplation, that of the restrictions of subject-matter in art, and that of the possible kinds and degrees of aesthetic feeling are virtually but three aspects of one and the same problem. That problem arises from the fact that in each of us other interests, such as the practical, the scientific, the sportive, etc., compete with that which manifests itself in aesthetic contemplation. The various interests of man have but limited independence, and usually they are not equally strong. In most of us, probably, the practical man is the strongest and the aesthetic man the weakest. . . . the aesthetic man is therefore allowed by the others to appear, only when there is no temptation or no great temptation for those others to come forward. But in this respect individuals differ greatly both by nature and by training. In artists the capacity to take the contemplative attitude is usually much more highly developed than in other persons. Unfortunately, artists often overlook this and leave in or about their work handicaps to contemplation that cannot be overcome by the public to whom they exhibit it.

§ 3

The nature of the conditions of aesthetic feeling. If we ask for the conditions, in terms of kind and degree of feeling, which facilitate the taking or the maintaining of the aesthetic attitude, i.e., the obtaining of aesthetic feelings, we note that any of the feelings which by instinct or by habit are intimately connected with an important practical reaction may not be aroused in any but a mild degree if the contemplative attitude is not at once to be displaced by the practical. Examples of such feelings would be fear, disgust, horror, lust, greed, hunger, and so on. The temptation to give up

---

[2] *Principles of Psychology*, Vol. II, p. 646.

contemplation, which the arousing of such feelings furnishes, can, as already pointed out, to some extent be counteracted by the introduction of positive inducements to maintain it. Tragedy is the outstanding example of this possibility. The tragic emotions are unpleasant and therefore closely connected with the practical reactions of avoidance of, or interference with, the situation from the presence of which those emotions arise. If in spite of this temptation to practical action, contemplation is maintained, it is because the positive values present at the same time in contemplation are sufficient to overcome that temptation. As Santayana points out in his excellent discussion of tragedy, these positive values are found not only in beauty of form and in the nobility of characters and setting, but also and perhaps chiefly in the felt value of the wisdom which may be garnered from the presentation of a case of some typical problem of human life. As he says, "However unpleasant truth may prove, we long to know it, partly because experience has shown us the prudence of this kind of intellectual courage, and chiefly because the consciousness of ignorance and the dread of the unknown is more tormenting than any possible discovery" (*Sense of Beauty*, p. 230).

It is not to be forgotten in the present connection, however, that while some measure of beauty is as we have seen almost a condition of the aesthetic "visibility" of works of art to most persons, such "visibility" and therefore such beauty nevertheless are no necessary constituents of the work of art. The importance which they undoubtedly have, concerns not the nature of art, but its social services and rewards. As already stated, no contradiction is involved in speaking of something as being both a work of art and irredeemably ugly.[3] But aesthetic contemplation of such a work of art, though possible, and indeed necessary to the apprehension of its ugliness, would under normal circumstances be abandoned at once.

§ 4

"Feeling" does not mean merely pleasure and displeasure. Feeling, whether aesthetic or not, does not consist of mere pleasure or displeasure. Most feelings, indeed, are either pleasurable or the reverse, but there is much to a feeling beside pleasure or displeasure. Each feeling has its essence in a unique qualitative residuum which differentiates it from all others; whereas, in respect to pleasurableness or the reverse, it is like numberless others. Therefore the nature of love, fear, hatred, jealousy, or of any other feeling whether named or nameless, is something that no description can impart. Just because a feeling is, as already pointed out, not a resultant

---

[3] See Chapter I, Section 3, pp. 16–18 of *The Philosophy of Art*. (Eds.)

but an emergent, one necessarily has to experience it either at first hand, or not at all.

If there were to a feeling nothing more than its pleasantness or unpleasantness, then, since the beauty of an object consists in the pleasantness of it to contemplation, any two equally beautiful objects would be interchangeable as modes of expression for the artist and as objects of contemplation for the beholder. But obviously this is not the case. Casanova says that "Love is not like some merchandise that one desires, and for which one substitutes another more or less similar when one cannot get that which one covets. Love is a sentiment or caprice of sympathy; only the object which inspires it can extinguish it or make it burn.[4] It is the same in art. Painting a landscape, or a figure, is not for the artist a possible substitute for the painting of a bowl of pansies, even though the beauty of the landscape or the figure be in its way as great as that of the pansies, or greater. His endeavor is to express objectively the particular feeling he happens to have, and this can be done only by the constructing of the one particular object which is for him the aesthetic symbol of that feeling. From the standpoint of the beholder instead of the creator, the same unsubstitutability holds. To suppose otherwise would be much like supposing that any piece of information can be substituted for any other if only both are equally true.[5]

It is interesting, however, to ask why this unsubstitutability is a fact even from the standpoint of a merely hedonistic "consumer." The answer is that it is a matter of context. We speak of exchanging one beauty, or one experience of beauty, for another; but this can be done only indirectly. What we do directly is to exchange one beautiful *thing* for another. And a beautiful thing, is almost invariably only a part of the total aesthetic object contemplated, which includes more or less of the context in which the thing is. When we declare the things exchanged to be equally beautiful, we probably assume a context appropriate to each; and therefore if we exchange the things without the contexts, we destroy the equality. The case is the same here as with the pleasures of eating. The most delicious soup ceases to be such if served after dessert. And if the attempt were made to substitute the pleasure of a symphony for that of our dinner, the pangs of hunger would prevent the pleasure which otherwise we should find in the music.

However, if the matter of contexts is eliminated by speaking not of equally beautiful *things,* but of equally beautiful *aesthetic objects* (which, by definition, have no contexts); and by supposing the emotional blankness specified in the definition of the aesthetic attitude, to be attained *perfectly,*—then, for a purely hedonistic "consumer," equally beautiful aesthetic objects *are*

---

[4] *Mémoires,* Vol. V, p. 273.
[5] This should not be taken to imply a complete analogy between beauty and truth, in their respective realms.

strictly interchangeable. Different but equally true pieces of information are not interchangeable for any purpose except that of having equally true propositions. But Beauty (unlike truth), being an *immediate* value, can involve no differences of ulterior purposes; and a consistently hedonistic theory of values must insist on the fact that, not pleasant feelings, but the feeling called pleasure, always remains qualitatively the same whatever the object that gives it (e.g., whether a piece of candy or a sonata); and is susceptible only of quantitative variations, for instance, of volume, intensity, and duration.[6]

§ 5

The feelings experienced by human beings are endlessly various, and only a very few, such as love, fear, anger, etc., have received names. There is a fact which it is most important to realize clearly and to bear constantly in mind throughout the present volume, for otherwise the philosophy of art set forth in its pages is bound to be completely misunderstood. The fact referred to is that *the feelings experienced by human beings are endlessly numerous and various, and that the immense majority of them cannot be referred to by name because they have received none.*

Only a very few feelings, such as those already alluded to,—love, anger, fear, jealousy, anxiety, etc.,—have names. They are feelings which are closely connected with typical, recurrent situations in life, and are usually accompanied by overt and easily recognizable modes of behavior. The terms "the emotions," and "the passions," designate principally those standard, labelled feelings, and indeed those feelings primarily as out of the aesthetic status, that is to say, as mere accompaniments or incidents of practical endeavor of one sort or another. But to one such named feeling, there are a thousand that have received no name, but which are none the less real experiences of the very same general sort, viz., emotional.

Unfortunately, in our inner experience still more than in outer, what is not labelled commonly escapes our notice. As La Rochefoucauld almost says, some people would never have known love, had they not heard of it.

---

[6] Although I am convinced that none but a hedonistic theory of values is sound, I am also convinced that any hedonistic calculus that involves the notion of sums of pleasures, is nonsense because that notion is itself nonsense. Pleasures are what logicians call "intensive" qualities, not "extensive"; that is to say, there is no known operation by means of which any two pleasures uniquely determine a third greater than either,—which is what summation means. Pleasures can be compared as to intensity and duration, but we cannot *add* them any more than, to use one of Royce's examples, we can "add" together the excellence of Byron's poetry and the excellence of Shelley's and get thereby a third factual excellence greater than either. The additive "program," in such cases, remains but empty words. It denotes no actual operation yielding facts.

Those of our feelings for which no names exist are so easy to overlook that when much is made of them, as in these pages, many persons are likely to be somewhat bewildered, and, as with the aesthetic attitude, to think that some quasi-mystical sort of experience must be in question, which they themselves do not have. But this is not so. Almost every one has feeling-responses, i.e., experiences emotional in kind but quite distinct from love, fear, anger, or other namable emotions, in the presence of such things as patches of colors, bits of lines, single tones, the patterns of rugs, lace, wallpaper, and so on. These emotional experiences are not merely experiences of pleasure or displeasure. Each of them has, in addition to its pleasurableness or the reverse, its individual feeling-tang, or emotional "taste," different with each color, tone, line, etc. For the purpose of bringing to awareness the often unsuspected abundance and variety of the emotional states we experience, such simple sources of unlabelled feelings as just suggested are better than more elaborate objects; for the latter, although even more fertile of such feelings, also in many cases touch off to some extent one or another of the labelled feelings, which, because of its familiarity and its label, we at once notice to the probable exclusion of the unlabelled.

The feelings which are unlabelled, are so for various reasons. They are commonly of lower intensity than "the passions"; they do not last so long; and do not recur so often. They have no immediate and obvious practical manifestations. The chief reason, however, is probably that they are *individuals without a kind*. The names Anger, Love, Anxiety, etc., are not proper names but names of kinds, and the cases of those kinds are not noticed by us as individuals but as cases-of-a-kind. The *individuality* of each is overlooked by us as generally as are the unlabelled feelings. This overlooking is due to the fact that most of the time we are living practically, ectotelically, and that for this sort of living, *kinds,* which have laws that we can apply (while individuals as such have not), are alone important, alone noticed, and alone given names.

The deliberate aesthetic contemplation of the objects of the unlabelled feelings, makes the noticing of those feelings very much easier. Even then, however, one is usually not to expect an experience comparable in intensity to the experiences we spontaneously think of when "the emotions" are mentioned. Moreover, the unlabelled feelings (or indeed any feeling), in so far as then having the aesthetic status, will not, like "the emotions," be apprehended as *in us;* but will on the contrary be objectified, i.e., apprehended as emotional qualities of the aesthetic objects contemplated.

Failure to recognize that the realm of feeling contains not merely love, fear, anger, and so on, but a vast wealth of other unnamed but just as truly emotional experiences, is I believe the principal explanation of such opposition as there has been to "emotionalist" theories of art. The so-called formalists, like Hanslick,[7] seem wholly blind to the fact that form is important in aesthetic objects for the very reason that it itself, in contemplation, is the source of certain aesthetic *emotions* which nothing else can objectify. And they are blind also to the fact that *contents* as well as forms, and in abstraction from forms, e.g., single tones and stray patches of color, are *also* sources of certain aesthetic emotions, which nothing else can yield. A statement such as that "A tone becomes musical material only by association with other tones," [8] should therefore be recognized for what it is, namely, a piece of sheer formalistic dogmatism, and not at all a report of empirical fact.

§ 6

Aesthetic feeling distinguished from sensation. It is important not to confuse aesthetic feeling with sensation. When a content of attention is referred to as "a sensation," it is usually then being regarded as an object *of cognition.* An object of cognition is essentially something which comes to us, as it were, with an introduction. Thus if the color blue is at a given time for us an object of cognition, it is so in virtue of its coming introduced, for instance, as "the color of the sky," or as "a color like or unlike the color of this or that," or as "something we desired to see," etc. In short, we meet it as *object of a reference of some sort, past or about to come,* i.e., as answering, or forestalling, a question; or satisfying or anticipating a perhaps unformulated curiosity. It thus functions as an element in a judgment whether explicit or not, and belongs to the realm of information.

But if on the contrary a patch of blue is out of relation to our curiosity, and constitutes only a content of attention from which in aesthetic contemplation a feeling is obtained, then the patch of blue is no longer object of knowledge, but aesthetic object. It functions as aesthetic symbol of a certain feeling,—of a somewhat different one with each distinguishable shade of blue. Since such a feeling has no proper name, we are able to refer to it when occasion arises to do so, only by either pointing to its aesthetic symbol or by naming that symbol when it has a name, saying, for instance, *the feeling of* cerulean blue. But a source of confusion is latent in this mode of speech, due to the ambiguous manner in which the word Feeling has been used, viz., sometimes, as by William James, to denote any psychological state, and sometimes to denote only states of the nature of emotion. As already stated, it is in the latter sense that the word Feeling is used in these

---

[7] *The Beautiful in Music.*
[8] *How to Listen to Music,* by H. E. Krebiehl, 2nd Ed., p. 17.

pages, so that by "the feeling of cerulean blue" is not here meant the *color,* cerulean blue, but the *emotion* of which we become conscious when, attending to that color, we take toward it the attitude which we have called the aesthetically contemplative. That emotion or feeling is a fact distinct from and additional to the mere blueness, for at least in the case of so trivial a content of attention as a mere patch of color, no noticeable feeling usually arises unless we deliberately "listen" for it, i.e., unless we take the aesthetic attitude towards the blue attended to.

§ 7

Aesthetic feeling, passion, and artistic feeling or inspiration. A question which presents itself here is how to describe, not the feeling that the spectator obtains in contemplation, but the feeling which possesses an artist at the time he is attempting to create an objective expression of it. We cannot speak of it as aesthetic feeling, since aesthetic feeling, by definition, presupposes the contemplative attitude, and what we are now considering is the feeling at the moment when the artist's attitude is creative, viz. effective. We may designate it *Artistic feeling,* remembering that, as with passion and aesthetic feeling, the term refers not to a qualitative difference, but to a difference in external relations. Artistic feeling, which is what most often is called *artistic inspiration,* is like passion in that both express themselves in action, i.e., in the case of each, the attitude is effective; but in the case of passion it is ectotelically effective, and in that of artistic feeling on the contrary, endotelically so. Passion expresses itself by dealing with the facts that constitute the reason for its existence, destroying or preserving them. Artistic feeling or inspiration does nothing of the sort, but expresses itself by creating what we may call a mirror of itself.

It might be objected, however, that in some cases the distinction above between aesthetic feeling and artistic feeling cannot be maintained. One might urge, for instance, that in painting the artist almost always has a model, from the contemplation of which, or of some aspect of which, arises the feeling he attempts to express, which is therefore aesthetic feeling. But it must be remembered that the distinction between aesthetic and artistic feeling is not based on any internal difference between the two, but solely on a fact external to the feeling itself, viz., on the attitude at the time, of the person having the feeling. And it is obvious that when the artist's attitude changes from the contemplative to the effective, the *status* of his feeling automatically changes also from the "aesthetic" to the "artistic," even if the feeling happens to remain wholly unchanged in point of intrinsic quality. Thus, from the standpoint of the feeling itself, the distinction between aesthetic and artistic feeling is factitious and of no importance. But from the standpoint of the total state constituted by the feeling *and* the attitude at the time, it is on the contrary a very real and necessary one: the state of aesthetic receptiveness is a very different state from that of artistic inspiration.

AS EMOTION

CONTROLLED EMOTION

STEPHEN C. PEPPER

Emotion [1]

EMOTION IS THE MOST intimately felt and the least satisfactorily understood of all objects of experience. Everyone knows emotion, yet no one seems to know what it is. It baffles analysis and yet lies in our bosoms. The paradox, I suggest, disappears, if we recognize that emotion is the very essence of quality. It is the very quality of the event itself when this event is voluminous, intense, and highly fused. It is, in short, a relative term and its correlate is analysis.

At one extreme is cold analysis, which drains the quality out of an event and leads off into the compartments of systematized conceptual schemes. At the other extreme is pure fusion of quality which insulates an event from other events, as far as such insulation is possible. We do not, however, generally call a fused quality an emotion unless the event in which it occurs is massive and intense—unless, that is, many strands are involved and driven well up into the focus of the event. An extensive fusion spread out over the fringe and lacking in intensity and concentration, we are likely to call a mood. If there is concentration of quality, but no great massiveness or intensity, we call it sensuous feeling. Absorption in the violet of a night sky would be sensuous feeling. The spell of a soft evening saturating thought, movement, and utterance would be a mood. A surge of passion such as inspired Shelley's "Swiftly walk o'er the western wave, Spirit of Night" would be an emotion. If sensuous feeling acquires intensity, it rapidly gathers up extensity and turns into emotion. The same with mood. There is only a difference of degree among them.

---

[1] Reprinted from *Aesthetic Quality,* by Stephen C. Pepper, pp. 89–113; copyright, 1937, by Charles Scribner's Sons; used by permission of the publishers. (Eds.)

We accept, therefore, James's theory of the emotions, only enlarging the theory to take in not only bodily sensations but any sensations, and insisting more explicitly than he does on the fusion. "What kind of an emotion of fear," he writes, "would be left if the feeling neither of quickened heart-beats nor of shallow breathing, neither of trembling lips nor of weakened limbs, neither of goose-flesh nor of visceral stirrings, were present, it is quite impossible for me to think. Can one fancy the state of rage and picture no ebullition in the chest, no flushing of the face, no dilation of the nostrils, no clenching of the teeth, no impulse to vigorous action, but in their stead limp muscles, calm breathing, and a placid face? The present writer, for one, certainly cannot. The rage is as completely evaporated as the sensation of its so-called manifestations, and the only thing that can possibly be supposed to take its place is some cold-blooded and dispassionate judicial sentence, confined entirely to the intellectual realm, to the effect that a certain person or persons merit chastisement for their sins" (Psych. vol. ii, p. 452).

The emotion of fear and the emotion of anger are the fusions of these sensations. That is to say, fear and anger are fused qualities which upon analysis resolve themselves into these elements of discriminated sensations. We must add, however, that is is not only these internal sensations and muscular sensations that are involved in the quality of the emotion but quite as much the external visual, tactual, auditory, olfactory, and gustatory sensations in so far as these do enter into any simple event. Fear of a bear, fear of thunder, and fear of a worm in an apple, are quite specific emotions in which the qualities of the so-called external sensations are as intimately involved as the so-called internal sensations. Moreover, if we are going to be thoroughly analytical about the matter it is not only the sensations that are involved but also their relations to one another in the total situation. As someone has pointed out in this very context, a chained bear does not stimulate fear.

The internal and muscular sensations do, however, seem to have a certain preponderant importance in the analysis of emotion, in that these are the sensations of drive and activity. They seem to be the source of that intensity and concentration which are essential to emotion as distinct from mere sensuous immediacy. And those emotions are particularly powerful which have developed within certain patterns of action essential to the life of the organism. McDougall's attempt to pair off emotions with instincts was based on an important insight, however unacceptable the theory in detail. For patterns of action are purposive organizations of strands drafting in not only the energies of the organism but the structure of its environment, and concentrating these upon an end. Here is massiveness of material, concentration, and potential intensity—the very substance of emotion. The more highly practical and essential to the life of the organism is the pattern of action, so much the greater the potentiality of emotion.

Once more we meet that insistent paradox, that the most powerful aesthetic material is to be found in those activities intrinsically most hostile to aesthetic quality. For there is nothing more practical than a pattern of action vital to the preservation and well being of an organism—nothing more practical than love, hate, jealousy, fear, disgust, pride, anxiety, and in another way shame, contrition, sorrow, despair.

How are these materials to be brought into the service of aesthetic quality? Of course, through the agency of conflict. This is another factor in emotion which James's theory does not sufficiently stress. Once the emotion is upon us in its full intensity, we may be able to analyze it conceptually into its sensational and relational constituents. But how did it acquire that intensity? A pattern of action is a habit and tends to run itself off and be done. It acquires volume and qualitative intensity—in a word, emotion—only through obstruction. Block a vital pattern of action, and emotion emerges. To be sure, no sooner does the emotion arise than the natural onrush of the pattern of action tends to drain off the quality of the emotion in the pursuit of the practical end. But the emotion has been created, and thereafter all that needs to be done is to hold the habit or the instinct back so that the emotion may flame. Conflict is the source of emotion, and in the previous chapter we were talking about emotion all the time without naming it.

There we were watching the appearance of emotion as conflict brought it to the surface in the stream of time. That is why music and the drama so well served our purpose. But emotion wells up equally in static pools. There is emotion in pictures felt at the first glance, and in lyrics which do not seem to move into conflicts. What is the source of these emotions, and where are the conflicts hidden?

The answer is a reference to those patterns of action, about which we were just speaking. We call these patterns of action expressions of emotion. They are really, as we saw, the emotion or part of the emotion itself. They are exhibitions of conflict. A child in a tantrum shows by his bodily attitudes, his cries, and the sort of things he says, the kind of conflict going on in him. These patterns of action become as familiar to us all as the patterns of colors and shapes which we call animals, trees, and insects. We learn them partly out of ourselves and partly out of our environment. When they occur in our environment, we are frequently drawn into them ourselves. An angry man makes us angry, and we wallow in a community of anger, and the patterns of action mesh into one another and constitute a mutual pattern which is not easily disentangled into two.

The learning of these patterns is of great practical importance, for they are our guides to social action. They tell us whether we can count on cooperation, or must nerve ourselves up to opposition, whether we should offer comfort, or ridicule, or encouragement, or rebuke. We become very adept at interpreting little signs—the dilation of the eye, the curling of a lip, the contraction of a jaw, the tip of the head, the tapping of a finger, and all the modulations and rhythms of the voice. Many of these signs are the same the world over and we call them instinctive, but many differ from culture to culture. They are details in patterns of action. They betray, often with great accuracy, complicated conflicts of purposes. Assisted by other confirmatory signs, we can often sympathetically reconstruct the conflict involved and enter into it and feel it ourselves.

Added to these bodily expressions are great quantities of what we call emotional stimuli—objects, which either through our biological make-up or through our social habits, normally enter into action patterns. Such are sudden loud noises, sudden movements, a violent aggressive jar, soft noises, gentle touches, warmth, a clear blue sky, great clouds, heavy surf, moonlight, a calm lake, a sword, a gun, a thimble, a flag, a party slogan, and all so-called emotive words. Also, there is a fine emotional discrimination among colors and combinations of colors; lines whether short and thick and jagged, or slim and sinuous; shapes whether square or blunt or pointed; tones; chords; scales whether the major or the minor mode or some exotic mode. How far these are learned or natural, no one knows, but in every culture they constitute an emotional language of great reliability for those who have been brought up in it.

Now, the point we are heading for is this, that an artist does not need a stretch of time in which to develop a conflict and its resultant emotion. Through the agency of these details of action patterns, he can plunge the spectator immediately into a violent purposive conflict and a strong emotion. And the fact that there is no temporal movement in the work of art, if, for instance, the work is a picture or a statue, acts in and of itself as a means of suspense holding the observer in the conflict without power of escape other than his own voluntary decision to turn away and look at something else. Furthermore, it permits of an intensive development of the emotion to a degree of refinement that a temporal work of art cannot ordinarily afford to make. A dancer cannot stop to realize an attitude as a sculptor can. The emotion of a dance is superficially more obvious and compelling than that of a statue. But in the end the statue may for a sensitive man actually develop the more intense emotion.

It is not, therefore, the obvious elements of a great picture or of a musical composition that account for the enhancement of quality found there—not the mere colors, and forms, and lines, and represented figures, nor the mere pitches, and intensities, and durations—but what these carry along with them as biological and social action patterns. Under the surface, sometimes clearly seen, sometimes only felt, impulses meet and intrude upon one another or conflict and the waters of experience are filled with a radiant fusion of quality, with an emotion.

There are three technical modes of producing emotion through a work of art: first, direct stimulation; second, representation; and third, expression. In the first, stimuli are directly evocative of emotion, or details detached from action patterns are set into a composition, which as a total stimulus arouses an emotion. This is the method of abstract design. We think at once of music and architecture. In the second, men and women expressing emotions are represented, and our emotions are stirred at perceiving the expressions of these represented emotions. Here we think of the novel, the drama, the representative picture, and the statue. In the third, signs of the artist's own emotions appear in his work of art, and our emotions are stirred at the exhibition of his emotions. Perhaps here we think particularly of the lyric.

All three modes may be mingled in one work of art. But the first two modes used alone or preponderantly produce art which we call objective, the third art which we call subjective. There is no good aesthetic ground that I can see for preferring one mode to another. There are great works in each mode and in all sorts of combinations of them.

Furthermore, the emotion evoked in the spectator through any of the foregoing modes may be either an emotion *with* or *at* the emotions exhibited in the work of art, or may be a combination of the two. To feel emotions *with* the emotion exhibited is, of course, to accept the direct stimulation of the first mode; to sympathize with the emotions represented according to the second mode (feel angry as the characters show anger, feel a little afraid as they show fear, etc.); or, according to the third mode, to enter into the expressed emotions of the artist.

To feel emotion *at,* however, is a more complicated activity in each case. To feel emotion *at* directly stimulated emotion, according to the first mode, is likely to be detrimental to the appreciation of the work of art concerned; as also to feel emotion *at* the expression of the artist according to the third mode. For in each of these cases, the activity seems usually to involve a retreat of the spectator from the work of art and a critical judgment whether of admiration or irritation or disgust or even moral indignation. But the quality of these emotions is not a realization of the event of the work of art but of another event, merely instigated by the work of art. Furthermore, they are all highly practical activities, leading rapidly off into action. Except in the humorous and the comic, an artist cannot safely lead his audience to feel emotion *at* the emotions he evokes according to the first and third modes.

But in the case of the second mode, that of represented emotion, feeling *at* the emotions represented is often necessary, for several different emotions may be simultaneously represented, and it would be impossible to sympathize with all of them at once. Generally the artist leads the spectator to feel *with* the emotions of one character, the principal one, and *at* the emotions of the others. But sometimes the artist may lead the reader or spectator to feel emotion *at* even the principal character. This is indeed the very point of Flaubert's "Madame Bovary," as Lubbock so penetratingly shows.[2] Flaubert keeps muttering to his reader, so to speak, "Look at her! See how she acts! What a silly woman!" An extreme appearance of objectivity is obtained by this treatment of emotion.

Sometimes feeling *at* and feeling *with* are combined. Painting particularly lends itself to such a combination, because being a spatial art emotions may overlay one another within the work and be separately and successively felt. I have in mind a picture of Daumier's representing a woman and a child with a basket of clothes climbing the steps of an embankment of the Seine. It is painted in somber browns and cream. The figures are modeled in heavy simple masses, and the bright apartment houses across the river glare in contrast with the murky shadows through which the figures are moving. A dull sense of sadness first emerges from the painting, then pity, and then indignation. There is no doubt that these layers of emotion were intended by the artist and lie within the picture. It is a picture with a definite social comment, something profounder than irony because of the very richness and variety of emotions underlying the irony. Furthermore, these different emotions at once intrude upon and restrain one another, so that we feel the event deeply and yet do not take the picture as a piece of propaganda or begin to think about practical action. On the contrary, the social conflict suggested becomes itself a factor of enhancement fusing with the contrasts of color and line and mass. And at the same time (art is so full of paradoxes) the full realization of this event because of its restraint and because of its very intrinsic beauty acts in the long run as more powerful propaganda than propaganda.

If, then, emotion, as we have described it, is so important in art, why do artists so often disparage it? Why is an emotional appreciation so often regarded as weak and superficial? Because the objectionable gushing emotion is often not an emotion in the work of art, or at least not the full realization of the work of art. Because the emotion is false to the work of art, and in that sense a false emotion. Because, in one word, it is sentimentality.

James's often quoted anecdote of the old couple before Titian's "Assumption" exemplifies the reason: "I remember seeing an English couple sit for more than an hour on a piercing February day in the Academy at Venice before the celebrated 'Assumption' by Titian; and when I, after being chased from room to room by the cold, concluded to get into the sun-

---

[2] See Percy Lubbock, *The Craft of Fiction* (New York: Jonathan Cape and Harrison Smith, 1931), pp. 60ff. (Eds.)

shine as fast as possible and let the pictures go, but before leaving drew reverently near to them to learn with what superior forms of susceptibility they might be endowed, all I overheard was the woman's voice murmuring: 'What a *deprecatory* expression her face wears! What *self-abnegation!* How *unworthy* she feels of the honor she is receiving!' Their honest hearts had been kept warm all this time by a glow of spurious sentiment that would have fairly made old Titian sick" (Psych. vol. ii, pp. 471–2). There is, to be sure, a touch of this emotion integral to the picture, but the old couple taking this touch as their cue went off into far distant events on an emotional spree of their own. Their enjoyment was, of course, aesthetic of a kind, but not of Titian's kind nor approximating the depth and breadth of Titian's kind. In a word, they did not understand the picture, and the artist naturally resents it—the more so as he is generally justified in believing that his work of art is a basis for a richer experience than their spontaneous gushes.

If it is an orgy of blind emotion that is wanted, the bones of a saint, a blessed biscuit, or two sticks crosswise would do as well. To the same tenor, James remarks in the very sentence after the foregoing quotation that "Mr. Ruskin somewhere makes the (for him terrible) admission that religious people as a rule care little for pictures, and that when they do care for them they generally prefer the worst ones to the best." It is, moreover, a point made by the modern Irish mystics, that if one is a saint he is not a poet. Mystic absorption may be the summit of realization; but it is beyond art, and as the mystics themselves aver, it is ineffable. Our problem here is not to estimate the aesthetic value of a mystic experience, or of any blind emotional experience. The value may be very high. But we can with assurance state that a person who wanders with his thoughts or his images or his emotions away from the work of art he is contemplating, is not realizing the event there presented, and we are free to suspect that he lacks the cultivation to do so.

Much has been written about the aesthetic emotion. There is no specifically aesthetic emotion, but from the discussion into which we have been led, it is clear that there is a distinction between what may be called an artistic and an unartistic emotion. The one rises out of and is the direct fusion of the details of the work of art. If momentarily a complete fusion occurs—what Dewey calls a seizure, which is a sort of ecstasy of appreciation—diffusion will follow and let one down into the discriminated details of the very work of art. But an unartistic emotion is one set off possibly by a work of art, but based upon conflicts not integral to the work. It may lead off into practical action, or it may be more or less objectless in the sense that it is undirected and uncontrolled. I see no reason why an objectless emotion might not through its intensity of quality have considerable beauty. It is likely, however, to lack the spread of quality which a discriminable structure lends to a work of art.

A certain balance of emotional fusion and analytic discrimination is the normal aesthetic experience. A man who habitually flies off into emotional ecstasy in the presence of a work of art is likely to lack depth of appreciation, even if the emotion is relevant. But it is better to do this than drift into the opposite habit of considering a work of art only in a cold, analytic way. This hard-boiled attitude is very disconcerting to a novice who is eager to appreciate, and full of potential enthusiasm. The calm technical judgments of a connoisseur, especially when flavored with sarcastic innuendoes about callow ebullitions, is stifling to emotion and the young man becomes afraid to enter into the work he wants to appreciate. He begins insincerely to emulate the manner of the expert, and to imitate his witticisms. Actually, if he but knew it, his natural effusions, thin as they may be, are closer to a realization of the work, than the erudite comments of such an expert.

For a description of the frigidity of the jaded critic, from whom all warmth of appreciation and sense of beauty has vanished and has been displaced by a mechanical clicking of habitual judgments, I turn again to James: "Where long familiarity with a certain class of effects, even aesthetic ones, has blunted mere emotional excitability as much as it has sharpened taste and judgment, we do get the intellectual emotion, if such it can be called, pure and undefiled. And the dryness of it, the paleness, the absence of all glow, as it may exist in a thoroughly expert critic's mind, not only shows us what an altogether different thing it is from the 'coarser' emotions we considered first, but makes us suspect that almost the entire difference lies in the fact that the bodily sounding-board vibrating in the one case, is in the other mute. 'Not so very bad,' is, in a person of consummate taste, apt to be the highest limit of approving criticism. 'Rien ne me choque' [nothing jars me] is said to be Chopin's superlative praise of new music. A sentimental layman would feel, and ought to feel, horrified on being admitted to such a critic's mind to see how cold, how thin, how void of human significance, are the motives for favor and disfavor that there prevail. The capacity to make a nice spot on the wall will outweigh a picture's whole content; a foolish trick of words will preserve a poem; an utterly meaningless fitness of sequence in one musical composition set at naught any amount of 'expressiveness' in another" (Psych. vol. ii, p. 471).

Better to remain like the old couple before Titian's "Assumption" than become like this. It is the balance between these opposites that gives real good taste, and makes the genuine expert. Not that we can always appreciate a work of art at this balance. We slip back and forth from a more emotional to a more analytical attitude towards the work before us. The realization of the work is increased by these changing attitudes. But if we have lost the capacity for "seizure," for rich emotional fusion and ecstasy in a work, we have lost something precious. We have lost the power of full realization. We cannot be too far emotionally carried away by a work of art, as long as the emotion is the relevant emotion, that actual fusion of all the strands of that individual event.

Emotion is the culmination of vitality in art, of those factors which strip away habit and reveal the quality of the event. It is also the beginning of organization. It is not only a factor for increasing the intensity of quality, but also for enlarging its spread. The two chief methods of organization through emotion may be called the principle of dominant emotion, and that of natural emotional sequence.

The principle of dominant emotion is very simple. We noticed earlier the connection of emotions with action patterns. The elements of these patterns become then stimuli for specific emotions, which acquire individualities of their own. Furthermore, alternative stimuli develop. There are not only sad tones, but sad combinations of colors and lines, and sad words, and sad rhythms. The emotion of sadness has a specific individuality, but with many alternative strands. And all these strands or stimuli are schematically organized in that they constitute interlocking action patterns specific to that emotion. Now, the principle of dominant emotion is the selection, for a single work of art or section of a work, of stimuli belonging to one emotional scheme of action patterns. The specific quality of that emotion will then be echoed and reechoed through all parts of the work; and all details, diverse in other respects as they may be, become organized and unified through the simple emotion evoked by them. Furthermore, the expressive power of each detail becomes intensified by the repeated evoking of the same emotion. The principle is too well known to need exemplification.

But the principle of natural emotional sequence is not so well known. In our commerce with our environment, we find ourselves confronted by situations which call out regular sequences of emotions. A man meets a stranger in a lonely spot, or he is caught in the rain, or his boat capsizes, or he is handed bad news, or he sees a friend after long absence, or he finds a rival with his girl. There is a somewhat limited sequence of actions with corresponding emotions which we expect a man to follow under each of these circumstances. One of these normal sequences of emotion, I call a natural emotional sequence. A literary or dramatic narrative following one of these sequences is obviously unified to a high degree by the organization of action and emotion involved in such an anticipated sequence. Here is a very short and powerful instance of such emotional organization:

THE REAR GUARD [3]

By Siegfried Sassoon

Groping along the tunnel, step by step,
He winked his prying torch with patching glare
From side to side, and sniffed the unwholesome air.
Tins, boxes, bottles, shapes too vague to know,
A mirror smashed, the mattress from a bed;
And he exploring fifty feet below
The rosy gloom of battle overhead.
Tripping, he grabbed the wall; saw someone lie
Humped at his feet, half-hidden by a rug,
And stooped to give the sleeper's arm a tug.
"I'm looking for headquarters." No reply.
"God blast your neck!" (For days he'd had no sleep.)
"Get up and guide me through this stinking place."
Savage, he kicked a soft, unanswering heap,
And flashed his beam across the livid face
Terribly glaring up, whose eyes yet wore
Agony dying hard ten days before;
And fists of fingers clutched a blackening wound.
Alone he staggered on until he found
Dawn's ghost that filtered down a shafted stair
To the dazed, muttering creatures underground
Who hear the boom of shells in muffled sound.
At last, with sweat of horror in his hair,
He climbed through darkness to the twilight air,
Unloading hell behind him, step by step.

In this instance the physical circumstances which account for the sequence of the emotions are described step by step. But the principle becomes particularly interesting when there is a separation between the description of the circumstances and the sequence of the emotions, as in program music; or where there is no description of circumstances, but only the sequence of emotions. The sense of rightness or inevitability of emotional sequence in much pure music, especially when it is of a rather dramatic type like Beethoven's, is due to the sequence being a natural one such as would accompany a physical situation, but without the situation. The unity is then just as firm, and much more subtle, than in the case of the poem quoted. Something closely approximating such pure emotional sequence occurs frequently in poetry, as in Keats' "Ode to a Nightingale," or Shelley's "Adonais."

---

[3] Reprinted by permission of the author. (Eds.)

Changing circumstances are hinted at, but for the most part the emotions are nearly as disembodied from their physical accompaniments as in pure music.

Emotions are also organized by the regular design principles of contrast and gradation. But in these rôles the emotions are not active principles of organization but passive materials organized.

AS ORGANIZATION OF IMPULSES

I. A. RICHARDS

The Aesthetic Response as

Organization of Attitudes[1]

THE INTERVENTIONS of memory are not confined to sensation and emotion. They are of equal importance in our active behaviour. The acquisition of any muscular accomplishment, dancing or billiards, for example, shows this clearly. What we have already done in the past controls what we shall do in the future. If the perception of an object and the recognition that it is a tree, for example, involve a poise in the sensory system concerned, a certain completeness or "closure," to use the term employed by Köhler, so an act, as opposed to a random movement, involves a similar poise in a motor system. But sensory and motor systems are not independent; they work together; every perception probably includes a response in the form of incipient action. We constantly overlook the extent to which all the while we are making preliminary adjustments, getting ready to act in one way or another. Reading Captain Slocum's account of the centipede which bit him on the head when alone in the middle of the Atlantic, the writer has been caused to leap right out of his chair by a leaf which fell upon his face from a tree. Only occasionally does some such accident show how extensive are the motor adjustments made in what appear to be the most unmuscular occupations.

---

[1] From *Principles of Literary Criticism*, by I. A. Richards, pp. 107–113, 243–252. Reprinted by permission of Harcourt, Brace and Company, Inc., and of Routledge and Kegan Paul, Ltd. Title by the editors. (Eds.)

This incipient activity stands to overt action much as an image stands to a sensation. But such "imaginal" activity is, by its very nature, extraordinarily hard to detect or to experiment upon. Psychology has only dealt with fringes of the mind hitherto and the most accessible fringe is on the side of sensation. We have therefore to build up our conjectures as to the rest of mental happenings by analogy with the perhaps not entirely representative specimens which sensation supplies. This limitation has led the majority of psychologists to see in imaginal movement no more than images of the *sensations* from muscle, joint, and tendon, which would arise if the movement were actually made.

It is certain that before any action takes place a preliminary organisation must occur which ensures that the parts do not get in one another's way. It appears to the writer that these preliminaries in his case make up part of consciousness, but there is a heavy weight of authority against him. The point is no doubt exceptionally hard to determine.

In any case, whether the consciousness of activity is due to sensations and images of movements alone, or whether the outgoing part of the impulse and its preparatory organisation help to make up consciousness, there is no doubt about the importance of incipient and imaginal movement in experience. The work done by Lipps, Groos and others on *einfühlung,* or empathy, however we may prefer to restate their results, shows that when we perceive spatial or musical form we commonly accompany our perception with closely connected motor activity. We cannot leave this activity out of our account of what happens in the experiences of the arts, although we may think that those who have built upon this fact what they have put forward as a complete aesthetic—Vernon Lee, for example—have been far from clear as to what questions they were answering.

The extent to which any activity is conscious seems to depend very largely upon how complex and how novel it is. The primitive and in a sense natural outcome of stimulus is action; the more simple the situation with which the mind is engaged, the closer is the connection between the stimulus and some overt response in action, and in general the less rich and full is the consciousness attendant. A man walking over uneven ground, for example, makes without reflection or emotion a continuous adjustment of his steps to his footing; but let the ground become precipitous and, unless he is used to such places, both reflection and emotion will appear. The increased complexity of the situation and the greater delicacy and appropriateness of the movements required for convenience and safety, call forth far more complicated goings on in the mind. Besides his perception of the nature of the ground, the thought may occur that a false move would be perilous and difficult to retrieve. This, when accompanied by emotion, is called a "realisation" of his situation. The adjustment to one another of varied impulses—

to go forward carefully, to lie down and grasp something with the hands, to go back, and so forth—and their co-ordination into useful behaviour alters the whole character of his experience.

Most behaviour is a reconciliation between the various acts which would satisfy the different impulses which combine to produce it; and the richness and interest of the feel of it in consciousness depends upon the variety of the impulses engaged. Any familiar activity, when set in different conditions so that the impulses which make it up have to adjust themselves to fresh streams of impulses due to the new conditions, is likely to take on increased richness and fullness in consciousness.

This general fact is of great importance for the arts, particularly for poetry, painting and sculpture, the representative or mimetic arts. For in these a totally new setting for what may be familiar elements is essentially involved. Instead of seeing a tree we see something in a picture which may have similar effects upon us but is *not* a tree. The tree impulses which are aroused have to adjust themselves to their new setting of other impulses due to our awareness that it is a *picture* which we are looking at. Thus an opportunity arises for those impulses to define themselves in a way in which they ordinarily do not.

This, of course, is only the most obvious and simple instance of the way in which, thanks to the unusual circumstances in which things depicted, or in literature described, come before us, the experiences that result are modified. To take another obvious example, the description or the theatrical presentation of a murder has a different effect upon us from that which would be produced by most actual murders if they took place before us. These considerations, of vast importance in the discussion of artistic form, will occupy us later (pp. 145, 237). Here it is sufficient to point out that these differences between ordinary experiences and those due to works of art are only special cases of the general difference between experiences made up of a less and of a greater number of impulses which have to be brought into co-ordination with one another. The bearing of this point upon the problem of the aesthetic mode with its detachment, impersonality, etc., . . . will be apparent.

The result of the co-ordination of a great number of impulses of different kinds is very often that no *overt* action takes place. There is a danger here of supposing that no action whatever results or that there is something incomplete or imperfect about such a state of affairs. But imaginal action and incipient action which does not go so far as actual muscular movement are more important than overt action in the well-developed human being. Indeed the difference between the intelligent or refined, and the stupid or crass person is a difference in the extent to which overt action can be replaced by incipient and imaginal action. An intelligent man can "see how a thing

works" when a less intelligent man has to "find out by trying." Similarly
with such responses as are aroused by a work of art. The difference between
"understanding" it and failing to do so is, in most cases, a difference between being able to make the required responses in an imaginal or incipient
degree, adjusting them to one another at that stage, and being unable to
produce them or adjust them except overtly and at their fullest development. Though the kinds of activity involved are different, the analogy with
the case of the mathematician is not misleading. The fact that he will not
make half so many marks on paper as a schoolboy does not show that he
is any less active. His activity takes place at an earlier stage in which his
responses are merely incipient or imaginal. In a similar manner the absence
of any overt movements or external signs of emotion in an experienced
reader of poetry, or concert-goer, compared to the evident disturbances
which are sometimes to be seen in the novice, is no indication of any lack
of internal activity. The response required in many cases by works of art
is of a kind which can only be obtained in an incipient or imaginal stage.
Practical considerations often prevent their being worked out in overt form,
and this is, as a rule, not in the least to be regretted. For these responses are
commonly of the nature of solutions to problems, not of intellectual research,
but of emotional accommodation and adjustment, and can usually be best
achieved while the different impulses which have to be reconciled are still
in an incipient or imaginal stage, and before the matter has become further
complicated by the irrelevant accidents which attend overt responses.

These imaginal and incipient activities or tendencies to action, I shall call
attitudes. When we realise how many and how different may be the tendencies awakened by a situation, and what scope there is for conflict, suppression and interplay—all contributing something to our experience—it
will not appear surprising that the classification and analysis of attitudes
is not yet far advanced. A thousand tendencies to actions, which do not
overtly take place, may well occur in complicated adjustments. For these
what evidence there is must be indirect. In fact, the only attitudes which
are capable of clear and explicit analysis are those in which some simple
mode of observable behaviour gives the clue to what has been taking place,
and even here only a part of the reaction is open to this kind of examination.

Among the experiences which are by the nature of the case hidden from
observation are found almost all those with which criticism is concerned.
The outward aspect and behaviour of a man reading *The Prioresses' Tale*
and *The Miller's Tale* may well be indistinguishable. But this should not
lead us to overlook how great a part in the whole experience is taken by
attitudes. Many experiences which, if examined by introspection for their
actual content of sensation and imagery, differ very little, are totally diverse
in the kind and degree of implicit activity present. This aspect of experiences

as filled with incipient promptings, lightly stimulated tendencies to acts of one kind or another, faint preliminary preparations for doing this or that, has been constantly overlooked in criticism. Yet it is in terms of attitudes, the resolution, inter-inanimation, and balancing of impulses—Aristotle's definition of Tragedy [2] is an instance—that all the most valuable effects of poetry must be described.

. . . In describing the poet we laid stress upon the availability of his experience, upon the width of the field of stimulation which he can accept, and the completeness of the response which he can make. Compared with him the ordinary man suppresses nine-tenths of his impulses, because he is incapable of managing them without confusion. He goes about in blinkers because what he would otherwise see would upset him. But the poet through his superior power of ordering experience is freed from this necessity. Impulses which commonly interfere with one another and are conflicting, independent, and mutually distractive, in him combine into a stable poise. He selects, of course, but the range of suppression which is necessary for him is diminished, and for this very reason such suppressions as he makes are more rigorously carried out. Hence the curious local callousness of the artist which so often strikes the observer.

But these impulses active in the artist become mutually modified and thereby ordered to an extent which only occurs in the ordinary man at rare moments, under the shock of, for example, a great bereavement or an undreamt-of happiness; at instants when the "film of familiarity and selfish solicitude," which commonly hides nine-tenths of life from him, seems to be lifted and he feels strangely alive and aware of the actuality of existence. In these moments his myriad inhibitions are weakened; his responses, canalised—to use an inappropriate metaphor—by routine and by practical but restricted convenience, break loose and make up a new order with one another; he feels as though everything were beginning anew. But for most men after their early years such experiences are infrequent; a time comes when they are incapable of them unaided, and they receive them only through the arts. For great art has this effect, and owes thereto its supreme place in human life.

The poet makes unconsciously a selection which outwits the force of habit; the impulses he awakens are freed, through the very means by which they are aroused, from the inhibitions that ordinary circumstances encourage; the irrelevant and the extraneous is excluded; and upon the resulting simplified but widened field of impulses he imposes an order which their greater plasticity allows them to accept. Almost always too the chief part of his work

---

[2] "Tragedy is an imitation of an action . . . effecting through Pity and Terror the correction and refinement (κάθαρσις) of such passions." *Poetics,* VI.

is done through those impulses which we have seen to be most uniform and regular, those which are aroused by what are called the "formal elements." They are also the most primitive, and for that reason commonly among those which are most inhibited, most curtailed and subordinated to super-imposed purposes. We rarely let a colour affect us purely as a colour, we use it as a sign by which we recognise some coloured object. Thus our re-sponses to colours in themselves become so abbreviated that many people come to think that the pigments painters use are in some way more colourful than Nature. What happens is that inhibitions are released, and at the same time mutual interactions between impulses take place which only sunsets seem to evoke in everyday experience. We have seen in discussing com-munication one reason for the pre-eminence of "formal elements" in art, the uniformity of the responses which they can be depended upon to produce. In their primitiveness we find another. The sense that the accidental and ad-ventitious aspect of life has receded, that we are beginning again, that our contact with actuality is increased, is largely due to this restoration of their full natural powers to sensations.

But this restoration is not enough; merely looking at a landscape in a mirror, or standing on one's head will do it. What is much more essential is the increased organisation, the heightened power of combining all the several effects of formal elements into a single response, which the poet bestows. To point out that "the sense of musical delight is a gift of the imagination" was one of Coleridge's most brilliant feats. It is in such resolu-tion of a welter of disconnected impulses into a single ordered response that in all the arts imagination is most shown, but for the reason that here its operation is most intricate and most inaccessible to observation, we shall study it more profitably in its other manifestations.

We have suggested, but only by accident, that imagination characteristi-cally produces effects similar to those which accompany great and sudden crises in experience. This would be misleading. What is true is that those imaginative syntheses which most nearly approach to these climaxes, Tragedy for example, are the most easy to analyse. What clearer instance of the "balance or reconciliation of opposite and discordant qualities" can be found than Tragedy. Pity, the impulse to approach, and Terror, the impulse to retreat, are brought in Tragedy to a reconciliation which they find no-where else, and with them who knows what other allied groups of equally discordant impulses. Their union in an ordered single response is the *catharsis* by which Tragedy is recognised, whether Aristotle meant anything of this kind or not. This is the explanation of that sense of release, or repose in the midst of stress, of balance and composure, given by Tragedy, for there is no other way in which such impulses, once awakened, can be set at rest without suppression.

It is essential to recognise that in the full tragic experience there is no suppression. The mind does not shy away from anything, it does not protect itself with any illusion, it stands uncomforted, unintimidated, alone and self-reliant. The test of its success is whether it can face what is before it and respond to it without any of the innumerable subterfuges by which it ordinarily dodges the full development of experience. Suppressions and sublimations alike are devices by which we endeavour to avoid issues which might bewilder us. The essence of Tragedy is that it forces us to live for a moment without them. When we succeed we find, as usual, that there is no difficulty; the difficulty came from the suppressions and sublimations. The joy which is so strangely the heart of the experience is not an indication that "all's right with the world" or that "somewhere, somehow, there is Justice"; it is an indication that all is right here and now in the nervous system. Because Tragedy is the experience which most invites these subterfuges, it is the greatest and the rarest thing in literature, for the vast majority of works which pass by that name are of a different order. Tragedy is only possible to a mind which is for the moment agnostic or Manichean. The least touch of any theology which has a compensating Heaven to offer the tragic hero is fatal. That is why *Romeo and Juliet* is not a Tragedy in the sense in which *King Lear* is.

But there is more in Tragedy than unmitigated experience. Besides Terror there is Pity, and if there is substituted for either something a little different —Horror or Dread, say, for Terror; Regret or Shame for Pity; or that kind of Pity which yields the adjective "Pitiable" in place of that which yields "Piteous"—the whole effect is altered. It is the relation between the two sets of impulses, Pity and Terror, which gives its specific character to Tragedy, and from that relation the peculiar poise of the Tragic experience springs.

The metaphor of a balance or poise will bear consideration. For Pity and Terror are opposites in a sense in which Pity and Dread are not. Dread or Horror are nearer than Terror to Pity, for they contain attraction as well as repulsion. As in colour, tones just not in harmonic relation are peculiarly unmanageable and jarring, so it is with these more easily describable responses. The extraordinarily stable experience of Tragedy, which is capable of admitting almost any other impulses so long as the relation of the main components is exactly right, changes at once if these are altered. Even if it keeps its coherence it becomes at once a far narrower, more limited, and exclusive thing, a much more partial, restricted and specialised response. Tragedy is perhaps the most general, all-accepting, all-ordering experience known. It can take anything into its organisation, modifying it so that it finds a place. It is invulnerable; there is nothing which does not present to the tragic attitude *when fully developed* a fitting aspect and only a fitting aspect. Its sole rivals in this respect are the attitudes of Falstaff and of the Voltaire of *Candide*. But pseudo-tragedy—the greater part of Greek Tragedy as well as almost all Elizabethan Tragedy outside Shakespeare's six masterpieces comes under this head—is one of the most fragile and precarious of attitudes. Parody easily overthrows it, the ironic addition paralyses it; even a mediocre joke may make it look lopsided and extravagant.

This balanced poise, stable through its power of inclusion, not through the force of its exclusions, is not peculiar to Tragedy. It is a general characteristic of all the most valuable experiences of the arts. It can be given by a carpet or a pot or by a gesture as unmistakably as by the Parthenon, it may come about through an epigram as clearly as through a Sonata. We must resist the temptation to analyse its cause into sets of opposed characters in the object. As a rule no such analysis can be made. The balance is not in the structure of the stimulating object, it is in the response. By remembering this we escape the danger of supposing that we have found a formula for Beauty.

Although for most people these experiences are infrequent apart from the arts, almost any occasion may give rise to them. The most important general condition is mental health, a high state of "vigilance"; the next is the frequent occurrence of such experiences in the recent past. None of the effects of art is more transferable than this balance or equilibrium.

Despite all differences in the impulses concerned, a certain general similarity can be observed in all these cases of supremely fine and complete organisation. It is this similarity which has led to the legends of the "aesthetic state," the "aesthetic emotion" and the single quality Beauty, the same in all its manifestations. We had occasion in Chapter II to suggest that the characteristics by which aesthetic experience is usually defined—that impersonality, disinterestedness and detachment so much stressed and so little discussed by aestheticians—are really two sets of quite different characters. One set we have seen (Chapters X and XXIV) to be merely conditions of communication having nothing essentially to do with value, conditions involved in valueless and valuable communications alike. We have suggested above, however, that this kind of detachment and severance from ordinary circumstances and accidental personal interests may be of special service in these supremely valuable [3] communications, since it makes the breaking down of inhibitions more easy. This same facilitation of response is also, it should be added, the explanation of the peculiarly pernicious effect of bad but competent art.

We may now turn to consider that other set of characters which have

---

[3] It may perhaps be desirable to point out that this description of the effects of art follows from the theory of value outlined in Chapter VII. They are the most valuable experiences because they are the least wasteful. Thus the place assigned to them is not a mere personal expression of preference.

been confused with these communicative conditions, and which may justifiably be taken as defining a special field for those interested in the values of experience. There are two ways in which impulses may be organised; by exclusion and by inclusion, by synthesis and by elimination. Although every coherent state of mind depends upon both, it is permissible to contrast experiences which win stability and order through a narrowing of the response with those which widen it. A very great deal of poetry and art is content with the full, ordered development of comparatively special and limited experiences, with a definite emotion, for example, Sorrow, Joy, Pride, or a definite attitude, Love, Indignation, Admiration, Hope, or with a specific mood, Melancholy, Optimism or Longing. And such art has its own value and its place in human affairs. No one will quarrel with "Break, break, break," or with the *Coronach* or with *Rose Aylmer* or with *Love's Philosophy*,[4] although clearly they are limited and exclusive. But they are not the greatest kind of poetry; we do not expect from them what we find in the *Ode to the Nightingale*, in *Proud Maisie*, in *Sir Patrick Spens*, in *The Definition of Love* or in the *Nocturnall upon S. Lucie's Day*.

The structures of these two kinds of experiences are different, and the difference is not one of subject but of the relations *inter se* of the several impulses active in the experience. A poem of the first group is built out of sets of impulses which run parallel, which have the same direction. In a poem of the second group the most obvious feature is the extraordinary heterogeneity of the distinguishable impulses. But they are more than heterogeneous, they are opposed. They are such that in ordinary, non-poetic, non-imaginative experience, one or other set would be suppressed to give as it might appear freer development to the others.

The difference comes out clearly if we consider how comparatively unstable poems of the first kind are. They will not bear an ironical contemplation. We have only to read *The War Song of Dinas Vawr* in close conjunction with the *Coronach*, or to remember that unfortunate phrase "Those lips, O slippery blisses"! from *Endymion*, while reading *Love's Philosophy*, to notice this. Irony in this sense consists in the bringing in of the opposite, the complementary impulses; that is why poetry which is exposed to it is not of the highest order, and why irony itself is so constantly a characteristic of poetry which is.

These opposed impulses from the resolution of which such experiences spring cannot usually be analysed. When, as is most often the case, they are aroused through formal means, it is evidently impossible to do so. But sometimes, as in the above cited cases, they can, and through this accident

---

[4] May I assume that references here will not distress the reader? Tennyson, Scott, Landor, Shelley, Keats, Scott, Anon; Marvell, Donne, Peacock. I am anxious to facilitate the actual detailed comparison of these poems.

literary criticism is able to go a step further than the criticism of the other arts.

We can only conjecture dimly what difference holds between a balance and reconciliation of impulses and a mere rivalry or conflict. One difference is that a balance sustains one state of mind, but a conflict two alternating states. This, however, does not take us very far. The chief misconception which prevents progress here is the switchboard view of the mind. What conception should be put in its place is still doubtful, but we have already (Chapters XIV and XX) discussed the reasons which make a more adequate conception imperative. The rest of the difficulty is due merely to ignorance; we do not yet know enough about the central nervous system.

With this preliminary disavowal of undue certainty we may proceed. The equilibrium [5] of opposed impulses, which we suspect to be the ground-plan of the most valuable aesthetic responses, brings into play far more of our personality than is possible in experiences of a more defined emotion. We cease to be oriented in one definite direction; more facets of the mind are exposed and, what is the same thing, more aspects of things are able to affect us. To respond, not through one narrow channel of interest, but simultaneously and coherently through many, is to be *disinterested* in the only sense of the word which concerns us here. A state of mind which is not disinterested is one which sees things only from one standpoint or under one aspect. At the same time since more of our personality is engaged the independence and individuality of other things becomes greater. We seem to see "all round" them, to see them as they really are; we see them apart from any one particular interest which they may have for us. Of course without some interest we should not see them at all, but the less any one particular interest is indispensable, the more *detached* our attitude becomes. And to say that we are *impersonal* is merely a curious way of saying that our personality is more *completely* involved.

These characters of aesthetic experiences can thus be shown to be very natural consequences of the diversity of their components. But that so many different impulses should enter in is only what may be expected in an experience whose ground-plan is a balance of opposites. For every impulse which does not complete itself in isolation tends to bring in allied systems. The state of irresolution shows this clearly. The difference between any such welter of vacillating impulses and the states of composure we are considering may well be a matter of mediating relations between the supporting systems brought in from either side. One thing only perhaps is certain; what happens is the exact opposite to a deadlock, for compared to the experience of great poetry every other state of mind is one of bafflement.

---

[5] This topic is discussed from a slightly different angle in *The Foundations of Aesthetics* (Allen and Unwin, 1922).

AS DISTANCE

EDWARD BULLOUGH

Psychical Distance as a Factor in Art and an Aesthetic Principle[1]

§ 1

THE CONCEPTION OF "Distance" suggests, in connection with Art, certain trains of thought by no means devoid of interest or of speculative importance. Perhaps the most obvious suggestion is that of *actual spatial* distance, *i.e.,* the distance of a work of Art from the spectator, or that of *represented spatial* distance, *i.e.,* the distance represented within the work. Less obvious, more metaphorical, is the meaning of *temporal* distance. The first was noticed already by Aristotle in his *Poetics;* the second has played a great part in the history of painting in the form of perspective; the distinction between these two kinds of distance assumes special importance theoretically in the differentiation between sculpture in the round, and relief-sculpture. Temporal distance, remoteness from us in point of time, though often a cause of misconceptions, has been declared to be a factor of considerable weight in our appreciation.

It is not, however, in any of these meanings that "Distance" is put forward here, though it will be clear in the course of this essay that the above mentioned kinds of distance are rather special forms of the conception of Distance as advocated here, and derive whatever *aesthetic* qualities they may possess from Distance in its general connotation. This general connotation is "Psychical Distance."

A short illustration will explain what is meant by "Psychical Distance." Imagine a fog at sea: for most people it is an experience of acute unpleasantness. Apart from the physical annoyance and remoter forms of discomfort

---

[1] From *British Journal of Psychology,* V (1912), 87–98. Reprinted by permission. (Eds.)

such as delays, it is apt to produce feelings of peculiar anxiety, fears of invisible dangers, strains of watching and listening for distance and unlocalized signals. The listless movements of the ship and her warning calls soon tell upon the nerves of the passengers; and that special, expectant, tacit anxiety and nervousness, always associated with this experience, make a fog the dreaded terror of the sea (all the more terrifying because of its very silence and gentleness) for the expert seafarer no less than for the ignorant landsman.

Nevertheless, a fog at sea can be a source of intense relish and enjoyment. Abstract from the experience of the sea fog, for the moment, its danger and practical unpleasantness, just as every one in the enjoyment of a mountain-climb disregards its physical labor and its danger (though, it is not denied, that these may incidentally enter into the enjoyment and enhance it); direct the attention to the features "objectively" constituting the phenomenon—the veil surrounding you with an opaqueness as of transparent milk, blurring the outline of things and distorting their shapes into weird grotesqueness; observe the carrying-power of the air, producing the impression as if you could touch some far-off siren by merely putting out your hand and letting it lose itself behind that white wall; note the curious creamy smoothness of the water, hypocritically denying as it were any suggestion of danger; and, above all, the strange solitude and remoteness from the world, as it can be found only on the highest mountain tops; and the experience may acquire, in its uncanny mingling of repose and terror, a flavor of such concentrated poignancy and delight as to contrast sharply with the blind and distempered anxiety of its other aspects. This contrast, often emerging with startling suddenness, is like a momentary switching on of some new current, or the passing ray of a brighter light, illuminating the outlook upon perhaps the most ordinary and familiar objects—an impression which we experience sometimes in instants of direst extremity, when our practical interest snaps like a wire from sheer over-tension, and we watch the consummation of some impending catastrophe with the marveling unconcern of a mere spectator.

It is a difference of outlook, due—if such a metaphor is permissible—to the insertion of Distance. This Distance appears to lie between our own self and its affections, using the latter term in its broadest sense as anything which affects our being, bodily or spiritually, *e.g.,* as sensation, perception, emotional state or idea. Usually, though not always, it amounts to the same thing to say that the Distance lies between our own self and such objects as are the sources or vehicles of such affections.

Thus, in the fog, the transformation by Distance is produced in the first instance by putting the phenomenon, so to speak, out of gear with our practical, actual self; by allowing it to stand outside the context of our personal needs and ends—in short, by looking at it "objectively," as it has often been called, by permitting only such reactions on our part as emphasize the "objective" features of the experience, and by interpreting even our "subjective" affections not as modes of *our* being but rather as characteristics of the phenomenon.

The working of Distance is, accordingly, not simple, but highly complex. It has a *negative,* inhibitory aspect—the cutting-out of the practical sides of things and of our practical attitude to them—and a *positive* side—the elaboration of the experience on the new basis created by the inhibitory action of Distance.

2. Consequently, this distanced view of things is not, and cannot be, our normal outlook. As a rule, experiences constantly turn the same side towards us, namely, that which has the strongest practical force of appeal. We are not ordinarily aware of those aspects of things which do not touch us immediately and practically, nor are we generally conscious of impressions apart from our own self which is impressed. The sudden view of things from their reverse, usually unnoticed, side, comes upon us as a revelation, and such revelations are precisely those of Art. In this most general sense, Distance is a factor in all Art.

3. It is, for this very reason, also an aesthetic principle. The aesthetic contemplation and the aesthetic outlook have often been described as "objective." We speak of "objective" artists as Shakespeare or Velasquez, of "objective" works or art forms as Homer's *Iliad* or the drama. It is a term constantly occurring in discussions and criticisms, though its sense, if pressed at all, becomes very questionable. For certain forms of Art, such as lyrical poetry, are said to be "subjective"; Shelley, for example, would usually be considered a "subjective" writer. On the other hand, no work of Art can be genuinely "objective" in the sense in which this term might be applied to a work on history or to a scientific treatise; nor can it be "subjective" in the ordinary acceptance of that term, as a personal feeling, a direct statement of a wish or belief, or a cry of passion is subjective. "Objectivity" and "subjectivity" are a pair of opposites which in their mutual exclusiveness when applied to Art soon lead to confusion.

Nor are they the only pair of opposites. Art has with equal vigor been declared alternately "idealistic" and "realistic," "sensual" and "spiritual," "individualistic" and "typical." Between the defense of either terms of such antitheses most aesthetic theories have vacillated. It is one of the contentions of this essay that such opposites find their synthesis in the more fundamental conception of Distance.

Distance further provides the much needed criterion of the beautiful as distinct from the merely agreeable.

Again, it marks one of the most important steps in the process of artistic creation and serves as a distinguishing feature of what is commonly so loosely described as the "artistic temperament."

Finally, it may claim to be considered as one of the essential characteristics of the "aesthetic consciousness"—if I may describe by this term that special mental attitude towards, and outlook upon, experience, which finds its most pregnant expression in the various forms of Art.

§ 2

Distance, as I said before, is obtained by separating the object and its appeal from one's own self, by putting it out of gear with practical needs and ends. Thereby the "contemplation" of the object becomes alone possible. But it does not mean that the relation between the self and the object is broken to the extent of becoming "impersonal." Of the alternatives "personal" and "impersonal" the latter surely comes nearer to the truth; but here, as elsewhere, we meet the difficulty of having to express certain facts in terms coined for entirely different uses. To do so usually results in paradoxes, which are nowhere more inevitable than in discussions upon Art. "Personal" and "impersonal," "subjective" and "objective" are such terms, devised for purposes other than aesthetic speculation, and becoming loose and ambiguous as soon as applied outside the sphere of their special meanings. In giving preference therefore to the term "impersonal" to describe the relation between the spectator and a work of Art, it is to be noticed that it is not impersonal in the sense in which we speak of the "impersonal" character of Science, for instance. In order to obtain "objectively valid" results, the scientist excludes the "personal factor," *i.e.*, his personal wishes as to the validity of his results, his predilection for any particular system to be proved or disproved by his research. It goes without saying that all experiments and investigations are undertaken out of a personal interest in the science, for the ultimate support of a definite assumption, and involve personal hopes of success; but this does not affect the "dispassionate" attitude of the investigator, under pain of being accused of "manufacturing his evidence."

1. Distance does not imply an impersonal, purely intellectually interested relation of such a kind. On the contrary, it describes a *personal* relation, often highly emotionally colored, but of a *peculiar character*. Its peculiarity lies in that the personal character of the relation has been, so to speak, filtered. It has been cleared of the practical, concrete nature of its appeal, without, however, thereby losing its original constitution. One of the best-known examples is to be found in our attitude towards the events and characters of the drama: they appeal to us like persons and incidents of normal experience, except that that side of their appeal, which would usually affect

us in a directly personal manner, is held in abeyance. This difference, so well known as to be almost trivial, is generally explained by reference to the knowledge that the characters and situations are "unreal," imaginary. . . . But, as a matter of fact, the "assumption" upon which the imaginative emotional reaction is based is not necessarily the condition, but often the consequence, of Distance; that is to say, the converse of the reason usually stated would then be true: viz., that Distance, by changing our relation to the characters, renders them seemingly fictitious, not that the fictitiousness of the characters alters our feelings toward them. It is, of course, to be granted that the actual and admitted unreality of the dramatic action reënforces the effect of Distance. But surely the proverbial unsophisticated yokel whose chivalrous interference in the play on behalf of the hapless heroine can only be prevented by impressing upon him that "they are only pretending," is not the ideal type of theatrical audience. The proof of the seeming paradox that it is Distance which primarily gives to dramatic action the appearance of unreality and not *vice versa,* is the observation that the same filtration of our sentiments and the same seeming "unreality" of *actual* men and things occur, when at times, by a sudden change of inward perspective, we are overcome by the feeling that "all the world's a stage."

2. This personal but "distanced" relation (as I will venture to call this nameless character of our view) directs attention to a strange fact which appears to be one of the fundamental paradoxes of Art: it is what I propose to call "the antinomy of Distance."

It will be readily admitted that a work of Art has the more chance of appealing to us the better it finds us prepared for its particular kind of appeal. Indeed, without some degree of predisposition on our part, it must necessarily remain incomprehensible, and to that extent unappreciated. The success and intensity of its appeal would seem, therefore, to stand in direct proportion to the completeness with which it corresponds with our intellectual and emotional peculiarities and the idiosyncrasies of our experience. The absence of such a concordance between the characters of a work and of the spectator is, of course, the most general explanation for differences of "tastes."

At the same time, such a principle of concordance requires a qualification, which leads at once to the antinomy of Distance.

Suppose a man who believes that he has cause to be jealous about his wife, witnesses a performance of *Othello.* He will the more perfectly appreciate the situation, conduct and character of Othello, the more exactly the feelings and experiences of Othello coincide with his own—at least he *ought* to on the above principle of concordance. In point of fact, he will probably do anything but appreciate the play. In reality, the concordance will merely render him acutely conscious of his own jealousy; by a sudden reversal of perspective he will no longer see Othello apparently betrayed by Desdemona, but himself in an analogous situation with his own wife. This reversal of perspective is the consequence of the loss of Distance.

If this be taken as a typical case, it follows that the qualification required is that the coincidence should be as complete as is compatible with maintaining Distance. The jealous spectator of *Othello* will indeed appreciate and enter into the play the more keenly, the greater the resemblance with his own experience—*provided* that he succeeds in keeping the Distance between the action of the play and his personal feelings: a very difficult performance in the circumstances. It is on account of the same difficulty that the expert and the professional critic make a bad audience, since their expertness and critical professionalism are *practical* activities, involving their concrete personality and constantly endangering their Distance. [It is, by the way, one of the reasons why Criticism is an art, for it requires the constant interchange from the practical to the distanced attitude and *vice versa,* which is characteristic of artists.]

The same qualification applies to the artist. He will prove artistically most effective in the formulation of an intensely *personal* experience, but he can formulate it artistically only on condition of a detachment from the experience *qua personal.* Hence the statement of so many artists that artistic formulation was to them a kind of catharsis, a means of ridding themselves of feelings and ideas the acuteness of which they felt almost as a kind of obsession. Hence, on the other hand, the failure of the average man to convey to others at all adequately the impression of an overwhelming joy or sorrow. His personal implication in the event renders it impossible for him to formulate and present it in such a way as to make others, like himself, feel all the meaning and fullness which it possesses for him.

What is therefore, both in appreciation and production, most desirable is the *utmost decrease of Distance without its disappearance.*

3. Closely related, in fact a presupposition to the "antinomy," is the *variability* of Distance. Herein especially lies the advantage of Distance compared with such terms as "objectivity" and "detachment." Neither of them implies a *personal* relation—indeed both actually preclude it; and the mere inflexibility and exclusiveness of their opposites render their application generally meaningless.

Distance, on the contrary, admits naturally of degrees, and differs not only according to the nature of the *object,* which may impose a greater or smaller degree of Distance, but varies also according to the *individual's capacity* for maintaining a greater or lesser degree. And here one may remark that not only do *persons differ from each other* in their habitual measure of Distance, but that the *same individual differs* in his ability to maintain it in the face of different objects and of different arts.

There exist, therefore, two different sets of conditions affecting the degree of Distance in any given case: those offered by the object and those realized by the subject. In their interplay they afford one of the most extensive explanations for varieties of aesthetic experience, since loss of Distance, whether due to the one or the other, means loss of aesthetic appreciation.

In short, Distance may be said to be *variable both according to the distancing-power of the individual, and according to the character of the object.*

There are two ways of losing Distance: either to "under-distance" or to "over-distance." "Under-distancing" is the commonest failing of the *subject,* an excess of Distance is a frequent failing of Art, especially in the past. Historically it looks almost as if Art had attempted to meet the deficiency of Distance on the part of the subject and had overshot the mark in this endeavor. It will be seen later that this is actually true, for it appears that over-distanced Art is specially designed for a class of appreciation which has difficulty to rise spontaneously to any degree of Distance. The consequence of a loss of Distance through one or other cause is familiar: the verdict in the case of under-distancing is that the work is "crudely naturalistic," "harrowing," "repulsive in its realism." An excess of Distance produces the impression of improbability, artificiality, emptiness or absurdity.

The individual tends, as I just stated, to under-distance rather than to lose Distance by over-distancing. *Theoretically* there is no limit to the decrease of Distance. In theory, therefore, not only the usual subjects of Art, but even the most personal affections, whether ideas, percepts, or emotions, can be sufficiently distanced to be aesthetically appreciable. Especially artists are gifted in this direction to a remarkable extent. The average individual, on the contrary, very rapidly reaches his limit of decreasing Distance, his "Distance-limit," *i.e.,* that point at which Distance is lost and appreciation either disappears or changes its character.

In the *practice,* therefore, of the average person, a limit does exist which marks the minimum at which his appreciation can maintain itself in the aesthetic field, and this average minimum lies considerably higher than the Distance-limit of the artist. It is practically impossible to fix this average limit, in the absence of data, and on account of the wide fluctuations from person to person to which this limit is subject. But it is safe to infer that, in art practice, explicit references to organic affections, to the material existence of the body, especially to sexual matters, lies normally below the Distance-limit, and can be touched upon by Art only with special precautions. Allusions to social institutions of any degree of personal importance —in particular, allusions implying any doubt as to their validity—the questioning of some generally recognized ethical sanctions, references to topical subjects occupying public attention at the moment, and such like, are all dangerously near the average limit and may at any time fall below it, arousing, instead of aesthetic appreciation, concrete hostility or mere amusement.

This difference in the Distance-limit between artists and the public has been the source of much misunderstanding and injustice. Many an artist has seen his work condemned, and himself ostracized for the sake of so-called "immoralities" which to him were *bona fide* aesthetic objects. His power of distancing, nay, the necessity of distancing feelings, sensations, situations which for the average person are too intimately bound up with his concrete existence to be regarded in that light, have often quite unjustly earned for him accusations of cynicism, sensualism, morbidness or frivolity. The same misconception has arisen over many "problem plays" and "problem novels" in which the public have persisted in seeing nothing but a supposed "problem" of the moment, whereas the author may have been—and often has demonstrably been—able to distance the subject-matter sufficiently to rise above its practical problematic import and to regard it simply as a dramatically and humanly interesting situation.

The variability of Distance in respect to Art, disregarding for the moment the subjective complication, appears both as a general feature in Art, and in the differences between the special arts.

It has been an old problem why the "arts of the eye and of the ear" should have reached the practically exclusive predominance over arts of other senses. Attempts to raise "culinary art" to the level of a Fine Art have failed in spite of all propaganda, as completely as the creation of scent or liquor "symphonies." There is little doubt that, apart from other excellent reasons of a partly psycho-physical, partly technical nature, the actual, *spatial distance* separating objects of sight and hearing from the subject has contributed strongly to the development of this monopoly. In a similar manner *temporal remoteness* produces Distance, and objects removed from us in point of time are *ipso facto* distanced to an extent which was impossible for their contemporaries. Many pictures, plays and poems had, as a matter of fact, rather an expository or illustrative significance—as for instance much ecclesiastical Art—or the force of a direct practical appeal—as the invectives of many satires or comedies—which seem to us nowadays irreconcilable with their aesthetic claims. Such works have consequently profited greatly by lapse of time and have reached the level of Art only with the help of temporal distance, while others, on the contrary, often for the same reason have suffered a loss of Distance, through *over*-distancing.

Special mention must be made of a group of artistic conceptions which present excessive Distance in their form of appeal rather than in their actual presentation—a point illustrating the necessity of distinguishing between distancing an object and distancing the appeal of which it is the source. I mean here what is often rather loosely termed "idealistic Art," that is, Art springing from abstract conceptions, expressing allegorical meanings, or illustrating general truths. Generalizations and abstractions suffer under this disadvantage that they have too much general applicability to invite a personal interest in them, and too little individual concreteness to prevent them applying to us in all their force. They appeal to everybody and therefore to none. An axiom of Euclid belongs to nobody, just because it compels every one's assent; general conceptions like Patriotism, Friendship, Love, Hope, Life, Death, concern as much Dick, Tom and Harry as myself, and I, therefore, either feel unable to get into any kind of personal relation to them, or, if I do so, they become at once, emphatically and concretely, *my* Patriotism, *my* Friendship, *my* Love, *my* Hope, *my* Life and Death. By mere force of generalization, a general truth or a universal ideal is so far distanced from myself that I fail to realize it concretely at all, or, when I do so, I can realize it only as part of my *practical actual being, i.e.,* it falls below the Distance-limit altogether. "Idealistic Art" suffers consequently under the peculiar difficulty that its excess of Distance turns generally into an *under*-distanced appeal—all the more easily, as it is the usual failing of the subject to *under*-rather than to *over*-distance.

The different special arts show at the present time very marked variations in the degree of Distance which they usually impose or require for their appreciation. Unfortunately here again the absence of data makes itself felt and indicates the necessity of conducting observations, possibly experiments, so as to place these suggestions upon a securer basis. In one single art, viz., the *theater,* a small amount of information is available, from an unexpected source, namely the proceedings of the censorship committee,[2] which on closer examination might be made to yield evidence of interest to the psychologist. In fact, the whole censorship problem, as far as it does not turn upon purely economic questions, may be said to hinge upon Distance; if every member of the public could be trusted to keep it, there would be no sense whatever in the existence of a censor of plays. There is, of course, no doubt that, speaking generally, theatrical performances *eo ipso* run a special risk of a loss of Distance owing to the material presentment[3] of its subject-matter. The physical presence of living human beings as vehicles of dramatic art is a difficulty which no art has to face in the same way. A similar, in many ways even greater, risk confronts *dancing:* though attracting perhaps a less widely spread human interest, its animal spirits are frequently quite unrelieved by any glimmer of spirituality and consequently form a propor-

---

[2] Report from the Joint Select Committee of the House of Lords and the House of Commons on the Stage Plays (Censorship), 1909.

[3] I shall use the term "presentment" to denote the manner of presenting, in distinction to "presentation" as that which is presented.

tionately stronger lure to under-distancing. In the higher forms of dancing technical execution of the most wearing kind makes up a great deal for its intrinsic tendency towards a loss of Distance, and as a popular performance, at least in southern Europe, it has retained much of its ancient artistic glamour, producing a peculiarly subtle balancing of Distance between the pure delight of bodily movement and high technical accomplishment. In passing, it is interesting to observe (as bearing upon the development of Distance), that this art, once as much a fine art as music and considered by the Greeks as a particularly valuable educational exercise, should—except in sporadic cases—have fallen so low from the pedestal it once occupied. Next to the theater and dancing stands *sculpture*. Though not using a *living* bodily medium, yet the human form in its full spatial materiality constitutes a similar threat to Distance. Our northern habits of dress and ignorance of the human body have enormously increased the difficulty of distancing Sculpture, in part through the gross misconceptions to which it is exposed, in part owing to a complete lack of standards of bodily perfection, and an inability to realize the distinction between sculptural form and bodily shape, which is the only but fundamental point distinguishing a statue from a cast taken from life. In *painting* it is apparently the form of its presentment and the usual reduction in scale which would explain why this art can venture to approach more closely than sculpture to the normal Distance-limit. . . . *Music* and *architecture* have a curious position. These two most abstract of all arts show a remarkable fluctuation in their Distances. Certain kinds of music, especially "pure" music, or "classical" or "heavy" music, appear for many people over-distanced; light, "catchy" tunes, on the contrary, easily reach that degree of decreasing Distance below which they cease to be Art and become a pure amusement. In spite of its strange abstractness which to many philosophers has made it comparable to architecture and mathematics, music possesses a sensuous, frequently sensual character: the undoubted physiological and muscular stimulus of its melodies and harmonies, no less than its rhythmic aspects, would seem to account for the occasional disappearance of Distance. To this might be added its strong tendency, especially in unmusical people, to stimulate trains of thought quite disconnected with itself, following channels of subjective inclinations—day-dreams of a more or less directly personal character. *Architecture* requires almost uniformly a very great Distance; that is to say, the majority of persons derive no aesthetic appreciation from architecture as such, apart from the incidental impression of its decorative features and its associations. The causes are numerous, but prominent among them are the confusion of building with architecture and the predominance of utilitarian purposes, which overshadow the architectural claims upon the attention.

AS INTRANSITIVE ATTENTION

ELISEO VIVAS

A Definition of the Esthetic Experience [1]

THIS PAPER PROPOSES a definition of the esthetic experience that will satisfy elementary logical requirements. Such a definition should not only distinguish the esthetic from other modes of experience, but should be based not upon subjective data gathered solely from introspection, but upon as broad a factual basis as is available. And once arrived at, such a definition should throw light on the problems of esthetics. It is unfortunate that the time at my disposal allows me only to present a very succinct and perhaps hermetic sketch of something which demands fairly extended treatment.[2]

Our first step must be to take issue with those writers who give the emotion the central rôle in their account of the esthetic experience. There are in this respect two theories worth considering. One holds that the esthetic object arouses emotion in the spectator; and the other that the content or meaning of art, objectively speaking, is emotion. Both propositions seem to be maintained by Mr. Dewey while only the latter is maintained by Mr. Prall.[3] The first, however, is in conflict with experimental esthetics, the results of which, I take it, indicate that the emotion is an accidental consequence of esthetic apprehension. This being the case, it should not be included in its definition. The crucial proof that it is so lies in the fact that the same esthetic object (or even the same object of fine art) is capable of arousing different

---

[1] From *Journal of Philosophy*, XXXIV (1937), 628–634. Reprinted by permission. (Eds.)

[2] A more complete treatment is to be found in Eliseo Vivas, "A Natural History of the Aesthetic Transaction," *Naturalism and the Human Spirit,* ed. Yervant H. Krikorian (New York: Columbia University Press, 1944), pp. 96–120. (Eds.)

[3] John Dewey, *Art As Experience* (Minton Balch and Company), pp. 67, 68, 79, 91, 237, 238. The treatment of the emotion by Mr. Dewey is extremely baffling. See "A Note on the Emotion in Mr. Dewey's Theory of Art," *The Philosophical Review*, Sept. 1938. D. W. Prall, *Aesthetic Judgment* (Thomas Y. Crowell Company), pp. 213ff. *Aesthetic Analysis* (Thomas Y. Crowell Company), Chapter V, especially pp. 141ff.

emotional reactions in different spectators or even in the same spectator at different times. Again, competently trained persons in music and in poetry are found who deny that the adequate esthetic experience involves the presence of the emotion. In poetry the mention of only one name should suffice—that of T. S. Eliot. In music the evidence which Vernon Lee has recently offered us is overwhelming. And her evidence is confirmed by previous empirical investigations.[4]

These observations can not be refuted with the retort that emotion *should* be aroused by the esthetic object, for that calls for a justification of the prescription, which an empirical definition could not furnish us with. Nor can we refute them with the retort that if there are any such differences of opinion as regards the presence of emotion, these differences point to the fact that there are at least two "varieties of the esthetic experience" radically different from one another in one of which emotion plays the central rôle and another of which it does not play any rôle at all.[5] For this last retort would still leave us with the question as to what is common between these two types of experience, and obviously it would be this common element which alone should be included in our definition.

To the definitions of the experience grounded on the assertion that the objective meaning of art is emotion the following objections must be raised: First, as yet no adequate explanation has been given of the means by which the object expresses "emotion." In his last book Mr. Prall tries to tell us how; but his explanation, careful reading will show, does not go beyond the statement that objects do as a fact express emotion.[6] Empathy theory was, in part at least, an effort to explain this phenomenon. But empathy is not an explanation but a mystification of which Reid and Dewey have effectively disposed.[7] The second objection is much stronger: the assertion that the objective content of art—or as Mr. Prall puts it, its meaning—is emotion, fails to distinguish between objective characters in things and the objective-subjective complex which is the emotion and which has, so to speak, its center of gravity in the subjective. Objective characters of things are what they are, and when Mr. Prall maintains that they are "feeling" or that they

---

[4] The evidence alluded to is to be found in Vernon Lee, *Music and its Lovers* (E. P. Dutton and Co.), Chapters I and II, and corroborating evidence will be found conveniently summarized in Albert R. Chandler, *Beauty and Human Nature* (D. Appleton–Century Company), Chapter 6, Chapter 12, pp. 230–236. T. S. Eliot, *The Sacred Wood, Essays on Poetry and Criticism* (Alfred A. Knopf, Inc.). "The end of the enjoyment of poetry is a pure contemplation from which all the accidents of personal emotion are removed . . ." (p. 15).

[5] This is the conclusion to which Vernon Lee arrives, *op. cit., passim,* especially pp. 543ff. Note how subjectivism as regards esthetic judgments follows naturally from this position.

[6] *Op. cit., loc. cit.*

[7] Dewey, *op. cit., passim,* but particularly pp. 16 and 249. Louis Arnaud Reid, *A Study in Aesthetics* (The Macmillan Company), pp. 85ff.

have "a feel," so far as the careful reader is able to make out this contention can only mean that when language seeks to denote the untranslatable characters of an esthetic object it sometimes chooses for the task terms which are often used to denote emotional states.[8]

If emotion can not be used as a defining trait of the experience, how shall the experience be defined? In our attempt to answer that question it would be advisable to bear in mind that no definition is worth considering which is not resolutely grounded on the assumption that the esthetic experience is an experience of an esthetic object, and that an esthetic object is an object—any object—grasped in such a way as to give rise to an esthetic experience. The assumption is necessary if we are to avoid the isolation of the self from the world which Mr. Dewey has so vigorously shown to have such dire consequences for esthetic theory.[9]

Grounded on this assumption the esthetic experience can be defined, I submit, in terms of attention. The advantages of such definition are manifold, and the only difficulty it presents is the rather easy task of distinguishing *esthetic* attention from that involved in other modes of experience. A brief statement of such definition would read as follows: "An esthetic experience is an experience of rapt attention which involves the intransitive apprehension of an object's immanent meanings in their full presentational immediacy."

This does not mean that the experience is one of direct intuition, if "intuition" be used to signify the prehension of objective meanings by a mirror-mind. The esthetic experience is the result of an interaction in time between a mind and an object, and to say a mind is to say a system of meanings in terms of which the objective presentation is apprehended for what it is. This in turn must be taken to imply that the meanings and characters of the object are in the object for a mind, in such a way that they can be pointed out to others of a similar equipment. The word "immanent" seeks to signify that the meanings are immediately and directly in the object; or in other words that the object is not a mnemonic device or a stimulus of associative processes or a referential sign, but a direct and immediate carrier of meanings. But the important word in our formula besides attention is the word "intransitive." And this word means to signify that attention is esthetic when it is so controlled by the object that it does not fly away from it to meanings not present immanently in the object; or in other words that attention is so

---

[8] Carroll C. Pratt, *The Meaning of Music. A Study in Psychological Aesthetics* (McGraw-Hill Book Company, Inc.). Parts II and III, esp. pp. 157ff. and his article "Objectivity of Esthetic Value" in *The Journal of Philosophy,* Vol. XXXI (1934), pp. 38–45.

[9] *Op. cit., passim,* particularly Chapters I–VI, XI–XIII.

controlled that the object specifies concretely and immediately through reflexive cross-references its meanings and objective characters.[10] And thus we may contrast esthetic with all other modes of attention by noting that other modes of attention discover in objects not immanent but referential meanings, which is to say, meanings which carry us beyond the object to other objects or meanings not present upon it.

We ruled out emotion above on the basis of unexplained data. But our definition now enables us to account for this data. For rapt attention on an object excludes self-consciousness, and emotion can not be present without the latter. True it is that experiences in which self-consciousness completely disappears must be fairly rare, since seldom do we have the energy, interest, or training which are their necessary conditions. But that sometimes we do have them, and that we frequently are able to approach them is a verified matter of fact.[11]

A warning is at this point necessary. Although sometimes almost totally devoid of emotion, the esthetic experience need never be a cold experience. For if we distinguish, as we should, between emotion and feeling, it will be readily seen that it is the feeling that gives the glow to the experience and not the emotion.[12] But the feeling is a by-product of the experience and is a concomitant not only of esthetic but of any other activity which is successful. Again, our definition does not mean to suggest that exclusive emphasis is to be put upon analysis. There is no question that the esthetic experience involves a preparation which can be achieved only through analytic effort. But the experience proper is an experience of adequate and full apprehension of an intransitive kind. It is a having, not a cutting up.

I should now like to suggest some of the advantages of our definition. Our definition throws light on that most important feature of the esthetic experience which has been so loosely termed its "autonomy," and which has often served as its defining trait. The autonomy of the esthetic experience follows from the fact that to the degree to which it is controlled fully and adequately by the object, to that degree does it seem after its enjoyment to have been thoroughly disengaged from the rest of our experience and to possess a *sui generis* character. It also throws light on a phenomenon which has been the spring board for a great deal of mysticism, namely, the deep conviction of the superior reality of the object in which the experience often leaves us. This conviction springs from the intransitive nature of our attention, since

---

[10] The position here taken will be recognized as that of *"objective relativism."*

[11] Compare Vernon Lee, *op. cit., loc. cit.,* with Reid, *op. cit.,* who denies this: "But consciousness of ourselves . . . can probably never disappear. It is a matter of degree and focus" (p. 80).

[12] Pratt, *op. cit.,* p. 177.

during the experience the object remains in complete monopolistic possession of consciousness.[13]

There are other important questions of esthetics on which our definition also throws light. But among these there is one to which I should like to call your especial attention:—our definition enables us to relate the perceiver with the object in a detailed, specific, and verifiable manner. It is not merely a question of asserting in general terms that the object controls the experience, but one of showing a more intimate and detailed relation.[14] For it can be shown that the so-called "factors of advantage," widely recognized by psychologists as controlling attention, are the very factors which under more appropriate names are discovered by analysis to be the generic traits of esthetic objects. A list of these factors of advantage in attention usually include the following: *change, strength, striking quality,* and *definiteness of form.* Now take a representative list of the generic traits discovered by esthetic analysis. *Unity in variety, theme, thematic variation, emphasis,* and *evolution* according to a *rhythmic pattern.* It is, of course, claimed that any other list of truly generic traits would do; but this one is a usual one. Our task is to show how the generic traits of esthetic objects are, under different names, the very factors which psychologists discover are of advantage to attention.

Attention is described by psychologists as exploratory and restless unless somehow controlled, hence the importance of *definiteness of form* in the object which elicits it. This factor of advantage corresponds to *the unity* of the esthetic object, without which divagation easily occurs. But attention requires *change,* or it tires and lapses. In the esthetic object, *the variety* which is unified, carries attention from any one of its aspects reflexively to another, providing change and permitting their free apprehension, while the *unity* which relates them guides attention intransitively within the whole. Again, it is the *unity in variety* of the object which gives attention the needed rest and relief in change, which is a condition of intensity and of prolonged duration. Interpreted broadly, then, the principle of *unity in variety* corresponds to those factors of advantage which hold attention on an object. But the other generic traits of esthetic objects mentioned above—*theme, thematic variation, emphasis,* and *evolution*—in so far as they are distinct from the widest and most generic of these, *unity in variety,* also can be shown to correspond to the factors of advantage to which reference was made. *The theme,* for instance, arrests our attention and is thus seen to correspond to

---

[13] Cf. William James, *Principles of Psychology,* Vol. II, Chapter XXI, pp. 287ff. See a brief study of this question by the author under the title of "Reality in Art" in *The University Review* (The University of Kansas City), Vol. IV (1937), No. 1.

[14] Cf. E. A. Shearer's criticism of Dewey's assertion of correspondence between perceiver and object in "Dewey's Esthetic Theory," *The Journal of Philosophy,* Vol. XXXII (1935), p. 651.

the striking quality which is said by psychologists, in their own terms, to perform the same function. Again *the emphasis* with which the theme is elaborated corresponds to *the strength* demanded by the psychologists. And the need for *change,* although already referred to, is not only provided by the unified variety, but is provided in a manner which more exactly controls the attention by the way in which the artist develops his theme in *a rhythmic scheme.* The *variation* of the theme aids it in providing the striking quality required to shock attention, to surprise it, and to present it with some degree of difficulty, without which it would become lax through boredom.

These remarks do not mean to exhaust the subject. It is hoped, however, that they have enabled us to see that those traits which analysis finds in all esthetic objects are really factors which facilitate attention while retaining it within the object.

Why, it may be asked, is it necessary to relate the object to the experience in the concrete and detailed manner here attempted? Is it not enough to assert—and this, of course, would require no proof—that the object is the stimulus to which the experience is the response? The reason why it is necessary to go beyond this assertion is that if the experience is controlled by the object, it is of interest to know exactly what point by point correspondence is there between the object and the experience. Through a detailed correlation between object and experience it can be shown that the subjective state is not a purely arbitrary affair, but depends, to some extent at least, on the structure of the object which determines that state. Since the structure is an objective affair, to the extent to which the object determines the state, to that extent have we grounds on which to base judgments of esthetic value.

It is time to come to a conclusion, and in view of the variety of related subjects discussed in the brief compass of this paper, a summary of the high points of these notes would be perhaps advisable. The esthetic experience was defined as an experience of intransitive attention, to which, if the empirical evidence is examined, the emotion will be found to be a widely variable concomitant and therefore unavailable as its defining term. Indeed when the self disappears in an intense experience of attention, the emotion is hardly present. In the light of our definition a good number of the problems of esthetics are elucidated which otherwise remain opaque and stubborn. But among these, the problem of correlating object and experience was given especial attention, on account of the importance such correlation would have for the problem of the esthetic judgment.

THE AESTHETIC
JUDGMENT

We HAVE NOW WITNESSED many examinations of the relation between the aesthetic object and the observer. Before we leave the group of problems which arise when we consider the relationships among the creator, the object, and the observer, there is still another which must be proposed. The response of the spectator to the work of art is a response to an object of value; the availability of this value makes aesthetic experiences worth having. It is therefore important that we try to discover how this value is assigned, where it is said to reside, and what validity evaluation may claim. While still remaining on the aesthetic level and, in accordance with the advice given us earlier by L. A. Reid, refraining from indulging the critical level, we must find a theoretical justification for criticism. It is at this point that the aesthetician must take part in the heated disputes currently being carried on in the field of value theory.

We cannot justify criticism on the theoretical level, however, without first proposing some idea of what criticism is and what it is capable of doing. Recently, with the advent of a school of literary critics popularly called the "new critics," it has been especially recognized that an attempt to define the function of criticism can, by placing the proper limitations, clear the ground for effective practical criticism in the arts. Although there are many differing conceptions of the function of criticism, so that disagreements occur even within the ranks of the so-called "new critics," we have included only two of the many possible discussions of this issue in order to allow more space for problems of value, which many consider to be more central to the

412

study of aesthetics. Thus the selections by Greene and Blackmur, which introduce this section, attempt to define the nature and function of criticism in the arts. By affirming the social as well as the aesthetic importance of the critical act, they make crucial the consideration of the authority or validity which each of us, as critic, may claim for his aesthetic judgments.

This is the problem investigated by the authors who follow. If the object of the aesthetic experience is an object of value, we must discover the locus or seat of this value. Is it in the mind of the spectator, in the object, or in the relation between the two? Does the spectator create or project the value himself, does he share with the object in creating it, does he share with other spectators in its creation, or does he merely discover the value, which was there before his arrival and remains unchanged after his departure? We have included here four selections, representing different shadings in theory of value from the extreme of subjectivism to the extreme of objectivism. For Boas, value is completely contingent upon the particular interests which the spectator brings with him, while for Joad it is an objective essence in the Platonic sense. Child and Heyl maintain positions in which relativism has been variously modified in the direction of objectivity, in order to allow for some agreement and some corrigibility in aesthetic judgments without removing value from the human realm. Joad, denying the legitimacy of such qualifications, insists that once a theorist rejects the complete objectivity of value, he cannot logically escape unmitigated subjectivism. In any case, the student has here some of the principal alternatives in value theory from which he must choose. And, with these discussions, we complete the problems which can be raised about the triad (artist-object-observer) which constitutes the normal aesthetic process.

The Function of Criticism

THEODORE MEYER GREENE

The Three Aspects of Criticism[1]

A WORK OF ART is a unique, individual whole—a self-contained artistic "organism" with a "life" and reality of its own. But it is also an historical phenomenon—the product of a specific artist in a specific school, period, and culture, and an exemplification of stylistic characteristics which it shares with other works by the same artist and of the same school, period, and culture. Finally, works of art vary in artistic excellence, truth, and significance: every work of art possesses its own degree of perfection and its own measure of truth or falsity, triviality or greatness.

The competent critic takes all three aspects of the work of art into account, and so, though with less systematic and historical rigor, does the artistically sensitive layman.[2] He apprehends the individual work of art in all its self-contained uniqueness through sensitive artistic re-creation. But to re-create it adequately he must understand the artist's "language," and this implies familiarity with the generic style of the composition and its cultural setting. Historically oriented re-creation, in turn, does not exhaust critical response,

---

[1] From Theodore Meyer Greene, *The Arts and the Art of Criticism* (Princeton: Princeton University Press, 1940), pp. 369–373. Copyright, 1940, by Princeton University Press. Reprinted by permission. (Eds.)

I am especially indebted to Professor A. E. Hinds for the following analysis of artistic and literary criticism. Professor Hinds is at present engaged in writing a book on literary criticism in which these distinctions will be examined both systematically and historically (T.M.G.).

[2] The difference between lay and critical response to art is one of degree rather than of kind. Ideally, at least, the critic differs from the layman merely in possessing greater artistic sensitivity, a more accurate and a richer historical orientation, and a capacity for more objective judicial appraisal. That some laymen surpass some professional critics in one or other of these respects is irrelevant to my argument. My only concern is to formulate the basic principles of artistic response as these are exemplified in artistic and literary criticism at its best.

for such response also implies appraisal of the work of art with respect both to its artistic quality and to its truth and spiritual significance. Criticism has therefore three aspects, the historical, the re-creative, and the judicial. Each aspect relates itself to a corresponding aspect of the work of art itself—historical criticism, to the work's historical character and orientation; re-creative criticism, to its unique artistic individuality; and judicial criticism, to its artistic value. These aspects of criticism are mutually conditioning factors of a single organic process: their relation to one another is strictly analogous to the interrelation of style, individuality, and value in the work of art itself.

The special task of historical criticism is that of determining the nature and expressive intent of works of art in their historical context. It involves, on the one hand, the authentication of texts and monuments, and, on the other, their interpretation in the light of available biographical, social, cultural, and other types of evidence. It is only thus that we can hope to understand what it was that the authors or makers of works of art intended to express, and to interpret this intention in the light of *their* interests and cultural background.

The special task of re-creative criticism is that of apprehending imaginatively, through sensitive artistic response, what the artist has actually succeeded in expressing in a specific work of art. The re-creative critic will inevitably, and quite properly, *also* relate what he thus apprehends to his own interests and needs. But this act is not in itself integral to re-creative criticism, save in so far as it contributes positively to the critic's understanding of the work of art itself and *its* expressed content. The prefix "re," in the term "re-creation," is of crucial importance.

The special task of judicial criticism is that of estimating the value of a work of art in relation to other works of art and to other human values. This determination of value involves, as we shall see, an appeal to at least three distinguishable normative criteria—a strictly aesthetic criterion of formal artistic excellence, an epistemic criterion of truth, and a normative criterion of larger significance, greatness, or profundity.

It must be emphasized that these three aspects of criticism are in reality three complementary approaches to the work of art, and that each approach can be explored effectively only in conjunction with the other two. Historical inquiry divorced from sensitive re-creation and judicial appraisal can merely produce an uninspired chronicle of "objective" historical "facts" which, by themselves, must fail to determine the artistic nature and value of the works of art under consideration. The effort to re-create a work of art without any understanding of its historical context must fail to be truly *re*-creative and must remain a purely subjective reaction. And man's aesthetic response to art must lack all artistic significance if it is not accompanied by an appraisal of it in terms of appropriate artistic standards. But this evaluation of a work of art must remain purely academic, scientific, or moralistic, if it is undertaken without historical perspective and without artistic sensitivity.

Thus, re-creative apprehension and judicial appraisal are both conditioned by historical orientation. Really to *re*-create a work of art is to apprehend the content which its author actually expressed in it, i.e., to interpret it correctly as a vehicle of communication. Such apprehension implies not only a general understanding of the medium employed but a familiarity with the artist's language and idiom, and these, in turn, are determined by his school, period, and culture as well as by his own personality. It also implies a knowledge of the artist's times and of his intellectual and spiritual environment. Without such historical orientation no critic, however artistically sensitive, can escape critical "sentimentality," that is, an illegitimate intrusion into the work of art of what does not exist in it and a failure to apprehend certain of its essential ingredients. Judicial appraisal, in turn, must be arbitrary and unfair unless it is based upon an historically objective understanding of what is appraised. The question, What is it worth? presupposes the question, What is it? and this question can be answered only within an historical frame of reference.

Similarly, the re-creation of a work of art in all its individuality is essential to both historical and judicial criticism. It conditions the work of the historian of art and literature because the subject-matter of such historical study can be determined only in terms of immediate artistic response. Only man's artistic sensitivity can reveal what is and what is not a "work of art," and so, what does and what does not constitute the appropriate subject-matter of artistic and literary history. On the other hand, only that can be subjected to valid artistic appraisal [3] which has been faithfully re-created. Appraisal cannot be based on rules or principles permitting of a purely mechanical application. We must "feel" what we would judge; our appraisal must be based upon an immediate artistic experience in the presence of the work of art itself.

Finally, though judicial appraisal is in a sense the culmination of criticism, it actually pervades the entire critical enterprise. Try as we may to postpone appraisal until the historical and re-creative tasks have been completed, we shall discover that we have been appraising the objects of artistic contemplation from the very outset. We are inescapably normative in all our thought and conduct. No sooner are we confronted with what purports to be a work of art than we evaluate it, however incipient may be this evaluation and how-

---

[3] i.e., appraisal which purports to be an objectively valid estimate of the work of art itself. Without such re-creation, appraisal is irrelevant to the work of art in question and records either a merely subjective preference or a merely mechanical application of academic rules.

ever often this preliminary judgment may be revised in the light of new historical evidence and fresh re-creative discovery. This normative compulsion is not only inescapable; it is essential to profitable historical inquiry and to fruitful artistic re-creation. For historical investigations which are not guided throughout by a sense of values and standards, both artistic and non-artistic, i.e., which lack normative perspective, tend to be trivial and inconsequential.[4] Significant historical research, in art as in other fields, must be guided by normative principles if it is to produce significant results. Artistic re-creation, in turn, can be no more than idle, self-indulgent play if the artistic quality and the truth and significance of art are ignored. Even the aesthete, who deprecates the categories of artistic truth and greatness, is, at his best, aware of "pure" artistic quality and prides himself on the refinement of his aesthetic taste.

The ideally all-round critic, then, is equally proficient in orienting himself historically to the work of art, in re-creating it, and in appraising it; and no critic can afford to be entirely deficient in any one of these three respects. But critics tend, as the result of temperament and training, to be predominantly historical, re-creative, or judicial in their basic approach to works of art in the several media. This predominant critical aptitude and interest, in turn, tends to identify them more or less closely with one or other of the great critical movements of a given culture. These movements, distinguished from one another by a major emphasis upon some aspect of the critical enterprise, may persist for centuries, but they acquire special importance during certain periods in history. Thus, in our modern European culture, "neoclassic" criticism, which was preponderantly judicial and which was distinguished for its allegiance to Aristotelian principles derived from the *Poetics,* flourished in the seventeenth and eighteenth centuries. "Romantic" criticism, which was preponderantly re-creative and which was distinguished for its interest in original genius, its emphasis upon the conceptually unanalyzable character of artistic quality, and its belief in the intuitive character of artistic apprehension, was the dominant critical movement of the first half of the nineteenth century. Finally, modern historical scholarship in literature and the fine arts achieved increasing importance during the second half of the nineteenth century and is still the dominant critical approach to art. These movements, I must repeat, differ from one another only in major emphasis, and the greatest figures in each movement owe their distinction to their unusual aptitude for all three types of criticism. But even the greatest critics tend to reflect the intellectual climate of their period and culture and to exhibit an affinity with one or other of the great critical movements.

---

4 When the minute researches of a factually-minded scholar unearth facts which more synoptic minds can use and interpret profitably, these discoveries must be regarded as happy accidents. It is clear that the best historical research is not conducted in this way.

If the ultimate interdependence of these three aspects of criticism is stead-fastly borne in mind, it is profitable to note that their logical order of priority differs from their psychological order of priority. Historical inquiry logically precedes artistic re-creation as its necessary (though insufficient) condition, because a work of art, especially when it belongs to another age or culture, simply cannot be understood without the requisite historical orientation. Re-creation, in turn, is the necessary (though insufficient) condition of judicial appraisal, since only that can be significantly appraised whose nature has been re-creatively apprehended. Psychological interest tends to reverse this order. We normally take pains to re-create what, at first glance, arouses our artistic interest (i.e., elicits a preliminary, more or less favorable, judicial estimate), and historical research in the realm of art is usually motivated by the desire to understand more adequately what we have already partially re-created and enjoyed.[5]

R. P. BLACKMUR

A Burden for Critics [1]

WHEN GEORGE SANTAYANA made his apology for writing a system of philosophy—one more after so many, one more after a lifetime of self-denial—he put his plea for forgiveness on the ground that he was an ignorant man, almost a poet. No doubt there was some reservation in Santayana's mind when he made that plea; no doubt there is some in mine when I adapt it to myself. This essay does not introduce a system of criticism; it is only a plea that criticism take up some of its possibilities that have been in abeyance, or in corruption, for some time; and it may be that like San-

---

[5] It might perhaps be argued that the professional critic's special prerogative is to offer and defend judicial estimates, and that the layman's chief interest in art is properly confined to artistic re-creation and enjoyment. But such a distinction between the lay-man and the critic would, if pressed, radically distort the unitary nature of man's response to art. In actuality, the layman is continually appraising what he apprehends and enjoys, and most professional critics have chosen to be critics, partly at least, be-cause of their unusual capacity for artistic re-creation and enjoyment. The more we consider the matter, the more inescapable is the conclusion that everyone who approaches art seriously, i.e., both re-creatively and judicially, is really a "critic," even though his critical equipment be more or less deficient.

[1] This essay, originally published in *The Hudson Review*, I (1948), 170–185, was reprinted in *Lectures in Criticism*, Bollingen Series XVI (New York: Pantheon Books, 1949). Reprinted by permission of the Bollingen Foundation, Inc. (Eds.)

tayana's philosophy it will look like an approach to a system. If so, it is the system of an ignorant man, and there is nothing in it that does not remind itself at every turn that it is the kind of ignorance which goes with being almost a poet. Poetry is one of the things we do to our ignorance; criticism makes us conscious of what we have done, and sometimes makes us conscious of what can be done next, or done again.

That consciousness is the way we feel the critic's burden. By a burden, I mean both a weight and a refrain, something we carry and something that carries us along, something we have in possession and something that reminds us what we are. It is the burden of our momentum. In relation to it we get work done. Out of relation to it we get nothing done, except so far as we are swept along; and of course we are mainly swept along. The critic's job is to put us into maximum relation to the burden of our momentum, which means he has to run the risk of a greater degree of consciousness than his mind is fit for. He risks substituting the formulas of relation for the things related. I take it the critic is a relativist; but his relativism does not need to be either deterministic or positivistic, as in our time it usually is; he may rather be the relativist of insight, aspiration, vision. He is concerned with choice, not prescription, with equity, not law; never with the dead hand, always with the vital purpose. He knows that the institution of literature, so far as it is alive, is made again at every instant. It is made afresh as part of the process of being known afresh; what is permanent is what is always fresh, and it can be fresh only in performance—that is, in reading and seeing and hearing what is actually in it at this place and this time. It is in performance that we find out relation to momentum. Or put another way, the critic brings to consciousness the means of performance.

Perform is a word of which we forget the singular beauty. Its meaning is: to furnish forth, to complete, to finish, in a sense which is influenced by the ideas clustered in the word *form;* so that *performance* is an enlightening name for one of our richest activities, rich with extra life. If it is the characteristic intent of the critic to see about the conditions of performance, it is his characteristic temptation to interfere with those conditions. He will find substitutes; he will make one condition do for every condition; he will make precedent do for balance, or rote for authority; and, worst of all, he will impose the excellence of something he understands upon something he does not understand. Then all the richness of actual performance is gone. It is worth taking precautions to prevent that loss, or at any rate to keep us aware of the risk.

The precautions of the past come down to us as mottoes; and for the critic of literature in our time I would suggest three mottoes—all Latin—as exemplary. *Omnis intellectus omniformis est:* every mind is omniform, every mind has latent in it all possible forms of the mind, even one's own mind.

The temptation is to make some single form of the mind seem omnicompetent; omnicompetence becomes omniscience and asserts for itself closed authority based upon a final revelation. *Omnis intellectus omniformis est.* This is a motto of the Renaissance, and leads us directly to a motto of the high Middle Ages, which preceded, or initiated, rather than followed, an era of absolute authority: *Fides quaerens intellectus.* If the temptation of the Renaissance was to put one's own version of the mind in first place, the temptation of the Middle Ages was to identify God with either one's own knowledge of him or with one's particular form of faith. *Fides quaerens intellectus* is a motto meant to redeem the temptation; for it is faith alone that may question the intellect, as it is only the intellect that can curb faith. The very principle of balance, together with the radical precariousness of its nature, lies in the reversibility of this motto. Just so, the value of both these mottoes is heightened by putting them into relation with a third, which is classical in its time, and which has to do primarily neither with intellect nor faith but with the temptation of the moral sensibility. *Corruptio optima pessima:* in corruption the best is the worst. Here, in this motto, is that hard core of common sense—Cochrane's phrase—of which the Christian world has never got enough in its heritage from classical culture. It reminds the moral ego of its fatal temptation to forget that the ground it stands on is not its own, but other, various, and equal. Surely we have made the best in us the worst when we have either pushed an insight beyond its field or refused, when using one insight, to acknowledge the pressure of all those insights—those visions of value—with which it is in conflict. If we do not see this, we have lost the feeling of richness, the sense of relation, and the power of judgment; and without these we cannot, as conscious critics, bring our experience of literature to actual performance. We should know neither what to bring, nor what to look for.

All this is generality; it applies to literature chiefly in the sense that literature is one aspect among many of the general human enterprise. The horror, for critics, of most aspects of that enterprise, is that they are exigent in action and will by no means stand still for criticism until they are done for. The beauty of literature is that it is exigent in the mind and will not only stand still but indeed never comes fully into its life of symbolic action until criticism has taken up the burden of bringing it into performance and finding its relation to the momentum of the whole enterprise. Both what constitutes performance and the very nature of relation—that is to say, what must be done and what may be taken for granted—change from time to time. It seems likely that one reason there has been so little great literature is that at most times so little has been required of it: how often has a Virgil felt obligated to create the myth of imperial culture? It is even more likely that the ability to cope with the task was wanting when required: how often has a Dante turned up to put into actual order all that had been running into the disorder of the rigid intellect and the arbitrary will? Ordinarily, past times have required little of literature in the way either of creating or ordering a culture. The artist's task was principally to express the continuity of his culture and the turbulence that underlay it. That is perhaps why we find the history of criticism so much concerned with matters of decorum: that is to say, with conformity, elegance, rhetoric, or metrics: matters not now commonly found or considered in the reviews. In our own time—if I may be permitted the exaggerations of ignorance and of poetry—almost everything is required of the arts and particularly of literature. Almost the whole job of culture, as it has formerly been understood, has been dumped into the hands of the writer. Possibly a new form of culture, appropriate to a massive urban society, is emerging: at any rate there are writers who write with a new ignorance and a new collective illiteracy: I mean the Luce papers and Hollywood. But the old drives persist. Those who seem to be the chief writers of our time have found their subjects in attempting to dramatize at once both the culture and the turbulence it was meant to control, and in doing so they have had practically to create—as it happens, to re-create—the terms, the very symbolic substance, of the culture as they went along.

I do not mean that this has happened by arrogation on the part of the writers; I mean they have been left alone with this subject as part of the actual experience of life in our time: which is always the subject which importunes every serious writer if he is honest and can keep himself free of the grosser hallucinations. The actual is always the medium through which the visitation of the Muse is felt. Perhaps a distinction will clarify what is meant. It is getting on towards a century since Matthew Arnold suggested that poetry could perhaps take over the expressive functions of religion. Possibly Arnold only meant the functions of the Church of England and the lesser dissenting sects. Whatever he meant, it did not happen, it could not and it cannot happen. All poetry can do is to dramatize, to express, what has actually happened to religion. This it has done. It has not replaced or in any way taken over the functions of religion; but it has been compelled to replace the operative force of religion as a resource with the discovery, or creation, of religion as an aesthetic experience. The poet has to put his religion itself into his poetry along with his experience of it. Think, together, of the religious poetry of George Herbert and of T. S. Eliot: of how little Herbert had to do before he got to his poetry, of how much Eliot is compelled to put into his poetry before he is free to write it. Consider too—and perhaps this is more emphatic of what has happened—the enormous mass of exegetical criticism it has seemed necessary and desirable to apply to Eliot's poetry and indeed to the whole school of Donne. This criticism neither compares, nor judges; it elucidates scripture.

Let us put the matter as a question. Why do we treat poetry, and gain by doing so, after much the same fashion as Augustine treated the scriptures in the Fifth Century? Why do we make of our criticism an essay in the understanding of words and bend upon that essay exclusively every tool of insight and analysis we possess? Why do we have to re-create so much of the poem in the simple reading which is only the preface to total performance? Do we, like Augustine, live in an interregnum, after a certainty, anticipating a synthesis? If so, unlike Augustine, we lack a special revelation: we take what we can find, and what we find is that art is, as Augustine sometimes thought, a human increment to creation. If this is so, how, then, has it come about?

We know very well how it has come about, and we come late enough in the sequence of our time so that we can summarize it in what looks like an orderly form—or at any rate a poetic form. It composes into something we can understand. We come late in a time when the burden of descriptive and historical knowledge is greater than any man or group of men can encompass; when the labor by which our society gets along from day to day is not only divided but disparate and to the individual laborer fragmentary; and when, in an effort to cope with the burden of knowledge and the division of labor, we have resorted to the adulterative process called universal education.

As a natural effect of such a situation we have the disappearance or at least the submergence of tradition in the sense that it is no longer available at either an instinctive or a critical level but must be looked for, dug out, and largely re-created as if it were a new thing and not tradition at all. We have also a decay of the power of conviction or mastery; we permit ourselves everywhere to be overwhelmed by the accidents of our massive ignorance and by the apparent subjectivity of our individual purposes. Thus we have lost the field of common reference, we have dwindled in our ability to think symbolically, and as we look about us we see all our old unconscious skills at life disappearing without any apparent means of developing new unconscious skills.

We have seen rise instead a whole series of highly conscious, but deeply dubious and precarious skills which have been lodged in the sciences of psychology, anthropology, and sociology, together with the whole confusion of practices which go with urbanization. Consider how all these techniques have been developed along lines that discover trouble, undermine purpose, blight consciousness, and prevent decision; how they promote uncertainty, insecurity, anxiety, and incoherence; how above all they provide barriers between us and access to our common enterprise. Perhaps the unwieldy and unmanipulable fact of urbanization does more of the damage than the conscious techniques.

But this is not a diagnosis, it is a statement of sequence, a composition of things in relation. At the point where we arrest this sequence, and think in terms of what we can remember of our old culture, does it not seem plain to us what we have? Do we not have a society in which we see the attrition of law and rational wisdom and general craft? Do we not have an age anti-intellectual and violent, in which there is felt a kind of total responsibility to total disorder? Who looks ahead except to a panacea or a millenium which is interchangeable with an invoked anarchy, whether in the world or in the individual personality? Do we not above all each day wonderfully improve our chances of misunderstanding each other? These are the questions we ask of a living, not a dead, society.

They become more emphatic when we ask them about the schools of art and criticism which accompanied this shift in the structure of society. If we begin with Arnold's effort at the secularization of the old culture, it is easy to remind ourselves of the sequence which it began. Here it is, in very rough order. The hedonism in Pater, the naturalism of Zola, the impressionism of Anatole France, Art for Art as of the 90's, the naturalistic relativism of de Gourmont, the aestheticism of the psychologists, the rebirth of symbolism (as in Mallarmé and Yeats), the private mind, Imagism and Free verse, futurism, expressionism and expressive form, Dada and surrealism, dream literature, spontaneous or automatic form, anti-intellectual form, the school of Donne in English and American poetry, the stream of consciousness (that libel on Joyce), the revolution of the word, the new cult of the word. Some of these phrases will carry different meanings to different people; let us say that the general sequence runs towards some kind of autonomous and absolute creation and therefore towards total literalism.

That is on the positive side. On the negative side, every school on the list except Arnold's secularism, which was less a school than a plea for one, is an attack on disinterestedness of mind and imagination, though none of them meant to be so. And Arnold, who meant just the opposite, helped them at their business by seeing too much necessity in the offing. All of them either accepted or revolted violently against a predetermined necessity; none of them was able to choose necessity or to identify it with his will. None of them was apparently acquainted with the sense of our Latin mottoes. Their only causes were Lost Causes; their only individuals were atoms; they reflected their time, as schools must.

The world has about now caught up with these trains of ideas, these images, trends, habits, patterns, these tendencies towards either mass action or isolated action—equally violent whether in attraction or repulsion. It is a world of engineers and anarchs; rather like the Roman world when the impulse of Virgil and the Emperor Augustus had died out and the impulse of Benedict and Augustine had not yet altered the direction and aspect of the general momentum. It is a world alive and moving but which does not understand itself.

Of this world individual artists have given a much better account than the doctrines of their schools would suggest, and they have done so for two reasons. The arts cannot help reacting directly and conventionally to what is actual in their own time; nor can the arts help, whether consciously or not, working into their masterpieces what has survived of the full tradition—however they may contort or corrupt it. They deal with life or experience itself, both what is new and what is accumulated, inherited, still living. They cannot come *de novo*. They cannot help, therefore, creating at a disinterested level, despite themselves. That is why they constitute a resource of what is not new—the greater part of ourselves—and a means of focusing what is new, all that necessarily aggravates us and tears at our nerve ends in our friction with it. That is why Chartres Cathedral survives better than the schools of the Bishop of Chartres; though both were equally vital in their time.

Consider in this light what seem to be the masterpieces of our time. Consider the poetry of Eliot, Yeats, Valéry, Rilke; the novels of Joyce, Gide, Hemingway, Proust, Mann, Kafka; the plays of Shaw, Pirandello, O'Neill; the music of Stravinsky, Bloch, Bartok, Ravel, Satie, Schoenberg; the painting of Matisse, Picasso, Rouault, Marin, Hartley; the sculptor of Maillol, Brancusi, Faggi, LaChaise, Zorach, Archipenko, Moore. Think also, but at another level, not easy to keep in strict parallel, of the architecture of Leviathan: the railway station at Philadelphia, the Pentagon, the skyscrapers, the gasoline stations, the highway systems, the east and west side highways, apartment houses each a small city, and the interminable multiple dwellings. Think too of the beautiful bridges which connect or traverse eyesores: the Washington Bridge, the Pulaski Skyway. Lastly, for architecture, think of the National Parks, with their boulevards running at mountain peak.

What an expression of an intolerable, disintegrating, irrational world: a doomed world, nevertheless surviving, throwing up value after value with inexhaustible energy but without a principle in sight. And how difficult to understand the arts which throw up the values. Only Hemingway and Maillol in the roster above perhaps made works which seem readily accessible when seriously approached. Shaw is as difficult as Joyce, Mann as Kafka, if you really look into them. The difficulties arise, it seems to me, partly because of the conditions of society outlined above as they affect the audience and partly because of these same conditions as they affect the artist at his work. The two are not the same, though they are related. The audience is able to bring less to the work of art than under the conditions of the old culture, and the artist is required to bring more. What has changed its aspect is the way the institutions, the conceptions, the experience of culture gets into the arts. What has happened is what was said above: almost the whole job of culture has been dumped on the artist's hands.

It is at this point that we begin to get at the burden of criticism in our time. It is, to put it one way, to make bridges between the society and the arts: to prepare the audience for its art and to prepare the arts for their artists. The two kinds of preparation may sometimes be made in one structure; but there is more often a difference of emphasis required. Performance, the condition we are after, cannot mean the same thing to the audience and the artist. The audience needs instruction in the lost skill of symbolic thinking. The arts need rather to be shown how their old roles can be played in new conditions. To do either, both need to be allied to the intellectual habits of the time. Besides analysis, elucidation, and comparison, which Eliot once listed as the functions of criticism, criticism in our time must also come to judgment.

If we look at the dominant development in criticism in English during the last thirty years—all that Mr. Ransom means by the New Criticism—with its fineness of analysis, its expertness of elucidation, and its ramifying specialization of detail—we must see how natural, and at bottom how facile, a thing it has been. It has been the critics' way of being swept along, buoyed more by the rush than by the body of things. It is a criticism, that is, which has dealt almost exclusively either with the executive technique of poetry (and only with a part of that) or with the general verbal techniques of language. Most of its practitioners have been men gifted in penetrating the private symbolisms and elucidating the language of all that part of modern poetry we have come to call the school of Donne. With a different criticism possibly another part of modern poetry might have become dominant, say the apocalyptic school—though of course I cannot myself think so. In any case, it was a criticism created to cope with and develop the kind of poetry illustrated by Eliot's *Wasteland* and Yeats' *Tower,* two poems which made desperate attempts to reassert the tradition under modern conditions: Eliot by Christianity, Yeats by a private philosophy. Eminently suited for the *initial* stages of the criticism of this poetry, it has never been suited to the later stages of criticism; neither Eliot nor Yeats has been compared or judged because there has been no criticism able to take those burdens. For the rest, the "new criticism" has been suited for *some* older poetry, but less because of the nature of the poetry than because of the limitation of the modern reader. For most older poetry it is not suited for anything but sidelights, and has therefore made misjudgments when applied. It is useless for Dante, Chaucer, Goethe, or Racine. Applied to drama it is disfiguring, as it is to the late seventeenth and all the eighteenth century poetry. Yet it has had to be used and abused because there has seemed no other way of re-creating—in the absence of a positive culture outside poetry—a verbal sensibility capable of coping with the poetry at all. In a stable society with a shared culture capable of convictions, masteries, and vital dogmas, such a criticism might have needed only its parallel developments for the novel and the play and the older forms of all literature; such a society does not need much criticism. But in an unstable society like ours, precisely because the burden put upon the arts is so unfamiliar and so extensive (it is always the maximum burden in intensity) a multiple burden is put upon criticism to bring the art to full performance. We have to compare and judge as well as analyze and elucidate. We have to make plain not only what people are reading, but also—as Augustine and the other fathers had to do with the scriptures—what they are reading about.

Here I do not wish to be misunderstood. Critics are not fathers of a new church. I speak from a secular point of view confronting what I believe to be a secular world which is not well understood; and I suppose what I want criticism to do can as well as not be described as the development of aesthetic judgment—the judgment of the rational imagination—to conform with the vast increase of material which seems in our time capable only of aesthetic experience. This is not to define a revelation or create a society. It is to define and explore the representations in art of what is actually going on in existing society. I see no reason why all forms of the word *aesthetic* cannot be restored to good society among literary critics by remembering its origin in a Greek word meaning to perceive, and remembering also its gradual historical limitation to what is perceived or felt—that is, what is actually there—in the arts. I have here the company of Bergson who thought that the serious arts gave the aesthetic experience of the true nature of what the institutions of society are meant to control. And in another way, I have more support than I want in the philosophy of Whitehead, who found that the sciences in new growth, far from giving us knowledge with relation among its parts, give us instead abstractions good for practical manipulation but comfortable only to a mystery. As a consequence, his philosophy of organism, with its attribution of feeling relations everywhere, is an aesthetic philosophy; in which knowledge comes to us as an aesthetic experience.

We do not need to go so far as Whitehead. The sort of thing that is wanted here to go on with seems to show clearly in James Joyce, whose *Ulysses* is the direct aesthetic experience of the breakdown of the whole Graeco-Christian world, not only in emotion but also in concept. Or again, Mann's *Magic Mountain* is the projected aesthetic experience of both that whole world and the sickness which is breaking it down. And again, Gide's *Counterfeiters* is a kind of gratuitous aesthetic experience—a free possibility—of what is happening along with the breakdown. Lastly, Eliot's religious poetry is a partly utopian and partly direct aesthetic experience of the actual Christian life today. That is what these works are about, and they cannot be judged aesthetically until full stock has been taken of what they are about. For us, they create their subjects; and indeed it is the most conspicuous thing about them that they do so. On each of these authors—even Eliot in his kind of reference—the whole substance of his subject is a necessary part of the aesthetic experience of it. It is for that reason that we have to judge the subject as well as what is done with it. To exaggerate only a little, in the world as it is, there is no way to get a mastery of the subject except in the aesthetic experience. How do we go about doing so?

That is, how does criticism enlarge its aesthetics to go with the enlargement of aesthetic experience? Here we must take again the risk of generalization, and we must begin with a generalization to get what the sciences have done with aesthetics out of the way. If we do not get rid of them by generalization we cannot get rid of them at all, for in detail their techniques are very tempting. Let us say then that psychology turns aesthetics into the mechanics of perception, that scientific logic turns it into semasiology, just as technical philosophers had already turned it into a branch of epistemology. All these studies are troublemakers and lead, like our social studies, to the proliferation of a sequence of insoluble and irrelevant problems so far as the critic of literature is concerned. Let us put it provisionally, that for the literary critic aesthetics comprises the study of superficial and mechanical executive techniques, partly in themselves, but also and mainly in relation to the ulterior techniques of conceptual form and of symbolic form. I do not say that one of these is deeper or more important than another, certainly not in isolation. But let us take them in the order given, and generalize a program of work.

By superficial and mechanical executive techniques I mean the whole rationale of management and manipulation through more or less abitrary devices which can be learned, which can be made elegant, and which are to some extent the creatures of taste or fashion so far as particular choice is concerned. In some lucky cases they may be the sole preoccupation of the working artist, as in some unlucky cases they may be the one aspect of his work to which he seemingly pays least attention. In our own day they are troublesome to the extent that they are ignored in an abeyance from which they ought to be redeemed. It would seem to me, for example, that a considerable amount of potentially excellent verse fails to make its way because the uses of metre—in the sense that all verse has metre—are not well understood, though they are now beginning again to be played with: Mr. Eliot has just resorted to the metrics of Johnson and Milton. The critic who is capable of doing so ought to examine into the metres of his victims. Similarly, the full narrative mode is in little use by serious novelists, and the full dramatic mode is not in much more use; yet these are the basic modes of a man telling a story. If only because they are difficult, the critic ought to argue for them when he sees a weakness which might have been turned into a strength by their use. Again, and related to the two previous examples, there is a great deal of obscurity in modern writing which could be cleared up if writers could be forced (only by criticism) to develop a skill in making positive statement, whether generalized or particular, whether in verse or in prose. Statement may make art great and ought not to be subject to fashion.

And so on. The critic can have little authority as a pedagogue. The main study of executive techniques will always be, to repeat, in relation to the ulterior techniques of conceptual and symbolic form. By conceptual techniques I mean the rationale of what the artist does with his dominant convictions, or obsessions, or insights, or visions, and how they are translated into major stresses of human relations as they are actually experienced. Here we are concerned with the aesthetics of the idea in relation to the actual, of the rational in relation to what is rationalised. In Dostoevsky, for example, we are interested in his conception of the Double only as we see what happens to it in the character of Versilov, or Raskolnikov, or Dmitri Karamazov. In Joyce's *Ulysses* it is not the Homeric pattern of father and son that counts, but what happens to the conception of intransigence in Stephen in concert and conflict with that transigent man Bloom. So in the later poems of Yeats, the concepts of the Phases of the Moon are interesting as they work or fail to work in the chaos and anarchy and order of actual lyric emotions. On a more generalized level, it is through concern with conceptual techniques that one notes that the European novels of greatest stature seem to follow, not the conceptual pattern of Greek tragedy but the pattern of Christian rebirth, conversion, or change of heart; which is why novels do not have tragic heroes. But examples are endless.

And all of them, as those just cited, would tend if pursued to lead us into the territory of symbolic techniques which underlies and transcends them. I am not satisfied with the term. By symbolic techniques I mean what happens in the arts—*what gets into the arts*—that makes them relatively inexhaustible so long as they are understood. I mean what happens in the arts by means of fresh annunciations of residual or traditional forces, whether in the language, culture, or institutions of the artist's society. I mean those forces that operate in the arts which are greater than ourselves and come from beyond or under ourselves. But I am not satisfied with the definitions any more than I am with the term. It may be I mean invokable forces, or raw forces, the force of reality, whatever reality may be, pressing into and transforming our actual experience. It is what bears us and what we cannot bear except through the intervention of one of the great modes of the mind, religion, philosophy, or art, which, giving us the illusion of distance and control, makes *them,* too, seem forces greater than ourselves. It is in the figure of Dante himself in the *Divine Comedy,* Faustus in *Faustus,* Hamlet and Lear in *Hamlet* and *Lear,* Emma Bovary in *Madame Bovary,* all the brothers in *The Brothers Karamazov*. It is in the conjunction of the gods of the river and of the sea with the Christian gods in Eliot's *Dry Salvages*. It is the force of reality pressing into the actuality of symbolic form. Its technique is the technique of so concentrating or combining the known techniques as to discover or release that force. It is for this purpose and in this way that the executive, conceptual, and symbolic techniques go rationally together: the logic, the rhetoric, and the poetic; they make together the rationale of that enterprise in the discovery of life which is art. But the arts are not life, though in the sense of this argument they may make a rationale for discovering life. Whether they do or not, and how far, is the act of judgment that is also the last act in bringing particular works of art to full performance. Because the arts are imperfect, they can be judged only imperfectly by aesthetic means. They must be judged, therefore, by the declaration and elucidation of identity in terms of the whole enterprise which they feed, and of which they are the play, the aesthetic experience. There is a confusion here that cannot be clarified for it is a confusion of real things, as words are confused in a line of verse, the better the line the more completely, so that we cannot tell which ones govern the others. The confusion is, that it is through the aesthetic experience of it that we discover, and discover again, what life is, and that at present, if our account of it is correct, we also discover what our culture is. It is therefore worthwhile considering the usefulness of a sequence of rational critical judgments upon the art of our time as an aid in determining the identity, the meaning in itself, of present society. Such a sequence of judgments might transform us who judge more than the art judged.

Here perhaps is a good point to sweep some bad rubbish into the bins. Critical judgment need not be arrogant in its ambitions, only in its failures. Nor is it concerned with ranks and hierarchies, except incidentally. What I mean by judgment is what Aristotle would have meant by the fullest possible declaratory proposition of identity. Again, the ideal of judgment—no more to be reached by critics than by other men—is theological: as a soul is judged finally, quite apart from its history, for what it really is at the moment of judgment. Our human approximation of such judgment will be reached if we keep the ideal of it in mind and with that aid make our fullest act of recognition. Judgment is the critic's best recognition.

Thus it is now clear that my purpose in proposing a heavy burden for criticism is, to say the least of it, evangelical. What I want to evangelise in the arts is rational intent, rational statement, and rational technique; and I want to do it through technical judgment, clarifying judgment, and the judgment of discovery, which together I call rational judgment. I do not know if I should have enough eloquence to persuade even myself to consider such a burden for criticism, did I not have, not this time as precautions but as mentors, my three Latin mottoes. *Omnis intellectus omniformis est. Fides quaerens intellectus. Corruptio optima pessima.* They point the risk, and make it worth taking.

The Validity of the Aesthetic Judgment

GEORGE BOAS
The Authority of Criticism[1]

So FAR WE HAVE been talking about what critics find in works of art and artistry; the question will be immediately asked, What ought they to find? Ought they like Muther to see in Daumier simply a caricaturist or like Meier-Graefe the precursor of the Post-impressionists? Ought they to see in *Hamlet* the triumph of thought over action or the technical difficulties of making the tragedy last for five acts? Ought they to see in Matisse the culmination of Ingres or the decay of capitalism?

There are two outstanding meanings of the word "ought" as it is used. The first signifies the rule as given in natural science: a falling body ought to increase its velocity according to a well known mathematical formula; the temperature and pressure of a gas ought to vary according to another. It would appear as if in such sentences "ought" were superfluous. But as a matter of fact it is not. For scientific laws are not descriptive of natural events as they actually occur, but of natural events as they would occur under highly simplified and controlled conditions. The simplification and control are undertaken with a view to keeping the scientific account of things consistent. Thus the law of falling bodies is strictly true only in a vacuum and Boyle's law is true only of "perfect" gases—which may be defined circularly as gases which obey it. Nevertheless, the scientist knows and can measure the influences which cause reality to deviate from perfection, and consequently though he is describing what has been called ideal, as con-

---

[1] From George Boas, *A Primer for Critics* (Baltimore: The Johns Hopkins Press, 1937), pp. 138–148. Reprinted by permission. (Eds.)

trasted with real, situations, he is not dealing with fancies, dreams, or fictions. He knows that when things do not obey the laws which they ought to obey, either they are not the things he thought they were or that some circumstance is present which deflects them from strict obedience.

The second meaning of "ought" reduces to prediction. If certain things are done, then certain desirable effects will follow; therefore these things "ought" to be done. A man "ought" to obey the Ten Commandments, for, if he did, he would please God, or be happy, or go to Heaven, or what not. A sonnet "ought" to have fourteen lines, for if it does, it will be like all other sonnets. When a discussion arises over whether a given act ought to be performed, it will be seen upon scrutiny always to rest upon the question of its desirability. But sometimes it is asked whether one "ought" to desire certain results, as if there were an immutable and universal rule prescribing human wishes. Riches, for instance, are admitted to be desirable in the sense of being desired, but "ought" people to desire them? Fame, pleasure, power, too, are frequently criticised as unwarranted desires; no one denies that people do desire them, but many have denied that people "ought" to desire them.

What such criticism means is that if people did not desire riches, fame, pleasure, and power, but something else—not necessarily poverty, obscurity, pain, and weakness,—the effects of their acts would be the realization of their critic's desires. Thus when a Christian preaches meekness, on the ground that the meek shall inherit the earth, he means first that if one were meek, one would inherit the earth—a simple prediction—and second, that everyone actually does desire to inherit the earth. For if no one desired to inherit the earth, it would never be advanced as a good. We must assume, that is, that complete hypocrisy has never obtained in human history and that, for instance, even the saints actually and honestly desired the saintly life, however bizarre it may seem to sinners.

Now no one ever questioned the legitimacy or the universality of his own desires. A child is surprised and affronted when his parents tell him that learning is more to be desired than play; neither its instrumental nor its terminal values appeal to him. So a dog seems to agree with Plato that the pleasures of smell are the highest than any animal can attain. One's desires, it will be noticed, are always questioned by others, never by oneself. One might outgrow one's desires as new instincts and appetites develop with maturity, but within any one period of one's taste, it would be impossible for an individual to stand outside himself and say, "What I desire is not desirable." Self-criticism arises out of the criticism of others; one's own desires are standards until someone questions them.

They are standards not only for ourselves but for everyone else. For we naturally believe others to be like ourselves until their difference is proved. When proved, it is first not evidence of diversity, but of abnormality. It requires a certain education to be willing to admit that human nature is not all of a piece and that one's own nature is not a fair sample of all humanity. There are to be sure some desires and interests which are fairly pervasive though apparently none,—not even those needed for self-preservation— which cannot be eradicated. And the discovery in others of desires similar to one's own is always treated as evidence of the essential rightness of their value. For it is proof of the normality of one's character, both in the sense of its usualness and of its typicality.

Yet an objective study of the history of taste, both within the growth of any individual and that of the race, shows that no desires are eternal and no standards universal. Standards emerge out of the confusion of appetites and acquire authority; they are neither omnipresent nor omnipotent. Their compulsive force is achieved by historical accident—in the Aristotelian sense of "accident"—and is not inherent in their essential nature. Thus people at all times and in all societies have treated the most diverse satisfactions as if they were rooted in the very nature of humanity, logically deducible from it, and necessary to its happiness. But as a matter of fact, even in primitive societies, there is conflict of ideals and whatever uniformity has been attained is due to various repressive means, varying from taboos to moral suasion.

Within the lives of individuals we can observe even biologically harmful acts taking on compulsive force. The psychiatric clinics are full of people who cannot help performing rites which seem to those of us who do not share their feelings as trivial, nonsensical, vicious, shameful, childish, perverse. They are in the clinics because they feel the necessity of performing these rites, not because they share society's opinion of them. That feeling of necessity is as strong as the saint's and the hero's. Consequently the appeal to conscience, common-sense, and general practice proves nothing more about values than the extent of their appeal.

One might lay down as the first principle of the history of taste—moral taste as well as aesthetic and group as well as individual—the necessity of the habitual. That habit is second nature is a platitude dating at least from Aristotle, and one's second nature is as strong, if not so ineradicable, as one's first. We know that since habit is acquired and not innate it might be different from what it is; we also know that when it is once established, it operates unconsciously; we know finally that it has the same compulsive force which reformers would like to see resident in the acts of which they approve.

When several people, or a social group, have the same interests, it is clear that they will share the same habits and that their social habits will be unquestioned until someone arises who finds them unsatisfactory or until the environment changes to the point of making them inconvenient. Thus peace could become an ideal in a militaristic society only if someone actually found war unsatisfactory; but the dissatisfaction would have to be very great to overcome the dislike of deviating from the habitual, for the very fact of being habitual confers unquestionable sanctity. In the case of war, we know that people have lamented its existence since the days of Hesiod, but no one tried to depreciate the values upon respect for which its existence depends until modern times. Hesiod bewailed the fact of war but he was not a pacifist; war to him was probably a necessary evil. Even now the men who benefit from war do not deprecate it. They tend on the contrary to range between lamenting its existence while pleading for its inevitability and praising it to the skies as the father of all the manly virtues. When no one benefits from war and everyone knows and feels the harm it does, then only can there be a genuine revulsion from it. But until that time the inertia of custom plus the actual benefits it confers will keep it alive and flourishing.

The necessity of the habitual accounts for the turning of instrumental into terminal values. For what is felt to be necessary—felt, not merely known—is retained in the social order and that which is good-in-itself is that which is no longer good-for-anything-else. However useful certain practices may have been in their origin, one cannot argue to their continued usefulness because of their survival. Antiquity itself is considered valuable and the very fact that a practice or object is ancient is considered evidence of its worth. This is the explanation, as we have tried to suggest above, for the rise of the fine out of the useful arts. And this is also the reason why the fine arts are especially cultivated in wealthy societies and at times when the leisure class can afford to pay for the useless. We do not mean to deny that in any society an object which pleases the senses may not be preferred to one which does not; we mean simply to say that great wealth alone permits the encouragement of the fine arts on a grand scale, though what the patron really is buying is flattery.

One can no more give a reason why society should retain so many obsolete and obsolescent institutions than one can explain the retention of vestigial organs in animals and plants. One can trace their history and demonstrate their quondam utility but that gives no reason for their retention, if by "reason" one mean "present utility." Their survival must simply be accepted as a fact and along with their survival must be accepted the reverence and love which human beings have for them. The problem is one for the psychologist, not for the philosopher, for nothing is easier for the philosopher than to demonstrate the uselessness—and hence, as he is likely to believe, the stupidity—of whatever has no purpose. But if one began to legislate against the useless, one would begin with the world as a whole.

Every appetite, desire, velleity, confers value upon its object. But just as there emerges sooner or later within the same individual some order which reconciles or integrates his interests, so in society there is a dominant group whose interests give character to the whole. Thus when we speak of "the Greeks" we usually mean a small group of Athenians living in the fifth and fourth centuries B. C.; we seldom mean the Spartans or Thebans, and never the slaves or peasants. When we speak of the Renaissance Italians, do we ever mean the working class upon whose shoulders—if not upon whose brains—rested the burden of the courtly magnificence? Historians of the future speaking of present-day Russians will not mean the surviving nobles of the Old Regime nor the thousands of unabsorbed tradesmen and farmers; they will mean the leaders of the Communist Party. Consequently when we read histories of the various arts, we find their subject matter to have been taken from those objects approved by the social group whose tastes are harmonious with the historian's. But as taste changes, new figures appear in the histories, obscure personages emerge into the foreground and artists who were popular in their time drop into the background. Thus people like William Blake, Daumier, Melville, are considered much more important by people of a later day than by their contemporaries, and the latter are blamed for not appreciating their greatness; Tupper, Bouguereau, Longfellow, who produced works eminently satisfying to their contemporaries, are either omitted from the histories or held up as horrible examples of the bad taste of their times. But taste in itself can be neither good nor bad, and the task of the historian of art is not to praise or blame but to analyse and record and, if possible, explain.

The reconciliation of conflict is effected in a variety of ways. The most potent is *snobisme,* either up or down. By *snobisme* I mean the acceptance of the values of people one admires. The average student in an art school, for example, will graduate having absorbed all the standards of his teachers; he will apologize for his judgments on several grounds: the authority of teachers, the eternality of the beautiful, tradition, progress. What such arguments turn into when analysed is a statement of one's taste in abstract terms accompanied by the belief that an abstract statement is an explanation. Thus when one says one admires Renoir for his opulent line, one thinks one has explained why Renoir is admirable; but suppose an opulent line disgusts someone? Again, the neo-classic artists—Pope, David, Canova—are often reproached for their "coldness"; why should one not be cold? The truth is that the leading critics, who are men of learning (Sainte-Beuve), or of artistic reputation (Coleridge), or brilliant journalists (Mencken), or influential teachers (Brunetière), utilize their prestige and their forensic ability to present their taste in a form which turns out to be persuasive. Their arguments fall to pieces when analysed by people who do not share their tastes, but to people who do, they seem to rest upon self-evident truths.[2]

Snobisme, though the most important reconciler of conflict, is supplemented by force. This force may be economic pressure, (in the form of advertising), propaganda, and persecution. One has only to think of such terms as "the American scene," "art for the people," "Christian art," "modernism," as terms of praise, to appreciate the effectiveness of force. One could make out as good a case for the picturesque non-American scene, art for the élite, pagan art, and classicism, as for these. But since taste is not exclusively aesthetic, but also ethical, political, even scientific, changing as civilization changes, certain phrases and rhetorical themes will have a power which their opposites will not have. It is no accident that the absorption of a time-dimension into mathematical physics, the growth of the biological sciences, the spread of statistics, all occurred contemporaneously with the vogue for the dynamic, the vital, the original, the novel. For science and philosophy are the most fertile sources of principles of approbation, and in the seventeenth century when clock-work was the model of the universe, mechanical properties permeated all fields of taste down to social etiquette.

There are some interests, however, which are never reconciled. Their sponsors, like Greuze and Rudyard Kipling, live on to see their ideals superseded and their devils become gods. But they still have their admirers and patrons. People still read Kipling and Whistler's *Mother,* as it is popularly called, drew record crowds on its recent tour of America. Yet no one would say that either Kipling or Whistler were representative of our times. Taste is stratified in every era, the taste of a generation ago, of to-day, of to-morrow, existing in layers. The partizans of each declare it to be eternal, as lovers swear that their love is eternal each time that it shifts.

What then the critic can authoritatively do in the field of terminal values is somewhat limited. He can make predictions based upon his own experience and that of people of his sort. He can predict the relative intensity of the aesthetic experience and its probable duration. He can also point out the novelty, or lack of it, which he believes the work of art to possess and classify the type of value: beauty, grotesqueness, sublimity, etc. In each of these investigations he is measuring the worth of the work of art, for the most intense and the more enduring are both terms of praise in the minds of some people and the novel in the present age is at a premium. Finally, to perceive the conformity of a work of art to type has always been the special delight of human beings, who still are likely to shun the

---

[2] See the quotations from Gérard de Lairesse and Tieck in Muther's *The History of Modern Painting,* II, 33f., and *The Foundations of Aesthetics* by Ogden, Richards, and Woods, *passim.*

peculiar and individual because it is by its very nature *sui generis*. Every-thing, *sui generis* or not, has some form, but to be able to see it when no text-book has told one its name, is too much to ask of most of us. Thus we rest content when we know what "the" fugue is, or "the" sonnet, or "the" novel, and can see these Platonic essences embodied in some particular; our powers of perception are limited by our powers of reasoning, and, as Aris-totle remorselessly dismissed the unusual as the monstrous, the perverse, or the unnatural, we are willing to dismiss what we can only enjoy without classification as the trivial or the exceptional. Plato and Aristotle explained the unintelligible as the mischievous effect of matter; the dream of a work of art, one might expect, would be—and indeed it usually is—more perfect than the reality. If we accept the metaphysics which lies behind this, our impatience with what we cannot understand is reasonable. But to accept the metaphysics involves such enormous commitments, that most of us would perhaps prefer to admit the existence of individuals and their respectabil-ity.

BERNARD C. HEYL

Relativism Again[1]

> "As there are different beauties, all of equal grace, in different
> bodies, different judges of like intelligence will judge them to be of
> great variety among themselves, each according to his predilection."
> Dürer.

A PERNICIOUS AND PREVALENT idea claims that there are only two possible critical positions toward evaluation. Accordingly we must either be subjectivists or objectivists, nihilists or absolutists. No middle ground is possible. This idea, which has been the major source of criticism of my book, *New Bearings in Esthetics and Art Criticism,* needs refutation.

In the following pages I hope to show that a third position, relativism, is

---

[1] From Bernard C. Heyl, "Relativism Again," *Journal of Aesthetics and Art Criticism,* V (1946), 54–61. Reprinted by permission. (Eds.)

The problems discussed in this essay are by no means new. Because of their impor-tance, however, and because contemporary art criticism is, in the main, undistinguished, a reconsideration of critical theories seems desirable and timely. (B.C.H.)

one that presents basic differences from both subjectivism and absolutism.[2] An understanding of these differences should prove that relativism is the most satisfactory theory for the formulation of value judgments and should thus eliminate the alleged necessity for accepting either of two unsound alternatives.

Relativism and Subjectivism

According to subjectivism, value is best defined in terms of an individual response which, in the case of aesthetic value, ordinarily is an immediate emotional state that delights. It follows that the critic's evaluations are matters of individual tastes which are at once self-justifying and incapable of justification. They are unreasoned, arbitrary, intuitive preferences or likings. What *I* like is good and what *I* prefer is better. De gustibus non est disputandum. Thus subjectivist criticism is purely personal and impressionistic in that it aims to record in writing sensations experienced in the presence of a work of art.

According to relativism, value may also be defined in psychological terms. Like subjectivism, that is to say, one aspect of relativism holds that value exists, not ontologically, but psychologically—as, for example, "the qualitative content of an apprehending process." Though this similarity between their theories allies relativism with subjectivism and differentiates both from absolutism, relativism, unlike subjectivism, insists upon the necessity and importance, when evaluating, of deliberation and reflection. Mere preference and liking, though an essential condition, is an insufficient one for the activity of valuing, since that activity should in large measure depend upon the rational factor of thoughtful inquiry. This distinction between subjectivist and relativist theory—a distinction that one may also apply when differentiating "taste" and "judgment"—may be further elucidated, following John Dewey, by contrasting certain words in pairs, the first word indicating the preference of subjectivism, the second, the conclusion of relativism: desired and desirable, satisfying and satisfactory, admired and admirable. Thus relativist criticism is largely based upon cognitive judgment, upon a serious, reasoned discrimination between good and bad, better and worse.

The significance of these differences between subjectivism and relativism appears in the divergent answers these positions give to such crucial critical questions as the following: are some appreciations better than others? can

---

[2] Throughout I shall use the word "absolutism" rather than "objectivism" since the latter seems peculiarly subject to ambiguous interpretations. If anyone prefers to call *either* the absolutism *or* the relativism here discussed "objectivism," he is raising, of course, only a verbal problem.

superior artistic judgments be cultivated? is education in the Fine Arts possible?

The subjectivist critic, if he is consistent, must answer these questions negatively. Since value for him is an immediate and emotional, an unreasoned and unreflective state, he cannot show *why* one taste is superior to another, or *how* tastes may improve. Thus he cannot sensibly maintain that an unsophisticated, untutored evaluation is worse than his own. He can merely point out that it is different. These, then, are the disastrous consequences of subjectivism; for, as John Dewey explains, "The conception that mere liking is adequate to constitute a value situation makes no provision for the education and cultivation of taste and renders criticism, whether aesthetic, moral or logical, arbitrary and absurd." [3]

The relativist critic takes a very different stand. Believing that value is conditioned to a considerable extent by deliberation and reflection, he affirms that artistic sensitivity and appreciation may be enormously enhanced, perhaps even acquired, through training and experience. He is convinced, for example, that the change from one's youthful appreciations to those of maturity reflects genuine improvement: that, in some significant sense, Dickens is superior to Dreiser, Giotto to Taddeo Gaddi, Beethoven to Bruckner. Again, he claims that the judgment of the expert critic is superior to that of the naive amateur who "knows what he likes," in that the critic's choice has been made through enlightened artistic knowledge and experience. He will therefore attempt to explain, as specifically as possible, why the evaluations of the mature man and of the expert are the finer ones. Unlike subjectivism, then, relativism recognizes and elucidates the important fact of growth and education in artistic sensitivity.

In at least one other important critical respect subjectivism and relativism notably differ. Subjectivist criticism, being wholly personal, intuitive and impressionistic, does not require standards. How, indeed, could standards of any sort be useful to a type of criticism which evaluates solely by expressing immediate pleasures and displeasures? Since standards cannot serve its aims, subjectivism is logically correct in repudiating them.

Relativism, on the other hand, finds critical standards of the utmost importance. [4] Though these differ markedly, as I shall later explain, from the standards of absolutism, they nonetheless give relativist criticism a special and important sort of objectivity totally absent from subjectivism. They form, that is to say, a specific frame of reference toward which specific evaluations are directed. If, then, relativist standards are clearly expounded, specific value judgments become universally comprehensible. By elucidating

---

3 "The Meaning of Value," *Journal of Philosophy,* February, 1925, p. 131.

4 For a more complete analysis of relativist standards, see the author's *New Bearings in Esthetics and Art Criticism* (New Haven, 1943).

his standards the critic enables his audience at least to *understand* his evaluations. This principle, which I call "Logical Relativism," is perhaps the most
stabilizing one in criticism.

We may cite an example to illustrate the efficacy of logical relativism by
noting diverse ratings accorded Bramantino's Adoration of the Magi in the
National Gallery, London. Adolfo Venturi admires the picture greatly, finding in it an effect of "regal splendour" and a supreme example of the art of
balancing cubistic masses. This judgment is based upon a standard which
values highly formal compositional effects. Berenson, on the contrary, though
granting that the picture is "winning," finds in it no evidence of serious art.
This verdict is readily comprehensible too, since we know that, for Berenson,
serious art must present notable tactile values, movement and space composition. A third, and still less exalted appraisal of the painting, will be given
by one who, like myself, considers the standard of "associative form" a
basic one. According to this standard, the painting is inferior since certain
gestures, postures and expressions seem affectedly conceived and ill related
to the given theme, The Adoration of the Magi. All three judgments are comprehensible since we know the standards upon which they are based.

A more extended discussion of relativism than is necessary for my specific
aim would show that values are conditioned by, and relative to, specific
cultural groups and periods. This conviction of the relativist further distinguishes his position from subjectivism by the spread and duration of its
values. Whereas subjective evaluations are logically binding only for the
individual and for the moment, relative ones are binding, *ordinarily,* for
particular groups of people during a particular cultural age. Ordinarily, that
is to say, since some few evaluations are agreed upon by many types of people in many different ages. This occasional widespread agreement in no
sense, however, proves that values have absolute subsistence; rather, it is
the natural consequence of certain rare emotional and intellectual qualities
that are common to the majority of mankind.

Since the foregoing critical positions differ in these several ways, it seems
reasonable to differentiate them by using different terminology. If he wishes
to do so, one is at perfect liberty, to be sure, to call relativism a "type of subjectivism" or an "enlightened subjectivism," but by doing so he would be
muddling, in a field where lucidity is all too rare, vital critical distinctions.

Relativism and Absolutism

According to absolutism, value is best defined as a quality that is
intrinsic to the object in the sense that it has ontological subsistence and is
independent of any relation to the mind. It follows that the absolutist critic
will believe in the existence of absolute, ultimate standards and will hold

that there is one and only one "correct taste," "right judgment," "real estimate," or "true verdict." His concern, therefore, will be to strive to achieve
that perfect and infallible evaluation which, given his assumptions, must
exist.

Relativism, we have seen, accepts, as one of its aspects, a psychological
definition of value. It also accepts, however, a definition of value which
centers one's attention primarily on the object and which, therefore, *seems*
to associate it with absolutism. This definition considers value as a *relational*
property of an object or as the *capacity* of an object to produce an effect
upon someone. It is a *potential* quality which becomes actual only in a
transaction with an individual. To explain this meaning concretely: a work
of art is valuable in the same sense in which milk is nourishing and cyanide
poisonous.

Now some *"objectivists"* will assert that *their* notion of value is precisely
this relational one. Realizing that values are in some way connected with
human relationships, and being unwilling, therefore, to contend that they
exist in a realm of pure and eternal forms, these objectivists will repudiate
absolutism and will claim that the relational interpretation of value, since
it correctly explains their views, should be called "objective" rather than
"relative." Or, instead of distinguishing between absolutism and relativism,
they will prefer to distinguish between "absolute and relative objectivism."
This preference, I must insist, is essentially a verbal one which should in
no serious way affect the present discussion. Anyone who wishes for the
remainder of this paper to substitute for the term "relativism" either "objectivism" or "relative objectivism" is entirely free to do so.

The relativist further believes that values are significantly dependent upon
one's culture and environment, upon one's temperament and experience.
His standards, contrasting with the allegedly fixed and infallible ones of the
absolutist, are flexible and tentative. As a critic, he denies that there are
unchangeable and absolute evaluations and urges, rather, that value judgments are largely conditioned by individual attitudes, particular social groups
and specific civilizations.[5] His theory and practice, unlike those of absolutism,
make no pretensions to timelessness and to universality.

Though to attempt with any fulness either to challenge absolutism or to
defend relativism is a task beyond the scope of this essay, we may point up
the foregoing paramount distinctions between them by trying to understand what each position entails in the light of concrete illustrations.

What stand shall we take, for example, toward the acceptance of certain
well known opposed cultural ideals? Is Communism right for Russia and

[5] Though one may effectively argue that much modern art is created as a reaction
against contemporary capitalist society, this very reaction indicates the great influence
of that society upon the art that rejects it.

wrong for America? Is suicide honorable in Japan and dishonorable in America? Is polygamy good in Islam and bad in Christendom? Is homosexuality justifiable in ancient Greece and unjustifiable in America? Was Plato right or wrong in condemning the family as a legal and ethical institution and in abolishing it from his republic? Was the Paideia of the Greeks correct and the Paideia of the Persians incorrect? Are Quakers right or wrong in condemning the use of alcohol?

The absolutist, affirming that moral codes are unchangeable, will assert that there is one, and only one, correct or true attitude toward communism, suicide, polygamy and so forth. The relativist, affirming that the values of moral codes vary with the varying ideals of society and surroundings, may accept as a positive value for its own culture many divergent creeds, though he may himself reject one or all of them. He will be impressed, moreover, by the absurd spectacle of absolutists of different times and places fundamentally disagreeing and will draw the conclusion that the absolutist position is, in fact, a decidedly provincial one.

We may further contrast absolutism and relativism by considering the types of standards to which each subscribes. For the absolutist critic these standards are universal, fixed and eternal. But what examples may one name? What standards of this sort can one apply? Surely they cannot, in any significant sense, be concrete. For if a critic cites as his absolute standards certain reasonably specific qualities which seem to him of ultimate value— for example, plastic form and rhythmic movement in painting—he at once encounters another critic who evaluates these qualities quite differently. If he should claim that *his* particular standards alone characterize all painting that is genuinely art, he is being at once presumptuous and question-begging. If one selects standards of a more abstract nature, there will not, to be sure, be such disagreement. If one asserts, for example, that "unity" or "harmony" or "communication" or "beauty" or "expression" is essential to the best art, there would be quite general agreement, *provided* the meanings of these terms were not too carefully defined but were left sufficiently general and vague. But is it not obvious that, as the specific applicability of standards to works of art diminishes, their critical usefulness and significance diminish also? The most abstract standards are surely the most empty, therefore the most futile.

There is one standard, currently accepted by Crocean critics, which, if satisfactory, would staunchly support the absolutist position toward evaluation. According to Lionello Venturi, the absolute standard of judgment is to be found, not in any object, but in the soul, imagination, or artistic personality of the painter. Here we find, he claims, an absolute, intrinsic value. Critical conclusions are right or wrong since they are based upon this quality, that is, upon the personality or imagination of the artist. The aim of criticism is to reconstruct artistic personalities and to discover whether they have expressed themselves well or badly. In Croce's terminology, the absolute or objective value of a work of art depends upon the degree of harmony between the artist's intuition and expression, or "between the poet's vision and his handiwork." In simpler language, has the artist successfully fulfilled his intention?

Unfortunately for the absolutist position, this supposedly ultimate standard has proved vulnerable for two principal reasons. First, how is the intention of the artist and its success to be accurately determined? No lesser names than Henri Focillon, T. S. Eliot and Roger Fry have in recent years asserted that the critic and the artist often find different meanings in a work; [6] and, as John Dewey remarks: "It is absurd to ask what an artist 'really' meant by his product; he himself would find different meanings in it at different days and hours and in different stages of his own development." [7] Second, by so stressing the importance of an exact balance between the intuition and expression of the artist, Crocean critics seem to put at a premium sheer technical perfection and to ignore distinctions in value between the important and unimportant, between the major and the minor. Artistic perfection becomes the sole criterion, artistic greatness or significance is ignored. In addition to these two general objections to the standard in question, a highly concrete and personal one may be added. When Lionello Venturi concludes, specifically on the basis of his own theses, that the Bathers by Renoir in the Tyson Collection is "anti-artistic" and lacks "the creative spirit of Renoir, his joy, his grace, his animation," [8] he vitiates, for one critic at least, his entire argument.

In a number of ways the standards of relativist criticism differ basically from those of absolutism. They are, to begin with, empirical criteria, not rigid rules, which have been evolved from human choice and experience. They are working hypotheses or codified principles which critics formulate as they study and appreciate works of art. Unlike the unalterable prescriptions of absolutism, they are tentative and flexible, as already pointed out, in that they may at any time be revised.

Again, relativist standards differ greatly from absolutist ones in respect to their specificity. Because of the underlying assumptions of absolutism, that position, we saw, reasonably necessitates critical standards that are abstract rather than concrete, vague rather than definite. According to relativism, on the other hand, standards may be as specific as one chooses to make them. The varying ideals of diversely constituted critics may all be used as frameworks for their particular evaluations, one critic establishing

[6] *New Bearings in Esthetics and Art Criticism,* pp. 113–114.
[7] *Art as Experience,* New York, 1934, pp. 108–109.
[8] *The Art Bulletin,* December, 1944, p. 273.

a criterion of "significant form," another of "life-communicating quality," a third of "simplicity and restraint," a fourth of "realism" and so on. *Provided they are reflected upon and intelligently formulated,* these and many other principles are acceptable to relativist theory.

That diverging or even opposed standards are tenable in relativist criticism should surprise no one. Whereas absolutism claims that, if one of two contradictory criteria is to be accepted, the other is to be rejected, if one is right, the other is wrong, relativism, recognizing the dependence of values upon differing cultures and temperaments, asserts the legitimacy of many different claims. Relativism believes, that is to say, that ideals, hence values, of all sorts change from period to period and that, within one period, there are differently constituted yet equally sensitive and cultured critics who naturally subscribe to varied, yet equally valuable standards and judgments. These beliefs, which one may conveniently term "Psychological Relativism," are corner stones of relativist theory and practice.

An enormous amount of empirical critical evidence supports the contentions of psychological relativism.[9] While the presentation of any substantial portion of this evidence is clearly impossible in a short essay, the citation of a few characteristic samples will at least indicate what kind of critical facts impress the relativist.

A historical study of the ratings accorded any artist or his work, for example, will in all probability reveal remarkably diverse value judgments, not only between the most sensitive critics of different periods but between those of the same period. For Leonardo's contemporaries, his caricatures seemed typical of his art, his S. John a success; for us, the caricatures are decidedly exceptional in his *oeuvre,* the S. John a failure. For Dr. Mather, The Last Supper "is perhaps the most impressive picture in the world"; for Langdon Douglas it is unconvincing in its artificiality, exaggeration, bombast. Differences of critical opinion today are equally striking in regard to more recent art. Though an absolutist might argue that diversity in evaluations upon painting, say, since 1870 may be accounted for because the closeness and newness of this art make its meanings for us difficult, should he not be uneasy when confronted with the bewildering diversity of evaluations upon earlier 19th century art? The work of Gericault, according to Wilenski, is "coarse and derivative," yet Fry tells us that this painter "was almost the most gifted artist of the 19th century." Professors A. M. Friend and P. J. Sachs, the two most gifted teachers of French painting I have known, evaluate the art of Delacroix in opposite ways: for Friend this art is exaggerated,

---

[9] Some of this evidence is cited in the following works: F. P. Chambers, *The History of Taste,* New York, 1932; E. E. Kellett, *The Whirligig of Taste,* London, 1929; E. E. Kellett, *Fashion in Literature,* London, 1931; Joan Evans, *Taste and Temperament,* New York, 1939; B. C. Heyl, *New Bearings in Esthetics and Art Criticism,* New Haven, 1943; Henri Peyre, *Writers and Their Critics,* Ithaca, 1944.

artificial and unimportant; for Sachs it is vital, stirring and great. Whereas some of the best contemporary critics sum up their views upon Millet by the terms "insincere" and "sentimental," others conclude that he is a convincing and profound artist. Such diversity of opinion, I submit, may be multiplied almost indefinitely. For, as Hume somewhere remarks, "As the variety of taste is obvious to the most careless enquirer; so will it be found, on examination, to be still greater in reality than in appearance."

Does not this psychological relativism, the absolutist will surely ask, make knowledge impossible, judgment pointless and value illusory? Only, we reply, to those who, because of their persistent demand for absolutes, blindly deny, misinterpret or attempt to explain away critical empirical facts. To all others the recognition of relativity and of multivalence is both realistic and reasonable. "It shifts the issues to firmer grounds, in fact removes the issues from the realm of illusion—the realm of eternal truths that turn out to be so strangely contradictory and so temporal—by bringing them within the scope of intelligent inquiry into actual conditions." [10] In short, the irreducible critical differences which make absolutism seem unintelligible and absurd, are readily accounted for by psychological relativism.

What bearing will this relativism have upon the critic's attitude toward his evaluations? I would emphasize two prime considerations. First, each critic should realize, deep down, that his appraisals are markedly relative since they depend in part upon his particular psychological make-up, philosophical outlook and cultural environment. He should therefore remember that equally competent, though differently constituted critics, may disagree with his evaluations, and he should recognize as fully as possible, difficult though it may be to do so, the reasons for and the reasonableness of other claims. Second, he should affirm his judgments with the full realization that, *for himself and for others with comparable background and basic attitudes,* they are the accepted and correct ones. They are not the unarguable preferences of the subjectivist, but are thoughtful, reasoned appraisals. They are as binding and as true for him as any evaluations subscribed to by an absolutist.

The foregoing considerations evidently determine in large measure the policy that a *teacher* should employ. Recognizing the validity or truth of his opinions *from one point of view,* he will communicate them as convincingly, persuasively and enthusiastically as he can. Recognizing also, however, their relativity, he will never attempt to force their acceptance, but will rather explain in what sense differing judgments may be correct and why the quest for the values of absolutism is a foolish and futile one.

In conclusion I wish to urge that critical relativism is not merely a cau-

---

[10] H. J. Muller, *Science and Criticism,* New Haven, 1943, p. 17.

tionary attitude evolved in order to avoid certain difficulties inherent in
other theories. It is a distinctive position which differs radically from subjectivism and absolutism and which, therefore, should be carefully distinguished from both. It cannot, to be sure, be formulated with exactitude. Thus,
for example, since the relativist cannot define with finality the competent,
cultured, sensitive or expert critic, his position is, to a degree, unavoidably
imprecise. But as Aristotle insists, the accuracy of conclusions necessarily
varies according to the field under investigation. In his own words, "Our
discussion will be adequate if we are content with as much precision as is
appropriate to the subject-matter; for the same degree of exactitude ought
no more to be expected in all kinds of reasoning than in all kinds of handi-
craft. . . . Let each of the views put forward be accepted in this spirit,
for it is the mark of an educated mind to seek only so much exactness in
each type of inquiry as may be allowed by the nature of the subject-matter."

ARTHUR CHILD

The Social-Historical Relativity

of Esthetic Value[1]

THE CONSISTENT EMPLOYMENT of the social context as a cate-
gory of philosophic interpretation requires an acknowledgement of the social-
historical relativity of esthetic value. Now and again, indeed, over a period
of centuries, various social-historical factors have been granted some sort
of esthetic relevance. But even such recent theorists as Boodin and Dewey,
both of whom employ explicitly the category of the social context, have
failed to develop in any detail the implications of the social-contextualist
approach to esthetic value. It seems important, therefore, to begin work
on a detailed development, and in the present paper we propose to attempt
such a beginning.

First, however, we must set forth a few definitions and explanations.
Esthetic value, as we understand it, is that unique felt quality of the esthetic
experience which is marked by the fact that one likes it. It is a value because
one does value it. And an object is termed "beautiful" when the experience

---

[1] Arthur Child, "The Social-Historical Relativity of Esthetic Value," *Philosophical
Review*, LIII (1944), 1–22. Reprinted by permission. (Eds.)

of it is qualified in this particular liked and valued manner. Esthetic dis-value, on the other hand, is that felt quality of the esthetic experience which is marked by the fact that one dislikes it, and it is a disvalue because one dislikes it. The felt quality of the esthetic experience varies in two senses: first, in intensity or in regard to the strength or the weakness of the feeling; and, second, in what for lack of a better word we might call extensity or in regard to the breadth and depth, the comprehensiveness of meaning, the area of contextual implications. One could argue that the term "extensity" should apply only to the experience and not to its felt quality. To our introspec-tion, however, there seems to be an indefinite number of determinate forms of this felt quality—forms determined by the experience of which they are the felt qualities. In other words, the nature of the felt quality of the esthetic experience is intrinsically affected by the nature of the esthetic experience itself; and by extensity we mean simply to refer to the reflection, in the felt quality, of the breadth and depth of the experience. Since, then, the felt quality possesses these variable characteristics of intensity and extensity, it is possible for esthetic value itself (and not merely the esthetic experience) to vary with the social-historical context.

We shall now proceed to develop our theme of the social-historical relativ-ity of esthetic value under the topics of the contextual reference of the esthetic judgment, the interaction of objective and social-subjective factors in the esthetic experience, and social standards and esthetic value.

§ *1*

Social-historical relativism mediates, in the theory of the esthetic judgment, between the polar errors of absolute universalism and absolute relativism. On the one hand, in order to reconcile the asserted universality of esthetic judgment with the actual particularity of esthetic judgments, common and even popular opinion holds that the genuine esthetic judgment affirms, essentially, an injunction valid for every individual. But this primary universal Ought presupposes not only an absolute esthetic object but also a secondary universal Ought, namely, that every subject *ought* to possess (since, obviously, every subject does not possess) a psychic structure which, in respect to the esthetic demands of that supposedly absolute esthetic ob-ject, is identical with the psychic structure of every other subject. And one must admit that, if a subject does feel a compulsion to take some standpoint other than its present standpoint (and thus to alter its psychic structure), there is some Ought involved. The Ought, however, is the subject's own, for either the subject makes a deliberate effort to change or else, passively, it consents to the intersubjective influences which must otherwise constitute the agency of change. Every subject, in this sense, is a law unto itself. And we can see no way, therefore, to derive the universal Ought.

On the other hand, disillusioned with this axiological universalism of popular theory, one might attempt to maintain the theory that beauty is only a name for a collection of phenomena which possess, for all one can know, a quite disparate character; that each epoch, each period, each contemporary society, perhaps even each individual subject, attaches the name "beauty" to some peculiar experience of its own. But it seems clear that this absolute relativism of kind would fall into the errors of nominalism in general and would lie open, therefore, to the corresponding criticisms. The mere fact that the term "beauty" has such common use and that people understand each other in using the term, even if they do not agree with each other's judgments, appears to indicate that the phenomena to which the term refers are simply not altogether disparate and unique. Moreover, we do not see how such a relativism could allow, with consistency, of any esthetic Ought, yet an esthetic Ought there certainly is. And a clear distinction between this absolute relativism of kind and our social-historical relativism of degree, as two totally incompatible sorts of relativism, is fundamental to any appreciation of the meaning and any assessment of the validity of the present study.

Examining the esthetic judgment, then, from a social-contextual standpoint, we must go on to consider how one might legitimately derive an esthetic Ought. If, when one asserts flatly that "this is beautiful," one cannot legitimately refer to a universal subject, one does refer, nevertheless, to some subject. Unquestionably, one refers at least to oneself. But it would seem also legitimate to extend this reference to all other subjects who, because of their innate capacities, their environment, their education, their self-development, whatever the relevant character and magnitude of such factors, possess that subjective similarity to oneself which is necessary (or, as the case may be, necessary and sufficient) for the esthetic response in question. And this transegoistic reference constitutes a reference to a group of men in society.

But here the universalist might raise an objection. In point of fact, he might claim, the esthetic judgment presupposes not only those who now belong to the given group but also those who might be brought into the group. Upon the present or possible members of this group, the universalist might contend, the recognition of an absolute Ought is incumbent; and since the possibility of inclusion extends to all men, the absolute Ought has validity for all men. But we cannot admit the justice of this objection. Would there not be as many claimants to the rank of absolute Ought as there are groups with different experiences of beauty? In so far, of course, as anyone from outside the particular group in question should become capable of the distinctive response of that group, he would no longer (in the relevant respect, at the very least) stand outside of the group. But he would now have distinguished himself from those who do remain outsiders and who, as outsiders, continue to make esthetic judgments in conflict with the judgments of that group. In concrete fact, therefore, a conflict would still exist between the esthetic judgments of one group of men and the esthetic judgments of another group of men.

An opponent might also object that the group we speak of constitutes a mere aggregation of individuals and that it is not, therefore, in any structural sense, a true social group .And we admit the seeming justice of this objection. However, one must remember that our interpretation proceeds in terms of the category of the social context and thus that it presupposes, as a correlative implication of that category, a social-contextual theory of mind. And, for a social-contextual theory of mind, a similarity of minds must derive (to neglect the biotic ground of its possibility) either from an identity or from a similarity of social contexts. Hence we can justifiably regard those individuals who, because of a subjective similarity, respond or are capable of responding to the same esthetic object in the same way either as in some sense composing an empirical social group or as belonging to groups which, as groups, possess a sociologically intelligible similarity to each other.

We return, then, to the social-contextual derivation of the esthetic Ought. Unless there exists a desire, an aspiration, a conative tendency, a willed possibility, which the subject feels as an imperative, there can exist nothing of the compulsive nature that we associate with an Ought. But from the standpoint of social-contextualism such an imperative is easy to find: it consists in the desire, conscious or unconscious, to belong to (or, alternatively, to be regarded as belonging to) some certain social group. And in order, in some cases, to satisfy the requirements for belonging (or, at least, for seeming to belong) to some certain group, one must respond esthetically in a certain manner to some certain object or objects or class of objects. If, therefore, a subject feels as a compulsive ideal the belonging (or the seeming to belong) to such a group, then, certainly, one may justifiably describe the esthetic situation as characterized by an Ought with reference to that ideal. Thus social-contextualism can derive the Ought of the esthetic judgment from the requirements of group membership.

Admittedly, one cannot have a desired esthetic response purely by willing to have it. But, given the ideal of membership in a particular group, if one cannot have the appropriate response one must at all events and all costs seem to have it. And from the resultant pretense, engendered by the desire to be regarded as belonging to the "right" group, to the "superior" group, to the group with the greater prestige, arises the stereotyped character of much pseudo-esthetic judgment. But the importance of this pretense passes beyond the mere fact of pretense itself. For, precisely by pretending to respond in the approved manner to the relevant objects and, underneath that response, by actually attempting so to respond, one facilitates the assumption of those group predispositions which make the approved response at least possible. And, moreover, one possesses in the desire to belong to the particular group a stimulus to the acquisition of the technical knowledge necessary for a genuine response in harmony with the predispositions of that group. In this way, therefore, by a concomitant absorption of culture-attitudes and development of technical knowledge, one often comes, in the end, to respond genuinely with a response of the approved order and thus actually to experience beauty in the proper degree in the presence of the relevant esthetic objects. And in this process we find the cultural genesis of no small measure of the agreement of authentic judgments of beauty.

It should be clear from our discussion of the Ought involved in the esthetic judgment that, in order to undertake a legitimate inquiry as to the truth or falsity of a judgment that "this is beautiful," one must specify, at least implicitly, the subjective reference of the judgment. If "this idea is true" means that this idea corresponds with the cognitive object which it intends, "this object is beautiful" means that the idea that this object is beautiful corresponds with the state of affairs constituted by the positive response, actual or potential, of some person or of the members of some group to the esthetic object in question. For practical purposes, it is true, the problem of subjective reference can be (or, at all events, is) largely neglected; for, despite any explicit claim to universality, judgments contain an implicit reference to their own particular circumambient context. But from a theoretical standpoint the determination of the correct subjective reference becomes, clearly, an extremely important problem in esthetic criticism and, especially, historico-criticism.

In conclusion, then, a brief consideration of possible causes of error in making a critical or an historico-critical esthetic judgment with reference to a definite social context should prove worthwhile. One might, in the first place, misjudge the attitudes (that is, the socially derived predispositions) of the group, so that one's judgment of its responses would also be wrong. Since, moreover, individual variations occur within any group, the esthetic judgment must refer to a more or less typified response; and one's judgment might not come close enough to the center of the responses as typified. The relative integration or relative unintegration of a particular group affects the measure in which the typified response can represent adequately the concrete responses of that group, and the comprehensiveness (that is, the proportion of truth or falsity) of the esthetic judgment will vary with the representational adequacy of the typified response. And if the typified response should represent a rather inchoate, undeveloped, unrefined mass of feelings, any esthetic judgment with reference to the group in question would necessarily prove rather misleading. Thus far we have been speaking of responses, but mistakes are also possible with respect to the groups or to the groupings of which one makes an esthetic judgment. For instance, one might select a group so large that the excessive breadth and pervasiveness, the excessive generality, of the esthetically relevant predispositions would exclude the legitimate imputation to them of any concrete and particular esthetic response. Or the group, finally, while an important grouping from some points of view and for some purposes, might not form what one could call a concrete group, might not objectively constitute a social context, or, at all events, might not constitute that kind of social context out of which esthetic predispositions would develop.

§ 2

Two factors enter constitutively into the esthetic experience: the objective ground of esthetic value (or that in the object which universally tends to call forth the esthetic response) and the esthetic subjectivity (or that in the subject which is capable of responding esthetically).

These factors equally underlie the esthetic experience as the conditions of its existence and the determinants of its nature, and the experience of esthetic value arises as a result of their ineluctably preconscious interaction. To suggest that the esthetic interaction occurs, not within, but as a precondition of, the esthetic experience, we employ the term "subgression." The esthetic interaction is a subgressive interaction because the esthetic experience, like bare perception, appears in the form of an accomplished fact. Moreover, it is just because the objective and the subjective do interact beyond the realm of consciousness that the esthetic experience possesses an integral character. Now frequently an esthetic experience contains subjective elements, anomalous to common theory, which nevertheless, in Veblen's words, are "inextricably blended" with the objective ground. The ulterior esthetician, indeed, finding these elements irrelevant to his own analysis of esthetic appreciation and offensive to his own good taste, will deny them a role in the esthetic experience; but his denial proceeds from an arbitrary dogmatism. Experience is what it is lived as being. And if an integral experience blends inextricably an appreciation of the expensive, say, with an appreciation of the objective ground of esthetic value, then precisely that inextricable blend is what the particular subject experiences in its particular esthetic experience. Within the esthetic experience one neither does nor can distinguish between the objective side and the subjective side.

Although men do not always agree as to what is beautiful or as to the degree in which beautiful things are beautiful, yet a comparatively large measure of agreement as to esthetic value—and, therefore, as to esthetic objects—does exist. Moreover, the mere possibility of a disagreement as to the precise esthetic value of esthetic objects presupposes some generic similarity in the various objects that men apprehend as beautiful. This common objective nature, corresponding to a generic subjectivity, is what we refer to as the objective ground of esthetic value. In our opinion (though we cannot here argue the point) the objective ground consists in quality and in organized relationships or form. Form and quality, then, entering into the typical esthetic experience from the object, universally tend to call forth the esthetic response. But the objective ground does not enter into the esthetic experience abstractly and generically; on the contrary, it enters experience as discriminated, selected, and concretized. And in which specific esthetic objects the concretized characters of form and quality shall be created or apprehended—how, that is, they shall be concretized, and what concretion shall be recognized—depends on the specific social-subjective constitution of particular groups of men. An artist, for instance, will not create the sort of object which will not be found beautiful by the group to which he at least ultimately appeals; the sort of object he will create is determined by the predisposition of some group, actual or projected, to discover therein the concretized ground of beauty. Hence, the objective ground in the abstract is determined selectively by the generic nature of man as a particular sort of living creature on the level of social existence, while the objective ground in the concrete is selectively determined by some specific social context.

Clearly, then, we hold that the objective ground, though indeed a necessary, does not constitute a sufficient ground for the experience of esthetic value. To this contention the following protest might be entered: that actually the objective ground is both necessary and sufficient, for the only problem involved is, essentially, one of recognition, and this recognition is indicated by the appreciations of those persons who possess superior taste. When persons of superior taste respond esthetically, this argument would run, their response establishes the theoretical sufficiency of the objective ground in question to elicit the esthetic response from anyone whomsoever. Nonetheless, we must insist that this argument is wholly untenable, for the preferences of the so-called "superior" persons vary from time to time, from place to place, from context to context, and are thus themselves characterized by a social-historical relativity. And this relativity makes it absurd to claim that the tastes of the "superior" persons are certain and absolute.

From such specific considerations as the following, in any case, one must realize the intrinsic relevance of social-subjective factors to the esthetic experience. In the first place, the social-subjective factors may so obliterate or may so distort the objective ground, for the subject, that the object will appear either as not possessed of any esthetic character at all or as qualified by an actual esthetic disvalue. And this obliteration or distortion can occur in spite of the fact that, analytically and objectively, the subject may have to concede the existence of that objective ground which the nature of his own social subjectivity prevents him from appreciating. In the second place, on the basis of an objective ground which, from an objective and analytical standpoint, constitutes the slightest, most trivial, most tenuous ground, the social-subjective factors peculiar to one context may create an esthetic experience of such depth and intensity as, from another context, to seem altogether fantastic, grossly sentimental, or ridiculously affected. Here, indeed, there might be some question about the assertedly objective and analytical standpoint. And we declare, rather than grant, that social-subjective factors do enter into what claims to be objective and analytical. Nevertheless, there is here a significant difference between analysis and appreciation. And in the first instance mentioned above it is the person contextually incapable of appreciation who himself, nothwithstanding, admits the presence of an objective ground. In the second instance, therefore, there would seem to be no impossibility in principle (however rare in fact) that the criticism of the objective ground as insignificant in respect to form and quality should come from within the appreciating context itself. And certainly, at all events, the import of our two considerations cannot be escaped through the contention, in the first instance, that the person who denied an experience of beauty actually had the denied experience or, in the second instance, that actually the experience of beauty was not an experience of the depth and intensity claimed for it by the persons who underwent the experience. For, in the nature of the situation, as against the claimed quality of an immediate experience there can be slight evidence other than the behavior of the subject of the experience. And even a revised judgment by the subject, made, as it must be, at a further remove from the original experience than the original judgment, might result from such irrelevant influences as a temporal weakening of the impression derived from the experience or a disapproval of the impression because of attitudes extraneous to the original experience. Hence we insist that, in the absence of behavior-evidence to the contrary, the esthetic value experienced, if any, must be taken for approximately what it is originally reported to be and that, in consequence, our illustrations of the intrinsic relevance of social-subjective factors possess validity.

We go on to the components of the esthetic subjectivity. By the esthetic subjectivity we refer to the mind in so far as it is oriented toward the objective ground of esthetic value, in so far, in other words, as it engages (or, sometimes, refuses to engage) in the esthetic experience. Within the esthetic subjectivity, then, we must distinguish the following factors.

First, there are the universal characters possessed by all men in their quality as human beings or socialized men. It is these primarily physical and more elementary psychic predispositions which determine the objective ground universally tending to arouse an esthetic response and which thus make possible any esthetic experience at all. These predispositions are probably as inexplicable as life itself, and they are obviously related to characteristics of the lower animals. Because (whatever, precisely, they might be) the permanent and racial predispositions are presupposed by all esthetic experience, they must simply be accepted, like the esthetic experience itself, as a presupposition of esthetic inquiry.

Second, superimposed on the psycho-biotic foundation, there are the specifically social factors, the socio-historically evolved, accumulated, adapted, and modified predispositions which, in the interaction between the individual and the social groups in which and through which the individual exists, become incorporated into, and thereby co-constitute, the mind of the individual social-historical human being. It is the group predispositions to which the social-historical relativity of esthetic value has reference. It is the group predispositions, moreover, which concretize the objective ground in general. In respect to creation, therefore, the group predispositions condition the concrete specification which the artist will give to the objective ground; and in respect to appreciation, the group predispositions determine the sort of concrete specification to which the members of the group will respond esthetically. Hence it is that our chief interest lies with the social-subjective factors.

Third, there are the individual factors, the characters of the individual human being. These characters may be sterile eccentricities, incapable of any contribution to culture; they may be genuine creative powers; or they may be simply the social factors considered as incorporated into the individual mind. This last possibility necessitates a further discussion of the individual factors in relation to the social factors. While the individual relativity of esthetic value does exist in its own right, yet the apparent relativity to the individual is not, to any significant degree, a relativity merely to the individual. For, in large measure and even in general, the individual represents some stratum, layer, current, tendency, of social-historical existence. In so far as the individual does, then, either symptomize or lead, he possesses more than a mere individual significance; and he cannot otherwise possess, properly speaking, any significance at all. But, from the other side, the social context depends just as much on the individual as the individual on the social context, for the social-historical factors are only active in, only exist in, and, indeed, only exist *as* individual factors. Thus the individual, on the one hand, even if the social-historical is something above and beyond any particular individual, constitutes the very mode of existence of the social-historical. The social-historical factors as such, on the other hand, constitute a norm of the individual structures as those structures are interrelated within a particular social context. And these normal structures, these group predispositions, could hardly become incorporated into the structure of any particular individual mind without some variation (even if, as in the majority of cases, an essentially nonsignificant variation) in consequence of the variation in the biotic individuality of all the disparate individuals whose minds are co-constituted by the group predispositions. When we speak of individual factors, therefore, we refer to a behaviorally significant deviation from the contextual norm.

As we have observed, some particular social subjectivity might inhibit any esthetic response to an object in reference to which a different subjectivity would allow, or even require, an esthetic response. But, after all, it is with notable rarity that there occurs either a total inhibition of a positive response or a substitution of a negative for a positive response where a positive response would seem indicated. (By using the term "inhibition" we mark as irrelevant any failure of response due to the absence of the object or to the inability to understand it.) The influence of the social subjectivity in respect to the rejection of an objective ground is, by and large, either to create an indifference to that ground or else to weaken the response into a quite negligible quantity. In such cases one simply makes a selective preferential response to other objects than the object in question. That is, out of the class of objects determined, by the socio-biotic nature of man as man, as in general qualified for the production of an esthetic experience, men as group men—thinking, feeling, and willing in terms of group predispositions—select those particular objects which best conform to these predispositions and to which, therefore, they will in actuality respond with an esthetic response. And when the predispositions of a certain group do not dispose the attention of the typified mind of the group to a given object, that object will not appear, to the normal members of the particular group, as possessed of a high degree of beauty; yet this fact, it seems clear, does not imply that such an object will appear as ugly. Thus the contextual relativity of esthetic value is not, in general, a matter of beauty against ugliness or of esthetic experience against a refusal to experience esthetically: partly it is a matter of esthetic experience against an indifference to the esthetic quality and form of a given object or class of objects, but still more it is a matter of the varying degrees of experienced beauty.

Nevertheless, one might protest that we do not account adequately for the universal element which, in some sense and in general, does seem to characterize the esthetic experience. But our theory provides in two ways for any such "universal" element that might exist. We have insisted, first, that the esthetic object does present, in its characters of form and quality, an objective ground of esthetic value. We have insisted, second, that social man (whatever the nature of a quite hypothetical nonsocial man) does possess a tendency to respond to these characters of form and quality in the manner known as esthetic. And these two theses, it seems to us, would suffice to account for whatever element of universality one might discover in the esthetic experience. In any case, "universality" is only a manner of speech, for not everyone does respond esthetically to every esthetic object. If all men possessed essentially the same social subjectivity, then, indeed, art would become universal. And this possibility is not in principle excluded for some remote future time. At present, however, and for a future of unforeseeable length, the social subjectivities of men do and will differ; and we must therefore insist, for such time as this condition obtains, that the intensity and extensity, as well as the very existence, of esthetic value depend on many and disparate social-historical factors.

Again, inasmuch as the esthetic quality, like any immediate quality, is intrinsically incommunicable, one might inquire after the evidence that the felt quality of the esthetic experience does in fact vary. And, of course, with esthetic experience as with any other form of immediate experience, we must rely on the indirect evidence drawn from social behavior and its results. When some person declares that he finds a given object only moderately beautiful, while another person insists that he finds the same object surpassingly beautiful, we must accept these statements, in the absence of evidence to the contrary, as reports of divergent experiences of the object. And behavior of a nonlingual kind often supplements the behavior of language. However, the objection is not yet conclusively met, for what of the cases in which a person from a remote context (the remoteness being either historical or contemporary) appears to have just as intense an experience of esthetic value in the presence of a given object as a person native to the context of that object? Here, we answer, even if there should be no difference in intensity, there must, in any event, be a difference in extensity, that is, in the reflected breadth and profundity of the felt contextual periphery of the experience. And there must also be a reason for the existence, rather than the non-existence, of the esthetic value. In regard to the creative experience we find direct evidence in the facts of creative work. Though it can be imitated, though sometimes it can be reproduced even with technical perfection, neither primitive art nor any other art can be created with real success in a context essentially different from that to which it is proper. Even in a single tradition, in the portrayal of a single conventionalized object, such as the Buddha, the art of one period will show a marked difference in attitude, feeling, spirit, from that of another. But if such social-historical differences exist in the creative experience, as shown by its manifestations, will they not also exist in the appreciative experience? It is the social-historical mind that appreciates no less than it is the social-historical mind that creates; and the merely appreciative mind is bound far more closely to the social-historical context than is the original and creative mind. We cannot believe, therefore, that the appreciative mind could overpass the creative mind by any universal freedom from the conditions and determinations of a specific time and place and association.

§ 3

Social standards, though derived from the more fundamental experiences of associative living, constitute the most explicitly important of the social-subjective factors that determine esthetic value. A significant discussion of the relationship between a certain class of social standards, on the one hand, and esthetic experience and esthetic taste, on the other, occurs in the chapter on "Pecuniary Standards of Taste" in Thorstein Veblen's *Theory of the Leisure Class*. Previously we have referred to the statement made there that an "inextricable blend" takes place between the social and the esthetic in the production of certain esthetic experiences. Nevertheless, Veblen also remarks that one may declare something to be "perfectly lovely" when an esthetic analysis would allow one to say only that it is pecuniarily honorific. And here Veblen seems to forget about the inextricable blending. For it is hard to believe that anyone would normally declare something to be lovely (and Veblen is obviously speaking of normal experience) if there did not actually exist in the object *some* ground of esthetic value. And if there existed in the object itself not even the slightest such ground, then we should say that at least the simulacrum of an objective ground entered into the experience by projection from the subject. In something that is "perfectly lovely," therefore (unless the particular commendation, indeed, should prove perfectly vacuous), the pecuniary honorificabilitude must itself be interfused, within the esthetic experience, with some esthetic character, actual or projected, of the object. We must insist on the possible subgression of social standards into the esthetic experience—and even of such standards as expensiveness and reputability.

In disagreeing with Veblen, however, we do not contend that such social standards as those he mentions must, where they obtain, enter integrally into the esthetic experience. They may enter, or they may not enter; and if they do enter, they may enter in various degrees. The relationship between these social standards and the esthetic experience should be further clarified by an explicit statement of all the principal alternatives.

First, one may appreciate an object purely with respect to its expensiveness or reputability, say, without any esthetic response to the objective ground which the object really possesses. Second, while appreciating the object with respect to its expensiveness or reputability, one may still experience it esthetically without the entrance of these particular standards into the actual esthetic experience. Or in the third place (and this seems the most common alternative) the social standards may subgress into the esthetic experience directly, as a part not merely of the general subjectivity but of the esthetic subjectivity itself. And when this third alternative is the case, then, whether the esthetician likes it or not, these standards are themselves esthetic and are themselves integral to the integral esthetic experience. That is, they are not distinguished, within the experience, from the rest of the experience, and they are therefore integral; while they affect the intensity and either by expansion contribute to, or by limitation detract from, the extensity of the experienced value, and they are therefore esthetic.

Beyond the ironic values that interest Veblen, in any event, stand the more inevitable types of cultural values. And these values, in one social-historical form or another, through and through pervade all social subjectivities—and hence all esthetic subjectivities—whatsoever. As to the esthetic relevance of these values, there can be no alternatives.

This position leads us to the following conclusion: *Because men prefer that which they approve, beauty will vary, in general, with the variation in the approach of any given work of art toward the perfection of the social standards—that is, the customary, the ethical, the political, the religious standards—of the percipient. Since, in other words, beauty involves the social standards of the percipient, the perfect portrayal of what one feels to be in itself more perfect by the criterion of one's social standards is, other things being equal, more beautiful than the perfect portrayal of what, by that same criterion, one feels to be in itself less perfect.*

For it is an empirical fact that, whereas a work of art may be exceedingly beautiful in relation to the social-historical context in which it arose, yet in relation to other social-historical contexts, with different social-historical standards, it may be much less beautiful, may have no esthetic value at all, or may even be ugly. And who is to say which judgment, if any, is wrong? From a given social perspective one could, indeed, criticize the social subjectivity of another perspective as deficient in regard to perceptiveness, in regard to the quality or the type of its social standards, etc. But from the second perspective, in turn, one could make the identical criticism of the first perspective. And neither representative could actually refute the esthetic experience, the esthetic judgment, the esthetic taste, of the other: each could only *reject* the experience, the judgment, the taste, that conflict with his own. Rejection, however, is not disproof.

It follows that one cannot discuss in general whether social standards ought to enter or ought not to enter into esthetic experience and esthetic judgment. They do enter. And it is only with reference to some particular set of contextually derived ideals that one can argue for the thesis that social standards ought not to enter. Even here, fundamentally, the argument is probably more an argument against certain social standards to which one objects than an argument (and, of course, an utterly futile argument) against the subgression of social standards in general. Moreover, we cannot doubt that, to a greater or less extent, perhaps for the most part unconsciously, those who uphold the thesis themselves apply social standards in the judgment of esthetic value; for into their minds, too, as minds of men—and therefore into their experience—the norms and the ideals of social groups must enter as one of the most decisive factors in the historical matrix.

Social standards, then, have a constitutive relevance to esthetic value through their subgression into the esthetic experience. But they also have a selective relevance through their determination of esthetic tastes, for it is (at all events on the more or less conscious level) that aspect of the esthetic subjectivity known as taste which selects those esthetic objects to which an esthetic response—or to which one degree or another of the esthetic response—shall be made, or from which an esthetic response shall be withheld, or in the presence of which the experience shall be that of an actual esthetic disvalue. And we must now consider social standards in relation to esthetic taste.

Here, of course, the chief question is that ancient one: Can there be any legitimate disputation about tastes? Our relativization of esthetic value to social-historical contexts might seem, at first thought, to make any such disputation totally illegitimate. But this, we shall now see, is not actually the case.

As we have shown, disputes about tastes are disputes not, in the main, as to whether a given object possesses esthetic value but rather as to the nature of the esthetic value that it is admitted to possess. In the very fact of a disputation about tastes, therefore, some measure of agreement is presupposed, for it is in general agreed that the objects under consideration are esthetic objects. And in general, after all, disputations about tastes do occur within a primary context that rather closely unites the disputants in spite of the differences of secondary context that may somewhat separate them. That is, the disputants commonly partake of the same broad culture whatever the differences between the respective cultural subgroups to which they belong. And even in regard to very dissimilar primary contexts of great scope, such as the European and the Chinese, our contention as to some measure of esthetic agreement would still hold.

If agreement exists, however, so does that disagreement which we have referred to the subjective factors. And we must now go further into the interpretation of esthetic disagreement from the social-contextual standpoint. Often what appears as a dispute about absolute esthetic merit is, in actuality, a dispute about esthetic merit in relation to two different contexts; and this could hardly be called a dispute, properly speaking, at all. It is only a quarrel. And the appearance even of an esthetic quarrel is, in the end, no more than a superficial appearance; for, in the end, the supposedly esthetic disagreement reduces to an advocacy, however implicit, of the habits, modes of thinking and acting, attitudes, standards, ideals, worldviews, of different social contexts. From the divergence in social context results the divergence in esthetic taste, and nothing could ever be done about the second without some sort of resolution of the first.

In connection with such contextual divergences disputes about tastes are illegitimate, for then they do not proceed with reference to that common social-subjective presupposition which alone could legitimatize them. When, on the contrary, a dispute occurs within a common secondary context and in relation, within that context, to common elements, the dispute is legitimate. For here not only does there exist the objective ground about which there could be no argument not resolvable in principle (since within the common context the objective ground is, as objective, the same for all disputants) but there also exists a common and accepted standard of subjective reference. And not merely within but also across secondary contexts, in spite of their social-subjective and therefore esthetic disagreement, one will ordinarily find, as we saw, a large measure of agreement that derives from their compresence within a common primary context. Across such secondary contexts, disputation about tastes is legitimate in reference to those primary social-subjective predispositions which the particular secondary contexts happen to share.

Cross-contextual argument occurs most frequently when the contextual difference is relatively slight, for here the broad predispositions of the mutual primary context tend to obscure the disparity in the more restricted predispositions of the divergent secondary contexts, and this obscuring of differences makes it easy to assume that the argument pertains to esthetic validity in general rather than to specific social subjectivities. The futility of arguing across contexts becomes evident to almost anyone, on the other hand, when the contextual difference is relatively great, for here the divergence in social subjectivities stands out stark and plain. But there is also appreciation across great contextual differences. And it is an interesting fact that an appreciation from a primary context very remote from the primary context within which a given disparity of socio-esthetic subjectivities occurs may have an effect— either from some social cause or for some relatively pure esthetic reason—

within the latter primary context, so that the members of one of its secondary contexts may become able to penetrate to an objective ground which previously was blocked from them by their own secondary subjectivity.

An important aspect of the problem of tastes concerns the general resistance to the esthetic acceptance of novel works of art. Often, certainly, this resistance follows from the origin of an artist with a new inspiration in some group of a lower social status than the groups with which the dominant critics and patrons of art are associated. And in many cases the new art does represent—and may openly express—a social protest against these groups of a higher status. But even where no special protest exists, a stultified conservatism will tend to identify any change at all with an attack on its own interests. It is when the issues which divided the secondary contexts from each other lose their compulsive reality or when these issues take on a different form or when the protestant artists rise personally to the dominant group or when the group represented by these protestant artists itself achieves social dominance, that the objective ground in the once-resisted works of art becomes more easily recognized and the works themselves are at last accepted into the corpus of socially approved works within the larger social context. The acceptance of the erstwhile subversive art then seems a matter of course, and the erstwhile resistance to this art then seems stupid and even incredible. Actually, however, within the original primary context the adverse esthetic valuation had a serious social significance; it constituted, in the esthetic field, a defence of definite social ideals, standards, attitudes. And this adverse valuation can appear stupid or incredible only from the standpoint of some very different primary context or else of the primary context that has superseded the antagonisms within the original primary context which it succeeds in an essential continuity.

What can be done in respect to the cultivation of tastes? For social-contextualism, clearly, the problem of intellectual training in the more abstract sense is logically subsequent to the problem of the inculcation of culture-attitudes. It is only because the cultural problem is taken, in the main, for granted, that the intellectual problem has acquired its predominance in theory. In the absence of the same cultural predispositions, then, the educational problem is, in the first place, the problem of inculcating them; and only when the same relevant attitudes are already present does the educational problem become, in the first place, the problem of refining and developing them as tools of analysis. The basic cultivation of tastes concerns those predispositions which pertain to the most inclusive context effectively acknowledged by the educators themselves—that is, to the pragmatically primary context—for the predispositions pertaining to the more limited contexts might inhibit that appreciation of beauty which would accord with the predispositions of the more inclusive context. If the mind is, in essence, an organization of predispositions, it is nevertheless possible to alter certain variable (because socially derived) predispositions; it is possible to bring to the esthetic level of the mind the more generalized characteristics of the more generalized world-view of the larger context and to enforce these characteristics, instead of the predispositions of some narrower context, as the directly selective principles of the socio-esthetic subjectivity. But since often the secondary contexts possess peculiar values without the possession or preservation of which the primary context would remain or become the poorer, this process must not constitute a mere negation; it must take the form, rather, of a reduction to moments, a sublation.

The justification for the concept of a more generalized world-view inherent in the primary context reveals itself in the contrast of any two primary contexts. Such a contrast discloses that within any primary context there are general predispositions which pervade or persist beneath the disparate and often conflicting predispositions of its secondary contexts. We must point out, however, that the inherence of predispositions in the primary context does not by any means, even for that context, entail the corresponding existence of absolute Oughts. To the person who does not wish to accept these attitudes, who resolutely prefers, say, the sentimental, the expensive, the bizarre, the revolutionary, the counter-revolutionary, whatever the case may be, there is nothing more to be said. He can only be left alone—or liquidated. Nevertheless, it is difficult to resist the generalized attitudes when accompanied by the proper prestige; for, as we showed earlier, a relative and contextual Ought becomes attached to them precisely through the intermediation of that social prestige.

The problem of education leads inevitably to the question of the relationship between esthetics and the political context. In order to clarify issues, let us take the national-political context of a dictatorship that deliberately attempts to control the esthetic realm for the sake of political expediency. Although absolute control of art would destroy art, since it would destroy that element of spontaneity which is essential to the creative process, certain political states do insist on at least the orientation both of art and of the appreciation of art to certain social standards and social ideals. From outside those political contexts, one might indeed object on various grounds to the regulation of art by politics: on the basis of one's own esthetic preferences, one might object to the proscription of this type of music and the prescription of that; from the standpoint of one's own political ideal of freedom of thought and expression, one might censure the refusal of a state to publish, to screen, to exhibit, works that do not accord with the tenor of official doctrine; because of one's own ethical beliefs, one might abhor the persecution of artists who reject the demands of political coordination. Realistically considered, however, all such objections are irrelevant to the political context within which the dictation occurs. From its own standpoint, a political state has the right to dictate methods, styles, contents, attitudes, tastes, because it has the power to do so. And education functions, of course, as part of the mechanism of dictation, for it is above all through education that the state can impose its will in any other than a repressive sense.

Political power, then, is an aspect of the larger context to which esthetic activity, esthetic appreciation, and esthetic education, are often relativized. Whether or not, that is, one approves of a particular organization of political power or of its cultural effects, one must recognize the political aspect of the larger context as a brute (and sometimes a brutal) fact. If one does disapprove of a certain political organization, one may seek to alter or to destroy it; and many artists at many periods have exerted themselves politically—often, at least in part, because of the attempt of the state to control their art with reference to political ideals which they did not and could not share. In so far, however, as they oppose a given political context, they place themselves morally outside of that context; and not seldom, if they have regard for their personal safety, they must place themselves outside of that context physically. For, from the standpoint of the political context in question, any objection to its esthetic activities is not only irrelevant but may even be subversive. And the best proof of this irrelevance, perhaps, is the fact that the political context actually does educate esthetically according to its political ideals, that it actually does inculcate those predispositions necessary for the esthetic condemnation of what is politically condemned and for the esthetic approval of what is politically approved.

But relativity to a political context is only one of the senses—and in the end, it may be, only one of the minor senses—in which esthetic value possesses a social-historical relativity. For, in reference to mind, any specific organization of political power constitutes a comparatively extraneous influence as against the profounder and more pervasive cultural realities. It is these realities, the elemental relationships between man and man as socialized men, the social group interactions that alone allow men to sustain their character as men—it is these realities in and through and as a part of which the individual mind itself arises. And it is these more basic realities, therefore, which in the long term, their infinite potentialities undamming themselves, incontrovertibly affirm to the group that in which, for that group, beauty is to be found and that in which, in that group, beauty is to be created.

C. E. M. JOAD

The Objectivity of Beauty[1]

IT IS, I THINK, in our experience of music that the clearest evidence for the uniqueness of aesthetic emotion and for the objective character of that upon which it is directed is to be found. Before, however, we can proceed to consider this evidence, it is necessary to establish the objectivity of beauty as a general concept. By the phrase "objectivity of beauty as a general concept" I wish to imply that beauty is an independent, self-sufficient object, that as such it is a real and unique factor in the universe, and that it does not depend for being what it is upon any of the other factors in the universe. I mean further that when I say that a picture or a piece of music is beautiful, I am not making a statement about any feeling that I or any other person or body of persons may have or have had in regard to it, or about a relation subsisting between my mind or the mind of any other person or body of persons and the picture or piece of music in question, but that I am making an assertion about a quality or property possessed by the picture or piece of music itself; and that the assertion is to be taken to imply that in virtue of the possession of this quality or property, the picture or piece of music stands in a certain special relationship hereafter to be defined to the world of value in general and to beauty in particular.

With a view to establishing this position it will be desirable to consider two alternative views which are frequently put forward in explanation of what it is that we mean when we say that a work of art is beautiful, and to indicate the objections to which they are exposed. If these views can be satisfactorily disposed of, I shall have advanced some way in the direction of proving by process of elimination that the meaning which I wish to give to the statement "this work of art is beautiful" is the right meaning.

1. Subjectivist Accounts of Beauty

The antithesis of the view that I am advocating is the extreme subjectivist position which is adopted by Tolstoy in *What is Art?* Tolstoy identi-

---

[1] From C. E. M. Joad, *Matter, Life and Value* (London: Oxford University Press, 1929), pp. 266–283. Reprinted by permission. (Eds.)

fies art with the communication of emotion. When a man tells a story, composes a song, or paints a picture with the object of communicating an emotion to others, then there is art; when the emotion is new and springs from a fresh religious attitude to the world, then there is good art. The effect of this is clearly to make the value of a work of art depend at least in part upon the receptivity of its audience. Tolstoy is careful to guard himself against the (Crocean) view that art is expression of emotion; the emotion of the artist must, he says, be *communicated;* if it is not, then the art is poor.[2] Now the extent to which an emotion can be communicated to others is clearly dependent upon the receptivity of those who experience it, and if you proceed, as Tolstoy does, to make the merit of a work of art proportional to the amount and intensity of the emotion it calls forth, the criterion of its value must be sought not in some intrinsic characteristic of the work itself but in the nature of the feelings entertained in regard to it.

This would mean that beauty is not an objective and inherent quality of works of art, but is resolved, in so far as the word "beauty" retains any meaning at all, into a type of emotional effect, this effect consisting in the feelings which persons who appreciate the work of art which is said to be beautiful entertain in regard to it; the more people like it, in fact, the better it is. Tolstoy, as is well known, did not shrink from this conclusion, affirming that, inasmuch as Russian peasant songs have a wider appeal than *Hamlet,* producing, that is to say, a feeling of pleasurable emotion in more persons than *Hamlet* does, they are superior to *Hamlet* as works of art. This is in effect to make the criterion of beauty consist in a counting of heads.

It is to be noticed that no considerations of quality are permitted to enter into this assessment. To say that one work of art is better or of higher quality than another is meaningless, unless it means that the first work succeeds in communicating more emotion than the second. Similarly "more emotion" cannot be interpreted as meaning aesthetically more valuable emotion, since no meaning is assigned to aesthetic value except in terms of communicated emotion, and the only standard by which we are entitled to assess communicated emotion is a quantitative one. Thus once again the only criterion of aesthetic value is the quantity of pleasurable feeling aroused in the audience or spectators, from which it follows that the most valuable work of art is that which is most liked. It is customary to make a distinction between what is good and what we like, and most people would admit, at any rate

---

2 Tolstoy, *What is Art* (Oxford, 1924), pp. 171–174. See especially the definition on p. 173: "To evoke in oneself a feeling one has experienced and, having evoked it in oneself, then by means of movements, lines, colours, sounds or forms expressed in words, so to transmit that feeling that others experience the same feeling—this is the activity of art." (C.E.M.J.) See our selection from this essay, p. 483. Although this selection primarily concerns the relation between art and society and art and religion, there are several statements in it which parallel this definition. (Eds.)

in theory, that because of a deficiency in taste they may fail to like that which they know to be good, and like that which they know to be bad. But for Tolstoy's theory no such distinction exists; there is no difference between liking a work of art and knowing it to be good. To say that we know it to be good is merely another way of saying that we like it, the former statement being in fact incapable of any other meaning. This theory is the exact counterpart of those hedonistic theories of ethics which abolish the common distinction between what is desirable and what is desired, by denying to the word "desirable" any meaning except in terms of what actually is desired. Just as for this type of theory the statement "you *ought* to do this because it is good" has no meaning in ethics, so the statement "you *ought* to like this because it is beautiful" has no meaning in aesthetics.

It is not possible to refute extreme positions of this type by logical argument, any more than it is possible to disprove the somewhat similar hypothesis of the solipsist in metaphysics. Although irrefutable by argument, the Tolstoyan theory possesses nevertheless considerable importance from the dialectical point of view. Its importance arises in this way: there are a number of theories of aesthetics which look for the criterion of value to the effect produced by a work of art upon the mind or minds of some person or body of persons, or which find it in a particular kind of relationship between the work in question and some mind or body of minds. These theories, like the Tolstoyan, issue in the conclusion that beauty is subjective; but the conclusion is not so easily detected. It is exceedingly important, therefore, to be able to show that these theories whose subjectivist tendency is disguised do in fact reduce themselves to this Tolstoyan position whose subjectivism is open and avowed. Having effected this reduction, we may then proceed to point to the obvious fact that each and all of these positions, including both the extreme subjectivist view and the disguised, do in fact totally fail to explain or to provide for the unique character of our feeling for beauty.

This, indeed, is so obvious that, so far as the extreme Tolstoyan view is concerned, few people to-day would venture to defend it. There are, however, many who, in order to avoid committing themselves to the admission of the objective and independent status of beauty and the unanalysable character of the emotion we feel for it, adopt one or other of the various theories of disguised subjectivism which, by disavowing the crude simplicity of the Tolstoyan view, seek to evade the charge of having analysed beauty into pleasurable states of feeling. It is important, therefore, that we should be able to show that these alternative positions do in fact reduce themselves to the complete subjectivity which Tolstoy frankly embraced. I will consider two of them from this point of view.

(a) It may be said that although the value of a work of art is ultimately to be assessed in terms of the feelings which it arouses, it does not, therefore, follow that we have simply to count heads. If, for example, we take a Bach fugue, which we will call (x), as an example of good art, and a drawing-room ballad (y) as an example of inferior art, it may be admitted that (y) causes pleasurable feelings to numerically more people than (x). But (y) is not, therefore, proved to be superior to (x), since those in whom (x) causes pleasurable feelings are more entitled to judge of the comparative merits of the two works of art than those who prefer (y). It may and can be shown that those who possess a technical knowledge of music, who have spent their lives in its study and whose experience enables and entitles them to sift the valuable from the worthless, who have, moreover, listened both to (x) and to (y) on numerous occasions, unanimously prefer the former. For this reason, therefore, we are justified in saying that (x) is superior to (y) since it is preferred by those of mature taste. It may further be urged in support of this view that with regard to all the greatest works of art, the plays of Shakespeare, the Preludes and Fugues of Bach, the paintings of Cezanne, there is a sufficient consensus of opinion among experts to justify us in un-hesitatingly asserting their value. There is also an appeal to the effect of time and the judgment of posterity.

The argument, therefore, amounts to this: (x) is preferred by those who are entitled to judge; it is, moreover, preferred by them throughout a longer period, being still admired when (y) is forgotten: therefore, since it is more liked in the long run and appeals to a better taste at any given moment, it is superior to (y). In other words, although more people may prefer (y) at any given moment, they are not the right kind of people, and they are probably fewer in the long run.

Thus the ability to evoke pleasurable feelings in persons of good taste is substituted for the ability to evoke the greatest quantity of pleasurable feelings on the whole as the standard of beauty.

There are two difficulties about this view. The first is that the consensus of opinion among experts to which appeal is made is non-existent. There is no work of art whose value is admitted to-day which has not at some time or other been roundly condemned by experts, just as there is no canon of morality that has not been questioned by good men. Experts of the same generation are in perpetual controversy with one another over contemporary work, and at perpetual variance with experts of the preceding generation over the works of the past. Tastes change, and the consensus of one generation, in so far as it exists, is often diametrically opposed to that of another. Speaking broadly, we may say that each generation of experts tends to take the gods of its grandfathers off the shelf upon which its fathers have placed them. We cannot, therefore, define our expert simply as one who knows what is valuable in art and who in virtue of his knowledge subscribes to an admitted consensus of opinion.

How, then, and this is our second difficulty, are we to define the expert, by an appeal to whose good taste the merit of a work of art, or in other words, the criterion of beauty is to be established? Training and experience, which might have been expected to assist us in framing a definition, prove but halting guides; men who have had the advantages of both frequently prefer (*y*) to (*x*) and show their preference by visiting and praising musical comedies and going into raptures over dance-music, drawing-room ballads, or tone-poems. Nor does agreement with the assumed good taste of others provide the hall-mark we require; the obligation to define good taste in others by agreement with which the taste of an expert is to be authenticated, is rapidly found to involve us in a vicious circle, apart from the fact that, as we have already pointed out, such agreement is noticeably to seek.

Failing a satisfactory definition from other sources, we are forced in the long run to define the expert by reference to the judgments in which his taste expresses itself. The expert, we shall say, is the man who recognizes what is good and likes it; he is, in other words, the sort of person who prefers (*x*) to (*y*). Thus in attempting to escape from the impasse of complete subjectivism by the appeal to experts, we find ourselves completing a vicious circle. The argument now runs as follows. By what criterion are we to judge (*x*) to be superior to (*y*)? Answer, by the consensus of opinion among persons of good taste, who unanimously prefer (*x*). By what characteristic are we to recognize these experts whose judgment is to be trusted to establish the superiority of (*x*)? Answer, they may be known by the fact of their universal preference for (*x*).

If, then, the appeal to quality of taste as a criterion of aesthetic value breaks down owing to the impossibility of defining what we mean by quality except in terms of judgments about the works of art whose value is in question, we are reduced to the crude subjectivist position of assessing the value of a work of art in terms of the amount of pleasurable feeling it excites.

(b) It may be said that aesthetic value is not to be assessed in terms of the feelings which any person or body of persons entertains towards a work of art, but is a quality of the relation which subsists between knowing mind and object known. If *A* is a picture, *B* the knowing or appreciating mind, and *R* the relation which subsists between them when *B* knows *A*, we may say (i) that beauty or aesthetic value cannot be a quality of *A* taken alone, since this would be tantamount to asserting the objectivity of beauty in the sense for which I am contending; (ii) that it is not a quality of *B* taken alone, since this, like the view already considered that aesthetic value depends upon or is relative to *B*, leads to a crude and unacceptable subjectivism, and that, therefore, (iii) aesthetic value must be a quality of *R*.

This view is frequently found in conjunction with an Idealist theory of knowledge. It is inconceivable to many that there should be beauty in a world of objects which is not and never has been perceived by any mind. Objects, it may be said, cannot be beautiful independently of minds to appreciate them, just because they cannot exist independently of such minds. Even if we were to suppose that they could exist independently of knowledge, they are nevertheless insensibly transformed in the process of being known, so that the object as known is different from the object prior to its entry into knowledge. It is only of the object as known that beauty can be affirmed, of the object, that is to say, as standing in a certain relation to the knowing mind. Hence it is of the object as related to mind that we predicate aesthetic value, or in other words, beauty only comes into existence when there is a certain relation R between A and B, namely, the relationship which consists in A being known by B. We may further refine on this, and say that beauty is an epiphenomenon that supervenes upon the union of mind and object, when the object is of a certain class and the mind in a certain state or condition.

This view seems to be open to a number of objections, of which I will mention three.

(i) It is not asserted that it is upon the union of mind with any known object that beauty supervenes, but only upon the union with objects of a certain class, those, namely, which, when rightly appreciated by a mind in a certain condition or state of development, are capable of entering into a relation of which aesthetic value can be predicated. Now the property of belonging to a certain class is a property which the object possesses in its own right, independently, that is to say, of its entry into the knowledge relation. If we call the property (x), we may say that it is only objects which are independently qualified by (x) which are capable of entering into the aesthetic relation. But in thus postulating the independent possession by an object of a property which is essential to the occurrence of what is called aesthetic experience, we are in fact affirming the objective basis of aesthetic value.

(ii) The view in fact reduces itself to the subjectivism which it seeks to avoid. We are asked to believe that beauty is a property neither of A (the picture) nor of B (the mind), but of R when R is the relation between A and B. Now the relation of the mind to a picture which it appreciates is obviously different from its relation to a picture which it dislikes. R therefore varies as A varies; it also varies as B varies, since the same mind may entertain different feelings towards the same picture at different times. Since R varies with B, it is partly dependent for its characteristics upon the characteristics of B; beauty, therefore, which on this view only comes into existence when R is of a certain kind, which is, in other words, one of the characteristics of R, is itself dependent at least in part upon the characteristics of B. Beauty, therefore, is not an objective entity existing independently of mind in its own right; it is a characteristic of a relation, which varies with and is therefore dependent upon the existence of a certain attitude of mind, or, more accurately, of certain states of feeling. Aesthetic value, in other words, is subjective; the extent to which it will characterize the relation between a mind and a particular work of art depends at least in part upon the sentiments which the perceiver experiencing the work in question entertains in regard to it; if these sentiments are hostile, or if they do not exist, the relation will not be the required character, and we are not entitled, therefore, to say that the work of art is beautiful.

(iii) The third objection is one of a general character which springs directly from and presupposes a realist theory of knowledge. It is only valid, therefore, in so far as we have on other grounds adopted a realist theory. The view we are considering appears to rest upon a confusion between object and apprehension of object. An object apprehended is . . . necessarily different from the apprehension of it; it is indeed only because it is different that it can be apprehended. If, therefore, the knowledge of (x) is different from (x), the elimination of the one cannot affect the other; the presence or absence of knowledge cannot, that is, affect the qualities of the object known. If, therefore, the object possesses the quality of being beautiful, nothing that happens in or to any mind that may be apprehending the object can possibly affect its beauty, which will be no more enhanced by appreciation than it will be diminished by disparagement. That which is affected by the presence or absence of mind is not beauty, but the appreciation of beauty. Unless, therefore, we identify apprehension of object with object apprehended, it will follow that it is the appreciation of beauty only which is subjective, and that beauty itself, being unaffected by the presence or absence of appreciation, is objective.

Nor is it only theory of knowledge that shows such an identification to be inadmissable; the language of ordinary aesthetic experience testifies to its impracticability. If there is no ultimate distinction between aesthetic object and apprehension of aesthetic object, we can for beauty read "appreciation of beauty." It follows that when we admire a beautiful sunset, we are in fact admiring our admiration of a beautiful sunset; that when we pass strictures about a work of art for lack of design, it may be, or faults of perspective, we are in fact making uncomplimentary remarks about a process which is going on in our own heads, and that when we praise a piece of music, the object of our regard is really our own sentiments. It follows, too, that we are precluded from having a direct experience of any aesthetic object, since our appreciation of that object insists on intervening between us and the experience, and becoming itself the object of experience.

Thus the position that the existence of beauty is or is dependent upon the existence of a mind to enter into relation with the so-called beautiful object leads to results which amount to a *reductio ad absurdum* of the subjectivist position.

Let us, finally, suppose that all the people in the world are abolished but one. Let the sole survivor of humanity—and for the moment we will assume that there is no such thing as a divine mind—be confronted with the Sistine Madonna of Raphael. This picture, it will be said by the subjectivists, is still beautiful because it is being appreciated. Suppose further that in the midst of the last man's contemplation of the picture he too is abolished. Has any alteration occurred in the picture? Has it experienced any change? Has in fact anything been done to it? The only change that has occurred is that it has ceased to be appreciated. Does it therefore automatically cease to be beautiful? Those who hold the subjectivist position must maintain that it does, and, as I pointed out above, there is no logical disproof of their contention. Yet, although it cannot be disproved I maintain that it fails to make provision for the undoubted fact that we all of us do think that it is better that an uncontemplated Madonna should exist than an uncontemplated cesspool. It is the existence of this undeniable human sentiment which suggests that it is only through confusion between the appreciation of beauty and the beauty appreciated that philosophers have been led to think that it is impossible to conceive of beauty which is not perceived by mind.

It is sometimes urged at this point that although beauty may still attach to the uncontemplated Madonna, the beauty has lost its value. It is no longer significant. What non-significant beauty can mean, if it is not an alternative expression for non-contemplated beauty, it is not easy to discover. But in what sense can it be maintained that no value attaches to uncontemplated beauty? Professor G. E. Moore has dealt with the point in his *Principia Ethica,* chap. iii, p. 83, § 50.

> Let us imagine one world [he says] exceedingly beautiful. Imagine it as beautiful as you can: put in whatever in the world you most admire—mountains, rivers, the sea, trees, sunsets, stars, and moon. Imagine all this combined in the most exquisite proportions, so that no one thing jars against another, but each contributes to increase the beauty of the whole. And then imagine the ugliest world you can possibly conceive. Imagine it simply as a heap of filth, containing everything that is most disgusting to us for whatever reason, and the whole, so far as may be, without one redeeming feature. . . . The only thing we are not entitled to imagine is that any human being ever has or ever by any possibility can see and enjoy the beauty of the one or hate the foulness of the other. . . . Is it irrational to hold that it is better that the beautiful world should exist than the one which is ugly?

To answer that it is irrational, is a hard saying, and it is one to which most subjectivists seem averse from committing themselves. Whatever be the meaning of beauty, we must, I think, answer that it is better that a supremely beautiful world should exist than a supremely ugly one, even if we can never behold either of them. And this, I think, constitutes a cogent argument against those who hold, either that objects which are not perceived cease to be beautiful, or that, even if they are still beautiful, their beauty has no value.

For these reasons I contend that beauty is not a quality of nor is it dependent upon a relation between an object and a mind or a group of minds. The position that beauty is a quality of or is dependent upon a certain feeling or set of feelings entertained by a mind or body of minds, has already been discussed under (*a*) above, and although we have not been able to bring forward arguments of a logical character against this position, we have convicted it of inability to explain the uniqueness of our feeling for aesthetic value. If, then, beauty is not a quality of a knowing mind nor dependent upon a knowing mind, nor a relation between knowing mind and object known, the only alternative seems to be that it is a quality of the object known. This, then, is the position that I propose to maintain.

2. Beauty as Objective

That we commonly make statements such as "this picture is beautiful" or "this picture is better than that" is undoubted. Now the plain man would certainly maintain that his intention in making statements of this kind is to describe some quality possessed by the picture. It would also appear prima facie that since the quality in question is believed to be an attribute of the picture, the attitude of mind implied by such statements is one of discovery or of recognition; on coming to look at it, he *realizes* or *notices* that the picture is beautiful, and in saying that his realization that the picture is beautiful involves an attitude of discovery, we are implying also that what is discovered exists independently of the discovery. What I maintain is that these common-sense assertions do represent a truth concerning aesthetic emotion and the object upon which it is directed; I believe, that is to say, that beauty is as truly a quality of a picture as its shape, and that whatever reasons there are for regarding the latter as independent of the observer apply also to the former. We have already advanced some way towards this conclusion by a discussion and elimination of alternative views; we have now to consider the positive reasons for it.

The best positive statement of the grounds for the position advocated is that given by Plato; it constitutes part of the general argument for the theory of Ideas. This argument falls into two parts. First, for reasons into which it is not necessary to enter, the sensory world is shown to be in a constant state of change or flux. Nothing in it completely *is;* it is always halfway on the road to being something else. Further, no two persons entertain the same opinion about it, the qualities which it is thought to exhibit being relative to the state of the perceiver's mind and also of his body: it is therefore, according to Plato, impossible to obtain certain and agreed knowledge about the sensory world. Yet science and still more mathematics show that certain and agreed knowledge is possible; it cannot, therefore, be about the changing qualities of the sensible world but about the perfect archetypes of which the sensible qualities are but imperfect models.

Secondly,[3] if we consider such an entity as "whiteness," it is clear that it is not of any white object, snow or cream, of which we are thinking; nor is it of the sum total of all such white objects. Yet in considering whiteness we are clearly thinking about something, both because it is impossible to think about nothing and because a thought of whiteness is different from a thought of blackness. Nor can it be said that this "something" is merely a mental concept, an idea in our own minds, dependent on our minds for its existence. Snow would still be white, or would still be qualified by that property in virtue of which we call it white, even if no mind were aware of the fact. Since, therefore, whiteness would still be predicable of snow even in the absence of minds to be aware of the fact, we may say that whiteness is not dependent for its existence upon mind. But if whiteness is other than white objects, if it is also non-mental and independent of mind, and if nevertheless it is clearly something, there seems to be no alternative but to place it in the category of real objects to which Plato assigns the Forms; it is, that is to say, a permanent and immutable object, non-mental and non-material, which is the cause of the common quality which different white objects possess, and in virtue of which we call them white. Hence, we arrive at the world of Forms which are objects of thought and not of sense, and stand in the same sort of relation to mind as the subsistent objects described in Chapter III.[4] The subsistent objects differ from the Forms in three important respects.

---

[3] I am combining a number of different arguments scattered up and down the *Dialogues*. The argument in the actual form in which it is here given does not occur anywhere in Plato.

[4] Mr. Joad's definition of subsistent objects in Chapter III (p. 124) follows:

"Thus we are driven to postulate the presence in the universe of objects which have neither physical nor mental existence, but which are discovered by mind as forming part of the external world. It is customary to say of these objects not that they exist, but that they subsist. Subsistent objects are, I think, what many realists have meant to designate by the term 'concept,' although I am not sure that they would attribute to the concept precisely the same status and function as those with which I endow the subsistent object. For me, however, subsistent objects and concepts are identical. I believe that subsistent objects are exceedingly numerous, far mor numerous than either physical objects or mental acts. There is a subsistent object for every physical object considered

They are not, in virtue merely of the fact that they are subsistent, objects of value and entitled therefore to reverence, although some of them may in fact be valuable; they do not own a higher reality than that of the physical world, and they are not the cause of the existence of physical objects.

Although, however, beauty is a subsistent object so far as its relation to the sensible world is concerned, it belongs to a special class of subsistent objects which are distinguished from the main company of such objects in that they are recognized as possessing value. In respect of its possession of value, beauty may be included among Plato's Forms as an object of reverence revealed to insight. To the question of the relationship between subsistent objects, physical objects, and objects of value I shall return in a later chapter, where I hope to discuss the general questions involved.[5] In the present chapter I shall be concerned with the special case of the relation of the Form of Beauty to aesthetic objects.

Applying Plato's theory of Forms to aesthetic objects, we are enabled to give a meaning to statements such as those made above to the effect that (x) is a good picture, or that (x) is a better picture than (y). By the first statement we shall mean that there attaches to the picture (x) a definite quality or property in virtue of which it arouses a certain kind of emotion in us as a result of which we call it beautiful; by the second, that one picture possesses this quality in a more eminent degree than another. The pictures do not, however, depend for their possession of this property upon any mind or body of minds either in the present, past, or future, nor is the property relative to any mind or body of minds. It follows first, that it is not necessary that a picture should be appreciated by mind in order that it may have the property; secondly, that its possession of the property is not affected by the various judgments that may be passed in regard to it in different generations or by different people in the same generation, as to whether it has the property or not. I wish to emphasize this second point, because the notorious differences of aesthetic valuation which amply justify the generalization that there is no single work of art of first-rate importance that has not been frequently condemned by competent persons, are often advanced as an argument in favour of the view that beauty is subjective, or is at any rate relative to taste. On the theory here put forward, however, it is clear that the different estimates of the value or beauty of a picture that may be advanced no more imply that the picture has no aesthetic value in its own right, than the varying guesses that may be made as to the temperature of a

---

as a set of sense data, and there is also one for each sense datum in the set. Subsistent objects include everything that can be thought of and also all the relations between the things that can be thought of; they include the counterparts of everything that exists, and of everything that may or might have existed but does not." (Eds.)

[5] The student who is interested in following this argument, as presented by Mr. Joad, is directed to *Matter, Life and Value,* Chap. IX, pp. 380–384. (Eds.)

room prove that the room has not a temperature which is independent of and unaffected by the guesses. But just as it is possible for some of the guesses to be more correct than others, so will some of the judgments of the aesthetic value of a picture be nearer the truth than others. This assertion is perfectly compatible with the further assertion that it is impossible to know with certainty which of the conflicting judgments is in fact nearer to the truth, impossible, that is to say, except to a mind which has a direct knowledge of the Form of beauty itself, and the possessor of such a mind will not, for reasons into which we shall enter later, be in a position to explain the grounds upon which he pronounces one of the conflicting judgments to be more correct than another.

We define a person who consistently passes judgments on the aesthetic value of works of art which are reasonably near the truth or which are nearer the truth than those of most, as a person of good taste. It follows from what has just been said that it is not possible to decide with certainty who is a person of good taste and who is not. This result appears to be borne out by experience. Certain broad generalizations as to the conditions necessary to the passing of reasonably accurate judgments have, however, been established by the experience of mankind. There are times with all of us when we are blind to beauty; a certain tranquillity, an even temper of mind must first be achieved. All the religions and all the philosophies have insisted that we must somehow escape from the turmoil to catch a vision of beauty; while the water is troubled it cannot reflect the sky, but that does not prevent the sky being there for reflection.

The possession by the picture of the quality in virtue of which we say that it is beautiful or has aesthetic value is due, then, to a special kind of connexion between the picture and the Form of Beauty. As stated above, I propose to discuss in a later chapter the nature of this connexion, and hope to advance reasons against the Platonic view in so far as it represents the picture as *participating* in the Form of Beauty. For the present it will be sufficient to anticipate the result of this discussion by asserting, without attempting to defend the assertion, that, in my view, the connexion is one which can best be expressed by saying that the object of art is beautiful in so far as it copies or reproduces the patterns and arrangements that subsist in the real world. It is these patterns and arrangements of the real world which are the source of aesthetic value and which I conceive after the model of Plato's world of Forms as immutable, eternal, and self-subsistent, that we may suppose Plato to have compendiously described by the expression "the Form of Beauty."

Since the criterion of the beauty or aesthetic value of a work of art is to be found in its possession of a quality which belongs to it in virtue of its special connexion with the Form of Beauty, it is clear that it is not to be sought in any relation which the picture may or may not have to the purpose of the artist, or in his success in executing that purpose. All questions relating to the power and originality of the artist's conception, to the extent to which he has succeeded in embodying his conception in the work of art, to the nature of the effect which he may have intended to produce or to his success or failure in producing that effect, to the ability of his work to arouse emotion in the spectators, whether it be the emotion which the artist himself has felt and which is, therefore, communicated emotion, or some other emotion, are, therefore, irrelevant to the question of the beauty of the work of art. Considerations of this kind neither constitute a criterion of beauty nor do they provide a meaning for the term. The only consideration that is relevant to the value of the work of art under discussion, the only question that we are entitled to ask in respect of it is, Does it or does it not exhibit the quality in question? If, as Plato would say, it participates in the Form of Beauty, or if, as I should prefer to put it, it possesses significant form, by virtue of the fact that it reproduces the structure of reality, it is beautiful and has value; if it does not, it has none. And the reason why aesthetic criticism is relative and empirical and lacks the authority and precision of science, is simply that no certain or agreed pronouncement can be made on this question.

Such is the bearing of Plato's general theory of Forms upon the meaning of the assertion that a particular work of art is beautiful or has aesthetic value. But Plato has something to add with particular reference to the Form of Beauty. He describes this Form in greater detail than any of the others, and asserts . . . in the Phaedrus . . . that beauty alone among the Forms is apprehended by the soul in the world of becoming as she really is.[6] What he has to tell us on the subject amounts nevertheless to little more than a series of hints. These hints are chiefly concerned to throw light upon the nature of our appreciation of beauty, both as she is manifested in works of art and other material media, and as she is revealed direct to the philosopher. First there is the famous account in the *Symposium* of the grades or stages in the apprehension of the Form.[7] Plato describes the ascent of the soul from the apprehension of beauty in the sensible world, to the direct vision of the Form of Beauty in the intelligible world. In this ascent there are three stages. A man begins by appreciating the beauty of one beautiful object or shape; he then advances to the stage in which he can appreciate several beautiful objects and realizes that beauty is a common property belonging to many different things. The next stage is the apprehension of abstract

---

[6] *Phaedrus,* 250. "But of beauty I repeat again that we saw her there shining in company with the celestial forms; and coming to earth we find her here too, shining in clearness through the clearest aperture of sense. . . . But this is the privilege of beauty, that she is the loveliest and also the most palpable to sight."

[7] Plato, *Symposium,* 210.

beauty, that is, the beauty of laws and institutions. But the knowledge of the Form of Beauty is not yet. Perseverance and aptitude in the study of the abstract beauty of stage three are required. We learn, moreover, in the seventh book of the *Republic* that the method by which a man approaches nearer to the true vision of the Form is by an arduous study in that branch of knowledge which is farthest removed from illusion, that is, in the exact sciences of measuring, weighing, and counting, namely, the Theories of Number, Geometry, Stereometry, and Astronomy; [8] and it is for the reason that he has had no training in weighing and measuring and calculating that it is said of the artist in the tenth book that he will never attain to a perception of the Form itself.[9] After prolonged study of this kind will come the sudden apprehension of the Form. This is described in the *Symposium* in the language of a mystical vision. "And at last the vision is revealed to him of a single science which is the science of beauty everywhere." [10] In the seventh epistle Plato says that the knowledge of the Forms cannot be put into words like other kinds of learning, but that suddenly, after much study and familiarity with the pursuit of them, light whereby they may be beheld springs up in the soul like flame from a fire. This final apprehension is a kind of intuition, a mystical flash entirely divorced from the purely logical and mathematical processes of study which necessarily precede it. The vision follows logically from and is conditioned by the leading-up process; but in itself it is distinct and unique, involving both immediacy and separation from self. Then will it be seen that all other beautiful things are beautiful only in so far as they participate in the true being of beauty.[11]

Two conclusions emerge. The first reveals the Form of Beauty as the origin of the aesthetic value which belongs to the objects of the sensible world; this I have already discussed, and have attributed the aesthetic significance of sensible objects to their ability to reproduce the forms or patterns of the real world. According to the second, the extent to which a particular work will or will not have that relation with the Form of Beauty which Plato variously describes as participation by the work of art in the Form and as manifestation of the Form in the work of art, depends upon the vision of the artist. If he has himself seen the Form, then the work will possess the quality of significant form in virtue of which we say that it has aesthetic value; if he has not, no amount of training, no mastery over technique will enable him to create beautiful works. It does not therefore follow that training and technique are useless; on the contrary the best recipe for ensuring the revelation of the vision of the Form, and the consequent

---

8 Plato, *Republic,* Book VII, 525–528.
9 *Ibid.,* Book X, 602, 603.
10 Plato, *Symposium,* 210.
11 Cf. Plato, *Symposium,* 211.

creation of works of art, is for the artist to discipline himself strictly in the exact sciences of measuring, weighing, and counting recommended by Plato.

Translated into modern terms, this means that an artist who has perfected himself in the technique of drawing and painting, or in the theory of harmony and the details of orchestration, or who pays strict attention to the rules of rhythm and metre, will be more likely to produce a work of beauty than one who sets about his task uninstructed and without study. But such training and study will not enable the artist to command the Form, or to ensure that beauty will clothe his work. The coming of the Form knows no law. It is the incalculable element in all art; it can neither be compelled nor cajoled.

And this would seem to be the reason for the fact so often noted that works of the greatest elaboration and technical skill are yet not great works of Art. This explains also why beauty attaches to the work of some men who, like Walt Whitman, disregard all rules, and throw all canons of taste overboard, whilst it eschews the laboured productions of those who, like some of the Augustan poets, follow rigorously and with perfect taste the best traditions of the elders. But it is equally true that the Form of beauty is more likely to be attracted by a knowledge of rules and of technique than where such knowledge is absent, and that, other things being equal, erudition and skill are more likely to produce works of beauty than so-called inspiration which is devoid of them.

This is as far as Plato takes us. In the last resort the apprehension of the Form in virtue of which an artist is enabled to produce work of aesthetic value is left unexplained. Effort and training help, but they are not sufficient; whether the artist philosopher's search will be rewarded by a vision of reality lies upon the knees of the gods. But this at least is certain, that if his vision is not refreshed by the Form of Beauty, however fleeting the glimpse, then, although he may by accident produce works of value, he will not know that they are beautiful. It is with this somewhat arbitrary revelation of the Form to the artist as the origin and source of aesthetic value in the work of art that Plato leaves us. Can we not, in the light of [my] theory of evolution sketched in Part I, carry our account a stage further? [12] I think that we can; in making the attempt, however, I shall be content at this stage merely to state a position to be defended in later chapters.

The evolution of life I have defined in terms of an advance in the scope and subtlety of awareness. Beginning with an awareness of the constituents of the physical universe, life has already reached a level at which it is in thinking more or less permanently aware of subsistent objects. During the period of recorded history the possibility of a further advance has become

---

[12] This theory is sketched in Part I of *Matter, Life and Value*. (Eds.)

apparent; there begin, that is to say, to be fleeting intimations of a new type of object of which life is now for the first time aware. Like the subsistent object this new type of object is eternal, non-material, and self-sufficient; but it is differentiated from the subsistent object by its possession of what we call value. Of its company are beauty, goodness, and truth. Plato was the first to recognize that these three entities were in some unexplained way different from the other Forms, and was constrained to give them a place at the head of his hierarchy of reals, thus making a distinction for which no adequate ground can be found in his philosophy. To me they seem to be differentiated from all other subsistent objects in respect of this quality of possessing value, and to be the source (in a manner to be hereafter explained) of such value as is found to attach to sensible objects.

Following up Plato's hint as to the superior accessibility of the Form of Beauty, we may say that life having emerged at a level at which it becomes for the first time capable of the awareness of value, finds the medium in which value is chiefly manifested to be those works of art which we call beautiful. This at least is true of the ordinary man who is capable of apprehending only such value as the artist makes plain for him. But in the artist himself life expresses itself at a higher level as a capacity for apprehending value in the world of nature and the forms of sound. Of the artist's apprehension at the present stage of life's development two conclusions may be affirmed. First, it is fleeting and intermittent and can neither be commanded nor retained; secondly, it is attained only by those whom I have likened to evolutionary "sports" on the mental plane, in whom the capacity for awareness has emerged at a higher level than in the rest of the species.

There are in the sensible world combinations, whether of line and colour or of sound, which reproduce albeit obscurely the patterns and arrangements that characterize the real world. The perception of these combinations by the artist is attended by the thrill of excitement which Plato describes in his mystical account of the manifestation of the Form of beauty. The vision passes, but the artist recalling its outlines sets to work to reproduce in a material medium, either in paint, in stone, or in sound, the forms and patterns which he has momentarily glimpsed. Hence pictures and statues and pieces of music have value in proportion as the artist's vision has enabled him to grasp, his memory to retain, and his skill to reproduce or copy the patterns and forms of the world of value whose copies he has perceived in the sensible world. When this reproduction has been achieved, the work of art is, to use Plato's language, made in the likeness of the Form of beauty. Further, the artist, in virtue of his skill, enables the spectator to recognize in his work the outlines and patterns of the world which he, the artist, has first apprehended in a material medium. And the spectator, viewing for the first time, though in the copy of a copy, the image and likeness of the real world, is thrilled with the same emotion as that which was excited in the artist by his perception of value in natural objects.

> For, don't you mark, we're made so that we love
> First when we see them painted, things we have passed
> Perhaps a hundred times nor cared to see.[13]

The spectator experiences vicariously the emotion which the artist has felt for the likeness of reality; to use Plato's language, art turns the eye of the soul round to reality. It is to this emotion that we give the name of aesthetic emotion, and the work of art arouses this emotion in proportion as it succeeds in reproducing the forms and arrangements of the world of value.

---

[13] Browning, *Fra Lippo Lippi.*

Section Seven

THE FUNCTIONS
OF ART

THE INTERACTIONS among the artist, the object of art, and the observer take place within a social context; and the relation of these three factors, which make up the aesthetic process, to the environment in which the process occurs, raises a complex array of problems for the aesthetician. Each of the factors—artist, object, and observer—serves and is served by the pressures of religion, politics, morality, and truth. The total psychology which the artist and the observer bring to the aesthetic process is largely formed by these surrounding social pressures, and it may be claimed, in turn, that the artist and observer, both of whom affect their society by their commerce with art, owe certain obligations to this society. Similarly, the values in the aesthetic object bear some relation to those extra-aesthetic values within whose shelter the aesthetic object is produced and appreciated. Limitations of space prevent the editors from including selections which would do complete justice to all the relationships which analysis shows to be possible between the three factors of the aesthetic process and the four extra-aesthetic aspects of the outside world which we have listed above. Thus, for purposes of keeping this section within reasonable bounds, the editors have collapsed the factors, artist, object, and observer, into the single term, "art." And without considering singly any of the three factors which make up this term, we shall study the relation between art and religion, beween art and society or politics, between art and morality, and between art and truth.

There are three general attitudes which most writers have toward the

480

function of art considered from the standpoint of the audience. Art has been considered solely an end in itself, the pleasure it gives the spectator being sufficient justification for its existence. Or art has been considered a means to either private or public improvement, or both, in the sphere of religion, politics, morality, or truth. Finally, writers have considered that art can be a unique means to private or public improvement only if it is first conceived as an end in itself. The editors have not organized this section in terms of these distinctions—distinctions which may seem too fine and too difficult to trace closely—but, rather, have chosen the more obvious divisions based on the nonaesthetic interest to which art is being related. Yet they have tried also to provide for what seems to them to be the significant light which these distinctions throw on the problems of this section. Thus selections have been included which argue for the autonomy of art, the first of the positions outlined above. And, as we shall see later in this preface, the other selections, whether they concern the relation of art to religion, society, morality, or truth, may be seen to illustrate either of the other two positions we have distinguished: art may be treated solely as it affects the nonaesthetic activity, or it may be treated first in its own terms so that its purely aesthetic function can allow it to perform an indispensable service for the more practical world within which it flourishes.

Our main emphasis in this section nevertheless falls on the other kinds of human activity with which, it is claimed, art has important relations. Tolstoy considers the religious function of art. But since his conception of religion is so largely social, this selection points the way to the Marxist view of art and society which Bukharin presents to us. Santayana also examines the relation of art to society, but he conceives the problem from the standpoint of the moralist rather than from that of the revolutionist. His selection, then, leads us to consider the relation of art to morality. Wimsatt and Zink, who follow, show us different treatments of this latter problem. Bell and Bradley are introduced after them to offer positions which deny the positive claims made by the others about the relationship between art and nonaesthetic interests. Both of these writers insist that art be independent, that it serve no end extrinsic to itself.

The last four articles deal with the relation of art to truth. This problem stands apart from the others and even, perhaps, above them; or at least it would seem to be logically prior to them. For what we think about the religious, the social, or the moral function of art depends largely on what we conceive to be the capacity of art to make meaningful statements about these spheres of human activity; and to determine this capacity we must know whether art can make meaningful statements about anything.

For contemporary aesthetics the problem is defined by I. A. Richards in *Principles of Literary Criticism* (1924). The selection here given from

Science and Poetry is a more succinct statement of the ideas developed in the earlier book. Richards distinguishes between referential and emotive discourse, and, allowing propositional truth only to the former, denies it to art, which he classifies as purely emotive. It is in the light of Richards' definition of the problem that Weitz claims that art does involve propositional statements which may be true or false. Walsh and Leon, instead of arguing for the propositional truth of art, try to show that it offers its own special, nonphilosophical form of knowledge.

As we have anticipated above, it is possible to see in these selections yet another set of distinctions which a complete organization of the problems of this section would have to reveal and to which the editors cannot do full justice because of limitations of space. Some of the authors simply abstract from art meanings and values which they wish to relate directly to the nonaesthetic interest—life, as it is usually called—which concerns them. Others undertake the more complex task of approaching the object as aesthetic and yet insisting that, while remaining an aesthetic object, it has the capacity (and a unique capacity) to influence life. The former authors emphasize the effect of art on life by picking some aspect of the aesthetic object—some of its meanings and values—regardless of the way these are related to the other aesthetic factors which make up the object. The other authors, while recognizing that the aesthetic object has nonaesthetic effects, maintain that these can be produced, or can only be properly produced, when the object first functions in its aesthetic capacity. In other words, in order to relate the aesthetic function of the object to the nonaesthetic, some writers consider only its extrinsic relations, while others dwell on its intrinsic relations.

Thus Tolstoy treats the object as a tool of religion, Bukharin treats it as a device of political interests, Santayana as a means to his proposed morality. Similarly, it is abstract and propositional truth to which Richards and Weitz immediately relate art, whether negatively or positively. On the other hand, Winsatt and Zink would give art a moral function, and Walsh and Leon would give it a cognitive function, but only after an intense study of art as art. And of course, Bell and Bradley, fighting for the autonomy of art, do not, in their selections, allow for any function except the aesthetic. It is perhaps for this reason that they are especially useful to the student of the aesthetic object. (Thus, in our section on the object, an earlier selection from Bell's *Art* was included, and the student was referred to the selection from Bradley, which in many ways serves the objectives of that section.) Indeed, many discussions of the problems raised in this section may refer to problems which we considered earlier. We should have expected this in discussions which relate the components of the aesthetic process to the other aspects of human activity. Thus we end much as we began, by seeing the place of art in the total human economy. But if we sought to differentiate and isolate art at the beginning of our study (see Section II), we learn here at the end, after having found the isolation of art useful for our study of it, that art must finally in some way be restored to its place amid the cluster of interests that characterize man at the human level.

Christian Art

LEO TOLSTOY

The Religious Function of Art [1]

ART IN OUR SOCIETY has become so perverted that not only has bad art come to be considered good, but even the very perception of what art really is has been lost. In order to be able to speak about the art of our society it is, therefore, first of all necessary to distinguish art from counterfeit art.

There is one indubitable sign distinguishing real art from its counterfeit —namely, the infectiousness of art. If a man without exercising effort and without altering his standpoint, on reading, hearing, or seeing another man's work experiences a mental condition which unites him with that man and with others who are also affected by that work, then the object evoking that condition is a work of art. And however poetic, realistic, striking, or interesting, a work may be, it is not a work of art if it does not evoke that feeling (quite distinct from all other feelings) of joy and of spiritual union with another (the author) and with others (those who are also infected by it).

It is true that this indication is an *internal* one and that there are people who, having forgotten what the action of real art is, expect something else from art (in our society the great majority are in this state), and that therefore such people may mistake for this aesthetic feeling the feeling of diversion

---

[1] Leo Tolstoy, *What is Art? and Essays on Art,* tr. Aylmer Maude (London: Oxford University Press, World's Classics Series, 1938), pp. 227–250. Reprinted by permission. Title by the editors. (Eds.)

and a certain excitement which they receive from counterfeits of art. But though it is impossible to undeceive these people, just as it may be impossible to convince a man suffering from colour-blindness that green is not red, yet for all that, this indication remains perfectly definite to those whose feeling for art is neither perverted nor atrophied, and it clearly distinguishes the feeling produced by art from all other feelings.

The chief peculiarity of this feeling is that the recipient of a truly artistic impression is so united to the artist that he feels as if the work were his own and not some one else's—as if what it expresses were just what he had long been wishing to express. A real work of art destroys in the consciousness of the recipient the separation between himself and the artist, and not that alone, but also between himself and all whose minds receive this work of art. In this freeing of our personality from its separation and isolation, in this uniting of it with others, lies the chief characteristic and the great attractive force of art.

If a man is infected by the author's condition of soul, if he feels this emotion and this union with others, then the object which has effected this is art; but if there be no such infection, if there be not this union with the author and with others who are moved by the same work—then it is not art. And not only is infection a sure sign of art, but the degree of infectiousness is also the sole measure of excellence in art.

The stronger the infection the better is the art, as art, speaking of it now apart from its subject-matter—that is, not considering the value of the feelings it transmits.

And the degree of the infectiousness of art depends on three conditions:—

(1) On the greater or lesser individuality of the feeling transmitted; (2) on the greater or lesser clearness with which the feeling is transmitted; (3) on the sincerity of the artist, that is, on the greater or lesser force with which the artist himself feels the emotion he transmits.

The more individual the feeling transmitted the more strongly does it act on the recipient; the more individual the state of soul into which he is transferred the more pleasure does the recipient obtain and therefore the more readily and strongly does he join in it.

Clearness of expression assists infection because the recipient who mingles in consciousness with the author is the better satisfied the more clearly that feeling is transmitted which, as it seems to him, he has long known and felt and for which he has only now found expression.

But most of all is the degree of infectiousness of art increased by the degree of sincerity in the artist. As soon as the spectator, hearer, or reader, feels that the artist is infected by his own production and writes, sings, or plays, for himself, and not merely to act on others, this mental condition of the artist infects the recipient; and, on the contrary, as soon as the spectator, reader, or hearer, feels that the author is not writing, singing, or playing, for his own satisfaction—does not himself feel what he wishes to express, but is doing it for him, the recipient—resistance immediately springs up, and the most individual and the newest feelings and the cleverest technique not only fail to produce any infection but actually repel.

I have mentioned three conditions of contagion in art, but they may all be summed up into one, the last, sincerity; that is, that the artist should be impelled by an inner need to express his feeling. That condition includes the first; for if the artist is sincere he will express the feeling as he experienced it. And as each man is different from every one else, his feeling will be individual for every one else; and the more individual it is—the more the artist has drawn it from the depths of his nature—the more sympathetic and sincere will it be. And this same sincerity will impel the artist to find clear expression for the feeling which he wishes to transmit.

Therefore this third condition—sincerity—is the most important of the three. It is always complied with in peasant art, and this explains why such art always acts so powerfully; but it is a condition almost entirely absent from our upper-class art, which is continually produced by artists actuated by personal aims of covetousness or vanity.

Such are the three conditions which divide art from its counterfeits, and which also decide the quality of every work of art considered apart from its subject-matter.

The absence of any one of these conditions excludes a work from the category of art and relegates it to that of art's counterfeits. If the work does not transmit the artist's peculiarity of feeling and is therefore not individual, if it is unintelligibly expressed, or if it has not proceeded from the author's inner need for expression—it is not a work of art. If all these conditions are present even in the smallest degree, then the work even if a weak one is yet a work of art.

The presence in various degrees of these three conditions: individuality, clearness, and sincerity, decides the merit of a work of art as art, apart from subject-matter. All works of art take order of merit according to the degree in which they fulfil the first, the second, and the third, of these conditions. In one the individuality of the feeling transmitted may predominate; in another, clearness of expression; in a third, sincerity; while a fourth may have sincerity and individuality but be deficient in clearness; a fifth, individuality and clearness, but less sincerity; and so forth, in all possible degrees and combinations.

Thus is art divided from what is not art, and thus is the quality of art, as art, decided, independently of its subject-matter, that is to say, apart from whether the feelings it transmits are good or bad.

But how are we to define good and bad art with reference to its content or subject-matter?

How in the subject-matter of art are we to decide what is good and what is bad?

Art like speech is a means of communication and therefore of progress, that is, of the movement of humanity forward towards perfection. Speech renders accessible to men of the latest generations all the knowledge discovered by the experience and reflection both of preceding generations and of the best and foremost men of their own times; art renders accessible to men of the latest generations all the feelings experienced by their predecessors and also those felt by their best and foremost contemporaries. And as the evolution of knowledge proceeds by truer and more necessary knowledge dislodging and replacing what was mistaken and unnecessary, so the evolution of feeling proceeds by means of art—feelings less kind and less necessary for the well-being of mankind being replaced by others kinder and more needful for that end. That is the purpose of art. And speaking now of the feelings which are its subject-matter, the more art fulfils that purpose the better the art, and the less it fulfils it the worse the art.

The appraisement of feelings (that is, the recognition of one or other set of feelings as more or less good, more or less necessary for the well-being of mankind) is effected by the religious perception of the age.

In every period of history and in every human society there exists an understanding of the meaning of life, which represents the highest level to which men of that society have attained—an understanding indicating the highest good at which that society aims. This understanding is the religious perception of the given time and society. And this religious perception is always clearly expressed by a few advanced men and more or less vividly perceived by members of the society generally. Such a religious perception and its corresponding expression always exists in every society. If it appears to us that there is no religious perception in our society, this is not because there really is none, but only because we do not wish to see it. And we often wish not to see it because it exposes the fact that our life is inconsistent with that religious perception.

Religious perception in a society is like the direction of a flowing river. If the river flows at all it must have a direction. If a society lives, there must be a religious perception indicating the direction in which, more or less consciously, all its members tend.

And so there always has been, and is, a religious perception in every society. And it is by the standard of this religious perception that the feelings transmitted by art have always been appraised. It has always been only on the basis of this religious perception of their age, that men have chosen from amid the endlessly varied spheres of art that art which transmitted feelings making religious perception operative in actual life. And such art has always been highly valued and encouraged, while art transmitting feelings already outlived, flowing from the antiquated religious perceptions of a former age, has always been condemned and despised. All the rest of art transmitting those most diverse feelings by means of which people commune with one another was not condemned and was tolerated if only it did not transmit feelings contrary to religious perception. Thus for instance among the Greeks, art transmitting feelings of beauty, strength, and courage (Hesiod, Homer, Phidias) was chosen, approved, and encouraged, while art transmitting feelings of rude sensuality, despondency, and effeminacy, was condemned and despised. Among the Jews, art transmitting feelings of devotion and submission to the God of the Hebrews and to His will (the epic of Genesis, the prophets, the Psalms) was chosen and encouraged, while art transmitting feelings of idolatry (the Golden Calf) was condemned and despised. All the rest of art—stories, songs, dances, ornamentation of houses, of utensils, and of clothes—which was not contrary to religious perception, was neither distinguished nor discussed. Thus as regards its subject-matter has art always and everywhere been appraised and thus it should be appraised, for this attitude towards art proceeds from the fundamental characteristics of human nature, and those characteristics do not change.

I know that according to an opinion current in our times religion is a superstition humanity has outgrown, and it is therefore assumed that no such thing exists as a religious perception common to us all by which art in our time can be appraised. I know that this is the opinion current in the pseudo-cultured circles of today. People who do not acknowledge Christianity in its true meaning because it undermines their social privileges, and who therefore invent all kinds of philosophic and aesthetic theories to hide from themselves the meaninglessness and wrongfulness of their lives, cannot think otherwise. These people intentionally, or sometimes unintentionally, confuse the notion of a religious cult with the notion of religious perception, and think that by denying the cult they get rid of the perception. But even the very attacks on religion and the attempts to establish an idea of life contrary to the religious perception of our times, most clearly demonstrate the existence of a religious perception condemning the lives that are not in harmony with it.

If humanity progresses, that is, moves forward, there must inevitably be a guide to the direction of that movement. And religions have always furnished that guide. All history shows that the progress of humanity is accomplished no otherwise than under the guidance of religion. But if the race cannot progress without the guidance of religion,—and progress is always going on, and consequently goes on also in our own times,—then there must be a religion of our times. So that whether it pleases or displeases the so-called cultured people of to-day, they must admit the existence of religion—not of a religious cult, Catholic, Protestant, or another, but of religious perception—which even in our times is the guide always present where there is any progress. And if a religious perception exists amongst us, then the feelings dealt with by our art should be appraised on the basis of that religious perception; and as has been the case always and everywhere, art transmitting feelings flowing from the religious perception of our time should be chosen from amid all the indifferent art, should be acknowledged, highly valued, and encouraged, while art running counter to that perception should be condemned and despised, and all the remaining, indifferent, art should neither be distinguished nor encouraged.

The religious perception of our time in its widest and most practical application is the consciousness that our well-being, both material and spiritual, individual and collective, temporal and eternal, lies in the growth of brotherhood among men—in their loving harmony with one another. This perception is not only expressed by Christ and all the best men of past ages, it is not only repeated in most varied forms and from most diverse sides by the best men of our times, but it already serves as a clue to all the complex labour of humanity, consisting as this labour does on the one hand in the destruction of physical and moral obstacles to the union of men, and on the other hand in establishing the principles common to all men which can and should unite them in one universal brotherhood. And it is on the basis of this perception that we should appraise all the phenomena of our life and among the rest our art also: choosing from all its realms and highly prizing and encouraging whatever transmits feelings flowing from this religious perception, rejecting whatever is contrary to it, and not attributing to the rest of art an importance that does not properly belong to it.

The chief mistake made by people of the upper classes at the time of the so-called Renaissance,—a mistake we still perpetuate,—was not that they ceased to value and attach importance to religious art (people of that period could not attach importance to it because, like our own upper classes, they could not believe in what the majority considered to be religion), but their mistake was that they set up in place of the religious art that was lacking, an insignificant art which aimed merely at giving pleasure, that is, they began to choose, to value, and to encourage, in place of religious art, something which in any case did not deserve such esteem and encouragement.

One of the Fathers of the Church said that the great evil is not that men do not know God, but that they have set up instead of God, that which is not God. So also with art. The great misfortune of the people of the upper classes of our time is not so much that they are without a religious art as that, instead of a supreme religious art chosen from all the rest as being specially important and valuable, they have chosen a most insignificant and, usually, harmful art, which aims at pleasing certain people and which therefore, if only by its exclusive nature, stands in contradiction to that Christian principle of universal union which forms the religious perception of our time. Instead of religious art, an empty and often vicious art is set up, and this hides from men's notice the need of that true religious art which should be present in life to improve it.

It is true that art which satisfies the demands of the religious perception of our time is quite unlike former art, but notwithstanding this dissimilarity, to a man who does not intentionally hide the truth from himself, what forms the religious art of our age is very clear and definite. In former times when the highest religious perception united only some people (who even if they formed a large society were yet but one society among others—Jews, or Athenian or Roman citizens), the feelings transmitted by the art of that time flowed from a desire for the might, greatness, glory, and prosperity, of that society, and the heroes of art might be people who contributed to that prosperity by strength, by craft, by fraud, or by cruelty (Ulysses, Jacob, David, Samson, Hercules, and all the heroes). But the religious perception of our times does not select any one society of men; on the contrary it demands the union of all—absolutely of all people without exception—and above every other virtue it sets brotherly love of all men. And therefore the feelings transmitted by the art of our time not only cannot coincide with the feelings transmitted by former art, but must run counter to them.

Christian, truly Christian, art has been so long in establishing itself, and has not yet established itself, just because the Christian religious perception was not one of those small steps by which humanity advances regularly, but was an enormous revolution which, if it has not already altered, must inevitably alter the entire conception of life of mankind, and consequently the whole internal organization of that life. It is true that the life of humanity, like that of an individual, moves regularly; but in that regular movement come, as it were, turning-points which sharply divide the preceding from the subsequent life. Christianity was such a turning-point; such at least it must appear to us who live by the Christian perception of life. Christian perception gave another, a new, direction to all human feelings, and therefore completely altered both the content and the significance of art. The Greeks could make use of Persian art and the Romans could use Greek art, or, similarly, the Jews could use Egyptian art—the fundamental ideals were one and the same. Now the ideal was the greatness and prosperity of the Persians, now the greatness and prosperity of the Greeks, now that of the Romans. The same art was transferred to other conditions and served new nations. But the Christian ideal changed and reversed everything, so that, as the Gospel puts it, "That which was exalted among men has become an abomination in the sight of God." The ideal is no longer the greatness of Pharaoh or of a Roman emperor, not the beauty of a Greek nor the wealth of Phoenicia, but humility, purity, compassion, love. The hero is no longer Dives, but Lazarus the beggar; not Mary Magdalene in the day of her beauty but in the day of her repentance; not those who acquire wealth but those who have abandoned it; not those who dwell in palaces but those who dwell in catacombs and huts; not those who rule over others, but those who acknowledge no authority but God's. And the greatest work of art is no longer a cathedral of victory [2] with statues of conquerors, but the representation of a human soul so transformed by love that a man who is tormented and murdered, yet pities and loves his persecutors.

And the change is so great that men of the Christian world find it difficult to resist the inertia of the heathen art to which they have been accustomed all their lives. The subject-matter of Christian religious art is so new to them, so unlike the subject-matter of former art, that it seems to them as though Christian art were a denial of art, and they cling desperately to the old art. But this old art, having no longer in our day any source in religious perception, has lost its meaning, and we shall have to abandon it whether we wish to or not.

The essence of the Christian perception consists in the recognition by every man of his sonship to God and of the consequent union of men with God and with one another, as is said in the Gospel (John xvii. 21 [3]). Therefore the subject-matter of Christian art is of a kind that feeling can unite men with God and with one another.

The expression *unite men with God and with one another* may seem obscure to people accustomed to the misuse of these words that is so customary, but the words have a perfectly clear meaning nevertheless. They indicate that the Christian union of man (in contradiction to the partial, exclusive, union of only certain men) is that which unites all without exception.

Art, all art, has this characteristic, that it unites people. Every art causes those to whom the artist's feeling is transmitted to unite in soul with the artist and also with all who receive the same impression. But non-Christian art while uniting some people, makes that very union a cause of separation between these united people and others; so that union of this kind is often a source not merely of division but even of enmity towards others. Such is all patriotic art, with its anthems, poems, and monuments; such is all

---

[2] There is in Moscow a magnificent "Cathedral of our Saviour," erected to commemorate the defeat of the French in the war of 1812.—A.M. [Translator].

[3] "That they may all be one; even as thou, Father, art in me, and I in Thee, that they also may be in us."

Church art, that is, the art of certain cults, with their images, statues, processions, and other local ceremonies. Such art is belated and non-Christian, uniting the people of one cult only to separate them yet more sharply from the members of other cults, and even to place them in relations of hostility to one another. Christian art is such only as tends to unite all without exception, either by evoking in them the perception that each man and all men stand in a like relation towards God and towards their neighbour, or by evoking in them identical feelings, which may even be the very simplest, provided that they are not repugnant to Christianity and are natural to every one without exception.

Good Christian art of our time may be unintelligible to people because of imperfections in its form or because men are inattentive to it, but it must be such that all men can experience the feelings it transmits. It must be the art not of some one group of people, or of one class, or of one nationality, or of one religious cult; that is, it must not transmit feelings accessible only to a man educated in a certain way, or only to an aristocrat, or a merchant, or only to a Russian, or a native of Japan, or a Roman Catholic, or a Buddhist, and so on, but it must transmit feelings accessible to every one. Only art of this kind can in our time be acknowledged to be good art, worthy of being chosen out from all the rest of art and encouraged.

Christian art, that is, the art of our time, should be catholic in the original meaning of the word, that is, universal, and therefore it should unite all men. And only two kinds of feeling unite all men: first, feelings flowing from a perception of our sonship to God and of the brotherhood of man; and next, the simple feelings of common life accessible to every one without exception—such as feelings of merriment, of pity, of cheerfulness, of tranquillity, and so forth. Only these two kinds of feelings can now supply material for art good in its subject-matter.

And the action of these two kinds of art apparently so dissimilar, is one and the same. The feelings flowing from the perception of our sonship to God and the brotherhood of man—such as a feeling of sureness in truth, devotion to the will of God, self-sacrifice, respect for and love of man— evoked by Christian religious perception; and the simplest feelings, such as a softened or a merry mood caused by a song or an amusing jest intelligible to every one, or by a touching story, or a drawing, or a little doll: both alike produce one and the same effect—the loving union of man with man. Sometimes people who are together, if not hostile to one another, are at least estranged in mood and feeling, till perhaps a story, a performance, a picture, or even a building, but oftenest of all music, unites them all as by an electric flash, and in place of their former isolation or even enmity they are conscious of union and mutual love. Each is glad that another feels what he feels; glad of the communion established not only between him and all present, but also with all now living who will yet share the same impression; and, more than that, he feels the mysterious gladness of a communion which, reaching beyond the grave, unites us with all men of the past who have been moved by the same feelings and with all men of the future who will yet be touched by them. And this effect is produced both by religious art which transmits feelings of love of God and one's neighbour, and by universal art transmitting the very simplest feelings common to all men.

The art of our time should be appraised differently from former art chiefly in this, that the art of our time, that is, Christian art (basing itself on a religious perception which demands the union of man), excludes from the domain of art good in its subject-matter, everything transmitting exclusive feelings which do not unite men but divide them. It relegates such work to the category of art that is bad in its subject-matter; while on the other hand it includes in the category of art that is good in subject-matter a section not formerly admitted as deserving of selection and respect, namely, universal art transmitting even the most trifling and simple feelings if only they are accessible to all men without exception, and therefore unite them. Such art cannot but be esteemed good in our time, for it attains the end which Christianity, the religious perception of our time, sets before humanity.

Christian art either evokes in men feelings which through love of God and of one's neighbour draw them to closer and ever closer union and make them ready for, and capable of, such union; or evokes in them feelings which show them that they are already united in the joys and sorrows of life. And therefore the Christian art of our time can be and is of two kinds: first, art transmitting feelings flowing from a religious perception of man's position in the world in relation to God and to his neighbour—religious art in the limited meaning of the term; and secondly, art transmitting the simplest feelings of common life, but such always as are accessible to all men in the whole world—the art of common life—the art of the people—universal art. Only these two kinds of art can be considered good art in our time.

The first, religious art—transmitting both positive feelings of love of God and one's neighbour, and negative feelings of indignation and horror at the violation of love—manifests itself chiefly in the form of words, and to some extent also in painting and sculpture: the second kind, universal art, transmitting feelings accessible to all, manifests itself in words, in painting, in sculpture, in dances, in architecture, and most of all in music.

If I were asked to give modern examples of each of these kinds of art, then as examples of the highest art flowing from love of God and man (both of the higher, positive, and of the lower, negative kind), in literature I should name *The Robbers* by Schiller; Victor Hugo's *Les Pauvres Gens* and *Les Misérables;* the novels and stories of Dickens—*The Tale of Two Cities, The Christmas Carol, The Chimes,* and others—*Uncle Tom's Cabin;* Dostoévski's works—especially his *Memoirs from the House of Death*—and *Adam Bede* by George Eliot.

In modern painting, strange to say, works of this kind, directly transmitting the Christian feeling of love of God and of one's neighbour, are hardly to be found, especially among the works of the celebrated painters. There are plenty of pictures treating of the Gospel stories; these however, while depicting historical events with great wealth of detail, do not and cannot transmit religious feelings not possessed by their painters. There are many pictures treating of the personal feelings of various people, but of pictures representing great deeds of self-sacrifice and Christian love there are very few, and what there are are principally by artists who are not celebrated, and they are for the most part not pictures but merely sketches. Such for instance is the drawing by Kramskóy (worth many of his finished pictures), showing a drawing-room with a balcony past which troops are marching in triumph on their return from the war. On the balcony stands a wet-nurse holding a baby, and a boy. They are admiring the procession of the troops, but the mother, covering her face with a handkerchief, has fallen back on the sofa sobbing. Such also is the picture by Walter Langley to which I have already referred, and such again is a picture by the French artist Morlon, depicting a lifeboat hastening in a heavy storm to the relief of a steamer that is being wrecked. Approaching these in kind are pictures which represent the hard-working peasant with respect and love. Such are the pictures by Millet and particularly his drawing, "The Man with the Hoe," also pictures in this style by Jules Breton, Lhermitte, Defregger, and others. As examples of pictures evoking indignation and horror at the violation of love of God and man, Gay's picture "Judgment" may serve, and also Leizen-Mayer's "Signing the Death Warrant." But there are very few of this kind also. Anxiety about the technique and the beauty of the picture for the most part obscures the feeling. For instance, Gérôme's "Pollice Verso" expresses, not so much horror at what is being perpetrated as attraction by the beauty of the spectacle.[4]

To give examples from the modern art of our upper classes, of art of the second kind: good universal art, or even of the art of a whole people, is yet more difficult, especially in literature and music. If there are some works which by their inner contents might be assigned to this class (such as *Don Quixote,* Molière's comedies, *David Copperfield* and *The Pickwick Papers* by Dickens, Gógol's and Púshkin's tales, and some things of Maupassant's), these works for the most part—owing to the exceptional nature of the feelings they transmit, and the superfluity of special details of time and locality, and above all on account of the poverty of their subject-matter in comparison

---

[4] In this picture the spectators in the Roman Amphitheatre are turning down their thumbs to show that they wish the vanquished gladiator to be killed.—A.M.

with examples of universal ancient art (such, for instance, as the story of Joseph)—are comprehensible only to people of their own circle. That Joseph's brethren, being jealous of his father's affection, sell him to the merchants; that Potiphar's wife wishes to tempt the youth; that having attained to highest station he takes pity on his brothers, including Benjamin the favourite—these and all the rest are feelings accessible alike to a Russian peasant, a Chinese, an African, a child, or an old man, educated or uneducated; and it is all written with such restraint, is so free from any superfluous detail, that the story may be told to any circle and will be equally comprehensible and touching to everyone. But not such are the feelings of Don Quixote or of Molière's heroes (though Molière is perhaps the most universal, and therefore the most excellent, artist of modern times), nor of Pickwick and his friends. These feelings are not common to all men but very exceptional, and therefore to make them contagious the authors have surrounded them with abundant details of time and place. And this abundance of detail makes the stories difficult of comprehension to all who do not live within reach of the conditions described by the author.

The author of the novel of Joseph did not need to describe in detail, as would be done nowadays, the blood-stained coat of Joseph, the dwelling and dress of Jacob, the pose and attire of Potiphar's wife, and how adjusting the bracelets on her left arm she said, "Come to me," and so on, because the content of feeling in this novel is so strong that all details except the most essential—such as that Joseph went out into another room to weep—are superfluous and would only hinder the transmission of emotion. And therefore this novel is accessible to all men, touches people of all nations and classes young and old, and has lasted to our times and will yet last for thousands of years to come. But strip the best novels of our time of their details and what will remain?

It is therefore impossible in modern literature to indicate works fully satisfying the demands of universality. Such works as exist are to a great extent spoilt by what is usually called "realism," but would be better termed "provincialism," in art.

In music the same occurs as in verbal art, and for similar reasons. In consequence of the poorness of the feeling they contain, the melodies of the modern composers are amazingly empty and insignificant. And to strengthen the impression produced by these empty melodies the new musicians pile complex modulations on each trivial melody, not only in their own national manner, but also in the way characteristic of their own exclusive circle and particular musical school. Melody—every melody—is free and may be understood of all men; but as soon as it is bound up with a particular harmony, it ceases to be accessible except to people trained to such harmony, and it becomes strange, not only to common men of another nationality, but to all who do not belong to the circle whose members have accustomed themselves to certain forms of harmonization. So that music, like poetry, travels in a vicious circle. Trivial and exclusive melodies, in order to make them attractive, are laden with harmonic, rhythmic, and orchestral complications and thus become yet more exclusive, and far from being universal are not even national, that is, they are not comprehensible to the whole people, but only to some people.

In music, besides marches and dances by various composers which satisfy the demands of universal art, one can indicate very few works of this class: Bach's famous violin *aria,* Chopin's nocturne in E flat major, and perhaps a dozen bits (not whole pieces, but parts) selected from the works of Haydn, Mozart, Schubert, Beethoven, and Chopin.[5]

Although in painting the same thing is repeated as in poetry and in music—namely, that in order to make them more interesting, works weak in conception are surrounded by minutely studied accessories of time and place which give them a temporary and local interest but make them less universal—still in painting more than in other spheres of art may be found works satisfying the demands of universal Christian art; that is to say, there are more works expressing feelings in which all men may participate.

In the arts of painting and sculpture, all pictures and statues in so-called genre style, representations of animals, landscapes, and caricatures with subjects comprehensible to every one, and also all kinds of ornaments, are universal in subject-matter. Such productions in painting and sculpture are very numerous (for instance, china dolls), but for the most part such objects (for instance, ornaments of all kinds) are either not considered to be art or are considered to be art of a low quality. In reality all such objects if only they transmit a true feeling experienced by the artist and comprehensible to every one (however insignificant it may seem to us to be), are works of real, good, Christian, art.

I fear it will here be urged against me that having denied that the conception of beauty can supply a standard for works of art, I contradict myself by acknowledging ornaments to be works of good art. The reproach

---

[5] While offering as examples of art those that seem to me best, I attach no special importance to my selection; for, besides being insufficiently informed in all branches of art, I belong to the class of people whose taste has been perverted by false training. And therefore my old, inured habits may cause me to err, and I may mistake for absolute merit the impression a work produced on me in my youth. My only purpose in mentioning examples of works of this or that class is to make my meaning clearer and to show how, with my present views, I understand excellence in art in relation to its subject-matter. I must moreover mention that I consign my own artistic productions to the category of bad art, excepting the story *God sees the Truth but Waits,* which seeks a place in the first class, and *A Prisoner of the Caucasus,* which belongs to the second.—L.T.

(Both the stories mentioned are included in *Twenty-Three Tales* in the "World's Classics" Tolstóy series.—A.M.)

is unjust, for the subject-matter of all kinds of ornamentation consists not in the beauty but in the feeling (of admiration at, and delight in, the combination of lines and colours) which the artist has experienced and with which he infects the spectator. Art remains what it was and what it must be: nothing but the infection by one man of another or of others with the feelings experienced by the artist. Among these feelings is the feeling of delight at what pleases the sight. Objects pleasing the sight may be such as please a small or a large number of people, or such as please all men—and ornaments for the most part are of the latter kind. A landscape representing a very unusual view, or a genre picture of a special subject, may not please every one, but ornaments, from Yakútsk ornaments to Greek ones, are intelligible to every one and evoke a similar feeling of admiration in all, and therefore this despised kind of art should in Christian society be esteemed far above exceptional, pretentious, pictures and sculptures.

So that in relation to feelings conveyed, there are only two kinds of good Christian art, all the rest of art not comprised in these two divisions should be acknowledged to be bad art, deserving not to be encouraged but to be driven out, denied, and despised, as being art not uniting but dividing people. Such in literary art are all novels and poems which transmit ecclesiastical or patriotic feelings, and also exclusive feelings pertaining only to the class of the idle rich: such as aristocratic honour, satiety, spleen, pessimism, and refined and vicious feelings flowing from sex-love—quite incomprehensible to the great majority of mankind.

In painting we must similarly place in the class of bad art all ecclesiastical, patriotic, and exclusive pictures; all pictures representing the amusements and allurements of a rich and idle life; all so-called symbolic pictures in which the very meaning of the symbol is comprehensible only to those of a certain circle; and above all pictures with voluptuous subjects—all that odious female nudity which fills all the exhibitions and galleries. And to this class belongs almost all the chamber and opera music of our times,—beginning especially with Beethoven (Schumann, Berlioz, Liszt, Wagner),—by its subject-nature devoted to the expression of feelings accessible only to people who have developed in themselves an unhealthy nervous irritation evoked by this exclusive, artificial, and complex music.

"What! the *Ninth Symphony* not a good work of art!" I hear exclaimed by indignant voices.

And I reply: Most certainly it is not. All that I have written I have written with the sole purpose of finding a clear and reasonable criterion by which to judge the merits of works of art. And this criterion, coinciding with the indications of plain and sane sense, indubitably shows me that that symphony of Beethoven's is not a good work of art. Of course to people educated in the worship of certain productions and of their authors, to people whose taste has been perverted just by being educated in such worship, the acknowledgement that such a celebrated work is bad, is amazing and strange. But how are we to escape the indications of reason and common sense?

Beethoven's *Ninth Symphony* is considered a great work of art. To verify its claim to be such I must first ask myself whether this work transmits the highest religious feeling? I reply in the negative, since music in itself cannot transmit those feelings; and therefore I ask myself next: Since this work does not belong to the highest kind of religious art, has it the other characteristic of the good art of our time—the quality of uniting all men in one common feeling—does it rank as Christian universal art? And again I have no option but to reply in the negative; for not only do I not see how the feelings transmitted by this work could unite people not specially trained to submit themselves to its complex hypnotism, but I am unable to imagine to myself a crowd of normal people who could understand anything of this long, confused, and artificial production, except short snatches which are lost in a sea of what is incomprehensible. And therefore, whether I like it or not, I am compelled to conclude that this work belongs to the rank of bad art. It is curious to note in this connexion, that attached to the end of this very symphony is a poem of Schiller's which (though somewhat obscurely) expresses this very thought, namely, that feeling (Schiller speaks only of the feeling of gladness) unites people and evokes love in them. But though this poem is sung at the end of the symphony, the music does not accord with the thought expressed in the verses; for the music is exclusive and does not unite all men but unites only a few, dividing them off from the rest of mankind.

And just in this same way, in all branches of art, many and many works considered great by the upper classes of our society will have to be judged. By this one sure criterion we shall have to judge the celebrated *Divine Comedy* and *Jerusalem Delivered,* and a great part of Shakespeare's and Goethe's work, and in painting every representation of miracles, including Raphael's Transfiguration, etc.

Whatever the work may be and however it may have been extolled, we have first to ask whether this work is one of real art, or a counterfeit. Having acknowledged, on the basis of the indication of its infectiousness even to a small class of people, that a certain production belongs to the realm of art, it is necessary on this basis to decide the next question, Does this work belong to the category of bad exclusive art opposed to religious perception, or of Christian art uniting people? And having acknowledged a work to belong to real Christian art, we must then, according to whether it transmits feelings flowing from love of God and man, or merely the simple feelings uniting all men, assign it a place in the ranks of religious art, or in those of universal art.

Only on the basis of such verification shall we find it possible to select from the whole mass of what in our society claims to be art, those works which form real, important, necessary, spiritual food, and to separate them from all the harmful and useless art and from the counterfeits of art which surround us. Only on the basis of such verification shall we be able to rid ourselves of the pernicious results of harmful art and avail ourselves of that beneficent action which is the purpose of true and good art, and which is indispensable for the spiritual life of man and of humanity.

The Social Responsibility of Art

NIKOLAI BUKHARIN

Poetry and Society[1]

1. Poetry

THE FINAL SUBJECT of this report is that of the problems of poetic creation in the U.S.S.R. But before proceeding to an analysis of these problems, it will be worth our while critically to examine a number of general questions connected with poetic creation—the more so since there is still a great deal that is not clear here, and this lack of clarity is reflected above all in our literary criticism, which has a great task to perform and does not always perform it well.

Here I must ask my hearers to excuse me. For a certain period of time they may find it rather boring, but boredom, like evil, will the better set off the good that will follow in the latter part of my report, where it will not be so boring, and where I shall, perhaps, encounter violent objections. Here I may invoke the authority of the blessed Augustine, who said that evil exists only in order to set off the good. Having cited such a powerful authority as this, let me ask you to have patience for a little.

---

[1] From Nikolai Bukharin, "Poetry, Poetics and the Problems of Poetry in the U.S.S.R.," *Problems of Soviet Literature,* ed. in English by H. G. Scott (New York: International Publishers, n.d.), pp. 187–210. Title by the editors. (Eds.)

Let us first consider poetry as such. The *Encyclopaedia Britannica* says: "Absolute poetry is the concrete and artistic expression of the human mind in emotional and rhythmical language."

It is easy to see that this definition suffers from the fundamental defect that it defines poetry, that is, a concrete form of art, by means of artistic activity, which itself must be defined from the point of view of the specific character of art. The definition is therefore tautological. Moreover, it is obviously necessary somehow to differentiate the special properties of poetic speech, of poetic language and of the corresponding poetic thought, because thought is firmly and indissolubly linked up with language. Ancient Hindu poetics had already developed the Anandavardhana doctrine (tenth century B.C.) of the twofold, "hidden" meaning of poetic speech. According to this doctrine, language in which words are used solely and exclusively in their direct, "customary" sense cannot be called poetic speech. Whatever such speech may convey, it will be prose. Only when the words, by various associations, evoke other "pictures, images, feelings," when "poetic thoughts glimmer, radiate, as it were, through the words of the poet, but are not expressed directly by him," do we have authentic poetry. Such is the doctrine of the *"dhvana,"* of the poetic innuendo, of the hidden meaning of poetic speech. Similar theories have often been associated with a mystic interpretation of poetry and poetic experience, as of something touching the fringe of "other worlds." In ancient China we find, for example, a whole brilliant poetic treatise, the poem *Categories of Verse* by Ssŭ-K'ung T'u (837–908 A.D.), on the theme of divine poetic inspiration, where the "True Lord," the "Prime Ancestor," the "Creator of Transformations," the "Spirit-like Transmogrifier," the "Heavenly Loom," the "Wondrous Mechanism," the "Highest Harmony" and, finally, the "Black Nothing"—the Great Tao— lives in a state of inexpressible poetic "inspiration." Having their roots deep in the idea of the magic of the word, such ideas often led to the direct deification of the word, which became a mystic essence. Thus, we find in one Arab philosopher the interpretation of the "Word" with a capital W, the Greek Logos, not as reason raised to the degree of the world's Demiurge, but as the embodiment of volition creating the world. Yet strange as it may seem, it is a highly characteristic fact that this magical or semi-magical interpretation of the art of words and the art of poetry, after a long cycle of ages, has once more gained currency in our own era; it was comparatively recently that we had a similar interpretation of poetry in bourgeois literary theory and bourgeois poetics.

In our own times Gumilev [2] has expressed this idea in poetic form:

---

[2] Gumilev, Nikolai Stepanovich (1886–1921). Russian poet, prose writer and critic. Shot in 1921 for participation in a whiteguard plot. The verses here quoted are from his last book, *The Pillar of Fire.* (H.G.S.)

In days of yore, when o'er a world still new
God leaned his head, it was a word
Which made the sun stop in his course,
And towns were ruined by a word.

But we forgot the word alone is blessed
'Mid terrors that are sent us for a rod,
And in the Gospel that was writ by John
'Tis said the word—is God.

In his day Balmont,[3] an unquestioned master of language, attempted to provide a "theoretical" basis for this fetishization of speech-reflexes in his book, *Poetry as Magic,* the very title of which clearly indicates the author's trend of ideas. "The world needs the creation of images," he declared. "The world has its magicians, who broaden and enrich the circle of existence by the magic of their will and the music of their words." This poet, who was organically incapable of logical thinking, produces nothing to "prove" his argument but a long succession of carefully chosen and impressive images, which are intended to take the place of thought. Andrey Biely,[4] on the other hand, once made an attempt to give philosophic depth to the same subject, and word fetishism with him reached truly Himalayan heights. "If there were no words, there would be no world," he wrote. "My Ego, apart from its surroundings, does not exist at all. The world, apart from me, does not exist either. 'I' and 'the world' spring to life only in the process of their union in sound."

Thus, authors of various theories have lapsed into pure mysticism in their attempts to approach the problems of poetic speech. This, of course, had its causes—causes of a social and historical nature which are not far to seek. But at present this does not concern us. We only want to point out the *existence* of such a way of putting the question, and that at different periods and in different countries.

Such points of view, inasmuch as they are idealistic and mystical, are of course unacceptable to us. They are a sort of refined barbarism, crudely contradictory to all scientific experience. But their very existence emphasizes the problem of the specific character of poetic thought and poetic speech, of that "mystery," "sorcery," and "magic," in which the mystics seek to envelop their readers' minds as in a veil, locking all the doors of rational perception.

But there is nothing mystic in phenomena themselves. The process of

---

[3] Balmont, Constantine Dmitrievich (b. 1867). Well-known Russian poet. One of the four chief representatives of Russian symbolism—Bryussov, Blok, Balmont and Biely. Emigrated after the October Revolution of 1917. (H.G.S.)

[4] Russian poet, prose writer and critic (1880–1934). The passage quoted is from an article entitled "The Magic of Words" in his book *Symbolism.* (H.G.S.)

life, taken as "experience," has its intellectual, emotional and volitional sides. We make a conventional distinction between logical thought, thought in terms of concepts, and "thought in terms of images," the so-called "realm of emotion." True, in actual life the stream of experience is integral and undivided; nevertheless, in this very unity, we have the intellectual pole and the emotional pole, even though they may not exist in their "pure form," even though they may merge into one another. But it would be entirely and essentially wrong to make an absolute mechanical subdivision of the so-called "spiritual life" into water-tight compartments of feeling and intellect, or of the conscious and the unconscious, or of the directly sensory and the logical. These are not separate domains of abstract categories. They are dialectical magnitudes composing a unity. At one and the same time we are confronted with differences and even with opposites, though these opposites also merge into one another. This likewise gives rise to a certain difference in types of thinking.

Logical thinking employs concepts, which range themselves into a whole ladder of thought, with various rungs, or degrees, of abstraction. Even when we are dealing with the highest type of logical thought—dialectical logic— where the abstract concept includes its concrete attributes, the very concept, as such, causes sensory colours, sounds and tones to lose their vividness. Moreover, perceptive action oversteps the bounds of the senses, although it has its source in them; in summarizing human experience, it perceives, for instance, the subjectivity of colour, and coming closer to a real perception of the world, of its objective nature, independent of the subject, it "replaces" colour by a light wave of definite length. In science, the entire qualitative diversity and multiformity of the world take on other forms, quite distinct from immediate sensation, but giving a much more adequate reflection of reality—that is, more true.

On the other hand, the entire world of emotions—love, joy, terror, grief, rage, and so on to infinity—the entire world of desire and passion, not as the object of research, but as experience, as well as the whole world of immediate sensations, also have their points of condensation—thought in terms of images. Here there is no abstraction from what is directly experienced. Here the process of generalization does not take us beyond its limits (as is the case in logical thought and in its highest product, scientific thought). Here this very sensory experience—doubly concrete and doubly "alive"—is itself condensed. Here we have, not a scientific reflection of real existence, but a sensorily generalized picture of a phenomenological series, not of the "essence," but of the "phenomenon." This does not by any means signify that we are dealing with an illusion or a dream. Nothing of the sort! This essence appears in the phenomenon. The essence merges into the phenomenon. The senses do not fence us off from the world.

But objective reality is here "reflected" differently. In science, it is reflected as a world of qualitatively diverse forms of matter; in art, as a world of sensory images; in science, as electrons, atoms, species, value, etc.; in art, as colours, odours, hues, sounds, images. The type of thinking here is not the same as in logical thought. Here generalization is achieved not by extinguishing the sensory, but by substituting one complex of sense symbols for a great multitude of other complexes. This "substitute" becomes a "symbol," an "image," a type, an emotionally coloured unity, behind which and in the folds of whose garments thousands of other sensory elements are concealed. Every such unity is sensorily concrete. To the extent that such unities are selected and fixated, *i.e.,* that these experiences are constructively, creatively reproduced, to this extent we have art.

The word itself is a highly complex magnitude. Being the product of many thousands of years of development, it embraces, like some cell of a "spiritual organism," all the problems of thought with both its principles—image and concept. In scientific terminology, it grows as a symbol of the "pure concept"; in poetical speech, it is imagery first and foremost. Consequently, the laws governing both the selection of words and their combination will differ, or, to express it otherwise, poetical speech will inevitably have its specific peculiarities. That remarkable investigator of these problems, Potebnia,[5] who while essentially developing the theory of Humboldt,[6] arrived at a number of most original solutions, formulates the polarity of art and science as follows:

> Alike in the broad and in the strict sense, all that pertains to thought is subjective; that is to say that, even though conditioned by the external world, it is yet the product of personal creation. But within this all-embracing subjectivity, we can distinguish the objective and the subjective, and refer science to the first and art to the second. The basis for this is as follows: in art, only the image is the common property of all; it is understood differently by everyone, and the understanding of it can consist only of unanalysed (real and wholly personal) feeling, such as is evoked by the image; in science, however, there is no image, and feeling cannot enter save as a subject of research; the sole building material of science is the concept, composed of symbols of the image already objectivized in the word. If art is a process of objectivized primary data of spiritual life, then science is a process of objectivizing art. The difference in degree of

---

[5] Potebnia, Alexander Aphanasyevich (1835–1891). Russian linguist, philologist and writer on the theory of poetry. The passage here quoted is from a work by him entitled *Thought and Language.* (H.G.S.)

[6] Humboldt, Karl Wilhelm von (1767–1835). German philologist. Author of *The Heterogeneity of Language and its Influence on the Intellectual Development of Mankind.* (H.G.S.)

objectivity of thought is identical with the difference in the degree of its abstractness: the most abstract of sciences, mathematics, is at the same time the most unquestionable one in its principles, the one that least of all admits the possibility of personal views.

It is easy to see that these formulations contain a number of errors. The author does not present any clearly defined ideas on the truthfulness, the objectivity of perception, and a loophole is left open for idealism; he obviously underestimates the social character of language, of the entire creative process, etc.; he draws too sharp a line of demarcation, metaphysically separating different aspects of thought. In consequence there is little that is dialectic here. At the same time there is much that is true and unquestionably deserving of attention. To continue the broken thread of our argument, we may say that the system of concepts proceeds outward through science: taking the sensations as our starting point, we advance further and further beyond their borders, where we perceive the objective character of the world, continually studying new facts and perfecting science, moving along the endless path of converting relative truth into absolute truth, destroying antiquated systems of science as we proceed on our way. In the field of art we do not go beyond the limits of the phenomenological series; here, as we said before, the objective world is reflected differently; here emotions are not made the object of scientific research; here even nature is "humanized." Here, therefore, the "warm," emotional, vivid and metaphorical principle is placed in relative contrast to the "cold," intellectual, logical principle:

> Water and stone,
> Verse and prose,
> Ice and fire. (*Pushkin.*)

Poetry is understood both in the broad and in the narrow sense of the word. All speech in terms of images is poetical speech; from this point of view Gogol's *Dead Souls* or Pushkin's *The Captain's Daughter* are poetical works. By poetry in the narrow sense is understood not simply the fixation of sensory images in words, but, in addition, rhythmical speech and even rhymed speech. It must not be thought, however, that there are any hard and fast lines of demarcation. The rhymed, rhythmical rules of arithmetic in India have only the sound image; they thus possess one element of poetry, but that does not make them poetry. The philosophical treatise of Lucretius, *De Rerum Natura* (*On the Nature of Things*), presents not only sound images but many others besides, and is therefore poetry. Here too, then, one element merges into the other.

Poetic creation and its product—poetry—represent a definite form of social activity, and are governed in their development, regardless of the specific nature of poetic creation, by the laws of social development. As we shall see later, when we go into this question in detail, the "verbal" character of poetic creation is no argument whatever against the sociological treatment of poetry. On the contrary: only by a Marxian analysis of poetry can we understand it in its full scale, in all the totality of its attributes. True, the Marxists have paid but little attention to the specific problems of language. But a deeper analysis of its phenomena inevitably leads to a sociological treatment of the word itself. And indeed it could not be otherwise. Examine a word, and you discover the palaeontology of language. Words are the depository of the whole previous life of mankind, which has passed through various social-economic structures, with diverse classes and groupings, different spheres of experience, labour, social struggle, culture. That which Potebnia calls "the heredity of words," and which can be developed into the evolution of language (or languages), is the reflection of actual social-historical life. Within the microcosm of the word is embedded the macrocosm of history. The word, like the concept, is abridged history, an "abbreviature," or epitome, of social-historical life. It is a product of this life, not a Demiurge of history, not a Logos creating a world out of nothing.

We have seen how poetry, as the fixation of sensory images in words, summarizes the world of emotion in its own peculiar way. But these emotions, these experiences are in themselves experiences of the social-historical man, and in a class society, of the class man. For even such emotions as have their roots in the fathomless biological depths of man, like emotions of an erotic nature, are modified in the course of the historical process. Fixated, selected images therefore cannot but come within the spheres of sociological analysis; they are social phenomena, phenomena of social life. Finally, thinking in terms of imagery is none the less thinking. The emotional element here merges with its opposite. On the other hand, a tremendous wealth of ideas, concepts, standards, ideologies, systems of philosophy enters bodily into poetic unity as an inseparable part of it. Here the intellectual merges with the emotional, that is, with its opposite. The poetic image, as an integral unity, is therefore not "purely" emotional; much less is the unified system of images purely emotional. Hence it follows that poetry, when considered from this angle, is a social product; it is one of the functions of a concrete historical society, reflecting and expressing in a specific form the specific features of its time and—in so far as we are dealing with a class society—of its class.

It is highly ridiculous how certain bourgeois theoreticians, giving a rehash of idealist, philosophical aesthetics or aesthetic philosophy, which has been represented by very great names, by such giants of bourgeois thought as Kant, Schopenhauer and Hegel, keep reiterating surprisingly vapid and tedious arguments to the effect that art in general and poetry in particular have no relation at all to practice, to "interest," to will. Kant, for example, in his *Critique of Judgement,* asserted this principle with all his force. Schopenhauer contrasts "disinterested" artistic contemplation to the ancillary character of science.[7] According to Hegel, "the object of art should be contemplated in itself, in its independent objectivity, which, though existing for the subject, does so only in a theoretical, intellectual way, not practically, and without any reference whatever to desire or will." [8] All this is utter nonsense. Take the art of ancient Greece. The comedies of Aristophanes are political journalism, but at the same time admirable works of art. There you will find the struggle of parties, definite political tendencies, ridicule of political opponents, etc. And the tragedians—Sophocles, Aeschylus, Euripides?

Everyone will understand the significance of the poetic contests that were held there, when the poets were awarded crowns by the crowd. If we went a step further, and if the crowd in the Park of Culture and Rest were to crown with laurels, let us say, Sasha Bezymensky, as the best popular bard, that would be something taken right out of the ancient Greek world.

The objective, and also active, significance of the social function of poetry —if we are to give it a more general formulation—is to assimilate and transmit experience and to educate character, to reproduce definite group psychologies. This peculiarly perceptive, peculiarly educative and peculiarly effectual function of poetry is truly tremendous, and at times it turns into that of an extraordinarily active militant force.

Here we must emphasize once again that the subjective experience even of a "purely scientific" worker may be just as completely disinterested, in the sense of its remoteness from all practice, as that of the creative artist; that "contemplation" of the astronomical map may, subjectively, be void of any element of self-interest or practicality. But objectively, in the total social relation, *i.e.,* when regarded as a social function, both science and art in general and poetry in particular play, as has been pointed out, a tremendously vital and at the same time a practical role.

The cosmogonies of ancient India, the *Gilgamesh Epic* of Babylon, the Greek *Iliad* and *Odyssey,* the Chinese fables, Vergil's *Aeneid,* the works of the great Greek tragedians, the *Song of Roland,* the Russian folk-tales, etc.— were they not all mighty levers of a peculiar social pedagogy, forming people in accordance with their own commandments and canons? The ancient cosmogonies were veritable poetical encyclopaedias. Homer was a funda-

---

[7] Schopenhauer: *World as Will and Idea,* Section 36.

[8] Hegel: *Werke, Aesthetik, Dritter Teil: Das System der einzelnen Künste,* Berlin, 1843, Vol. X (2), 253–254 (N.B.)

In the English translation (*The Philosophy of Fine Art,* tr. F. P. B. Osmaston, London, G. Bell and Sons, Ltd., 1920, III, 15) the passage is rendered as follows: "An object of art, however, should be contemplated in its independent and self-contained objective presence, which no doubt is there for the mind that perceives it, but only as an appeal to soul and intelligence, not in some active relation, and with none whatever to the appetites and volition." (Eds.)

mental subject of so-called "school" tuition. In Rome the verses of Vergil were crammed and scanned by no means as an empty pastime. The society of those times and its social leaders were thereby reproducing themselves in the realm of ideas, in an idealized form, inculcating their ideas, thoughts, conceptions, feelings, characters, ambitions, ideals, virtues. Even the Aristotelian *catharsis* (purging of the emotions) is a method of peculiar moral and intellectual hygiene (*cf.* Lessing's arguments in his *Hamburgische Dramaturgie* regarding the ultimate moral aim of tragedy). Horace knew what he was doing when he wrote that the aim of poetry was to mingle the useful with the pleasant—*"miscere utile dulci."* The well-known Arab philosopher, Averrhoes, spoke of tragedy as the "art of praising" and comedy as the "art of censure." [9] Contrary to idealist philosophy, Chernyshevsky,[10] in his famous *Dissertation,* upheld the principle: "What is of general interest in life forms the content of art," and this somewhat crude formula is nevertheless infinitely closer to reality than are the pale shades of "disinterested" idealistic definitions, whose metaphysics carry us away into the almost airless void of an a-social "stratosphere."

The fact that words play a tremendous part in poetic creation, that the specific character of poetry is thought in terms of images, does not in any way run counter to a sociological treatment of poetry, because even the word itself is the product of social development and represents a definite condensing point in which a whole series of social factors find their expression. And for this reason we Marxists are faced with the task of subjecting this side of the matter, too, to a Marxist study, *viz.,* the question of language, the question of words, the question of word creation, of the evolution of language, etc.; and it seems to me that quite a considerable theoretical foundation for such a study has been laid in our Marxist and near-Marxist literature.

2. Poetics as the Technology of Poetic Craftsmanship

Here again we shall have to settle some theoretical scores with the formalists, at the same time assigning them to the place they have merited among researchers in art theory, and also with those in the sociological (including the Marxian) camp of literary theory who tend to over-simplify the question. We shall take our examples from comparatively early works written when the formalists were still such in the genuine sense of the word. The formalists were guided by considerations of the following nature: Poetic

---

[9] *Cf.* Ign. Kratschkovsky, *"Die Arabische Poetik im IX Jahrhundert"* in *Le Monde Oriental,* No. XXIII, 1929. Upsala.

[10] Chernyshevsky, Nikolai Gavrilovich (1829–99). Great Russian scholar and critic, publicist and revolutionary. (H.G.S.)

language, *i.e.,* in the final analysis, the word, is a constituent principle of poetry. It is therefore necessary to elucidate the laws of poetic word combinations (from various angles). Since "poetry is language in its aesthetic function," "language methods" represent "the sole hero" in the science of literature.[11] In other words: the specific nature of poetry requires the study of these methods, which constitute the only object of literary theory. From this point of view the Marxian way of putting the question becomes sheer nonsense—an irrelevant intrusion of alien problems and utterly inadequate methods. The question has been much more subtly dealt with by Zhirmunsky,[12] but in the final analysis even he did not deviate very widely from his colleagues. "Poetics," we read, "is a science which studies poetry as an art. . . . What is now the subject of the most animated scientific interest is not the evolution of a philosophical view of life or of the 'feeling of life' in the great monuments of literature, not historical development, and the changing of social psychology in its interaction with the individual psychology of the poet-creator, but the study of the poetic art—poetics, historical and theoretical."

The theoretical basis for this conclusion is provided by the author's argument regarding the real coalescence of so-called "form" and "content" in art. "In actual fact, such a division of the *what* and the *how* in art represents only a conventional abstraction. Love, grief, tragic struggles of the soul, philosophical ideas, etc., exist in poetry not by themselves, but in that concrete form in which they have been expressed in the given work." "All facts of 'content' also become phenomena of form." This is both true and not true. Not true, because the author sees only the unity, but does not see the contrariety; he regards the entire complex only from the angle of formal logic, and not dialectically. This is the first point. Secondly—and this is much more important in the present case—the author's reasoning is vicious at the root. In reality, we are here dealing with a science whose duty is to understand poetry (historically and theoretically—we will not here discuss the question of the arbitrariness of this antithesis) *as an art.* This vital and original unity, which is developing and evolving, contains elements of "love, grief . . . philosophical ideas." They are put into definite (poetic) form, but in their transformed aspect, they have entered into the "whole." How is this "whole" to be understood without touching on the genesis, origin, development, etc., of all these elements?

Evidently we must draw just the opposite conclusion to that arrived at by Zhirmunsky, namely, that since all the elements enumerated have entered

[11] R. Jacobson, *Latest Russian Poetry*. Prague, 1921, p. 11.
[12] Zhirmunsky, Victor Maximovich (b. 1891). Contemporary Russian literary critic, adhering to the formalist school of thought. The passages here quoted are from essays in his *Problems of Literary Theory*, Leningrad, 1928. (H.G.S.)

into some synthetic whole—a work of art—then, in order to understand this whole in all its aspects, we must go beyond its borders and reveal the sources of the entire morphological process. One cannot understand law without going beyond the borders of legal formulae. One cannot understand religion without going beyond the borders of dogmatic theology. One cannot understand art without analysing its connections with the entire life-activity of society, because art must not be transformed into a metaphysical "thing-in-itself." Furthermore, as we have seen above, the very "form" of the word itself "possesses content," and that not only as the morphological factor in every new poetic work. It "possesses content" in another sense as well—namely, as the condenser of social-historical experience. The selection of metaphors in their concrete form "comes" not as a result of the immanent logic of words: it is taken from the surroundings of life, just as is the *genre,* the style and a thousand other things.

The narrowness and one-sidedness of "pure formalism" compel Zhirmunsky to criticize, quite rightly, the theoretical structure of Eichenbaum's [13] arguments. However, he lapses from his position and inevitably begins to contradict himself. In another work, analysing the presence of "extraneous elements" in art, he concludes: "All these examples raise the question of the limits of historical (and, we may add, not only historical.—*N.B.*) poetics and the delimitation of its problems within the bounds of a broader science of literature." Very good. But in that case we are faced with the following conclusion: either this "broader science" deals with art—in which case the whole fundamental structure of the author's argument collapses; or it is a science whose object is much broader than art—in which case the author's argument regarding the coalescence of the so-called form with the so-called content falls to the ground, that is, the author's conception collapses at the other end.

Finally, Zhirmunsky makes a desperate attempt of a dualistic nature. He subdivides art into two sorts: 1) "pure, formal, objectless arts, like ornaments, music, dancing," where "the very material of which they are built is conventional to the core, abstract, aesthetic, not burdened (!!—*N.B.*) with meaning, material significance, practical tasks," and 2) arts "with an object or theme," "like painting, sculpture, poetry, theatrical art," "burdened with meaning" where "the material of art is not especially aesthetic. . . ." This attempt, however, is doubly fatal to the author. It is fatal because such a subdivision simply does not fit the facts. The ornament is an image of things, people, plants and animals, symbolized to a very high degree, or else it is directly and intimately connected with "practical life"

---

[13] Eichenbaum, Boris Mikhailovich (b. 1886). Literary critic. One of the leaders of the formalist school in Russia. (H.G.S.)

in another way (*e.g.,* pictures on clay vessels). Music, as such, is by no means "objectless"—it is enough to mention Beethoven, Wagner, church music; there is even such a thing as philosophical music—Scriabine, for instance. The dance possesses a very great vital significance (and even a purely practical one)—war dances, erotic dances, etc. Secondly, this attempt is fatal to the author because it decisively contradicts his ideas, for this time he quite inequitably tears away a number of elements from the aesthetic whole on the grounds that they are "burdensome" and unartistic.

We have selected Zhirmunsky because he is one of the subtlest art critics of the formalist or "near-formalist" camp. His spiritual *confrère* beyond our borders, Professor O. Walzel, flounders in the toils of approximately the same contradictions in his search for "synthetic literary research" (*synthetische Literaturforschung*).[14]

The foregoing analysis gives us the clue to the positive solution of the problem. An integral science of literature must include the elucidation of the laws of literature as a whole, as an active function in the life of society, as a "superstructure" of a peculiar kind, and this should include the laws, conditionally speaking, of the "formal elements" as well.

As a sub-species of such a literary science, as a conditionally specialized branch, we may have also a science of these formal elements, which must likewise have its sociological basis. All this does not preclude the possibility of special researches within limited and perhaps even narrower bounds. Hence valuable results can also be derived, for example, from work done to elucidate the special laws governing the technique of verse construction, or work devoted exclusively to the problem of imagery, or to the problems of sound in its relation to the image, etc., etc. These would all be special "branches," furnishing material for an integral science of literature. The tendency, therefore, which can frequently be observed in our own Marxian ranks—namely, a purely nihilistic attitude to the problem of form as such—is entirely wrong. In such an event literary research resolves itself into nothing but a superficial social-class characterization of the so-called ideological content of the poetic work, which, in its bare, rudimentary and over-simplified form, is carried over into the characterization of the poet as a poet. As we have seen above, however, form and content constitute a unity, but a unity of contradictions. Moreover, such an attitude leads people to understand by "content" what is, properly speaking, the ideological source of the content, and not its artistic transformation. Needless to say, this leads to quite incorrect conclusions.

It should be clearly and distinctly understood that there is a tremendous difference between formalism in art, which must be emphatically rejected,

---

[14] See O. Walzel, *Das Wortkunstwerk. Mittel seiner Erforschung.* Verlag Quelle u. Meyer, Leipzig. See especially pp. 20–21.

formalism in literary criticism, which is equally unacceptable, and the analysis of the formal elements in art (which is not formalism at all)—an analysis which is exceedingly useful and which at the present time, when we have to "master technique" in all fields, is absolutely indispensable.

Formalism in art denotes the self-emasculation of the art in question, the utter impoverishment of its component parts—a phenomenon connected with the extreme contraction of the circle upon which such *soi-disant* art exercises its influence. It is individualism bordering on solipsism, where sound almost ceases to be a form possessing any "content."

In poetry we have such a phenomenon in the shape of "irrational language." When one reads:

> Lulla, lolla, lalla-goo,
> Leeza, lolla, lulla-lee,
> Pines, shoo-yat, shoo-yat.
> Gee-ee, Gee-ee-oo-oo—

then the purely sound content (the musical melody of the verse) is in direct contrast to individual "human" words. The word ceases to be a word, because it is devoid of all meaning. All the living wealth of poetry disappears. Shklovsky [15] concluded his article "On Poetry and Irrational Language" with the "prophecy" of Slowacki [16] that: "A time will come when only the sounds in poetry will interest poets." This hope, expressed by one of the foremost theoreticians of formalism, fully explains why he has played such a negative role in regard to poetry as an art. When Paul Verlaine, that brilliant master of verse, poet of the subtlest and most delicate moods, demanded *"de la musique avant toute chose"* ("music before all else"), he never even dreamed of adopting the language of "Dyr bull shirr—ubeshur" *à la* Kruchenykh.[17]

The formalists have a peculiar logic of development. If the so-called "content" is to be considered as an "extraneous element," if all "meaning" is nothing but a "burdensome magnitude," if this meaning "blocks the road" of aesthetic emotion, then, of course, poetry's main line of development can be expressed in the slogan: "Down with *Faust* and long live 'Dyr bull shirr'!" Thus, the theoretical "emancipation" from "meaning" leads in practice to "irrationality." It must be borne in mind that we are not here speaking of "word-building" and that our standpoint is by no means that of the notorious Admiral Shishkov.[18] What we are discussing is a tendency to do away with

---

[15] Shklovsky, Victor Borisovich (b. 1891). Contemporary Russian critic. (H.G.S.)

[16] Slowacki, Juliusz (1809–49). Polish poet of the romantic school. (H.G.S.)

[17] Kruchenykh, Alexey Eliseyevich (b. 1886). One of the first Russian futurists. Inventor of the "irrational language." (H.G.S.)

[18] Shishkov, Alexander Semenovich (1754–1841). Reactionary writer; vice-admiral in the Russian fleet. Opposed the linguistic reform of Karamzin. Maintained that the Russian language was identical with Ecclesiastical Slavonic. (H.G.S.)

the word as such, to destroy all concepts, to debase imagery—in other words, to annihilate poetry as a verbal art. The dialectics of formalism develop as follows: they begin their "Gospel according to St. John" by promulgating the thesis: "In the beginning was the word," and define the essence of poetry by the word and the word alone—only to end by doing away with that word altogether, and thus demolishing their central principal. The extreme individualism of these arguments is also indicative of their social roots. They have their origin in abject fear of the flood of new "content" accompanying the revolution, which overturned the tea-tables in so many drawing-rooms, in the going into hermitage of "proud" bourgeois-intellectual "individuals," who want to creep away into the burrow of the professional anchorite ("And we, the poets wise" . . .).

It is interesting to trace the evolution of formalism in art as the evolution of decadence in bourgeois art. I have already had occasion to show once in print how in the epoch of universal decadence in which all bourgeois humanity is now living, the latter casts away the element of content from all art, *i.e.,* in the last resort, destroys art itself.

So it was with painting, when bourgeois artists, continually impoverishing the elements of "content," brought painting to the verge of a "pure," "decorative spot"; all that remains is the "spot" as a principle, and further progress is barred. The same thing happened in sculpture, through expressionism, when nothing was left but a curved line—and that was all. In architecture they began to be afraid of superfluous "content," reduced themselves to absolutely simple geometrical forms, and here too ended up in a blind alley.

The impoverishment of the elements of content brings its nemesis in the suicide of the given form of art. When the decadence of art reaches its last limits, there begins a process of frenzied casting around in different directions, and this will continue until the other half of mankind—the proletariat, the toiling population—succeeds in creating a synthetic art, which will gather together all the riches of human society and will create masterpieces of integral humanity; and this will have nothing in common with either physical or spiritual eunuchs, but will regard them with contempt and abhorrence.

Formalism in literary theory, as we have seen, is closely linked up with formalism in art itself. Its most glaring error is that it attempts, on principle, to tear art from its vital social context. It creates the illusion, or the fiction, of an entirely independent "series" of phenomena in art. The specific nature of art it confuses with its complete autonomy. As for the laws of art's development, it sees them only in the immanent laws of its morphology, quite devoid of any connection with the most important morphological problems of social life in general. This dry, vapid, lifeless conception must emphatically be rejected.

All this must not be confused with the task of analysing the formal elements in art. The latter, as we have seen above, is necessary and useful in the highest degree. The formalists considered this partial work to be everything; they deduced general principles from this material. This is wrong and harmful. But an analysis of the formal elements in art, a profound study of all problems of the structure of poetical speech, is an indispensable part of the broader field of work. And in this respect there is something to be learned even from the formalists, who investigated these problems, while Marxist literary critics have regarded them with complete disdain.

This question acquires a special importance and actuality just now, when the problem of the cultural heritage in general and the problem of mastering the technique of art in particular have been raised anew and in a serious light. But before discussing this question, it is first necessary to say a few words about the general problem, *viz.,* to answer the question of how, in general, it is possible to learn from the "old masters," the "classics," the "predecessors," etc.

This question is by no means an idle one, and clarity here will obviate many mistakes. The essence of the whole matter can be briefly summarized as follows: Every poetical work is an integral unity, in which sound, ideas, imagery, etc., are component parts synthetically united. On the other hand, it is also a unity from the sociological viewpoint, since all the component parts and their synthesis, taken together, are "ideological reflexes" of a definite period and a definite class. How, then, under such circumstances, is it possible to learn? Should we not, on the contrary, utterly reject all previous "contents," "forms," "methods," etc.? As is well known, such conclusions have actually been drawn, although their absurdity is self-evident. The general answer to this question has been given by materialist dialectics, according to which "negation" is not sheer destruction, but a new phase in which "the old" exists *in aufgehobener Form,*[19] to use Hegel's terminology. In such a type of "movement" we have the possibility of a succession which will dialectically combine both a rupture with the old and a peculiar continuation of it. A number of elements, when carried over into another combination, into another context, begin to live a new life, and thus a new "unity" is obtained. The reason for this is that a unity is not a monolithic magnitude, but contains inner contradictions. We may observe similar things in the field of material life: when we import a new machine, we introduce it into a new complex of technical-economic organization, and the "meaning" of the machine thereby becomes different. Approximately the same thing happens in the realm of ideas—*mutatis mutandis,* of course.

---

[19] Literally, "in suspended" or "abrogated form." (H.G.S.)

There is another and quite different side to this question. Is it possible to learn to be a poet at all?

A perfectly correct answer, as it seems to us, was given to this question by Valery Bryussov. "Ability for artistic creation," he said, "is an inborn gift, like beauty of face or a powerful voice; this ability can and should be developed, but by no amount of effort or study can it be acquired. *Poetae nascuntur* (poets are born)." The development of poetic ability is achieved with difficulty. "Truly great poets, endowed with a genius for creation, achieved technical mastery only by means of slow probation and long, patient labour." We are thus brought face to face with the problems of poetics, as the technology of poetic creation. In other words: elucidation of the laws governing the so-called formal elements can be presented in the form of definite standards. Poetics then appears not only as a part of the theory of literature but, when transposed to another logical key, acquires the significance of a system of rules. What we have in mind is not, of course, a school-book exposition of the subject, although even this is useful with a view to raising the general level of poetic culture, but a conscious understanding of the full importance of *this* factor too. Without a study of the technology of poetic creation, one cannot learn the specific "craftsmanship," "the poet's trade," as Bryussov expresses it, not very accurately, in his *Experiments*. Of course—and this seems to us axiomatic—the "studies" cannot and should not on any account be limited to this "technology." Even that part of the studies which relates to the problem of the "cultural heritage" cannot be confined within such limits. For the wider our horizons are in all directions, the more fruitful will be the process of making this heritage our own. Nevertheless a solution of this most elementary problem is quite indispensable, and this must be stressed with especial force, because the problem in question somehow or other has not and does not come within the range of vision of our poets and—which is also extremely important—of our duly impanelled critics. Problems of rhythm and metre, problems of verbal scoring, of stanza construction, etc.—all these must enter into the sphere of careful study, and the poet really must not resemble that character in Dmitryev [20] who

"Forgets his lack of knowledge when he passes into raptures."

Such, in our opinion, is the problem of poetics, as the technology of poetic creation.

It seems to me that our most serious attention must now be turned to this side of the matter. And this applies to criticism, too.

At the present time one of the main tasks of criticism is not only to give

[20] Dmitryev, Ivan Ivanovich (1760–1837). Russian poet, satirist and writer of fables. (H.G.S.)

an exact social-economic and social-political equivalent for the various poets, poetic tendencies, etc., but also to analyse these carefully from the viewpoint of the specific character of poetic creation, from the viewpoint of language, imagery, stanza construction, verbal scoring, etc.

Without such an analysis, literary criticism at the present time is not of full value. In the days when we were vanquishing bourgeois society, our criticism was a battering ram which smashed the enemy. We picked out the main thing, the sharpest point, *viz.,* the social-political factor, and this, in our hands, was a shaft which we shot against the bourgeois antagonist.

But when we ourselves are building, when we need to learn craftsmanship, when we know that a definite number of poets have already taken their stand on a definite political platform, when we know perfectly well that, ideologically, they are already close to us (of course, there will be backsliders, and we must be ruthless towards all enemies, nor must we relax our vigilance for an instant)—this, of course, is not everything. We must at the same time raise the problem of craftsmanship as never before, and criticism, in analysing the objects of its critical attention, must lay this very important and essential side of the matter under the microscope.

Such criticism, unfortunately, has not as yet grown up among us in its full stature. But this is one of the tasks confronting us at the present time on the literary front.

GEORGE SANTAYANA

Justification of Art [1]

IT IS NO LONGER the fashion among philosophers to decry art. Either its influence seems to them too slight to excite alarm, or their systems are too lax to subject anything to censure which has the least glamour or ideality about it. Tired, perhaps, of daily resolving the conflict between science and religion, they prefer to assume silently a harmony between morals and art. Moral harmonies, however, are not given; they have to be

---

[1] Reprinted from *Reason in Art,* Volume IV of *The Life of Reason,* by George Santayana; copyright, 1933, by Charles Scribner's Sons; pp. 166–190, 222–230. Used by permission of the publishers. (Eds.)

made. The curse of superstition is that it justifies and protracts their absence by proclaiming their invisible presence. Of course a rational religion could not conflict with a rational science; and similarly an art that was wholly admirable would necessarily play into the hands of progress. But as the real difficulty in the former case lies in saying what religion and what science would be truly rational, so here the problem is how far extant art is a benefit to mankind, and how far, perhaps, a vice or a burden.

That art is *prima facie* and in itself a good cannot be doubted. It is a spontaneous activity, and that settles the question. Yet the function of ethics is precisely to revise *prima facie* judgments of this kind and to fix the ultimate resultant of all given interests, in so far as they can be combined. In the actual disarray of human life and desire, wisdom consists in knowing what goods to sacrifice and what simples to pour into the supreme mixture. The extent to which aesthetic values are allowed to colour the resultant or highest good is a point of great theoretic importance, not only for art but for general philosophy. If art is excluded altogether or given only a trivial rôle, perhaps as a necessary relaxation, we feel at once that a philosophy so judging human arts is ascetic or post-rational. It pretends to guide life from above and from without; it has discredited human nature and mortal interests, and has thereby undermined itself, since it is at best but a partial expression of that humanity which it strives to transcend. If, on the contrary, art is prized as something supreme and irresponsible, if the poetic and mystic glow which it may bring seems its own complete justification, then philosophy is evidently still prerational or, rather, non-existent; for the beasts that listened to Orpheus belong to this school.

To be bewitched is not to be saved, though all the magicians and aesthetes in the world should pronounce it to be so. Intoxication is a sad business, at least for a philosopher; for you must either drown yourself altogether, or else when sober again you will feel somewhat fooled by yesterday's joys and somewhat lost in to-day's vacancy. The man who would emancipate art from discipline and reason is trying to elude rationality, not merely in art, but in all existence. He is vexed at conditions of excellence that make him conscious of his own incompetence and failure. Rather than consider his function, he proclaims his self-sufficiency. A way foolishness has of revenging itself is to excommunicate the world.

It is in the world, however, that art must find its level. It must vindicate its function in the human commonwealth. What direct acceptable contribution does it make to the highest good? What sacrifices, if any, does it impose? What indirect influence does it exert on other activities? Our answer to these questions will be our apology for art, our proof that art belongs to the Life of Reason.

When moralists deprecate passion and contrast it with reason, they do so, if they are themselves rational, only because passion is so often "guilty," because it works havoc so often in the surrounding world and leaves, among other ruins, "a heart high-sorrowful and cloyed." Were there no danger of such after-effects within and without the sufferer, no passion would be reprehensible. Nature is innocent, and so are all her impulses and moods when taken in isolation; it is only on meeting that they blush. If it be true that matter is sinful, the logic of this truth is far from being what the fanatics imagine who commonly propound it. Matter is sinful only because it is insufficient, or is wastefully distributed. There is not enough of it to go round among the legion of hungry ideas. To embody or enact an idea is the only way of making it actual; but its embodiment may mutilate it, if the material or the situation is not propitious. So an infant may be maimed at birth, when what injures him is not being brought forth, but being brought forth in the wrong manner. Matter has a double function in respect to existence; essentially it enables the spirit to be, yet chokes it incidentally. Men sadly misbegotten, or those who are thwarted at every step by the times' penury, may fall to thinking of matter only by its defect, ignoring the material ground of their own aspirations. All flesh will seem to them weak, except that forgotten piece of it which makes their own spiritual strength. Every impulse, however, had initially the same authority as this censorious one, by which the others are now judged and condemned.

If a practice can point to its innocence, if it can absolve itself from concern for a world with which it does not interfere, it has justified itself to those who love it, though it may not yet have recommended itself to those who do not. Now art, more than any other considerable pursuit, more even than speculation, is abstract and inconsequential. Born of suspended attention, it ends in itself. It encourages sensuous abstraction, and nothing concerns it less than to influence the world. Nor does it really do so in a notable degree. Social changes do not reach artistic expression until after their momentum is acquired and their other collateral effects are fully predetermined. Scarcely is a school of art established, giving expression to prevailing sentiment, when this sentiment changes and makes that style seem empty and ridiculous. The expression has little or no power to maintain the movement it registers, as a waterfall has little or no power to bring more water down. Currents may indeed cut deep channels, but they cannot feed their own springs—at least not until the whole revolution of nature is taken into account.

In the individual, also, art registers passions without stimulating them; on the contrary, in stopping to depict them it steals away their life; and whatever interest and delight it transfers to their expression it subtracts from their vital energy. This appears unmistakably in erotic and in religious art. Though the artist's avowed purpose here be to arouse a practical impulse, he fails in so far as he is an artist in truth; for he then will seek to move the given passions only through beauty, but beauty is a rival object of passion in itself. Lascivious and pious works, when beauty has touched them, cease to give out what is wilful and disquieting in their subject and become altogether intellectual and sublime. There is a high breathlessness about beauty that cancels lust and superstition. The artist, in taking the latter for his theme, renders them innocent and interesting, because he looks at them from above, composes their attitudes and surroundings harmoniously, and makes them food for the mind. Accordingly it is only in a refined and secondary stage that active passions like to amuse themselves with their aesthetic expression. Unmitigated lustiness and raw fanaticism will snarl at pictures. Representations begin to interest when crude passions recede, and feel the need of conciliating liberal interests and adding some intellectual charm to their dumb attractions. Thus art, while by its subject it may betray the preoccupations among which it springs up, embodies a new and quite innocent interest.

This interest is more than innocent, it is liberal. Not being concerned with material reality so much as with the ideal, it knows neither ulterior motives nor quantitative limits; the more beauty there is the more there can be, and the higher one artist's imagination soars the better the whole flock flies. In aesthetic activity we have accordingly one side of rational life; sensuous experience is dominated there as mechanical or social realities ought to be dominated in science and politics. Such dominion comes of having faculties suited to their conditions and consequently finding an inherent satisfaction in their operation. The justification of life must be ultimately intrinsic; and wherever such self-justifying experience is attained, the ideal has been in so far embodied. To have realised it in a measure helps us to realise it further; for there is a cumulative fecundity in those goods which come not by increase of force or matter, but by a better organisation and form.

Art has met, on the whole, with more success than science or morals. Beauty gives men the best hint of ultimate good which their experience as yet can offer; and the most lauded geniuses have been poets, as if people felt that those seers, rather than men of action or thought, had lived ideally and known what was worth knowing. That such should be the case, if the fact be admitted, would indeed prove the rudimentary state of human civilisation. The truly comprehensive life should be the statesman's, for whom perception and theory might be expressed and rewarded in action. The ideal dignity of art is therefore merely symbolic and vicarious. As some people study character in novels, and travel by reading tales of adventure, because real life is not yet so interesting to them as fiction, or because they find it cheaper to make their experiments in their dreams, so art in general is a rehearsal of rational living, and recasts in idea a world which we have no present means of recasting in reality. Yet this rehearsal reveals the glories of a possible performance better than do the miserable experiments until now executed on the reality.

When we consider the present distracted state of government and religion, there is much relief in turning from them to almost any art, where what is good is altogether and finally good, and what is bad is at least not treacherous. When we consider further the senseless rivalries, the vanities, the ignominy that reign in the "practical" world, how doubly blessed it becomes to find a sphere where limitation is an excellence, where diversity is a beauty, and where every man's ambition is consistent with every other man's and even favourable to it! It is indeed so in art; for we must not import into its blameless labours the bickerings and jealousies of criticism. Critics quarrel with other critics, and that is a part of philosophy. With an artist no sane man quarrels, any more than with the colour of a child's eyes. As nature, being full of seeds, rises into all sorts of crystallisations, each having its own ideal and potential life, each a nucleus of order and a habitation for the absolute self, so art, though in a medium poorer than pregnant matter, and incapable of intrinsic life, generates a semblance of all conceivable beings. What nature does with existence, art does with appearance; and while the achievement leaves us, unhappily, much where we were before in all our efficacious relations, it entirely renews our vision and breeds a fresh world in fancy, where all form has the same inner justification that all life has in the real world. As no insect is without its rights and every cripple has his dream of happiness, so no artistic fact, no child of imagination, is without its small birthright of beauty. In this freer element, competition does not exist and everything is Olympian. Hungry generations do not tread down the ideal but only its spokesmen or embodiments, that have cast in their lot with other material things. Art supplies constantly to contemplation what nature seldom affords in concrete experience—the union of life and peace.

The ideal, however, would not come down from the empyrean and be conceived unless somebody's thought were absorbed in the conception. Art actually segregates classes of men and masses of matter to serve its special interests. This involves expense; it impedes some possible activities and imposes others. On this ground, from the earliest times until our own, art has been occasionally attacked by moralists, who have felt that it fostered idolatry or luxury or irresponsible dreams. Of these attacks the most interesting is Plato's, because he was an artist by temperament, bred in the very focus of artistic life and discussion, and at the same time a consummate moral philosopher. His aesthetic sensibility was indeed so great that it led him, perhaps, into a relative error, in that he overestimated the influence which art can have on character and affairs. Homer's stories about the gods can hardly have demoralised the youths who recited them. No religion has ever given a picture of deity which men could have imitated without the grossest immorality. Yet these shocking representations have not had a bad effect on believers. The deity was opposed to their own vices; those it might itself be credited with offered no contagious example. In spite of the theologians, we know by instinct that in speaking of the gods we are dealing in myths and symbols. Some aspect of nature or some law of life, expressed in an attribute of deity, is what we really regard, and to regard such things, however sinister they may be, cannot but chasten and moralise us. The personal character that such a function would involve, if it were exercised willingly by a responsible being, is something that never enters our thoughts. No such painful image comes to perplex the plain sense of instinctive, poetic religion. To give moral importance to myths, as Plato tended to do, is to take them far too seriously and to belittle what they stand for. Left to themselves they float in an ineffectual stratum of the brain. They are understood and grow current precisely by not being pressed, like an idiom or a metaphor. The same aesthetic sterility appears at the other end of the scale, where fancy is anything but sacred. A Frenchman once saw in "Punch and Judy" a shocking proof of British brutality, destined further to demoralise the nation; and yet the scandal may pass. That black tragedy reflects not very pretty manners, but puppets exercise no suasion over men.

To his supersensitive censure of myths Plato added strictures upon music and the drama: to excite passions idly was to enervate the soul. Only martial or religious strains should be heard in the ideal republic. Furthermore, art put before us a mere phantom of the good. True excellence was the function things had in use; the horseman knew the use and essence of a bridle better than the artisan did who put it together; but a painted bridle would lack even this relation to utility. It would rein in no horse, and was an impertinent sensuous reduplication of what, even when it had material being, was only an instrument and a means.

This reasoning has been little understood, because Platonists so soon lost sight of their master's Socratic habit and moral intent. They turned the good into an existence, making it thereby unmeaning. Plato's dialectic, if we do not thus abolish the force of its terms, is perfectly cogent: representative art has indeed no utility, and, if the good has been identified with efficiency in a military state, it can have no justification. Plato's Republic was avowedly a fallen state, a church militant, coming sadly short of perfection; and the joy which Plato as much as any one could feel in sensuous art he postponed, as a man in mourning might, until life should be redeemed from baseness.

Never have art and beauty received a more glowing eulogy than is implied in Plato's censure. To him nothing was beautiful that was not beautiful to the core, and he would have thought to insult art—the remodelling of nature by reason—if he had given it a narrower field than all practice. As an architect who had fondly designed something impossible, or which might not please in execution, would at once erase it from the plan and abandon it for the love of perfect beauty and perfect art, so Plato wished to erase from pleasing appearance all that, when its operation was completed, would bring discord into the world. This was done in the ultimate interest of art and beauty, which in a cultivated mind are inseparable from the vitally good. It is mere barbarism to feel that a thing is aesthetically good but morally evil, or morally good but hateful to perception. Things partially evil or partially ugly may have to be chosen under stress of unfavourable circumstances, lest some worse thing come; but if a thing were ugly it would *thereby* not be wholly good, and if it were *altogether* good it would perforce be beautiful.

To criticise art on moral grounds is to pay it a high compliment by assuming that it aims to be adequate, and is addressed to a comprehensive mind. The only way in which art could disallow such criticism would be to protest its irresponsible infancy, and admit that it was a more or less amiable blatancy in individuals, and not *art* at all. Young animals often gambol in a delightful fashion, and men also may, though hardly when they intend to do so. Sportive self-expression can be prized because human nature contains a certain elasticity and margin for experiment, in which waste activity is inevitable and may be precious: for this license may lead, amid a thousand failures, to some real discovery and advance. Art, like life, should be free, since both are experimental. But it is one thing to make room for genius and to respect the sudden madness of poets through which, possibly, some god may speak, and it is quite another not to judge the result by rational standards. The earth's bowels are full of all sorts of rumblings; which of the oracles drawn thence is true can be judged only by the light of day. If an artist's inspiration has been happy, it has been so because his work can sweeten or ennoble the mind and because its total effect will be beneficent. Art being a part of life, the criticism of art is a part of morals.

Maladjustments in human society are still so scandalous, they touch matters so much more pressing than fine art, that maladjustments in the latter are passed over with a smile, as if art were at any rate an irresponsible miraculous parasite that the legislator had better not meddle with. The day may come, however, if the state is ever reduced to a tolerable order, when questions of art will be the most urgent questions of morals, when genius at last will feel responsible, and the twist given to imagination will seem the most crucial thing in life. Under a thin disguise, the momentous character of imaginative choices has already been fully recognised by mankind. Men have passionately loved their special religions, languages, and manners, and preferred death to a life flowering in any other fashion. In justifying this attachment forensically, with arguments on the low level of men's named and consecrated interests, people have indeed said, and perhaps come to believe, that their imaginative interests were material interests at bottom, thinking thus to give them more weight and legitimacy; whereas in truth material life itself would be nothing worth, were it not, in its essence and its issue, ideal.

It was stupidly asserted, however, that if a man omitted the prescribed ceremonies or had unauthorised dreams about the gods, he would lose his battles in this world and go to hell in the other. He who runs can see that these expectations are not founded on any evidence, on any observation of what actually occurs; they are obviously a *mirage* arising from a direct ideal passion, that tries to justify itself by indirection and by falsehoods, as it has no need to do. We all read facts in the way most congruous with our intellectual habit, and when this habit drives us to effulgent creations, absorbing and expressing the whole current of our being, it not merely biasses our reading of this world but carries us into another world altogether, which we posit instead of the real one, or beside it.

Grotesque as the blunder may seem by which we thus introduce our poetic tropes into the sequence of external events or existences, the blunder is intellectual only; morally, zeal for our special rhetoric may not be irrational. The lovely Phoebus is no fact for astronomy, nor does he stand behind the material sun, in some higher heaven, physically superintending its movements; but Phoebus is a fact in his own region, a token of man's joyful piety in the presence of the forces that really condition his welfare. In the region of symbols, in the world of poetry, Phoebus has his inalienable rights. Forms of poetry are forms of human life. Languages express national character and enshrine particular ways of seeing and valuing events. To make substitutions and extensions in expression is to give the soul, in her inmost substance, a somewhat new constitution. A method of apperception is a spontaneous variation in mind, perhaps the origin of a new moral species.

The value apperceptive methods have is of course largely representative, in that they serve more or less aptly to dominate the order of events and to guide action; but quite apart from this practical value, expressions possess a character of their own, a sort of vegetative life, as languages possess euphony. Two reports of the same fact may be equally trustworthy, equally useful as information, yet they may embody two types of mental rhetoric, and this diversity in genius may be of more intrinsic importance than the raw fact it works upon. The non-representative side of human perception may thus be the most momentous side of it, because it represents, or even constitutes, the man. After all, the chief interest we have in things lies in what we can make of them or what they can make of us. There is consequently nothing fitted to colour human happiness more pervasively than art does, nor to express more deeply the mind's internal habit. In educating the imagination art crowns all moral endeavour, which from the beginning is a species of art, and which becomes a fine art more completely as it works in a freer medium.

How great a portion of human energies should be spent on art and its appreciation is a question to be answered variously by various persons and nations. There is no ideal *à priori;* an ideal can but express, if it is genuine, the balance of impulses and potentialities in a given soul. A mind at once sensuous and mobile will find its appropriate perfection in studying and reconstructing objects of sense. Its rationality will appear chiefly on the plane of perception, to render the circle of visions which makes up its life as delightful as possible. For such a man art will be the most satisfying, the most significant activity, and to load him with material riches or speculative truths or profound social loyalties will be to impede and depress him. The irrational is what does not justify itself in the end; and the born artist, repelled by the soberer and bitterer passions of the world, may justly call them irrational. They would not justify themselves in his experience; they make grievous demands and yield nothing in the end which is intelligible to him. His picture of them, if he be a dramatist, will hardly fail to be satirical; fate, frailty, illusion will be his constant themes. If his temperament could find political expression, he would minimise the machinery of life and deprecate any calculated prudence. He would trust the heart, enjoy nature, and not frown too angrily on inclination. Such a Bohemia he would regard as an ideal world in which humanity might flourish congenially.

A puritan moralist, before condemning such an infantile paradise, should remember that a commonwealth of butterflies actually exists. It is not any inherent wrongness in such an ideal that makes it unacceptable, but only the fact that human butterflies are not wholly mercurial and that even imperfect geniuses are but an extreme type in a society whose guiding ideal is based upon a broader humanity than the artist represents. Men of science or business will accuse the poet of folly, on the very grounds on which he accuses them of the same. Each will seem to the other to be obeying a barren obsession. The statesman or philosopher who should aspire to adjust their quarrel could do so only by force of intelligent sympathy with both sides, and in view of the common conditions in which they find themselves. What ought to be done is that which, when done, will most nearly justify itself to all concerned. Practical problems of morals are judicial and political problems. Justice can never be pronounced without hearing the parties and weighing the interests at stake.

A circumstance that complicates such a calculation is this: aesthetic and other interests are not separable units, to be compared externally; they are rather strands interwoven in the texture of everything. Aesthetic sensibility colours every thought, qualifies every allegiance, and modifies every product of human labour. Consequently the love of beauty has to justify itself not merely intrinsically, or as a constituent part of life more or less to be insisted upon; it has to justify itself also as an influence. A hostile influence is the most odious of things. The enemy himself, the alien creature, lies in his own camp, and in a speculative moment we may put ourselves in his place and learn to think of him charitably; but his spirit in our own souls is like a private tempter, a treasonable voice weakening our allegiance to our own duty. A zealot might allow his neighbours to be damned in peace, did not a certain heretical odour emitted by them infect the sanctuary and disturb his own dogmatic calm. In the same way practical people might leave the artist alone in his oasis, and even grant him a pittance on which to live, as they feed the animals in a zoological garden, did he not intrude into their most inmost conclave and vitiate the abstract cogency of their designs. It is not so much art in its own field that men of science look askance upon, as the love of glitter and rhetoric and false finality trespassing upon scientific ground; while men of affairs may well deprecate a rooted habit of sensuous absorption and of sudden transit to imaginary worlds, a habit which must work havoc in their own sphere. In other words, there is an element of poetry inherent in thought, in conduct, in affection; and we must ask ourselves how far this ingredient is an obstacle to their proper development.

The fabled dove who complained, in flying, of the resistance of the air, was as wise as the philosopher who should lament the presence and influence of sense. Sense is the native element and substance of experience; all its refinements are still parts of it existentially; and whatever excellence belongs specifically to sense is a preliminary excellence, a value antecedent to any which thought or action can achieve. Science and morals have but representative authority; they are principles of ideal synthesis and safe transition; they are bridges from moment to moment of sentience. Their function is indeed universal and their value overwhelming, yet their office remains derivative or secondary, and what they serve to put in order has previously its intrinsic worth. An aesthetic bias is native to sense, being indeed nothing but its form and potency; and the influence which aesthetic habits exercise on thought and action should not be regarded as an intrusion to be resented, but rather as an original interest to be built upon and developed. Sensibility contains the distinctions which reason afterward carries out and applies; it is sensibility that involves and supports primitive diversities, such as those between good and bad, here and there, fast and slow, light and darkness. There are complications and harmonies inherent in these oppositions, harmonies which aesthetic faculty proceeds to note; and from these we may then construct others, not immediately presentable, which we distinguish by attributing them to reason. Reason may well outflank and transform aesthetic judgments, but can never undermine them. Its own materials are the perceptions which if full and perfect are called beauties. Its function is to endow the parts of sentience with a consciousness of the system in which they lie, so that they may attain a mutual relevance and ideally support one another. But what could relevance or support be worth if the things to be buttressed were themselves worthless? It is not to organise pain, ugliness, and boredom that reason can be called into the world.

When a practical or scientific man boasts that he has laid aside aesthetic prejudices and is following truth and utility with a single eye, he can mean, if he is judicious, only that he has not yielded to aesthetic preference after his problem was fixed, nor in an arbitrary and vexatious fashion. He has not consulted taste when it would have been in bad taste to do so. If he meant that he had rendered himself altogether insensible to aesthetic values, and that he had proceeded to organise conduct or thought in complete indifference to the beautiful, he would be simply proclaiming his inhumanity and incompetence. A right observance of aesthetic demands does not obstruct utility nor logic; for utility and logic are themselves beautiful, while a sensuous beauty that ran counter to reason could never be, in the end, pleasing to an exquisite sense. Aesthetic vice is not favourable to aesthetic faculty: it is an impediment to the greatest aesthetic satisfactions. And so when by yielding to a blind passion for beauty we derange theory and practice, we cut ourselves off from those beauties which alone could have satisfied our passion. What we drag in so obstinately will bring but a cheap and unstable pleasure, while a double beauty will thereby be lost or obscured—first, the unlooked-for beauty which a genuine and stable system of things could not but betray, and secondly the coveted beauty itself, which, being imported here into the wrong context, will be rendered meretricious and offensive to good taste. If a jewel worn on the wrong finger sends a shiver through the flesh, how disgusting must not rhetoric be in diplomacy or unction in metaphysics!

The poetic element inherent in thought, affection, and conduct is prior to their prosaic development and altogether legitimate. Clear, well-digested perception and rational choices follow upon those primary creative impulses, and carry out their purpose systematically. At every stage in this development new and appropriate materials are offered for aesthetic contemplation. Straightness, for instance, symmetry, and rhythm are at first sensuously defined; they are characters arrested by aesthetic instinct; but they are the materials of mathematics. And long after these initial forms have disowned their sensuous values, and suffered a wholly dialectical expansion or analysis, mathematical objects again fall under the aesthetic eye, and surprise the senses by their emotional power. A mechanical system, such as astronomy in one region has already unveiled, is an inexhaustible field for aesthetic wonder.

Similarly, in another sphere, sensuous affinity leads to friendship and love, and makes us huddle up to our fellows and feel their heart-beats; but when human society has thereupon established a legal and moral edifice, this new spectacle yields new imaginative transports, tragic, lyric, and religious. Aesthetic values everywhere precede and accompany rational activity, and life is, in one aspect, always a fine art; not by introducing inaptly aesthetic vetoes or aesthetic flourishes, but by giving to everything a form which, implying a structure, implies also an ideal and a possible perfection. This perfection, being felt, is also a beauty, since any process, though it may have become intellectual or practical, remains for all that a vital and sentient operation, with its inherent sensuous values. Whatever is to be representative in import must first be immediate in existence; whatever is transitive in operation must be at the same time actual in being. So that an aesthetic sanction sweetens all successful living; animal efficiency cannot be without grace, nor moral achievement without a sensible glory.

These vital harmonies are natural; they are neither perfect nor pre-ordained. We often come upon beauties that need to be sacrificed, as we come upon events and practical necessities without number that are truly regrettable. There are a myriad conflicts in practice and in thought, conflicts between rival possibilities, knocking inopportunely and in vain at the door of existence. Owing to the initial disorganisation of things, some demands continually prove to be incompatible with others arising no less naturally. Reason in such cases imposes real and irreparable sacrifices, but it brings a stable consolation if its discipline is accepted. Decay, for instance, is a moral and aesthetic evil; but being a natural necessity it can become the basis for pathetic and magnificent harmonies, when once imagination is adjusted to it. The hatred of change and death is ineradicable while life lasts, since it expresses that self-sustaining organisation in a creature which we call its soul; yet this hatred of change and death is not so deeply seated in the nature of things as are death and change themselves, for the flux is deeper than the ideal. Discipline may attune our higher and more adaptable part to the harsh conditions of being, and the resulting sentiment, being the only one which can be maintained successfully, will express the greatest satisfactions which can be reached, though not the greatest that might be conceived or desired. To be interested in the changing seasons is, in this middling zone, a happier state of mind than to be hopelessly in love with spring. Wisdom discovers these possible accommodations, as circumstances impose them; and education ought to prepare men to accept them.

It is for want of education and discipline that a man so often insists petulantly on his random tastes, instead of cultivating those which might find some satisfaction in the world and might produce in him some pertinent culture. Untutored self-assertion may even lead him to deny some fact that should have been patent, and plunge him into needless calamity. His Utopias cheat him in the end, if indeed the barbarous taste he has indulged in clinging to them does not itself lapse before the dream is half formed. So men have feverishly conceived a heaven only to find it insipid, and a hell to find it ridiculous. Theodicies that were to demonstrate an absolute cosmic harmony have turned the universe into a tyrannous nightmare, from which we are glad to awake again in this unintentional and somewhat tractable world. Thus the fancies of effeminate poets in violating science are false to the highest art, and the products of sheer confusion, instigated by the love of beauty, turn out to be hideous. A rational severity in respect to art simply weeds the garden; it expresses a mature aesthetic choice and opens the way to supreme artistic achievements. To keep beauty in its place is to make all things beautiful.

GEORGE SANTAYANA

Art and Happiness

THE VALUE OF ART lies in making people happy, first in practising the art and then in possessing its product. This observation might seem needless, and ought to be so; but if we compare it with what is commonly said on these subjects, we must confess that it may often be denied and more often, perhaps, may not be understood. Happiness is something men ought to pursue, although they seldom do so; they are drawn away from it at first by foolish impulses and afterwards by perverse laws. To secure happiness conduct would have to remain spontaneous while it learned not to be criminal; but the fanatical attachment of men, now to a fierce liberty, now to a false regimen, keeps them barbarous and wretched. A rational pursuit of happiness—which is one thing with progress or with the Life of Reason—would embody that natural piety which leaves to the episodes of life their inherent values, mourning death, celebrating love, sanctifying civic traditions, enjoying and correcting nature's ways. To discriminate happiness is therefore the very soul of art, which expresses experience without distorting it, as those political or metaphysical tyrannies distort it which sanctify unhappiness. A free mind, like a creative imagination, rejoices at the harmonies it can find or make between man and nature; and, where it finds none, it solves the conflict so far as it may and then notes and endures it with a shudder.

A morality organised about the human heart in an ingenuous and sincere fashion would involve every fine art and would render the world pervasively beautiful—beautiful in its artificial products and beautiful in its underlying natural terrors. The closer we keep to elementary human needs and to the natural agencies that may satisfy them, the closer we are to beauty. Industry, sport, and science, with the perennial intercourse and passions of men, swarm with incentives to expression, because they are everywhere creating new moulds of being and compelling the eye to observe those forms and to recast them ideally. Art is simply an adequate industry; it arises when industry is carried out to the satisfaction of all human demands, even of those incidental sensuous demands which we call aesthetic and which a brutal industry, in its haste, may despise or ignore.

Arts responsive in this way to all human nature would be beautiful according to reason and might remain beautiful long. Poetic beauty touches the world whenever it attains some unfeigned harmony either with sense or with reason; and the more unfeignedly human happiness was made the test of all institutions and pursuits, the more beautiful they would be, having more numerous points of fusion with the mind, and fusing with it more profoundly. To distinguish and to create beauty would then be no art relegated to a few abstracted spirits, playing with casual fancies; it would be a habit inseparable from practical efficiency. All operations, all affairs, would then be viewed in the light of ultimate interests, and in their deep relation to human good. The arts would thus recover their Homeric glory; touching human fate as they clearly would, they would borrow something of its grandeur and pathos, and yet the interest that worked in them would be warm, because it would remain unmistakably animal and sincere.

The principle that all institutions should subserve happiness runs deeper than any cult for art and lays the foundation on which the latter might rest safely. If social structure were rational its free expression would be so too. Many observers, with no particular philosophy to adduce, feel that the arts among us are somehow impotent, and they look for a better inspiration, now to ancient models, now to the raw phenomena of life. A dilettante may, indeed, summon inspiration whence he will; and a virtuoso will never lack some material to keep him busy; but if what is hoped for is a genuine, native, inevitable art, a great revolution would first have to be worked in society. We should have to abandon our vested illusions, our irrational religions and patriotisms and schools of art, and to discover instead our genuine needs, the forms of our possible happiness. To call for such self-examination seems revolutionary only because we start from a sophisticated system, a system resting on traditional fashions and superstitions, by which the will of the living generation is misinterpreted and betrayed. To shake off that system would not subvert order but rather institute order for the first time; it would be an *Instauratio Magna,* a setting things again on their feet.

We in Christendom are so accustomed to artificial ideals and to artificial institutions, kept up to express them, that we hardly conceive how anomalous our situation is, sorely as we may suffer from it. We found academies and museums, as we found missions, to fan a flame that constantly threatens to die out for lack of natural fuel. Our overt ideals are parasites in the body politic, while the ideals native to the body politic, those involved in our natural structure and situation, are either stifled by that alien incubus, leaving civic life barbarous, or else force their way up, unremarked or not justly honoured as ideals. Industry and science and social amenities, with all the congruous comforts and appurtenances of contemporary life, march on their way, as if they had nothing to say to the spirit, which remains entangled in a cobweb of dead traditions. An idle pottering of the fancy over obsolete forms—theological, dramatic, or plastic—makes that by-play to the sober business of life which men call their art or their religion; and the more functionless and gratuitous this by-play is the more those who indulge in it think they are idealists. They feel they are champions of what is most precious in the world, as a sentimental lady might fancy herself a lover of flowers when she pressed them in a book instead of planting their seeds in the garden.

It is clear that gratuitous and functionless habits cannot bring happiness; they do not constitute an activity at once spontaneous and beneficent, such as noble art is an instance of. Those habits may indeed give pleasure; they may bring extreme excitement, as madness notably does, though it is in the highest degree functionless and gratuitous. Nor is such by-play without consequences, some of which might conceivably be fortunate. What is functionless is so called for being worthless from some ideal point of view, and not conducing to the particular life considered. But nothing real is dissociated from the universal flux; everything—madness and all unmeaning crosscurrents in being—count in the general process and discharge somewhere, not without effect, the substance they have drawn for a moment into their little vortex. So our vain arts and unnecessary religions are not without real effects and not without a certain internal vitality. When life is profoundly disorganised it may well happen that only in detached episodes, only in moments snatched for dreaming in, can men see the blue or catch a glimpse of something like the ideal. In that case their esteem for their irrelevant visions may be well grounded, and their thin art and far-fetched religion may really constitute what is best in their experience. In a pathetic way

these poor enthusiasms may be justified, but only because the very conception of a rational life lies entirely beyond the horizon.

It is no marvel, when art is a brief truancy from rational practice, that the
artist himself should be a vagrant, and at best, as it were, an infant prodigy.
The wings of genius serve him only for an escapade, enabling him to skirt
the perilous edge of madness and of mystical abysses. But such an erratic
workman does not deserve the name of artist or master; he has burst convention only to break it, not to create a new convention more in harmony
with nature. His originality, though it may astonish for a moment, will in
the end be despised and will find no thoroughfare. He will meantime be
wretched himself, torn from the roots of his being by that cruel, unmeaning
inspiration; or, if too rapt to see his own plight, he will be all the more pitied
by practical men, who cannot think it a real blessing to be lost in joys that
do not strengthen the character and yield nothing for posterity.

Art, in its nobler acceptation, is an achievement, not an indulgence. It
prepares the world in some sense to receive the soul, and the soul to master
the world; it disentangles those threads in each that can be woven into the
other. That the artist should be eccentric, homeless, dreamful may almost
seem a natural law, but it is none the less a scandal. An artist's business
is not really to cut fantastical capers or be licensed to play the fool. His
business is simply that of every keen soul to build well when it builds, and
to speak well when it speaks, giving practice everywhere the greatest possible
affinity to the situation, the most delicate adjustment to every faculty it
affects. The wonder of an artist's performance grows with the range of
his penetration, with the instinctive sympathy that makes him, in his mortal
isolation, considerate of other men's fate and a great diviner of their secret,
so that his work speaks to them kindly, with a deeper assurance than they
could have spoken with to themselves. And the joy of his great sanity, the
power of his adequate vision, is not the less intense because he can lend it
to others and has borrowed it from a faithful study of the world.

If happiness is the ultimate sanction of art, art in turn is the best instrument of happiness. In art more directly than in other activities man's self-
expression is cumulative and finds an immediate reward; for it alters the
material conditions of sentience so that sentience becomes at once more
delightful and more significant. In industry man is still servile, preparing
the materials he is to use in action. In action itself, though he is free, he
exerts his influence on a living and treacherous medium and sees the issue
at each moment drift farther and farther from his intent. In science he is
an observer, preparing himself for action in another way, by studying its
results and conditions. But in art he is at once competent and free; he is
creative. He is not troubled by his materials, because he has assimilated

them and may take them for granted; nor is he concerned with the chance complexion of affairs in the actual world, because he is making the world over, not merely considering how it grew or how it will consent to grow in future. Nothing, accordingly, could be more delightful than genuine art, nor more free from remorse and the sting of vanity. Art springs so completely from the heart of man that it makes everything speak to him in his own language; it reaches, nevertheless, so truly to the heart of nature that it co-operates with her, becomes a parcel of her creative material energy, and builds by her instinctive hand. If the various formative impulses afoot in the world never opposed stress to stress and made no havoc with one another, nature might be called an unconscious artist. In fact, just where such a formative impulse finds support from the environment, a consciousness supervenes. If that consciousness is adequate enough to be prophetic, an art arises. Thus the emergence of arts out of instincts is the token and exact measure of nature's success and of mortal happiness.

Art and Morality

W. K. WIMSATT, JR.

Poetry and Morals: A Relation Reargued [1]

§ 1

THE ANCIENT QUESTION whether poetry can appear independently of morals has not lacked recent answers, both affirmative and negative, and both earnestly argued. "Can that be beautiful for man," asked Mr. Victor Hamm in these pages a few years ago—"Can that be beautiful . . . which is not ethically beautiful?" The answer for him was emphatically

---

[1] W. K. Wimsatt, Jr., "Poetry and Morals: A Relation Reargued," *Thought,* XXIII (1948), 281–299. Reprinted by permission. (Eds.)

that it could not. The artist "cannot disintegrate himself except . . . by a fundamental self-deception which vitiates and depraves the very center of his character, the fountains whence his energies as a human personality spring." [2] For this unified view of values I would at the outset confess my serious sympathy. It is difficult to dissent from it with thorough complacency. On the other hand the champions of the school attacked by Mr. Hamm— Messrs. Maritain and Adler—have assured us that "The artist is necessarily autonomous in his own sphere." [3] It is in this direction that I myself would argue, yet I should sympathize with a critic of poetry—Mr. Hamm or another —who might argue that the *necessity* of this view is far from clear, that the solution is too smooth and triumphant. The same view has been advanced with great delicacy (if some wavering) by at least one distinguished poet of our day, Mr. T. S. Eliot, yet it has suffered, I believe, on the whole from seeming to lack relevance to an art such as poetry, made of words and ideas, and notorious for imbroglios with all sorts of moral interest. It will be the purpose of this essay to inquire how in fact the doctrine of aesthetic autonomy *can* apply to poetry. And first by noticing some related but distinct issues, and then some alternative solutions to the proper issue.

Poetry, said Plato, in effect, is a kind of inspired ignorance; it stands at two removes from the truth; it is furthermore at fault in that it feeds and waters the passions. He drew a decided distinction between poetic quality and moral results. "The greater the poetic charm . . . the less are they meet for the ears of boys and men who are meant to be free." The conclusion was on the whole decidedly moral. Somewhere, in some Utopian state, a truthful and moral poetry might occur. But poetry as Plato had actually known it was intolerable. "And so when we have anointed him with myrrh and set a garland of wool upon his head, we shall send him away to another city." [4]

There, at the start of the tradition, we have at least three main propositions (or bundles of related propositions) which anyone entering upon a discussion of poetry and morals might well distinguish and number for convenient reference.

Ia. Poetry has philosophic content—images and their interpretation—possibly true and moral, usually false and immoral.
Ib. The poetic value of poetry is not the same as or even strictly determined by its truth or morality.
IIa. Poetry has moral power: i.e., it produces moral effects on those who hear it—possibly for good, mostly for evil.

---

[2] "Literature and Morality," *Thought*, XV (June, 1940), 278, 280.
[3] Mortimer Adler, *Art and Prudence* (New York, 1937), p. 448.
[4] *Ion; Republic*, iii, 387, 398; x, 862; *Phaedrus; Laws*, ii, 607; vii, 800; viii, 829.

IIb. The poetic value of poetry is not the same as or even strictly determined by its moral effect.

III. Both philosophico-moral content and moral effect have a claim on our allegiance which is prior to the claim of poetic value.

It will be observed that the second pair of propositions, IIa and IIb, concern what poetry *does,* its persuasory and contagious effect, but not as such what poetry *says* or is, poetry objectively considered as a body of cognitive and analyzable meaning. The first pair of propositions, Ia and Ib, consider just this body of meaning. Ib, asserting the difference between the poetic and the moral value of meaning, is the crucial proposition which a certain school of moralists, Mr. Hamm among them, would deny. Proposition III, the rule of arbitration between poetry and morals, follows from the concept of morals. Yet the very meaning of this proposition, it is worth noting, depends largely on Ib. If Ib is not true, III can relate only to what poetry *does.* If poetry is not cognitively separable from morals, if one makes no distinction between poetic meaning and moral meaning, there can be no cognitive and intrinsic conflict: the poet in being moral is only following the rule of his craft. Not III, of course, but the vindication of its premise in Ib is the concern of the critic. Let the moralist assert that poetry *should* be moral. The critic would ask whether poetry *need* be moral in order to be poetry.

Moral critique of poetry has often forced proposition III into close conjunction with the two affective propositions IIa and IIb. From poetry, said Stephen Gosson, the English Plato of 1579, we advance to piping, "from pyping to playing, from play to pleasure, from pleasure to slouth, from slouth to sleepe, from sleepe to sinne, from sinne to death, from death to the Divel." [5] Such complaints, it should be said at the start, are not what the theorist of poetry would discuss, nor any of the like moral and political issues which arise from propositions IIa, IIb, and III, the issues of conscience and censorship—the chief concern of Mr. Adler in his *Art and Prudence.* Again, it should be said that the issue for the theorist is not that of the author's personal morals or philosophy. It may be true, as Mr. Hamm has asserted, that "a literary work can never be indifferent morally in its origins." [6] It is certainly not true, as Mr. Adler has asserted, that "intrinsic" criticism of art is that which "regards the work in relation to the artist." [7]

[5] *The School of Abuse* (London, 1841), p. 14.

[6] *Thought,* XV (June, 1940), 270.

[7] *Art and Prudence,* p. 453. Mr. M. C. Beardsley and I have labored the distinction between poem and author in *A Dictionary of World Literature,* ed. Joseph T. Shipley (New York, 1943), s.v. "Intention"; and in "The Intentional Fallacy," *Sewanee Review,* LIV (Summer, 1946), 468–488.

Mr. Adler's moral concern parcels the work of art between author and audience, until what is strictly intrinsic is only technique. See below, notes 16 and 24.

We inquire now not about origins, nor about effects, but about the work so far as it can be considered by itself as a body of meaning. Neither the qualities of the author's mind nor the effects of a poem upon a reader's mind should be confused with the moral quality of the meaning expressed by the poem itself.

§ 2

To take up the issue between poetry and morals at the cognitive level, it is to be observed that if Platonic proposition Ib, asserting the separability of poetry and morals, is not true, then one of two extremely unified and simplified views or claims will follow—or have followed at various times. Either (1) morals reaches over and claims poetry—not simply as superior to poetry but as defining poetry; or (2) poetry reaches over and claims to define morals.[8] We have seen the second view in such romantic and postromantic statements as that of Shelley, "Poets are the unacknowledged legislators of the world," or in the system of Matthew Arnold, where poetry is a "criticism of life."

> More and more mankind will discover that we have to turn to poetry to interpret life for us, to console us, to sustain us. Without poetry, our science will appear incomplete; and most of what now passes with us for religion and philosophy will be replaced by poetry.[9]

A similar view appears in the more recent psychological theory of Mr. I. A. Richards, where poetry as pseudo-statement bolsters our morale undermined by science.[10] It is easy to see that a morality of this sort, determined by poetry, is not really a morality in the sense of a code, but a relative morality of almost indefinite diversity and flexibility—for such is poetry—and that hence what theorists of this school mean in the end is that they do not subscribe to a code.[11] For these we may say that in the large sense the problem to be discussed in this essay does not exist, since there is no distinction

---

[8] "Rival claims of annexation in which morality is reduced to beauty or beauty to morality," quotes Mr. Hamm from Ralph Barton Perry's *General Theory of Value* (New York, 1926), p. 8 (*Thought*, XV, 279). It is difficult to see why this upsetting fact should be introduced by Mr. Hamm in the "Conclusion" of an essay asserting the unity of literature and morals.

[9] "The Study of Poetry," *Essays in Criticism, Second Series* (London, 1888), p. 2.

[10] The affinity of Mr. Richards' views for the Arnoldian may be seen in his later statement: "Poems which have a destination, a final solution . . . have only a subordinate value. Instead of establishing, as the best poetry does, the norms of value, they have to be judged by standards more inclusive than themselves" (*Coleridge on Imagination*, New York, 1935, p. 213).

[11] "Modern thinking, in its effort to find a plausible substitute for dogmatic theology, has put upon literature a greater moral burden than it is actually fitted to bear" (F. A. Pottle, *The Idiom of Poetry* [Ithaca, 1946], p. 210, "The Moral Evaluation of Literature").

between, and hence no need of explaining the relation between, poetry and morals.

Nor does the problem really exist for those of the other school, who deny Platonic proposition Ib for an opposite reason and make poetic value depend upon moral value: Mr. Hamm, for instance, or Sir Philip Sidney when he answers Gosson with the argument that poetry is a "feigning notable images of virtues [and] vices," [12] or Rymer and Dennis a century later, the school of "poetic justice," or the Earl of Roscommon in his couplet:

> Immodest words admit of no Defence,
> For want of Decency is want of Sense.[13]

Among recent statements of the moral view the most extreme is perhaps that of Mr. Arthur Machen: "Literature is the expression, through the aesthetic medium of words, of the dogmas of the Catholic Church, and that which is out of harmony with these dogmas is not literature . . ." [14] More moderately the late Irving Babbitt and other neo-humanists have said that poetry gives ethical insight.[15]

If the Arnoldian view, as we have seen, leaves morals in a bad way, it should be equally clear that the rigorous moral view not only leaves very little to the critic of poetry in his own right (a loss which might perhaps have to be overlooked) but also makes a vast invasion into the usually recognized canon of the world's poetry—so much of it is in one way or another immoral. One cannot really refute Plato. Or to put this more moderately and without the unhappy implication that a great part of the world's best literature is substantially evil, let us say that a moral code must be by its nature too rigid to accommodate, or at least too rigid to account for or specifically sanction, the widely heterogeneous concreteness of the world's recognized poetry. There is no religion or philosophy that will embrace Homer's heroes and gods, the fatalism of Greek tragedy, the atomism of Lucretius, the Heaven, Purgatory and Hell of Dante, the Senecan Stoicism of Shakespeare, the occultism—what has seemed to many the diabolism—of Milton, the world soul of Wordsworth, the flowers of evil of Baudelaire. The choice between poetry and morals is not specifically a Christian one—though today in the Western world it may be felt most acutely by a serious Christian. It is the choice which appears for any moralist—for Plato banishing the poets from the city, for Tolstoy in his old age repudiating all of his own work ex-

---

[12] *The Defense of Poesy*, ed. A. S. Cook (Boston, 1890), p. 11. In other passages Sidney is more inclined to make a Platonic distinction between poetic and moral power. "Poesy may not only be abused, but . . . being abused, by the reason of his sweet charming force, it can do more than any other array of words" (p. 38).

[13] *Essay on Translated Verse*, ll. 23–24.

[14] *Hieroglyphics* (New York, 1923), p. 160.

[15] Cf. Norman Foerster, "The Esthetic Judgment and the Ethical Judgment," in *The Intent of the Critic*, ed. Donald Stauffer (Princeton, 1941), p. 69.

cept two of his simplest short stories, for the totalitarian Marxist—except that for the Marxist there is no very nice problem. He simply rejects—almost everything.

§ 3

This essay is an attempt to express the point of view of one who accepting a moral code would yet save poetic value—not as superior to moral value but as different from it. And it is not easy—in a full and thoughtful way—to affirm Platonic proposition Ib and escape between the relaxed simplification of the Arnoldian and the severe one of the moralist. A long tradition, beginning with Plato and with the separation by Aristotle of his *Poetics* from his *Ethics,* testifies to the utility of the distinction between poetry and morals. Today the moralist will often make the distinction quite casually:

> Just as an engineer may not construct and approve a bridge, the durability of which he doubts for the load he knows his clients will attempt to transport over it; and just as a chef may not serve food which he knows is even partially on the way to corruption and which might presently cause distress or worse to the consumer,—so also the poet or writer may not express anything, *however beautifully,* which both he and his critics have reason to believe will be subversive to thought or action on the part of him who reads it.[16]

Yet it is not easy, especially when the moralist phrases it, to see how this distinction can be seriously maintained. The bridge which was destined to fall might *look* well when inspected, but looks are surely not a very profound test of a bridge. The bridge would simply be a bad bridge. The food might *taste* well before making the eater ill, and here is a more plausible resemblance to what is maintained about beautiful but dangerous poetry. The food answers one important (if specious) requirement of good food. But how can poetry, which concerns good and evil, which is an intellectual art and which exists and has quality only in being understood, be both beautiful and morally destructive? Here one must indeed agree with Mr. Hamm: "Language, unlike marble, pigments and musical sounds, is immediately and essentially expressive of ideas. . . . The literary artist expresses implicit moral judgments." [17] Very few, if any, important poems

---

[16] Jerome Kobel, "Literature and Morality: A Prefatory Essay," *The Franciscan Educational Conference,* xxii (Dec., 1940), p. 267. The italics are mine. Father Kobel's essay (pp. 259–356) is an excellent survey of the subject.

[17] *Thought,* XV, 269, 274. I join Mr. Hamm in recommending to the reader P. H. Frye's cogent treatment of the intellectual character of literary art, in his *Romance and Tragedy* (Boston, 1922). Cf. Yvor Winters, *The Anatomy of Nonsense* (New Directions, 1943), p. 125.

are simply imagistic. The late Dr. Temple, Archbishop of Canterbury, in a lecture on literature found "Hardy's great masterpiece, 'Tess of the D'Urbervilles' " to be "among the worst books ever committed to paper." He was unable to yield "to the undoubted artistic power that is displayed by Hardy in that great artistic achievement." Upon which a writer in the *Times Literary Supplement* observed:

> The relationship of truth and beauty makes it impossible to accept that . . . a "great masterpiece" can be numbered among the "worst books ever committed to paper." A masterpiece is not made by phrases, decorations and patterns; these qualities are imposed by the wisdom in their content.[18]

This, one might say, is a pronounced step in the Arnoldian direction. Yet the point of it cannot be overlooked. The problem has been made more acute in our day by schools of psychological criticism and of exhaustive rhetorical exegesis which have taught us to find the beauty of poems by sifting them to their minutest scruples of meaning. What Plato saw as the evil of poetry, the mixture of its emotions and the confusion of its advice, has become now, under such names as ironic "tension" and "synaesthesis," the richness of aesthetic value.

A hint at a solution was offered by Aristotle in his *Rhetoric* when he said that imitation is pleasant "even if the object imitated is not itself pleasant; for it is not the object itself which here gives delight—the spectator draws inferences ('That is a so-and-so') and thus learns something fresh." [19] And the notion has been reiterated in diverse places—for example, in Plutarch's essay *How a Young Man Should Study Poetry,*[20] in the *Summa Theologica* of St. Thomas ("Imago dicitur esse pulchra, si perfecte repraesentat rem, quamvis turpem"),[21] in a *Spectator* on Imagination by Joseph Addison ("The Description of a Dunghill is pleasing . . . if the Image be represented to our Minds by suitable Expressions").[22] Today the same notion is invoked to justify the historical study of literature: the scholar, says Pro-

---

"It would seem," says Mr. Adler, "that the excellence of a work of art is due only to a technical mastery of materials by the artist and is unaffected by the direction of his moral character toward good or evil" (*Art and Prudence,* p. 443). But on the next page: "In the case of the fine arts, the situation is complicated by . . . the fact that for most of the fine arts, poetry and music certainly, the object of imitation is human action, the moral life."

[18] *Times Literary Supplement,* Dec. 4, 1943, p. 583.

[19] *Rhetoric,* I, 11.

[20] In F. M. Padelford, *Essays on the Study and Use of Poetry* (New York, 1902), p. 59.

[21] [An image is said to be beautiful if it represents a thing perfectly, even though that thing be ugly—Eds.] *Summa Theologica,* I, 39, 8.

[22] *Spectator* No. 418.

fessor H. N. Fairchild, "can admire a fine statement of a detestable fallacy in the spirit of a surgeon who speaks of a 'beautiful tumour.' " [23] A refined version of the theory is thus described by Mr. Maritain:

> The artist takes for stuff and substance of his work whatever is most profound, most exalted and most vile, the moral life of man, the heart of man "hollow and full of filth"—and the rarest passions and the life of the spirit itself, nay, the Gospel and sanctity, everything; but with it all an absolute prohibition, upon pain of committing a sacrilege against art, against pursuing any other end than the pure delight, order, richness, tranquillity and rapture, which the soul ought to savour in the work. This is no longer art *on nothing* as in the theory of gratuitousness in its first form; but art *for nothing,* for nothing but art's sake.[24]

Mr. Maritain does not subscribe to this view, but in another place he himself has said: "art . . . comes into the midst of our hierarchies like a moon prince. . . . It can be mad and remain art." This is all very well. It should be obvious from what has been said so far that the argument of this essay tends rather in this direction than in the opposite. Yet such an explanation certainly runs the risk of leaving the poem in a posture of serious embarrassment. If poetry can say what is vile and full of filth (or if poetry can be mad), then it would seem to make no difference what poetry says.

§4

The main thesis of Plato's *Phaedrus* is that an ideal rhetoric or art of using words would by dialectic and a certain inspiration rise to the level of philosophy—that is, would deal with truth. Actual rhetoric, that of the sophists, what was known to Socrates, was not an art—had no contact with the truth—for it could be put to purposes of deception. This view of rhetoric and implicitly of poetry followed from the Socratic ethic, where virtue was wisdom. If to know was to do, then that which did wrong (rhetoric) did not know. The ethic of Aristotle was, on the other hand, a step away from the ethic of sheer wisdom, and accordingly Aristotle is able, both in his *Poetics* and in his *Rhetoric,* to say more than Plato in favor of verbal art as it was actually practiced. Rhetoric is a power which, like all other powers except virtue itself, can be misused. The misuse lies not in the art but in the moral purpose. Book III, chapters 1–13, of Aristotle's

---

[23] *The Romantic Quest* (New York, 1931), p. 427.
[24] *Art and Scholasticism,* trans. J. F. Scanlan (New York, 1942), p. 131. Cf. Adler, *Art and Prudence,* pp. 438–444; Oliver de Selincourt, *Art and Morality* (London, 1935), pp. 128, 131.

Rhetoric, on the devices of verbal style, is the natural complement of this basic view.

An idea of verbal rhetoric as distinct from the pith and worth of what is meant by words is thus from the start intrinsic to the theory of separable poetic and moral values which we have sketched so far and which we are struggling to improve. And something indeed may be said on the score of merely verbal rhetoric, and should be said here, though with the distinct reservation that such rhetoric must be far from enough to permit any important or profound distinction between poetic and moral values. It is possible to name certain formal levels of expression which, though intimately bound up with and deriving their value only from their relation to the stated meaning, are yet not parts of this meaning in the sense that they always add to it or in their absence subtract from it. Under this head come the various forms of syntactic and phonetic support of statement (the *parisosis* [parallelism] and *paromoiosis* [alliteration] of Aristotle), to some extent the intimations of what is called prose rhythm, and, for certain kinds of writing and within limits, even correctness of diction—much, in short, though not all, of what is commonly thought of as "style." This might include the kind of values one may see in the prose of Edgar Allan Poe, where, though the message is often meretricious and merely lurid, yet a kind of cogent swing or rhythm of logic is felt. It might include what critics have alluded to as more music than sense in many lines of a decadent poet like Swinburne or Dowson. But if the nonmoral value of poetry lay only here, it would be a trivial thing, worth the contempt of Socrates. "The style is excellent," says Pope, alluding to the judgment of a certain kind of critics; "The sense they humbly take upon content." [25]

It is at deeper levels of meaning that more important distinctions must be sought. And if we understand the depth, subtlety and indirectness of the total and many-dimensional meaning which modern criticism rightly discerns as the poetic object, we shall not despair of distinctions.

We may first of all make short work of a case often described with approval by the moralist, where evil is represented *as* evil—in the novels, for example, of Mr. François Mauriac (if so simple a statement does them justice, or if so simple a case ever really occurs). Here, of course, there is no moral evil, and no problem. The effects of the presentation may be unhappy for this or that reader (a moral, not an artistic, issue), but the meaning itself, the interpretation, is moral. Whatever literary quality is present, it has its moral basis. If the theory of gratuitousness means vileness of this sort,

---

[25] *Essay on Criticism,* ll. 307–308. It is consistent with the general easy distinction between art and prudence seen by Mr. Adler that he should divide criticism of a work of art into [1] "artistic *or* technical" and [2] "moral" (*Art and Prudence,* p. 444). It is I who have italicized the word *or.*

the theory is really no different from that of the moral critic. The moral judgment fits the matter or the situation. If the theory is to be different from a moral theory, vileness must be vileness represented as attractive, vileness with an apology, or vileness recommended. In short, the poem must be vile.

There are two main ways in which a poem may approach vileness—that is, in which it may be ethically defective: (1) by asserting an unacceptable philosophy; (2) by approving, commending, or inviting an immoral choice or passion. It is perhaps easier to see that the first way will rarely of itself be incompatible with some wisdom and with some or even a great deal of poetic value. One may agree with Mr. T. S. Eliot that poetry does not characteristically state philosophies. "In truth," says Mr. Eliot, "neither Shakespeare nor Dante did any real thinking—that was not their job." [26] Poetry does not think, but presents the feelings connected with thinking, or thoughts as the grounds of feeling. It is perhaps true that, as Professor Norman Foerster says, Wordsworth's *Tintern Abbey* expresses a degree of "unwisdom." [27] But then this unwisdom—the fusion of teleological naturalism, associationism, and pantheism which pervades the poem and without which indeed the poem would not be—is unwise simply in that it is not enough, it comes short of being an acceptable philosophy. Indeed we know this deficiency not so much through the poem itself as through our knowledge of its philosophic antecedents in Hartley or in Cudworth. As a philosophy it is better than no philosophy, or better, say, than dialectical materialism—because it contains much larger elements of truth. As an idea in a poem, a semimetaphoric notion of a spirit pervading a landscape, it need be no more of a philosophy than one chooses to make it. It is one way of being inspired by a landscape, one approach, we may easily say, toward God. Poems, on the whole, as dramatic and specific utterances, here and now, tend to escape the defect of philosophic incompleteness. The philosophy need only be adequate to the situation in hand—or reach beyond that by symbolic extension.

A harder case is the second of the two named above, that of a poem which embodies a clear approval of an evil choice and its evil emotion. An answer to the question how we are to find poetic value in such a poem may be suggested in the statement that on the assumption of a Socratic ethic we might have more difficulty in doing so. On the Christian grounds of an ethic of will, we may find the distinction easier. The fact indeed that it seems to us possible to distinguish this class, the simply immoral, from the other, the philosophically wrong, marks the great difference between an ethic where

---

[26] "Shakespeare and the Stoicism of Seneca," *Selected Essays 1917–1932* (New York, 1932), p. 116.

[27] *The Intent of the Critic,* ed. Donald Stauffer (Princeton, 1941), p. 76.

the virtuous man is he who resists temptation and that where the virtuous man is he who is never tempted. But once admit temptation, and much is open to us—a wide realm of motives which may be profoundly moving and sympathetic though falling short of the morally acceptable. We have a question of how much good can be the cause of sin. Here I would be strictly Thomistic and would accept Mr. Maritain and Mr. Adler for a certain distance as my guides. The human sinner, so we are instructed in the classic explanation, does not choose evil *qua* evil—a contradiction, since *bonum* is defined as *terminus appetitus* [end of appetite]. He chooses a lower good or one inappropriate to the moment—*quod non est vel nunc vel hoc modo bonum.*[28] But of lower and inappropriate goods there are many levels, lower and higher, and in the gamut of human goods which in some situations the virtuous man foregoes, there is room for an indefinite range of complexity, richness and sympathy.[29]

As a ground on which to explore this principle I choose the *Antony and Cleopatra* of Shakespeare. "The tragedy of *Antony and Cleopatra*," says Benedetto Croce, "is composed of the violent sense of pleasure, in its power to bind and to dominate, coupled with a shudder at its abject effects of dissolution and of death."[30] If this is so, then of course there is no problem. *Antony and Cleopatra* is simply one of the easy cases, already alluded to, in which evil is represented as evil: the implications are basically moral. Again, there is the explanation of the theologically minded critic S. L. Bethell: according to which *Antony and Cleopatra* celebrates "affections rooted deep in the sensual nature," intuitive, spontaneous, and positive, with all their "moral and aesthetic corollaries." The antitype is Caesar, the cold politician whose heart is set entirely on the passing world. In the tragic denouement the "element of self-giving inherent in the sensual nature" is "purged of selfish fear" and "revealed in its eternal significance."[31] It is not my purpose to deny the availability of such views to the interpretation

---

[28] [which is not good either now or in this particular way—Eds.]. *Contra Gentiles,* III, cap. 10. See Mr. Maritain's *Saint Thomas and the Problem of Evil* (Milwaukee, 1942), p. 41. See *Summa Theologica,* II–II, 47, 13, and Adler, *Art and Prudence,* p. 438; I–II, 18, 1, and Étienne Gilson, *Moral Values and the Moral Life,* trans. Leo Ward (St. Louis, 1931), p. 81; *De Malo,* I, 3, c, and Leo Ward, *Values and Reality* (New York, 1935), p. 71.

[29] "Dans toute forme ou toute espèce d'art il y a comme un principe ou un germe secret d'immoralité" [in all forms or all kinds of art there is some sort of secret principle or germ of immorality—Eds.]. (Ferdinand Brunetière, *L'Art et la Morale* [Paris, 1898], p. 15.)

[30] *Shakespeare, Ariosto, and Corneille* (London, 1920), p. 241. Antony and Cleopatra, says Dryden, were "famous patterns of unlawful love; and their end accordingly was unfortunate" (*Preface to All for Love, Essays of John Dryden,* ed. W. P. Ker [Oxford, 1926], i, 191).

[31] S. L. Bethell, *Shakespeare and the Popular Dramatic Tradition* (Westminster, 1944), pp. 128–131.

of *Antony and Cleopatra* or in general of other poems which present similar moral problems. The solution of Mr. Bethell may, in fact, appear to differ only by a twist of emphasis from what I myself propose. The difference is that I seek a formulation which will enable us to say frankly that a poem is a great poem, yet immoral.

What is celebrated in *Antony and Cleopatra* is the passionate surrender of an illicit love, the victory of this love over practical, political and moral concerns, and the final superiority of the suicide lovers over circumstance. That is a crudely one-sided statement which makes the play as plainly immoral as it can be made. There is of course far more—the complex, wanton and subtle wiles of the voluptuary queen, her infinite variety which age cannot wither nor custom stale, the grizzled and generous manhood and the military bravery of Antony—the whole opulent and burnished panorama of empire and its corruptions. Such intricacies and depths surely at least add to the interest of immorality and—without making it any more moral—yet make it more understandable, more than a mere barren vileness, a filthy negation. It is to be noted that the reasons on the side of morality are so far as possible undercut, diminished or removed from the play. The politics from which Antony secedes are not a noble Roman republicanism, the ideals of a Brutus or a Cato, but the treacheries and back-stabbing of a drunken party on a pirate's barge. The victimized Octavia is a pallid and remote figure, never (as in Dryden's version) made to appear as a rival motive to the Egyptian seductions.[32] The suicides which provide the catastrophe have at least the subjective palliation that they are within the Stoic code which is the standard of the whole scene.[33]

> Give me my robe, put on my crown; I have
> Immortal longings in me; now no more
> The juice of Egypt's grape shall moist this lip.
> Yare, yare, good Iras; quick. Methinks I hear
> Antony call; I see him rouse himself
> To praise my noble act; I hear him mock
> The luck of Caesar, which the gods give men
> To excuse their after wrath: husband, I come:
> Now to that name my courage prove my title!
> I am fire and air; my other elements
> I give to baser life.

---

[32] "Though I might use the privilege of a poet, to introduce her into Alexandria, yet I had not enough considered, that the compassion she moved to herself and children was destructive to that which I reserved for Antony and Cleopatra" (Dryden, *Preface to All for Love,* Essays, i, 192).

[33] "Shakespeare nowhere approves suicide outside the Roman plays, but in them he seems to accept it, along with the pantheon, as data" (S. L. Bethell, *op. cit.* p. 129).

There is no escaping the fact that the poetic splendor of this play, and in particular of its concluding scenes, is something which exists in closest juncture with the acts of suicide and with the whole glorified story of passion. The poetic values are strictly dependent—if not upon the immorality as such—yet upon the immoral acts. Even though, or rather because, the play pleads for certain evil choices, it presents these choices in all their mature interest and capacity to arouse human sympathy. The motives are wrong, but they are not base, silly, or degenerate. They are not lacking in the positive being of deep and complex human desire. It is not possible to despise Antony and Cleopatra. If one will employ the classic concept of "imitation," the play imitates or presents the reasons for sin, a mature and richly human state of sin. Imitation, on this understanding, is not prior to and exclusive of interpretation, but follows it. The interpretation and judgment are taken as presented objects. This is the meaning of defense repeated in every generation by the poet. "I moot," says Chaucer, "reherce Hir tales alle. . . . Or elles falsen som of my mateere." [34] "Art," says William Butler Yeats, "is a revelation, and not a criticism." [35]

§ 5

Poetic value, though different from moral value, cannot thereby be considered as something antonomously remote from the rest of human experience. In the total of any concrete human situation—even that of the anchorite in his cell—there are multiple values inviting recognition or choice. The moral value in any given situation, what is right, is abstract; it is known by rule and conscience. By necessity it excludes. Neither a right nor a wrong choice, however, excludes the awareness of many values, some interrelated and supporting, some rival, some sacrificed by a choice, some in some situations held in ironic balance or entering into unresolved tensions. Poetry, by its concreteness and dramatic presentation of value situations, whether it inclines to a right answer or to a wrong answer—by the very fullness and hence imaginative power of its presentation—has the meaning and being which makes it poetry. This is the poetic value. It is a rhetorical value only inasmuch as the nuances of rhetoric, the symbolic complexities of a rhetorical unity, are the counterparts of the psychological complexities which make the meaning of a poem. Rhetoric, except in the most superficial sense, does not exist unless in a meaning of a certain stature.

It would seem to follow from what has just been said that there could be virtuous choices and right philosophy—or at least verbal descriptions of

---

[34] *The Miller's Prologue* [I must repeat all their tales. . . . Or else misrepresent some of my material—Eds.].

[35] *Essays* (New York, 1924), p. 243.

these—which would be too simple, severe and abstracted from living reality to have poetic interest. Certainly there can be verbal presentations of evil which are too simply negative or too naively mistaken to have this interest. With the immoral splendors of Cleopatra's suicide farewell, compare, for example:

FOR MY DAUGHTER

Looking into my daughter's eyes I read
    Beneath the innocence of morning flesh
Concealed, hintings of death she does not heed.
    Coldest of winds have blown this hair, and mesh
Of seaweed snarled these miniatures of hands;
    The night's slow poison, tolerant and bland,
Has moved her blood. Parched years that I have seen
    That may be hers appear: foul, lingering
Death in certain war, the slim legs green.
    Or, fed on hate, she relishes the sting
Of others' agony; perhaps the cruel
    Bride of a syphilitic or a fool.
These speculations sour in the sun.
I have no daughter. I desire none.[36]

What is wrong with this poem is that it is simply not enough. The poem does not do justice to the occasions and concrete character of bad feelings. This kind of vileness, one may suppose, was not what Mr. Maritain meant. One would be hard put to explain the "pure delight, order, riches, tranquillity and rapture, which the soul ought to savour" in this kind of evil.

The areas which are to be defined by such a conception of poetic badness will be at higher levels of course much disputed. It is with no thought of expressing an opinion about the poetry of Shelley that I cite here another of Mr. Eliot's delicate adjustments to the balance between poetry and doctrine. In his essay on Shakespeare and Seneca he believed it was not the job of the poet to think. Yet in his Harvard lectures on *The Use of Poetry and the Use of Criticism* he finds himself, for something like a philosophic reason, unable to accept the poetry of Shelley. For there are some beliefs which are acceptable (in these obviously a poetry can be grounded), others again which if not acceptable yet correspond so well to some large area of human experience that we may call them "tenable" (perhaps the Senecan stoicism and Lucretian atomism which he mentioned in his essay on Shakespeare)—but again others which are neither acceptable nor tenable. The poetry of Shelley, one would gather, is inextricably wound up in beliefs of the third class.

---

[36] From *The Fall of the Magicians,* by Weldon Kees, copyright, 1947, by Weldon Kees. Reprinted by permission of Harcourt, Brace and Company, Inc.

One of the faults which Plato found with poetry was [37] that in imitating the actions and feelings of men, poetry discovered the lack of unity in their lives, the strife and inconsistency. Recent schools of criticism, as we have said, have likewise noted the importance to poetry of the elements of variety and strife in human living and have seen the poem as a report made under tension or an ironically suspended judgment rather than a commitment to solutions. And this view would seem to put the poem clearly in the realm of the amoral or premoral. But again, recent criticism has noted with approval the Coleridgean doctrine of a resolution or *reconciliation* of opposites, a doctrine which may not read so well with the ironic. As Mr. J. C. Ransom has observed, elements are not reconciled merely by being got into the same poem. To the present writer it would seem that though poetry is inclusive, it is also exclusive in the sense that a poem has a presiding idea, attitude and coherence and thus at least a tendency to an assertion. As certain critics of a theological leaning have recently been saying, poetry, though it is not dogma and cannot take the place of dogma, yet finds in a frame of beliefs its "ultimate character" and "latent presuppositions." [38] If it is possible, as it has been the main burden of this essay to insist, that a poem, even a great poem, may fall short of being moral—or to put it another way, if it is true that starting with the fixity of dogma we cannot hope to define the content of poems—it is yet true that poems as empirically discovered and tested do tend, within their limits and given the peculiar *données* or presuppositions of each, to point toward the higher integration of dogma. The Christian critic, if he cares to insist to the full at all moments on his Christianity as well as on his critical discernment, may without doing violence to the latter, follow the direction recently pointed out to the poet: "Christian dogma will aid the artist not by giving him a privileged and special subject-matter but rather by defining for him a perspective from which 'full light' can be had on all subject matters." [39] Perhaps it follows that in this light the greatest poems for the Christian will never be that kind, the great though immoral, which it has been our labor to describe. *Antony and Cleopatra* will not be so great as *King Lear*. The testimony of the critical tradition would seem to confirm this. The greatest poetry will be morally right, even though perhaps obscurely so, in groping confusions of will and knowledge— as *Oedipus the King* foreshadows *Lear*. All this is but the consistent capstone which completes but does not contradict the system of values in which poetic is distinguished from moral and both are understood in relation to the master ideas of evil as negation or not-being, a gap in order, and of good

---

[37] *Republic*, x, 603.

[38] Roy W. Battenhouse, "Theology and Literary Criticism," *The Journal of Bible and Religion*, xiii (Feb., 1945), 21.

[39] Roy W. Battenhouse, *loc. cit.*, p. 20.

as positive, or being—in the natural order the designed complexity of what is most truly one or most has being.[40]

SIDNEY ZINK

The Moral Effect of Art [1]

This essay presupposes that art is a peculiar form of experience but not the sole or necessarily the highest form. The question it considers is what, within such presuppositions, is the relation of art to morality and the good life. I shall not discuss the peculiar value of art, or the total scheme of values: the first is the general subject of aesthetics, the second, of ethics. But presupposing certain things about art and about the good, I shall discuss possible relations between them.

An initial distinction ought to be made between the questions of art and the good, and of art and the moral. The problems of what is "good" and what is "moral" are distinct: the first consists in the description, definition, and gradation of all significant values; the second in the description of the attitude of the human valuer toward values. Utilitarian ethicists have been preoccupied with the first problem, whereas Kantian and idealistic philosophers have been preoccupied with the second. Both groups have used the term "good" for their two objects of concern and have mutually minimized the objects of the other's concern. For the utilitarian, what is "good" are the things that are possessed with satisfaction in experience; for the idealist, what is alone "good" is the attitude of the experiencer toward the content of experience. Thus the advocates of "pleasure" as against the advocates of the "good will." I mention the dispute only to clarify the above distinction, not to enter the debate. Adhering to the above definitions, I shall consider art chiefly, not in reference to the scheme of values, not as a kind of good among other goods, but in reference to the proper attitude of the human being toward values.

There is a possible objection: Isn't the proper or moral attitude simply

---

[40] "Without unity nothing could exist. To be is no other than to be one; the more unity a thing has, so much the more being does it possess" (St. Augustine, *De Moribus Manichaeorum*, II, vi, 8). "Unless a thing be one it cannot be: abstract its principle of unity and it is no longer the thing we say it is" (Plotinus, *Enneads*, VI, ix, 1).

[1] From *Ethics*, LX (1950), 261–274. Reprinted with permission of The University of Chicago Press and the author. (Eds.)

a theoretical and practical adherence to the correct scheme of values; and, if so, isn't the relation of art to this scheme identical with its relation to the moral attitude? I think not (this will become clearer in the sequel): for a man can both know and do what is good without having a moral experience or assuming a moral attitude. The moral attitude is possible only in a moral experience, and the moral experience is possible only in a moral conflict— that is, in a conflict of values such that the human agent is forced into a questioning of his knowledge about, and behavior in pursuit of, the good. The moral attitude is that of conscientious pursuit of the right solution to a moral conflict.

There is an essential conflict between the demands of morality and of art. Morality insists upon the interconnectedness of experiences; art insists upon the self-containedness of each particular experience. The moral man scrutinizes the given action for its relations to other actions; the aesthetic man absorbs himself in the immediate experience. Morality insists upon the inviolability of the man, art upon the inviolability of the experience. Morality recognizes the fact of dimensionality in life; art stresses the fact of qualitativeness. The first would make life consistent; the second would make it intense. Morality speaks in the interest of the whole, art in the interest of the part. Without conscience, a man would not be a man but only a series of unrelated experiences. Without art, or the character of art, life might be a pattern of parts perfectly consistent in relation to each other and perfectly insignificant within themselves.

It follows that life ought to find place for both morals and art: a man ought to be a unity and he ought also to contain something within this unity. Everyone who considers the question seems to presuppose this much, and so to take as the particular task the arbitration of these contrary demands. The solutions all seem to fall within some kind of compromise. It is true that philosophers usually assert the ultimate authoritativeness of morals, whereas the artists plead the all-sufficiency of art. The philosopher (like Plato) may place art under the direction of a social agency or limit art in the kind of effects possible to it (involving at the same time a limitation of the kinds of subject matter available for its use); while the artist (like Sidney) may argue that it is the essential nature of art to achieve in its own proper working every kind of effect—intellectual, volitional, emotional— which the moralist regards as desirable. Yet these extreme proponents of the contrary claims mutually recognize that they must somehow account for the demands of the other.

There are several possible conceptions of the relationship of morals and art which might serve as the basis for the solution of the problem of the reconciliation of their contrary claims. One view would make a reconciliation needless; another would make it impossible; while yet another would make it possible. The first is the view that art and the best life are identical; the second, that they are essentially opposed; the third, that they are causally but contingently related.

But before considering these three positions, there is another approach which ought to be mentioned. It discovers a likeness between art and the good life, and may be thought to provide thereby a reconciliation. The view is particularly prevalent in contemporary philosophy, but it seems to be based upon a figure of speech and to give little real insight into the relation of morality and art. It conceives the artwork as a kind of image or symbol of the good life.

An essential trait of the artwork is "harmony," and "harmony" is frequently taken as also describing the character of the good life. In the artwork many different qualities are united into a single harmonious whole; and, on one ethical view, the total span of the good life will combine into an orderly whole its several eras and interests.

This is an amiable view of the good—the view that the good is happiness. It is sunny and naturalistic. Life is an opportunity for accumulating a solid and sound stock of values. The principle of conduct is to maximize and harmonize: first maximize, but only so long as one can, at the same time, harmonize. Get as much as possible, but don't try for too much, else there will arise discord and consequent cancellation of part of what has been already accumulated. Harmony is required as a necessary support and safeguard of maximization.

The same principle applies in art (Croce has taught it). Of two artworks that are genuinely such, the better one is the one that has the most in it. The standard is strictly quantitative. But the material may be only so abundant as is comprehensible into unity. The work must, to be art, be an individual whole; and as this is the nature which no artwork can fail to possess, it is a nature which cannot distinguish one work of art from another. The further principle which enables such distinction is a principle of perfect generality in the field of value, applicable here as everywhere. It is, simply: The more of an identical good thing, the better. Thus harmony states the restrictive condition: Add nothing which cannot be genuinely added; introduce neither enemies of the existing members nor aliens which can only remain by setting up in the same physical area a distinct social unit.

This is the rule, likewise, in utilitarian ethics. The better life is that which is the more extensive in the several dimensions: the life which is broader, intenser, longer, provided always that the individual remain a single individual, the variety being brought into a single whole.

One need not challenge this view of the good as harmony to see that the relation which it would establish between the moral and the aesthetic is only external and symbolic. If the good is harmony, then any work of art is a charming image of the good. But it may be an image and nothing more: art may portray one character (even an essential one) of the good, without significantly influencing either our understanding or pursuit of it. Analogies are often most impressive when the total objects analogized are most diverse. It seems so in the case of art and the good life. Art is a single object of experience; life is a multitude of experiences. Harmony on the small scale will not insure harmony on the large, nor conversely: one would not suppose that an uninterrupted series of aesthetic experiences would constitute a harmonious life, or that a harmonious life must be composed of uniformly harmonious experiences. Indeed, those who live most exclusively the life of art are supposed to live in ways which the ethicist would judge highly intemperate and inharmonious. Artists are notoriously likely to deviate from the customary, the moderate, and the right. (Or is this chiefly true not of dramatic but of plastic or musical artists? Or is it true, in the dramatic arts, chiefly of the lyric poets, who are nearest to these other nonliterary arts?) And, on the other hand, most ethicists are inclined to require a certain amount of discord in a moral life—enough to arouse the moral perplexity and exercise the will. Thus, harmonious experiences of art are not enough for a good life; nor does the total harmony of a good life altogether exclude experiences that are internally discordant. Since no genuine relations between art and the moral are disclosed by an examination of the trait of harmony which they share, we must regard this relation as only metaphorical.

We encounter, however, literal assertions that art and the good converge, not merely in a single trait, but in essence and in entirety—the assertion, indeed, that the two are actually one. This view can be presented in contrary ways (and mean rather different things), according as the standard of this life is taken narrowly or broadly. Walter Pater and John Dewey have both proposed the ideal of making the experience of life a kind of experience of art, but Pater has taken "art" more narrowly than Dewey. Pater conceived art to be chiefly what goes by that name, and wished to give the quality of a painting or poem to ordinary experiences. Dewey interprets art in a more democratic and American fashion, and argues that any satisfactory experience of life is a kind of work of art. The difference of emphasis appears in the two sets of terms central to their different doctrines. Both regard art as a fusion of contrary things which in a less civilized life are separate; but for Pater these terms are "form" and "matter," which are more proper to art, whereas for Dewey they are most essentially "means" and "end," which refer more to the processes of practical life.

Both versions are, I think, very interesting and illuminating in their particular emphases, but also very extravagant. Dewey's warm nature would embrace everything in a brotherly union, without bothering too much as to whether the parties were compatible. In his amiable zeal he exaggerates the similarities of the phases of experience, and underrates their individualities. Pater, on the other hand, is so impressed with the refined delights of the aesthetic contemplation of individuals that to him nothing else seems greatly to matter. But looking at the phenomena prosaically we surely discover that life imposes moral demands which cannot be avoided (however unpleasant a distraction they might be for a Paterian sensibility) or transformed into an aesthetic fusion of "means and ends" (however democratically and optimistically Dewey might seek to point out such opportunities).

As Pater and Dewey regarded the good and best life as aesthetic in its very nature, Plato, on the contrary, regarded the two as naturally opposed. For Plato, the highest good is intellectual contemplation; and art he considered a distortion of the truth. Art is at a third remove from the truth; the artist copies physical objects, which are themselves but imitations of the real essences, and, moreover, he copies them imperfectly. For not only does his artistic medium limit him to the presentation of only a partial aspect of the total object of imitation, but his own fallibility and popular taste prompt him to the imitation of those aspects which are less worthy and which appeal to the passionate rather than the rational part of the soul. This second deficiency of popular art Plato believed capable of correction by political supervision of art production. And a suitably censored art he did admit into the state as an instrument of education. But though art may thus serve as a means to moral conduct, it offers only imperfect and limited guidance and must be a useless hindrance to the person who has reached moral maturity. The mature man will put aside these enchanting mirrors of the truth in order to behold the truth directly, and the truth will provide both direction in practical conduct and the object of his highest experience. Thus, while Plato, like Pater and Dewey, places his faith in a single kind of experience, within which he finds chiefly differences of degree or of purity, unlike these modern writers he submits the regular categories of experience to a severe judgment in terms of his standard, and emerges, not (like Dewey) with a formula for equating the several kinds of experience, but with a sharp differentiation of ranks and values. The highest good is the contemplation of the truth; those who are capable of it are few and their moments of full achievement are rare. It has its roots in ordinary experience, even in such experiences as those of art; but in its culmination it rises into another realm, and there its very intensity can be measured by the degree to which it becomes oblivious of its earthly origins. Dewey would have all experience so treated as to acquire a common character, and such experience would be "aesthetic" in the full sense of this word. Plato accepts the rarity and fugitiveness of the highest experience and sadly recognizes the vast inferiority of all else.

It is hard not to sympathize with the contrary ideals which motivate the contrary exaggerations of Dewey and Plato—with Dewey's democratic exaggeration in the interest of the quantity of good in experience, and Plato's aristocratic exaggeration in the interest of purifying the quality of the good in experience. But to adopt either is to impoverish art: art's peculiarity as a form of experience disappears in Dewey's ethical monism, and art's high worth is repudiated by Plato's ethical transcendentalism.

But these several views of art and morality—that they are essentially identical or essentially opposed or related only symbolically—though they have been influential, seem to have been less widely held than the less extreme position, that art and morality are related causally, and that art tends to instil virtue. The last thesis is usually accompanied by certain qualifications concerning the conditions under which this effect can be expected; but these conditions usually consist in the definition of the true subject-matter and scope of art, so that the best art is just that kind which is most morally beneficial. Such is the point in common among views as diverse as those of Aristotle, Sidney, Shelley, and I. A. Richards. These writers differ from Plato, Dewey, and Tolstoi, in that they recognize the right of art to produce an effect peculiarly its own, different from the effect of knowledge or virtue or piety. But while recognizing the peculiarity and autonomy of the aesthetic experience, they believe that this experience tends to have as a concomitant result the generation of virtue.

The variations among these writers may be viewed as differences as to the kind of artistic subject-matter which is productive of virtue and as to the parts of human nature on which art acts to produce this effect. I think all believe that art acts on the sensibility; but some stress feeling, whereas others stress imagination; and, further, some think that art also increases moral knowledge, whereas others neglect this. Aristotle (and I. A. Richards and DeWitt Parker) describes the aesthetic experience as emotional and finds this emotional experience of positive value to morality. Shelley describes the aesthetic experience as essentially imaginative and claims that by stimulating the imagination it engenders sympathy and extends the appreciator's capacity for moral discrimination. Philip Sidney argues that art provides both instruction as to the nature of the good and emotional incitement to do the good.

Two other kinds of differences in these positions are significant. Sidney and Shelley say that art provides positive guidance in morality, whereas Richards and Parker (and apparently Aristotle, though his position here is debatable) say that art helps morality in the negative fashion of removing tendencies to immorality, purging the organism of those impulses which, if neither suppressed nor sublimated, can lead to excess. A more significant difference for the definition of art concerns the role of the subject-matter of art in the achievement of the moral effect. Sidney held that poetry instructs men in virtue by presenting ethical rules and ethical examples, so that the moral viewpoint of the artist presumably should be definite and conventional. Shelley admits this function of art but stresses its operation in other ways and derives its moral effect more immediately from its aesthetic one. For Shelley, art works not chiefly by telling the reader what is good so much as by exercising his imagination and so making him more capable of sympathy, imagination being "the great instrument of moral good."

Of these several views I think Shelley's is the most positive, most tolerant, and most generally satisfactory. He allows more than the others both to morality and to art. He confines art less to the representation of a particular subject-matter and morality less to the adherence to a set of formal prescriptions. Most critics in their treatment of the subject seem to have assumed a static and conventional morality. This is shown in two features of their essays. One is their centering on the nature of art rather than on the nature of the morally good; the other is their assumption that the moral business of literature is to provide moral answers (rather than moral questions) and answers practically efficacious.

Most critics seem agreed not to ask what the good is. This suggests that, whatever the good may be, the critics will not disagree about it. And that may be because the nature of this thing is either unquestionably clear or impossibly vague. It cannot be that critics are lazy, or feel a philosophical incompetence. And if the nature of the good were impossibly vague, one could not profitably inquire into the efficacy of literature in promoting it. So the subject must be very clear.

It is doubtless clear in one sense, in that we can agree upon which general terms describe the good and, in important instances, even upon the kind of conduct to which these terms refer. For example, we can agree that it is good to be rational, and that to be rational is not, for instance, to indulge in food or drink to excess. Perhaps, as another example, we can agree that it is good to be charitable, and that to be charitable means to forgive the offenses of our neighbors. And agreeing on the goodness either of rationality or charity, we can yet disagree on the capacity of art to promote them. Plato and Aristotle were alike convinced that the good is the rational; but one thought that art usually conduced to it, whereas the other thought art conduced to its opposite. Likewise, Sidney and Shelley were agreed on the goodness of charity, and they agreed further upon the capacity of art to promote it; they differed on the way they conceived art to have this effect.

I think that—as a corollary of their agreement about the good—most of those who have asserted the moral value of literature have conceived it as providing not moral questions so much as moral answers. The critics who regard literature as giving moral knowledge seem to have conceived this knowledge very simply, either as a general precept or a particular example of such a precept or both. The end toward which they look is concrete action, and the problem is seen as the instigation of the proper courses of behavior rather than of the proper courses of thought. Sidney recommends poetry on the ground that it will furnish both the general precept which is peculiar to philosophy and the particular example which is peculiar to history, but, above all, that, as a result of this, it will move the appreciator to good conduct. Thus, when literature is viewed as a source of moral knowledge, the whole effectiveness of this knowledge is judged by its eventuation in practice, and the kind of knowledge which literature is thought properly to provide is that which will most readily "move" to conduct.

These assumptions seem to me to misconstrue the nature both of the moral, and of the aesthetic in so far as it is conceived as contributing to the moral. And art, though it may implant definite ethical precepts and cultivate definite practical habits, may also do the reverse. Thus we must ask: Is it in the nature of art to cause either the moral or its opposite, and, if it can achieve such precepts and habits as the above, is this result an essentially moral one?

One might wonder, on the basis of the above assumptions, whether, indeed, any moral contribution of art would not be superfluous. For if the nature of moral good is so clear that critics can agree about it, it must be sufficiently clear and unarguable to the less strenuous minds of ordinary mortals. Indeed, it is likely that the latter will have got their moral conceptions from just such nonartistic sources as the critics. Still, I suppose no one would question that this moral knowledge, though so generally available, is always capable of advantageous enforcement and development. One may possess a sound set of ethical precepts, yet feel uncertain of their theoretical foundation, or their particular application. Or his ethical knowledge may be complete, while he is insufficiently impressed with this knowledge. Art may serve to impress him further. It is not difficult to find novels and plays that seem to intend and do manifestly accomplish with particular readers, one or more of these purposes. One who reads *The Brothers Karamazov* may gain a new understanding of the Christian doctrine of love and pride; if he reads *The Grapes of Wrath,* he may be directed to apply the precept of neighborliness to a particular group of people; from *Madame Bovary* he may derive a new impression of the vicious consequences of romanticism. All these effects may occur; but they will depend upon the particular reader and the particular circumstances—the opposite effects may occur. A reader of *The Brothers Karamazov* may conclude that (the author's views to the contrary) the hero and the ethical truth which the book reveal are Ivan Karamazov and the philosophy of socialism; or he may read *The Grapes of Wrath* and only feel more strongly the necessity of totalitarian methods in handling such social problems; or he may find such a sympathy with the impulses of *Madame Bovary* that what impresses him is the attractiveness of her values and not the sordidness of her fate.

I think the same observation can be made of other views as to how art works its moral effect. Art may serve to remove excess emotion and quell riotous desires, or it may arouse emotion and inflame desire. And there are records of both criminal and humanitarian actions which have—according to the "appreciators' " confessions—resulted from the appreciation of a work of art.

This puts the matter on the basis of fact; and if it were to be settled in this way we should need a corps of sociologists to conduct a survey and determine whether the vicious or the virtuous results predominate. The philosopher, however, can reject this method on the ground that the statistician cannot determine whether the contact with art (which is followed by virtue or vice) is an aesthetic contact. I am here on the side of the philosophers and, in particular, on the side of those, such as Croce, who hold that any emotional effect is unessential to art. Croce also holds that *any* extension or application of the artwork is alien to the pure experiencing of it, so that art is inherently as incapable of aiding morality by intellectual as by emotional stimulation. I do not quite agree with Croce in this, for I think that dramatic literary art naturally encourages an intellectual activity which is essential to morality. Thus I must try to show that dramatic literature is not entirely free of effects outside the aesthetic experience, that these effects are intellectual, and that the moral experience is intellectual essentially and not merely instrumentally and contingently.

Croce holds that art is nonscientific, noninstructive in any sense, and, though he does not (to my knowledge) condemn the use of art for other purposes, one gathers from him that such a use does some violence to art. But I think that we can react to a work of art as art, and also give it other uses in other parts of experience. In its own nature any work of art is a self-contained individual, and to experience it in its proper nature is to experience it as an integral, self-subsistent whole. But this self-contained experience is itself a member of a varied field of experience, and the recognition of the autonomy of art as art should not obscure the relations of art to other things. Let us insist first, as Croce does, that although art incorporates into itself materials from the rest of life, it incorporates them completely, in such a way that these materials acquire a new nature and meaning, independent of their actual sources and potential references. But we should recognize, second, that this independence which the aesthetic experience insistently asserts is as insistently repudiated by the larger body of experience to which it belongs. In short, life will not allow art to exist merely as art. Men try to organize their lives, and to see the bearing of their experiences and kinds of experience on one another. The experience of art occurs in a field of experience; and, although it may try to plant its flag on a particular corner of that field, to assert its absolute autonomy and prohibit intercourse with the others, it cannot prevent its neighbors from clustering about its borders, and, if not making military invasions, at least paying visits as interested tourists. A man may be intensely interested in art, and care for nothing but the particular and isolated apprehensions of individuality which each work of art provides. But most persons who are seriously interested in art will also be seriously interested in the other spheres of life, and the force of interest in these separately will also be a force of interest in their relations. A man interested in painting and in history would be a strangely segmented creature who was not also interested in the history of painting and the influence of painting in history. And one interested in psychology and in the novel will find much to explore in their mutual relations.

All of this is not to deny the existence of a peculiarly aesthetic experience which makes no connections with the rest of experience. It is rather to assert its existence, as the primary phenomenon, and then to give heed to a different and equally palpable reality, the continuous and more or less consciously coherent stretch of experience in which the experience occurs. There is in the human being some tendency to make his life a unity, and this involves not merely the avoidance of conflicts but the establishment of common bonds. This does not mean the mixing of experiences. But different experiences can keep to their separate houses without ceasing to be friendly, and they need not go in for communism to permit their children to intermarry. We ought first to read a psychology as science and a novel as art. But it is no disrespect to either to compare them afterward. It is in the interest of a coherent life to do so, and it is to contribute, moreover, to the enrichment of their separate experiences. For however self-contained a thing may be in its own right, its materials are the materials of a common world; its appreciation in its peculiarity therefore depends upon the widest appreciation of these materials of which it is composed. A man who has looked with attention at visual materials in life will be better able to appreciate the particular transformation which such materials undergo to constitute a new individuality in art; and the man who has observed his fellowmen attentively will be better able to appreciate the peculiar unity of action in a drama. And as an extra-aesthetic experience serves to enrich aesthetic experience, so aesthetic experience may help the student of art to a keener understanding of life. This can be seen in some obvious examples.

Art is capable of theoretic enlightenment in that it presents general elements in new relations (and the most complex knowledge can do nothing else). In the tragedy of *Hamlet,* for example, we may gain new insight into the relation of sensibility and intelligence to what may be called a skepticism of practice; in *Othello* we see into the relation of the active and practical virtues to intellectual and moral unsoundness. The general principle is well illustrated by these two instances because of their contrariety: they show us, at the same time, how literary works may promote understanding, not merely by themselves, but in comparison. Othello and Hamlet exhibit opposite sets of virtues and opposite moral inadequacies; Othello's virtues are active, and, accordingly, he acts on insufficient evidence; Hamlet's virtues are reflective, and, to make him act, no amount of evidence is sufficient. The sort of understanding which we gain from these plays does not enable us to formulate general principles connecting, by a necessary rule, a kind of temperament with a kind of behavior; but that is precisely because no kinds of materials—actual or fictive— enable us to formulate such principles. Still we do gain some kind of understanding from our observation of uniformities and connections in the actions of particular persons, and we learn also from our observation of characters in fiction. What we obtain are not rules but hypothetical formulas, asserting that when one trait or action is present, another is likely to be present. This is not an understanding of what actions are good and bad but of the connections of actions subject to judgments of good and bad. It may be that an understanding of the relation of temperaments and actions is the nearest we can get to a knowledge of the good; but if it be only preliminary or complementary to this knowledge, it is nonetheless necessary and important.

In fact, I think the moral life is theoretic essentially. Theory perhaps should eventuate in practice, but practice can be morally good only when it is preceded by reflection. Action undetermined by reflection may be "good" in a utilitarian sense (bringing pleasant consequences to one's self or to others); but it will be without moral quality, for it will have been without moral effort. Good things may be produced by any kind of action whatever— whether it be one of unthinking habit or of pure accident; even an intentionally evil action may have good consequences. But what makes an action morally good is the exertion of moral effort—that is, the effort deliberately to ascertain and do what is good. Goodness is entirely proportionate to the effort. The good man is the man who tries to be good; and no man is wholly good who is not trying to be better. In this effort reflection is needed as an instrument of consistency and caution in behavior, and also of clarity and assurance in understanding. Because no action is morally good which is not done because it is morally good, there is no moral action which does not arise out of deliberate reflection. Pascal said: "Let us endeavor to think well: this is the principle of morality." It is much easier to do what seems to be good than to seek to know what is certainly and really good. But a man cannot be truly good until he has called into doubt what customarily goes by that name; and he owes it to his rational nature to persist in his inquiry as long—even if it be a lifetime—as it requires to answer it. (I do not say that certainty in this field is possible: let him then cease thinking when by thinking he has seen the rational necessity of skepticism or faith.) There are perhaps few genuinely moral agents: most of us are social animals, agreeably doing what society requires without asking whether society requires what is right.

This makes clear the moral deficiency of such results as other writers have ascribed to literature in praise of its moral efficacy. The results achievable by the books above mentioned—the theoretical acceptance of a moral precept of Christian love; the practical recognition of the need for a particular form of social action; or an emotional impulsion to reject a certain form of experience—these would be moral in an only superficial sense. For morality is not chiefly an affair of the affirmation of a belief, or the performance of a particular act, or movement by an emotional tendency; rather is it a conscientiousness of mind and will in the scrutiny and actualization of values. Neither belief nor action nor feeling possesses moral value until it is rationally developed and deliberately intended. What chiefly needs moral direction is not the course of behavior so much as the course of thought; and for this, moral questions are more useful than moral answers. To show that art can contribute not merely to the good life of action but to the best life of moral reflection, we should show that art encourages rather than curtails the activity of thinking.

This indicates the need for qualifying the views of Shelley and Sidney. Agreeing that art strengthens imagination, that imagination fosters sympathy, and that sympathy widens our appreciation of values, we have to add that this immediate appreciation must, to become moral, be subjected to a critical reflection and issue in an intellectual clarity. And Sidney's view, which would ostensibly make such a clarity an office of art, would in fact give a poor substitute. The highly generalized emotional proclivities toward charity, bravery, etc., or the conventional intellectual formulas about these virtues (which Sidney represented art as furnishing) are indeed positively dangerous to reflection, whereas sensibility may be a step toward it. Shelley's expanded sympathy may promote heterogeneity and confusion of purpose, but that would be better, on the whole, than the narrowness and rigidity, and the supplanting of reflection, which are latent in Sidney's methods.

Croce has criticized such views as failing to treat art as art, but they are equally liable to the charge of failing to treat the moral agent as moral. The only significant morality is conscious: a person who needs moral instruction from others is still incapable of strictly moral action. His improvement should be self-improvement and if art is a means to this, it is one that he should deliberately use as such.

This disqualifies political or pedagogical applications of art. The statesman can indeed use art to strengthen nationalism, and the teacher can use art to foster good habits, such as fairness, caution, fortitude. But such virtues are rudimentary, proper to children and childish adults, who, being unable to choose rationally and for themselves, may be provided with art to direct their choice for them. If art is to contribute to the best life, it must be used deliberately by the moral agent for his own good, not practiced on him by some ministerial authority who acts in his interest. The former is the only way in which respect can be shown for the moral agent, just as it is the only way in which justice is done to the work of art. To justify art as an effective device in propaganda and exhortation is to justify not art but propaganda and exhortation, and not the use but the aesthetic and moral abuse of art.

The manner in which dramatic art can provide stimuli for moral inquiry and moral insight can be briefly illustrated by the same obvious examples. *Hamlet* exhibits the tragedy of a man unable squarely to face the moral question or fully to ignore it, and it is scarcely possible for the appreciator to feel the drama of this problem in Hamlet without the exercise of his own moral and reflective powers; and he cannot do this without an increase of moral insight. Hamlet's tragedy is a stimulus to moral reflection, and Hamlet's character is an opportunity for psychological enlightenment.

It sometimes requires considerable exertion of will to recognize the presence of a moral problem, for this often involves both sustained effort of thought and the painful renunciation of familiar values. Hamlet could not quite face the problem, and he could not quite act without facing it. He could not act on the demands imposed by the accepted standard of filial obligation, requiring the revenge of his father's murder, nor could he formulate a different standard. In immediate physical crises he lacked neither readiness nor fortitude, but he could not summon the moral effort to determine what he ought to do; and his failure, or "tragic flaw," concerns not at all his delay in taking the physical action but his delay in settling the question of what action is right. Had he really been convinced he ought to kill Claudius, we must suppose he would have done so with the address he shows in boarding the pirate ship, in struggling with Laertes in Ophelia's grave, or in the final duel with Laertes. What he cannot do is to decide what he ought to do, and so his eventual resolution is one of fatalism and resignation. The moral weakness we can charge to Hamlet is, then, in a way just the reverse of that which Coleridge alleged, although it also involves Coleridge's point—it was a weakness in firmly hewing to the deliberate problem until it has been resolved, a weakness which arose, however, from a strength of intellect and tenderness of sensibility which could discern situational complexities to which a grosser mind would be oblivious. Had Hamlet only been able to accept conventional prescriptions as to the son's filial duties to a murdered father, there would have been no tragedy; and this makes us wonder whether the critical moral struggle is not in the working-out of decisions rather than their practical application. That is to see differently the Platonic notion that virtue is knowledge.

One can, however, question whether the chief part of the moral life is the reflective scrutiny of values. Surely, the objector would say, the best part of life is not the questioning but the enjoying of values. This seems obvious; and in a different world it might be true. Thinking—about values or anything else—is not its own justification: the justification of thinking is the pressure of questions, and one who has no questions about what is good should not think about it. But perhaps he ought to try to have questions. For the questions are there. A man should not try to make problems, but he should try to react to those that exist. The questions are a more inherent part of the physical, and social, and personal universe than any answers this same universe provides. Evil is a part of the fabric of things, just as good is: the entire problem is their intermixture and (at least, apparent) mutual dependence. There are innumerable things—"values"—to enjoy, and a rational animal might make a life which was a happy succession of values, untroubled by the demon of conscience. One of the insights of Christianity is that it is better to be troubled. This same doctrine, however, seems to premise this on the occurrence of an unfortunate action and accident, in which man, by a rebellious choice, brought into existence the kind of world fraught with such problems.

Plato has noticed more clearly the dubious blessedness of the life of innocence and unalloyed happiness: Socrates, speaking in his playful manner, says in the *Statesman:*

> "Suppose that the nurslings of Cronos, having this boundless leisure, and the power of holding intercourse, not only with men, but with the brute creation, had used all these advantages with a view to philosophy, conversing with the brutes as well as with one another, and learning of every nature which was gifted with any special power, and was able to contribute some special experience to the store of wisdom, there would be no difficulty in deciding that they would be a thousand times happier than the men of our own day. Or, again, if they had merely eaten and drunk until they were full, and told stories to one another and to the animals—such stories as are now attributed to them—in this case also, as I should imagine, the answer would be easy. But until some satisfactory witness can be found of the love of that age for knowledge and discussion, we had better let the matter drop . . ." [272B–D, Jowett trans.].

For man, a paradise would scarcely be a paradise in which he could not think. And if he had an occasion to think, then he could not be in paradise. The paradox is that man's highest activity—moral reflection—is called forth by his lowest impulses, and (to wind paradox within paradox) by the intimate union in him of the lower and higher impulses—only the greatly good man being capable of the greatly evil action.

To moral reflection there are direct and indirect, real and fictive, painful and pleasant, stimuli. The direct, real, and painful route is the actual situation which demands a critical moral decision. The indirect, fictive, and pleasant stimulus is observation of another person in such a situation. It it such a situation which all serious literature presents, and which is most intensely presented by the most intense and the highest literary form—tragedy.

One of the intellectual effects of tragedy is to make the observer question the meaning of life, and it does this in two conspicuous ways. It directly exhibits (as A. C. Bradley has noticed) the close interrelation of good and evil, and it presents characters who at some point in their struggle call into doubt themselves and their lives and the worth of those things to which they have devoted their greatest energies. If Othello and Antony are exceptions, this only helps explain their slighter tragic stature. They are noble men who are ruined, but they would be nobler if they better understood their ruin. Othello at the last can but resort to the kind of outward bravery which is the best part of him; and instead of taking in the meaning of his action, confesses his incapacity to cope with it. Macbeth commits a worse crime, but he recovers from it better; if he is a worse man, he is also a more complex one, and, for the spectator, more impressive and more instructive.

Othello evokes our immediate sympathy; but I think Macbeth wins our deeper respect, and this because his conflict occurs on a more ultimate and reflective level. It is in its irresistible might that evil triumphs over Macbeth, in its corrosive insidiousness that it overcomes Othello. Evil confronts Macbeth with almost entire frankness, and he yields to its powerful attractions. He faces the moral problem squarely—and squarely makes the immoral choice. Othello's problem is less tormented and less prolonged, and more emotional; and it is his mind (for evil makes its attack at the weakest point) that falls prey to Iago and that brings on his disaster. In Macbeth it is conscience that succumbs, in Othello it is only simplicity. The witness of Macbeth observes evil enter unadorned and work the destruction of a noble man; in Othello he sees evil forced to assume disguises and working under cover of darkness. Thus it is the purer and sublimer nature of evil that is exhibited in *Macbeth*. Simplicity is surmountable, and we can imagine a slight change of circumstance or the good offices of a discerning friend as a way of averting the fate of Othello. But the force by which evil destroys

Macbeth is one which neither accident nor external aid can dispel. The clear recognition of this force—and no spectator of Macbeth's tragedy can fail of some dim groping toward such a recognition—is a first condition of moral reflectiveness.

I have taken these examples from tragedy because I think the moral potentialities of art are greatest in tragedy and are in fact limited to literature—and, specifically, to dramatic literature (meaning by this, however, the creative presentation of character, whatever the specific literary devices —that is, whether the method be chiefly dialogue, narrative, or stream-of-consciousness description; whether it be staged, read, or heard; and whether it be in prose or verse). The particular means to the moral effect are the vivid depiction of evil (and good) and the penetrating analysis of character. In such means tragedy is rich, comedy poor; while the means of music and painting are of entirely another sort, and lyric poetry deliberately rejects the means available to it in order to associate itself with, and achieve the kind of effect of, these latter nonliterary arts. This raises the new, important question of the classes and relations of the arts, which is not in place here but which I must touch briefly and dogmatically.

Comedy, dealing (as Bergson has shown) with the type rather than the individual, exposes character instead of analyzing it, and, conformably to its more superficial treatment, has an effect more momentary and faint. It presents human foibles, not human crimes: it discloses conflicts which are social and remediable rather than psychical and universal. Thus its affinities are to sociology more than to morality, and it is more capable of generating a social consciousness than a moral conscience.

Music and painting, on the other hand, are without the most elementary means of moral efficacy. Morality is reflective; and reflection can only be promoted by intellectual materials, of which literature has the sole artistic use. Words, which are this art's most elementary subject-matter, are, in ordinary use, instruments of knowledge and reference; and although they may be artistically transformed to serve a new and noncognitive, nonreferential end, this transformation is in the case of dramatic literature not so complete as to prevent the appreciator's retranslating them into the symbols of knowledge. This translation is not possible with the musical and the plastic arts, whose sounds and colors are not terms of knowledge—not in ordinary life and, so, even less in art.

Nor is this translation possible (or, at least, natural or likely) in the kind of literature that is called "lyrical." The literary expression of a natural scene, as in the song about winter in *Love's Labour's Lost,* or of a single emotion, as in the profession of devotion in Shakespeare's Sonnet 57, contain as little material for thinking as a piece of music or a painting.

Support for this view can be found even among those aestheticians who think that all genuine art is lyrical. Croce and Pater assert that *all* art *ought* to be lyrical, i.e., self-contained and nonreferential, a fusion of matter and form such that the identification of anything within the artwork with anything outside it is impossible; but Pater recognizes that the ideal is perfectly attained only in music and is almost necessarily violated in literature. The literary form which does approach this musical ideal is lyric poetry. Pater (and also A. E. Housman to much the same effect in *The Name and Nature of Poetry*) cites Mariana's song from *Measure for Measure* as an example of this perfect fusion of literary matter and form, the matter of the words being so informed by a new aesthetic spirit and so transformed from their ordinary prosaic meanings that a literal statement of the poem's meaning is impossible. It must follow that whatever the values of such art, they are not moral. Such works are jewels which shine by their own light and adorn nothing but themselves. They are perhaps more perfect in beauty than their more ponderous dramatic rivals, and they may or may not be greater art. But they do not move to awe or wonder, unless at their own technical perfection. They provide us with a joyous moment, rather than an urge to reflection. They do so just because of their self-containedness. No conflict is developed within their pattern, which it is the very life of the drama to do, and no problem is stimulated in the reader, which is the essence of the moral attitude to ponder. They live serenely apart from the world, and what they offer the appreciator is a kind of blessed retreat. Thus their preponderant concern with nature, which in actuality is wont to minister to the same monastical need.

It is true that such effects *may* confer positive ethical benefits, which various critics would recognize as true promotions of the moral. I have argued above the advantageousness of recognizing the possibility (and this only) of such effects, and of designating them as distinctly nonmoral. Lyrical poetry may (or may not) eliminate emotional excesses and may (or may not) strengthen the imagination as an agent of moral sympathy; but if it does not arouse moral reflection, its moral function is but accidental and suspect. And we can scarcely seek such a function in an art which refuses all contact with knowledge.

Art as Autonomous

A. C. BRADLEY

Poetry for Poetry's Sake [1]

THE WORDS "Poetry for poetry's sake" recall the famous phrase
"Art for Art." It is far from my purpose to examine the possible meanings
of that phrase, or all the questions it involves. I propose to state briefly what
I understand by "Poetry for poetry's sake," and then, after guarding against
one or two misapprehensions of the formula, to consider more fully a single
problem connected with it. And I must premise, without attempting to justify
them, certain explanations. We are to consider poetry in its essence, and
apart from the flaws which in most poems accompany their poetry. We are
to include in the idea of poetry the metrical form, and not to regard this
as a mere accident or a mere vehicle. And, finally, poetry being poems, we
are to think of a poem as it actually exists; and, without aiming here at
accuracy, we may say that an actual poem is the succession of experiences—
sounds, images, thoughts, emotions—through which we pass when we are
reading as poetically as we can. Of course this imaginative experience—if
I may use the phrase for brevity—differs with every reader and every time
of reading: a poem exists in innumerable degrees. But that insurmountable
fact lies in the nature of things and does not concern us now.

What then does the formula "Poetry for poetry's sake" tell us about this
experience? It says, as I understand it, these things. First, this experience
is an end in itself, is worth having on its own account, has an intrinsic value.
Next, its *poetic* value is this intrinsic worth alone. Poetry may have also an
ulterior value as a means to culture or religion; because it conveys instruction, or softens the passions, or furthers a good cause; because it brings the

---

[1] From A. C. Bradley, *Oxford Lectures on Poetry*, copyright, 1909, by Macmillan
and Company, Ltd., and used with The Macmillan Company's permission, pp. 4–25,
30–32. (Eds.)

poet fame or money or a quiet conscience. So much the better: let it be valued for these reasons too. But its ulterior worth neither is nor can directly determine its poetic worth as a satisfying imaginative experience; and this is to be judged entirely from within. And to these two positions the formula would add, though not of necessity, a third. The consideration of ulterior ends, whether by the poet in the act of composing or by the reader in the act of experiencing, tends to lower poetic value. It does so because it tends to change the nature of poetry by taking it out of its own atmosphere. For its nature is to be not a part, nor yet a copy, of the real world (as we commonly understand that phrase), but to be a world by itself, independent, complete, autonomous; and to possess it fully you must enter that world, conform to its laws, and ignore for the time the beliefs, aims, and particular conditions which belong to you in the other world of reality.

Of the more serious misapprehensions to which these statements may give rise I will glance only at one or two. The offensive consequences often drawn from the formula "Art for Art" will be found to attach not to the doctrine that Art is an end in itself, but to the doctrine that Art is the whole or supreme end of human life. And as this latter doctrine, which seems to me absurd, is in any case quite different from the former, its consequences fall outside my subject. The formula "Poetry is an end in itself" has nothing to say on the various questions of moral judgment which arise from the fact that poetry has its place in a many-sided life. For anything it says, the intrinsic value of poetry might be so small, and its ulterior effects so mischievous, that it had better not exist. The formula only tells us that we must not place in antithesis poetry and human good, for poetry is one kind of human good; and that we must not determine the intrinsic value of this kind of good by direct reference to another. If we do, we shall find ourselves maintaining what we did not expect. If poetic value lies in the stimulation of religious feelings, *Lead, kindly Light* is no better a poem than many a tasteless version of a Psalm: if in the excitement of patriotism, why is *Scots, wha hae* superior to *We don't want to fight*? if in the mitigation of the passions, the Odes of Sappho will win but little praise: if in instruction, Armstrong's *Art of preserving Health* should win much.

Again, our formula may be accused of cutting poetry away from its connection with life. And this accusation raises so huge a problem that I must ask leave to be dogmatic as well as brief. There is plenty of connection between life and poetry, but it is, so to say, a connection underground. The two may be called different forms of the same thing: one of them having (in the usual sense) reality, but seldom fully satisfying imagination; while the other offers something which satisfies imagination but has not full "reality." They are parallel developments which nowhere meet, or, if I may use loosely a word which will be serviceable later, they are analogues.

Hence we understand one by help of the other, and even, in a sense, care for one because of the other; but hence also, poetry neither is life, nor, strictly speaking, a copy of it. They differ not only because one has more mass and the other a more perfect shape, but because they have different *kinds* of existence. The one touches us as beings occupying a given position in space and time, and having feelings, desires, and purposes due to that position: it appeals to imagination, but appeals to much besides. What meets us in poetry has not a position in the same series of time and space, or, if it has or had such a position, it is taken apart from much that belonged to it there; and therefore it makes no direct appeal to those feelings, desires, and purposes, but speaks only to contemplative imagination— imagination the reverse of empty or emotionless, imagination saturated with the results of "real" experience, but still contemplative. Thus, no doubt, one main reason why poetry has poetic value for us is that it presents to us in its own way something which we meet in another form in nature or life; and yet the test of its poetic value for us lies simply in the question whether it satisfies our imagination; the rest of us, our knowledge or conscience, for example, judging it only so far as they appear transmuted in our imagination. So also Shakespeare's knowledge of his moral insight, Milton's greatness of soul, Shelley's "hate of hate" and "love of love," and that desire to help men or make them happier which may have influenced a poet in hours of medita- tion—all these have, as such, no poetical worth: they have that worth only when, passing through the unity of the poet's being, they reappear as quali- ties of imagination, and then are indeed mighty powers in the world of poetry.

I come to a third misapprehension, and so to my main subject. This formula, it is said, empties poetry of its meaning: it is really a doctrine of form for form's sake. "It is of no consequence what a poet says, so long as he says the thing well. The *what* is poetically indifferent: it is the *how* that counts. Matter, subject, content, substance, determines nothing; there is no subject with which poetry may not deal: the form, the treatment, is every- thing. Nay, more: not only is the matter indifferent, but it is the secret of Art to 'eradicate the matter by means of the form,' "—phrases and statements like these meet us everywhere in current criticism of literature and the other arts. They are the stock-in-trade of writers who understand of them little more than the fact that somehow or other they are not "bourgeois." But we find them also seriously used by writers whom we must respect, whether they are anonymous or not; something like one or another of them might be quoted, for example, from Professor Saintsbury, the late R. A. M. Stevenson, Schiller, Goethe himself; and they are the watchwords of a school in the one country where Aesthetics has flourished. They come, as a rule, from men who either practise one of the arts, or, from study of it, are interested in its methods. The general reader—a being so general that I may say what I will of him—is outraged by them. He feels that he is being robbed of almost all that he cares for in a work of art. "You are asking me," he says, "to look at the Dresden Madonna as if it were a Persian rug. You are telling me that the poetic value of *Hamlet* lies solely in its style and versification, and that my interest in the man and his fate is only an intellectual or moral interest. You allege that, if I want to enjoy the poetry of *Crossing the Bar,* I must not mind what Tennyson says there, but must consider solely his way of saying it. But in that case I can care no more for a poem than I do for a set of nonsense verses; and I do not believe that the authors of *Hamlet* and *Crossing the Bar* regarded their poems thus."

These antitheses of subject, matter, substance on the one side, form, treatment, handling on the other, are the field through which I especially want, in this lecture, to indicate a way. It is a field of battle; and the battle is waged for no trivial cause; but the cries of the combatants are terribly ambiguous. Those phrases of the so-called formalist may each mean five or six different things. Taken in one sense they seem to me chiefly true; taken as the general reader not unnaturally takes them, they seem to me false and mischievous. It would be absurd to pretend that I can end in a few minutes a controversy which concerns the ultimate nature of Art, and leads perhaps to problems not yet soluble; but we can at least draw some plain distinctions which, in this controversy, are too often confused.

In the first place, then, let us take "subject" in one particular sense; let us understand by it that which we have in view when, looking at the title of an un-read poem, we say that the poet has chosen this or that for his subject. The subject, in this sense, so far as I can discover, is generally something, real or imaginary, as it exists in the minds of fairly cultivated people. The subject of *Paradise Lost* would be the story of the Fall as that story exists in the general imagination of a Bible-reading people. The subject of Shelley's stanzas *To a Skylark* would be the ideas which arise in the mind of an educated person when, without knowing the poem, he hears the word "skylark." If the title of a poem conveys little or nothing to us, the "subject" appears to be either what we should gather by investigating the title in a dictionary or other book of the kind, or else such a brief suggestion as might be offered by a person who had read the poem, and who said, for example, that the subject of *The Ancient Mariner* was a sailor who killed an albatross and suffered for his deed.

Now the subject, in this sense (and I intend to use the word in no other), is not, as such, inside the poem, but outside it. The contents of the stanzas *To a Skylark* are not the ideas suggested by the word "skylark" to the average man; they belong to Shelley just as much as the language does. The subject, therefore, is not the matter *of* the poem at all; and its opposite is not the *form* of the poem, but the whole poem. The subject is one thing; the poem, matter and form alike, another thing. This being so, it is surely obvious that the poetic value cannot lie in the subject, but lies entirely in its opposite, the poem. How can the subject determine the value when on one and the same subject poems may be written of all degrees of merit and demerit; or when a perfect poem may be composed on a subject so slight as a pet sparrow, and, if Macaulay may be trusted, a nearly worthless poem on a subject so stupendous as the omnipresence of the Deity? The "formalist" is here perfectly right. Nor is he insisting on something unimportant. He is fighting against our tendency to take the work of art as a mere copy or reminder of something already in our heads, or at the best as a suggestion of some idea as little removed as possible from the familiar. The sightseer who promenades a picture-gallery, remarking that this portrait is so like his cousin, or that landscape the very image of his birthplace, or who, after satisfying himself that one picture is about Elijah, passes on rejoicing to discover the subject, and nothing but the subject, of the next—what is he but an extreme example of this tendency? Well, but the very same tendency vitiates much of our criticism, much criticism of Shakespeare, for example, which, with all its cleverness and partial truth, still shows that the critic never passed from his own mind into Shakespeare's; and it may be traced even in so fine a critic as Coleridge, as when he dwarfs the sublime struggle of Hamlet into the image of his own unhappy weakness. Hazlitt by no means escaped its influence. Only the third of that great trio, Lamb, appears almost always to have rendered the conception of the composer.

Again, it is surely true that we cannot determine beforehand what subjects are fit for Art, or name any subject on which a good poem might not possibly be written. To divide subjects into two groups, the beautiful or elevating, and the ugly or vicious, and to judge poems according as their subjects belong to one of these groups or the other, is to fall into the same pit, to confuse with our pre-conceptions the meaning of the poet. What the thing is in the poem he is to be judged by, not by the thing as it was before he touched it; and how can we venture to say beforehand that he cannot make a true poem out of something which to us was merely alluring or dull or revolting? The question whether, having done so, he ought to publish his poem; whether the thing in the poet's work will not be still confused by the incompetent Puritan or the incompetent sensualist with the thing in *his* mind, does not touch this point: it is a further question, one of ethics, not of art. No doubt the upholders of "Art for art's sake" will generally be in favour of the courageous course, of refusing to sacrifice the better or stronger part of the public to the weaker or worse; but their maxim in no way binds them to this view. Rossetti suppressed one of the best of his sonnets, a sonnet chosen for admiration by Tennyson, himself extremely sensitive about the moral effect of poetry; suppressed it, I believe, because it was called fleshly. One may regret Rossetti's judgment and at the same time respect his scrupulousness; but in any case he judged in his capacity of citizen, not in his capacity of artist.

So far then the "formalist" appears to be right. But he goes too far, I think, if he maintains that the subject is indifferent and that all subjects are the same to poetry. And he does not prove his point by observing that a good poem might be written on a pin's head, and a bad one on the Fall of Man. That truth shows that the subject *settles* nothing, but not that it counts for nothing. The Fall of Man is really a more favourable subject than a pin's head. The Fall of Man, that is to say, offers opportunities of poetic effects wider in range and more penetrating in appeal. And the fact is that such a subject, as it exists in the general imagination, has some aesthetic value before the poet touches it. It is, as you may choose to call it, an inchoate poem or the débris of a poem. It is not an abstract idea or a bare isolated fact, but an assemblage of figures, scenes, actions, and events, which already appeal to emotional imagination; and it is already in some degree organized and formed. In spite of this a bad poet would make a bad poem on it; but then we should say he was unworthy of the subject. And we should not say this if he wrote a bad poem on a pin's head. Conversely, a good poem on a pin's head would almost certainly transform its subject far more than a good poem on the Fall of Man. It might revolutionize its subject so completely that we should say, "The subject may be a pin's head, but the substance of the poem has very little to do with it."

This brings us to another and a different antithesis. Those figures, scenes, events, that form part of the subject called the Fall of Man, are not the substance of *Paradise Lost;* but in *Paradise Lost* there are figures, scenes, and events resembling them in some degree. These, with much more of the same kind, may be described as its substance, and may then be contrasted with the measured language of the poem, which will be called its form. Subject is the opposite not of form but of the whole poem. Substance is within the poem, and its opposite, form, is also within the poem. I am not criticizing this antithesis at present, but evidently it is quite different from the other. It is practically the distinction used in the old-fashioned criticism of epic and drama, and it flows down, not unsullied, from Aristotle. Addison, for example, in examining *Paradise Lost* considers in order the fable, the characters, and the sentiments; these will be the substance: then he considers the language, that is, the style and numbers; this will be the form. In like manner, the substance or meaning of a lyric may be distinguished from the form.

Now I believe it will be found that a large part of the controversy we are dealing with arises from a confusion between these two distinctions of substance and form, and of subject and poem. The extreme formalist lays his whole weight on the form because he thinks its opposite is the mere subject. The general reader is angry, but makes the same mistake, and gives to the subject praises that rightly belong to the substance.[2] I will read an example of what I mean. I can only explain the following words of a good critic by supposing that for the moment he has fallen into this confusion: "The mere matter of all poetry—to wit, the appearances of nature and the thoughts and feelings of men—being unalterable, it follows that the difference between poet and poet will depend upon the manner of each in applying language, metre, rhyme, cadence, and what not, to this invariable material." What has become here of the substance of *Paradise Lost*—the story, scenery, characters, sentiments, as they are in the poem? They have vanished clean away. Nothing is left but the form on one side, and on the other not even the subject, but a supposed invariable material, the appearances of nature and the thoughts and feelings of men. Is it surprising that the whole value should then be found in the form?

So far we have assumed that this antithesis of substance and form is valid, and that it always has one meaning. In reality it has several, but we will leave it in its present shape, and pass to the question of its validity. And this question we are compelled to raise, because we have to deal with the two contentions that the poetic value lies wholly or mainly in the substance, and that it lies wholly or mainly in the form. Now these contentions, whether false or true, may seem at least to be clear; but we shall find, I think, that they are both of them false, or both of them nonsense: false if they concern anything outside the poem, nonsense if they apply to something in it. For what do they evidently imply? They imply that there are in a poem two parts, factors, or components, a substance and a form; and that you can conceive them distinctly and separately, so that when you are speaking of the one you are not speaking of the other. Otherwise how can you ask the question, In which of them does the value lie? But really in a poem, apart from defects, there are no such factors or components; and therefore it is strictly nonsense to ask in which of them the value lies. And on the other hand, if the substance and the form referred to are not in the poem, then both the contentions are false, for its poetic value lies in itself.

What I mean is neither new nor mysterious; and it will be clear, I believe, to any one who reads poetry poetically and who closely examines

---

[2] What is here called "substance" is what people generally mean when they use the word "subject" and insist on the value of the subject. I am not arguing against this usage, or in favour of the usage which I have adopted for the sake of clearness. It does not matter which we employ, so long as we and others know what we mean. (I use "substance" and "content" indifferently.)

his experience. When you are reading a poem, I would ask—not analysing it, and much less criticizing it, but allowing it, as it proceeds, to make its full impression on you through the exertion of your recreating imagination —do you then apprehend and enjoy as one thing a certain meaning or substance, and as another thing certain articulate sounds, and do you some-how compound these two? Surely you do not, any more than you apprehend apart, when you see some one smile, those lines in the face which express a feeling, and the feeling that the lines express. Just as there the lines and their meaning are to you one thing, not two, so in poetry the meaning and the sounds are one: there is, if I may put it so, a resonant meaning, or a meaning resonance. If you read the line, "The sun is warm, the sky is clear," you do not experience separately the image of a warm sun and clear sky, on the one side, and certain unintelligible rhythmical sounds on the other; nor yet do you experience them together, side by side; but you experience the one *in* the other. And in like manner, when you are really reading *Hamlet,* the action and the characters are not something which you con-ceive apart from the words; you apprehend them from point to point *in* the words, and the words as expressions of them. Afterwards, no doubt, when you are out of the poetic experience but remember it, you may by analysis decompose this unity, and attend to a substance more or less isolated, and a form more or less isolated. But these are things in your analytic head, not in the poem, which is *poetic* experience. And if you want to have the poem again, you cannot find it by adding together these two products of decom-position; you can only find it by passing back into poetic experience. And then what you recover is no aggregate of factors, it is a unity in which you can no more separate a substance and a form than you can separate living blood and the life in the blood. This unity has, if you like, various "aspects" or "sides," but they are not factors or parts; if you try to examine one, you find it is also the other. Call them substance and form if you please, but these are not the reciprocally exclusive substance and form to which the two contentions *must* refer. They do not "agree," for they are not apart: they are one thing from different points of view, and in that sense identical. And this identity of content and form, you will say, is no accident; it is of the essence of poetry in so far as it is poetry, and of all art in so far as it is art. Just as there is in music not sound on one side and a meaning on the other, but expressive sound, and if you ask what is the meaning you can only answer by pointing to the sounds; just as in painting there is not a meaning *plus* paint, but a meaning *in* paint, or significant paint, and no man can really express the meaning in any other way than in paint and in *this* paint; so in a poem the true content and the true form neither exist nor can be imagined apart. When then you are asked whether the value of a poem lies in a substance got by decomposing the poem, and present, as such, only in reflective analysis, or whether the value lies in a form arrived at and existing in the same way, you will answer, "It lies neither in one, nor in the other, nor in any addition of them, but in the poem, where they are not."

We have then, first, an antithesis of subject and poem. This is clear and valid; and the question in which of them does the value lie is intelligible; and its answer is, In the poem. We have next a distinction of substance and form. If the substance means ideas, images, and the like taken alone, and the form means the measured language taken by itself, this is a possible distinction, but it is a distinction of things not in the poem, and the value lies in neither of them. If substance and form mean anything *in* the poem, then each is involved in the other, and the question in which of them the value lies has no sense. No doubt you may say, speaking loosely, that in this poet or poem the aspect of substance is the more noticeable, and in that the aspect of form; and you may pursue interesting discussions on this basis, though no principle or ultimate question of value is touched by them. And apart from that question, of course, I am not denying the usefulness and necessity of the distinction. We cannot dispense with it. To consider separately the action or the characters of a play, and separately its style or versification, is both legitimate and valuable, so long as we remember what we are doing. But the true critic in speaking of these apart does not really think of them apart; the whole, the poetic experience, of which they are but aspects, is always in his mind; and he is always aiming at a richer, truer, more intense repetition of that experience. On the other hand, when the question of principle, of poetic value, is raised, these aspects *must* fall apart into components, separately conceivable; and then there arise two heresies, equally false, that the value lies in one of two things, both of which are outside the poem, and therefore where its value cannot lie.

On the heresy of the separable substance a few additional words will suffice. This heresy is seldom formulated, but perhaps some unconscious holder of it may object: "Surely the action and the characters of *Hamlet* are in the play; and surely I can retain these, though I have forgotten all the words. I admit that I do not possess the whole poem, but I possess a part, and the most important part." And I would answer: "If we are not concerned with any question of principle, I accept all that you say except the last words, which do raise such a question. Speaking loosely, I agree that the action and characters, as you perhaps conceive them, together with a great deal more, are in the poem. Even then, however, you must not claim to possess all of this kind that is in the poem; for in forgetting the words you must have lost innumerable details of the action and the characters. And, when the question of value is raised, I must insist that the action and characters, as you conceive them, are not in *Hamlet* at all. If they are, point them out. You cannot do it. What you find at any moment of that succession of experiences called *Hamlet* is words. In these words, to speak loosely again, the action and characters (more of them than you can conceive apart) are focussed; but your experience is not a combination of them, as ideas, on the one side, with certain sounds on the other; it is an experience of something in which the two are indissolubly fused. If you deny this, to be sure I can make no answer, or can only answer that I have reason to believe that you cannot read poetically, or else are misinterpreting your experience. But if you do not deny this, then you will admit that the action and characters of the poem, as you separately imagine them, are no part of it, but a product of it in your reflective imagination, a faint analogue of one aspect of it taken in detachment from the whole. Well, I do not dispute, I would even insist, that, in the case of so long a poem as *Hamlet,* it may be necessary from time to time to interrupt the poetic experience, in order to enrich it by forming such a product and dwelling on it. Nor, in a wide sense of 'poetic,' do I question the poetic value of this product, as you think of it apart from the poem. It resembles our recollections of the heroes of history or legend, who move about in our imaginations, 'forms more real than living man,' and are worth much to us though we do not remember anything they said. Our ideas and images of the 'substance' of a poem have this poetic value, and more, if they are at all adequate. But they cannot determine the poetic value of the poem, for (not to speak of the competing claims of the 'form') nothing that is outside the poem can do that, and they, as such, are outside it." [3]

Let us turn to the so-called form—style and versification. There is no such thing as mere form in poetry. All form is expression. Style may have indeed a certain aesthetic worth in partial abstraction from the particular matter it conveys, as in a well-built sentence you may take pleasure in the build almost apart from the meaning. Even so, style is expressive—presents to sense, for example, the order, ease, and rapidity with which ideas move in the writer's mind—but it is not expressive of the meaning of that particular sentence. And it is possible, interrupting poetic experience, to decompose it and abstract for comparatively separate consideration this nearly formal element of style. But the aesthetic value of style so taken is not considerable; [4] you could not read with pleasure for an hour a composition which had no other merit. And in poetic experience you never apprehend this value by itself; the style is here expressive also of a particular meaning, or rather is

---

[3] These remarks will hold good, *mutatis mutandis,* if by "substance" is understood the "moral" or the "idea" of a poem, although perhaps in one instance out of five thousand this may be found in so many words in the poem.
[4] On the other hand, the absence, or worse than absence, of style, in this sense, is a serious matter.

one aspect of that unity whose other aspect is meaning. So that what you apprehend may be called indifferently an expressed meaning or a significant form. Perhaps on this point I may in Oxford appeal to authority, that of Matthew Arnold and Walter Pater, the latter at any rate an authority whom the formalist will not despise. What is the gist of Pater's teaching about style, if it is not that in the end the one virtue of style is truth or adequacy; that the word, phrase, sentence, should express perfectly the writer's perception, feeling, image, or thought; so that, as we read a descriptive phrase of Keats's, we exclaim, "That is the thing itself"; so that, to quote Arnold, the words are "symbols equivalent with the thing symbolized," or, in our technical language, a form identical with its content? Hence in true poetry it is, in strictness, impossible to express the meaning in any but its own words, or to change the words without changing the meaning. A translation of such poetry is not really the old meaning in a fresh dress; it is a new product, something like the poem, though, if one chooses to say so, more like it in the aspect of meaning than in the aspect of form.

No one who understands poetry, it seems to me, would dispute this, were it not that, falling away from his experience, or misled by theory, he takes the word "meaning" in a sense almost ludicrously inapplicable to poetry. People say, for instance, "steed" and "horse" have the same meaning; and in bad poetry they have, but not in poetry that *is* poetry.

> "Bring forth the horse!" The horse was brought:
> In truth he was a noble steed!

says Byron in *Mazeppa*. If the two words mean the same here, transpose them:

> "Bring forth the steed!" The steed was brought:
> In truth he was a noble horse!

and ask again if they mean the same. Or let me take a line certainly very free from "poetic diction":

> To be or not to be, that is the question.

You may say that this means the same as "What is just now occupying my attention is the comparative disadvantages of continuing to live or putting an end to myself." And for practical purposes—the purpose, for example, of a coroner—it does. But as the second version altogether misrepresents the speaker at that moment of his existence, while the first does represent him, how can they for any but a practical or logical purpose be said to have the same sense? Hamlet was well able to "unpack his heart with words," but he will not unpack it with our paraphrases.

These considerations apply equally to versification. If I take the famous line which describes how the souls of the dead stood waiting by the river, imploring a passage from Charon:

Tendebantque manus ripae ulterioris amore;

and if I translate it, "and were stretching forth their hands in longing for the further bank," the charm of the original has fled. Why has it fled? Partly (but we have dealt with that) because I have substituted for five words, and those the words of Virgil, twelve words, and those my own. In some measure because I have turned into rhythmless prose a line of verse which, as mere sound, has unusual beauty. But much more because in doing so I have also changed the *meaning* of Virgil's line. What that meaning is *I* cannot say: Virgil has said it. But I can see this much, that the translation conveys a far less vivid picture of the outstretched hands and of their remaining out-stretched, and a far less poignant sense of the distance of the shore and the longing of the souls. And it does so partly because this picture and this sense are conveyed not only by the obvious meaning of the words, but through the long-drawn sound of "tendebantque," through the time occupied by the five syllables and therefore by the idea of "ulterioris," and through the identity of the long sound "or" in the penultimate syllables of "ulterioris amore"—all this, and much more, apprehended not in this analytical fashion, nor as *added* to the beauty of mere sound and to the obvious meaning, but in unity with them and so as expressive of the poetic meaning of the whole.

It is always so in fine poetry. The value of versification, when it is indis-solubly fused with meaning, can hardly be exaggerated. The gift for feeling it, even more perhaps than the gift for feeling the value of style, is the *specific* gift for poetry, as distinguished from other arts. But versification, taken, as far as possible, all by itself, has a very different worth. Some aesthetic worth it has; how much, you may experience by reading poetry in a language of which you do not understand a syllable. The pleasure is quite appreciable, but it is not great; nor in actual poetic experience do you meet with it, as such, at all. For, I repeat, it is not *added* to the pleasure of the meaning when you read poetry that you do understand: by some mystery the music is then the music *of* the meaning, and the two are one. However fond of versi-fication you might be, you would tire very soon of reading verses in Chinese; and before long of reading Virgil and Dante if you were ignorant of their languages. But take the music as it is *in* the poem, and there is a marvellous change. Now

> It gives a very echo to the seat
> Where love is throned;

or "carries far into your heart," almost like music itself, the sound

Of old, unhappy, far-off things
And battles long ago.

What then is to be said of the following sentence of the critic quoted before: "But when any one who knows what poetry is reads—

Our noisy years seem moments in the being
Of the eternal silence,

he sees that, quite independently of the meaning, . . . there is one note added to the articulate music of the world—a note that never will leave off resounding till the eternal silence itself gulfs it"? I must think that the writer is deceiving himself. For I could quite understand his enthusiasm, if it were an enthusiasm for the music of the meaning; but as for the music, "quite independently of the meaning," so far as I can hear it thus (and I doubt if any one who knows English can quite do so), I find it gives some pleasure, but only a trifling pleasure. And indeed I venture to doubt whether, considered as mere sound, the words are at all exceptionally beautiful, as Virgil's line certainly is.

When poetry answers to its idea and is purely or almost purely poetic, we find the identity of form and content; and the degree of purity attained may be tested by the degree in which we feel it hopeless to convey the effect of a poem or passage in any form but its own. Where the notion of doing so is simply ludicrous, you have quintessential poetry. But a great part even of good poetry, especially in long works, is of a mixed nature; and so we find in it no more than a partial agreement of a form and substance which remain to some extent distinct. This is so in many passages of Shakespeare (the greatest of poets when he chose, but not always a conscientious poet); passages where something was wanted for the sake of the plot, but he did not care about it or was hurried. The conception of the passage is then distinct from the execution, and neither is inspired. This is so also, I think, wherever we can truly speak of merely decorative effect. We seem to perceive that the poet had a truth or fact—philosophical, agricultural, social—distinctly before him, and then, as we say, clothed it in metrical and coloured language. Most argumentative, didactic, or satiric poems are partly of this kind; and in imaginative poems anything which is really a mere "conceit" is mere decoration. We often deceive ourselves in this matter, for what we call decoration has often a new and genuinely poetic content of its own; but wherever there is mere decoration, we judge the poetry to be not wholly poetic. And so when Wordsworth inveighed against poetic diction, though he hurled his darts rather wildly, what he was rightly aiming at was a phraseology, not the living body of a new content, but the mere worn-out body of an old one.[5]

In pure poetry it is otherwise. Pure poetry is not the decoration of a preconceived and clearly defined matter: it springs from the creative impulse of a vague imaginative mass pressing for development and definition. If the poet already knew exactly what he meant to say, why should he write the poem? The poem would in fact already be written. For only its completion can reveal, even to him, exactly what he wanted. When he began and while he was at work, he did not possess his meaning; it possessed him. It was not a fully formed soul asking for a body: it was an inchoate soul in the inchoate body of perhaps two or three vague ideas and a few scattered phrases. The growing of this body into its full stature and perfect shape was the same thing as the gradual self-definition of the meaning. And this is the reason why such poems strike us as creations, not manufactures, and have the magical effect which mere decoration cannot produce. This is also the reason why, if we insist on asking for the meaning of such a poem, we can only be answered "It means itself."

And so at last I may explain why I have troubled myself and you with what may seem an arid controversy about mere words. It is not so. These heresies which would make poetry a compound of two factors—a matter common to it with the merest prose, *plus* a poetic form, as the one heresy says: a poetical substance *plus* a negligible form, as the other says—are not only untrue, they are injurious to the dignity of poetry. In an age already inclined to shrink from those higher realms where poetry touches religion and philosophy, the formalist heresy encourages men to taste poetry as they would a fine wine, which has indeed an aesthetic value, but a small one. And then the natural man, finding an empty form, hurls into it the matter of cheap pathos, rancid sentiment, vulgar humour, bare lust, ravenous vanity —everything which, in Schiller's phrase,[6] the form should extirpate, but which no mere form can extirpate. And the other heresy—which is indeed rather a practice than a creed—encourages us in the habit so dear to us of putting our own thoughts or fancies into the place of the poet's creation. What he meant by *Hamlet,* or the *Ode to a Nightingale,* or *Abt Vogler,* we say, is this or that which we knew already; and so we lose what he had to tell us. But he meant what he said, and said what he meant.

Poetry in this matter is not, as good critics of painting and music often affirm, different from the other arts; in all of them the content is one thing with the form. What Beethoven meant by his symphony, or Turner by his

---

[5] This paragraph is criticized by the writer of this essay in the note which follows this selection.

[6] Not that to Schiller "form" meant mere style and versification.

picture, was not something which you can name, but the picture and the symphony. Meaning they have, but *what* meaning can be said in no language but their own: and we know this, though some strange delusion makes us think the meaning has less worth because we cannot put it into words. Well, it is just the same with poetry. But because poetry is words, we vainly fancy that some other words than its own will express its meaning. And they will do so no more—or, if you like to speak loosely, only a trifle more—than words will express the meaning of the Dresden Madonna. Something a little like it they may indeed express. And we may find analogues of the meaning of poetry outside it, which may help us to appropriate it. The other arts, the best ideas of philosophy or religion, much that nature and life offer us or force upon us, are akin to it. But they are only akin. Nor is it the expression of them. Poetry does not present to imagination our highest knowledge or belief, and much less our dreams and opinions; but it, content and form in unity, embodies in its own irreplaceable way something which embodies itself also in other irreplaceable ways, such as philosophy or religion. And just as each of these gives a satisfaction which the other cannot possibly give, so we find in poetry, which cannot satisfy the needs they meet, that which by their natures they cannot afford us. But we shall not find it fully if we look for something else.

Note

This paragraph has not, to my knowledge, been adversely criticised, but it now appears to me seriously misleading. It refers to certain kinds of poetry, and again to certain passages in poems, which we feel to be less poetical than some other kinds or passages. But this difference of degree in poeticalness (if I may use the word) is put as a difference between "mixed" and "pure" poetry; and that distinction is, I think, unreal and mischievous. Further, it is implied that in less poetical poetry there necessarily is only a partial unity of content and form. This (unless I am now mistaken) is a mistake, and a mistake due to failure to hold fast the main idea of the lecture. Naturally it would be most agreeable to me to re-write the paragraph, but if I reprint it and expose my errors the reader will perhaps be helped to a firmer grasp of that idea.

It is true that where poetry is most poetic we feel most decidedly how impossible it is to separate content and form. But where poetry is less poetic and does not make us feel this unity so decidedly, it does not follow that the unity is imperfect. Failure or partial failure in this unity is always (as in the case of Shakespeare referred to) a failure on the part of the *poet* (though it is not always due to the same causes). It does not lie of necessity in the nature of a particular kind of poetry (*e.g.* satire) or in the nature of a particular passage. All poetry cannot be equally poetic, but *all* poetry ought to maintain the unity of content and form, and, in that sense, to be "pure." Only in certain kinds, and in certain passages, it is more difficult for the poet to maintain it than in others.

Let us take first the "passages" and suppose them to occur in one of the more poetic kinds of poetry. In certain parts of any epic or tragedy matter has to be treated which, though necessary to the whole, is not in itself favour-able to poetry, or would not in itself be a good "subject." But it is the busi-ness of the poet to do his best to make this matter poetry, and pure poetry. And, if he succeeds, the passage, though it will probably be less poetic than the bulk of the poem, will exhibit the complete unity of content and form. It will not strike us as a mere bridge between other passages; it will be enjoy-able for itself; and it will not occur to us to think that the poet was dealing with an un-poetic "matter" and found his task difficult or irksome. Shake-speare frequently does not trouble himself to face this problem and leaves an imperfect unity. The conscientious artists, like Virgil, Milton, Tennyson, habitually face it and frequently solve it.[7] And when they wholly or partially fail, the fault is still *theirs*. It is, in one sense, due to the "matter," which set a hard problem; but they would be the first to declare that *nothing* in the poem ought to be only mixedly poetic.

In the same way, satire is not in its nature a highly poetic kind of poetry, but it ought, in its own kind, to be poetry throughout, and therefore ought not to show a merely partial unity of content and form. If the satirist makes us exclaim "This is sheer prose wonderfully well disguised," that is a fault, and *his* fault (unless it happens to be ours). The idea that a tragedy or lyric could really be reproduced in a form not its own strikes us as ridiculous; the idea that a satire could so be reproduced seems much less ridiculous; but if it were true the satire would not be poetry at all.

The reader will now see where, in my judgment, the paragraph is wrong. Elsewhere it is, I think, right, though it deals with a subject far too large for a paragraph. This is also true of the next paragraph, which uses the false distinction of "pure" and "mixed," and which will hold in various degrees of poetry in various degrees poetical.

It is of course possible to use a distinction of "pure" and "mixed" in an-other sense. Poetry, whatever its kind, would be pure as far as it preserved the unity and content of form; mixed, so far as it failed to do so—in other words, failed to be poetry and was partly prosaic.

---

[7] In Schiller's phrase, they have extirpated the mere "matter." We often say that they do this by dint of style. This is roughly true, but in strictness it means, as we have seen, not that they decorate the mere "matter" with a mere "form," but that they produce a new content-form.

CLIVE BELL

Art and Ethics [1]

Between me and the pleasant places of history remains, however, one ugly barrier. I cannot dabble and paddle in the pools and shallows of the past until I have answered a question so absurd that the nicest people never tire of asking it: "What is the moral justification of art?" Of course they are right who insist that the creation of art must be justified on ethical grounds: all human actvities must be so justified. It is the philosopher's privilege to call upon the artist to show that what he is about is either good in itself or a means to good. It is the artist's duty to reply: "Art is good because it exalts to a state of ecstasy better far than anything a benumbed moralist can even guess at; so shut up." Philosophically he is quite right; only, philosophy is not so simple as that. Let us try to answer philosophically.

The moralist inquires whether art is either good in itself or a means to good. Before answering, we will ask what he means by the word "good," not because it is in the least doubtful, but to make him think. In fact, Mr. G. E. Moore has shown pretty conclusively in his *Principia Ethica* that by "good" everyone means just good. We all know quite well what we mean though we cannot define it. "Good" can no more be defined than "Red": no quality can be defined. Nevertheless we know perfectly well what we mean when we say that a thing is "good" or "red." This is so obviously true that its statement has greatly disconcerted, not to say enraged, the orthodox philosophers.

Orthodox philosophers are by no means agreed as to what we do mean by "good," only they are sure that we cannot mean what we say. They used to be fond of assuming that "good" meant pleasure; or, at any rate, that pleasure was the sole good as an end: two very different propositions. That "good" means "pleasure" and that pleasure is the sole good was the opinion of the Hedonists, and is still the opinion of any Utilitarians who may have lingered on into the twentieth century. They enjoy the honour of being the only ethical fallacies worth the powder and shot of a writer on art. I can

---

[1] From Clive Bell, *Art* (London: Chatto & Windus, Ltd., 1914), Section III, Chap. II. Reprinted by permission. The argument which follows assumes the reader's acquaintance with the first chapter of *Art*, the heart of which is reprinted in our section on the object (see p. 208). (Eds.)

imagine no more delicate or convincing piece of logic than that by which Mr. G. E. Moore disposes of both. But it is none of my business to do clumsily what Mr. Moore has done exquisitely. I have no mind by attempting to reproduce his dialectic to incur the merited ridicule of those familiar with the *Principia Ethica* or to spoil the pleasure of those who will be wise enough to run out this very minute and order a masterpiece with which they happen to be unacquainted. For my immediate purpose it is necessary only to borrow one shaft from that well-stocked armoury.

To him who believes that pleasure is the sole good, I will put this question: Does he, like John Stuart Mill, and everyone else I ever heard of, speak of "higher and lower" or "better and worse" or "superior and inferior" pleasures? And, if so, does he not perceive that he has given away his case? For, when he says that one pleasure is "higher" or "better" than another, he does not mean that it is greater in *quantity* but superior in *quality*.

On page 7 of *Utilitarianism*, J. S. Mill says:—"If one of the two (pleasures) is, by those who are competently acquainted with both, placed so far above the other that they prefer it, even though knowing it to be attended with a greater amount of discontent, and would not resign it for any quantity of the other pleasure which their nature is capable of, we are justified in ascribing to the preferred enjoyment a superiority in quality, so far outweighing quantity as to render it, in comparison, of small account."

But if pleasure be the sole good, the only possible criterion of pleasures is quantity of pleasure. "Higher" or "better" can only mean containing more pleasure. To speak of "better pleasures" in any other sense is to make the goodness of the sole good as an end depend upon something which, *ex hypothesi,* is not good as an end. Mill is as one who, having set up sweetness as the sole good quality in jam, prefers Tiptree to Crosse and Blackwell, not because it is sweeter, but because it possesses a better kind of sweetness. To do so is to discard sweetness as an ultimate criterion and to set up something else in its place. So, when Mill, like everyone else, speaks of "better" or "higher" or "superior" pleasures, he discards pleasure as an ultimate criterion, and thereby admits that pleasure is not the sole good. He feels that some pleasures are better than others, and determines their respective values by the degree in which they possess that quality which all recognise but none can define—goodness. By higher and lower, superior and inferior pleasures we mean simply more good and less good pleasures. There are, therefore, two different qualities, Pleasantness and Goodness. Pleasure, amongst other things, may be good; but pleasure cannot mean good. By "good" we cannot mean "pleasureable"; for, as we see, there is a quality, "goodness," so distinct from pleasure that we speak of pleasures that are more or less good without meaning pleasures that are more or less pleasant.

By "good," then, we do not mean "pleasure," neither is pleasure the sole good.

Mr. Moore goes on to inquire what things are good in themselves, as ends that is to say. He comes to a conclusion with which we all agree, but for which few could have found convincing and logical arguments: "states of mind," he shows, alone are good as ends.[2] People who have very little taste for logic will find a simple and satisfactory proof of this conclusion afforded by what is called "the method of isolation."

That which is good as an end will retain some, at any rate, of its value in complete isolation: it will retain all its value as an end. That which is good as a means only will lose all its value in isolaticn. That which is good as an end will remain valuable even when deprived of all its consequences and left with nothing but bare existence. Therefore, we can discover whether honestly we feel some thing to be good as an end, if only we can conceive it in complete isolation, and be sure that so isolated it remains valuable. Bread is good. Is bread good as an end or as a means? Conceive a loaf existing in an uninhabited and uninhabitable planet. Does it seem to lose its value? That is a little too easy. The physical universe appears to most people immensely good, for towards nature they feel violently that emotional reaction which brings to the lips the epithet "good"; but if the physical universe were not related to mind, if it were never to provoke an emotional reaction, if no mind were ever to be affected by it, and if it had no mind of its own, would it still appear good? There are two stars: one is, and ever will be, void of life, on the other exists a fragment of just living protoplasm which will never develop, will never become conscious. Can we say honestly that we feel one to be better than the other? Is life itself good as an end? A clear judgment is made difficult by the fact that one cannot conceive anything without feeling something for it; one's very conceptions provoke states of mind and thus acquire value as means. Let us ask ourselves, bluntly, can that which has no mind and affects no mind have value? Surely not. But anything which has a mind can have intrinsic value, and anything that affects a mind may become valuable as a means, since the state of mind produced may be valuable in itself. Isolate that mind. Isolate the state of mind of a man in love or rapt in contemplation; it does not seem to lose all its value. I do not say that its value is not decreased; obviously, it loses its value as a means to producing good states of mind in others. But a certain value does subsist—an intrinsic value. Populate the lone star with one human mind and every part of that star becomes potentially valuable as a means,

---

[2] Formerly he held that inanimate beauty also was good in itself. But this tenet, I am glad to learn, he has discarded.

because it may be a means to that which is good as an end—a good state of mind. The state of mind of a person in love or rapt in contemplation suffices in itself. We do not stay to inquire "What useful purpose does this serve, whom does it benefit, and how?" We say directly and with conviction—"This is good."

When we are challenged to justify our opinion that anything, other than a state of mind, is good, we, feeling it to be a means only, do very properly seek its good effects, and our last justification is always that it produces good states of mind. Thus, when asked why we call a patent fertiliser good, we may, if we can find a listener, show that the fertiliser is a means to good crops, good crops a means to food, food a means to life, and life a necessary condition of good states of mind. Further we cannot go. When asked why we hold a particular state of mind to be good, the state of aesthetic contemplation for instance, we can but reply that to us its goodness is self-evident. Some states of mind appear to be good independently of their consequences. No other things appear to be good in this way. We conclude, therefore, that good states of mind are alone good as ends.

To justify ethically any human activity, we must inquire—"Is this a means to good states of mind?" In the case of art our answer will be prompt and emphatic. Art is not only a means to good states of mind, but, perhaps, the most direct and potent that we possess. Nothing is more direct, because nothing affects the mind more immediately; nothing is more potent, because there is no state of mind more excellent or more intense than the state of aesthetic contemplation. This being so, to seek any other moral justification for art, to seek in art a means to anything less than good states of mind, is an act of wrong-headedness to be committed only by a fool or a man of genius.

Many fools have committed it and one man of genius has made it notorious. Never was cart put more obstructively before horse than when Tolstoi announced that the justification of art was its power of promoting good actions.[3] As if actions were ends in themselves! There is neither virtue nor vice in running: but to run with good tidings is commendable, to run away with an old lady's purse is not. There is no merit in shouting: but to speak up for truth and justice is well, to deafen the world with charlatanry is damnable. Always it is the end in view that gives value to action; and, ultimately, the end of all good actions must be to create or encourage or make possible good states of mind. Therefore, inciting people to good actions by means of edifying images is a respectable trade and a roundabout means to good. Creating works of art is as direct a means to good as a human

---

[3] See the selection from Tolstoy given above in this section, p. 483. (Eds.)

being can practise. Just in this fact lies the tremendous importance of art: there is no more direct means to good.

To pronounce anything a work of art is, therefore, to make a momentous moral judgment. It is to credit an object with being so direct and powerful a means to good that we need not trouble ourselves about any other of its possible consequences. But even were this not the case, the habit of introducing moral considerations into judgments between particular works of art would be inexcusable. Let the moralist make a judgment about art as a whole, let him assign it what he considers its proper place amongst means to good, but in aesthetic judgments, in judgments between members of the same class, in judgments between works of art considered as art, let him hold his tongue. If he esteem art anything less than equal to the greatest means to good he mistakes. But granting, for the sake of peace, its inferiority to some, I will yet remind him that his moral judgments about the value of particular works of art have nothing to do with their artistic value. The judge at Epsom is not permitted to disqualify the winner of the Derby in favour of the horse that finished last but one on the ground that the latter is just the animal for the Archbishop of Canterbury's brougham.

Define art as you please, preferably in accordance with my ideas; assign it what place you will in the moral system; and then discriminate between works of art according to their excellence in that quality, or those qualities, that you have laid down in your definition as essential and peculiar to works of art. You may, of course, make ethical judgments about particular works, not as works of art, but as members of some other class, or as independent and unclassified parts of the universe. You may hold that a particular picture by the President of the Royal Academy is a greater means to good than one by the glory of the New English Art Club, and that a penny bun is better than either. In such a case you will be making a moral and not an aesthetic judgment. Therefore it will be right to take into account the area of the canvases, the thickness of the frames, and the potential value of each as fuel or shelter against the rigours of our climate. In casting up accounts you should not neglect their possible effects on the middle-aged people who visit Burlington House and the Suffolk Street Gallery; nor must you forget the consciences of those who handle the Chantry funds, or of those whom high prices provoke to emulation. You will be making a moral and not an aesthetic judgment; and if you have concluded that neither picture is a work of art, though you may be wasting your time, you will not be making yourself ridiculous. But when you treat a picture as a work of art, you have, unconsciously perhaps, made a far more important moral judgment. You have assigned it to a class of objects so powerful and direct as means to spiritual exaltation that all minor merits are inconsiderable. Paradoxical as it may seem, the only relevant qualities in a work of art, judged as art, are artistic qualities: judged as a means to good, no other qualities are worth considering; for there are no qualities of greater moral value than artistic qualities, since there is no greater means to good than art.

Art and Truth

I. A. RICHARDS
Poetry and Beliefs [1]

THE BUSINESS OF THE POET, as we have seen, is to give order and coherence, and so freedom, to a body of experience. To do so through words which act as its skeleton, as a structure by which the impulses which make up the experience are adjusted to one another and act together. The means by which words do this are many and varied. To work them out is a problem for linguistic psychology, that embarrassed young heir to philosophy. What little can be done shows already that most critical dogmas of the past are either false or nonsense. A little knowledge is not here a danger, but clears the air in a remarkable way.

Roughly and inadequately, even in the dim light of present knowledge, we can say that words work in the poem in two main fashions. As sensory stimuli and as (in the *widest* sense) symbols. We must refrain from considering the sensory side of the poem, remarking only that it is *not* in the least independent of the other side, and that it has for definite reasons prior importance in most poetry. We must confine ourselves to the other function of words in the poem, or rather, omitting much that is of secondary relevance, to one form of that function, let me call it *pseudo-statement*.

It will be admitted—by those who distinguish between scientific state-

[1] From I. A. Richards, *Science and Poetry,* 2nd ed., rev. and enl. (London: Kegan Paul, Trench, Trubner & Co., Ltd., 1935), pp. 61–74, 92–94. Reprinted by permission. The Appendix, pp. 92–94, is included at the request of Mr. Richards. (Eds.)

ment, where truth is ultimately a matter of verification as this is understood in the laboratory, and emotive utterance, where "truth" is primarily acceptability *by* some attitude, and more remotely is the acceptability *of* this attitude itself—that it is *not* the poet's business to make scientific statements. Yet poetry has constantly the air of making statements, and important ones; which is one reason why some mathematicians cannot read it. They find the alleged statements to be *false*. It will be agreed that their approach to poetry and their expectations from it are mistaken. But what exactly is the other, the right, the poetic, approach and how does it differ from the mathematical?

The poetic approach evidently limits the framework of possible consequences into which the pseudo-statement is taken. For the scientific approach this framework is unlimited. Any and every consequence is relevant. If any of the consequences of a statement conflicts with acknowledged fact then so much the worse for the statement. Not so with the pseudo-statement when poetically approached. The problem is—just how does the limitation work? One tempting account is in terms of a supposed universe of discourse, a world of make-believe, of imagination, of recognized fictions common to the poet and his readers. A pseudo-statement which fits into this system of assumptions would be regarded as "poetically true"; one which does not, as "poetically false." This attempt to treat "poetic truth" on the model of general "coherence theories" is very natural for certain schools of logicians but is inadequate, on the wrong lines from the outset. To mention two objections, out of many; there is no means of discovering what the "universe of discourse" is on any occasion, and the kind of coherence which must hold within it, supposing it to be discoverable, is not an affair of logical relations. Attempt to define the system of propositions into which

> "O Rose, thou art sick!"

must fit, and the logical relations which most hold between them if it is to be "poetically true"; the absurdity of the theory becomes evident.

We must look further. In the poetic approach the relevant consequences are not logical or to be arrived at by a partial relaxation of logic. Except occasionally and by accident logic does not enter at all. They are the consequences which arise through our emotional organization. The acceptance which a pseudo-statement receives is entirely governed by its effects upon our feelings and attitudes. Logic only comes in, if at all, in subordination, as a servant to our emotional response. It is an unruly servant, however, as poets and readers are constantly discovering. A pseudo-statement is "true" if it suits and serves some attitude or links together attitudes which on other grounds are desirable. This kind of "truth" is so opposed to scientific "truth" that it is a pity to use so similar a word, but at present it is difficult to avoid the malpractice.[2]

This brief analysis may be sufficient to indicate the fundamental disparity and opposition between pseudo-statements as they occur in poetry and statements as they occur in science. A pseudo-statement is a form of words which is justified entirely by its effect in releasing or organizing our impulses and attitudes (due regard being had for the better or worse organizations of these *inter se*); a statement, on the other hand, is justified by its truth, *i.e.,* its correspondence, in a highly technical sense, with the fact to which it points.

Statements true and false alike do, of course, constantly touch off attitudes and action. Our daily practical existence is largely guided by them. On the whole true statements are of more service to us than false ones. None the less we do not and, at present, cannot order our emotions and attitudes by true statements alone. Nor is there any probability that we ever shall contrive to do so. This is one of the great new dangers to which civilization is exposed. Countless pseudo-statements—about God, about the universe, about human nature, the relations of mind to mind, about the soul, its rank and destiny—pseudo-statements which are pivotal points in the organization of the mind, vital to its well-being, have suddenly become, for sincere, honest and informed minds, impossible to believe as for centuries they have been believed.[3] The accustomed incidences of the modes of believing are changed irrecoverably; and the knowledge which has displaced them is not of a kind upon which an equally fine organization of the mind can be based.

This is the contemporary situation. The remedy, since there is no prospect of our gaining adequate knowledge, and since indeed it is fairly clear that scientific knowledge cannot meet this need, is to cut our pseudo-statements free from that kind of belief which is appropriate to verified statements. So released they will be changed, of course, but they can still be the main instruments by which we order our attitudes to one another and to the world. This is not a desperate remedy, for, as poetry conclusively shows, even the most

---

[2] A pseudo-statement, as I use the term, is not necessarily false in any sense. It is merely a form of words whose scientific truth or falsity is irrelevant to the purpose in hand.

"Logic" in this paragraph is, of course, being used in a limited and conventional, or popular, sense.

[3] See Appendix. For the mind I am considering here the question "Do I believe *x?*" is no longer the same. Not only the "What" that is to be believed but the "How" of the believing has changed—through the segregation of science and its clarification of the techniques of proof. This is the danger; and the remedy suggested is a further differentiation of the "Hows." To these differences correspond differences in the senses of "is so" and "being" where, as is commonly the case, "is so" and "being" assert believings. As we admit this, the world that "is" divides into worlds incommensurable in respect of so called "degrees of reality." Yet, and this is all-important, these worlds have an order, with regard to one another, which is the order of the mind; and interference between them imperils sanity.

important among our attitudes can be aroused and maintained without any believing of a factual or verifiable order entering in at all. We need no such beliefs, and indeed we must have none, if we are to read *King Lear*. Pseudo-statements to which we attach no belief and statements proper, such as science provides, cannot conflict. It is only when we introduce inappropriate kinds of believing into poetry that danger arises. To do so is from this point of view a profanation of poetry.

Yet an important branch of criticism which has attracted the best talents from prehistoric times until to-day consists of the endeavour to persuade men that the functions of science and poetry are identical, or that the one is a "higher form" of the other, or that they conflict and we must choose between them.

The root of this persistent endeavour has still to be mentioned; it is the same as that from which the Magical View of the world arose. If we give to a pseudo-statement the kind of unqualified acceptance which belongs by right only to certified scientific statements—and those judgments of the routine of perception and action from which science derives—, if we can contrive to do this, the impulses and attitudes with which we respond to it gain a notable stability and vigour. Briefly, if we can contrive to believe poetry, then the world *seems,* while we do so, to be transfigured. It used to be comparatively easy to do this, and the habit has become well established. With the extension of science and the neutralization of nature it has become difficult as well as dangerous. Yet it is still alluring; it has many analogies with drug-taking. Hence the endeavours of the critics referred to. Various subterfuges have been devised along the lines of regarding Poetic Truth as figurative, symbolic; or as more immediate, as a truth of Intuition transcending common knowledge; or as a higher form of the same truth that science yields. Such attempts to use poetry as a denial or as a corrective of science are very common. One point can be made against them all: they are never worked out in detail. There is no equivalent of Mill's *Logic* expounding any of them. The language in which they are framed is usually a blend of obsolete psychology and emotive exclamations.

The long-established and much-encouraged habit of giving to emotive utterances—whether pseudo-statements simple, or looser and larger wholes taken as saying something figuratively—the kind of assent which we give to unescapable facts, has for most people debilitated a wide range of their responses. A few scientists, caught young and brought up in the laboratory, are free from it; but then, as a rule, they pay no *serious* attention to poetry. For most men the recognition of the neutrality of nature brings about—through this habit—a divorce from poetry. They are so used to having their responses propped up by beliefs, however vague, that when these shadowy supports are removed they are no longer able to respond. Their attitudes to so many things have been forced in the past, over-encouraged. And when the world-picture ceases to assist there is a collapse. Over whole tracts of natural emotional response we are to-day like a bed of dahlias whose sticks have been removed. And this effect of the neutralization of nature is perhaps only in its beginnings. However, human nature has a prodigious resilience. Love poetry seems able to out-play psychoanalysis.

A sense of desolation, of uncertainty, of futility, of the groundlessness of aspirations, of the vanity of endeavour, and a thirst for a life-giving water which seems suddenly to have failed, are the signs in consciousness of this necessary reorganization of our lives.[4] Our attitudes and impulses are being compelled to become self-supporting; they are being driven back upon their biological justification, made once again sufficient to themselves. And the only impulses which seem strong enough to continue unflagging are commonly so crude that, to more finely developed individuals, they hardly seem worth having. Such people cannot live by warmth, food, fighting, drink, and sex alone. Those who are least affected by the change are those who are emotionally least removed from the animals. As we shall see at the close of this essay, even a considerable poet may attempt to find relief by a reversion to primitive mentality.

It is important to diagnose the disease correctly and to put the blame in the right quarter. Usually it is some alleged "materialism" of science which is denounced. This mistake is due partly to clumsy thinking, but chiefly to relics of the Magical View. For even if the Universe were "spiritual" all through (whatever that assertion might mean; all such assertions are probably nonsense), that would not make it any more accordant to human attitudes. It is not what the universe is made of but how it works, the law it follows, which makes verifiable knowledge of it incapable of spurring on our emotional responses, and further, the nature of knowledge itself makes it inadequate. The contact with things which we therein establish is too sketchy and indirect to help us. We are beginning to know too much about

---

[4] My debt to *The Waste Land* here will be evident. The original footnote seems to have puzzled Mr. Eliot and some other readers. Well it might! In saying, though, that he "had effected a complete severance between his poetry and all beliefs" I was referring not to the poet's own history, but to the technical detachment of the poetry. And the way in which he then seemed to me to have "realized what might otherwise have remained a speculative possibility" was by finding a new order through the contemplation and exhibition of disorder.

"Yes! Very funny this terrible thing is. A man that is born falls into a dream like a man who falls into the sea. If he tries to climb out into the air as inexperienced people endeavour to do, he drowns—*nicht wahr?* . . . No! I tell you! The way is to the destructive element submit yourself, and with the exertions of your hands and feet in the water make the deep, deep sea keep you up. So if you ask me how to be? In the destructive element immerse . . . that was the way." *Lord Jim*, p. 216. Mr. Eliot's later verse has sometimes shown still less "dread of the unknown depths." That, at least, seems in part to explain to me why *Ash Wednesday* is better poetry than even the best sections of *The Waste Land*.

the bond which unites the mind to its object in knowledge [5] for that old dream of a perfect knowledge which would guarantee perfect life to retain its sanction. What was thought to be pure knowledge, we see now to have been shot through with hope and desire, with fear and wonder; and these intrusive elements indeed gave it all its power to support our lives. In knowledge, in the "How?" of events, we can find hints by which to take advantage of circumstances in our favour and avoid mischances. But we cannot get from it a *raison d'être* or a justification of more than a relatively lowly kind of life.

The justification, or the reverse, of any attitude lies, not in the object, but in itself, in its serviceableness to the whole personality. Upon its place in the whole system of attitudes, which is the personality, all its worth depends. This is as true for the subtle, finely compounded attitudes of the civilized individual as for the simpler attitudes of the child.

In brief, the imaginative life is its own justification; and this fact must be faced, although sometimes—by a lover, for example—it may be very difficult to accept. When it is faced, it is apparent that all the attitudes to other human beings and to the world in all its aspects, which have been serviceable to humanity, remain as they were, as valuable as ever. Hesitation felt in admitting this is a measure of the strength of the evil habit I have been describing. But many of these attitudes, valuable as ever, are, now that they are being set free, more difficult to maintain, because we still hunger after a basis in belief.

Appendix

Two chief words seem likely occasions of misunderstanding in the above; and they have in fact misled some readers. One is *Nature,* the other is *Belief.*

Nature is evidently as variable a word as can be used. It senses range from the mere inclusive THAT, in which we live and of which we are a part, to whatever would correspond to the most detailed and interconnected account we could attain of this. Or we omit ourselves (and other minds) and make Nature *either* what influences us (in which case we should not forget our metabolism), *or* an object we apprehend (in which case there are as many Natures as there are types of apprehension we care to distinguish). And what is "natural" to one culture is strange and artificial to another. (See *Mencius on the Mind,* chap. III.) More deceptively, the view here being inseparable from the eye, and this being a matter of habitual speculation, we may talk,

---

[5] Verifiable scientific knowledge, of course. Shift the sense of "knowledge" to include hope and desire and fear as well as reference, and what I am saying would no longer be true. But then the relevant sense of "true" would have changed too. Its sanction would no longer be verifiability.

as we think, the same language and yet put very different things into Nature; and what we then find will not be unconnected with what we have put in. I have attempted some further discussion of these questions in Chapters VI and VII of *Coleridge on Imagination*.

Belief. Two "beliefs" may differ from one another: (1) In their objects (2) In their statements or expressions (3) In their modes (4) In their grounds (5) In their occasions (6) In their connections with other "beliefs" (7) In their links with possible action (8) And in other ways. Our chief evidence usually for the beliefs of other people (and often for our own) must be some statement or other expression. But very different beliefs may fittingly receive the same expression. Most words used in stating any speculative opinion are as ambiguous as "Belief"; and yet by such words belief-objects must be distinguished.

But in the case of "belief" there is an additional difficulty. Neither it nor its partial synonyms suggest the great variety of the attitudes (3) that are commonly covered (and confused) by the term. They are often treated as though they were mere variations in degree. Of what? Of belief, it would be said. But this is no better than the parallel trick of treating all varieties of love as a mere more or less only further differentiated by their objects. Such crude over-simplifications distort the structure of the mind and, although favourite suasive devices with some well-intentioned preachers, are disastrous.

There is an ample field here awaiting a type of dispassionate inquiry which it has seldom received. A world threatened with ever more and more leisure should not be too impatient of important and explorable subtleties.

Meanwhile, as with "Nature," misunderstandings should neither provoke nor surprise. I should not be much less at my reader's mercy if I were to add notes doubling the length of this little book. On so vast a matter, even the largest book could contain no more than a sketch of how things have seemed to be sometimes to the writer.

MORRIS WEITZ

Art, Language and Truth [1]

The "Emotive-Referential" Dispute: Literature and Truth Claims

IN CONTEMPORARY AESTHETIC INQUIRY there is a good deal of discussion about the linguistic character of art. Morris, Langer, Cassirer, Richards, Burke, Blackmur, Panofsky, Ducasse, Freud, and others have dealt extensively with this aspect of art. Parker has pointed out that, historically speaking, this is a rather new approach. Two other basic interpretations of art preceded this linguistic one, the dominant view of our era. First was the doctrine that art is essentially imitation, either of the universal features of reality, including human experience, or of the beautiful in nature. This doctrine, whose hegemony lasted some two thousand years and which was known as classicism, was unable to explain much of art, especially fantastic art; consequently, it was succeeded by the romantic theory, according to which art is essentially imagination. Further probings into the nature of art, especially in the last one hundred years or so, disclosed the social and communicative character of art, and led eventually to the contemporary view that art is essentially a language.[2]

The organic theory concurs with this prevalent conception of art. Because it stresses the expressive dimension of art, that is, the fact that all of its constituents may function as icons, indices, or symbols to spectators, it accepts the thesis that art is a language.

But to affirm that art is a language immediately provokes the query, what *kind* of language? The most imposing, perhaps even the most accepted, view today is that art is an *emotive* language. Ducasse and I. A. Richards are among the champions of this view. Ducasse writes: *"Art is essentially a form of language—namely, the language of feeling, mood, sentiment, and emo-*

---

[1] Reprinted by permission of the publishers from Morris Weitz, *Philosophy of the Arts* (Cambridge, Mass.: Harvard University Press, 1950), pp. 134–152. (Eds.)

[2] DeWitt H. Parker, "Aesthetics," *Twentieth Century Philosophy,* ed. Dagobert D. Runes, New York, Philosophical Library, pp. 42–45.

tional attitude. It is thus to be distinguished from the language of assertion." [3]

However, it is Richards who has offered the details of the emotive theory. According to him (and C. K. Ogden), at least in *The Meaning of Meaning,* which constitutes the prolegomenon to Richards' later work, language has many functions. It symbolizes thought, expresses attitudes of the speaker, evokes attitudes in the listener, and promotes certain effects. But these can be sharply divided into two main functions, the symbolic and the emotive. Symbolic language, or the symbolic use of words, is the statement, recording, support, and communication of thought, whereas emotive language, or the emotive use of words, is the evocation, expression, or excitation of feelings and attitudes.

To illustrate: Suppose I say, "This painting is the work of Picasso." My statement is informative, referential, and true or false, depending upon whether or not the painting *is* Picasso's. But if I say, "This painting is excellent," then, according to Richards, I am not really saying anything *about* the painting; instead I am articulating or expressing my feelings of approval toward it, perhaps even in the hope of evoking similar feelings in my listeners.

This distinction between the emotive and the symbolic (referential) uses of language Richards regards as basic to the distinction between art, especially literature, which is his main problem, and science. To understand the emotive use of language and to use it exclusively is the function of art. Art ought to abandon its quest for knowledge and truth, for it is not necessary to know *what* things are in order to express our feelings toward them. [4]

In its semantical dimension, the emotive theory of Ducasse and Richards is the view that art, as a system of signs, does not embody propositions or referential assertions, that is, *truth claims,* but serves only as the expression or excitation of feelings, emotions and attitudes. Carnap has supplemented this view, which is essentially positivistic, by affirming the kinship of artistic (also metaphysical and ethical) language and certain body gestures. I laugh, I cry, I yell, or I stamp my feet. My laughing, crying, yelling, or stamping my feet expresses my feelings and attitudes. Linguistically, when I perform in these ways, I communicate something to my audience; and I may even inspire them to similar body activity. But I do not say anything; I state no fact; I make no claim. What I do is not true or false, but an expression of feeling. So too with art; it is also a form of emotional gesture, a kind of stamping of one's feet or clapping of one's hands, but ever so nicely! Thus,

---

[3] C. J. Ducasse, *Art, the Critics, and You,* New York, Oskar Piest, 1944, pp. 52–53 (italics in original).

[4] C. K. Ogden and I. A. Richards, *The Meaning of Meaning,* New York, Harcourt, Brace and Company, 1923, esp. pp. 123–126, 147–151, 227–229, and 230–236.

the language of art, from literature to music, is closer to body gestures than it is to the language of science or empirical statements.[5]

This theory raises an extremely important question, one which is central to the contemporary doctrine that art is a language. Is art merely an emotive language or is it referential and assertive as well? *Can art embody truth claims?*

Among contemporary aestheticians who have been engaging in debate on this issue, T. M. Greene has offered the most extensive defense of the doctrine that art does embody truth claims, and he maintains that all of the arts, not only literature, embody "propositional truth." His theory has been discussed in two recent books, by B. C. Heyl and by John Hospers. Both of these critics, I think, have succeeded in exposing the inadequacies of Greene's position, so that there would be no point here in entering into *their* particular dispute, especially if one, like myself, does not accept the premises of either side of the dispute.[6] Instead, we shall present a different solution.

Hospers, in his critique of Greene, comments: "Professor Greene might have sought a way out which in fact he does not, namely, to say that works of art are *implied* assertions (or else that they imply assertions)." [7]

This "way out" has already been indicated by DeWitt Parker, in his formulation of the concept of "depth meaning."

> Many poems and some works of plastic art possess what I like to call "depth meanings"—meanings of universal scope underneath relatively concrete meanings or ideas. Thus in the following line of one of Frost's little poems
>
> Nothing gold can stay
>
> the word "gold" has its usual surface meaning, but underneath that is its depth meaning, precious; so in addition to saying that nothing golden can endure, the poet is saying that nothing valuable can abide —a more universal statement.[8]

In my opinion, the introduction of Parker's concept of depth meaning offers us a new way of analyzing the problem of truth in art. I do not think that it solves the whole problem for us but it does seem to solve at least part of it, and in the following way. Let us, for the moment, grant the positivistic thesis that literature (with the trivial exception of those statements in it that

---

[5] Rudolf Carnap, *Philosophy and Logical Syntax,* London, Kegan Paul, Trench, Trubner and Company, 1935, Chap. 1.

[6] T. M. Greene, *The Arts and the Art of Criticism,* Princeton, Princeton University Press, 1940, Chap. xxiii; B. C. Heyl, *New Bearings in Esthetics and Art Criticism,* New Haven, Yale University Press, 1943, Chap. iii; and John Hospers, *Meaning and Truth in the Arts,* Chapel Hill, University of North Carolina Press, 1946, Chaps. v–vi.

[7] John Hospers, *op. cit.,* p. 160 (italics in original).

[8] DeWitt H. Parker, *The Principles of Aesthetics,* second edition (New York: F. S. Crofts and Company, 1946), p. 32.

are about historical figures and places, etc.) is primarily emotive. Still, it does not follow that none of it is also referential. For if we employ Parker's concept of depth meaning, we may assert that literature is emotive on one linguistic dimension, the surface meanings, and referential on the other, the depth meanings. We can then point out that the emotive theory possesses an initial credibility only because it neglects the entire realm of depth meanings in literature by confining itself to the meanings presented immediately through the *printed* page.

As an example of a work in literature that embodys certain truth claims through the presence of depth meanings, I will choose the recent American novel, *Native Son,* by Richard Wright.[9] The novel deals with a young Negro, Bigger Thomas, who is without faith in his poverty-stricken, frustrated life. His feelings and attitudes toward life are inchoate except that he deeply resents his status as a Negro. His tragedy begins when he accepts a charity job as a chauffeur given him by one of the millionaire landlords of Chicago's South Side slums, where Bigger lives. The millionaire has a daughter, Mary Dalton, who is having her fling with Communism. Naturally, she becomes interested in Bigger and desires to get a glimpse into his way of life. She and her boy friend trick him into acting as their guide to the Negro dives of the South Side.

During the course of the evening, Mary gets drunk and, after persuading her boy friend to leave her alone with Bigger on her way home, she makes advances to him. Bigger is not interested, knowing well the penalty that would be meted out to him if he accepted her invitation. Instead he takes her home and carries her into her bedroom, trying to keep her quiet and put her to sleep. Mary's mother, who is blind, hears the noises of her daughter and enters the room. Bigger, terrified at her presence, is forced to put a pillow over Mary's head, to stop her mumbling. Mrs. Dalton finally leaves and Bigger removes the pillow, only to discover that Mary has suffocated. Desperate, Bigger decides to burn his victim rather than to try to explain what happened. The rest of the story concerns the discovery of Bigger's guilt, his escape and second murder, then his arrest, trial, and finally his execution.

So much for the story. As a story it is all that an emotionalist could wish for: it is exciting and beautifully written, at a kind of white heat that keeps up with the plot. The question now arises, are there any truth claims in the novel? The answer, according to our hypothesis, depends upon the presence and nature of the depth meanings.

The first thing we notice as we read the novel is that it is not about an isolated Negro but about all Negroes and group minorities in America.

---

[9] This example and its analysis constitute a revision of the author's articles, "Does Art Tell the Truth?" and "The Logic of Art," *Philosophy and Phenomenological Research,* III (March, 1943), no. 3; and V (March, 1945), no. 3.

Bigger Thomas, the subject of the novel, in the course of his experiences, epitomizes and embodies the truth claim that individual freedom is still an abortive ideal in America, since our social injustices cancel out individual development.

As contemporary novels go, however, this is a rather trivial thematic truth claim, and one might be led to infer from it that even if some novels do contain truth claims through their depth meanings, they are trivial and consequently aesthetically insignificant.

But a careful reading of Wright's novel will, I believe, reveal another depth meaning and truth claim that is far from trivial; in fact, it is so poignant that it saves the work from being merely another proletarian novel. It is to be found in the final pages of the novel where Bigger, having been sentenced to die, is talking with his lawyer, Mr. Max. Mr. Max is trying to soothe Bigger. He tells him that he will not die in vain, that he will be remembered as another martyr of exploitation. But all of this means nothing to Bigger, who is preoccupied with his own fate and his own life's meaning. The last paragraphs are especially significant:

> "Mr. Max, you go home. I'm all right . . . Sounds funny, Mr. Max, but when I think about what you say I kind of feel what I wanted. It makes me feel I was kind of right . . ." Max opened his mouth to say something and Bigger drowned out his voice. "I ain't trying to forgive nobody and I ain't asking for nobody to forgive me. I ain't going to cry. They wouldn't let me live and I killed. Maybe it ain't fair to kill and I reckon I really didn't want to kill. But when I think of why all the killing was, I begin to feel what I wanted, what I am . . ."
>
> Bigger saw Max back away from him with compressed lips. But he felt he had to make Max understand how he saw things now.
>
> "I didn't want to kill!" Bigger shouted. "But what I killed for, I *am!* It must've been pretty deep in me to make me kill! I must have felt it awful hard to murder . . ."
>
> Max lifted his hand to touch Bigger, but did not.
>
> "No; no; no . . . Bigger, not that . . ." Max pleaded despairingly.
>
> "What I killed for must've been good!" Bigger's voice was full of frenzied anguish. "It must have been good! When a man kills, it's for something . . . I didn't know I was really alive in this world until I felt things hard enough to kill for 'em . . . It's the truth, Mr. Max. I can say it now, 'cause I'm going to die. I know what I'm saying real good and I know how it sounds. But I am all right when I look at it that way . . ."
>
> Max's eyes were full of terror. Several times his body moved nervously, as if he were about to go to Bigger, but he stood still.

"I'm all right, Mr. Max. Just go and tell Ma I was all right and not to worry none, see? Tell her I was all right and wasn't crying none . . ."

Max's eyes were wet. Slowly, he extended his hand. Bigger shook it.

"Good-bye, Bigger," he said quietly.

"Good-bye, Mr. Max." [10]

This scene, especially as it is read in its relations to the rest of the novel, contains a depth meaning that is a profound truth claim concerning the present state of man. Through Bigger, and in this speech, especially, Wright is *claiming* that the only freedom left to man is the freedom to destroy, first others and finally oneself. No other novelist or poet has articulated this idea, so far as I know. Nor even has any contemporary sociologist or philosopher. Here, then, is an example where the artist not only asserts something important (which is true or false) but is the only intellectual to have done so.

It is only when one comes to discern this depth meaning that the novel takes on its basic significance. Until it becomes clear that Bigger is more than a symbol of exploitation and represents *all* men who struggle to realize themselves in a world full of evil, the novel remains a mere adequate proletarian one. But it is this meaning that gives the novel its universality. The symbol of Bigger, the killer of white women, who is modern man in his own tortured self-destructiveness, vivifies the whole work and makes of each scene, especially the courtroom scene, something much deeper than it could possibly be when the novel is analyzed in terms of the other depth meanings alone. The novel rises above the truth claim concerning the exploitation of minorities in America to signify what Wright regards as the tragedy of modern man, that he can attain autonomy only by destruction and eventual self-destruction.

It is important to point out that the truth claims of literature are not always true. Like the truth claims of science, they may be false, too. Consequently, when we say that *Native Son* contains truth claims, we do not mean to be asserting that it contains a number of *truths*. It may very well be that the depth meanings of *Native Son* are all false. But so far as our problem is concerned, that would make no difference at all. The important thing is that much of literature contains truth claims, hence is as linguistically referential as science.

In fact, I find it incredible that aestheticians who read contemporary fiction should support the emotive theory of the language of art. A survey of our own American realistic fiction, especially the novels of Dos Passos, Hemingway, Faulkner, Steinbeck, and Farrell, cannot but reveal the presence

---

[10] Richard Wright, *Native Son*, New York, Harper and Brothers, 1940, p. 358; reprinted by courtesy of the publishers. (Eds.)

of truth claims in the depth meanings of their work. The Farrell trilogy, *Studs Lonigan,* for example, contains as its basic depth meaning and truth claim the judgment that American life, dominated by bourgeois values, is vacuous and spiritually sick to the core.

What does it mean to say that a work of literature contains a depth meaning? That is to say, what is the logical status of a depth meaning and artistic truth claim? This is a large question, but at least part of the answer, I believe, is the following.

In *some* works of literature, where there are these depth meanings which do function as truth claims, there appear black marks on paper. These marks serve as signs of concepts or ideas of one sort or another to readers; and these ideas, in syntactical juxtaposition to each other, comprise the sentences and meanings of the work. But these are its surface or printed meanings, and they are, logically speaking, what we may call, according to the terminology of Russell's theory of logical types, "first-order" meanings. And if we grant the positivist his thesis that art is initially an emotive language, we may refer to these as emotive first-order meanings.

Now, besides these meanings, these works contain certain depth meanings which, logically speaking, are "second-order" in character. These meanings may be propositional in nature and function as truth claims. They are contained in the work of art even though they do not appear in print. To assert that they are contained in the work is to say that they are *implied* by the first-order meanings, where by implication we do not mean Russell's material or Lewis's strict implication, since neither of these conceives correctly our nonmathematical, ordinary sense of implication. Part of what is meant by implication in the sense in which we are using it has been formulated best by G. E. Moore when he writes, for example, "There seems to me to be nothing mysterious about this sense of 'imply,' in which if you assert that you went to the pictures last Tuesday, you *imply,* though you don't *assert,* that you believe or know that you did." [11] Thus, when we say that a literary work, such as *Native Son,* contains a second-order truth claim, what is meant is that some of the printed meanings imply the truth claim even though it is not expressed in the sense of appearing in print. Truth claims are second-order, then, because they depend upon and cannot exist without the printed first-order meanings. They are logical functions of the first-order meanings in the way that "Napoleon had all the characteristics of a great general" would be a second-order logical function of the first-order sentences, "Napoleon had courage," "Napoleon had cunning," "Napoleon had loyalty," etc., were these latter sentences to appear in a book on the printed page and the former not to appear in print at all but still be part of the total book.

---

[11] *The Philosophy of G. E. Moore,* ed. P. A. Schilpp (Evanston: Northwestern University Press, 1942), p. 542 (italics in original).

Alfred Ayer, who supports the positivist position in its general orientation, has challenged its interpretation of the language of art. He denies that the language of art is emotive. In literature, even in poetry, the sentences are to be construed as linguistically referential in character. But, with the trivial exception of references to historical events, persons, etc., they are all false.[12]

This is an improvement upon the positivist theory of art, I think; but it, too, is incorrect, since not *all* the truth claims or referential statements of literature *are* false. There is more reason to believe that some of them (for example, that race prejudice in America thwarts individual growth) are true than there is for believing that all of them are false.

The emotive theory aside, the situation regarding the language of literature in relation to truth claims seems to me to include at least three different categories. First—and let us use examples from poetry throughout for the sake of simplicity, although let it be understood that the same analysis is applicable to drama, the novel, and the short story—there are many poems that contain truth claims as surface sentences, and not necessarily as depth meanings. Longfellow's "A Psalm of Life" contains the following lines:

> Life is real! Life is earnest!
>   And the grave is not its goal;
> Dust thou art, to dust returnest,
>   Was not spoken of the soul.
>
> Not enjoyment, and not sorrow,
>   Is our destined end or way;
> But to act, that each tomorrow
>   Find us farther than today.

Whatever we may think of this specimen, and it *is* pretty bad, we cannot deny that it makes a number of truth claims about the nature of life directly through the printed sentences of the poem.

So does this example from Shakespeare:

> Blow, blow, thou winter wind!
> Thou art not so unkind
> As man's ingratitude.

Or this one:

> Let me not to the marriage of true minds
> Admit impediments. Love is not love
> Which alters when it alteration finds,
> Or bends with the remover to remove:
> O, no! it is an ever-fixèd mark
> That looks on tempests and is never shaken.

---

[12] A. J. Ayer, *Language, Truth and Logic* (New York: Oxford University Press, 1936), pp. 37–39.

In both of these the poet is actually stating something that purports to be as much a revelation of certain aspects of reality (namely, the world of human experience) as any statement in science. In neither of these examples is it even necessary to paraphrase the claim since it is made so clearly; and in each case, if we wish to do so, or if we regard it as aesthetically relevant to do so, we may raise the question of the actual truth or falsity of the claim.

Poetry affords us many, many examples of printed truth claims. It is futile to deny it and I think the reason distinguished readers of poetry like Richards have denied it is that they did not want the truth claims of poetry to enter into our evaluation of the poetry. But we must keep our problems separate. Our immediate problem is whether or not poetry is able to embody truth claims. The examples given show that some poems, good and bad, do embody these claims, and within the surface-printed sentences. In no way does it follow from the presence of these truth claims that they constitute the most important element in poetry; or that they are the whole of any poetic communication; or even that they are important or aesthetically relevant at all. All of these are quite different considerations. In fact, there are at least four different questions to keep straight, and we are at present dealing only with the first. These questions are: (1) does some or all art embody truth claims? (2) ought any art to embody truth claims? (3) does the presence of truth claims make a difference to our appreciation of those works that have them? (4) ought the presence of truth claims to make a difference in our appreciation of those works that contain them? If critics and aestheticians had kept these questions distinct, we might have avoided a great deal of unnecessary debate during the last twenty-five years.

We shall discuss the last three questions in our next chapter.[13] Let us now continue with the first and the enumeration of the categories of the language of poetry. Poetry can embody truth claims within the printed sentences; this is the first category. It can also embody truth claims as depth meanings. The truth claim of "Prufrock," namely, that there are two kinds of life and two kinds of death, is never stated as a printed sentence anywhere in the entire poem; yet it is part of the total poem as surely as the connotative overtones of coffee spoons are within the poem, even though they are never printed either.

Another example of a poem that contains a truth claim presented as a depth meaning is Yeats's "A Deep-Sworn Vow." [14]

This is an extremely poignant communication, full of passion and paradox. Among its constituents is the depth meaning, not printed but present

---

[13] This chapter is not included in this selection. (Eds.)

[14] From W. B. Yeats, *The Wild Swans at Coole,* New York, The Macmillan Company, 1919. The text of the poem, included in Mr. Weitz's essay, is here omitted (Eds.).

nevertheless, that one cannot erase the memory of true love; this constituent functions as a truth claim about the content of human experience.

One could with no difficulty at all list hundreds of examples of poetic communications in which depth meanings embody truth claims that serve as artistic commentaries on human experience by the poet. I conclude, therefore, that the emotive theory is simply false in its assertion that no art contains referential meanings.

The only element of truth in the emotive theory, at least so far as literature is concerned, lies in the third of our classifications. There are many poems in which there are no printed or implied truth claims, but instead articulations of wishes or commands or expressions of attitudes.

In Longfellow's "A Psalm of Life," we have the following combination of a wish and a command:

> In the world's broad field of battle,
>   In the bivouac of Life,
> Be not like dumb, driven cattle!
>   Be a hero in the strife!

> Trust no Future, howe'er pleasant!
>   Let the dead Past bury its dead!
> Act,—act in the living Present!
>   Heart within, and God o'erhead!

In Elizabeth Barrett Browning's "How Do I Love Thee," we have a pure expression of an attitude—of love—toward some object—the beloved:

> How do I love thee? Let me count the ways.
> I love thee to the depth and breadth and height
> My soul can reach, when feeling out of sight
> For the ends of Being and ideal Grace.
> I love thee to the level of everyday's
> Most quiet need, by sun and candle-light.
> I love thee freely, as men strive for Right;
> I love thee purely, as they turn from Praise.
> I love thee with the passion put to use
> In my old griefs, and with my childhood's faith.
> I love thee with a love I seemed to lose
> With my lost saints,—I love thee with the breath,
> Smiles, tears, of all my life!—and, if God choose,
> I shall but love thee better after death.

Finally, consider E. E. Cummings's "Portrait," in which the poet expresses his cavalier, flippant attitude toward death, and in which there is no truth claim stated or implied:

Buffalo Bill's
defunct
         who used to
         ride a watersmooth-silver
                            stallion
and break onetwothreefourfive pigeonsjustlikethat
                                              Jesus

he was a handsome man
                      and what i want to know is
how do you like your blueeyed boy
Mister Death [15]

Painting and Truth Claims

So much for the emotive theory and the problem of artistic truth
as it applies to literature. What can we say of painting and truth? Can paintings make truth claims?

Erwin Panofsky, one of the leading exponents of the iconological approach
to painting, has written about painting in such a way as to leave no doubt
that he believes it does contain certain truth claims or propositional assertions about the world. In his famous essay, *"Et in Arcadia Ego,"* which is
a model of the sort of analysis he engages in as an iconologist, Panofsky is
concerned with the Death theme in Watteau and Poussin. Here are a number of quotations from this essay:

> (1) [He says of Poussin's painting, *"Et in Arcadia Ego":*] The
> transformation of a mere *memento mori* into the revelation of a meta-
> physical principle which connects the present and the future with the
> past and overthrows the limits of individuality, means that "Life"
> is conceived as transitory yet blessed with indestructible beauty and
> felicity; on the other hand, "Death" is seen as a preserver as well as a
> destroyer. From this emerges the magnificent conception of a cyclical
> succession which subordinates the existence of individuals to the in-
> exorable laws of cosmic principles, both natural and moral, endow-
> ing every stage of this existence, however transitory, with a sub-
> stantial value of its own.

> (2) [In summary of Poussin's art:] Thus Poussin's conception of
> life as a condition free though fatebound, dignified though pathetic,
> imperishable though variable, transpires even in a composition which
> seems to be nothing but the offshoot of a rather conventional allegori-
> cal tradition.

> (3) Watteau's *Fêtes Champêtres,* too, may be called allegories of

---

[15] From *Collected Poems,* published by Harcourt, Brace and Company; copyright,
1923, by E. E. Cummings. Reprinted by permission. (Eds.)

transience; however, they neither visualize the annihilation of the past, nor the persistence of ideal forms outlasting the destruction of matter. They depict the fading away of reality as such. Existence itself seems to be subject to transience; past, present, and future fuse into a phantasmagoric realm in which the border-line between illusion and reality, dream and wakefulness, nature and art, mirth and melancholy, love and loneliness, life and the continuous process of dying, are thoroughly obliterated.[16]

It is clear, I think, from the above quotations, that Panofsky believes that paintings embody not only single truth claims but even systems of them as they become basic *Weltanschauungen*. It may be that Panofsky is too grandiloquent in his reflections upon the truth claims of paintings; but there seems to be some sense in which these truth claims can be made in painting. The problem for aesthetics, which curiously enough is similar to Kant's problem of justifying science, is to show *how* these truth claims are possible.

In order to do this, I am convinced, we must give up the positivistic version of the distinction between emotive and referential language. Perhaps the whole distinction should be repudiated, but I should not like to commit myself on this point.

There are certain kinds of activity that the positivists have traditionally classified as *pure* emoting but that upon analysis can be seen to embody referential propositional assertions about the world that are true or false in the way in which ordinary empirical judgments are. Consider as an example the Christian ritualistic act of kneeling in prayer. Now, according to the positivist view, this act is pure emoting, the expression of feelings and attitudes, and an act which, linguistically, may enter into communication, but only in the sense of inducing similar feelings and attitudes (or perhaps even opposing ones) in the spectators around the worshiper. And, most importantly, the positivist maintains, there is nothing in the act that asserts anything or constitutes a truth claim.

That kneeling in prayer is the expression of a feeling or attitude, or that it can induce others to act, need not be denied; but that it is pure emoting, completely nonassertive and nonreferential in character can be denied. Kneeling in prayer in a Christian ritualistic context includes also a referential propositional assertion or truth claim about the world. Specifically, the act itself includes, as *one* of its constituents, the assertion or claim that *there is a God Who is worthy of human respect*. Instead of affirming the proposition, "That God exists and is worthy of our respect," in ordinary verbal ways (i.e., in English, French, German, etc.), the worshiper gestures it as part

[16] Erwin Panofsky, "Et in Arcadia Ego," *Philosophy and History, Essays Presented to Ernst Cassirer,* ed. Raymond Klibansky and H. J. Paton (Oxford: The Clarendon Press, 1936), pp. 240, 242, 247–248. Reprinted by permission. (Eds.)

of his total act of kneeling in prayer. His action is the medium of conveying the asserted proposition; and the assertional part of the action may be construed as a truth claim about the existence and nature of God. It will not do to say that the whole action is true or false, just as one cannot say that the usual method of speaking, which is after all an act, too, is true or false. It is only one aspect of the act, namely, the asserted proposition, spoken or gestured as the case may be, that is true or false.[17]

I should like to propose that in paintings where there are truth claims they are presented in ways that resemble the truth claims offered in certain ritualistic acts like kneeling in prayer in a Christian society. Painting can make certain truth claims mainly through its constituents of the symbol, the subject, or both working in relation to the plastic expressive elements.

Consider, to begin with, one of Hobbema's landscapes in which, it is said, there is being asserted that nature is the conflict between the old and the new. Is this a valid conception of the capacities of painting? I think that it is. In Hobbema, it is the subject and its traditional transparently symbolic associations that embody the truth claim. The subject of the landscape is usually the representation of old, decaying trees being contrasted with the representation of young, powerful-looking, new trees. We interpret this subject as a sign of certain objects and concepts; these concepts have certain traditionally associated meanings; these meanings comprise the assertional propositional claim that nature is the struggle between the old and the new, the decaying and the living.

In the "Resurrection," by Piero della Francesca, there is present, as one of the constituents, the truth claim that man is in ignorance and darkness whereas God is in Truth and Light. Without raising any question about the whole problem of verifying such a claim, which would constitute a problem even in the prose statement of such a claim, we may say that the picture contains this truth claim through the very simple device of flooding the representations of Christ and the sky with tremendous light, and leaving the representation of man on the earth in relative shadow and darkness. All of these elements, with their transparently symbolic associations, add up to the assertional truth claim.

In the "Guernica," by Picasso, there is being asserted, among other things, that the victory of Fascism is the brutal destruction of everything. The painting asserts this through the bull, who symbolizes Fascism and who is relatively intact, and the other subjects—the soldier, the horse, the women, the children, and the houses—which are torn to pieces. All of these elements

---

17 We follow Sheffer and Lewis in distinguishing between propositions and assertions, and in regarding truth and falsity as attributes of assertions, not of propositions. See C. I. Lewis, *An Analysis of Knowledge and Valuation* (La Salle: The Open Court Publishing Company, 1946), pp. 48ff.

serve as a collective sign of the assertional proposition or truth claim regarding the nature of Fascism. One need only look at the painting to see that the artist is not wondering about the destructive character of Fascism, or denying it, or wishing it, or supposing it, but *asserting it*. The whole force of the painting leaves no doubt about the assertional character of the proposition, "That Fascism means the brutal destruction of everything."

Finally, one may say of Picasso's "Man with an All-Day Sucker" that it contains as one of its elements the truth claim that Fascism is the return to the infantile. This claim is made through the representation of a brutal-looking soldier (who is a transparent symbol of the Fascist), who is holding a sucker in the shape of a spear. The fact that the adult soldier is holding the weapon enables us to interpret the picture as claiming that Fascism is the return to the infantile, that is, the stage in which we lick all-day suckers.

Music and Truth Claims

So much for the arts of literature and painting as they relate to the problem of referential language or truth claims. Our primary aim has been to offer a refutation of the extravagant views of the emotive theory. We have no desire to demonstrate that all art embodies truth claims; in fact, in our discussion of poetry, we presented certain examples of poetry in which no truth claims were made. Stated in its positive form, our thesis has been that in some of the arts, especially in literature and painting, among the many elements there are to be found, either directly or indirectly, either stated or gestured, certain asserted propositions which are true or false. The extent of these truth claims in the arts is still an open question, and an invitation to further aesthetic analysis. The whole problem of truth claims in music, for example, needs a tremendous overhauling along the lines we have suggested or perhaps along other lines made possible by the continuing growth of the discipline of semiotic. The present writer, unfortunately, has doubts about the linguistic capacities of music. That music is a language in the sense of a system of signs that has meaning to listeners, we have already shown,[18] but that music is a language in the sense of a system of signs that contains propositions in the ways that literature or painting do, we do not feel ready to accept. The position of J. W. N. Sullivan, in his book, *Beethoven: His Spiritual Development,* to the effect that music can embody a philosophy and that Beethoven's music does, while it is attractive and one would like to believe it, is open to serious criticisms of the sort mentioned already in our previous discussions of extreme heteronomy in music.[19] The most I am

---

[18] See pp. 110ff. of *Philosophy of the Arts.* (Eds.)
[19] See pp. 112ff. of *Philosophy of the Arts.* (Eds.)

prepared to say, and this very tentatively, is that some music does contain *musical analogues* of assertions or truth claims. Consider, for example, Beethoven's last quartet, Opus 135. Many critics, even the composer himself, find in it the assertion that life is good or that affirmation of life is the answer to doubt. Perhaps this is too much to find in the music, but what one does find is the sequence of *musical* doubt and affirmation. The fourth and final movement begins slowly and is characterized in this beginning section by irresolution and hesitation within the musical sounds; this is followed by an allegro section in which all the musical doubt and irresolution give way to musical materials that are completely affirmative in their expressive character. Now, if we accept musical hesitation and affirmation as transparent symbols, we may say that this fourth movement embodies the contrast between doubt and affirmation, in which the latter comes after the former, as a kind of *reply* to it. But this is a musical reply, and the whole movement is at most an analogue of the claim that in life affirmation is the answer to doubt.

DOROTHY WALSH

The Cognitive Content of Art [1]

THE ARTS HAVE customarily been regarded as a source of intellectual nourishment. They have been accepted as vehicles of insight, revelation, and enlarged comprehension. Dissenting voices have, however, been raised from time to time, voices which express with indignation a denial of the value of art as a means to any adequate knowledge. The denial is, indeed, false, but the indignation is something with which we should sympathize. It springs from a profound and serious moral foundation. It expresses the protest of the disinterested, modest, disciplined, scientific consciousness against something which has all the appearance of highhanded, irresponsible, *ex cathedra* pronouncement by those confirmed individualists who are artists. How impressive, from this point of view, is that passage in the tenth book of Plato's *Republic* where, by means of a poetic simile, the simile of the mirror, Plato indicates the cognitive irresponsibility of artists. The representational artist reproduces nature and man by the simple and

---

[1] Dorothy Walsh, "The Cognitive Content of Art," *Philosophical Review*, LII (1943), 433–451. Reprinted by permission. (Eds.).

easy trick of catching their image in a mirror. This, Plato suggests, should deceive only the intellectually incompetent. Yet from Plato's time on defenders of art, as a vehicle of serious knowledge, have not been wanting. They have insisted that, though the purpose of art be to hold as it were the mirror up to nature, still this artistic mirror image provides the revelation of something otherwise not capable of being known.

These old quarrels are still with us and they threaten in our contemporary civilization to be a locus of bitter antagonism. Anyone who reads the current literary journals or who converses with literary artists and critics must be aware that they are today militant. Their campaign is part of a general offensive for the vindication of the humanities. The recent preoccupation with semantics has, moreover, intensified the conflict, for it has produced, in the person of the logical positivist, a new type of intellectual puritan whose passion for the antiseptic and the sterilized leads him to disinfect language and thought of their germinal ideas. When poetry is pronounced to be nonsense or, at best, emotive utterance, literary critics, who cannot but listen attentively when anyone speaks of language, have felt that it was time to take the offensive. But any defence of the cognitive content of art which is developed for the single art of literature will not suffice for philosophical purposes. The whole problem requires to be treated with greater generality.

It may prove useful to begin with the elimination of certain current misconceptions regarding the nature of art considered as a vehicle of insight and knowledge. Two such misconceptions have been revived and advanced by Professor F. S. C. Northrop in a recent article in *Furioso* (Vol. I, No. 4). Mr. Northrop first makes it clear that it is science and scientifically oriented philosophy which are the custodians of knowledge in the proper sense. Art, he thinks, can fulfill only two cognitive functions. First, art as it is autonomous, "in and for itself," can perform the function of making us aware of the immediacy of sensuous aesthetic surface. Practical life is dominated by utilitarian interests, and scientific knowledge is preoccupied with abstractions; and, due to the pressure of both, we cease to attend to the sensuously given for its own sake. The artist points it out to us in an arresting way. The purpose of a poem might be, for example, to make us see just how the sunlight sparkles on the water of a brook. Of course, if we are capable of seeing this for ourselves, we do not need the poem. Nature can give us everything that art can give if only we will open our eyes. Artists perform the altruistic function of drawing our attention to what we might otherwise fail to notice. And, since the sensuous is an ingredient of experience, art, in indicating it, denotes reality. Surely such a doctrine as this will not suffice. It must, of course, be acknowledged that all art has a sensuous embodiment for perception and imagination, but the recognition of this should not mislead us into the supposition that art is nothing but the presentation of the sensuous. Surely only someone who has never understood the complicated and really elaborate character of artistic expressiveness through sensuous material can suppose that the opening of our eyes or ears or nostrils on any sensuous content which nature is in fact pleased to afford will do for us what art will do. Artists do often attend with concentrated intensity to the sensuous aspect of experience, and they always reverence with peculiar piety the sensuous nature of the material of their special art, but sensuous material is never for any artist an end in itself. It is something to be exploited; it is raw material. No artist is content merely to reproduce for the careless observer the exact character of the sensuously given.

Mr. Northrop recognizes a second cognitive function of art: the expression for easier comprehension of an intellectual content borrowed from some other source. This is the famous fallacy of art's being philosophy or science or theology made easy for popular consumption through sensuous embodiment. The example given in this case is that Dante's *Commedia* is St. Thomas' *Summa Theologica* made easy. The author adds that, since St. Thomas has nothing to say to the modern world, so Dante, apart from the sensuous vividness of his expression, has nothing to communicate either. It is further suggested that, if we could get a work of art, presumably literature, which popularized modern scientific theory, it would be, until it became out of date, of great cultural utility.

Now here again we have a doctrine which is clearly not in accordance with the data of our experience of art and artists. In the first place, it assumes that, although the construction of works of art may be difficult, the understanding of them is somehow easy. But the plain fact is that the comprehension of works of art is not easy. Let anyone undertake a thorough understanding of Dante's *Commedia* and he will discover that he has about as much chance of reading this as he runs as he has of reading the *Summa Theologica*.

In the second place, what grounds have we for supposing that artists are conscientious and careful purveyors, without distortion, of other people's ideas? The very opposite seems to be the case. Artists are notoriously high-handed even when they are not ill informed. Dante, who was, with respect to the theological material which he used, one of the most conscientious, followed St. Thomas only when it suited his purpose, which was not always. You cannot expect an artist to be a faithful reporter; he has something else to do. It is indeed true that, in certain historical periods, literary and plastic artists were expected to convey information as well as to create works of art. But, since the work of art always had its own unique intellectual content, the accuracy of the information it was supposed to convey was always in jeopardy. This was no less the case when the given material was mythological than when it was scientific, philosophical, historical, or political. The Church had every reason to be nervous when it confined the task of the pictorial teaching of scripture to artists, and the orthodox followers of Marx or Lenin have the same reason for apprehension when modern poets undertake to spread the gospel.

The fact is that natural piety toward the experientially given, whether it be a theoretical conception, a human experience, or a material object, is foreign to the artist, who is not a reporter but a creator. Anything that God or nature, philosophy or science, politics or history, or art itself, can give him is not going to be accepted as something finished and as such to be respected. It is going to be reduced to the level of raw material for a new creation. Certainly works of art may and do exhibit the influence of ideas derived from non-artistic intellectual disciplines, but art is not a satisfactory method for popularizing such ideas. The sensuous embodiment which they receive at the hands of art does not make them easy; it makes them different.

So far, then, we may conclude that, whatever be the cognitive content of art, it is not satisfactorily interpreted as the mere transmission for easy comprehension of either the sensuous or the intellectual components of experience. A work of art always involves the imaginative transformation of the given.

It is, however, possible to regard the artistic transformation of the given in various ways. We turn now to those theories concerning the cognitive content of art which hold that such transformations are in the interest of expressing the fundamental and inner nature of the actual. There are two radically opposed variants of this doctrine. One is the view that every work of art is the expression of the personality of the artist. The other is the view, in opposition to this, that art is the revelation of the objective truth about man or nature, the physical or psychical, but in some profound visionary sense impossible to the superficial investigations of science.

The notion that art is the expression of the personality of the artist derives its plausibility from the fact that artists are generally uncooperative and sometimes highly eccentric and that many works of art seem to be concerned with the expression of the emotional implications of something. In addition, there is the fact that literary and artistic critics are concerned with the biography of artists in a way in which few scientists are concerned with the biography of scientists. But I doubt if all this warrants the conclusion that art is predominantly the expression of the personality of artists. In the first place, it must be remembered that curiosity about the biography of artists is often an impertinent indulgence in gossip and sometimes a tacit confession on the part of the critic of inability to elucidate a work of art without recourse to extraneous and usually irrelevant material. Furthermore, it may be asked, what is the artist to us or we to him that we should care about the revelation of his idiosyncratic personality? Putting aside the interest of friends, it would seem that we could be concerned only on the supposition that artists are unusual persons; but it is doubtful that we should judge them to be such except as they are the creators of works of art which are independently valuable. The works of an artist may, of course, be used as data for the interpretation of his personality; but it seems evident that his hastily written letters also provide data, often more revealing, and probably the psychiatrist at least would prefer to either of these the data provided by the unguarded flow of free association.

Unfortunately, however, those who defend the objectivity of artistic content incline to an error of an opposite sort. The escape from the personal heresy has resulted more often than not in a flight into unsubstantiated claims. Critics begin to talk about the insight of artists: insight into the heart of reality, insight into deeper meanings than any grasped by science. The sciences most commonly depreciated by literary critics are the young social sciences, and that commendable modesty which prompts such scientists to admit with candor the limitations of their knowledge to date is actually used as a weapon against them.

Because science proceeds slowly and cautiously in the interests of precision, it is falsely and hastily assumed that scientists are content with their present knowledge, whereas, as we know, every scientist's face is resolutely turned toward the future. But because the artist seems to be bold where the scientist is cautious he is credited with some mysterious power to penetrate to the heart of things. By individual insight he is supposed to know more about the actual world or at least about the nature of man than the disinterested cooperative labor of generations of scientists has uncovered.

Clearly we must discriminate between the artistic and the scientific enterprises. The realm of art presents a pluralism of self-sufficient expressive utterances while science comprises an ever widening continuity of discourse. The activity of the artist, even though he may grow in power and wisdom, is, nevertheless, a discontinuity of excursions, while the activity of the scientist, even though he attacks new problems, is a single one-directional march. The failure to grasp these differences naturally results in our admiration for the artist with his goal achieved and our pity for the scientist who knows that he will never live to see even the frontiers of the promised land.

But all attempts to seek, in the expressions of art, a deeper revelation of man or nature which escapes science and philosophy, must pause with some embarrassment before the phenomenon of artistic autonomy. The plain fact is that works of art are never competitive in the sense in which scientific hypotheses and philosophical theories may be. There is no doubt that it is possible to accept both Lucretius and Dante in a sense in which we cannot accept both Democritus and St. Thomas. Similarly, there is no catholicity of taste which can make it legitimate for a scientist to accept, without some higher synthetic principle of mediation, opposing interpretations of the same data.

No doubt it sometimes seems as if philosophical discourse were identical with creative literature. We are all aware of the tendency of such philosophers as Schopenhauer, Nietzsche, Bergson, and Mr. Santayana, to flee from the controversial battle into the sanctuary of poetic statement. But Nietzsche's attack on Schopenhauer and Santayana's attack on Bergson are evidence of the recognition that contradiction in philosophical doctrine does indeed necessitate choice, whereas radical diversity, amounting to incompatibility, in the content of two different works of art does not necessitate rejection of either.

No student of science or of philosophy would think of practising that "willing suspension of disbelief" which is generally recognized as suitable in the approach to art. What does this suspension involve? It is not an uncritical acceptance of anything, for works of art must fulfill certain requirements though they are not those which we make of philosophical theories or scientific hypotheses. We expect a work of art to convince us, but not by argument and not by evidence. Its authenticity must be internal to its concrete sensuous presence. Given this authenticity, we accept it, and it seems that what we willingly suspend is not only our awareness of the lack of correspondence of the content to actuality but also our knowledge that other works of art express, with similar authentic voices, different and often incompatible things. It is, of course, not only the poets who say incompatible things without mutual contradiction. Cézanne's vision of three-dimensional space and of the objects in that space is radically incompatible with the vision of Turner. In passing from the music of Bach to the music of Debussy we realize that we have made a transition from one world into another. We experience a like transition in passing from the cosmogony of Spinoza to that of Leibniz, but we know that the latter transition generates an intellectual problem which the former does not.

That art is no simple imitation or reproduction of nature is abundantly acknowledged. The legitimacy, indeed the desirability, of distortion in the interest both of design and of interpretation is freely conceded. What fails to be recognized in many critical quarters is the full consequence of this acknowledgment. It is repeatedly suggested that the infidelity to nature of the work of art as a whole is the very condition of its fidelity with regard to that particular aspect of actuality which it has chosen for emphasis or elaboration. The false assumption underlying this doctrine is that the articulations of art are all positive though partial. This would be plausible if art were abstract, but art is concrete and this involves outright negation rather than mere absence. In the visual world of Cézanne's creation the graceful vistas of Watteau's landscapes are not merely absent or neglected; they are specifically rejected. Sufficient attention to the negative as well as to the positive assertions of works of art eliminates the error of supposing that artists, like scientists, aim at cooperative synthesis of knowledge.

Since the actual world is in fact what it is, if works of art reveal its nature, they must be either mutually compatible or mutually contradictory. If they are the latter, the acceptance of one must necessitate the rejection of others. If they are the former, they must be capable of synthesis into larger more adequate or more inclusive wholes. But is it not equally implausible to say either that in accepting Lucretius we must reject Dante, or that we must seek some higher synthesis in which the partial but compatible truths of both poets can find expression? Salvador Dali tells us that the two artists who have most influenced him are Vermeer and da Vinci,—the luminous precision of Vermeer and the enigmatic suggestiveness of da Vinci. But it is clear that whatever be our high or low estimation of Dali, we do not expect to find in his work any synthesis which will enable us to transcend a thesis and an antithesis in the sense in which we might expect a scientific or a philosophical doctrine to include the partial insights of earlier theories. In art we do not look for or believe in any such synthesis.

The only escape between the horns of the dilemma which tries to compel our assent either to the theory that art is subjective and the expression of the personality of the artist, or that art is objective and a revelation of the actual world, is to recognize that art is really neither of these, but the delineation of the possible.

Of course "possibility" is a rather inclusive term. The statement that art is the delineation of the possible requires to be supplemented by some differentiation of the various meanings of possibility. Terms such as actual, possible and impossible are adverbial expressions and refer to a mode of being of one entity considered in relation to others. A mode of being of entities in a togetherness implies, of course, a contextual situation. But what is a context? It is sometimes held that a context must be a context of discourse, which is to say that a context must be a conceptual context. This assumption, when developed, leads either to Hegelian idealism or to one or another variety of epistemological scepticism. I confess I see no compelling reason for the assumption, and I suggest that we may recognize two quite different types of context, conceptual contexts and existential contexts. A conceptual context is a context of meanings related by some sort of logical order. An existential context is a context of active substances or of events related by causal efficacy. It is true that existential contexts are known by means of conceptual contexts, but the description of a thing is not identical with the being of a thing. It is also true that a conceptual context, as it is part of the awareness of some mind or minds, is included in an existential context, but what is known is not identical with the knowing or with the effect of the knowing. Thus conceptual and existential contexts are not reducible one to the other.

To be actual is to be operative within an existential context, that is, to be influenced and to exert influence in the sense of causal efficacy. To be possible is to be compossible with some existential or with some conceptual context. The possible, as it relates to an existential context, is the potential: the potential as capacity or tendency. This actually possible is sometimes called real possibility. The possible, as it relates to a conceptual context, may be called ideal possibility. I suggest that such ideal possibility may be classified as follows: (1) the formally possible, as, for example, in pure mathematics; (2) the hypothetical, as, for example, in scientific theory—this is the statement of what is probably actual; (3) the alternative, presented as I believe in art—this is an internally coherent or compossible scheme presented as alternative to the actual.

A great deal of time and an enormous amount of human energy have been devoted to the development of all three of these. If we ask why, the answer as it relates to inquiries of which science is representative is clearest and most obviously satisfactory. Man wishes to know the nature of things for the sake of orientation, prediction and control as well as for the satisfaction of curiosity. But what can be said about such enterprises as, for example, pure mathematics on the one hand, and art, as I have interpreted it, on the other? What is the justification for a preoccupation with possibility for its own sake? Nothing is so unfashionable today as the "art for art's sake" doctrine, since it is considered immoral to be caught anywhere in the vicinity of an ivory tower. Perhaps the pure mathematician has escaped denunciation only because the shocking extent of his purity has evaded popular notice. The answer regarding both mathematics and art could be: "but for delight their sole compulsion." This answer, however, though true, is not complete. The full answer is that the delight in question is a cognitive satisfaction since insight regarding the possible is insight into reality.

Both artistic and mathematical possibilities, as ideals of orderly structure, can furnish norms for practical life: schemes and patterns in terms of which man can organize his emotions or his thoughts, control behavior or build bridges. But it must be emphasized that this value in application requires that these possibilities be initially developed without regard for such application. Accommodation to the actual does not constitute the only disciplinary influence upon the human imagination. In fact, freedom from such accommodation engenders its own responsibilities.

Mr. G. H. Hardy in a recent book, *A Mathematician's Apology* (Cambridge University Press, 1940), has presented criteria for mathematical excellence which, I think, apply equally to art. These are seriousness and beauty. Seriousness means generality and depth; beauty means unexpectedness combined with inevitability and economy. Obviously, if what is presented to us purports to be a true account of some phase or aspect of the actual, we will be interested in it even if it seems to be something unimportant, such as the color of the tip of the wing of a certain species of bird. But if what is presented to us is something which makes no claim to describe the actual, it must be intrinsically interesting; the prime requirement is that it be, or appear to be, non-trivial.

With regard to art, requirements of beauty mean that, for one thing, a work of art must have novelty and freshness. If we find these lacking, we accuse the artist of failure in originality. Then it must have inevitability; that is, it must seem convincing as a possibility; it must have the appearance of authenticity. If we find this lacking, we say that it is false; but obviously we do not mean false to the actual, since what we know to be false in this sense can still have artistic authenticity. Finally, it must have economy: every element included must make its contribution to the effect of the whole. If we find this lacking, we say that it is disorganized. Seriousness is a criterion which differentiates greater from lesser works of art. Serious does not, of course, mean solemn. It implies range and depth. Range is richness and variety of included content. Depth is concentration of meaning in such a way as to provide levels of meaning within the same work of art. Depth is complexity on a vertical scale as range is complexity on a horizontal scale. The criteria of seriousness and beauty are not independent, since the artistic ideal is the achievement of novelty *with* generality and of inevitability and economy *with* depth.

The analogy, which I have drawn, between fine art and pure mathematics is intended to emphasize that the knowledge of the possible can be interesting and important in its own right and that although both art and mathematics are free from the requirement of accommodation to the actual, which is characteristic of science, nevertheless they must satisfy criteria of their own which, though different, are no less rigorous. Analogy, however, does not imply identity, and it is essential to indicate the important difference between art and mathematics both as to method and as to purpose. Mathematics is formal and abstract; art is sensuous and concrete. The former is expressible in signs while the latter commonly employs symbols.

To understand the sensuous symbolic expressions of art, it is important to distinguish the genuine symbol from the mere sign. Mathematics commonly uses the visual presentation of numbers, letters, and diagrams. These are sometimes called symbols but they are not genuine symbols; they are merely signs. A sign is a passageway to something else; it is a selfeffacing means to some insight which lies beyond it. It is diaphanous and transparent. A symbol is substantial and opaque. It does not point to something else; it holds its meaning within itself. The relation of the sign to what it signifies is a matter of convention, whereas the symbol must be, or at least appear to be, the suitable and natural vehicle of the meaning which it embodies; that is, it must in some sense resemble what it means. This is why signs function most effectively when they efface themselves, when they are as transparent as possible, allowing the perceiver to pass directly to the meaning. But symbols, being vessels and repositories of meaning, demand attention; their presentational appearance is important. Further, signs commonly belong within a system such that some signs may be substituted for others without loss of meaning, as $1 + 2$ is equivalent in meaning to 3, and a technical term is equivalent to its definition. But symbols are commonly solitary and cannot be substituted for one another without radical change of meaning.

The artist must exert a highly sustained creative energy to prevent his symbols from degenerating into mere signs. In poetry this is the effort to keep metaphor alive. The struggle of the poet is to maintain language full-bodied, solid, and inescapably present. The creative effort for sustained symbolic expression in plastic art is manifest in the effort to resist iconographical reduction. For once a work of plastic art becomes an icon, whether religious or secular, the observer tends to look through the sensuous material to grasp some meaning which lies beyond.

It is the nature of abstract signs that they can be used again and again without alteration and impoverishment, but it is the nature of concrete sensuous symbols that they must be constantly and freshly recreated for each individual work of art. It is true, of course, that creative advance in mathematics often necessitates the invention of new signs, but once these signs have been invented they become the common property of all mathematicians and can be used over and over indefinitely. Symbols reemployed must wear their symbolic expressiveness with a difference. If the artist can achieve this difference, the imaginative invocation of former artistic expressions which can be effected through the employment of similar symbols is a common method of increasing the seriousness, that is, the range and depth, of artistic expression. An example of this is the rose of Dante's *Paradiso*. But this manner of handling symbols, although it is perhaps the best means of creating complicated fusions of expressive meaning, is not indispensable. Artists, like cultural epochs, differ with respect to the value which they place upon tradition. And, although this is a factor which is reflected in their work, it is irrelevant to the question of their importance as artists. Thus novel and isolated symbols will function just as effectively if they fulfill the essential requirements of symbols, that is, if they are made to appear as the natural, necessary and inevitable sensuous vehicles of the meaning which they express.

This discrimination between sign and symbol provides the key to the differentiation between mathematical and artistic possibilities. Mathematical possibilities, being communicated and developed by signs, are both formal and systematic. The pure mathematician is one who spreads his wings, ascends to his Platonic heaven and remains there. His interest is confined to a highly abstract order of the possible, namely, the logical order of manifolds. His interest is satisfied by intellectual intuition, and he experiences no urge to actualize these insights in concrete sensuous material.

The artist, however, is, or aspires to be, a demiurgos. He seeks to create some ideal possibility by the process of working through some sensuous material. He cannot create a world, but he can create, in a work of art, an isolated selfsufficient structure which often impresses us as being a windowless monad which mirrors a world. Of course the consequence of this appetite in the artist for actualization is that the realm of art cannot hope to rival the systematic character of mathematics but presents an irreducible pluralism of unique visions.

The independent individuality of art-objects has always been recognized, but it is important to notice that this independence is twofold. In the first place, in spite of the integrating influence of artistic tradition, works of art are independent of one another. They cannot be synthesized and they cannot be rigorously systematized. The internality of relations within the work of art is in sharp contrast to the externality of relations of the art-object as a whole to other works of art. In the second place, the work of art is independent of the actual world of which, by virtue of its sensuous embodiment, it seems to be a part. In a sense it may appear paradoxical to urge this, for, if the aim of the artist has been properly described as the attempt to actualize a possibility in sensuous material, then surely, as actualized, it becomes a part of the actual world. In one way it does, but in another way it does not.

It is of the first importance to recognize this distinction. In so far as we consider a work of art either as a physical thing or as a product of human activity and an object of human appreciation, it certainly belongs to the context of nature or to the context of social culture. The recognition that a picture is also paint and canvas and so a natural object capable of physical and chemical analysis and subject to natural changes is current and hardly needs elaboration. But the recognition that a work of art is a cultural product has often been a source of considerable misunderstanding. Of course the artist is a human being and a social creature. Of course the culture of his period influences him; his imagination has to work within the limits set by the raw material, physical and social, available to him. Obviously, works of art are cultural products which, in turn, produce effects on audiences and are causally efficacious in modifying social life. A social psychologist, sociologist or historian would be bound to regard works of art as cultural data. It would be ridiculous to deny either the propriety of this or its importance.

Nevertheless it is essential to differentiate the question: What is a work of art and what does it express? from the question: What influences of the cultural period are reflected in this work of art and how did this work of art influence those who knew it? It is evident that these are different questions. It must further be remembered that the second question can be appropriately asked with regard to any intellectual product: the differential calculus, the Nicean creed, the theory of relativity. To say, correctly, that all this is cultural data is not to say that this is nothing but cultural data. It is surely obvious that before one can deal with Aristotelian philosophy, Christian theology or Newtonian science as cultural patterns, one must first understand them as philosophy, as theology, as science. The same is true with regard to art. A work of art may be regarded specifically as a work of art, or it may be regarded as a cultural or as a physical thing. From either of the latter points of view, it is a part of the context of the world, but considered specifically as a work of art it is an isolated structure which, though present in the actual world, is not of it.

One of the most impressive characteristics of the art-object is its boundary. Such an object may appear to possess an indefinite richness of internal depth and range, but it always has a boundary which isolates it from all other entities including other works of art. The so called temporal works of art are no exception. Every musical composition and every poem begins and ends and so returns upon itself. It never just commences and ceases. When it is thoroughly understood, every part is heard in the totality of the whole. It is surrounded by silence or at least by irrelevancy as pictures are surrounded by their frames. Thus works of art, present as physical things and present as cultural products, are, nevertheless, as works of art, imaginative vistas out of the actual. To enter into the contemplation of a work of art is to pass through the context of the actual to the appreciation of a unique, discontinuous possibility.

That works of art, though present in the actual world, are not really of it, is not always recognized. This is because of the fact that many of the possibilities revealed by art are fairly close to actuality. The imaginative possibility may vary from actuality very conspicuously or only slightly. Fantastic art differs from so called realistic art only in this sense. The criteria by which works of art are judged more or less excellent should be irrelevant to the consideration of how close or how remote they are to the actual. The development of photography has brought this matter vividly home to the pictorial artist. It is unfortunate that there is no comparable invention capable of making it equally impressive to the literary artist. Poets have always known it, but prosewriters of fiction do not always understand what fiction is. The modern world is full of novelists who are not artists. They want to write sociological treatises without submitting to the discipline of science. Thus they produce ambiguous works which make no attempt to meet either the rigorous requirements of art or the rigorous requirements of science.

A work of art presents a possibility which, because it is not abstract but concrete, must be regarded not as a schematism of or for the actual, but rather as an alternative to it. However, I do not think that we can insist that it must be conceived as an alternative to one aspect of the actual rather than another. Of course it is man who creates art and man is, naturally, interested in himself. It is a fact that perhaps the majority of works of art are concerned with the revelation of possibilities of human experience. The greater part of literature is concerned with what men might say and feel and think if they were unusually articulate or unusually sensitive or unusually representative in some way, and if the world that surrounded them and the events which influenced them were, whether fantastic or naturalistic, at any rate subject to a rigorous economical selfenclosed organization. Similarly, some music is expressive of what joy and sorrow would be like if it sounded in complicated harmonious patterns, and so forth. But I think that theorists who insist that artistic insight is always *sub specie humanitatis* are committed to too extreme a position. It is true that certain works of plastic art which present an artistic alternative to the non-human world of nature are elaborate experiments in anthropomorphism,—nature as it might be if it had human purpose and were subject to human emotion. But this is not always the case. Many such works of art have no humanistic reference and are the presentation of how some aspect of the natural world might have appeared if it were simply more rigorously organized, more selfsufficient, and, as a mere spectacle, more interesting.

Finally, we must remember that there are works of art which present artistic possibilities not capable of being considered as imaginative reconstructions of man or nature in any obvious sense: arabesque designs, so called abstract pictorial art, and a good deal of music. This is the exploitation of sensuous materials for the presentation of intricate, elaborate, autonomous schemes of order. Such works of art seem more analogous to the patterns of mathematical structure than to anything in the actual world. But these patterns are not formal possibilities; they are not variables which might be satisfied by any one of a range of values. They are sensuous symbols of what might have been a causally efficacious, integrated part of the natural world if nature had seen fit to achieve something more than crystal-formation or birdsong.

Artistic possibilities may be developed for the realization of a variety of ends and the expression of a variety of values. An artist may have a moral purpose which he presents positively, through idealization, or negatively, through satire. He may wish to offer a commentary on life or on the civilization of his time, or he may wish merely to liberate a fantastic imagination. His work may involve an act of religious devotion or the vicarious gratification of a thwarted desire. There is no limit or end to the secondary purposes which may be involved.

The primary purpose, however, is to create an object which has artistic value. It is exclusively by reference to this value that art may be said to be "a spirited protest against nature" and to present a concrete alternative to the actual which is intrinsically significant and valuable because it is better than the actual. To be better, by this standard, is to achieve plenitude and richness with structural selfsufficiency. Otherwise expressed, it means to achieve intensional depth and concentration of expressive meaning with extensional limitation and isolated finality. The Leibnizian God no doubt intended that his best of all possible worlds should achieve this unity in variety and be a work of art, but no actual world containing real individuals and changing through time can fulfill this aesthetic ideal. The compossible schemes, which are works of art, must remain possibilities, and possibilities isolated and irreducibly plural.

Possibility as it enters into the structure of such discourse as science, philosophical cosmology, and natural theology, is an entirely different matter. All three enterprises are concerned with what is taken to be actual. Consequently, in all three, reference must be made, at some point, to empirical data. Of course nobody supposes that knowledge of matter of fact concerning the actual is to be found neat, pure and uncontaminated through some translucent form of empirical observation. Facts are never discovered except under the illumination of some guiding theoretical conception. But theoretical conceptions must prove their explanatory adequacy by saving the phenomena of experience. In attempting to disclose the nature of the actual, science has its useful fictions, its ideal constructs, its norms of reference, and its imaginative flights. Cosmology and theology may use metaphor and symbol and the imaginative schemes of either may outrun the empirical evidence. Even if all meaningful statement in any of these disciplines embraces both logical structure and hypothetical formulation and hence contains some ineradicable reference to possibility, nevertheless there remains a great difference between the exploitation of the possible as a means of arriving at the description, explanation, prediction, or control of the actual, and the exploitation of the actual as a means of arriving at the delineation of the possible.

The argument of this paper may be summarized as follows. In the first place, it seems evident that art does reveal something to us; it has a cognitive content; it affords knowledge. The fact that art moves us, that we respond emotionally to it, cannot, I think, be interpreted to mean either that art is a mere emotional stimulant or that it is the mere expression of emotion.

For many things are efficacious in producing emotion—bombs and whisky no less than art—and, though art may indeed express emotion, no artist can express emotion *à propos* of nothing. There must be some cognitive core, some insight as a focus for emotion. But if we ask: What is it that art reveals?, and if, in seeking an answer, we turn as we should to the scrutiny of works of art, we find that we are confronted by an irreducible pluralism of selfsufficient, independent visions. There is neither community of discourse, on the one hand, nor conflict and competition, on the other. If art were, fundamentally, a revelation of the actual world, it would seem that we should find in our attitude toward it the tendency, evident in our attitude toward science, metaphysics, and theology, to seek some intelligible unity either by rejection and selection or by a higher synthesis which transcends and supplants what it absorbs. Yet it seems to be an empirical fact that in art we experience no urge in this direction. Art is welcomed in its pluralistic diversity. This being so, we could consider the hypothesis that art is pluralistic because each work of art is the expression of a purely individual and personal point of view. But though in some cases we can find the artist in his work, in many cases we cannot, and the chief fact which discredits the hypothesis is that an interest in art seems to be qualitatively quite a different thing from an interest in personality. Any interest we may have in the personality of an artist is derived from our initial interest in the work of art for itself.

Hence I suggest that, although a work of art is made out of sensuous material, which, as such, belongs to the actual world, and although it exhibits traces of the influence of the artist's life and his culture, nevertheless its prime purpose is to present to us, through sensuous symbolism, an ideal possibility. A work of art is, in a way, an addition to the actual, but an addition which, however it may be integrated as a cultural product, resists integration specifically as a work of art. As a work of art it is a selfenclosed isolated structure. To enter into the contemplation of it is to leave the context of the actual and to comprehend a concrete alternative as a possibility.

The ultimate object of philosophical inquiry is reality. Unless the real is construed as the perishing occurrence of the moment, it must embrace the possible as well as the actual. Consequently, an interest in the possible for its own sake should be recognized as philosophically justified. A liberal mind is surely one which is not tied irrevocably and exclusively to the present or to the actual. One of the valuable functions of history is that it is a means of freeing us from a too exclusive concern with the present. But pure mathematics and fine art are, in their different ways, even more significant as freeing us from an exclusive preoccupation with the actual. It is not a question of a mere happy escape from the slings and arrows of our immediate fortune. It is a question of a philosophic comprehension of the real in its manifestation as the intrinsically interesting possible.

PHILIP LEON

Aesthetic Knowledge[1]

To EXPERIENCE COLOUR, sound, taste, a new thrill, to appreciate and enjoy the light, movement of life, to gauge its seriousness, savour
its joy and penetrate its gloom is, I take it, to have knowledge, and the
object of this knowledge is constitutive of the world. We shall scarcely deny
this if we consider what kind of knowledge and what sort of a world we
should be left with if we removed from them the experience of the so-called
secondary and tertiary qualities; if we were left only with the comfortless
company of the dreary formulae of mathematics, the sciences and philosophy. The above experience may be distinguished as knowledge of quality:
its objects are the entities to which the term qualities secondary or tertiary
are applied, in it alone do we know what anything is like, *quale sit,* all other
knowledge being knowledge only *about* a thing, knowledge of its relations.

Aesthetic or imaginative knowledge, the experience we have with the
help of works of art, both in their creation and their appreciation which is
re-creation, is knowledge of quality. Through works of art we know serenity,
majesty, mysteriousness, pathos, tragedy, the gorgeous gloom and splendour
which is the Agamemnon of Aeschylus, the serene and tranquil horror which
is the Oedipus Tyrannus of Sophocles, the bright speed of Homer, the brood-
ing pathos of Virgil. Be it well understood that any of these words and
phrases is general and consequently inadequate; for the full realization of
a unique quality it is necessary to have a whole work of art, the Agamemnon
or the Oedipus Tyrannus which is both the full description of the quality
and the quality itself. The essence of a work of art, whatever its subsidiary
aspects, such as those of representation or imitation and of theory or doctrine, is that it is a synthesis which is the revelation of a new quality such
as we should have if we could suddenly become aware of the colour of ultra-
violet rays. The converse, I think, can also be maintained, namely, that all
knowledge of quality, when adequate and complete is art, the awareness of
a bare secondary quality being a limiting case or an abstraction from a richer
experience.

---

[1] Philip Leon, "Aesthetic Knowledge," *Proceedings of the Aristotelian Society,* XXV
(1925), 199–208. Reprinted by permission. (Eds.)

In this paper I should like to examine briefly the formal characteristics of aesthetic knowledge mainly with a view to testing its claims to being absolute knowledge. These claims are often conceded to it by philosophers who, weary themselves of their own search for the absolute, end up by saying that it is perhaps to be found by the artist and poet more than by anyone else; these claims are also implicit in our feeling about any great compelling work of art, the feeling that however broken and confused the light we get from theories, however futile our efforts to realize goodness, here we have something final, ultimate, something that we shall meet with as such in heaven, something without which, at any rate, heaven would be but a sorry place.

The first characteristic of aesthetic knowledge is the oneness in it of subject and object, of the knowing and the known. Even if as idealists we hold that that is the real mark of all knowledge, we must admit that in other knowledge the separation between subject and object, even though ultimately erroneous, does arise, whereas in aesthetic knowledge it is not present and cannot be present. Aesthetic knowledge is essentially a living through. Its object, quality, can be indifferently called the quality of the world or of our minds or souls. We may therefore speak of the aesthetic experience, meaning to indicate by experience the oneness of the knower, the knowing and the known.

Secondly, the aesthetic experience is knowledge in which there is not present the distinction or separation between subject and predicate. It is all subject or all predicate, and there is no assertion or predication. A poem or a piece of music may be considered as an adjectival texture, as quality enjoyed, realized, contemplated, but not predicated of anything. It is never "about" anything. True, a literary work of art is made up of propositions, but that these are not real assertions or judgments can be seen when we reflect that the import of a work of art would be epitomized in a descriptive phrase, a description of a quality, rather than in a proposition or judgment as would be the case, say, with a book of science, history or philosophy. A poem can be merely exclamatory, and in its real import always is a mere exclamation, which you cannot meet with "Yes" or "No," or with argument, as you can a judgment.

As there is no assertion, so neither is there the distinction between truth and error, appearance and reality. The aesthetic object, the aesthetic experience is essentially appearance and essentially real. There can be no argument about its reality, just as there can be no argument about the reality of any apprehended colour. Argument in such a case, I take it, can only arise when we start attributing the colour and attributing it to one thing rather than to another. But the aesthetic experience as such is merely apprehension of quality, free from every act of attribution. Being non-assertive, it in itself does not contain the assertion of the reality or un-reality of its object or of itself. But looking at that object and experience from a point of view other than the aesthetic, say as philosophers, I do not see how we can ever deny reality to it. A work of art either helps us to appre-hend something or it fails to do so. But what we apprehend must be real, it being the same as the apprehension. It is imaginary because grasped by the imagination, but nothing is added or taken away from its status by saying that it is merely imaginary. That holds true if we remember that what a work of art really gives us is what I have called a quality and not anything else. I do not mean that Centaurs are to be found in the animal kingdom because someone has painted them, or that the exploration of the skies or of Mount Olympus will reveal to us gods leading a riotous and immoral life because we read of them in Homer.

The aesthetic object *qua* aesthetic object, is, and is always apprehended as, essentially one, free internally from relations. It is an immediate unity or unity of quality and is thus distinguished from other unities, *e.g.,* the unity of a thing, a system, a universal, teleological unity. All these latter can only be apprehended by thought and their apprehension is the apprehension of relations. A work of art when not enjoyed as a work of art, when conse-quently it is not an aesthetic object, can of course be analyzed into parts and their relations to each other: a tragedy is divided into acts and scenes and sentences, a picture into different figures and colours uniting in a harmony, a temple into innumerable parts. But in the moment of aesthetic enjoyment there are not parts seen or rather thought in their relations. The relations denoted by balance, harmony, proportions, contract, form, are relations apprehended in immediacy, *i.e.,* such that both the relations and the relata are all one quality. I mean that in spite of all diversity discoverable by analysis, in spite of its being somehow dependent on the apprehension of diversity and on different acts of apprehension, the enjoyment of the Agamemnon is essentially the apprehension of one quality "gorgeous gloom," or whatever we may call it, and that we have here essentially the same unity as there is in the apprehension of a flash of light though physical analysis reveals the multeity of billions of vibrations, or in the apprehension of "glittering sharpness" analyzable psychologically into visual sensations and tactile images, or in that of genial light, warmth and freshness, analyzable into organic, kinaesthetic and many other sensations and images.

Free in this sense from relations internally, the aesthetic object is also free from relations externally, from relations to another. It is complete, self-sufficient, isolated, a universe, and true individual. It is this which gives the aesthetic activity its repose and perfection. Any aesthetic object must obey the law which Aristotle lays down for a tragedy: it must have a proper beginning and a proper end; nothing outside it leads to it and it leads on to nothing outside itself. There is nothing else which is an "it," or is called an individual, that possesses this individuality and self-subsistence. Everything else exists in an infinite environment and has its being in its relations and interactions with this environment, never completely within itself. Consequently, no other knowledge has the completeness and satisfactoriness of the aesthetic experience. It is this which chiefly gives it its claim to being absolute or typical of the absolute. That claim has by some been made for history. But history, it has to be admitted, is knowledge of an infinite whole whose parts are infinitely inexhaustible or unknowable, *i.e.,* it is a knowledge which can never be complete or proper knowledge. All knowledge other than the aesthetic experience suffers from this infinity. Whether it be a single judgment, a whole book, or department of science, it is never self-subsistent. It is predicational: it attaches a predicate to a subject, the nature of which is apprehended in part at least elsewhere, outside the judgment or book or system. A judgment or system of judgments consequently always refers us outwards, to other apprehension: it forms part of a larger context to which both its beginning and its end point; in fact it has not properly either a beginning or an end. Its interests depend upon questions asked and answers given elsewhere; the dwelling in it is a continual excursion from it, and such excursion, such questioning, and endless reference and discursiveness is what constitutes the apprehension, the understanding, the knowing.

But it is not so with the aesthetic experience; the latter is an absorption; it is complete and self-contained; it is marked by repose and finality. It has these characteristics because its object is a complete self-subsistent universe. We do not come to a poem with questions, and its interest does not depend on answers given elsewhere; the asking of any questions does not constitute the aesthetic apprehension, but on the contrary, like any reference to anything outside the poem, song or picture, it is fatal to the aesthetic attitude. Of course, the aesthetic object can, when we are not appreciating it as such, be related to others. We can give the sources of a drama, compare it to others and make it the subject of an infinite series of judgments. But the point is that such knowledge does not constitute the act of apprehending the drama *qua* drama, *i.e.,* seeing it acted and enjoying it, but is on the contrary incompatible with it and impossible till after the aesthetic apprehension proper is over.

I have emphasized the unity of the aesthetic object, but it is a unity which covers a rich variety or multiplicity, discoverable by analysis though not aesthetically apprehended as a many. This manyness in one is most obviously realized as a synthesis of the senses. Art is said to be sensuous, to appeal primarily through one of our senses, through hearing or sight. But then we must say that one of the senses does the work of all the rest, and all in one act. So in music we can be said to hear wetness, hear colour, a perfume,

a taste. In a picture, we see warmth, we see loudness, sweetness and freshness, sharpness, etc. Hence it is that critics tend to speak of music in terms
of colour and of painting in terms of music.

But the elements which enter into the aesthetic synthesis are not merely
sensuous. It is all experience that may enter into it. Art, in the words of
Pater, "presents us with a kind of profoundly significant and animated
instants, a mere gesture, a look, a smile perhaps—some brief and wholly
concrete moment—into which, however, all the motives, all the interests and
effects of a long history have condensed themselves, and which seem to
absorb past and future in an intense consciousness of the present." It is this
characteristic which Coleridge marks by calling the Imagination "esem-
plastic," and "coadunative." It is best illustrated again from Pater in his
description of the Mona Lisa. The Mona Lisa is primarily colour; but it
is colour which "is expressive of what in the ways of a thousand years men
had come to desire . . . It is wrought of strange thoughts and fantastic
reveries and exquisite passions . . . All the thoughts and experiences of
the world have etched and moulded there . . . the animalism of Greece,
the lust of Rome, the mysticism of the Middle Age, with its spiritual ambition
and imaginative loves, the return of the Pagan world, the sins of the Borgias."
We may not all accept this particular analysis as authentic; but we must
admit that some such "coadunation" is effected by all great art. Such synthesis points to some experience where all the past, all experience is resumed
and preserved all in one in an immediate unity. That experience cannot be
anything other than the Absolute, but its type and the approximation to it
is to be found in the aesthetic experience only.

The aesthetic experience also presupposes and synthetizes all other types
of experience. "Poetry," Coleridge says, "is the blossom and fragrancy of
all human knowledge, human thoughts, human passions, emotions, language." "It is," according to Shelley, "the perfect and consummate surface
and bloom of all things; it is as the odour and colour of the rose to the texture
of the elements which compose it; as the form and splendour of unfaded
beauty to the secrets of anatomy and corruption." To be less poetical, the
aesthetic experience presupposes perception: to appreciate an aesthetic
object we must perceive a picture, hear a poem, etc., to create an aesthetic
object we must have lived through at least ordinary perceptual experience.
While not itself conceptual, it presupposes the concept and indeed it contains
it, though not explicitly in the form of argument or doctrine, but in an implicit immediate form as a philosophy may be contained in a drama of
Aeschylus. It is not in itself ethical, and its value is not ethical, but it presupposes the ethical experience in the sense that no art, at any rate, no great
art and least of all great poetry can be produced or appreciated except by
men who are sensitive to good and evil. Like the absolute, though in itself

neither true nor false, since it is not judgment or assertion, the aesthetic experience contains both truth and error. The doctrines or judgments which we may extract from a poem, and which we say are contained in it implicitly, may be either true or false without affecting its own value which is beauty. For error we must find a place in the universe since it is a fact. It is difficult to see how it can find a place in truth itself even though we call it a "negative moment" in it. That place it can find in a value other than that of truth, in beauty, in the aesthetic experience. Errors like the mythology of paganism or the cosmography of the Middle Ages cannot *qua* errors be resolved in the complete body of truth, if such there be. But they gave a special colouring to men's minds, produced a special quality, a special immediate experience, expressed in art and in this guise they find their place in the whole.

Similarly, though in itself neither ethically good or bad, the aesthetic experience contains both good and evil in the way in which the Mona Lisa may be said to express spiritual ambition and imaginative loves, as well as the sins of the Borgias and the lust of Rome. Just as for error so for evil we must find a place in the whole, and this can only be done because the value of the whole is not ethical but beauty. That the world as a moral phenomenon is a deception, and can only be justified as an aesthetic phenomenon, was a view at one time held by Nietzsche. Because this view seems singular and rather mad, some expressions of it are worth quoting. The following is from Joseph Conrad:

> "The ethical view of the universe involves us at last in so many cruel and absurd contradictions . . . that I have come to suspect that the aim of creation cannot be ethical at all. I would fondly believe that its object is purely spectacular: a spectacle for awe, love, adoration, or hate, if you like . . . Those visions, delicious or poignant, are a moral end in themselves."

Another modern writer says: "Every great artist, a Dante or a Shakespeare, a Dostoievsky or a Proust, thus furnishes the metaphysical justification of existence by the beauty of the vision he presents of the cruelty and the horror of existence. All the pain and madness, even the ugliness and the commonplace of the world, he converts into shining jewels. By revealing the spectacular character of reality he restores the serenity of its innocence." Such a view can only seem singular and mad if we forget that beauty, "the spectacular," is a value.

Because of the above characteristics we may say that the aesthetic experience is above all other types or forms of experience or knowledge, it is that to which the others lead up, in which they are resolved, and in which they find their reality. It is the unification and reconciliation of them. Its features and functions are those which are attributed to the absolute: immediacy, the fusion of relations, self-subsistence or individuality, the character of a universe, the synthesis of subject and object, subject and predicate, appearance and reality, the one and many, truth and error, good and evil.

It would be tempting to say that in art we have absolute experience itself. But this would leave us with the Absolute as a plurality of the worst kind, a multitude of unrelated members, since there are many aesthetic objects each autonomous and completely independent. Or we might speak of the Absolute as continually making and unmaking itself, re-creating itself into fresh aesthetic objects, through the conflicts and contradictions of other forms of experience. But whereas the aesthetic experience itself does present the characteristics which we require of the Absolute, the process from one aesthetic moment to another does not, though no doubt our own experience is such a process.

We must therefore be content with saying that aesthetic experience alone does not possess the unsatisfactoriness of all other knowledge, *i.e.,* knowledge which is judgment or predicational and that therefore it alone reveals reality satisfactorily. Beauty is the highest category and alone applicable to the Absolute, *i.e.,* to the unity of all experience or all experience in a unity. Actual aesthetic objects are only types of this absolute or partial revelations of it.

Index

Abell, W., 212
Abercrombie, L., 141–142
Absolutism, and aesthetic experience (Child), 454–456
    and relativism (Heyl), 439–445, (Child), 446–450
    See also Objectivism
Abstraction, criticized (Gotshalk), 200–201
    and subject matter (Isenberg), 217–218
    See also Design; Form
Action and impulse (Richards), 387–390
    incipient and overt (Richards), 387
    and knowledge (Hulme), 128–131
    and morality (Maritain), 53
    practical (Dewey), 328
    See also Activity; Experience
Activity and empathy (Langfeld), 317
    justification of (Bell), 581
    See also Action, Experience
Actuality and Art (Walsh), 611
    See also Reality
Addison, J., 536
Adler, M., 531, 532, 536, 540
Aesthetic (Croce), 69
Aesthetic, the, its enemies (Langfeld), 320
Aesthetic experience, and aesthetic object (Vivas), 410–411
    as attention (Isenberg), 225, (Ducasse), 363–364, (Vivas), 406–411
    autonomy of (Vivas), 409–410
    Bradley on, 562
    and conflict (Dewey), 330
    and creative act (Editors), 278–279, (Collingwood), 350–356, (Ducasse), 359–360, 375–376
    defined (Bullough), 396–405, (Ducasse), 358–376, (Pepper), 376–386, (Richards), 386–395, (Vivas), 406–411

Aesthetic experience (*cont'd*)
    Delacroix on, 361
    as distance (Ducasse), 366, (Bullough), 396–405
    as emotion (Collingwood), 343–358, (Ducasse), 358–376, (Pepper), 376–386, (Vivas), 406–408
    extensity of (Child), 454–456
    its factors (Marshall), 311, (Child), 450
    and interest (Ritchie), 229–232
    interpretations of (Marshall), 304–311
    Lee on, 361
    Leon on, 620–624
    and non-aesthetic (Dewey), 341, (Zink), 554
    as organization of impulses (Richards), 386–395
    and other experiences (Isenberg), 214–218, (Richards), 388–389, (Ducasse), 365–368, (Santayana), 522–526
    and passion (Dewey), 336
    and perception (Hungerland), 235–236
    its phases (Parker), 99
    as pleasure (Marshall), 309, (Ducasse), 370–372
    Schopenhauer on (Ducasse), 361
    Spencer on (Ducasse), 361
    and senses (Prall), 187
    ubiquity of (Santayana), 522–526
    universality of (Child), 454–456
    varieties of (Editors), 15, (Parker), 90, (Child), 446
    See also Experience; Hearer; Listener; Observer; Response
Aesthetic feeling (*see* Emotion; Feeling)
Aesthetic judgment, absolutism and relativism in (Child), 446–450
    Boas on, 430–436

627